BURROUGHS WELLCOME & CO.

Burroughs Wellcome & Co.: Knowledge, Trust, Profit and the Transformation of the British Pharmaceutical Industry, 1880–1940

by Roy Church and E. M. Tansey

Crucible Books

Also from Crucible Books

'Factory of Dreams': A History of Meccano Ltd
Kenneth D. Brown, 2007
ISBN 978-1-905472-00-0

Ferranti: A History. Volume 2: From family firm to multinational company,
1975–1987
John F. Wilson, 2007
ISBN 978-1-905472-01-7

Seminal Inventions: Science, Technology and Innovation in the Modern World
John Pitts, 2007
ISBN 978-1-905472-05-5

The Strange Death of the British Motorcycle Industry
Stever Koerner, 2007
ISBN 978-1-905472-03-1

www.cruciblebooks.com

Burroughs Wellcome & Co.: Knowledge, Trust, Profit and the Transformation
of the British Pharmaceutical Industry, 1880–1940

© Roy Church and E. M. Tansey, 2007

First published in 2007 by
Crucible Books,
Carnegie House,
Chatsworth Road,
Lancaster LA1 4SL
www.cruciblebooks.com

British Library Cataloguing-in-Publication data
A catalogue record for this book is available from the British Library

ISBN 978-1-905472-04-8 *hardback*
ISBN 978-1-905472-07-9 *softback*

Designed, typeset and originated by Carnegie Book Production, Lancaster
Printed and bound by Cromwell Press, Trowbridge, Wilts

Contents

List of illustrations

All images, unless otherwise acknowledged, are taken from the Wellcome Foundation Archives (WFA), as is the original artwork for advertisements. All are reproduced courtesy of the Wellcome Photographic Library. Tables, flow-charts and diagrams have been compiled by the authors.

List of tables

Acknowledgements

In addition to generous funding support from the Wellcome Trust, we are pleased to acknowledge assistance and advice from many people. We benefited from the expertise and support of the archival and library staff of the Wellcome Library for the History and Understanding of Medicine, especially Dr Richard Aspin, Ms Teresa Doherty and Mr Adrian Steel, and also Mrs Eileen Maugham in the Glaxo Wellcome archives at Greenford. Past archivists of the Wellcome Foundation, Mrs Rosemary Milligan and Mr John Davies, helped guide one of us (EMT) through the records in their charge in the late 1980s and early 1990s. We are particularly grateful to the staff of the Wellcome Photographic Library for their considerable help in producing the images used in this volume, especially Mr Chris Carter and Mr Clive Coward. Drs Trevor Baldwin, Declan O'Reilly and Mike Collins assisted one of us (RAC) with research into the business. Thanks are also due the Librarian and staff of the Royal Society for their assistance with material in their care; and similarly to the Librarian and staff of the National Institute for Medical Research, and to the Director Sir John Skehel FRS for permission to use their records; to Edwin Green, archivist of the HSBC, and to Judy Burg, formerly archivist at Boots, and in the United States to Glenn Burchett and Kelly Eubank at the Glaxo Wellcome Heritage Center, Raleigh Durham, North Carolina, and to Mignon Adams of the Joseph W. England Library, University of the Sciences in Philadelphia. Research on the Australian business was facilitated by Ann Lewis at the Glaxo Wellcome archives in Melbourne.

Mrs Lois Reynolds and Mrs Wendy Kutner helped in the preparation of the final manuscript, Cath Topliffe prepared the index, and Mr Tony Corley, Professor Anne Hardy, Mrs Lois Reynolds and Dr Lise Wilkinson are to be thanked for reading and criticising draft chapters and Mrs Gwenllian Church for editorial assistance. We are also greatly indebted to Professor Derek Oddy, who read and commented critically on the entire manuscript, and Sir William Castell for his comments and generous foreword to the book.

Archives, locations and abbreviations

The main archive collections upon which this book is based are those of Burroughs Wellcome & Co., the Wellcome Foundation, and Sir Henry Wellcome. When Sir Henry Wellcome died in 1936 he left a mass of records, both personal and professional which were, in his mind, completely inter-related. Until 1990 the majority of these papers were held in the Wellcome Foundation Archive in the Wellcome Building, 183 Euston Rd. The Wellcome Foundation Limited and the Wellcome Trust had shared the Wellcome Building, originally built by Sir Henry Wellcome to house his historical collections, since the company was bombed out of its headquarters at Snow Hill in the City of London in 1942. At the time of the physical division of the two organisations in 1990 the records were split to create two rather artificially separate collections.

One, largely relating to the commercial side of the company, was retained by the Wellcome Foundation Limited and these form what is referred to in this volume as the Wellcome Foundation Archive (WFA) collection. On the Wellcome Foundation's merger with Glaxo in 1996, WFA were removed to the Glaxo Wellcome campus at Greenford, becoming part of an uncompleted re-cataloguing exercise of the corporate archives of Glaxo Wellcome. Following the merger of Glaxo Wellcome with Smith Kline Beecham the archives remained at what became the GlaxoSmithKline (GSK) site at Greenford. In 2001 most pre-Second World War records were returned to the Wellcome Trust, where they are now housed in the Wellcome Library for the History and Understanding of Medicine (the Wellcome Library for short, and the successor body to the Library of the Wellcome Institute for the History of Medicine). GSK retain the remaining, post-war Wellcome Foundation records, and some scattered pre-war records. Where we have consulted these, they are clearly identified in the text as remaining with GSK.

The second part of the collection split in 1990, those papers predominantly relating to Sir Henry Wellcome, his laboratories and his museums, moved to the Library of the Wellcome Institute for the History of Medicine, then part of the Wellcome Trust. These are now catalogued as 'Wellcome

Archives' (WA). Additionally, we have consulted some of the private records held by the Wellcome Trust.

Inevitably the distinctions between the two major collections are blurred and inconsistent, and there is considerable overlap. Some original material, examined and sometimes copied in the 1980s and used in this book, has been missing for several years During the course of the re-cataloguing of the WFA collection, and the re-assessment of WFA and WA duplication and overlap, we hope these records will come to light. To avoid confusion, we have identified these documents as 'Wellcome Missing Papers'.*

WA	Wellcome Archives, Wellcome Library London
WFA	Wellcome Foundation Archives, Wellcome Library London
	Wellcome Missing Papers
WT	Wellcome Trust Archives, Wellcome Trust London

Several other archival collections have been consulted, as listed below, with abbreviations used in the footnotes, where appropriate.

Archives of the University of the Sciences, Wellcome Collection, Philadelphia.
Boots Pure Drug Co. Archives, Nottingham

| BW (USA) Inc | at the Glaxo Wellcome Heritage Center, Research Triangle, Raleigh Durham, NC, USA |

Glaxo Wellcome Archives, Melbourne, Australia

| GWHC | Glaxo Wellcome Heritage Center |

HSBC Archives, London
Imperial College Archives, F. H. Carr Papers, London.

MRC	Medical Research Committee (1913–1922)
	Medical Research Council (1923 onwards)
NIMR	National Institute for Medical Research, London
PP/ARC	Papers of A. R. Cushny, Wellcome Library
PP/ROG	Papers of Sir Leonard Rogers, Wellcome Library
PP/SMB	Papers of Silas Mainville Burroughs, Wellcome Library
RPS	Royal Pharmaceutical Society
RS	Royal Society
SA/LIS	Records of the Lister Institute, Wellcome Library
TNA	The National Archives, formerly the Public Record Office

Other abbreviations

ABCM	Association of British Chemical Manufacturers
AGM	Annual General Meeting
BDH	British Drug Houses
BEF	British Expeditionary Force
BELRA	British Empire Leprosy Relief Association
BIPM	British Institute for Preventive Medicine

---

* As this book goes to press, the relevant files have been found in the archives of the Wellcome Trust. These records will gradually be re-integrated into the appropriate parts of either WFA or WA.

BMJ	*British Medical Journal*
BW&Co.	Burroughs Wellcome & Co.
CC	Chemotherapy Committee (of the MRC)
CRL	Chemical Research Laboratories
DSIR	Department of Scientific and Industrial Research
HSBC	Hong Kong Shanghai Banking Corporation
HSW	[Sir] Henry Solomon Wellcome
KME	Kepler Malt Extract
KMEC	Kepler Malt Extract Company
LB	Letter Book (in WFA Archives).
LSHTM	London School of Hygiene and Tropical Medicine
MRC	Medical Research Council
NHI	National Health Insurance
NIMR	National Institute for Medical Research
OTC	Over the Counter (medicines)
PATA	Proprietary Articles Trade Association
PP	Parliamentary Papers
RAMC	Royal Army Medical Corps
R&D	Research and Development
RS	Royal Society
SMB	Silas Mainville Burroughs
SMB&Co.	S. M. Burroughs & Co.
STC	Scientific and Technical Committee
TAF	Toxoid anti-toxin floccules
TTC	Therapeutic Trials Committee (of the MRC)
WBSR	Wellcome Bureau of Scientific Research
WCRL	Wellcome Chemical Research Laboratories
WCW	Wellcome Chemical Works
WF	Wellcome Foundation
WHML	Wellcome Historical Medical Library
WHMM	Wellcome Historical Medical Museum
WPRL	Wellcome Physiological Research Laboratories
WRI	Wellcome Research Institution
WTRL	Wellcome Tropical Research Laboratories

Foreword

The Wellcome Trust is one of the world's leading funders of medical research. Between 1936, when it was formed, and 1995, the Trust was the sole owner of the Wellcome Foundation which included the commercial partnership founded as Burroughs Wellcome & Company in 1880. Although the Trust has provided the funding for the research behind this study, following the usual process of peer review, the work is a completely independent scholarly account of the pharmaceutical firm of Burroughs Wellcome & Co. during its first sixty years. It is not simply a 'company history'. I am pleased to declare a special interest in this book, both as Chairman of the Trust and also as one whose career began in the company thirty years ago.

Silas Burroughs and Henry Wellcome were ambitious young American pharmacists who set up their pharmaceutical business in London, the capital of a major trading empire. Their success provided the original source of wealth which ultimately enabled the Trust to achieve the aims laid down by Sir Henry Wellcome before he died in 1936, including the funding and advancement of medical research for the benefit of mankind. It is important, therefore, that Professor Church and Dr Tansey have undertaken the first comprehensive investigation of the process by which that wealth was created. This begins with the tempestuous partnership between the flamboyant Americans and ends with the intervention by the Wellcome Trust into the management of the Wellcome Foundation which, by the 1930s, had begun to lose its way. It is at the end of that decade, following Henry Wellcome's death and the subsequent creation of the Wellcome Trust in 1936, that this volume closes. Much more remains to be written of the later history of the company in the UK, and especially in the US. However, it was the early company, despite its chequered history, which provided the financial basis from which eventually the Wellcome Trust could make a major and enduring contribution to the transformation of medical research and the development of medical science.

The business is placed in the context of the international pharmaceutical industry between 1880 and 1940, when research and development gradually became central to the business of medicine. The project has been possible thanks to Glaxo-Wellcome plc, which, since its formation in 1995, held the business archives relating to Burroughs Wellcome & Co., the Wellcome

Foundation and Wellcome plc, for donating to the Wellcome Trust's Library the records on which this study is based, and for allowing the authors access. These documents complement the large collection of Sir Henry Wellcome's private papers, already held by the Wellcome Library, which have also been used extensively.

My impression is that rarely has a medium-sized company in modern British economic history exercised such a dominant influence on an industry, and specifically also on medical research in Britain, as did Burroughs Wellcome & Co. The history reveals the importance of the company in advancing medical knowledge through research and development as a distinctive route to making profits. The quality of that research was recognised when the future Nobel Laureate Henry Dale, then the Director of the Wellcome Physiological Research Labotatories, was elected a Fellow of the Royal Society in 1914. He was the first scientist associated with the pharmaceutical industry to be so honoured, and of the scientific staff appointed during Wellcome's lifetime, another sixteen also became Fellows. During the second quarter of the twentieth century, however, the human consequences of the ever-present tensions among business managers and scientists (between profit-making and marketing on the one hand, and research and scientific reputation on the other) proved to be a source of difficulties for the company. The authors develop these themes, which have a wider significance for the understanding of the rise, decline, and possible resurrection of organizations.

For this reason, I am confident that in addition to academic scholars in the fields of business and medical history, this handsomely illustrated volume will interest a much wider audience. I hope that all those associated with the Wellcome Trust and the many past and present friends, customers, and employees of the Wellcome companies – and indeed of Glaxo Wellcome and GlaxoSmithKline – will enjoy this book.

Sir William Castell,
Chairman, The Wellcome Trust

Preface

When Silas Mainville Burroughs invited Henry Wellcome to join him
in forming a pharmaceutical enterprise in London in 1880, it was an
auspicious period. The young American pharmacists were embarking on
an enterprise in the capital city of the British empire, with trade routes and
connections to every part of the world. They were imbued with knowledge
of the new pharmacy and pharmacology which had developed in the
German-speaking countries, and which had spread across most of Europe
and into North America. Equally important, they were enthused with and
by new American techniques of selling and promotion. Given their powerful
characters – frequently flamboyant, talented and similar, although tragically
different and flawed – the various pieces were in place for an important
new venture in pharmaceutical history: the firm of Burroughs Wellcome
& Co.

The firm was to become the most significant company in the development
of the pharmaceutical industry in the United Kingdom before the Second
World War. Its pre-eminence and influence were established on two major
fronts. First, in its incorporation and advancement of business methods,
especially those associated with marketing. Second – and perhaps more
important – in its recognition of, investment in, and promotion of, innovative
scientific research. These latter activities not only enhanced and extended
product quality and range, but also contributed to remarkable scientific
advances which won the company unique prestige establishing, especially
among the medical community that used and recommended its products,
an unrivalled reputation.

Burroughs Wellcome & Co. became the largest manufacturer of pharmaceuticals in Britain. It was an innovator in creating policies, institutions,
and practices, unique at the time and which are necessary to gain an
understanding of the history of the pharmaceutical industry in Britain in
the nineteenth and twentieth centuries. The significance of this central role
derives from the perception among historians that the modern pharmaceutical industry, which established a spectacular record in the global
history of the industry during the second half of the twentieth century,
originated with the development of sulphonamides shortly before the Second

World War. This success could not have been achieved, however, without the contributions of Burroughs Wellcome & Co.

Among the major themes in economic and business history to which this book offers a novel contribution the most important is marketing, especially product development, branding, advertising, selling and salesmanship, market research, and the origins of resale price maintenance of which BW&Co. was a successful pioneer during the 1880s.

Uniquely, it was the establishment of research laboratories in the 1890s that distinguished BW&Co., and which provided a model for industrial R&D that was emulated by rival companies in the following decades, especially after the First World War. The tension between marketing for profit as an objective and the advancement of medical research is explored in detail, assessing evidence of the relationship between owners and managers in the office and factory on the one hand, and scientists in the laboratories on the other. Close examination is made of the problems which arose in this novel situation, and of the mechanisms that the company evolved to promote and develop scientific research. Of particular note is the personal success of Henry Wellcome in achieving registration under the 1876 Cruelty to Animals Act, to allow staff in the research laboratories to perform animal experiments. That permission, achieved after considerable effort, was the single most important factor in promoting innovative research within the company, and was to serve to a great extent as the pattern for pharmaceutical research in the UK. The wider impact of much of BW&Co.'s research is assessed and it is clear, for example, that at a time when the government was largely indifferent to instituting large-scale immunisation and vaccination campaigns, it was the company that assumed the pioneering role in the UK to implement such measures.

After the First World War there was considerable growth in competition as other British pharmaceutical firms followed BW&Co.'s precedent by linking scientific research with manufacturing. Not only did BW&Co. provide the example to be followed; it also provided many of the managers, scientists, and engineers, as members of its staff were enthusiastically recruited by other companies and the newly created Medical Research Committee, to create further new laboratories and institutes. This contributes to an understanding of the process by which skills and knowledge were diffused across an industry.

The tension between marketing and research intensified as the company's relative position in the industry declined. The nature and causes of business failure are examined in the context of trust in organisations, a concept which has produced a limited empirical literature, building on that generated by studies of entrepreneurship and management and of corporate and organisational culture. Before 1914 the trust relationship between the firm and consumers and clients emerges as a central factor explaining its success.

After 1914 the erosion of trust between managers and scientists pursuing sometimes conflicting priorities – and between managers in overseas subsidiary companies and London – are also central to an interpretation of the company's difficulties from the 1920s onwards.

Roy Church and E. M. Tansey, 2006

PART ONE
1878–1914

CHAPTER ONE

❧

From trading to manufacturing;
S. M. Burroughs & Co. and
Burroughs Wellcome & Co.,
1878–1888

American origins; Silas Burroughs and John Wyeth & Brother

Silas Mainville Burroughs first arrived in London from Philadelphia in the spring of 1878. Born in rural Medina, NY, on 24 December 1846, son of a congressman who had formerly been a merchant, Burroughs enjoyed the advantages of a prosperous and influential family which had trading and metropolitan connections. Little is known of his early education. Sometime in 1865, he found employment as a clerk and counter salesman in a drug store in Lockport, NY, moving after a year to similar employment in Albion, NY, where he stayed for two years before spending about six months in Buffalo, NY. In October 1869 he joined John Wyeth & Brother (in which John, a graduate of Philadelphia College of Pharmacy, managed the business while Frank was the chemist). Burroughs became one of their salesmen drumming up business travelling on the road.[1] The new appointment brought Burroughs to Philadelphia, the historic centre of American pharmacy. This was the location where the jobbing business of George K. Smith commenced trading in 1830. Later, he was joined in partnership by Mahlon Kline, bookkeeper and salesman for the firm; in 1929 Smith & Kline combined with the perfume manufacturer, Harry B. French, to form Smith Kline & French. Another important firm which also survived in some form into the late twentieth century was the retailing enterprise set up by another Philadelphia College graduate, William R. Warner (later part of the Warner-Lambert pharmaceutical company).[2] Shortly before the Civil War Warner perfected a process for coating pills with sugar, and after the war ended he commenced the manufacture of drugs under his own name.[3]

Other important firms that were to be major competitors when regional markets were transformed into a national market included the leading New York wholesaler, McKesson & Robbins. Formed in 1833, this firm introduced gelatine-coated pills to the market in the 1870s. In the Midwest during the immediate post-Civil War decades, enterprising physicians and pharmacists started drug firms which, like McKesson & Robbins, remained in business until the late twentieth century: Parke-Davis (1866), Eli Lilly (1876), Upjohn (1885), Abbott (1888) and G. D. Searle (1888).[4] Unlike the research-led manufacturing activities of the leading large German fine chemical producers,[5] the business of American pharmaceutical firms consisted of importing vegetable and mineral materials for extraction and purification. Subsequently the goods were distributed to wholesalers, to physician-entrepreneurs who prescribed and dispensed drugs, and to druggists. Among American physicians, one effect of the first US *Pharmacopaeia* published in 1835 had been a trend, increasingly marked from the mid-nineteenth century, away from prescribing and dispensing the ubiquitous bolus, the large pill for every ill which had remained the norm hitherto in Britain and Continental Europe.

The new trend was towards dispensing smaller doses of commercial preparations, carefully prescribed and specifically targeted. These consisted mainly of natural products of plant origin and salts formulated into pills, powders, or syrups. Because it was not possible to patent such items, the scope for competition between firms was limited to reducing production costs through technology and adopting new methods of marketing proprietary drugs as specialities. A movement towards greater standardisation as a consequence of larger scale production, part of a more general trend in American manufacturing, is discernible already from the mid-century,[6] manifestly in the application of machinery to the production of opium, quinine, and ergot during the Civil War.[7]

Applying steam to production processes, developing new types of grinders and pulverisers, rotating blades for mixing dry or fluid materials, and more powerful distilling and evaporating equipment contributed further to increasing the potential for profit in the industry.[8] The production of stronger extracts of more uniform strength that could be manufactured at lower costs was one important outcome. These technical, institutional, and environmental factors provided a context in which a handful of chemists began to integrate wholesaling supply with manufacturing on larger (though not large) scale. The peculiarly American transformation of the industry beginning in the 1870s consisted of mechanisation, standardisation, the establishment of proprietary brands of 'ethical medicines' (to distinguish them from patent and proprietary medicines widely promoted to the public), the building of an extensive distribution network, and intensive advertising directed at medical and pharmacy professionals. Simple mechanisation and marketing became the distinctive method by which American companies competed.[9] Cost reductions and the manufacture of standardised high-quality products enabled innovators and imitators alike to build on their local markets to grow into nationally competing companies.[10]

In the 1870s, the trend towards mechanisation and standardisation of products was combined in a single innovation. Designed and developed by John Wyeth and an employee named Henry Bower, the rotary tablet press was patented in 1872, the first commercially successful press in the US, which quickly transformed a large part of the pharmaceutical industry. Originally the rotary press was an English invention patented by William Brockedon in 1843. However, the improved machine compressed precise weights of ingredients into granules or pills which were smaller, superior in taste and effectiveness, disintegrated more rapidly, and rendered the administration of medicine easier for patient and physician. Following the commencement of manufacture in 1873, the manufacture and sale of a range of novel compressed products facilitated by the press soon included medicinal powders in tablet form, hypodermic tablets, triturates and medicinal lozenges.[11] The endorsement given to the pills by Professor Joseph Remington during his address at the meeting of the American Pharmaceutical Society in 1875 when he demonstrated Wyeth's compressed medicine proved to be an important turning point commercially for the brothers.[12]

S. SOLOMON — ADELAIDE

FIGURE 1.1
Silas Burroughs in Adelaide, Australia c.1882, while on a world-wide sales and marketing tour for BW&Co.

Witnessing the birth of this successful innovation and the training and experience he gained in selling the compressed goods for the Wyeths from 1870 proved to be equally significant for Burroughs' career. Perhaps his approach to business was also influenced by John Wyeth's motto: 'We do not do business for honour and glory, but for profit'.[13] Burroughs studied at the Philadelphia College between 1870 and 1877, though at the same time working for the Wyeths,[14] presumably on a part-time basis. His teachers regarded him as an outstanding student. Within months of graduation, he was elected to membership of the American Pharmaceutical Association and resumed his role as full time salesman for the Wyeths.[15]

Burroughs had chosen for his 'Inaugural Essay [graduating dissertation]' a detailed examination of the history and potential of compressed medicine manufacture. Based on published sources in the US, Germany, and Britain, it reviewed the history, the state of the art, current methods of production, and the extent of the practice of making compressed medicines.[16] His account of Brockedon's patent of 1843 and its failure to impress medical men in London led Burroughs to conclude that Brockedon's error lay not so much in the machine's design but was attributable to his attempts to sell the pills as *patented* products. This attracted scepticism among the medical profession which showed reluctance to use or recommend them. Herein lies a clue to his own approach to marketing compressed medicines.

Thus, when he left Philadelphia for London in the spring of 1878, Burroughs was expert in both the theory and practice of all aspects of the production of compressed medicines and possessed experience in selling them. This combination provided a perfect springboard for creating a trade in Britain. On his arrival, he proceeded to exploit this knowledge in markets where the new products were unknown. From May 1878 until September 1880, S. M. Burroughs & Co. (SMB&Co.) traded in London as an independent agency possessing sole rights outside the US to sell the products supplied by John Wyeth & Brother.[17]

Why did Burroughs take this momentous step? Rhodes James explains it as the consequence of the high regard in which he was held by the Wyeth enterprise which was 'so impressed with him that it sent him to London as its representative; it is not clear whether this was on its initiative or his'.[18] An obituary writer presented a detailed appreciation of his complex character:

> Rapid and keen in perception, candid and outspoken to the extent of bluntness, argumentative and tenacious in his opinions, without the offensiveness usually begotten by the last-named qualities; quick in his decisions and to the verge of impulsiveness; generous, with a strong sense of justice; careful of others in many respects and careless of himself; untiring in his energy, and unconventional in almost everything, self reliant and enthusiastic in all his undertakings, he presented without a remarkable presence, a distinct personality.[19]

Emphasising the positive qualities possessed by Burroughs, the obituarist did not pursue the implications of such a forceful personality. It is true that at some time the Wyeths must have been impressed with aspects of Burroughs' performance as a traveller, otherwise why would he have received from them 'more liberal compensation than any other ...'?[20] However, in 1881, John Wyeth reminded him: 'We were forced to tell you that you gave us more bother than all our travellers combined – too hasty arrangements with our customers, often in a manner prejudicial to our interests, making statements and promises we could not fulfil.'[21] With the intention of reducing the inflated costs of employing Burroughs and removing the problem of controlling his waywardness, the Wyeths suggested that he should move to England to set up as an independent agent for Wyeth's goods. They expressed their conviction that by canvassing chemists and visiting doctors, leaving samples to try, and advertising, Wyeth products would 'meet with favour'. This followed their own practice in the US, known as 'detailing', which John Wyeth believed correctly to be completely unknown in Britain.[22] Detailing involved salesman visiting doctors, explaining the products which the company could supply, and leaving samples in the hope that they would be tested and lead to orders.[23]

The trading agency of S. M. Burroughs & Co., 1878–1880

Commencing business as S. M. Burroughs & Co. in a small rented office on Southampton Street near the Strand, in June 1878 Burroughs obtained stocks of chlorate of potash pills, dialysed iron (both Wyeth specialities), pepsin, and Parker's lint. The specific advantages of the compressed medicines of which he sought to convince his prospective purchasers were 'accuracy of dose, ready and entire solubility, and perfect preservation of drug'.[24] Burroughs soon recognised the greater acceptability of the term 'tablets' in Britain compared with American goods with such names as Wyeth's Pepsonic Pills. Consequently before he began to sell compressed medicines he registered 'tablet' as a trade mark.[25] Subsequently he removed reference to their American origin from labels.[26]

Another significant step was the registration of trade-marked products under his *own* name: Burroughs Bromide of Potassium Elixir, Dextra Quinine, Pepsin, and Hazeline, for example. His introduction of 'Burroughs Beef and Iron Wine (*improved*) as A HIGHLY CONCENTRATED STRENGTH GIVING FOOD TONIC' caused particular offence to the Wyeths, whose own beef and iron mixture Burroughs was supposed to be promoting. Under the terms of the agreement with the Wyeths, Burroughs acquired additional agencies, mostly from other firms in the US; for such products as Professor Horsford's Acid Phosphate ('a remedy for physical exhaustion, headaches, and stomach disorders'), and Fellows' Compound Syrup and hypophosphites (a popular American all-purpose remedy). The agency for Bishop's Granular Effervescent Citrate of Caffeine ('the best known remedy for headache') was acquired from an English firm. After testing, the *British Medical Journal* reported: 'We have administered it in nervous headache and in the malaise following an alcoholic debauch with benefit.'[27] Nubian Waterproof Blacking, advertised as 'THE NEW DISCOVERY. A profitable addition to a druggist's business', was a product supplied to Burroughs by the Blake & Goodyear Boot and Shoe Machinery Co.

In swift succession, Burroughs moved to larger offices in Great Russell

FIGURE I.2
Nubian
waterproof
blacking, a
waterproof
leather polish
marketed by
SMB&Co.
and later by
BW&Co.
(*Chemist &
Druggist*, 15
March 1879)

A Profitable Addition to a Druggist's Business.

THE NEW DISCOVERY.

TRADE   MARK.

NUBIAN WATERPROOF BLACKING

Is an Oily Liquid Preparation, entirely free from Acid.

Will NOT INJURE the Leather; gives a PERMANENT POLISH of great brilliancy (without brushing), which does not rub off or soil the clothing; is Waterpoof; and through RAIN, SNOW, and MUD will last a Week.

Mud when dry may be brushed off with a stiff brush, or may be washed off, and the polish will remain the same.

NUBIAN BLACKING

Is suitable for LADIES' and GENTLEMEN'S BOOTS and SHOES of every description; also BELTS, PURSES, and TRAVELLING BAGS, HARNESS, MILITARY ACCOUTREMENTS, &c.

Easily applied with Sponge attached to the Cork, and should NOT be used more than once or twice a week.

THE DRUG TRADE SUPPLIED BY

S. M. BURROUGHS & CO.,

No. 8 Snow Hill, London, E.C.

The Leather Trade supplied by The Blake & Goodyear Boot and Shoe Machinery Co., No. 1 Worship St., Finsbury, London.

4

Street and in November to Snow Hill, Holborn. A rented basement in Cock Lane in the City was used as a warehouse and packing department.[28] SMB&Co. possessed space for expansion. Burroughs was convinced that growth potential existed for a product which was becoming popular in the US but was still hardly known in Britain. Already in the summer of 1878, Burroughs had contacted Wyeth requesting assistance in securing an agency from an American producer of 'some first-class malt extract' which could be mixed with other compounds to add digestive value. Within months, however, Burroughs became connected with a new enterprise whose operations were based in London and Jersey. An agreement to which Burroughs was a signatory in December 1878 saw the formation of the The Kepler Malt Extract Company (KMEC). This firm was about to enter into a market on the verge of development in Britain in which, however, with the exception of Allen & Hanburys,[29] American and German companies were taking the initiative.

The Kepler Malt Extract Co.

Kepler Malt Extract (KME) was based on patents to protect the invention of the formulae and mashing apparatus to make a product in the category 'new or improved medicinal compounds'.[30] Burroughs' connection began following an approach by Philip Lockwood, chairman of the Condensed Beer Company and owner of a patent for a malt extract, whose operations were located in Jersey. The proposal put to Burroughs was that he should become the managing director of KMEC. He would use his own company's London premises for mixing, bottling, and 'putting-up' (labelling

FIGURE 1.3 Kepler improved malt extract, Kepler Malt Extract Company, (*Chemist & Druggist*, 15 Feb. 1879). Medical authority in the form of Ziemssen's cyclopaedia of medicine is invoked to promote the therapeutic value of malt extract.

FEB. 15, 1879.   THE CHEMIST AND DRUGGIST.   63

KEPLER MALT EXTRACT COMPANY LIMITED LONDON.

IMPROVED MALT EXTRACT

(EXTRACTUM MALTI "KEPLER"),

Containing all the valuable Nutritive and Digestive Properties of the Best Malted Barley, Wheat, and Oats concentrated in vacuo.

FREE FROM ALCOHOL.

Possesses from FIVE to TEN times more value than any Alcoholic or Fermented Extract of Malt.

From "ZIEMSSEN'S CYCLOPÆDIA OF MEDICINE."

"During the last few years MALT EXTRACT has almost entirely taken the place of COD LIVER OIL in the treatment of phthisis and other wasting diseases at the BASLE HOSPITAL, and we have as yet found no reason for returning to the use of the latter remedy."

and packing) the cod liver oil and malt extract. This would be made from a mixture of cod liver oil with malt and glycerine spirit or alcohol, a mixture designed to disguise the nauseous characteristics of the oil. Burroughs was also to be responsible for the marketing of the product. The patent malt extract was to be supplied by Lockwood's Condensed Beer Company. Burroughs agreed to the proposal, a decision which proved to be the most important diversification of his own company's product range. Lockwood secured financial backing from two London merchants: Theo Y. Kelley, who was to assist Burroughs as company secretary and director,[31] and Charles F. Gardner, who became company chairman. When the enterprise was registered as a joint stock company in January 1879 at the Russell Street office,[32] authorised capital was £3,000 issued in £10 shares. Paid-up capital amounted to £2,030, of which Burroughs held shares to the value of £1,000 and was the largest shareholder. Lockwood and Gardner each held 50 shares, while the remainder belonged to nine other shareholders.[33] These included the company's chemists, E.R. Southby (formerly a chemist employed by Allsopp's, the brewers who owned a patent for the mashing apparatus) and L. Briant.[34] Under a legal agreement between Lockwood and the company, the patent on his 'secret process' became the property of the KMEC for which Lockwood would receive royalties. Two-thirds of those royalties were then assigned to Burroughs and Kelley. In addition Burroughs was to receive 5 per cent on sales.[35]

The scale of Burroughs' investment compares with his £1,200 share in the £2,000 equity capital of the partnership with Henry Wellcome which he was to enter in September 1880.[36] The relative importance of Burroughs' capital in the two companies suggests that his fertile mind may already have turned to extend his control of KMEC to add to that of SMB&Co. Protected by patent and marketed under a registered trademark, Kepler goods were suitable for promotion by detailing.[37] Promotion and sales were also conducted through a small number of commission agents and salesmen who were difficult to recruit. Burroughs told Wyeth: 'It is almost impossible in this country, the commercial traveller is a stereotyped man ... Men who can do what we want are not to be had and would be too expensive even if we could find them; we are, therefore, doing it ourselves'.[38] Kelley appears to have possessed some experience of the drug trade. Burroughs thought that travelling in the provinces had resulted in Kelley becoming 'knowledgeable about goods so that he can talk intelligently about them'; John Wyeth, however, was sceptical.[39] By March 1879, Burroughs reported having five travellers on the road all the time.[40]

Little has survived which might throw light on the measurable commercial and financial outcome of Burroughs' ventures. In 1879 he referred to KME as 'selling more than all the rest together', at a time when KMEC's sales were £1,515 in a six-month period. They rose to £5,150 in the accounting year beginning 1 April 1879, to £6,541 in the following year, and £10,223 by 1882.[41] Trading profits for the years between 1879 and 1882 were £2,879, £3,480, and £5,046. These amounted to an average return on sales of 53 per cent. Gross sales revenues of the partnership between Burroughs and Wellcome were £17,811 in 1880/81 and £33,158 in 1881/82.[42] Financial pressure and the expansion of Burroughs' managerial responsibilities, which were to grow as a result of his association with KMEC, was the context in which in February 1879, he recruited Robert Clay Sudlow. An experienced clerk at the age of 33, he had worked for several city firms but lacked familiarity with the drug trade. However, the earnest, efficient and hard-working Sudlow quickly assumed the role of Burrough's assistant, a position which Kelley, who had left the business, had signally failed to fulfil. Sudlow's entry into the firm was to be important for he was soon to become, in effect, general manager of Burroughs Wellcome & Co. (BW&Co.).[43] In the meantime, Burroughs sought a senior manager or partner who possessed experience and skills similar to his own. He approached a former Philadelphia College graduate, Henry Wellcome, a traveller for McKesson & Robbins, drug manufacturers in New York, who already possessed a reputation for his knowledge of pharmacy, success as a salesman, and connections in the American trade.

FIGURE 1.4
Robert Clay
Sudlow,
BW&Co.'s
first General
Manager,
c. 1880.

While Burroughs was the first to introduce compressed medicines into the British market, Allen & Hanburys was the first to acquire the new American technology for their manufacture.[44] The novelty associated with Burroughs' innovation was his adoption of the American method of 'detailing'. None of the British pharmaceutical firms followed his lead, consequently for many years detailing remained the distinctive feature of his, and subsequently of BW&Co.'s, marketing strategy.[45] The combined effect of these developments was to set the business on a path of expansion which, within the decade, established the company's world-wide reputation for growth and innovation.[46]

Henry Wellcome and the formation of Burroughs Wellcome & Company

Wellcome's background, described in detail by his biographer,[47] was both similar to and different from that of his senior partner. Seven years younger than Burroughs, Wellcome was born in 1853, the son of Solomon and Mary, an impoverished farming couple living in the tiny settlement of Almond, Wisconsin. A poor background, a fundamentalist religious family, and an elementary education (basic but adequate) were the major formative influences in Wellcome's youth. After leaving school at the age of 13, by which time his family had moved to Garden City, Minnesota, he joined his pharmacist uncle as an assistant. He also became acquainted with an English chemist from Leeds who established a small pharmacy in Garden City.

Encouragement and informal instruction in chemistry stimulated Wellcome's interest as, it seems likely, did the Englishman's talk of his country as the hub of the world's trading network and of the unique advantages of London as a centre of commerce and finance. These influences later provided reference points for the momentous decision to migrate to England.[48] Another English migrant who influenced Wellcome's professional

FIGURE 1.5
Henry
Wellcome,
*c.*1882.

development was William Worrall Mayo, a friend and colleague of Jacob Wellcome, Henry Wellcome's uncle. He was a practising doctor and surgeon who took Wellcome under his wing as an informal student. Through Jacob Wellcome's connection with Mayo, Henry Wellcome, at the age of seventeen, became a prescription clerk with Poole & Geisinger, a firm of pharmaceutical chemists in Rochester. On the advice of his uncle Jacob and of Mayo, Wellcome resolved to obtain a professional qualification by attending the Chicago College of Pharmacy, one of the two leading institutions of its kind in the US.[49] There he met Frederick Belding Power who was also working in a drug store to finance his future studies at the Philadelphia College of Pharmacy. Wellcome left Chicago to join Power in Philadelphia in 1873 where he secured employment and enrolled as a student. He graduated a year later, having successfully presented his thesis on a new design for urethral suppositories.

In 1874 he proceeded to a position as a travelling salesman, first with Caswell Hazard & Co., where he stayed for two years, and subsequently – and more significantly – with McKesson & Robbins. One of the longest established and most important drug wholesalers in New York, the firm was managed by three principals, each of whom was an active member of the American Pharmaceutical Association. The proprietors claimed that their company was the greatest drug house in the world. Unusually at that time, McKesson & Robbins also built an analytical laboratory to facilitate the process of ensuring the highest standards of purity in the drugs they sold. The exercise of quality control was combined with an aggressive marketing policy on an international, as well as a national, scale. Wellcome contributed to this, leading campaigns in Canada and Central and South America. A highly successful salesman in a business which attached great importance to effective distribution, Wellcome also attracted the attention of the pharmacy

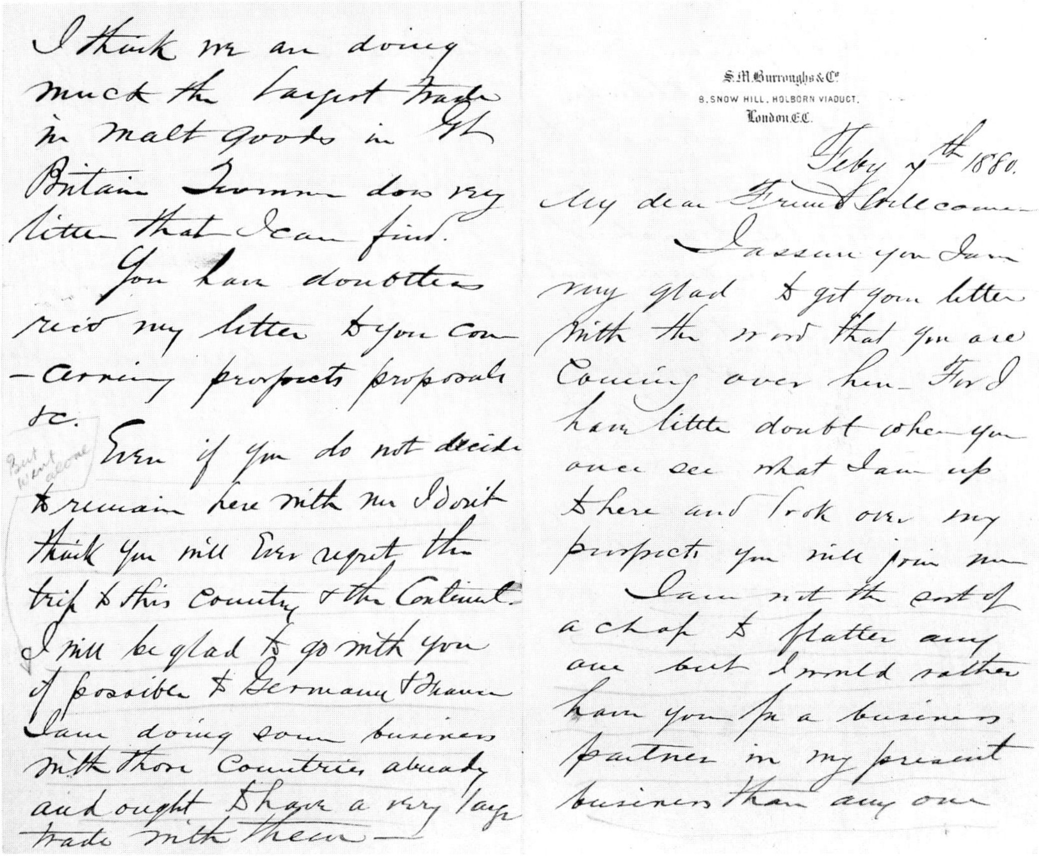
S. M. Burroughs & Co.
8, Snow Hill, Holborn Viaduct,
London E.C.

Feby 7th 1880.

My dear Friend Wellcome

I assure you I am very glad to get your letter with the word that you are coming over here. For I have little doubt when you once see what I am up to here and look over my prospects you will join me.

I am not the sort of a chap to flatter any one but I would rather have you as a business partner in my present business than any one

I think we are doing much the largest trade in Malt Goods in Gt Britain. Trommer does very little that I can find.

You have doubtless rec'd my letter to you concerning prospects proposals &c.

Even if you do not decide to remain here with me I don't think you will ever regret the trip to this Country & the Continent. I will be glad to go with you if possible to Germany & France. I am doing some business with those Countries already and ought to have a very large trade with them —

FIGURE 1.6

Letter from Silas Burroughs to Henry Wellcome, expressing his pleasure at Wellcome's forthcoming visit and that 'I am not the sort of chap to flatter any one but I would rather have you as a business partner in my present business than any other', 7 February 1880.

profession at large by his contributions to journals, notably a paper concerning 'the liquor question', and also because of publications dealing with the efficacy of plant-based drugs. His account of his exploration of the forests of Ecuador in search of Cinchona bark, then the prime source of pure quinine, brought him widespread recognition within the profession.[50]

It is not possible to describe exactly how Wellcome and Burroughs became acquainted, or the precise nature of their relationship, before they became partners in England. They knew each other in 1877 when, either through their shared occupation as salesmen for competing firms in Philadelphia or as graduates of the Philadelphia College of Pharmacy, they had become sufficiently acquainted for Burroughs to suggest a joint holiday or venture of some kind in England.[51] On Burroughs' death in 1895, Wellcome dwelt on the period (almost certainly before 1880) when the two were 'bosom friends'.[52]

The details of the courtship, which culminated in Wellcome joining Burroughs in partnership, have been described elsewhere.[53] Burroughs offered Wellcome the choice of becoming either a manager or a partner, adding: 'I think we would make a pretty lively team in the Pharmaceutical line'.[54] He also offered Wellcome the option of managing that part of the business dealing with new goods only, leaving himself, Burroughs, to manage and incur risks associated with existing products hitherto sold by SMB&Co. The alternative, an equal partnership and shared managerial responsibilities, was conditional on Wellcome securing the exclusive agency agreement to sell McKesson & Robbins's pills in Britain and the colonies. Initially, McKesson & Robbins offered an increase of 40 per cent salary which Wellcome declined. Thereupon, it was agreed that McKesson & Robbins would give him an exclusive 5 year agency for the sugar-coated pills and other products outside the Americas. The agreement, the details of which were the subject of protracted negotiations even after the partnership with Burroughs commenced, applied to Wellcome personally, though it also allowed him to associate with partners (not limited to Burroughs) in promoting a trade in their pills.[55] Wellcome embarked on a tour of England in April 1880 when he visited leading

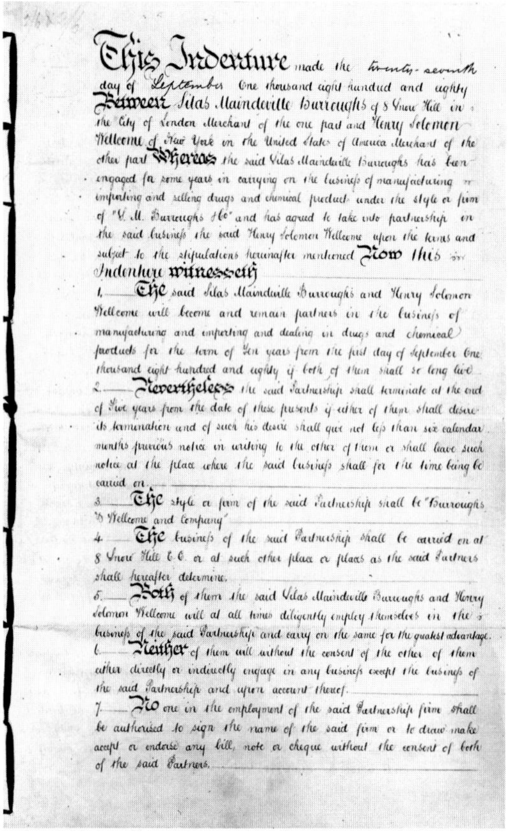

This Indenture made the twenty-seventh day of September One thousand eight hundred and eighty Between Silas Mainville Burroughs of 8 Snow Hill in the City of London Merchant of the one part and Henry Solomon Wellcome of New York in the United States of America Merchant of the other part Whereas the said Silas Mainville Burroughs has been engaged for some years in carrying on the business of manufacturing or importing and selling drugs and chemical products under the style or firm of "S. M. Burroughs & Co" and has agreed to take into partnership in the said business the said Henry Solomon Wellcome upon the terms and subject to the stipulations hereinafter mentioned Now this Indenture witnesseth

1. — The said Silas Mainville Burroughs and Henry Solomon Wellcome will become and remain partners in the business of manufacturing and importing and dealing in drugs and chemical products for the term of Ten years from the first day of September One thousand eight hundred and eighty if both of them shall so long live

2. — Nevertheless the said Partnership shall terminate at the end of Five years from the date of these presents if either of them shall desire its termination and of such his desire shall give not less than six calendar months previous notice in writing to the other of them or shall leave such notice at the place where the said business shall for the time being be carried on.

3. — The style or firm of the said Partnership shall be "Burroughs & Wellcome and Company"

4. — The business of the said Partnership shall be carried on at 8 Snow Hill E.C. or at such other place or places as the said Partners shall hereafter determine.

5. — Both of them the said Silas Mainville Burroughs and Henry Solomon Wellcome will at all times diligently employ themselves in the business of the said Partnership and carry on the same for the greatest advantage.

6. — Neither of them will without the consent of the other of them either directly or indirectly engage in any business except the business of the said Partnership and upon account thereof.

7. — No one in the employment of the said Partnership firm shall be authorised to sign the name of the said firm or to draw make accept or endorse any bill, note or cheque without the consent of both of the said Partners.

FIGURE 1.7 Articles of partnership between Silas Mainville Burroughs and Henry Solomon Wellcome, 27 September 1880.

dispensing chemists to assess trading prospects. After returning to the US, his second coming to Britain in August was followed in September by the formation of the partnership.[56]

The medical and economic environment

At the time when BW&Co. was formed the development of new drugs to cure specific diseases was limited and slow. Plants formed the basis of most prescriptions. Only a few specific therapies such as quinine for malaria were available. Opium from poppies was used as a general analgesic, sedative, and decongestant; common purgatives in use were aloes, senna, and rhubarb. Among the chemicals produced in the laboratory, mercury was to treat skin complaints and specific venereal infections, notably syphilis.[57] Chloroform anaesthesia, which had been used by surgeons since the mid nineteenth century, was heralded as the apotheosis of medicine enhancing the perception of the scientific authority of an emerging medical elite of consultants.[58] The discovery of morphine, an alkaloid derived from opium was important, not only as an analgesic but as an advance in scientific research. This led to further investigations to analyse other alkaloids to treat dysentery and vomiting, an avenue of research in which BW&Co. was to play a leading role. These developments signalled the origins of modern pharma-ceutical investigation and manufacture.[59] Several effective antipyretics and analgesics, developed as by-products of the German chemical industry, entered the market during the 1870s and 1880s.[60] However, symptomatic management rather than cure represented the realistic therapeutic limit of theory and practice in the 1880s. Patient care also included the admin-istration of arsenic as a common ingredient in the multitude of tonics available, while increasingly, cod liver oil (another product to be strongly associated with BW&Co.) was acknowledged in the medical profession as offering a supportive role in health care.[61]

Another building block in the modern pharmaceutical industry was the discovery that some simple organic chemicals derived or synthesized from coal tar contained medicinal properties, increasing the possibilities for the development of commercial processes.[62] Coal-tar chemicals and cellulose yielded chloral hydrate and amyl alcohol as anaesthetics or hypnotics. Of fundamental importance was the development of synthetic dyes which facilitated research by providing stains for bacteria and other micro-organisms. The demonstrations by Robert Koch in the 1870s and 1880s of causal links between specific organisms and disease were the theoretical basis for the subsequent development of the new field of serum therapy and bacteriology.[63] This required a completely new expertise in using animals for the production of pharmaceuticals, a field which BW&Co. became pre-eminent starting from the mid-1890s. In parallel with the application of germ theory, other important developments included synthesizing processes, chemical analysis and the investigation of chemical structure and associated physiochemical properties, laboratory methods, and the institutionalisation of research.[64] They were accompanied by the introduction of new clinical methods of studying disease and an improved medical understanding of the identities and characteristics of individual diseases.[65]

The market for health expanded during the late nineteenth century. Both death rates and infant mortality rates in England and Wales were higher in 1871/80 than in 1860, during a period when the public health movement exposed problems of a rapidly urbanising society.[66] After 1881, the mobilisation of resources at the local and national level increased investment in health, environment, and medicine. Indirectly this resulted in an increase in the number of doctors and a subsequent rise in the ratio of doctors to population from 1 to 1,723 to 1,439 by 1901.[67] The only measure (which offers dubious proxy for the market for health care products before 1907) is that for the value of output of patent and proprietary medicines, which increased from £0.6 million in 1875 to £1.5 million in 1900 (and roughly the same in 1907). The value of output of other fine chemicals and allied products separately recorded in 1907 was £3.4 million, indicating a ratio of fine chemicals to patent medicines of greater than two to one.[68] Other indicators of society's increasing demand for health care are the increased medical student registration figures and the numbers of medical practitioners.

Among the commonest ailments were digestive and alimentary disorders. Serious infectious diseases persisted: diphtheria and scarlet fever in all areas, tuberculosis in poorer districts. However, the most frequent illnesses, especially in urban industrial areas, were upper respiratory complaints: bronchitis and emphysema, colds, coughs, and influenza. During winter, bronchitis and pneumonia were especially prevalent, as were typhoid and diarrhoea in summer.[69] Endemic among the urban poor, rickets was a result partly of a specific nutritional deficiency (now known to be caused by a lack of vitamin D). The other contributory factor was a lack of sunlight (now known to be necessary for the natural production of vitamin D in the body) due to heavy air pollution and poor housing; the symptoms produced included softened bow legs, and a pigeon chest.[70]

Extensive nutritional deficiency revealed by investigators' surveys from the 1840s and the recognition at about the same time of chemistry as a significant and useful science, provided the basis for the emergence of a health food industry. The result was the advocacy of supplementing diets, particularly of convalescents and infants, either as hospital patients or receiving institutionalised care.[71] Cod liver oil had long been regarded as nutritious, but the deterrent to widespread consumption was that until the mid-1850s, it was available from suppliers (predominantly Norwegian) only in the form of evil-smelling, distasteful, brown oils prepared from putrefied livers. The introduction of steam-prepared oil, pale in colour, less odorous, and of weaker taste, rendered the oil, increasingly regarded as nutritious, more palatable.[72] From the 1870s, by the addition of malt extracts and other variants, innovators developed a growing market. Among the leaders in the British market were the American Maltine Manufacturing Co., and Allen & Hanburys, with whom BW&Co. entered into competition.[73] A comparable rise in popularity of meat extracts beginning in the 1860s also derived from the growing interest in food and nutritional science spearheaded by the German chemist, Justus von Liebig. The Liebig Extract of Meat Company was the commercial vehicle through which his theory which linked nutrition with chemical changes, soon to be discredited, exploited a growing market for nutritious food in a form which consumers were persuaded was portable, convenient, and of a high quality based on scientific criteria. Other chemists attracted to this market produced variants to compete with Liebig's beef teas and beef extracts.[74] One of the most successful was Beef and Iron Wine, introduced by the American, John Wyeth, in the 1870s and sold in Britain by Silas Burroughs & Co. from 1878.

The growth areas when BW&Co. began were in proprietary medicines that depended on aperient qualities (mainly compound pills and laxatives), 'tonic' wines and nerve medicines in liquid form, remedies for coughs and colds (mainly analgesic), and anti-pyretic preparations. Medicines for indigestion, anti-acid lozenges, and magnesium hydroxide suspensions also proliferated, as did dietetic foods including yeast preparations. As in the US, the absence of regulation over such products created opportunities for deception and downright fraud by those selling so-called 'patent' medicines, though patent protection for such preparations was rare.[75] Patent and proprietary medicines facilitated (doctors asserted that they encouraged) self medication, a practice that involved risk for the patient and adverse effects on practitioners' revenue from prescriptions. Increasingly during the nineteenth century, patent medicine manufacturers had offered ailing patients an alternative to a visit to the doctor. The view of this tripartite relationship was described in the *Chemist & Druggist* in 1886:

> The majority of people get to feel very bad before they go to the processes of being prescribed for and dispensed for in the orthodox fashion ... But something definite, tested by experience, something they can purchase at a fixed price and by just naming the article, without being catechized as to all their physical miseries, will always be popular.[76]

Chemists and druggists, like doctors, were critical of patent medicines and also of proprietary remedies which competed with their own specialities. This resistance posed a potential problem for the two young American pharmacists who, in 1880, employed American marketing methods to introduce American products to the British medical profession and to traditional chemists and druggists.

The professionalisation of doctors during the second half of the century and the enhanced authority of the medical profession, hospital consultants, private practitioners, and family doctors was accompanied by a growth in demand for medical provision and increased potential for ethical preparations on prescription. Both experienced growth in the late nineteenth century. From the 1860s an increase occurred in the number of hospital inpatients and outpatients in the voluntary hospitals of London and in the regions, as well as in the new specialist hospitals. Sick clubs, friendly and medical aid societies, and provident dispensaries widened access to medical treatment among the majority which could not afford the services of general practitioners. So, too, did the provision of dispensaries set up under the Poor Law in the 1870s to assist those who fell further below the poverty line. The growth in the number of specialist hospitals in London encouraged medical research and teaching, the techniques and equipment developed there becoming incorporated into reorganised general hospitals. The rise of the new specialist medicine created an incentive for pharmaceutical manufacturers to invest in the production of ethical medicines.[77] Undoubtedly, hospital consultants and hospital authorities possessed the greatest potential influence on which medicines were to be prescribed. However, general practitioners were also influential in affecting demand. Although payment for medicines was a declining practice as fees became a reward for the time, skill, or bedside manner of a practitioner, the individual prescription was regarded as an important asset in building a reputation as well as a list of patients who became consumers of ethical and other proprietary medicines. Both shared two important characteristics affecting the market. Neither patients nor practitioners could be certain of the effects of medicine after administration. This might induce the consumer to confuse output (evacuation or pain relief, for example) with outcome in the form of a cure which few preparations at that time could ensure. One effect was to provide scope for proprietary medicine manufacturers to exploit the gullible consumer and for the medical practitioner to satisfy the trusting patient. Such was the medical and social environment in which the partnership of Burroughs and Wellcome entered the British market in 1880.

The market environment at this time was also in flux, though it seems unlikely that either of the partners was aware of the changes taking place when they first set up business. Developments were occurring that were to have important consequences for the structure of the market for drugs, particularly affecting the trade in London and with the colonies.

Since the early seventeenth century, the licensing of apothecaries and the dispensing of physicians' medicines in the City of London had been a monopoly granted by Royal Charter to the Worshipful Society of

Apothecaries which was given a medical licensing role.[78] Members of staff of the laboratory at Apothecaries' Hall in Blackfriars were responsible for ensuring the quality of drugs (by inspection and seizure for destruction if necessary) supplied in the City by the Hall and by Society members; they provided a specialist service to public bodies and offered advice on chemical matters. As the arbiter of quality control, the Hall became the preferred supplier of drugs to government departments, hospitals, and other public bodies. By 1860 a protected, unrivalled reputation and personal connections had resulted in contracts which included those with the Royal Navy, the Army, Crown Agents, Greenwich, Chelsea, and St Bartholomew's Hospitals, and the East India Company. None of the contracts was open for tender. This monopoly of the bulk supply of packaged drugs formed the basis of a trade which during the 1860s was averaging roughly £60,000 of sales annually yielding almost £11,000 annual profit.[79] No evidence exists of a comparably large drug-producing enterprise in Britain at that time.

The degree of dominance derived from the important London market, public bodies and other leading institutions, however, began to diminish during the 1870s. Two important contributory factors originating from outside the organisation were competitive tendering and inspection applied by government to all contracts placed with public bodies. Pressure by the Treasury for accountability and greater cost effectiveness led to a sharp reduction in the lucrative contracts on which the Hall had relied for so long. Loss of the valuable Navy contract in 1870 was followed shortly by the East India Company contract. After a new inspectorate was established at the India Office in 1879 and tendering introduced, contracts began to dwindle; among the last to be affected in 1907 were those issued by the Crown Agents whose trade with the Hall fell from £17,000 to £4,000 by 1914.[80] The second external factor undermining the Hall's position was the emergence in the early nineteenth century of a division between apothecaries who concentrated either on medical practice, becoming surgeon apothecaries or 'general practitioners', or on dispensing and manufacture.[81] One result was the growth of a private commercial sector in which producers appealed increasingly to 'science' when advertising their claims for the quality of the drugs they offered. This contrasted with the Apothecaries' Society's presumption (the Hall did not advertise) to set standards and control quality which was based on royal privilege. The Hall's long-standing monopoly of trade with purchasers who until the 1870s had accepted high prices as necessary to ensure high quality, had created a market insensitive to cost considerations and made the Hall vulnerable to competition. The twin influences on the Hall's commercial predicament, one as a consequence of government policy, the other from competing firms producing drugs of acceptable quality while reducing prices by cutting costs, exposed the vulnerability of an obsolete quasi-commercial organisation. Its laboratories were dilapidated and ill-managed, shareholders and managers showing themselves to be incapable of responding to market pressures. By 1878 dividends had fallen steadily to one-fifth of the 1860 level; in 1880, the Hall declared its first financial loss and precipitated the dissolution of the joint stock that underpinned its activities.[82] By that time, the London market was diminishing in importance, as industrialisation in northern and midland regions was accompanied by a growth of population, an increase in the number of chemists and druggists, and an expansion of the retail trade.

Beyond the Apothecaries' Hall the industry consisted of small and medium sized, mainly family, firms possessing small analytical and works laboratories which supplied the medical profession and the trade with galenicals, fine chemicals, and proprietary goods. Typically staffed by no more than a single chemist, the laboratories were limited to routine sampling and testing; they did not undertake research that might lead to new products and allowed little scope for research and development.[83] Except for Allen & Hanburys and May & Baker, little is known about the history of these firms. Thomas Morson's well-established reputation for fine chemicals manufacture since 1821 did not produce commensurate commercial success.[84] Sales turnover of £27,265 in 1880 rose to £52,986 in 1891, a figure which BW&Co. exceeded after only six years in business.[85] The partnership between May & Baker originated in 1834. Initially supplying the trade with fine chemicals, diversification into fruit and alcoholic essences supplied to jam and other food manufacturers widened during the 1880s to include a patent-based trade in disinfectants, tungstic acid, and metallic sulphates for use by producers of varnish and linseed oil.[86] The net worth of the firm was £31,500 in 1880 which was also overtaken by BW&Co. by 1886.[87] Much less is known about other fine chemical producers which remained strictly within the traditional sector supplying specialist markets for alkaloids, such as quinine, metal salts, such as mercury and bismuth, and galenicals: Howard, Maw, Thomson & Son, and Whiffen & Sons, or of the Scottish wholesaling firms of J. F. Macfarlan, T. H. Smith, and Flockhart.[88] Almost certainly, the largest of the these traditional manufacturers was Allen & Hanburys, one of the oldest (originating in 1715) and BW&Co.'s principal competitor until the 1930s, in the market for traditional chemical and pharmaceutical products and also in the market for dietetic foods, notably cod liver oil and malt extract. The only measure of relative size available is the capital value of each firm; in 1893 the authorised capital of Allen & Hanburys was £75,000 compared with a capital value of BW&Co. of £56,030.[89]

The partnership's early financial difficulties

The initial Deed of Partnership of BW&Co. drawn up in September 1880 showed a capital of £2,000, of which Burroughs held £1,200 and Wellcome

£800. Unable to contribute his allotted share, Wellcome put up £400, exhausting his financial resources. To enable Wellcome to establish himself in London, Burroughs extended a loan of £550 at ten per cent interest.[90] Equity capital in the business grew rapidly to reach five figures in 1885. An almost sixfold increase in five years is explained for the first three years primarily by a growth in stocks of goods and packaging materials. Working capital at that time amounted to between three and five times the level of fixed assets. This dominance of working capital continued until the 1890s, when fixed capital rose from 50 per cent to 70 per cent of total assets.[91] This was the transitional period when manufacturing, on which the profitability of the business became increasingly dependent, was added to the firm's trading activity as an agency for American and some German goods.

The partner's first public display of the company's products occurred at the International Medical and Sanitary Exhibition in South Kensington in July 1881. The collection was praised in the *Medical Press and Circular* for the range and novelty of pharmaceutical products on display. These were supplied by leading American drug houses which represented 'new and practical improvements in medicine and pharmacy'.[92] Journal advertisements for

FIGURE 1.8
*Medical
Formulae
of New and
Improved
Chemical and
Pharmaceutical
Preparations*,
BW&Co.
1881.

the firm's products contained fulsome quotations commenting on the first price list issued by the partners in 1881: essentially products introduced by Burroughs to which were added the goods supplied by McKesson & Robbins. These elicited praise, too, in the columns of the *BMJ*, *Lancet*, *London Medical Record*, *Medical Times & Gazette*, and *Chemist & Druggist*. The Burroughs Ammonia Inhaler 'for inhaling the fumes of chloride of ammonium' was advertised as effective not only in removing catarrh, 'but ... after its use the patient is less susceptible to the weather than before'. In the *Lancet* the inhaler was described as an 'efficient apparatus', in the *Medical Press & Circular*, as 'an ingenious and convenient device'.[93]

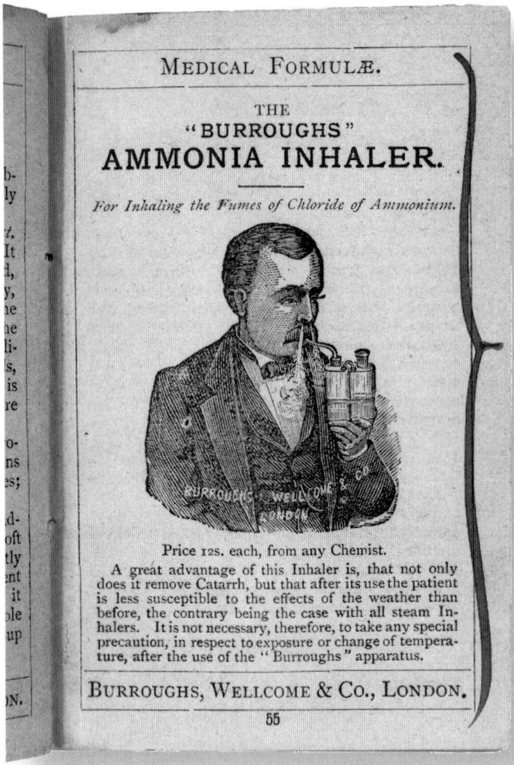

The balance sheets for the early years of the business obscure the profitability of trading. However, the financial basis in the first year of trading was sufficiently problematic for Sudlow to fear the need for external financing. In December 1881, Sudlow arranged a private loan from Charles F. Gardner (chairman of the Kepler business) to meet requirements for pay day.[94] In 1883 Wellcome succeeded in securing the extension of a £1,000 loan from a Mr Bishop,[95] probably the caffeine supplier for which BW&Co. was an agency. Persistent financial pressure was possibly one of the factors which in 1884 led Burroughs to consider either selling up or floating the business as a joint stock company.[96] Financial pressure, however, did not denote fundamental commercial weakness; it did not result from a failure of the company's products to sell. Following sales amounting to £17,811 in the first six months of trading, the figure for 1881/82 was £33,158, rising to £57,165 in 1882/83. From £55,724 in 1885/86, sales rose to £72,147 in 1886/87, £81,845 in 1887/88, and £74,550 in 1888/89.[97] The capital base increased from only £1,991 in 1880 to £7,002 by 1884; the rate of expansion in the level of activity, therefore, was considerable. Annual net profits were below £2,000 until 1885, an average of 4.4 per cent on sales.[98] These figures, however, are net, excluding partners' withdrawals, whether for travel costs connected with the business or for private expenditure. The scale of withdrawals and expenditure made by Burroughs earned him a reputation for profligate spending remarked upon by both Wyeth and

MEDICAL FORMULÆ.

THE
"BURROUGHS"
AMMONIA INHALER.

For Inhaling the Fumes of Chloride of Ammonium.

Price 12s. each, from any Chemist.

A great advantage of this Inhaler is, that not only does it remove Catarrh, but that after its use the patient is less susceptible to the effects of the weather than before, the contrary being the case with all steam Inhalers. It is not necessary, therefore, to take any special precaution, in respect to exposure or change of temperature, after the use of the "Burroughs" apparatus.

BURROUGHS, WELLCOME & CO., LONDON.

55

FIGURE 1.9 The 'Burroughs' ammonia inhaler, an early product promoted by BW&Co. Taken from BW&Co.'s 1881 price list.

Wellcome (and acknowledged by Burroughs to some degree).[99] An American obituarist referred to Burroughs' capacity for 'barbaric extravagances in all directions and an almost spendthrift disregard of money'.[100] There is little indication how he spent his money, but much of that withdrawn from the business between 1881 and 1884 was to meet travel and accommodation expenses overseas in the service of the firm. From the outset the volume of samples distributed in seeking to establish goodwill and the scale on which he ordered circulars to be printed drew criticism from his partner and from Wyeth.[101]

The sources of financial pressure were fourfold. One was the initial relatively low capitalisation of the firm and the burden which financing stock in trade imposed. Related to this (to the surprise of both partners) was the convention of long credits within the drug trade in Britain. This involved considerable delay between presenting invoices for goods and receiving payment from chemists and medical men, a system that diminished cash flow and which, unless turnover grew sufficiently rapidly to minimise the risk of insolvency, could threaten a firm's survival. Burroughs was particu-larly inclined to this practice, though in June 1882 he accepted Wellcome's argument that while such a policy might tempt custom initially, particularly in new markets overseas, the risks and costs involved were excessive and not in the best long-term interest of the business.[102] The third factor arose

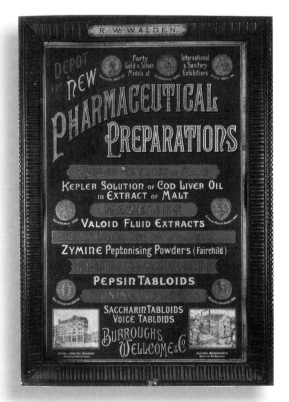

FIGURE 1.10
A pharmacy sign advert-ising BW&Co.'s 'new pharma-ceutical preparations', c. 1885.

from the partners' success in marketing the novel American products and the resulting requirement for further investment to expand production; hence the substantial growth in fixed assets especially from 1883. The fourth source of pressure on liquidity was the call for capital in order to acquire the KMEC in 1881/82, a short-term problem connected to an important long-term strategic investment.

One consequence of the central involvement of Burroughs in the KMEC was that BW&Co.'s premises were used for putting-up and selling malt extract. While the product was not new, the brand was novel; so too was the American approach Burroughs had adopted to sell Kepler goods as if they were ethical products, calling directly on medical men and on chemists and druggists to whom adver-tising was exclusively directed. In 1881 three travellers were selling Kepler goods which may have amounted to between one-fifth and one-third of all BW&Co.'s sales at that time. KMEC sales, therefore, eased cash flow for the parent company. It was not long, however, before KMEC was the source of severe financial burdens for BW&Co.

The acquisition of the Kepler Malt Extract Company

From the beginning of Burroughs' involvement with the Kepler enterprise other directors, notably Lockwood who held the patent to the extract process, had suspected him of duplicity. Friction revolved around payments made by the KMEC to BW&Co. The Memorandum of Association showed that originally the agreement was for one-third of the royalty income to be allocated each to Burroughs and Kelley as managers, plus a 5 per cent commission based on sales. SMB&Co. was to receive £125 as annual payment for use of the Snow Hill premises to which the mixing and getting up of the malt extract was removed in 1880.[103] Soon after Wellcome joined Burroughs in partnership, he succeeded Burroughs as general manager of the KMEC. This released Burroughs to travel overseas although he continued as a director.[104] Within months, however, Lockwood accused BW&Co. of loading disproportionate costs on the KMEC for the putting-up of goods by the partners' employees and of charging to the KMEC 50 per cent of the salaries of *ten* travellers. Lockwood complained to the chairman of the KMEC that such payments had not been authorised by the board. His request to be given access to the relevant data from the Kepler accounts kept at Snow Hill was refused by Burroughs and Wellcome. Subsequently, however (whether with or without the partners' approval is impossible to tell), Sudlow, practically involved in the production of the extract, prepared figures for Lockwood. These confirmed Lockwood's suspicions.[105] The data revealed that the putting-up costs for Kepler were almost twice those for Hazeline and Fellows' preparations, and more than twice the cost for Wyeth's Beef and Iron Wine, the other best-selling product. A parallel issue was the number of returns to the KMEC made by customers. The data Sudlow showed to Lockwood suggested that the problem of explaining returns lay not in quality, as Burroughs had alleged. He interpreted the data as showing that the explanation for excessive returns was the high rate of breakages and imperfect corking. Lockwood accused the partners of deceit and suspended royalty payments pending investigations.[106] Burroughs continued to insist that it was the formula which was the problem, that the extract was prone to decompose, and that this defect had only been overcome by the partners' introduction of salicylic acid into the formula to achieve stability. He told the board that he agreed with Kepler's competitors that Lockwood's 'secret process' of producing the extract was fictitious and of inferior quality. He maintained that it was remarkable that profit was being made at all and that it was only because of the modifications which he and his partner had made together with the careful supervision of the process conducted at Snow Hill, that 'thorough success' had been effected.[107] These exchanges were concurrent with the emergence of a further problem for Lockwood when the Malt Duty was removed in 1881. In effect, removal eliminated the advantage of securing the malt supply from Lockwood's plant in Jersey at a time when, partly as a result of the suspension of the duty, competition with Kepler goods was likely to increase.[108]

One month later, Lockwood wrote to the two partners saying that he was 'Furiously angry about your scheme of trying to obtain all the shares in the company'. He accused them of having met one half of its operating expenses from Kepler revenue and of turning other shareholders against Lockwood. He also referred to the 'grasping spirit which has been constantly shown in separately varying the contract to your advantage'.[109] Before Burroughs left England on his travels in October 1881, he sought legal advice from Augustine Birrell on how to terminate the agreement between the company and Lockwood, thereby ridding the partners of the obligations imposed by the original agreement. Birrell's opinion was that destroying the agreement was not straightforward, as the promoters had had the opportunity to examine Lockwood's product at the time of the agreement as well as the opportunity to be advised properly in that respect. Moreover, he observed astutely: 'However worthless these compounds may be it has not been impossible hitherto at all events to reap very large profits by their sale'. Should the majority shareholders achieve ownership of the company, the new owners would not be bound to obtain malt extract from Lockwood, nor to confine themselves to manufacture using his 'secret process'. The view was also expressed that the management fee and royalty agreement originally negotiated between Lockwood and Burroughs could be transferred to the partnership.[110] The vital question of the ownership of the Kepler trademark would remain. Importantly, unlike the patent, it would have no expiry date. The course Birrell recommended was a voluntary winding up of the company.[111]

Following Burroughs' departure, Wellcome was left to implement the agreed plan. This was to detach the Kepler brand, identified with the patent process and the name of the company, from its increasingly troublesome inventor. The plan was also to acquire ownership of the company and therefore the trademark brand name, after which an eventual winding up in due course would leave BW&Co. as owners of the brand. The proposal was the outright purchase of the patent for a payment of £2,000 to Lockwood ('rather than to a lawyer'), one half in cash, and the rest in bills over three years. An outflanking move made at the same time was an approach to other directors with a view to securing their shares in the business.[112] Wellcome struck the deal on behalf of the partnership which involved a payment of £9 per share for the Kepler business, including all stock in the pipeline from the Condensed Beer Co. The other directors having already accepted the offer, Kelley and Lockwood were the last to capitulate. From Ceylon, Burroughs wrote to his young partner: 'I am delighted that you are going to get rid of Lockwood on such favourable terms ... I wonder how you brought about this happy conclusion'.[113] Burroughs congratulated Wellcome: 'I am absolutely satisfied, would have been willing to take less even than this amount if Kelley had not in past times shown some "squeezing proclivities" towards us'.[114] Wellcome's relief that the outcome was successful was evident in his reply to Burroughs: '... must be watchful to safeguard against such entanglements in future ... shall feel younger and happier man when business is clear of complications and stock companies.'[115] Throughout Burroughs' lifetime, BW&Co. remained a private partnership and after his death, a personally owned private company.

The purchase was effected in two stages. The first occurred in December 1881 and was a private transaction by which Burroughs' shareholding increased to 168 shares and Wellcome's to 67 (rising to 132). Lockwood undertook not to manufacture any medical preparation or extract or to use the name Kepler.[116] In 1882 Sudlow (who as the general manager of BW&Co. from 1880, now also replaced Wellcome as manager of the KMEC) received 25 shares to qualify as a director, though all Kepler shares were held in trust by the partnership.[117] The KMEC continued to be operated as part of BW&Co. until the second stage of integration when it was finally wound up in 1909. The Kepler trademark, identified with malt extract, passed directly into the ownership of BW&Co.[118]

The pressure on the company's financial liquidity during the process of acquisition occurred at a time when, already alarmed, Sudlow alerted Wellcome to the adverse effect on the company's day to day working capital requirements imposed by incurring heavy liabilities on the Kepler account arising from 'heavy purchase of the malt shares'.[119] Liabilities on bills for purchasing the Kepler business totalled £4,000. This was at a time when additional space for bottling Kepler products led to the occupation of more premises in Cock Lane in 1881 and the renting of an additional floor in the Snow Hill building in 1882. Rumours of the partnership's financial weakness circulated in London.[120] Wellcome expressed the frustration created by events: '... we have worked like dogs over here & acquired far smaller results than we might have gained in America. The English people as a rule detest progress & novelty & whatever we have won here has been by persistent fighting.'[121]

Investment, growth and development

Expansion required space.[122] Burroughs hankered after obtaining what he referred to as 'the "Boss" premises of the drug business in London',[123] a goal which he thought could be achieved by the acquisition of a large new building at the corner of Snow Hill which would accommodate manufacturing and at the same time provide an elegant central city retailing and dispensing store. Wellcome was more cautious; he was concerned that a factory for malt production would probably require a £3,000 investment.[124] Using their personal shares in the KMEC as collateral, the partners obtained the loan of £1,000 at five per cent from Bishop, referred to above.[125] Burroughs made his Central Railroad shares available for Wellcome to sell.[126] Given limited resources, Wellcome persuaded Burroughs to opt for the cheaper option of a factory in a country location on a site south of the Thames at Bell Lane Wharf, Wandsworth. It consisted of buildings, a private dock for barges, and an abundant supply of fresh water from the River Wandle. Taken on a six year lease for £900 in the first year rising to £1,245 in the second,[127] this compared favourably with the annual rental, asked for the Snow Hill premises, of £1,800.[128] Ultimately, the narrow difference between the two rents suggests that the facilities offered by the Wandsworth plant

FIGURE 1.11
Exterior of BW&Co.'s (later the Wellcome Foundation's) headquarters, Snow Hill. Acquired in 1884, this building remained the company's headquarters until it was destroyed by a bomb in 1941.

FIGURE 1.12
The interior
of BW&Co.'s
headquarters
at Snow Hill
(from *Chemist
& Druggist*,
25 Jan. 1888),
showing a
prominent
model of the
Statue of
Liberty.

persuaded Wellcome of their superiority for the purpose of manufacture and distribution where 'the soot and smoke of London' would not contaminate tablet manufacture planned to begin in March 1883.[129]

On the move to Wandsworth, Kepler Manufacturing and Packing, Tabloid Manufacturing and Packing became separate departments. The functions of accounting, buying, sales, label printing and advertising remained at Snow Hill, as did leather working. Tablet production continued at Wandsworth until 1889, when a substantially larger factory was established at Dartford.[130] In addition to the acquisition of the Wandsworth lease in 1883 was the lease of the Snow Hill building so coveted by Burroughs. This decision was the result of Wellcome's change of mind which may have been influenced by securing slightly more favourable terms than previously offered, that is, for £900 in the first year and subsequently for an annual rental of £1,245 for 21 years.[131]

Other pressures on liquidity were also building up, not least due to the large purchases of cod liver oil, the price of which was rising.[132] Sudlow advised that a further £2,000 would be needed for expenditure on additional plant and equipment if production were to expand.[133] In 1884 Burroughs suggested capital for expansion could be raised if Wellcome were to increase his share of the equity in the business by borrowing from his friends and former employers, McKesson & Robbins, who knew and trusted him. An alternative was to float a company, limiting the issuance of shares to 'certain employees, drug houses, those in a position to push goods, and parties we co-operate with in this country selling their goods'.[134] These suggestions heralded the end of the first five years of the partnership agreement which,

despite Burroughs' musings about restructuring, was extended for a further
10 years with an option for either partner to terminate at the end of five and
the remaining partner to purchase. The renewed partnership agreement of
1885 increased the capital to £14,500, of which £10,500 was attributable to
Burroughs who also received a proportionate share of net profits. Reinvested

profit, which continued to be the main source of capital, was treated as a 5 per cent loan.[135]

During the early years of the business, growth in sales was not accompanied by high profitability. Burroughs' claim made in 1884, that 'business never was in such a promising and profitable condition' may have been true, though profits were low.[136] Wellcome's reference to the business in 1889, as having 'constantly increased and is very prosperous',[137] is not borne out by the accounts. Not until 1885 did average net profits exceed £2,000 or the ratio to sales average more than 5 per cent.[138] The figure rose to 7.8 per cent in 1885 and to a peak of 11.93 per cent in 1886,[139] but fell back to below 7 per cent in 1887 and 1888, and to only 2.7 per cent (explained by the disruption caused by the move to Dartford) in 1889.[140] Sales revenue, however, grew rapidly, rising from £52,184 in 1885 to almost £100,000 by 1888/89.[141] This expansion prompted Sudlow to warn the partners, only three years after moving into the Wandsworth premises, that already the factory lacked sufficient capacity to meet growing demand.[142] Heeding Sudlow's opinion, but against Wellcome's preference for the erection of temporary buildings

FIGURE 1.15 BW&Co.'s premises in Wandsworth, announcing their 'factory and laboratories', c. mid-1880s.

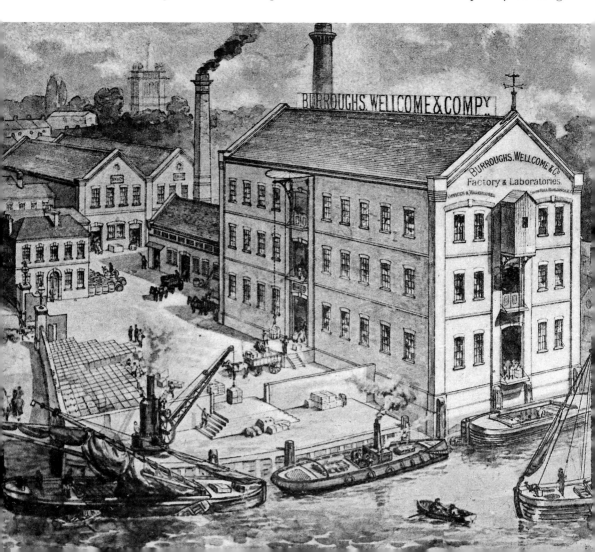

at Wandsworth, in Wellcome's absence in 1888, Burroughs instigated his own search for larger premises. The result was the purchase for £5,000, at Burroughs' personal expense, of the freehold of the former paper-making Phoenix Mills at Dartford.[143] The initial arrangement was that Burroughs would lease the premises to the partnership for 49 years for a £250 annual rental,[144] though seven years after purchase in 1893, the buildings were sold to the company at an independently valued price of £18,500. Meanwhile, again contrary to Wellcome's wishes, Burroughs issued instructions for a new building to be erected on the Dartford site.[145] Operating at full capacity within four years, expansion at Dartford was necessary to accommodate the continuing growth of the business following the transition of BW&Co. from being primarily a trading enterprise to being a manufacturing business.

Four factors explain the diversification into manufacturing. The first has its origins in the period before the partnership was formed and resulted from connections with the KMEC. Following the appointment of Burroughs as managing director of the KMEC, the transfer of the mixing and bottling of Kepler products to Snow Hill in 1879 had moved SMB&Co. on from being purely an agency to a processing, packaging, and sales enterprise. When the partnership was formed in 1880, those arrangements continued until the acquisition of the KMEC in 1881, when BW&Co. began to add manufacture to the processing and sale of Kepler goods. The repeal of the 1881 Malt Act provided a further incentive to develop the manufacture of malt extract by replacing the hitherto cheaper supplies from Jersey with English sources, henceforward free of duty. The second reason for adding manufacture to trading relates to the details of the agency agreement Burroughs had reached with Wyeth Bros. regarding compressed medicines. The third was the decision by the Commissioners of Customs and Excise to enforce the 1812 Stamp Act as it affected the production and sale of medicines. The fourth was the growth of competition. Each requires elaboration.

FIGURE 1.16 Storage warehouse, Hosier Lane, London EC (*Chemist & Druggist*, 30 May 1891).

Production and laboratory experimentation with Kepler Malt Extract; researching for quality

The production of cod liver oil and malt extract consisted of several processes. They involved mashing through a large cast iron vessel with mixing rakes

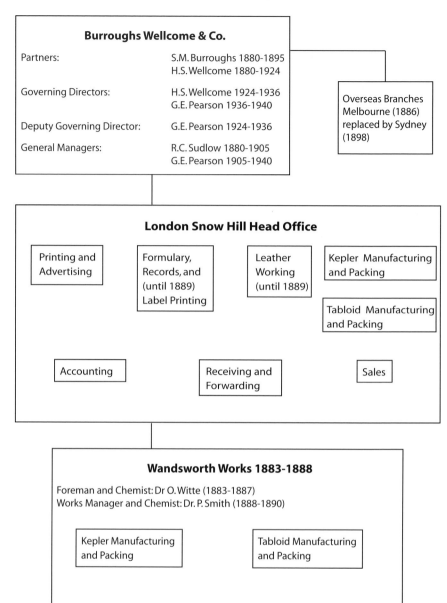

Burroughs Wellcome & Co.

Partners:	S.M. Burroughs 1880-1895
	H.S. Wellcome 1880-1924
Governing Directors:	H.S. Wellcome 1924-1936
	G.E. Pearson 1936-1940
Deputy Governing Director:	G.E. Pearson 1924-1936
General Managers:	R.C. Sudlow 1880-1905
	G.E. Pearson 1905-1940

Overseas Branches
Melbourne (1886)
replaced by Sydney
(1898)

London Snow Hill Head Office

Printing and
Advertising

Formulary,
Records, and
(until 1889)
Label Printing

Leather
Working
(until 1889)

Kepler Manufacturing
and Packing

Tabloid Manufacturing
and Packing

Accounting

Receiving and
Forwarding

Sales

Wandsworth Works 1883-1888

Foreman and Chemist: Dr O. Witte (1883-1887)
Works Manager and Chemist: Dr. P. Smith (1888-1890)

Kepler Manufacturing
and Packing

Tabloid Manufacturing
and Packing

FIGURE 1.17
BW&Co.
organisational
structure,
1880–89.

and slotted metal plates to run off the watery extract of malt leaving spent barley grains behind. However, the quantity and quality of malt produced in the mash-tun were dictated by temperatures and times taken in mashing and evaporation, in the process of concentrating the extract.[146] The low temperature evaporating process was the key to quality, taste, and colour. Finally, cod liver oil was mixed in pans with the extract and flavouring to produce an emulsion.[147] Marketability depended on the degree to which it was possible to ensure a sufficient level and stability of maltin (and therefore nutritive value) and consistency of quality. Flavour, colour, and density were other important attributes affecting palatability; the first depended on successful removal of fish taste, the others on achieving a liquid which was pale and exhibited a relatively low viscosity. Ensuring the extract's keeping quality was regarded as a priority with respect to the partners' ambition to develop markets in Australasia, India, and the Far East.[148]

Since early in 1881 Dr Otto Witte, a German chemist, had been employed as foreman.[149] Charged with the responsibility for quality control and improvement, by 1883, Wellcome referred to Witte as the firm's 'valued chemist'[150] whom he dispatched to the US, sworn to secrecy regarding BW&Co.'s practice of buying most malt extract from suppliers, and with instructions to learn as much as possible about American best practice in production and packaging, specifically the cork-cutting machines of McKesson & Robbins. Witte was given authority to purchase such equipment and supplies he considered necessary to improve production and boost sales.[151] On his return in 1884, new, larger, and more costly presses and condensing apparatus, designed to facilitate production in greater volume and obtain higher yield, were installed at the Wandsworth factory. Witte succeeded in increasing malt production by 50 per cent in 1886 compared with the previous year.[152] However, solidification of the product brought complaints from buyers. Wellcome accused Witte of making unauthorised alterations to the production process with the effect of 'disgracing us in every market', incurring costs through wastage, and resulting in minimal profitability.[153] Curiously, publicity in the medical press continued to be favourable towards the company. In 1887 the *Lancet* described KME as, 'the best known in this country, the largest used extract for a tonic, for dyspepsia, consumption, and wasting diseases'. The *London Medical Record* described it as 'unequalled … the extract which every physician prescribes'.[154] The *Lancet* referred to the long search for a true solution of cod liver oil and malt and to the many previous attempts which had been abandoned. BW&Co. was credited with having solved the problem.[155]

Witte returned to the US in 1887 when Wellcome instructed him to purchase more equipment to improve the quality and consistency of the Kepler products.[156] Unknown to Wellcome, Witte joined Burroughs to investigate setting up a factory there, an occurrence which on discovery intensified Wellcome's distrust of Witte (and of Burroughs). Worse was to come. In 1887 Witte was dismissed after he was discovered to have been offering BW&Co.'s secretly constructed tabletting machines to potential competitors.[157] His replacement was Dr A. P. Smith whose tenure in charge of the factory and 'research' was limited to months after he submitted a confused report on the biological activity of enzymes based on inappropriate tests. Furious at his own serious failure of judgement in appointing Smith, Wellcome was anxious to conceal the matter from the outside world.[158] However, on discovering that, without consultation, Burroughs had allowed Smith to sign cheques and draw on the firm's account, Smith was dismissed.[159] To changes in management personnel prompted by these dismissals were added others resulting from a reorganisation following the removal of production to Dartford in 1889 and the diversification into the production of chemicals.

The Stamp Act and the threat to the trade in American proprietary medicines

The decision to commence the manufacture of compressed medicine occurred in part as a reaction against the terms of the original agreement made by Burroughs with the Wyeths. This was the subject of a letter from Burroughs to Wellcome in 1882.

> Our mistake was to introduce them [Wyeth goods] into England as Wyeth's. We might continue to use Wyeth's name for 2 or 3 years and gradually drop it altogether if we don't we are making ourselves a catspaw. But if we are continuing to pay 20% let it be understood that we will make the goods ourselves as soon as it suits us to do so ... If we put them up in London there is no more necessity of having anything about 'manufactured in the US' on the goods. The London address should appear. And this would be better for the colonial trade too.[160]

The immediate plan was to purchase Wyeth's rights to elixirs, syrups, and iron pills,[161] and subsequently to manufacture tablets. This letter, written while Burroughs was in Australia, followed a lengthy attempt to renegotiate terms with John Wyeth who had proposed supplying preparations at 25 per cent above manufacturing costs, though he had refused to enter into a legal agreement, insisting 'trust is the key'.[162] Evidently, this did not exist so far as Burroughs was concerned. Following a visit to the Wyeths, Wellcome also expressed distrust, warning Burroughs not to succumb to the Wyeths' soft soaping, describing them as 'gushing and kind, but [with] the same old greedy spirit'.[163]

Dissatisfaction with the Wyeth agreement became a matter of serious concern at the same time that pressure on BW&Co. was exerted from another source in the form of the Commissioners of Customs and Excise based in Somerset House. To add to the difficulties resulting from a deteriorating relationship with the Wyeths in the US, the partners began to be affected by a change in policy in Britain. Beginning in the early 1880s, officials at Somerset House began to extend the applicability of the 1812 Stamp Act as it affected medicines which led to an intensification of efforts to detect and punish evaders.[164] Initially intended to prevent the import of quack medicines,[165] the Medicines Stamp Act of 1812 imposed an *ad valorem* duty on medicines adding approximately 12 to 15 per cent on retail prices. Henceforward, all imported drugs were deemed liable to stamp duty.[166] However, the Act exempted pure drugs: remedies 'known, admitted and approved in the prevention, cure or relief of any disorder, malady, or ailment'. The complaint by Wellcome and other manufacturers of such 'known, admitted and approved' medicines was that the exemption embodied in the Act had not been applied.[167] The justification of the Commissioners of Customs and Excise appears to have been based on a perception that medicines that were advertised were patent medicines, rather than, as the manufacturers and leading retailers were to argue, proprietary medicines which met the 'known remedy' criterion. Not until 1903, however, did the Commissioners accept the equation and the exemption, though only on condition that labels disclosed formulae and included a disclaimer of proprietary rights.[168] This marked a clearer distinction between quack patent medicine and proprietary medicines advertised by brand to the medical profession and to the trade.

Meanwhile, in 1882, Wellcome's argument (to be employed repeatedly and each time at length) was to the effect that the compressed medicines imported by BW&Co. were for the use of the medical profession and had not been advertised to the public in any way. Persistence by Wellcome in pressing Somerset House succeeded in securing a concession. In September 1882, officials agreed to the sale of compressed goods imported from America without a stamp 'for a short time' but only on condition that they should be manufactured in England as soon as possible.[169] Meanwhile, although a conditional exception had been made in the case of BW&Co.'s compressed goods, Somerset House proceeded to apply the Stamp Act to other imported proprietary as well as patent medicines. In 1883 Somerset House filed information regarding the sale of Hazeline ointment without a stamp. In defence, Wellcome explained to the solicitor acting for Customs that Hazeline consisted simply of the volatile principle distilled from the bark of Witch hazel. The spirit present was not active but merely a vehicle and preservative without which the product would decompose. If the presence of spirit placed Hazeline outside the category of simple drugs, then that objection applied equally to all chemically prepared drugs, including the active principles of plant extracts that were often produced in the form of salts or other chemical derivatives. It was not a patent or secret medicine and the procedure for making it was well known; it was not advertised to the public but only to medical practitioners and the wrapper contained only quotations from medical authorities extolling the virtues of the drug.[170] The last point was relevant because the duties were payable not only on foreign goods but also on all domestic or prepared drugs to which were attached any therapeutical notes.[171]

In 1883 Somerset House officials finally accepted the sustained repudiation of the nature of Hazeline, on condition that 'Burroughs' should be removed from the label. Wellcome conveyed the message to Burroughs, expressing relief: '... must thank our lucky stars we have got off so lightly'; even the authorities congratulated Wellcome on his 'ingenious and exhaustive defences'.[172] The application by Somerset House of a newly found vigilance in pursuit of infringers of the Act, induced in Burroughs an inclination to 'lie awake at nights fearing or dreading arrest in the morning'.[173] In 1884 McKesson & Robbins's capsulated pills were placed under order by the Board of Inland Revenue. Again, the arguments in defence of the sale of well-known drugs based on formulae contained in the British Pharmacopeia but prepared in an improved form for easier and more effective administration were rehearsed at length. The point was also made to the solicitor mounting the case against the firm:

> if compelled to stamp we may as well give up the agency, because members of the medical profession will not continue to use medicines with a government STAMP. English ASSISTANTS WOULD BE THROWN OUT OF WORK AND GOVERNMENT WOULD SECURE NO EXTRA REVENUE.[174]

He explained that the medical profession associated stamps with patent medicines and for that reason never prescribed *stamped* medicines. Hence, the threat to BW&Co.[175] The letter concluded by pleading for time should the case made in defence be rejected and the stamp requirement enforced: 'Burroughs Wellcome will get manufacture going as soon as possible, but some delay is inevitable as machinery has to be constructed which is quite elaborate and costly.'[176] Privately the partners despaired, accusing the laws of 'this stupid country [which] step in and rob us of our earned reward'.[177]

In 1884, the firm received a visit from the London Central District Supervisor. He reported that a sample of the company's Beef and Iron Wine had been analysed and found to contain spirit. Sudlow drew Burroughs' attention to this and to a related 'sudden awakening of the Inland Revenue to various preparations of beef wine now in the market, especially as regards the necessity of a wine licence for them.'[178] In fact, samples had been submitted to Somerset House when the product was first produced, to which the response had been that a licence was not required so long as the proportion of iron content was maintained.[179] It is hardly surprising that the partners felt embattled when in 1887, labels on cascara sagrada tablets were objected to because they were interpreted as claiming to be 'the most effective remedy' for constipation. The partners denied this, arguing that the company's precise description of the tablets as 'efficient' bore no relationship to the word 'curative' to which officials had objected.[180] The pursuit of this case was compounded by the Revenue's subterfuge (not dissimilar to that employed many times later by the partners in defence of their trademarks) which involved 'deception and misrepresentation', whereby multiple bottles of tablets of the firm's cascara sagarada were purchased by an official passing himself off as a member of the trade. Added to this, despite repeated correspondence with and visits to Somerset House, the partners could not discover the grounds on which the Revenue intended to impose a penalty for the sale. Personal inquiries from the company's office were described as having been treated with rudeness, offensiveness, and humiliating behaviour.[181] Wellcome's prominent role in orchestrating the campaign to exclude legitimate (proprietary) chemical and pharmaceutical products from the tax, strongly supported by the leading medical journals, lies beyond the scope of this study.[182]

Competition, costs, and the transition to manufacturing compressed medicines

The fourth factor explaining the investment in manufacturing was the impact of competition from American and European as well as British producers in the rapidly growing market for compressed goods. This development rendered the terms of agreement between BW&Co. and the Wyeths increasingly burdensome. The partners sought both to escape the attention of the Commissioners of Customs and Excise resulting from the importation of Wyeth's compressed medicines and to reduce costs to remain competitive. Wyeth's compressed medicines sold by BW&Co. found increasing difficulty in competing with lower priced goods then flooding the British market. The implication was that the arrangement proposed could offer only a short-term advantage which the royalty payments would nullify. The acquisition of the Wandsworth site in 1883 to accommodate enlarged production of malt extract proved to be timely and within months a new factory was erected which also included space that would facilitate the manufacture of compressed tablets.[183]

The argument repeated by Burroughs to the Wyeths many times, even before 1880 when he was a sole trader, was that he had invested heavily (especially through advertising estimated to account for one-half the cost) in creating a demand for Wyeth's goods in Britain and that an adequate return was justified. The same points were emphasized by Burroughs and Wellcome from 1880, also arguing that, unlike in America where the new machines had been patented, the Wyeths had not sought patent protection in Europe, an oversight which rendered their machine vulnerable to imitation.[184] The Wyeths did not object to local manufacture, a potential route for cost reductions available to BW&Co. benefiting from machines purchased at cost, but they insisted on the payment of royalties on tablet production in addition.[185] In Burroughs' absence in January 1883, Wellcome negotiated a provisional agreement with the Wyeths. In return for providing machinery at cost and exclusive rights to manufacture and supply tablets to all countries outside the Americas, the partners would pay a 20 per cent royalty (dubbed by Burroughs as 'tribute') on the cost of each tablet produced.[186] Burroughs remained opposed to the royalty on goods manufactured in England and urged termination of the agreement, whereas Wellcome objected to any such initiative unless the Wyeths first indicated their wish to withdraw.[187] In 1884 the partners proposed that the Wyeths would 'forgo' the tablet trade in return for supplying BW&Co. with fluid extracts.[188] Finally, John Wyeth refused to agree to outright sale of machinery without an agreement on royalty payments and expressed complete indifference to his firm's connections with BW&Co.[189]

During the summer of 1883 the partners commenced production of compressed pills using the primitive Brockedon punch and dies already installed in the new factory at Wandsworth. State of the art machinery was soon obtained from the US. Sam Fairchild, a Philadelphia drug manufacturer, business associate, and longstanding friend of Wellcome arranged the transactions secretly to conceal the identity of the purchaser from the increasing number of competitors entering the market for compressed goods.[190] These included American and German firms in addition to English fine chemical manufacturers who imported steam-powered machinery. They sold compressed goods at prices substantially below those at which BW&Co. could supply Wyeth's products. The partners viewed this development (led by English producers, Allen & Hanburys and Maws Sons & Thompson) as 'the greatest danger that has yet arisen.'[191] In 1883 Wellcome discovered that German makers were supplying compressed goods in bulk at substantially lower prices directly to some of BW&Co.'s regular customers who boxed them and promoted those instead of Wyeth's.[192] In 1884 Burroughs summed up the market situation: 'medics think other goods just as good as ours and cannot advise patients to get our tablets at double the price. Will have to halve prices in some instances or lose our trade'.[193] The threat to the partners was particularly serious because compressed goods had yielded relatively high profits, and competitors were aware of this.[194]

The strategy adopted to counter the problem of competition and diminishing profit margins consisted of three elements: selling in bulk and cutting prices; product development and promotion; and more efficient production. The first two elements are examined below.[195] Improved technology was part of the solution. Through substantial expenditure and the skill of the company's engineers in the design and construction of machinery, machinery of a superior kind became an important method of countering competition.[196]

Dr Witte was closely involved in managing the development of a prototype tablet machine, an operation so secret that in order to prevent any single engineer learning how the new model operated, Witte was entrusted to place various parts of the machinery into the hands of different men. In 1888, one such machine, capable of producing 600 high-quality tablets every minute, was patented worldwide.[197] This technological breakthrough, which strengthened the company's competitive position (by which time the trade in Wyeth's goods had dwindled to insignificance), coincided with the complete breakdown of negotiations with the Wyeth brothers. Their machines could not match the productivity and quality achieved by those being used by BW&Co. In the winter of 1888 the agreement ended at 30 days' notice.[198] By that time, too, the British company was producing tablets which, having already competed successfully with Wyeth goods in the home market, were about to be marketed in the US.[199] On termination of the contract Wellcome expressed his preference for not entering into competition with them in America. There the company had registered a patent for its new 'rapid-acting compressing machines', but had offered the Wyeths first refusal of the machine for use in the US. He added: 'As there has been considerable expense, expect you will be prepared to give a fair price for it'.[200] Wellcome concluded: 'You have been severe and unjust in your strictures against us, but [we] shall not cease to hold you in friendly regard and will be happy to place ourselves at your disposal'.[201] With agreed modifications, the original contract between Burroughs and the Wyeths, dating from 1878, appears to have survived the hostilities. In 1893 the two businesses appear to have resumed commercial relations, to be on the verge of a legal dispute over territory and infringement of trademarks, and to be discussing re-negotiation. This was symptomatic of the creative tension that had characterised the relationship between the two partners and the Wyeths from the beginning, but which ultimately failed.[202]

Within the first decade of the partnership's existence, the transition from trading to manufacture was marked by three related phases in the characteristics of the business. In the first phase, between 1880 and 1882 the partners enjoyed a virtual monopoly of the sale of compressed goods which Burroughs regarded as having been highly profitable. The second phase, between 1882 and 1884, saw the beginnings of competition, after which a third phase to 1887 was one in which competitors entered the market in considerable numbers. Monopoly and near-monopoly prices and profits were competed away, the new lower level of market prices compelling the partners to adjust, to match those of competitors and to accept lower profit margins. The significance of this development, driven primarily by mechanisation and low entry costs into the market for medicines and health foods, is an increase in the relative importance of marketing as the key to effective competition and profitability. Technical change and investment in buildings, plant, and equipment continued to be important, but these were open to any firm commanding financial resources. In a highly competitive market which had accompanied the evolution of 'modern'[203] or 'newer

FIGURE 1.18

The unicorn was the logo of BW&Co. and the Wellcome Foundation from 1908 until 1995. It is likely Wellcome was influenced in his choice of trademark by the popular legend that the unicorn horn possessed medicinal or magical properties, especially as an antidote to or preventive of poison. He gave clear instructions to his designers that he wanted 'delicacy and refinement, and grace with virility and verve'.

This design, by Mr Scobie of the College of Heralds, eventually met with Wellcome's approval, although initially he had remarked that, 'the horn is not quite as perfect as it was. The shaping of the upper part of the right hind leg is not quite satisfactory and the hooves require very slight modifications; the chest is a little exaggerated'. From *In Pursuit of Excellence* (Wellcome Foundation, 1980).

pharmacy' in Britain [204] in the 1880s, the 'creation of demand' had been the objective of Burroughs from 1878, and was subsequently pursued by his partner from 1880. This had been facilitated by the sheer innovative characteristics of American compressed goods and the relatively novel health food in the form of KME. During the second phase of market development, however, when novelty was reduced by the process of imitative investment by competitors, the process of establishing distinctive firm-specific advantages to secure monopoly or market niche through distinctive differences became both more complex and more important. That process involved decisions affecting product range and diversification, the establishment of brands and brand defence, advertising and public relations policy, the extension of American methods of selling medicines and health foods, treatment of chemists and druggists, and the building of reputation. The partners' success in those respects is crucial to any explanation of how, from small beginnings and within a decade, the partners achieved a place among the leaders of the trade in Britain and, as acknowledged by the *Chemist & Druggist*, an incomparable worldwide reputation. These marketing strategies are the subject of the next chapter.

CHAPTER TWO

Americanisation of the British drug trade: product innovation and 'creating a demand'

Products and agency agreements

The products sold by SMB&Co. formed the basis for the product range offered by BW&Co. in 1880, to which were added the ovid-shaped sugar-coated pills supplied from the US by McKesson and Robbins through the agency agreement negotiated with Wellcome.[1] Unlike the agreement with the Wyeths, McKesson & Robbins's agency rights (personal to Wellcome) in Britain were shared with Allen & Hanburys, Godfrey & Cooke, and Charles Symes & Co.[2] However, the high hopes for the commercial success of these pills entertained by Wellcome were dealt a serious blow. Independent tests organised by a group of Philadelphia manufacturers in 1883 on the quality of available compressed goods recorded an unfavourable verdict on those of McKesson & Robbins.[3] When three years later the initial agreement with BW&Co. lapsed there was no renewal.[4] Unfavourable publicity to which was added a lacklustre response in the market was the context in which even Wellcome admitted that the agreement had been unprofitable for both parties.[5]

Wyeth's compressed goods fared much better in both respects. Between 1880 and 1884, several chemical substances hitherto offered by the trade in the form only of elixirs were supplemented or replaced by compressed tablets. Wyeth's soluble-compressed hypodermic tablets were added to BW&Co.'s range in 1881. They consisted variously of morphine, strychnine, and atropine sulphate, for which was claimed 'absolute accuracy of dose, ready and entire solubility,' and 'perfect preservation'.[6] Compressed tablets containing pepsin, bismuth, and quinine were added to the list. These supplemented the growing list of products for which BW&Co. became agents for their mainly American suppliers: Fellows' Compound Syrup of Hypophosphites, Murray & Lanman's Florida Water, Lundborg's perfumes, and Murdoch's liquid foods (meat extracts). Agreements permitted sales in

Britain and in selected countries in Continental Europe, Australasia, Asia, and Africa.[7]

The most important of these additional agreements were those with Fairchild Brothers & Foster, manufacturing chemists of New York, whose principal, Sam Fairchild, was an old friend of Wellcome, and with the German firm of Benno Jaffe Darmstaedter (BJD). Beginning in 1884, BW&Co. secured an exclusive agency outside the American continent for the sale of Fairchild's digestive preparations which consisted mainly of pepsins and pancreatic extracts. The agreement also included a provision entitling BW&Co. to benefit from future improvements in Fairchild's products.[8] The connection with this firm proved to be enduring and profitable by introducing BW&Co.'s products into the US market, and because Sam Fairchild was alert to and became personally involved in the defence of the company's brands in that country.

BW&Co.'s commercial alliance with Benno Jaffe Darmstaedter began in 1886 when the English company secured a sole agency agreement to use and sell Lanoline, manufactured from pure wool fat intended for pharmaceutical, cosmetic, or toilet purposes. The agreement applied to sales in Britain and the colonies. Protected by a patent registered in England in 1882,[9] the German company owned the Lanoline trademark. Because of adverse effects of competition that included infringement of the patent, this agency arrangement proved to be less profitable and less enduring than that applying to Fairchild digestive preparations.

Products, brands and markets

Product diversification was not only secured by increasing the number of agency agreements. Simultaneously, a process of internal development was aimed at increasing the proportion of own brand products. During the early years, as the senior partner in the business, the extravagantly imaginative Burroughs was the most prolific source of ideas for new products or suggestions for novel uses for existing products. For example, the 1880 trade mark for Burroughs' Hazeline (also marketed briefly by a wholly owned Burroughs 'company' of the same name) was listed in the perfumery and toilet articles section of fine chemicals.[10] However, uses had to be specified in order to define a distinct product. Travelling through New Zealand in 1882, Burroughs discovered that Hazeline had been found cooling to the scalp and that when used by one young lady as a hair restorer had produced a fine head of hair within months; '... if it will do this', he wrote to Wellcome, 'every tin of Hazeline will sell. You bet!'[11] He urged Wellcome to persuade friendly doctors in London to experiment on patients with a view to marketing a Hazeline hair restorer. He also proposed that Hazeline should be presented as a treatment for piles and (perhaps by association) suggested extension of the product line by introducing a Hazeline Toilet Paper. With the addition of borax and glycerine he declared 'we should reasonably make a small fortune on a Hazeline soap for toilet, bath, and shaving purposes, perhaps scented with eucalyptus which is rapidly coming into use as an antiseptic' Hazeline for veterinary use was another suggestion.[12] An extract of lime juice, absorbent lint, essence of eucalyptus, 'tooth tablets', and 'tea berry' were among other products for which Burroughs thought profitable markets might be developed, though only one of which was taken further.[13] Typically, Wellcome's response was either silent or sceptical, drawing attention to the slim profit margins likely to result from such ventures and invariably, in those cases where development did proceed, only after questioning feasibility and counselling caution. In the event, after initial scepticism, essence of eucalyptus, for which Burroughs had detected large interest in Australia, won Wellcome's support as Eucalyptine. The 1884 trade mark listed it as a chemical preparation for medical, pharmaceutical, sanitary, and veterinary purposes, including as an antiseptic.[14] In India, Burroughs became excited about the prospects for phosphates from which he thought 'you can make a fortune ... There are so many temperance people here and nerve tonics are also much indicated. With an article like Phosphade you can gradually get a monopoly of such drinks',[15] though he thought that the flavour of the company's phosphates required improvement, perhaps by purchasing another company's formula.[16] From the beginning, Burroughs had been acutely aware of the importance of establishing a perception among potential consumers of distinctiveness for the firm's products. In 1878 he had secured trade mark protection for the name 'tablet' to be applied to Wyeth's products [17] because he felt that the British public and the medical profession particularly associated 'pills' with patent medicines. As a 'non-descriptive term of compressed drugs in the BI-convex form',[18] however, 'tablet' quickly revealed a vulnerability to international competition by a 'siege of imitators' at home and overseas, especially following the Patents, Designs, and Trademarks Act of 1883.[19] Establishing trademarks for products had been central to Burroughs' business before 1880 and continued to be so under the partnership. Some continued to be sold or introduced under the Burroughs name, some in Wellcome's and others in the name of the company, though from 1880 all were treated as if owned by the latter. Some were registered under a different company which was a fiction in all but name, presumably to conceal altogether the association with BW&Co. in certain markets, the Hazeline Co. and the Malt Jelly Co. (both in 1880), and the perfumery of the Bonita Sachet Co., registered in 1881, for example. First registered as a trademark in London in May 1879, by 1883 the Kepler Malt Extract Company Ltd had also been registered in nine Continental European countries, the US, Canada, India, and New South Wales. This was a pattern repeated for other products.

The creation of trade marks to compare with that of the successful Kepler brand became an objective of the partners immediately following the 1883 legislation. The Act prohibited 'word' trademarks if they referred to the character or quality of the goods to which they were attached (presumably reflecting the attitude of those involved in trade mark protection and hence the problem).[20] The legislation, which left considerable scope for confusion and problematical litigation, rendered the description 'tablet' vulnerable as a trade mark when applied specifically to compressed products.[21] 'Tablet' did not meet Burroughs' preference for creating distinctive and memorable product names. While in Australasia in 1883, he discovered a resistance among doctors to prescribing Burroughs' Beef & Iron Wine and suggested to Wellcome the adoption of a more 'professionally appealing 'Beef & Iron Elixoid'.[22] Simultaneously in England, Wellcome was searching for a 'pat name', a 'fancy' meaningless word to refer to the compressed tablets about to be manufactured. In 1884 he hit upon 'Tabloid', the name registered as a trade mark in the same year to describe the company's own new compressed tablets (though applicable also to other products such as lint and medical chests).[23] Each Tabloid contained an accurately measured single dose that was pure, stable and resistant to temperature, and in palatable and convenient form and received a favourable reception in the medical

press. Thorough reports on the physiological action and therapeutical uses of Cocaine Tabloids produced from coca leaves resulted in praise from the *Lancet* in which they were described as the best means of administration and unaccompanied by irritation when injected hypodermically: 'The anaesthesia they produce is so complete as to admit of the most serious operations without pain. They are far superior to any solution of cocaine, and their introduction has been the means of removing the great difficulty hitherto experienced in the use of this important drug'.[24] Cocaine was also an ingredient combined with chlorate of potash and borax in the manufacture of the company's new 'Voice Tabloid', advertised (especially to clergymen, singers, and public speakers) as effective in clearing a 'husky voice … as if by magic in the course of a few minutes'.[25] Combinations such as this were also produced to be incorporated in doctors' prescriptions, for example for an alkaline and antiseptic gargle or lotion to be mixed with water or wine. Not infrequently, medical

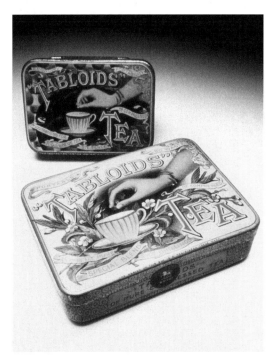

practitioners wrote to the company describing in detail a precise formula used in a treatment they had used successfully and frequently, suggesting this would be suitable for production in 'Tabloid' form. In some cases, specimens were prepared and dispatched to the doctor for testing before a decision as to whether to launch the product on a commercial scale or only to supply 'special orders' was made.[26] Tabloids were for internal application and included the commoner forms of medicine. Those for solution in water for external application, for example, quinine bismuth (for colds and headache) and mercuric potassium iodide used for disinfectant and in gynaecological cases, were advertised as Soloids. Other categories introduced during the 1880s[27] were ophthalmic Tabloids and Tabloids for hypodermic injections. By 1900 annual output of Tabloids and Soloids was roughly 260 million,[28] by which time the company's trademarks included Tabloid medicine chests and cases, Tea Tabloids, first manufactured in 1892 (the quality of which received endorsement by the Chairman of the National Health and Safety Committee),[29] and Tabloid photographic developer chemicals, exhibited at the Chicago Exposition of 1893.[30] Patent rights to produce compressed tea were acquired in 1892 from Mr Roger, a tea planter. Like compressed medicines, this form of instant tea was perceived by the partners to possess

FIGURE 2.2 BW&Co. advertisement for 'Tabloid' first aid kits and medicine chests. n.d.

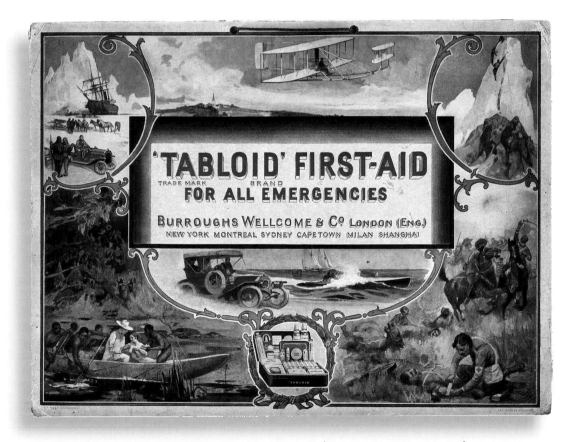

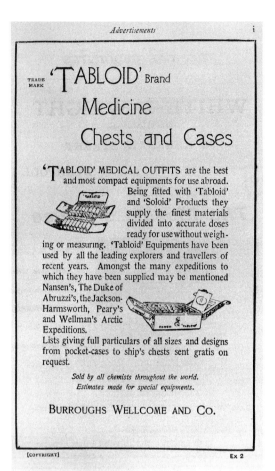
FIGURE 2.3 Advertisement for Tabloid medicine chests and cases 'from pocket cases to ship's chests' taken from Ronald Ross, *Malarial Fever, Its Cause, Prevention and Treatment* (Univ of Liverpool Press, 1900).

commercial potential for sale to travellers to whom medicine cases and chests would appeal, though there is little evidence that this proved to be the case.[31] Instant tea was a product roughly a century before its time in Britain.

Another innovation for which Burroughs can claim credit (albeit indirectly) and one of the few to achieve considerable long-term success was the conception of a small, carefully selected collection of medicines and first aid equipment packed in a portable case for the purpose of self medication in remote locations. The idea originated from Dr Valentine, superintendent of the mission at Agra which Burroughs visited whilst in India in 1882. He it was who drew attention to the value to medical missionaries of possessing a selection of compressed medicines in conveniently portable form put up in a small case for use in the field. Acting on this suggestion, Burroughs instructed Wellcome to arrange for the construction of such a prototype to be dispatched to the Agra mission for Dr Valentine's consideration. In addition to compressed medicines, including 'cholera tablet' and ipececac for dysentery,[32] the contents included bandages, absorbent cotton, adhesive plaster. Not all the products were made by BW&Co. though all contents featured in the practical advisory handbook supplied with each chest.[33]

From 1884, 'Tabloid' medical cases and chests became well-publicised products, the contents varying in accordance with precise local conditions and anticipated requirements in military campaigns, on expeditions, on plantations, or in dispensaries aboard ship, for the use of missionaries, travellers, sportsmen, yachtsmen, and adventurers of all kinds.[34] In 1885 Henry M. Stanley, the great explorer, placed the contract for the supply of medicines for his historic African expedition with BW&Co., recommending other explorers to do the same.[35] In purely commercial terms, however, the market created by missionaries and adventurers for medicine chests and cases cannot have been large. Much greater was the demand for 'Tabloid' medical equipment to equip armies and navies, though no data have survived to indicate the relative importance of medicine chests to the business.[36]

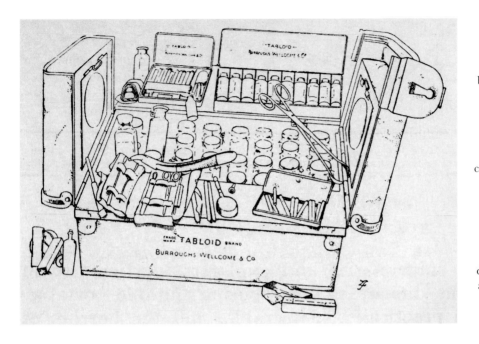

FIGURE 2.4
'Tabloid'
medicine
chest used
by Sir Henry
Stanley on
the Emin
Pasha Relief
Expedition.
BW&Co.
collected used
medicine
chests such
as these, to
examine the
remaining
contents for
deterioration,
and to use in
subsequent
promotional
material.
Taken from
Henry
Stanley *In
Darkest Africa*
(Sampson,
Low,
Marston,
Searle &
Rivington,
1890).

Scientific basis for diversification

Initiatives undertaken by Wellcome promised to take the company in a significantly different direction from that implied by most of the proprietary brand product developments proposed by Burroughs. In January 1883, Wellcome informed Burroughs that he had added phosphates of iron, quinine, and strychnine to the Price List, that they offered a wide profit margin, and that he was making arrangements to have sulphate and bisulphate of quinine put up. 'If possible we can then manufacture certain chemicals as an important part of future business and can begin with quinine'.[37] The plan was to purchase the drug in crude form and purify it, using a crystallisation process known to Wellcome to produce large feathery crystals.[38] Burroughs was enthusiastic. He emphasized the importance of establishing a distinctive product by naming it 'Quinine Soluble' and proposed that other chemicals should be imported from the US and Germany, put up with BW&Co. labels, and supplied on a comparable basis to that of the wholesale drug companies.[39] These exchanges marked the beginning of the company's trade in pure drugs for dispensing and for use by researchers and experimenters. Another of Wellcome's contributions to the product range was the 'Enule' line of suppositories that originated with his dissertation on urethral suppositories at the College in Philadelphia in 1878.[40]

Whereas proposals for product innovation from Burroughs derived primarily from his perceptions of potential markets overseas during this period, Wellcome's contribution to the process was influenced by his close attention to medical research reported in the medical and pharmaceutical journals and picked up during his attendances at conferences of professional bodies. One notable innovation illustrates this approach. In the 1860s, strophanthus, used in Africa for the preparation of poison arrows, had been brought to England and its properties subjected to analysis by Dr. William Sharpey. On the suggestion of the Africa explorer, David Livingstone, the poison was examined by Sir Thomas R. Fraser, Professor of Materia Medica at the University of Edinburgh. Wellcome spoke to Fraser at the Cardiff meeting of the BMA in 1885 when Fraser showed that strophanthus exercised a strong effect on the action of the heart. Wellcome dispatched an agent to Central Africa for the sole purpose of collecting strophanthus Kombe pods (at a cost of £20 per lb, unopened), buying up all supplies to secure a monopoly. The first tinctures manufactured by the company were presented to researchers and medical practitioners on request. By 1886 this novel treatment for cardiac patients was offered for sale at home and in the US at 7 shillings an ounce.[41]

Special orders initiated by individual customers continued to provide the basis for additions to Tabloid lines, including cotton wool and dressings from 1900. Until 1897 Tabloid hypodermics had only been supplied to individuals as special orders. The distribution of samples of Tabloid hypodermics to veterinary experts, however, resulted in the introduction of a new line into the market.[42] The process of product proliferation was haphazard, often consisting of a response to a formula requested by doctors.[43] The dissatisfaction of an Australian doctor with Parke Davis & Co's Acetozone used in the treatment of wounds led to experiments with a preparation based on hydrogen peroxide.[44] In 1897 Wellcome declared that 'from a practical business point of view' he had decided to give up all lines not of a pharmaceutical or chemical nature'.[45]

Broadening the product range; the innovation record

However, dietetic foods, notably Kepler goods and Beef & Iron Wine (later sold as Bivo[46]), Fairchild's digestive agents, and Hazeline and Lanoline products for toilet and cosmetic as well as medical use continued to figure among the products given prominence in the company's price lists and publicity during the twentieth century.[47] By 1907 Tabloid Laxative Fruit Pastilles (for children and delicate persons) increased the pastille line alone to 20. Additional lines were: Alaxa, described as an aromatic liqueur of cascara sagrada (another laxative to compete with Compark's Cascara Evacuant); menthol snuff; Xaxa, a preparation of salicylic acid identical with aspirin but offering 'guaranteed purity' at half the price; and Opa, an antiseptic mouth wash. New photographic lines included Tabloid Rytol, Tabloid Chromium Intensifier, and Tabloid Sulphiding Compound.[48]

Widening the Tabloid range of products was an important source of diversification; they numbered more than 100 in the 1890s. However, Kepler malt extracts were also developed to justify advertising some novelty in composition or value to consumers. The production of a Kepler Solution, a liquid preparation of barley malt (rather than an emulsion) in 1886 was well received by the medical press as was the improved Essentia Malti (Kepler) introduced in 1892.[49] After preliminary analysis in 1891, the *Lancet*'s verdict was favourable because of the high conversion ratio of extract into

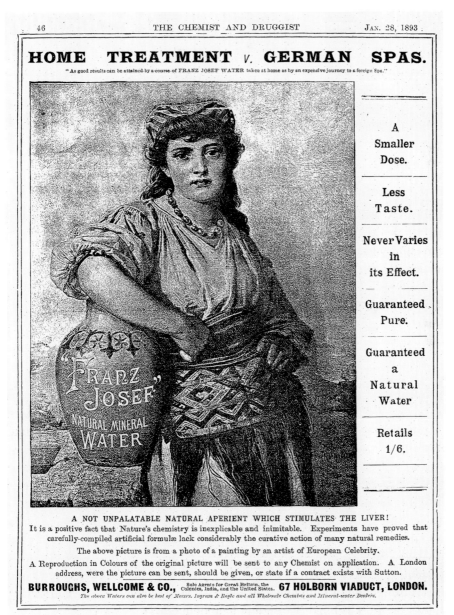

FIGURE 2.5 Advertisement for 'Franz Josef' natural mineral water by BW&Co. (*Chemist & Druggist*, 28 January 1893).

maltose and dextrin, indicative of a high diastatic value, and because of an attractive colour.[50] Not so sweet as the thicker extract, the new preparation put up in champagne bottles was considered suitable for administration in milk, aerated water, or wine and well-suited as a vehicle for other medicaments.[51] These new developments were aimed at those interested in 'sickroom dietetics and temperance as a non-alcoholic substitute for ale'. In 1891 Burroughs appeared before members attending the BMA's annual conference in Cardiff to demonstrate the process of producing Kepler Malto-Ricine, an extract consisting of 50 per cent castor oil. Advertised as a tasteless castor oil, the product was promoted as 'the perfect laxative for fastidious patients, delicate women, and children.'[52]

Through the company's association with the medical profession and its success in establishing a reputation as a reliable source of ethical medicines, the potential for expanding trade in medicines grew. Evidence for this is the approach made by Westminster Hospital in 1899 which, having supplied the company with its own pharmacopoeia, invited quotations for any preparation which the firm could put out under the Tabloid Brand. The urgency given by Snow Hill to researching the possibilities and producing a report reflects the importance attached to securing this contract.[53] Meanwhile, so successful were Tabloids that Wellcome added more branding categories: Soloids, which included effervescent products for use in public health, Elixoid fluid extracts, Vaporole and Vereneker inhalers, and Dartring lanoline. In 1905 a newly formed (and apparently short-lived) sales committee recommended entry (re-entry) into the pill trade which led to the preparation of samples of Tabloid coffee and milk and Tabloid milk compressed in cubes. The response at head office, conveyed to the manager at Dartford, was that: '... until we can develop something unique and original we should take orders for pills only from government, hospitals, and missionaries.'[54]

How innovative, through internal product development and the introduction of new products through agency agreements, was the company? It is impossible to answer this question with confidence, given the problematical nature of the evidence available. Beginning in 1879, the *BMJ* included an annual report of 'drug innovations', in which new drugs entering the market were described and commented upon. However, the reports relied on the drug companies themselves to provide the information. Scrutiny of the annual reports reveals BW&Co. to be introducing new drugs in numbers unmatched by the major competitors in the British market: Allen & Hanburys, May & Baker, and Parke Davis. Only Parke Davis announced as many as three in any one year (twice), whereas BW&Co. announced no fewer than two in 22 out of 24 years between 1879 and 1903, the total numbering 104. Thereafter, the numbers drop and few are recorded for any of the companies. It might be possible to interpret these figures as indicating a leading innovatory role for BW&Co., though the problematic characteristics of the series justify a degree of scepticism. Curiously, BW&Co.'s serum and antitoxins, a genuinely innovative product line,[55] receive no mention in the reports, yet the pages of the *BMJ* and of other journals regularly carried extensive advertisements that included detailed descriptions and advice on administration. None the less, it seems at least plausible to conclude that the partners themselves were more assiduous in reporting their other innovations, showing a greater awareness of the commercial importance of publicity as a form of advertising than their competitors.

Pricing policies

An essential element in the company's marketing policies was a flexible approach to pricing, on which during these early years Burroughs seems to have exercised the major influence. With the exception of Kepler goods, BW&Co. had begun as a company trading as an agency for goods manufactured by others. Under these circumstances, prices had been determined primarily by the suppliers with whom the partners then tried to negotiate modifications of supply costs, stock charges, discounts, and prices to meet British market conditions.[56] With respect to Kepler goods which were actually produced on the company's premises, prices were set to yield, in Burroughs' words, 'enormous profits'.[57] However, the opinions of medical men he met travelling at home and overseas led him to reflect on pricing policy. Doctors had expressed the view that while they wished to prescribe Kepler extract to poor people (noted to be those most in need of such a nourishing agent) prices were too high. A single bottle containing ¾ of a pound costing 2s. 9d. lasted five days; to achieve results in chronic cases dosage was required over a considerably longer period. In 1882 Burroughs suggested to Wellcome that they:

> … should begin to give more extract for the money and do the same with malt and oil … Such a policy would increase sales for doctors' prescriptions and immediately tend to give us a monopoly of the market in these goods. If we don't do it someone else will and thus sell a lot of goods on the demand we have created by our advertisements for it. It is easy for anyone to estimate the cost of extract of malt and see what enormous profits we are making'.[58]

From 1883, KME was sold in larger bottles containing an additional 25 per cent by weight but at the existing price. Similar drastic price reductions became necessary for compressed medicines, the profits on which were also described as enormous, as serious competition emerged in the market. In 1884 Godfrey & Cooke were offering compressed goods in bulk at half the price of those sold by BW&Co.[59] Burroughs feared that an association of the firm by the medical profession with 'outrageous margins' and excessive

FIGURE 2.6
Front cover of BW&Co.'s Price List, 1892.

profits would be extended to their other products and attract competitors. He instanced chlorate of potash as one of the most popular of the compressed goods. Purchased *by the gross* for one shilling, the price of *a dozen* Tabloid Chlorate of Potash was also one shilling. Burroughs reckoned that even if the tablets were sold at *only* six times the cost, sales would probably double. The method of price reduction favoured was to reduce the number of tablets per box and to sell at 50 per cent of current prices, with a fourfold increase in sales predicted as a result.[60]

Release from the Wyeth contract and the commencement of manufacture secured increased control over costs. The introduction of improved machinery made it possible to reduce the prices of some Tabloid compressed drugs (soluble quinine and saccharin, for example), to levels barely exceeding the cost of the crude drug making them highly competitive for dispensers.[61] However, the drastic reduction in prices necessary to compete in the market could not protect profits and did not remove the threat of serious injury from 'extravagant cutting'.[62] The policy to deal with the problem was to impose greater control in the market through agreements with the company's retailers. Part of a charm offensive to enlist their support, the introduction to the price list issued in 1887 promised chemists a 'very liberal profit' to the trade and assured them that BW&Co. would 'at all times endeavour to protect chemists in their legitimate profits and trust to their spirit of fair play to protect us by discouraging the sale of the various cheap imitations of our articles'.[63] From 1890 a series of agreements was established with chemists throughout the country. Each undertook not to sell the products of BW&Co. below those set down in the annual price lists. Retailers were also bound to inform the company of breaches of the agreement by others.[64] This was the origin of a major confrontation with many retailers who interpreted this not as a defence of retail chemists (as the partners presented it) but as an attack.[65]

While the overall trend of the price of drugs was downwards during the 1880s and 1890s, reliance on price lists to chart changes at the level of the firm can be misleading. Discount levels were crucial in striking contracts with agents, wholesalers, and government departments; orders from medical institutions often involved 'donations' as well as discounts. Typically, retailers received 20 per cent trade discount, wholesalers sometimes up to 50 per cent in the form of 'special and confidential discounts' on selected goods for newly appointed agents or for the best performers measured by volume and energy in pushing goods.[66] In negotiating with home or overseas government departments, discounts were 25 per cent plus a further 25 per cent on bulk orders.[67] Hospitals were particularly important, not least because doctors working there were predicted to become the largest prescribers of the firm's drugs elsewhere, both through private practice and their connections with other medical and non-medical institutions which provided medical services. When a hospital did not seem favourably disposed towards the company's goods and used competitors' products, the advice to a salesman was to 'please nurse this institution carefully and take every opportunity of remedying this state of affairs'.[68] This explains the 'special rates' sometimes allowed to hospitals and other charitable institutions that bore no relation to cost but were sometimes conditional on securing contracts for other products; for example, for both malt extract and cod liver oil. In the case of the Brompton Hospital for Consumption, the traveller was advised that should the price suggested not prove sufficiently low, he could reduce it further, 'even to gratis'.[69]

In the 1880s and 1890s it was customary for BW&Co. to offer confidential allowances, 'donations' of 33.3 per cent on orders supplied direct to hospitals and other charitable institutions, in effect concealing the ordinary net price from competitors. This changed from 1898, after one of the company's senior representatives reported that hospitals had begun to request net price quotations and yearly contracts. Another traveller reported that the Hospital Board of Halifax Royal Infirmary had forbidden the dispenser to order the company's products because the members objected to receiving the 33.3 per cent as a secret donation; they would, on the other hand, enter into a contract should the 33.3 per cent discount be deducted when quoting net prices. Pearson, BW&Co.'s most senior salesman, explained this as a result of dispenser and secretary to the Board omitting to inform members of the donation, the effect of which was to present members with inflated net prices shown on invoices, high compared with those submitted by competitors, some of which might be making an annual subscription, of which Board members would be informed. Pearson recommended that the company should adopt a similar policy.[70]

Concealed elements in pricing were not restricted to the home market. On his travels in the early 1880s, Burroughs discovered that colonial chemists strongly objected to the retail prices of goods being printed on wrappers or circulars and instructed discontinuance of the practice. The explanation was that almost invariably some duty was payable on importation in addition to carriage costs: '... when the customer sees a retail price printed on a wrapper and is charged more he thinks he is swindled and often refuses to take goods'.[71] He found that in India druggists did not pay much attention to price 'nor hardly grumble if anything is very dear saying that there is no difference to them as they add their profit on to the cost of the article whatever it was.'[72] Because of the long-established credit links with London merchants, they were also indifferent to the opportunity to buy goods on sale or return or on commission[73] After the reversal of Burroughs' easy credit policy towards the end of 1882, the travellers' task of selling in an increasingly competitive market became more difficult, success depending upon persuasion and support through advertising.

FIGURE 2.7
Malt
production
equipment,
Dartford,
1899.

Advertising ethical medicine: policy, contracts, and content

In 1881 expenditure on advertising may have reached 10 per cent of sales turnover.[74] This compared with roughly 25 per cent of sales spent by Thomas Beecham in 1892 in advertising patent medicines to the public.[75] Expenditure by BW&Co. on marketing (including travellers' salaries and expenses and advertising expenditure) increased sharply beginning in the early 1900s. That devoted to travellers' salaries rose roughly in line with sales and represented 6 per cent throughout the period between 1900 and 1914. The trend of advertising expenditure, however, rose from £15,335 in 1900 (£9,820 in 1899) to £95,918 in 1914. This represented 8.2 per cent of marketing expenditure in 1899, 10.9 per cent in 1905, 22 per cent in 1910 and 21 per cent in 1914.[76]

The product lines receiving most support were those introduced from the beginning of the partnership: Kepler, Wyeth, Fellows, and Hazeline. From 1884, with Kepler, the company's Tabloid lines received by far the most advertising support. In addition to the major British medical journals (national and regional) which charged most and in which more space was purchased, advertisements regularly appeared in the *Chemist & Druggist* and the *Pharmaceutical Journal*. The company pursued a strict policy of ethical advertising with respect to medicines, limiting promotion to the medical profession and to chemists and druggists through professional and trade

FIGURE 2.8
Advertisement
for BW&Co.'s
'Hazeline'
cream, n.d.

journals and avoiding direct advertising to consumers through newspaper advertising altogether. However, for Hazeline and Kepler goods especially, for which therapeutic claims were made but which were also suitable for general health-giving and cosmetic purposes, advertisements appeared in specialist magazines. Advertisements for Kepler goods were placed in the temperance organ, the *Band of Hope Reporter,* and in the *Baptist Visitor.* Lundberg perfumes and Hazeline advertisements appeared in ladies' and theatre magazines (and programmes selected on the basis of a particular actor's engagements), and in the *Hairdressers' Weekly Journal.* Other magazines included the *Illustrated London News, Cornhill Magazine, London Society,* and the *Graphic.* The entire range of products was also printed in various price lists issued by shipping companies and merchant wholesalers. The preferred precise locations for the company's advertisements in all journals and magazines were in front or back pages, inside front or back cover, facing leading article or editorial matter, and almost invariably covering a page or half page.[77] The March issue of the *Lancet* in 1883 contained no fewer than 27 such advertisements in the form of mostly new and original medical reports and therapeutical notes pertaining to BW&Co. products.

Distancing the company from media unrelated to medicine or pharmacy appears to have been due to Wellcome's influence on policy and in particular, his anxiety that compressed medicines should not be interpreted as an encouragement to 'self-prescription' (self-medication). In 1884 Burroughs wrote to Wellcome:

> I think you are strongly opposed to newspaper advertising to maintain the friendly support of the profession and their hearty goodwill as their friends and collaborators, not as their competitors in the field of prescribing for disease and thus by depriving them of their livelihood in a measure. Doctors have generally a pretty hard work in life and few get rich.[78]

Aware of doctors' hostility to self-medication, the partners' policy with respect to labelling was to ensure that nothing appeared but name, formula, and remarks on the form in which the drug was presented. No advice was given on administration.[79] Advertising was similarly aimed at creating trust among the medical profession regarding the quality of BW&Co.'s medicines.

Even some of the earliest advertisements in medical journals consisted of dense, technical descriptions of BW&Co.'s preparations which emphasised their scientific aspects or, in the case of KME, the scientific control exercised to ensure quality. Electrographically printed images were used to illustrate advertisements showing either products or, especially after the move to Snow Hill and subsequently to Dartford, buildings, projecting the scale and modernity of the company. The purity of Kepler Solution was advertised by the use of (unexplained) 'photomicrographs'.[80] Allusions to science and modernity are recurring themes in advertisements appearing from the beginning. Under the heading 'Progressive pharmacy', in 1888 one such advertisement referred to BW&Co.'s 'laboratories under the management of a distinguished practical and scientific chemist … assisted by a corps of thoroughly qualified pharmacists'; others appeared under such titles as 'Advanced pharmacy', 'Science in diet', Perfection in pharmacy' conveying the image the partners chose to project.[81] Advertisements intended for the trade retained informative text though also stressing the material benefit which selling the products would bring. One such advertisement directed 'to our friends, the drug trade' conveys the flavour: 'Caution. Chemists who do not wish to increase their business and profits are warned against reading these pages'. A caption accompanying a description of the qualities of KME encouraged chemists to 'Show this advertisement and you'll show profit.'[82]

Securing placements for advertisements was not always straightforward. A contract was sometimes conditional on the editor's undertaking to include frequent reports on the company's products in the body of the journal, a form of concealed advertising.[83] In 1881 a contract was placed with the *British Mercantile Gazette* for a one page advertisement opposite a leader in special issues priced at £10 per 15,000 copies plus two similar advertisements. The condition was that a report on the company's display at the International Medical and Sanitary Exhibition held in South Kensington should receive 'a liberal notice.'[84]

An indirect form of advertising was the distribution of *Medical Formulae of New and Improved Chemical and Pharmaceutical Preparations* first produced in 1881, which included a list of the company's products and an invitation to medical professionals to request specimens for delivery and trial. Free samples for doctors, and gifts in the form of blotters, medical diaries, and other items of professional interest, formed part of BW&Co.'s policy from the beginning. A major publicity campaign launched in 1882 originated from a suggestion made to Burroughs in India by a surgeon, General Moore, that a handbook of modern medicine (scientific and thorough but also simple and aimed primarily at doctors) would be well received.[85] The handbook included an index of medicines and diseases, descriptions of the advantages of compound drugs as well as the formulae for medicines sold by BW&Co., and articles which drew attention to conditions treatable with the company's products. The initial issue consisted of 20,000 formulae books bound in leatherette and 5,000 cloth editions. An enthusiastic response from the doctors who had received copies resulted in the printing of a further 20,000, half of which were sent to American and English consulates and the remainder to doctors, chemists, leading clergy, and plantations in the colonies. Wellcome told Burroughs that the campaign 'took the profession by storm'.[86] This marked the beginning of a series of publications of increasing complexity intended to combine the utility of a convenient source of reference for the medical profession with a reminder of the excellence of the products of BW&Co. Approximately 4,000 medical men in London was each sent a leatherette case of camphor, perceived to be 'at enormous expense'.[87] In addition to samples to well-placed senior medical professionals and influential doctors, elaborate leather cases containing free samples of Tabloids were offered as gifts to some of the most distinguished royal and political figures.

Beginning in 1890, the annual production of the *ABC Medical Diary* enlarged the subtle promotion aimed at the medical profession by providing useful information, such as pulse rates, and articles on specific conditions and therapeutic treatments in addition to a list of the company's preparations. In 1897 it was decided that the 'very best means of placing products before medical men and nurses'[88] was to issue, free of charge, medical and nurses' diaries (at least 35,000 for doctors and 20,000 for nurses) throughout the Empire and English-speaking communities, excepting the US and Canada. The expectation was that the diaries, which contained information of a medical nature but also the company's products, would be carried by the recipients all the year round and used as a handy source.[89] Policies of producing instructive publications, ethical advertising, and the distribution of samples on a large scale was to prove both commercially successful and strategically valuable when the company's pricing policy and the Tabloid brand came under attack from the retail trade beginning in the 1890s.

The partners placed a premium on securing expert endorsements, sometimes offered by medical professionals gratuitously in journal articles or conference addresses, and sometimes elicited from them as a request. These could be inserted both in journal advertisements and in circulars, diaries and other material issued to the medical profession and the trade. An example is provided by correspondence between Wellcome and a Mr Harwicker of Sheffield, thanking him for complimentary letters concerning the company's products: 'Would it be possible to write a letter to one of the medical journals [from which the firm intended to quote]?' Harwicker was asked to investigate other items and was sent £10 wherewith to purchase the publications.[90]

To persuade the medical profession of the value of products which the company also advertised in other magazines, the partners enlisted the aid of the medical profession itself. For example, Dr Murrell was asked to write two pages about Hazeline, paying special attention to its value as a treatment for various wounds, inflammations, and lung troubles, in time for an imminent issue of the *Lancet* in which the company had taken 19 pages. A relevant circular on Hazeline was enclosed together with an invitation to quote as much as the doctor thought proper.[91] On another occasion, an article written by Dr Whitmarsh for a similar purpose could not be used because of space constraints, but he was assured that it would be used in future; £5 was enclosed in the reply 'for professional services'.[92] Wellcome was also alive to the damage which other advertisers could inflict on the business presumably because Dr Luland (who was quoted in an advertisement for the Maltine Co., a competitor in the market for malt extracts) was known to Wellcome who wrote to him objecting to the quotation used by Maltine considered to be prejudicial to the partners' business interests. Describing Maltine as 'the most offensive competitor we have' Wellcome insisted that Dr Luland instruct Maltine Co. to withdraw his letter from their advertisements and to forbid them to publish again.[93] Burroughs urged Wellcome to contact Dr Prosser James (presumably known to Wellcome) to write an article for publication in the *Lancet* on extractions of maltin in all the varieties in which they appeared on the market. The plan was for Wellcome to carry out an analysis of Kepler which he would arrange for James to duplicate, to confirm its higher maltin content compared with all other malt extracts, and consequently to endorse Kepler.[94]

The ferocity of advertising competition is revealed in the correspondence between the company and the BMA treasurer, Dr Holman, in 1889. This referred to a previous period when the partners' relations with Fowke, business manager of the BMA, were considered to have been unfair, even leading to a two-year period when the company did not advertise in the *BMJ*. The two principal issues: the rejection of some of the firm's advertisements even though they proved acceptable to the editors of other journals, and the journal's inclusion of competitors' advertisements (Maltine & Co.) to which they objected for their 'very personal and aggressive character directed against us, and when we have attempted to reply in temperate, dignified and general terms in our advertisements, Mr Fowke has refused to insert our pages and declined to explain the basis of his objections'.[95]

Indirect and admittedly crude evidence suggesting some level of success in advertising may be deduced from the results of a competition arranged by the *Chemist and Druggist* in 1890. Chemists and druggists in Britain were issued with competition forms to vote for advertisements appearing in the journal's annual Diary supplement. Of the 1,040 votes cast, 477 considered the advertisements by BW&Co. to be the 'most generally effective' (the next best polled 247 votes); 498 regarded them as the most useful (second best 247), 482 believed they were the 'most high toned'. BW&Co.'s advertisements also ranked as the second best in the 'novel' category, fourth in the 'most amusing' and fourth in the 'best illustration' category.[96]

The competition to identify the article which chemists found 'the most popular in business', (presumably intended to test perceived selling power) however, showed BW&Co. trailing behind Beecham's pills (400 votes), Vaseline (made by the Cheeseborough Manufacturing Company), Pear's and Vinolia soaps (from Blondeau et Cie). Tabloids ranked fifth and Kepler Malt Extract eighth. When compared with the different character of Beecham's cheap all purpose pills, vaseline, the two toiletry items, and the competition from such varied advertisements for mineral waters, perfumes, and chocolate, the performance of BW&Co. in these competitions suggest success in establishing strong visibility in the market represented by retail traders. The outcome of a similar exercise held in 1895 when colonial and foreign retailers were invited to vote, showed a similar unanimity in placing BW&Co. first in the best price list category and leading or coming second in several others.[97]

Two other methods of advertising employed to create a high profile were the publicity associated with the use of medicine chests and cases, and the mounting of extravagant displays at exhibitions at home and overseas. As a source of advertising copy BW&Co.'s medicine chest and cases offered a large potential which BW&Co. exploited fully. International explorers, including Nansen, the Duke of Abruzzi, Jackson-Harmsworth, Scott, Shackleton, and Amundsen, and many early aviators including Beaumont, Vedrines, Pecquet, Bleriot, Wellman, and the balloonist, C.C.Turner took 'Tabloid' medical cases or chests with them, enthusiastic reports of their value quoted in advertisements and printed price list circulars and booklets.[98] Striking visual representation of the company's products were employed in a world-wide market and formed an essential part of the assiduous cultivation of a distinctive corporate image in which an international dimension was a major feature through which the company was associated with initiative, leadership, and achievements of a spectacular kind.

In addition to advertising in print, an important dimension of the partners' policy of promotion was through exhibitions, at home and overseas. The first exhibition at which the company's products were displayed proved to be a disaster, inasmuch as the International Medical and Sanitary Exhibition held in South Kensington in 1881 produced no awards. The company's exhibits elicited praise from the medical journals and its failure to win a single award evoked an outcry in the medical press which accused the executive committee responsible for organising the event of perpetrating a 'glaring injustice' against the American partners, one correspondent drawing attention to the award of a prize by one of the judges for an item for which he was the English agent. The organisers were also criticised for permitting (and making awards to) 'injurious quack articles', such as

'the infallible worm specific' and the 'marvellous Oriental Balsam'.[99] The partners ignored the calls for instant correction of the injustice, doubtless regarding the sympathy as well as praise extended by the press as an unexpected bonus and added publicity. In the future, the company's prizes were to accumulate in large numbers, the partners treating exhibitions as an opportunity to attract attention beyond the curiosity stimulated by new products. During the company's first quarter century, its products had received 190 highest awards for scientific excellence in international exhibitions across the world.[100] Presentation, informative but also ingenious and spectacular, was a method by which the company and its products would be remembered and would reinforce the efforts of the travelling representatives on the road.

FIGURE 2.9 Display of BW&Co.'s products at the International Medical and Sanitary Exhibition, London, 1881.

'Detailing' doctors to create a demand; sales representatives on the road

From the time Burroughs became an independent agent in London in 1878 he had adopted a marketing policy with which he had become familiar under the Wyeths in the US: 'detailing' doctors, issuing samples, and advertising.[101] While this policy was developed further under the partnership when Wellcome contributed his own ideas, the difficulties that Burroughs had encountered in recruiting sales representatives before 1880 persisted. This was manifested in the rapid turnover of salesmen during the 1880s. Between 1880 and 1886, no fewer than thirteen travellers were recruited at one time or another to maintain a sales force of four or five at any one time. Five of the travellers appointed between 1880 and 1886 remained with the company for less than a year.

Of three Americans appointed, only William Shepperson remained long with the company. Becoming one of its most effective salesmen during the 1880s, after two years in Britain he was sent to India where he was responsible for organising the company's display at the 1883 Calcutta Exhibition and for promoting the company's goods on that continent.[102] Nationality, though, was less important than qualifications. The partners' policy was to try to recruit only those possessing knowledge of medicine and/or pharmacy.[103] General practitioners, pharmacists, and a surgeon can be identified. Neither qualifications nor experience, however, guaranteed effective salesmanship; the surgeon, taken on for a month, was regarded as unsatisfactory, whereas Weld, of unknown experience but to become 'chief' of the travellers department, was one of the few representatives appointed in the early 1880s to stay with the firm. He became the first manager of the newly established Australian branch in 1886 before returning to the London office to fill an administrative role.[104] Experience of business was an additional advantage valued in travellers and reflected in the salary the partners were prepared to pay. Weld's starting salary in 1883 was £100, rising to £280 by 1895, the year when George Pearson, a young, qualified pharmacist with trade experience (and a future general manager of the company), joined the firm at a salary of £200.[105] This compared with a dispensing chemist's salary offered by the London Government Board of £120–£140, which the *Chemist & Druggist* considered average.[106] Salaries were regularly reviewed by the partners on the basis of travellers' sales records and the annual reports each was required to submit. In 1892 Wellcome noticed that Maddox – whose salary which exceeded £500 plus expenses implies the possession of most of the desirable attributes of a drug salesman – was receiving the same salary as another who had recorded five times the value of sales. This discovery led to a reduction in Maddox's salary to £500 plus expenses.[107] Several years earlier, when Burroughs wanted to appoint Dr Smith, a young physician, at a salary of £1,000, Wellcome considered that his lack of business experience justified no more than £800.[108] These salaries appear to define the upper limit of the salary range. Even after fourteen years experience with the firm, Weld's salary had risen to only £375 by 1897, a promotion to the office staff in the new sales department in 1898 increased that to £500.[109] These figures compare with estimated doctors' net annual income after 'expenses' of less than £500 for over 50 per cent of their number in an over-populated medical profession;[110] fewer than 18 per cent of general medical practitioners could earn more than £1,000.[111] The difficulty in recruiting satisfactory salesmen, therefore, is not explained by financial incentive but by the unusual and exacting requirement of a combination of some knowledge of medicine or pharmacy with business capability and personal sales drive. The partners did not always see eye to eye on this; Wellcome emphasised medical experience, Burroughs a commercial record. When in the US in 1883, Burroughs offered a position to H. John Van Schaack. Wellcome, who knew Schaack well, ruled this out. He described Schaack, who had previously worked in his father's business, as clever and active, but that 'his brusque harem scarum manner will never be accepted in this country'. Wellcome insisted that even if Schaack was to *pay the partners* $2,000 still he would not consider employing him.[112] Wellcome insisted that no travellers should be appointed who might push the company's goods as if they were patent medicines, a risk that he evidently felt Burroughs did not see. For that reason he vetoed appointments when the candidates' experiences were limited to that line of goods.[113]

The relatively strict criteria insisted upon when appointing the firm's representatives was crucial because of the precise character of the firm's innovative approach to marketing from the beginning. The *Medical Press & Circular*'s report on the firm in 1881 drew attention to the 'new line of practice not hitherto followed by English firms: of presenting samples of new preparations to practitioners who desire to test them, and by not advertising in any but medical and pharmaceutical journals'.[114] In 1888 the *Chemist & Druggist* remarked on those and other characteristics of the American practices the partners had introduced to Britain. They had taken up agencies of leading American firms, introducing their products in lavish style and adding their own specialities. By anticipating the demands of medical professionals, the partners had 'acted with the utmost loyalty to their pharmaceutical colleagues' by creating 'an entirely new class of business ... by methods and manners sufficiently novel to record'.[115] This was a remarkable tribute to the two Americans, for both the profession and many in the trade had been, and continued to be, deeply suspicious of proprietary medicines as an encouragement to self medication and a threat to trade. Evidence that this fear was slow to be allayed is found in a circular issued to all travellers in 1901 in which the question posed was:

'What is the state of medical men's bogey of self medication? Are more or less medical men mentioning it?'[116]

The partners' marketing policy and the philosophy that lay behind it were described in detail, with characteristic pomposity, by Burroughs in 1882.

This policy must evidently succeed a policy of demonstrations of facts showing that the dealers and merchants benefited to a proper extent as well as the consumer and prescriber. Thus by leading and not crowding, by inducing and not urging, by showing favours and not

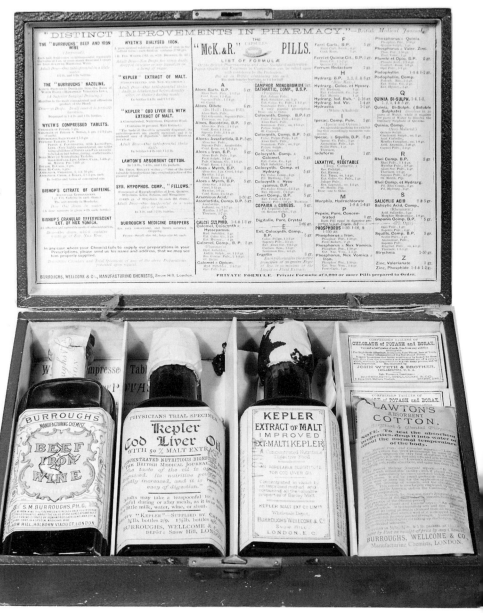

FIGURE 2.10
Early BW&Co. products: Burroughs beef and iron wine; Kepler cod liver oil with malt extract; Kepler extract of malt; Wyeth's compressed tablets of chlorate of potash and borax; and Lawton's absorbent cotton wool, in a sample case that also contains a price list of other products.

asking any, by proving our ability and purpose to benefit our customers as well as ourselves and make his interests our own and both mutual – thus will he effect to purchase instead of our asking him to order and encourage the sale of our own goods in every way. Such a policy gives one the right basis of equity, would make our business a mutual reciprocity of favours between our customers and ourselves – making it evident that we travel as much for their interests as our own and that in serving them and throughout the world we shall deserve to make through honesty of purpose and industry of conduct a competence for ourselves also.[117]

A note composed in 1883 headed 'Instructions to Travellers', probably sent to Wellcome by Burroughs, emphasised the importance of approaching the retailer before calling on doctors and persuading him to order so that the traveller could later refer to him as the company's agent when visiting the doctors. In the event of retailer's refusal to place an order, travellers were expected to try to secure an undertaking that he would order the company's goods if presented with prescriptions issued by doctors from a list which travellers supplied to retailers.[118] Retailers who stocked a full line of the company's principal goods were provided with circulars and pamphlets each bearing the retailer's name as 'agent' to BW&Co., the intention being to increase his authority to make recommendations.[119]

Burroughs also used his experience on the road before 1880 when advising Wellcome on the detailed logistics of enlisting the support of doctors. The somewhat didactic and repetitive manner in which the advice was delivered must have been irksome to Wellcome who also possessed experience as a sales representative, though he acknowledged Burroughs' expertise.[120] From Lahore early in 1883, Burroughs wrote to Wellcome recommending that he canvas doctors in the London hospitals, beginning with St Bartholomew's and the Royal Free, rather than at their homes where they saw private patients. He explained why Wellcome should 'go for the hospitals strong' for a few hours during afternoons. One reason was that the doctors and surgeons were assembled in the same place and therefore were more accessible, particularly if he gained entrance to the private room where they usually gathered to chat at the end of the day: 'The time of a London doctor which at hospital is nothing to him is worth a guinea a minute' [in private consulting rooms]. The second reason was that he had found doctors to be more likely to try novelties on hospital than on private patients, partly because of the hope that reports of tests might be published. He also urged Wellcome to 'get in with hospital surgeons' and to visit the hospital apothecary who would make appointments to see all the leading surgeons' others at convenient hours. Finally, he noted that Formula Lists should be given to students and that he should 'talk them up immensely'.[121] How much time Wellcome could afford to spend on these afternoon rounds in person is questionable during this particularly difficult period when Burroughs was abroad. However, four months later, Hill, one of the travellers, received special praise from Wellcome for his success in having introduced Hazeline into every hospital of note in London.[122] Hospitals continued to be a priority for the company's marketing strategy.

Researching the market for medicine

The partners' approach to countering potential hostility to the novelty of American preparations was a systematic sales campaign incorporating an early form of market research. The programme was introduced in August 1881, shortly before Burroughs left England on his worldwide sales tour. It is not clear which of the two partners was responsible for the initiative. It seems likely, however, that Wellcome was the architect. While Burroughs was responsible for introducing the personal visit to medical professionals in 1878, there is no evidence that he had adopted the systematic recording of data. His subsequent business career also suggests that the detailed preparation of the documentation required to implement the travellers' market research was uncharacteristic of Burroughs' typically broad brush approach. It seems likely also that the model for the scheme was American, possibly copied from Wellcome's former employers, Robbins & McKesson.

Under the new system every traveller was issued with a *pro forma* questionnaire which, on completion, was transformed into a consolidated compilation. Each time a traveller returned from a tour of his territory, the reports were submitted to the partners to assist with their analysis of the market and decisions on policy.[123] The questionnaires for doctors were slightly different from those issued for use when visiting chemists, but the intention behind both was the same. After entering the name of the town, its occupational characteristics, population, and the number of medical men resident in each location, travellers were asked to list the ages of those visited, their specialities, whether they wrote or dispensed prescriptions, and the class into which their practice (presumably judged by class of clientele) fell: 'common', 'moderate', or 'toney'. Presumably measured by size as well as clientele, travellers were also invited to rank doctors by 'class of practice' from A1 to 4. Questions were included to gauge doctors' responses to receiving a visit from the company's travellers, whether cordial, good, indifferent, uncivil, or refusing an interview. Similar questions elicited doctors' attitudes to the products offered by BW&Co., whether they were pleased, had used, would or would not use, indifferent – or whether a doctors' response merited the description 'old fogey'. Finally, the questionnaire sought to judge doctors' reactions to travellers who left samples. Were they pleased? Did they regard it as a questionable practice? Were they non-committal? Space was provided for general observations. Travellers differed in the exercising of diligence in completing the record sheets, while few added more than the briefest comment. An analysis of the questionnaires for the five years for which the records have survived is complicated by ambiguities contained in the returns (some travellers largely ignored some of the categories and some of the questions and the criteria employed to categorise responses differed). None the less, some of the results are interesting. The number of doctors visited between 1881 and 1885 was as follows: 1881, 994 (five months only); 1882, 1,919; 1883, 1,322; 1884, 1,359; 1885, 1,287. An indication of the coverage which these figures represent is that by October 1883 Wellcome claimed that in every town where at least two medical men resided, visits had been made by a traveller and samples had been distributed. Doctors in remoter parts had also received samples, though without a visit. Not surprisingly, the major proportion of practices was located in urban industrial areas, though the balance shifted from 1883 when the travellers fanned out into rural districts. Most doctors were described either as physician, surgeon (or a combination of both), or 'general'. Among the very small number of specialists visited were those associated with the treatment of nervous, women's, and venereal diseases, and homeopaths; most doctors visited offered a dispensing service, though the proportion of those limited to writing prescriptions rose from 1883.

Roughly one-third of the practices were described as either rich or 'toney'; adding those to whom the distinction of being a 'leading man' was allotted brings the percentage up to 45. Those described as common and moderate amounted to 41 per cent; the remainder were described as 'poor'. The reception given to travellers was overwhelmingly cordial. Few were refused an interview altogether, although a tiny minority of doctors expressed outright opposition to the introduction of new preparations, the reason for this in some cases explained by a clientele too poor to afford the firm's goods.[124] Age could also explain the conservative attitude towards the new products expressed by two practitioners in Newmarket aged 66 and 95.[125] Responses to BW&Co.'s products were most favourable to Wyeth's compressed tablets and hypodermics and McKesson & Robbins pills, Hazeline, and Kepler goods. The overall picture, measured by 'pleased' responses to the company's products by doctors who had either used or undertaken to use the company's goods is instructive. Those who neither used the company's goods nor intended to, accounted for roughly 60 per cent of all doctors visited in 1882 and 70 per cent in 1883. In 1884 and 1885 the proportions had changed; 66 per cent and 90 per cent were described as using, being pleased with, or intending to use the company's products. This is indicative of a profession willing to receive visits from travellers and willing to accept samples of new products, the main features of the new method of marketing drugs. Either this indicates a profession not resistant to innovation, or is a tribute to the effectiveness of the company's travellers.

Placing the practice of detailing in the contemporary medical context, the success of the company's representatives in overcoming a conservatism often attributed to the medical profession becomes comprehensible. So far as their receptivity to the new compressed medicines is concerned, during the late nineteenth century they were introduced at a time when contradictory ideas and ideals and extreme uncertainty prevailed among doctors regarding the nature, causes, and treatment of disease. This, together with a belief among doctors that it was as important to be a well-informed gentleman possessing social skills as it was to command technical expertise or medical knowledge, led them to regard clinical experience of whatever worked to be the guiding basis of medical practice – on which their living depended.[126] For this reason, it is not surprising that doctors were interested in new practices and therapies when their adoption promised to improve their market position. As for Kepler goods, the emphasis among the medical profession on the benefits to be obtained by patients through isolation, fresh air, good diet, and overfeeding[127] offered a favourable context in which the established value of cod liver oil in diminishing the effect of and building resistance to wasting diseases, the more palatable Kepler products could exploit.

In the case of chemists and druggists, travellers were asked to classify businesses according to whether the shop was 'fine' or 'common' (those categories visited were roughly equal in number) and whether they displayed

FIGURE 2.11 Record of a BW&Co's representative's calls on chemists in central London, 18 April 1882.

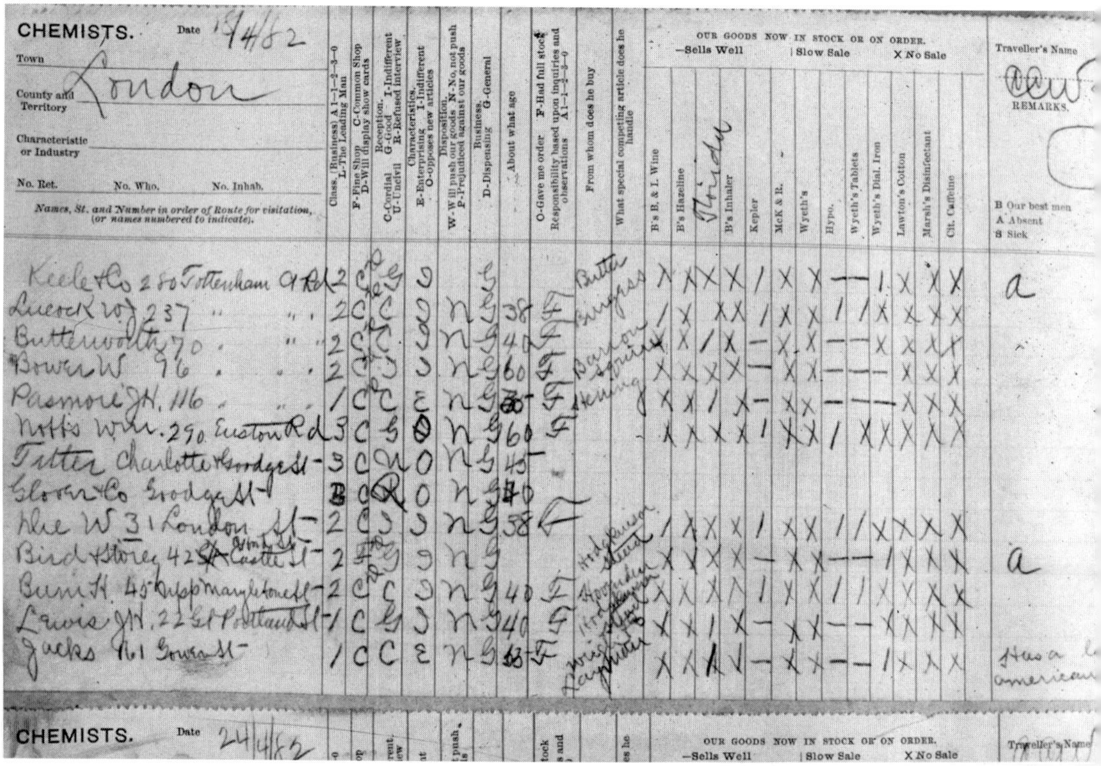
CHEMISTS. Date 18/4/82
Town London
County and Territory
Characteristic or Industry
No. Ret. No. Who. No. Inhab.
Names, St. and Number in order of Route for visitation, (or names numbered to indicate).
Class (Business) A1–1–2–3–0 L-The Leading Man
F-Fine Shop C-Common Shop D-Will display show cards
Reception. C-Cordial G-Good I-Indifferent U-Uncivil R-Refused Interview
Characteristics. E-Enterprising I-Indifferent O-Opposes new articles
Disposition. W-Will push our goods N-No. not push P-Prejudiced against our goods
Business. D-Dispensing G-General
About what age
O-Gave me order F-Had full stock
Responsibility based upon inquiries and observations A1–1–2–3–0
From whom does he buy
What special competing article does he handle
OUR GOODS NOW IN STOCK OR ON ORDER. —Sells Well | Slow Sale X No Sale
B's B. & I. Wine
B's Hazeline
B's Inhaler
Kepler
McK & R.
Wyeth's
Hypo.
Wyeth's Tablets
Wyeth's Dial. Iron
Lawton's Cotton
Marsh's Disinfectant
Cit. Caffeine
Traveller's Name
REMARKS.
B Our best men
A Absent
S Sick
CHEMISTS. Date 24/4/82
OUR GOODS NOW IN STOCK OR ON ORDER. —Sells Well | Slow Sale X No Sale
Traveller's Name

(or would be willing to display) BW&Co. showcards.[128] Chemists were ranked on a scale A1 to 4 to which was added the request to identify 'the leading man' in each district. Few chemists classed below 2 were among those visited, while from 1884 the proportion of first-class chemists visited exceeded those ranked as second class. As in the case of doctors, the travellers were well received; few chemists were 'uncivil' or refused an interview, although indifference was in greater evidence than among doctors. Few were opposed to introducing new products; moreover, the proportion of 'enterprising' chemists compared with those described as 'indifferent' was roughly seventy per cent in 1885 and 1886. Travellers were to ascertain attitudes towards the company's goods, as to whether they would push them or not. Travellers were instructed to check stock and record the orders of those customers who stocked the company's products.

The number of chemists visited between 1881 and 1886 was as follows: 1881, 350; 1882, 1,350; 1883, 880; 1884, 960; 1885, 1,030; 1886, 750. The responses from chemists displayed wide variations, the terms 'old fogey' and 'old duffer' figuring more frequently than in travellers' assessments of doctors. Not surprisingly, though with the important exception of the pills supplied by McKesson & Robbins, goods which sold well corresponded with those most favoured by the doctors: Wyeth's tablets and hypodermics, Kepler cod liver oil with malt extract, and Hazeline. By 1886 chemists also reported good sales of beef and iron wine and Wyeth's dialysed iron. However, very few chemists recorded sales of McKesson & Robbins pills in contrast to many doctors who gave them a positive response. The termination of the McKesson & Robbins agency in 1886, however, suggests that the views of the chemists and druggists prevailed.

It is possible to gain a rough idea of the workloads of travellers and the partners' expectations thereof, for each was closely monitored in connection with performance-related salaries. A complaint from traveller Francis Hastings for the absence of such an advance elicited from Wellcome the reply; '... the making of about 36 effective calls on doctors and chemists per week is not work which suggests a large outlay of energy and work'; Hastings was also accused of lacking in method and proper planning.[129] Similar admonishments were received by J.W. Hull and J.H. Francis, for whom 32 visits to doctors and 13 chemists were regarded as unsatisfactory: 'Remember that a doctor with a small practice now may have a large one in a few years, and goodwill of even small chemists is invaluable. The opponent of today can be converted into a future good customer'.[130] Just how many more than 45 calls per week were regarded as acceptable, however, is not recorded. The partners' policy was to ensure that travellers called on doctors and chemists between a maximum of three and a minimum of six months.[131]

Campaigning for contracts; tapping institutional sources of demand

The shops of retail chemists, doctors' surgeries, and hospitals were not the only targets for the partners' carefully constructed marketing strategy. A list of customers receiving between 20 and 33.3 per cent. discount on bulk orders by the 1890s also included infirmaries, hospital schools, orphanages, Poor Law Unions, prisons, Boards of Work and Guardian institutions, missions and missionaries, mining and exploration companies, and manufacturers or dealers in photographic goods.[132] One of the early tasks given to George Pearson was to expand the list of potential volume purchasers by gaining access to the P & O shipping line; he was advised to: '... understand that Dr Thin of Harley Street is old-fashioned, he is principal medical officer of P & O opposed to medical officers prescribing goods such as B&W. Please go and see him and send a detailed report'.[133]

Contacts for government departments, the Home Office, and the Local Government Board were sought through introductions by Professor Thane, Chief Inspector at the Home Office.[134] At the micro level, photographic societies were the object of a campaign to sell the newly introduced photographic chemicals. In 1900 the Australian branch manager was told that for a guinea plus expenses a very eminent member of staff from the Regent Street Polytechnic (evidently of some note in photographic circles) had given a series of 24 lectures in which he mentioned BW&Co.'s products.

> Only when he was approached by societies, who believed they would be getting a normal lecture, not a trade lecture, he mentioned products, said he used them, showed specimen case, and gave lantern demonstration of slides prepared using Tabloid chemicals. We obtained excellent results from his work.[135]

Almost certainly more important in the long term than any of these categories was the breakthrough when, after many years of patient and persistent effort by the partners, the Army Medical Department was persuaded to adopt Tabloid compressed goods and medical equipment for military campaigns. Orders appear to have begun on a small scale in 1892 when they were supplied to the British military expedition to Ashanti and to army hospitals in India. Surgeon T. H. Parke's letter to the *Chemist & Druggist* argued the case for the Medical Department of His Majesty's Services using Tabloids. He regarded the superiority of Tabloids for the army to be based on their consistency of strength, portability, and rapid dispensing facility. They were also cost effective, he argued, because they enabled one medical officer to do the work of two and rendered dispensers virtually redundant.[136] It was the substantial contract placed by the Army Medical Department in

1895 in connection with the Aconite Campaign in West Africa, however, which Wellcome regarded as an important turning point for the firm.

Wellcome urged Lloyd Williams, the factory manager, not to make the slightest slip that would result in 'grievous and incalculable loss. Deal with the matter with utmost intelligence and wisdom. Must not be made known outside that we are executing orders for the government.' This contract firmly established the firm as a permanent contractor of vital importance to the business from that time.[137] It also offered Wellcome an opportunity to offer the Army Medical Department six dozen free samples each of Wyeth Beef Juice and of 'Emol-Keleet'. The first was described as a stimulant recommended to relieve nervous and muscular fatigue consequent upon over-exertion by forced marches and during convalescence. The second as an invaluable treatment for healing open sores and as a balm for prickly heat, chafed skin, and swollen feet.[138]

In 1896, chests containing Tabloids were supplied to the British expedition in the Sudan. In 1898 the company received an order for more than 500,000 Tabloid compressed medicines from the army and from the Admiralty. The American army and navy were also supplied in support of their action against Spain in Cuba in 1898 and in 1899 in the Phillipines. The largest impact, however, was made by the orders the company received to supply the British colonial forces for the South African campaigns which commenced in 1899.[139] In 1900 the war in South Africa produced an order for more than 5 million followed by a further 6 million in 1901.[140] The land armies and the dispensaries of hospital ships were stocked with the firm's chests according to government regulations.[141] Conscious of the impact these would have on the business, Wellcome privately expressed the view to an American military surgeon that so long as the reverses suffered by the British army were temporary, they would prove 'a blessing' to BW&Co. because the more costly and trying the campaign, the more thorough and complete would the reorganisation and re-equipment of the British army be.[142] Firmly established as a major government supplier, the word 'government' was henceforward dropped from orders when recorded on receipt and the code 'AM' used to signify the formulae and the destination of orders, all of which was to remain strictly secret.[143]

Thus, conceived by a missionary for the use of missionaries, the commercial significance of Tabloids supplied in portable medicine chests achieved ultimate realisation on battlefields across the world. In an age of imperial expansion and military conflict culminating in the First World War, the market for compressed medicines particularly suitable for use in remote locations and under war conditions provided an important impetus contributing to the rapid growth in overseas sales between 1892 and 1914.

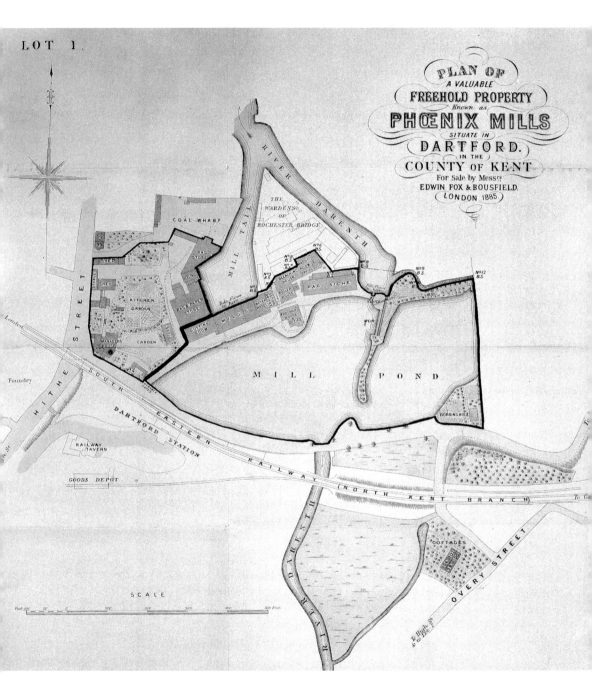

LOT 1.

PLAN OF
A VALUABLE
FREEHOLD PROPERTY
Known as
PHŒNIX MILLS
SITUATE IN
DARTFORD.
IN THE
COUNTY OF KENT
For Sale by Messrs
EDWIN FOX & BOUSFIELD.
LONDON 1885.

RIVER DARENTH

MILL TAIL

THE
WARDENS OF
ROCHESTER BRIDGE

COAL WHARF

RAG STORE

SHED

SHED

KITCHEN GARDEN

RAG & PAPER STORE

CUTTING ROOM

MILLS

GARDEN

MANAGERS HOUSE

No5 B.S.

No6 B.S.

No3 B.S.

BLEACHING ROOM

HOUSE

FOREMANS OFFICE

No8 B.S.

RAG STORE

No9 B.S.

No12 B.S.

SLUICE

WEIR

STREET

HITHE

Foundry

SOUTH EASTERN

DARTFORD STATION

RAILWAY TAVERN

GOODS DEPOT

RAILWAY (NORTH KENT BRANCH)

To London

MILL   POND

BOBBINS HOLE

RIVER DARENTH

COTTAGES

OVERY STREET

To High St
& Ch.

SCALE

Feet 100   50   0   100   200   300   400   500 Feet

'Quality for profit' through 'science and industry'; management and organisation, labour policies, and finance

Managers, management and organisation

The acquisition of Phoenix Mills at Dartford enlarged the company's capacity to grow and to increase productivity, a development to which an advertisement in the *Chemist & Druggist* drew attention: 'The increased scale of our production, greatly enlarged and improved facilities of new works, enlarged machines and apparatus allows us to manufacture on a larger scale and purchase crude drugs in much larger quantities, and in cost savings on materials and labour and a proportionate reduction in selling prices.'[1] How far those economies were actually realised is impossible to judge, though it is clear that securing such economies in a period of rapid growth also involved substantial reorganisation of production and intensification of management control during the twenty years after the move to Dartford in 1889. This process advanced further following Burroughs' death in 1895. The administration of finance, sales, and advertising, which continued to be carried on at the Snow Hill offices in London, was also subject to review and reorganisation.

Before that time, the partnership consisted of an uncomplicated, if less than satisfactory, management hierarchy in which both partners were fully engaged but were frequently at loggerheads. Increasingly during the 1880s, however, Wellcome was the partner most involved in organising production and managing home sales. From the beginning, he was assisted by Robert Clay Sudlow, who had been Assistant Manager of SMB&Co. During Burroughs' absence from the partnership while he was overseas between 1881 and 1883, Sudlow assumed increasing managerial responsibility, becoming *de facto* general manager under Wellcome's direction. Though lacking qualifications in pharmacy or medicine, his business

FIGURE 3.1
Plan of
Phoenix
Mills,
Dartford,
when the site
came up for
sale, 1885.

73

Pharmaceutical Laboratories of Burroughs Wellcome & Co. Dartford, Kent, Engl.
Offices and Warehouse, Snow Hill Buildings, London. E C

FIGURE 3.2
The 'Pharma-
ceutical
Laboratories'
of BW&Co.
the main
factory for
the company
on the site of
the Phoenix
Mills,
Dartford,
*c.*1890.

experience complemented the partners' knowledge. It enabled him to assist the considerably younger and less experienced Wellcome to manage a business which not only grew in size but accomplished the transition from trading to manufacturing. Sudlow's own capacities expanded with the firm. He proceeded to develop an interest in the specifics involved in the trade and manufacture of medical and pharmaceutical products. The central role he filled at BW&Co. in building the company's reputation associated with the success of Tabloids was acknowledged in 1901 when he was featured in a cartoon series appearing in the *Chemist & Druggist*. The cartoon was accom-panied by a light-hearted ditty linking him to the company's success: 'Loyal to his chieftain, master of the Craft.'[2] During this time, a level of mutual respect and trust developed between Sudlow and Wellcome. Two indications are Sudlow's introduction of Wellcome to freemasonry in 1885 (in which Wellcome was to become a senior figure) and Sudlow's deposition in defence of Wellcome during the legal action brought against him by Burroughs in 1888/89.[3] Sudlow's managerial authority in the enlarged organisation was also enhanced when he became the channel of communication between the partners. This occurred as a result of Burroughs' decision to terminate personal discourse with Wellcome completely, for a time communicating either through Sudlow or the partners' respective lawyers.[4] On the occasion of the firm's twenty-fifth anniversary, which coincided with Sudlow's retirement, a dinner was given in his honour. In addition to the encomiums with which he was presented, including one from Wellcome, a celebratory cartoon was produced that showed a beehive on top of which an angel held aloft a shining star, an image of Sudlow at its centre. Like Sudlow, William Henry Kirby, who had also been recruited from business by Burroughs in 1879, remained with the partnership until 1895 when he met an untimely death. Until that time he was Sudlow's Assistant General Manager and Chief Accountant. He was also a freemason and gave a deposition in Wellcome's defence in 1888.[5] Another employee close to Wellcome for many years was J. Collet Smith, another freemason. He had joined in 1881 as Private Secretary to the partners and was subsequently concerned primarily with estate development.

The unchanging composition of senior and office management contrasted with the turnover of managers and supervisory staff in the factory. Following Witte's dismissal from the post of Works Manager and Chemist in 1887 and the brief tenure of his successor, the role was divided into two. In 1892 Albert Searl was given responsibility for works administration and routine production while William Lloyd Williams was newly appointed to undertake 'superior technical and experimental work' including responsibility for all matters of 'commercial and scientific sensitivity', such as refining the formulae for government contracts.[6] This development marked the consolidation of laboratory experimental work hitherto conducted separately for pharmaceutical and Kepler goods and also separate from the development of chemical processes in preparation for production.[7] A visitor to Dartford in 1893 noted two hundred employees who were under the supervision of highly qualified analytical and pharmaceutical chemists. He also described an experimental laboratory used for testing as 'bringing medicine up to date' in a manner which 'would do credit to a university.'[8] Lloyd Williams was a key figure in this development. He was a prize-winning graduate of the Pharmaceutical Society's school, had worked in the Society's research laboratory, and subsequently became an associate of the Institute of Chemistry.[9] Williams' redefined role placed him alongside the emerging cadre of industrial chemists in Britain, for whom the analysis of their own firm's products and those of their competitors assumed increasing importance.[10] In 1896 he supervised the preparation

FIGURE 3.4
Packing girls
during a
recreational
break,
Dartford
c. 1910.

of animal product Tabloids (BW&Co.'s brand of compressed medicines) in a newly formed sub-department making Thyroid and Animal Products.[11] However, in 1897 a new post, Secretary of Works, was created with the intention of relieving Williams of 'business drudgery' to provide more time for scientific work. Aubrey Hill from the Pharmaceutical Department was appointed to the new role.[12] Consistent with practice prevailing at other pharmaceutical firms (notably Boots).[13] In 1898 he took charge of manufacturing in the new Chemical department until his premature death in 1899.[14] Meanwhile, Hill's move coincided with Wellcome's serious criticisms of Searl, the Works Manager of Dartford, regarding quality control and soon led to his replacement by Hill.[15] On Hill's resignation in 1906, Dr Hooper A. D. Jowett, a pharmaceutical chemist who had been appointed to the Wellcome Chemical Research Laboratories (WCRL) in 1896 at the age of 36, became Works Manager.[16] He was described by T. A. Henry of the WCRL as possessing a 'vigorous and inspiring personality', which he brought to bear in a position he occupied until his sudden death in 1936.[17]

The relocation of production to Dartford as a prelude to expansion and diversification was also the occasion for a reorganisation of production and involved changes in management personnel. The accounting, sales, printing and advertising, and leather working sections remained at Snow Hill until 1904 when thirty highly skilled, mainly Austrian, leather workers producing hand-made medical chests and first-aid cases moved to Dartford. Printing relocated to Dartford in 1907.[18] The preparation and packing of all Kepler and Hazeline lines, Enule products, dressings, pastilles, and capsules occurred in the Malt and Pharmaceutical Department, the latter consisting of medicines which were neither Tabloids nor Soloids. A new four storey building for the Malt and Pharmaceutical Department in 1894 was the first to be constructed at Dartford. This was followed in 1895 by a new two storey building to accommodate the Tabloid Manufacturing Department, the granulating, compressing, and sugar coating sub-departments, and another for triturating tinctures.[19] Separate sub-departments also existed for Hypodermic Tabloids and Soloids and for the production and packing of Tea Tabloids. The Tabloid Packing Department contained sub-departments for packing and labelling, and for dealing with stocks of advertising material. These departments moved into the Tabloid building to which a third storey was added three years later followed by an additional Tabloid building in 1900.[20]

Until 1901, when electric power was introduced to the works, steam powered and hand-operated compressing machinery (still necessary for a few drugs in the early twentieth century) and grinding mortar mills (princi-

FIGURE 3.5
Packing girls
during a
recreational
break,
Dartford
c. 1910.

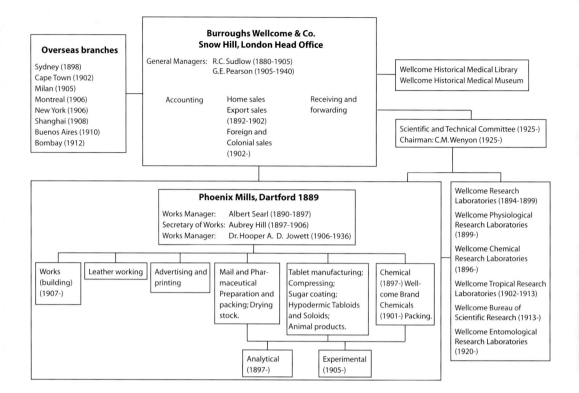

Overseas branches

Sydney (1898)
Cape Town (1902)
Milan (1905)
Montreal (1906)
New York (1906)
Shanghai (1908)
Buenos Aires (1910)
Bombay (1912)

Burroughs Wellcome & Co.
Snow Hill, London Head Office

General Managers: R.C. Sudlow (1880-1905)
G.E. Pearson (1905-1940)

Accounting

Home sales
Export sales
(1892-1902)
Foreign and
Colonial sales
(1902-)

Receiving and
forwarding

Wellcome Historical Medical Library
Wellcome Historical Medical Museum

Scientific and Technical Committee (1925-)
Chairman: C.M. Wenyon (1925-)

Phoenix Mills, Dartford 1889

Works Manager: Albert Searl (1890-1897)
Secretary of Works: Aubrey Hill (1897-1906)
Works Manager: Dr. Hooper A. D. Jowett (1906-1936)

Works
(building)
(1907-)

Leather working

Advertising and
printing

Mail and Phar-
maceutical
Preparation and
packing; Drying
stock.

Tablet manufacturing;
Compressing;
Sugar coating;
Hypodermic Tabloids
and Soloids;
Animal products.

Chemical
(1897-) Well-
come Brand
Chemicals
(1901-) Packing.

Analytical
(1897-)

Experimental
(1905-)

Wellcome Research
Laboratories (1894-1899)

Wellcome Physiological
Research Laboratories
(1899-)

Wellcome Chemical
Research Laboratories
(1896-)

Wellcome Tropical Research
Laboratories (1902-1913)

Wellcome Bureau of
Scientific Research (1913-)

Wellcome Entomological
Research Laboratories
(1920-)

FIGURE 3.6
BW&Co
organisa-
tional chart,
1889–1924.

pally used in the production of the new animal products) were the limits of mechanisation. Initially, preparation of these new products, which spawned the department of animal products, was located in the old Tabloid building. Limited at first to preparations of the thyroid gland, these were dissected by hand, mixed, dried, and ground. Orders during the experimental stage resulted from doctors' requests to supply preparations of various animal glands in Tabloid form.

In pursuit of quality; towards control and research

Facilities for quality control originated from the early production of malt products, a Kepler 'laboratory' having existed from the time production commenced.[21] Initially, the company's analyst was mainly concerned with testing supplies of raw materials and accepting only the highest quality. His responsibility was to decide whether a sample of cod liver oil fresh from a cask found by the Malt Department head to be unsatisfactory on grounds of taste, smell, or appearance, should be rejected.[22] On one occasion, the discovery of arsenic in samples from a large boatload of malt led to the rejection of the entire consignment.[23] Jowett believed that malt manufacturing was also instrumental in the evolution of experimentation. During the firm's earlier history the addition of a wide range of pharmaceutical

FIGURE 3.7
Packing girls
labelling
and boxing
medicines,
Dartford,
c. 1909.

preparations to diversify the Kepler line rendered the use of pure additives imperative. To achieve this, it became necessary to introduce strict scientific control into the organisation and to recruit highly trained chemists and pharmacists.[24]

A series of problems during the 1890s led to important changes in the organisation of the Works. In 1895 irregular working of the machines led to the loss of an entire blend of Tea Tabloids – the result, Wellcome concluded, of a defective system. This had failed to identify the problem soon enough to limit the scale of the loss.[25] These losses were symptomatic of the difficulty Wellcome faced in manufacturing products of the highest quality; 'BP or better', a reference to the standards set in the *British Pharmacopoeia*, was a claim made later in the company's advertisements. The trade-offs between production in greater volume, costs, and quality became recurrent concerns, especially following complaints from customers, competitors, imitators and other staff critical of increasingly defective products issued from Dartford. '… [N]ow is not the time for explanations and excuses', he told Searl, 'but for immediate remedying of undoubted defects.'[26] On discovering in 1898 that among a large and vital government order for Tabloid sodium bicarbonate, some were irregular and wrongly sized and the quinine was pink and crumbly, Wellcome issued an instruction to departmental heads that the firm should not only maintain its former standard 'but aim at much more – we must constantly advance, and always excel our rivals.[27] Our motto is not, and must not be, that "we have attained all" – but on the contrary, we must "unceasingly strive to improve and perfect". It will only be by redoubled vigilance, constant persevering experimentation, research and study, that the present defects can be overcome'.[28]

An important factor affecting the company's success in achieving this objective was the quality of chemicals from suppliers. Hinting at the difficulty of securing supplies of fine chemicals for the manufacture of high and consistent purity at a reasonable cost, Wellcome decreed that unless chemicals could be obtained to produce goods of the highest grade then, in future, Dartford must produce them of a superior quality, even if at higher costs than prevailing market prices. Applying the level of scientific control required to ensure purity and overall quality of products necessitated the appointment of scientists of the highest calibre. The importance of this pre-requisite was underlined in 1897 when the company faced potential embarrassment by the discovery of a wooden fragment contained in an enule morphine suppository. This coincided with concern expressed by the Pharmaceutical Society regarding variation in weight and content of suppositories, a subject widely reported in the medical and trade press. Immediate steps were taken with respect to enules and to the iron content in Blaud's pills which suggests Wellcome's sensitivity regarding the quality of these products, too. The measures specific to these products included the imposition of stricter rules regarding formulae and mixing and more frequent and more stringent testing.[29]

An Analytical Department was created in 1897 under the newly appointed Francis Carr. His training included chemistry, physics, and engineering though, like Jowett, he also possessed research experience in the laboratories of the Pharmaceutical Society. When, in 1898, a Chemical Department was opened in a new building at Dartford accommodating both the Experimental and Analytical Department as well as chemical manufacture it came under Carr's management,[30] as did the *Materia Medica* farm, begun in 1904. The function of the Analytical Department was 'to ensure purity, form, cleanliness, colour, and solubility of every drug and chemical which passed into stock'.[31] Safeguarding the secret formulae books and their secure storage was the responsibility of the Formulae Chemist; only he, a head of department, and the clerk at Dartford had access to the copy from the appropriate department. Before any order for an ingredient was issued for the production of any item, the working formula was checked and initialled by the departmental head against the official formula. Beginning in 1898, through a series of 'standing orders and departmental instructions' issued to department heads and updated on the basis of experience, strict control of every operation 'from manufacture to dispatch' was the responsibility of the analytical laboratories: 'Constant vigilance by all concerned in every stage of the operation is continually stressed and every discrepancy, however small, is immediately investigated.'[32]

Control measures regulating the production of Tabloids and Soloids required the labelling, recording, checking, and dating the name and weight at each stage of the production process. Where poisonous ingredients were used, initials of both weigher and checker were also entered in the poison book. A name and number was assigned to each batch to ensure identification in the event of complaints whether from customers or from inside the organisation. The final stage involved the Analyst examining the goods for identity, solubility, general excellence of finish, and for weight. Goods were not allowed to be packed until passed by the Analyst and labelled with an analytical number attached to all the goods packed from the same container, no goods were allowed to leave the packing room unless sealed by a signed band.[33] When occasionally customers returned batches of goods, they were tested by the Analytical Department before resubmitting them to manufacturing departments either for conversion into fresh drugs, reconditioning, or destruction. The Department repeated the testing process if manufacturing departments rejected the Department's requests.[34]

Similar printed Instructions to the Head of the Pharmaceutical Department underlined the personal responsibility of everyone working in the checking system for absolute accuracy and thoroughness: 'The only safe method of checking is to proceed on the assumption that everything is wrong until proved to be right'.[35]

The formation of an Analytical Department altered the function of the Experimental Department. Contents of a memorandum from head office were circulated to all departmental heads in 1897 suggesting that existing practice in regard to experimentation was unsatisfactory (though the proposed remedy was unclear). Citing the specific case of experiments with compound cube Tabloids, heads were informed:

> When [items for testing] were sent down to the Factory, it was never our intention that the experimenter should restrict himself to working it out on lines intended if by so doing he finds good results are not obtained. Of course every effort should be made to demonstrate the practicality of the original suggestion. We do not mean that any ideas not from the firm [i.e. head office] should be considered worthless or passed over without testing, but that the operator should not restrict himself to the original instructions.[36]

Trying to resolve the problem arising from departments' attempts to tread the fine line between observing instructions to the letter and experimenting pragmatically may explain the decision, taken in 1897, to concentrate responsibility within the Experimental Department in order to secure more effective control. It was divided into three sections: the chemical laboratory, the pharmaceutical laboratory, and the drawing office.[37] Its objectives were to improve existing products and processes, to develop new and marketable drugs, and to provide expert advice to all sections throughout the factory. Monthly reports on machinery and the monitoring of packed stock and pharmaceuticals provided departmental heads with information to assist with production planning and stock control.[38] Several other small departments or sub-departments existed for packing and bottling, labelling, maintaining records, receiving and forwarding stock, packing stock, engineering, and storing. Their precise location in the organisation changed little over time, though sub-division or re-absorption did take place. The malt and pharmaceutical department was split into separate sections in 1904. In 1907 the sub-sections within the departments were re-integrated to achieve flexibility between production lines in response to demand, a measure designed to raise productivity and reduce labour costs.[39]

Efficiency and cost control

In pursuit of Wellcome's policy of producing goods of 'quality for profit', an intensification of quality control was accompanied by efforts to contain costs. As in the case of quality control, containing costs involved reforms of organisation and working practices both in Dartford and at Snow Hill. Rising costs during the late 1890s were in part a reflection of a general trend in drug prices. However, the company's particular experience of a cost price squeeze became increasingly serious as the demand for the company's products grew rapidly before and especially during the Boer War. The problem of cost inflation, therefore, was the result of both general and specific factors peculiar to BW&Co. One response to generally high market prices had been to commence production of fine chemicals to replace those hitherto purchased from suppliers. The adoption of a more systematic approach to costing, measures intended to reduce lost working time, technical innovation, and reconsideration of the company's product range were other approaches to tackling the cost problem between 1890 and 1914.

A new system was introduced in 1898 under Fowkes, an accountant brought into the company as a consultant and alluded to by an insider as 'a reorganiser'[40]. Except in the chemical department, the principle adopted was that overhead charges borne by each department were to be based on hours worked rather than wage bills, the purpose being not to discriminate against low cost (primarily female) labour. The system was extended to the Tabloid department from 1901 and in a refined form was applied to pharmaceuticals from 1907 when, although hours worked continued to be the basis of costing, 'productive labour' costs were linked directly to product lines. Experimental work carried out was excluded from the company's overhead costs and debited to head office. The logic underlying this arrangement was that the works should be treated as if new lines had originated from an outside source from which they had also been purchased. In this case, the development costs would have been borne by that source. An adjunct to an attempt at greater cost control was the introduction of cards to systematise output data. The introduction in 1904 of clocks for job measurement was connected to Fowkes's reform of the accounting, costing, and data recording systems.[41]

Improving technology was the second approach to the company's productivity and capacity problems. Compressing and automatic corking machinery constructed in the firm's own workshops continued to be developed or improved and was regarded as giving the firm an advantage over others on the market.[42] This explains the high level of secrecy at Dartford where the contracts of key workers included a confidentiality clause. Cherkauer, the chief engineer from Continental Europe who in 1898 had designed a new and improved Tabloid machine, experienced the implementation of that policy when he submitted his resignation in 1901. Although Sudlow suspected that the reason Cherkauer was leaving was an aversion to vaccination introduced by the firm during a smallpox outbreak, Sudlow instructed Hill, Works Manager at Dartford, to 'Threaten strong punishment in any country in the world if he breaks the [secrecy] agreement. Demand all his papers, go fearlessly to his house. Do quickly. Do not allow him bluff or evasion. You can bluff and frighten if troublesome.'[43] During his interview with Cherkauer, Hill discovered that the reason why he was leaving was to take up another post. Cherkauer presented no objection to handing over papers and drawings. Even so, a home visit was arranged to remind Cherkauer 'of the penalties according to agreement if he transgressed.' Cherkauer expressed awareness of the agreement, referred to having taken legal advice, had no property belonging to the firm, and reported his intention to set up as a machinery repairer for large firms in Vienna. His speech and demeanour were interpreted by Hill as those of an honest individual and justified termination of pursuit.[44] In 1899, when Smart was offered a position as Cherkauer's successor and queried a secrecy clause in his contract, he was told that the firm relied on innovation and that any invention made in or out of company time would belong to the company.[45] In the short term, importing machinery made possible the rapid expansion in Tabloid production to meet government orders. In 1901 orders were placed with H.K. Mulford of Philadelphia which included a new granulating machine and compressing machines capable of producing 6 tablets at a stroke and turning out 360,000 tablets per 10-hour day as well. Continuing the practice of 'never under any circumstances' purchasing through regular channels, the order was placed through Sam Fairchild who agreed not to reveal BW&Co. as the buyer. All signs of identification were chiselled off the machines on delivery.[46] In the following year, a new German machine designed to dispense with granulation was investigated in secret by Hill and Raisin, the new chief engineer. Raisin was also sent to Paris to examine another machine with a view to adaptation for the production of compressed goods.[47] One consequence of obtaining increasingly productive machinery was that economies of large scale and continuous productions of a single product became potentially greater. This was important not only because of quicker action but because long runs reduced the amount of time and cost incurred by transferring from one tablet line to another. One estimate of the time taken to clean a machine producing 3,000 tablets was that it took ten times as long as it did to manufacture them.[48] The unexpectedly rapid increase in output necessitated by an unprecedented volume of orders from the Army Medical Department during the Boer War created other problems.[49]

A consequence of extensive sickness among the army, rather than of casualties from combat, the extraordinarily high demand for Tabloids (quinine especially), Soloids, and dressings, and the short delivery dates required compounded the difficulty of maintaining quality while manufacturing in substantially greater volume.[50] A breakdown in the health of a key female supervisor and large numbers of absentees as a consequence of the company's introduction of vaccination during the smallpox outbreak in the south-east in the autumn of 1901 intensified the problem.[51] In 1901 49 lines went out of stock and a further 41 were in short supply; others were late in delivery.[52] A head office memo to Dartford in March 1901, marked 'urgent', reported that the weekly production of Tabloids and Soloids (excluding Tabloid hypodermic and ophthalmic products) was 9 million plus 10 per cent for rejections. That figure was required to increase within six months to an output of 15 million including rejections,[53] a target which necessitated more machinery and an expansion of production capacity.[54]

In 1899, the manager of the Tabloid department was advised that because of the growing use and large size of many Tabloid effervescent products, the limits of accuracy to which other (more genuinely medicinal) products were manufactured should be relaxed to 'sensible limits'.[55] Meanwhile, Jowett prepared an initial report on the possible sources of cost inflation affecting Tabloids and Soloids. He concluded that especially in those lines for which costs had been excessive, the level of rejections of 'imperfect' products was 'unacceptably high' and consequently the cause of considerable financial cost. Phenacetin, one of the largest lines, suffered a particularly high level of rejections and cost inflation. One especially frustrating finding was that when presented with items they had rejected, some packers had admitted being unable to find any faults. The cost-increasing implications of high rejection levels arose from the additional heavy labour costs of recovery or of re-grinding, re-granulating, finishing, and cleaning of machinery before recommencing production. Several explanations were offered for the rejections, notably a 'lack of vigilance' among supervisory staff in the granulating and compressing departments where negligence was discovered to have been 'not infrequent'. For the first time, records of rejections were put in place, accumulated for a year in the first instance to facilitate analysis in preparation for another report to be submitted to Wellcome for action.[56] That report has not survived. However, the outcome may be inferred from correspondence between head office and Hector, manager of the Sydney branch; it implies that Wellcome's pursuit of quality was an important contributory factor to the problem of cost inflation. Hector was urged 'to intelligently interpret with prudence the stringent rules which have been in force in our works at Dartford in regard to rejections and ensure this whole question is put upon a rational basis as regards the manufacture of Tabloids and Soloids in Sydney.'[57] Significantly, Hector was advised that 'the system of rejecting products in force at the works has been carried to an unreasonable excess' and it was recommended that the overall Tabloid and Soloid rejection ratio should not exceed 5 per cent and should be 'ideally lower if possible.'[58] Reflecting the problems discovered in the works at Dartford in the first review, Hector was advised to pay particular attention to the prompt removal of initially damaged goods from machinery and to the observance of the strict conditions recommended, for example, the degree of fineness and dryness of powder in working certain drugs:

> These questions have been worked out more than once but no proper record has been made of the standard conditions and gradually operators have drifted backwards until attention has been drawn to defects, and then the standard conditions have to be rediscovered and at a frightful cost the defects are dealt with by rejecting enormous percentages – this is a short and easy way but it is ruinous.[59]

While offering potential scale economies in production, the higher speed new machinery also increased the costs of discontinuous working in the event of unsuitable raw materials fed into the machines.

A concern to contain costs was not confined to the popular general goods. In 1901 Carr was asked to explain why accounts relating to the chemical department showed that the amount of sulphate needed to produce one ounce of bisulphate had steadily increased. Fowkes's figures from the cost department revealed a loss on this line; output had fallen while costs had risen.[60] Carr emphasized the relationship between volume and cost of production. In response to a head office request, he compiled a list of chemicals showing minimum efficient levels of production of drugs and chemicals at lowest cost. He expressed concern that many products were being made in small quantities and at a loss; production, he believed, needed to be put on a 'more business like basis.' Carr was asked to provide current

VICTORIAN GUARDIANS OF THE WORKS

This classical photograph of the Wellcome Chemical Works Fire Brigade was taken in approximately 1898. Back row (left to right) : Third Officer Bargate and Firemen Purnett, Sloss, Spencer, Shackleton, Thomas, Taylor, Casey and Lepper. Middle row : Firemen Purton, Stacey and Dartnell, Second Officer Alderton, Fireman Neighbour, name not known, and Fireman Smith. Front row : Firemen Hardy and Ney, Chief Officer Morris, and Firemen Herbert and Brooker. Sons and daughters of some of these include Mr. W. Neighbour, compressing engineer with 43 years' service, Mr. C. W. Dartnell, shop foreman in the Engineers with 40 years' service, whose father gave this photograph some years ago to Captain Peters, and Miss J. Herbert (now Mrs. Fenner), of the Forwarding Department

FIGURE 3.8
The
Wellcome
Chemical
Works' Fire
Brigade,
*c.*1898,
(*Foundation
News*, Dec.
1958).

information concerning the length of time each product could be stocked, its approximate value, and where possible, an estimate of the optimal outputs for lowest cost. Head office expressed the view that the cheaper drugs, for which labour costs accounted for a high proportion of total costs, should be manufactured in very much larger quantities than hitherto. The production of expensive alkaloids and drugs were found to be economic in cost terms only if manufactured in a volume sufficient for several years' supply. The cost recorded for atropine sulphate was twice the market price and heralded a policy of buying in, re-crystallizing or purifying, and using for manufacture or sale.[61]

In the case of animal substances such as ox and pig bile, doubts were expressed as to the practicability for sufficient of the crude material to be dealt with at one time to make the quantities given, stability being the governing factor in deciding on the scale of manufacture.[62] Special formulae, typically made up in small quantities presented a special problem. Hitherto they had been accorded a priority because they were perceived to contribute to the extension of goodwill among the doctors who ordered them. However, they were difficult to make and 'costly in the extreme'. Head office asked for information on the volume prepared in a year before making a decision.[63]

Flirting with 'scientific management'

FIGURE 3.9
BW&Co.'s
first motorised
delivery van,
Dartford,
1906.

Coinciding with Sudlow's retirement in 1905, Wellcome engaged a business efficiency expert to report on various aspects of the company. One of these was the internal administration at head office which Wellcome considered to be in need of reorganisation in order to relieve him of detailed, executive duties.[64] In truth, since the death of Burroughs in 1895, Wellcome's frequent absences from England in pursuit of his archaeological interests, to collect and to travel, had inevitably reduced his capacity for face-to-face, day-to-day management, though the detail contained in his letters to Snow Hill reveals a remarkable ability to manage at arm's length. The other part of the brief given to the consultant and his team of accountants was to investigate possibilities for increasing the profitability of certain lines that currently were either unprofitable or less profitable. A year passed before Wellcome received any inkling of the contents of the long awaited report. In fact, no such report was forthcoming, merely advice to Wellcome that the company should concentrate production on Kepler goods and abandon some other lines. While conceding that the consultant may have been clever, Wellcome decided that it was 'a waste to employ him to do what our own staff can do … I do not relish paying big fees to men for the privilege of teaching them [our] systems'.[65] It seems likely, however, that for all his faults, the consultant had identified the product which was the most significant contributor to the firm's profitability. Wellcome may have been irked because the conclusion was perceived to conflict with his ambition for his firm to become a leader in the production of ethical pharmaceuticals of the highest quality based on laboratory research. Quality applied to science-based products, however, did not also guarantee profit, a possibility that Wellcome may have preferred to ignore.

A breathing space immediately followed the frenzied activity during the Boer War but soon disappeared. In 1903 mechanisation of the process of counting Tabloids into containers contributed to both the accuracy and speed with which the tablets left the line ready for packing and distribution. This stage of the process was further improved by the introduction of the first packing conveyors in 1905, both for Tabloids and goods made in the Pharmaceutical Department. A bottle washing conveyor, and a conveyer in the pharmaceutical department were introduced in 1907. In the Malt Department, corks were replaced by metal caps fitted by new bottling apparatus. In 1908 a malt extract was produced for the first time using vacuum pressure technology. An aerial conveyor to speed up the bottle-washing process was added in 1910 and a compressing machine fitted with counting and sorting apparatus was installed in 1912.[66] New technology was intended to raise productivity through facilitating larger scale production resulting in lower costs. These innovations occurred in response to rising costs and increasing difficulties in meeting customers' orders.

Concern over quality also resurfaced. In 1907 steps were taken to secure greater control over stocking. The packing of all goods was centralised under the charge of a chief storekeeper who was required to submit a daily report on progress.[67] Heads of departments were reminded that quality must not be sacrificed for efficiency in their efforts to increase rates of output or lower production costs.[68] Between 1908 and 1912 the production of Tabloids grew by 50 per cent to reach 470 million. In 1912 attention was drawn to standing order 57 to reiterate that nothing should be allowed to interfere with any detail in checking goods before delivery, either in the manufacturing or packing departments.[69] A scheme for increasing efficiency in the packing rooms (where unlike in the manufacturing departments pay was by rate rather than piecework) was also introduced. Based on principles of the new scientific management, under the new system an 'efficiency figure' was calculated by actual experiment in order to approximate a figure for each packing that an employee might reasonably be expected to achieve if working under optimal conditions, packing perfect products using perfect materials. This was compared with a four-year average for the line and the highest figure achieved. After the packing was completed, an analysis of 'packing tallies' carried out in the office was used to determine an individual's rate per hour. When that rate fell below the average, the head of department and works manager or superintendent were advised, explanations requested, and the fact recorded on the employee's efficiency card (rates above the average were also recorded). A report (probably by Jowett) on the preparation of the scheme at Dartford concluded: 'It is intended to gradually dispense with those below average and to pay those above the average a higher rate than those of the average rate. The result should be a gradual rise towards efficiency'.[70]

Symptomatic of the continuing tension between the drive for efficiency and the quality imperative, in 1909, the customary routine prior to placing new drugs or preparations on the market was reformed. New instructions specified the need for completeness of experiments to ensure perfect purity of drugs. In the case of preparations, their various possibilities should be explored thoroughly 'so that no improvement seems possible'. Thorough testing was the next stage to ensure that, where appropriate, each new substance possessed the highest degree of solubility and behaviour towards different solvents as well as permanence under tropical conditions. Long term keeping quality was the key test for preparations. The next stage for drugs was testing at the WPRL whose report (should it be favourable) should be followed by patenting. In fact, reform of the approach to patenting does not appear to have been implemented. Costing carried out by the works accountant was the next stage after consultation with departmental heads and the works manager. Probable first cost estimates 'with ample margin for contingencies' were to be prepared, as was a minimum efficient cost in the event that a large demand was anticipated. After goods had been approved for production and issued to head office, complete actual costs were to be substituted for estimates.

All goods proceeded to the Analytical Department; samples (and all possible information about the new products) were to be passed to Head Office where a decision would be made whether to proceed to testing on patients. Should such tests take place, even if prepared by the Experimental Department, samples must pass through analysis first. Subject to satisfactory trial and the decision by Head Office to market the preparation, henceforward the Experimental Department would advise the relevant department of the manufacturing process. While this took place, the Analytical Department had to formulate methods of control and specify standards; packings had to be prepared by the packing department. Finally, once the issue of the new product had been sanctioned, manufacturing, packing, and control were to be worked out simultaneously rather than consecutively.[71] Three years after these rules were introduced, Jowett drew attention to the continuing problem resulting from the development of new substances up to the production stages without, contrary to standing order 156, passing them through the Analyst. This meant that the exact formula of the substances were not on record and had to be ascertained afresh.[72] Jowett issued a general reminder notice a few months later to the effect that 'all instructions and systems which are put into force should be loyally observed and strictly carried out'. Department heads were invited to suggest modifications if at any time such regulations appeared to have become unnecessary. The notice ended: 'When a new system, or instruction, is issued the reason for its issue will not always be apparent to everyone … but it can be taken for granted that there are always good and sufficient reasons for the steps taken and that it is not a matter of red tape'.[73] The tone as well as content of this memorandum suggests that inter-departmental relations and relations between department heads and senior managers may have become less harmonious than hitherto.[74] In a relatively labour-intensive industry at this time, in which quality control at the shop floor level was so important, relations between employers, and managers, and labour also assume a special significance.

Disciplining the workers

The rapid expansion of production, especially from the 1890s, resulted in a substantial growth in employment. It is not possible to chart this development precisely in the absence of continuous series of employment data, though various estimates recorded by contemporaries provide some indication of timing and scale (Table 3.1).

FIGURE 3.10
Dining room,
Dartford,
c. 1900.

Table 3.1 *Employment at Burroughs Wellcome & Co., 1884–1932*

1884	101	25 young women and girls, 44 men, 32 office staff
1890	228	115 young women and girls, 85 men, 28 office clerks.
1892	600	
1899	721	Includes 329 young women and girls.
1900	1004	
1905	1300	
1930	2800	
1932	2600	

WFA, Acc 90/15: 01; WFA/GB/29/24, Dartford cuttings book 1, *Dartford Advertiser*, 1890; WFA, Acc. 82/1, Box 13, *Talk*, 21 July 1893; WFA, Wellcome LB 34, 194, Memo, 25 April 1899. It is not clear whether this figure includes salesmen, of whom there may have been a dozen, 1899. WFA, Wellcome LB 14, 503, BW&Co. to Wellcome, 23 Nov. 1900; Acc. 90/14:3.

In 1884, one year from the move to Wandsworth from Snow Hill, when manufacturing had begun, the firm employed 25 women, mostly 'young girls with nimble fingers' suited to packing, to whom should be added men employed in engineering and maintenance, printing and office staff, and salesmen, altogether possibly doubling the figure.[75] In 1890 the *Dartford Advertiser* referred to the employment of 115 women and 85 men at Dartford[76] to which should be added probably 37 clerks at Snow Hill (though excluding salesmen), implying possibly a doubling in the numbers employed between the relocations to Wandsworth and to Dartford. The enlarged capacity at Dartford, following the success of the Tabloid case, was accompanied by a threefold rise in employment which in 1892 exceeded 600, of whom

FIGURE 3.11
Packing girls in dining room, Dartford, *c.* 1900.

200 were making Tabloids. This also implies that, excluding office and sales staff, most of the remainder were manufacturing and packing malt products.[77] The first comprehensive figure compiled by Lloyd Williams in 1899 showed a total of 721 employees comprising 604 production workers at Dartford, 23 clerks at the Snow Hill head office, and 44 at the new research laboratories.[78] Another large increase occurred mainly as a result of the growth in demand for medicines during the Boer War though partly a consequence of expanding exports.

Increased numbers necessarily altered the conduct of relations between employers, managers, and workers. Equally important influences were the age, sex characteristics, and levels of skill of those employed at Dartford presented in Tables 3.2 to 3.4. Employment figures for 1890 and 1899 show ratios of females to males at Snow Hill and Dartford of roughly 60:40.

Table 3.2 *Number and average wages of male employees at BW&Co. in 1899*

Class (by skills)	Number	Average wages
A	5	36s. 8d.
B	26	28s. 2d.
C	48	20s. 11d.
D	4	15s. 3d.
E	19	11s. 2d.
F	55	7s. 1½d.
Sugar coating	1	54s.
Instrument dept	10	33s. 1d.
Engineers	38	33s. 1d.
Acacia Hall	7	21s.
Total	**213**	**20s. 6d.**

Table 3.3 *Number and average wages of female employees at BW&Co. in 1899*

Class (by skills)	Number	Average wages
A Forewomen	3	18s.
B	9 (minimum age 17)	17s. 6d.
C	21	16s. 1½d.
D	45	12s. 5d.
E	153	10s. 1d.
F	100	7s. 6½d.
Total (B to F)	**329**	**10s. 2½d.**

Table 3.4 *Building employees at BW&Co. in 1899*

FIGURE 3.12
Staff of the
Pharma-
ceutical
Department,
Dartford,
*c.*1900
(*Foundation
News*, May
1952).

Acacia Hall	50
Brockwell Hall	44
City	23
Works	62
Total	**179**

Based on WFA, LB 34, 194, Memo. (including tabulated
data) signed Wi. 25 April 1899.

In an industry which saw no truly radical technical changes in production
methods between the early 1880s and 1914, it is plausible to assume that this
ratio prevailed throughout. Lloyd Williams' detailed breakdown in 1899
reveals the extent to which BW&Co. depended upon lowly paid female
labour, two-thirds of whom earned an average weekly wage of 6*s.* 6*d.*
Girls became eligible to apply for work when aged 17 but on marriage
were discouraged from continuing in employment.[79] Limited opportunities
existed for promotion (if unmarried) to forewoman status which would be
rewarded by up to three times that figure. One quarter of male workers,
mostly boys, also fell into the unskilled and low paid category earning a
weekly average of roughly 9 shillings.

Another characteristic shared by the males and females recruited to work at BW&Co. was their lack of education especially in practical subjects. Wellcome was especially concerned that this deprived them of any ability to show initiative.[80] The firm did not accept apprentices as craft skills were not required to any great extent. Several positions requiring specific technical skills were filled by Austrian, German, and Swiss applicants whose education and training appears to have given them an advantage.[81] Such skills were not required for tasks performed by most of the large number of female workers who were required to exercise manual dexterity and to show diligence, application, and attention to detail. These characteristics are indicative of a susceptibility among the company's workers to a disciplinary approach by managers who perceived them as needing direction and motivation to fulfil the tasks required. An authoritarian, disciplinary approach was evident from the beginning, extending beyond factory workers to travelling representatives. Almost certainly, greater systematisation of the regime originated following the reorganisation during the mid-1890s, a time of rapid expansion when greater control over production costs and quality became an imperative. From 1898 these were presented as a series of numbered instructions and standing orders for issue to department managers by the Works Manager. They were comprehensive in scope and ranged from specification in detail of the methods to be observed in production and packaging procedures to requirements affecting employees' personal behaviour and hygiene. Conscientiousness, accuracy, and attention to detail in their work were persistent themes contained in the instructions. In 1909 the various rules and instructions added since 1898 were issued in a consolidated General Rules and Instructions document issued to all employees. These were linked to terms of agreement which each employee was required to sign, undertaking to guarantee observance of the rules and accept consequences in case of default.[82]

It is not surprising that punctuality was strictly enforced. A steam hooter marked the beginning and end of the working day. Working time was recorded by a system of numbered discs hung on boards in front of the gatehouse which were removed on entering and returned at lunchtime and again at the end of the day.[83] Once in the factory, regular inspection to ensure compliance was a task allocated to designated 'heads of rooms' and monitored at departmental level through an elaborate system of labelling, recordings in the work tally, and checking.[84]

Clothing was the subject of regulation for production workers from 1897 when, following the practice adopted in the research laboratories, females were required to wear blouses, caps, and overalls supplied by the firm. Males were issued with special jackets, overalls, and aprons, the Works Manager enjoining them to 'keep themselves ... clean and smart'. In 1904 new regulations regarding female clothing required the wearing of gowns which were either black or the standard shade of blue and made of serge or alpaca. Skirts were to be of walking length with a blouse or bodice of matching material. Plain white blouses were allowed for summer, though 'fancy ornaments and trimmings of all kinds must be dispensed with.'[85] 'Perfect cleanliness' also extended to the premises and machinery, operatives being expected to keep machines in perfect working condition and to take a pride in doing so.[86]

Regulations for working in the granulating department and compressing room illustrate the detailed instructions which employees were required to follow. Great care was to be taken to clean benches before work, to ensure all tools were clean and free from smell; scales and balances must be 'scrupulously clean and the surrounding bench free from dust, hands, *especially the fingernails*, should be cleaned when moving from one job to another, clothes should be well brushed with brush provided, gloves, goggles and muzzle should always be used when working on certain drugs, including hypodermic and ophthalmic preparations to avoid any effects from inhalation.'[87] These were reinforced when re-issued in 1905: '... Girls who do not conform to these regulations will be reported to management',

FIGURE 3.13
BW&Co.
Headquarters'
office staff,
c.1903.

while from 1907, 'transgression' was to result in immediate dismissal: 'Girls who do not observe these rules are not fit to carry out their duties ... [they] cause discomfort and inconvenience to other employees and cannot be considered suitable fellow workers'.[88]

Standing orders 'absolutely prohibited unnecessary talking between employees during business hours'; complete silence was to be observed while an employee was engaged in either weighing or compounding. Employees were warned not to drink from any vessel unless they had personally cleaned it first. Secrecy was also the subject of a standing order: 'Under no circumstances whatever is any specimen of any drug or chemical which is prepared in any special way or in any particular form for use in the Manufacturing Department of the Works, nor is any information whatsoever appertaining thereto, to be furnished to anyone outside the Works without the permission of the Works Manager'[89] Absence from work required immediate notification by letter or telegram.[90] Suspected malingerers were also subjected to scrutiny, one head of department was advised to avoid losing employees' time by using considerable discretion when presented by requests from his female workers to see the firm's doctor on account of slight morning ailments.[91] Lending or borrowing from other employees was banned and bad language punished by instant dismissal.[92] The number of rules increased from 36 in 1913 to 51 by 1917, when they included the injunction that employees should 'always be straightforward and sincere'.[93]

The application of some of these rules and instructions to office staff at Snow Hill in 1905, notably regarding dress and timekeeping, elicited an anonymous critique from one of those affected. As in the factory, henceforward overalls of different colours were to denote hierarchy, a change disliked as much as clocking in. The introduction of this system to staff at Head Office prompted the comment that the innovation was 'OK for factory employees but not for ladies and gentlemen engaged in a literary and mental occupation'. In 1910 the introduction of clocks and clocking-in superseded the previous system.[94] The self-styled 'Observer' criticised the rules generally as 'arbitrary and objectionable', undermining relations between Head Office and departmental heads, and between heads and subordinates.[95] He attributed what he perceived to be the imposition of increasingly strict codes of behaviour to the retirement of Sudlow and his replacement by Pearson in 1905, though it also appears to have coincided with the appointment of Jowett as Works Manager in the same year. An authoritarian approach to management throughout the organisation prevailed for many years before Pearson succeeded Sudlow. The style reflected Wellcome's own managerial philosophies; later these were endorsed by Pearson who, temperamentally averse to communication and loyal to Wellcome, invariably agreed with his employer on all matters regarding London and Dartford. Jowett, the Works Manager whose responsibilities included those of ensuring secrecy and safety affecting both consumers and workers, was unlikely to depart from their philosophy, though in later years he began to express concern about relations among managers.[96]

Labour recruitment and welfarism

If, as has been suggested, the sex and age composition of employees and their typically low level of education influenced the content and implementation of the company's labour disciplinary system, the same demographic features were likely to affect the employers' approach to recruitment and retention policies. Dartford was in a rural location where recruitment to factory work presented more difficulties than those which had occurred in Snow Hill and Wandsworth. It was important, therefore, to attempt to ensure that once employees had been hired, regardless of age or sex or whether employed in office, factory, or the laboratories, where appropriate they should attend the Dartford Technical Institute. From 1889 this became possible because of the introduction by the company of the eight-hour day. This innovation was mischievously introduced on Burroughs' initiative to coincide with the visit for the opening of the Dartford factory by Henry George, the leading American socialist and land reform advocate. Thereafter, employees were allowed time for attendance at evening classes in any subject, from building construction to French to dressmaking, the fees for which were paid by the company, though on condition that attendance was sufficient to qualify the student to sit examinations. In 1904 the company claimed some success in as much that workers had benefited, both through the content of their education (practical or otherwise), and by developing more self respect. A company view was that the results had 'increased direct value of some employees to the business … consequently their progress in the firm advanced'. However, a prevailing inertia and disinterest among most workers was also reported to show 'a lack of ambition which too frequently characterises the British working classes'.[97] Education and training formed part of a broader welfarist policy that claimed to bring capital and labour together, a goal that appears to have succeeded to some extent, though how far as an outcome of policy rather than the prospect of steady employment in a low wage rural area

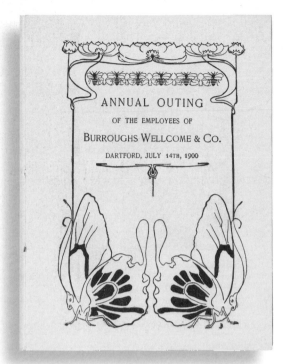

FIGURE 3.15
Title page of
commemo-
rative booklet
for employees'
annual
outing, 14 July
1900.

is not known.[98] One indicator of successful labour relations is the dominance of family employment, the firm giving preference to relatives of existing employees and the existence of many families at work in the factory. The receipt of applications from all parts of the country also suggests that the company was perceived as a desirable place for employment.[99] Those employees who belonged to societies and clubs favoured a friendly society and or medical club rather than a trade union. In response to a question in the Charles Booth survey in 1893, the firm was reported never to have had the slightest trouble with the unions. This was to prove the case also after the First World War.

A strike called by the Warehouse and General Union in 1920 attracted little support from Dartford workers who within days returned to work on inferior contracts containing an agreement to one hour's notice.[100] Even during the mid-1920s, including the period of the General Strike, Pearson reported that while various attempts had been made by the National Union of Drug and Chemical Workers to organise workers at Dartford, '... our people seem to have come to the conclusion that they gained nothing by listening to these paid organisers in the past and that they are much better off in remaining in direct contact with us as hitherto'.[101] This verdict confirmed a report contained in the Union's own bulletin issued to members to the effect that recruiting at Dartford had been a failure.[102] On that occasion, workers (the majority) who chose to continue working were transported in company vans and lorries to avoid interference from pickets. Notices were attached to the sides of vehicles normally used for the dispatch of goods to customers bearing the words: 'urgent medical supplies'.[103]

Other dimensions of the company's welfarist policy were annual outings and events, profit sharing, and the provision of facilities and financial support to encourage the formation and activities of clubs and societies. Annual fetes (in the preparation of which, in the early years, Wellcome took a detailed interest), day trips to the seaside, and events such as lectures and musical evenings, begun in 1884 continued into the post-war period.[104] These were aimed to cater for a wide range of activities: literary, dramatic, musical, and sporting, in addition to offering other leisure pursuits in the extensive landscaped gardens that included an artificial lake adjacent to

the factory. These developments were consolidated with the formation of
the Wellcome Club and Institute in 1898, which coincided with Wellcome's
acquisition of the lease of Acacia Hall in Dartford. A spacious manor house
set in nine acres of garden and meadow land, the Hall was quickly adapted
to accommodate a library, reading rooms, and club houses (separate for
men and women), gymnasium, and assembly hall suitable for orchestral,
dramatic, literary, and other cultural events and activities organised by
the Wellcome Club Committee.[105] Land was drained and laid out as a
sports ground, which, in addition to facilities for major sports, included
tennis courts. Evidence of a determined drive to establish a reputation
as a model employer was the staffing of Acacia Hall with a permanent
secretary, librarian, steward, gardeners, and a trained gymnastics instructor.
Clubs and societies proliferated in this well-resourced programme for the
promotion of healthy recreation, entertainment, and cultural fulfilment
among employees. By that time, societies and clubs existed to cater for the
needs of those interested in football, cricket, tennis, swimming, boating,
gymnastics, photography, and choral, orchestral, scientific and literary
activities. An Entertainments Committee was responsible for planning
and organising the firm's annual events programme.[106] Enlightened and
well-funded provision of such amenities and an employment policy which
minimised lay-offs even during the 1930s,[107] undoubtedly contributed to a
docile work force.

Following the commencement of annual events organised for employees

FIGURE 3.16
BW&Co.'s
works outing,
24 August
1886. Henry
Wellcome
is seated
slightly left
of centre, in
light suit and
cap. Second
on his left is
R. C. Sudlow.

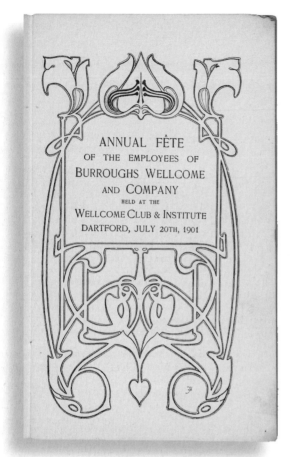

FIGURE 3.17
Title page of
commemo-
rative booklet
for employees'
annual fete,
20 July 1901.

ANNUAL FÊTE
OF THE EMPLOYEES OF
BURROUGHS WELLCOME
AND COMPANY
HELD AT THE
WELLCOME CLUB & INSTITUTE
DARTFORD, JULY 20TH, 1901

in 1884, the company introduced a plan for profit-sharing in 1885.[108] The philosophical foundations of this project, described initially as a bonus scheme, were the ideas of Henry George to which Burroughs was an enthusiastic adherent. The trigger, however, seems to have been the firm's liquidity crisis which in 1884 saw minimal pay increases for a second year, a problem which was explained to employees. The launch of the new scheme was inauspicious. The Snow Hill Office received complaints from twenty members of the packing and printing departments and from the office, claiming that the rates of pay proposed for 1885 (which the partners pointed out were higher than the 1884 levels) did not represent a pay rise. The bonus promised would be delayed for six months and, in effect, deprived them of 50 per cent of the proposed increase. Sudlow interceded with the partners, obtaining a 'substantial increase in pay', to which the Packing Department responded that employees were 'many times grateful and shall always make it our study to further the interest of the firm to the utmost of our abilities'.[109] The bonus system was re-launched in 1886 when distribution to employees was fixed at 5 per cent of the company's profits depending on their wages and salaries. The *Chemist & Druggist* expressed its approval of the scheme, interpreting the implication as a bonus of £300 in 1889 rising to more than £1,600 in 1893.[110] In 1899, four years after Burroughs' death, Wellcome terminated the profit-sharing scheme. He was opposed to George's political philosophy and shared Sudlow's preference for a method of offering incentives, adopting a more predictable formula to produce a more predictable outcome. The termination of the scheme, of course, also meant that Wellcome expunged a relic of his deceased partner's influence on the partnership. The nature of welfarism changed after Burroughs' death but did not diminish. The view that 'ritual aspects' of company life in England had been abandoned by the end of the nineteenth century[111] is wide of the mark. Traditional annual events and celebrations continued alongside the institutionalised activities designed to cement company-employee relations.

Finance, investment and profit

FIGURE 3.18
Maypole
dance at 25th
Anniversary
Fete in the
grounds of
the Wellcome
Club and
Institute,
Dartford, 15
July 1905.

One result of the efforts by partners, managers, and employees described above, resulted in a reputation for the company's products as of the highest quality, one of Wellcome's two principal objectives. The other was to build a profitable business. Both depended on innovation, organisation, and the exercise of control. Securing those objectives also required investment, in relation to which two questions are pertinent: how was the growth in production, sales, and employment financed, and how profitable was this investment?

Table 3.5 presents the composition of assets, sales, and profits. The acquisition of Phoenix Mills doubled fixed assets at a stroke, capital expenditure on reconstruction and plant resulting in an increase from £7,952 in 1888 to £16,658 in 1889. The appearance for the first time of 'Phoenix Mills and Premises' on the balance sheet in 1893, on repayment of the Burroughs purchase loan, added to continuing expenditure on plant and equipment which caused fixed assets to double again, reaching £33,982 in 1895. A revaluation (and the addition of £44,000 to take account of 'goodwill', first recorded in 1896 and remaining until 1912) explains the rise in the value of fixed assets to £80,537 in 1896. They rose to £120,727 in 1899, doubling by 1908 then rising to a pre-war peak in 1912 of £279,808; thereafter, goodwill disappeared from the balance sheet.

The figures presented in Table 3.5 reveal the changing relationship between fixed and working capital behind which lay the transformation of the business from a purely trading enterprise until 1883 into a manufacturing business. Before 1889, working capital exceeded fixed capital by a factor of between three and four to one. These ratios fell to one after the acqui-

sition of the Phoenix Mills. Revaluation in 1895 resulted in an increase in the fixed to working capital ratio of between three and four to one until 1906. The reversal of this trend thereafter occurred when sales expanded massively. Equity capital, representing the value of the partners' investment

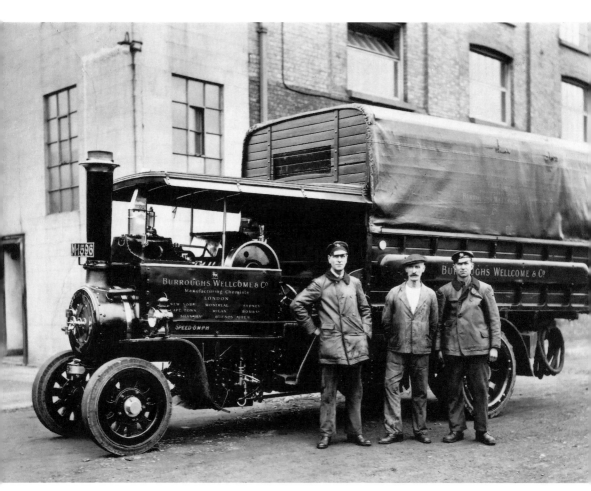

Table 3.5 BW&Co., financial data, 1880–1914 (£)*

Year ending August	Home and foreign sales	Net profit	Equity capital	Fixed assets	Working capital	Long-term debt	Profit/ sales	Profit/ capital
1880			1,991	463	1,528	0		
1881†	17,811	667	2,688	568	2,120	0		
1882	33,158	1,934	4,622	623	3,999	0	5.8	41.8
1883	57,165	2,038	6,660	2,832	3,828	0	3.6	30.6
1884		342	7,002	4,394	2,608	0		5
1885	52,184	4,078	11,080	3,395	7,685	0	7.8	36.8
1886	55,724	6,648	17,728	7,200	10,528	0	11.9	37.5
1887	72,147	4,543	22,271	7,534	14,737	0	6.3	20.4
1888	81,846	5,444	27,715	7,952	19,763	0	6.7	19.6
1889	74,550	2,348	30,063	16,658	13,405	0	3.1	7.8
1890		4,587	34,650	21,784	12,866	0		13.2
1891		5,280	39,930	19,824	20,106	0		13.2
1892		21,687	61,617	32,482	29,135	0		35.2
1893		−5,587	56,030	31,320	24,710	0		
1894		11,129	67,159	34,443	32,716	0		16.6
1895		22,005	66,158	33,982	32,716	0		33.3
1896		12,689	110,137	80,537	29,600	0		11.5
1897		12,926	84,589	85,172	29,759	30,342		15.3
1898		28,976	88,964	89,113	34,128	34,277		32.6
1899	175,701	25,637	112,366	120,727	37,003	45,364	14.6	22.8
1900	187,282	24,219	134,721	133,546	42,265	41,090	12.9	17.9
1901	204,690	18,589	153,310	139,896	42,352	28,938	9.0	13.1
1902	211,616	11,195	168,580	162,762	48,070	42,252	5.0	6.6
1903	220,439	21,909	192,871	166,259	69,987	43,375	10.0	11.4
1904	233,000	13,539	223,785	195,749	69,843	41,807	5.8	6.1
1905	246,020	11,506	226,787	213,456	66,641	53,310	4.7	5.1
1906	293,029	43,460	255,789	212,559	87,536	44,306	14.8	17.0
1907	314,228	56,183	293,023	214,990	121,831	43,798	17.9	19.2
1908	324,999	50,411	325,565	246,728	114,066	35,229	15.5	15.5
1909	327,119	43,416	353,479	246,986	139,874	33,381	13.3	12.3
1910	348,137	31,140	369,756	264,218	152,973	47,434	8.9	8.4
1911	372,149	42,109	391,653	277,182	179,053	64,582	11.3	10.75
1912	394,679	65,573	425,654	279,808	204,387	58,541	16.6	15.4
1913	417,312	85,321	425,292	239,163	222,969	32,840	20.5	19.9
1914	466,258	83,265	466,074	246,564	242,533	23,023	17.9	17.8

* The profit series before 1899 is net of proprietors' annual withdrawals. The fixed asset series between 1896 (following Burroughs' death) and 1912 includes 'goodwill' valued at £44,641.

† The sales figure for 1881 cited by Rhodes James (which implies an extraordinary high annual profit/sales ratio of 37 per cent.) probably refers only to part of the year. Rhodes James, *Henry Wellcome*, p. 141, footnote. WFA, Acc. 90/1, Box 149, account ledger, BW&Co.

in the company, reached five figures for the first time in 1885, rising from £11,080 to £66,158 in 1895. The rate of growth over the next ten years was slower. From the revalued figure of £110,137 in 1896, equity capital rose to £255,789 in 1906. This represented a similar growth rate to that of the company's close British rival, Allen & Hanburys. On conversion to becoming a limited company in 1893, that business had been capitalised at £75,000 which compared with the equity capital of BW&Co. at that time, of £56,030. Further investment at Allen & Hanburys brought the figure to £475,000 in 1912, when that of BW&Co. was £429,292, rising to £466,074 in 1914.[112] Between 1906 and 1914, therefore, while the capital of Allen & Hanburys remained marginally greater than that of BW&Co., the rate of growth of BW&Co. was faster.

The financing of activity was primarily a problem of balancing trade debts and credit which at times involved sacrifices among the managerial staff. Thus, in 1892, Wellcome reported that Sudlow had drawn attention to his not having received an increase in salary for two years and that the currently highly prosperous state of the business justified reward. Sympathetic to this request, Wellcome wrote to Burroughs remarking on the value of Sudlow and Searl which had 'constantly exceeded the amount we pay them', and to the great difficulty in finding replacements for either manager.[113] Similar financial stringencies prevailed in 1884 and 1885 and were followed by the introduction of a 'profit-sharing' scheme. These difficulties occurred at a time when although Burroughs' private wealth was sufficient to inject finance for long-term investment in plant and buildings by increasing equity capital, short-term debt had to be covered from trade credit and short-term loans.

In 1889 Burroughs' personal resources again provided the means by which production capacity could expand in the long term, this time in the form of a loan to the firm from which he received interest. One result was that in 1895, Burroughs owned 75 per cent of the partnership's assets. His death not only removed this source but also presented Wellcome with an immediate problem. Olive Burroughs contested the settlement and the date of the transfer of her late husband's share of the business.[114] Both the settlement sum and the date for payment were contested strongly in a protracted process that culminated in legal action against Wellcome. The dispute was resolved only after a court order was issued in July 1898. This gave Wellcome sole ownership of all partnership assets. Conveyance of the Phoenix Mills property to Wellcome was formally completed in April 1899. In addition to immediate repayment of £33,558 credited to Buroughs's drawing account, the cost to Wellcome in acquiring his erstwhile partner's assets was £97,906. The major proportion of this purchase money was transferred from the business, though £40,000 came from a loan from the City Bank, repayable in monthly instalments of £2,000.[115]

The figures showing the amounts Wellcome withdrew from the business in 1895, 1896, and 1897 (the year which coincides with the appearance of a substantial bank loan on the balance sheet) reveal the major source of funds which enabled Wellcome to buy the company. He withdrew £14,607 in 1895, £22,607 in 1896, and £1,298 in 1897 when net profits were respectively £22,005, £12,689, and £12,926. The initial bank loan in 1897 amounted to £30,342 after which the average level until 1913 was £39,059. When the loan began, the figure was equivalent to roughly 36 per cent of equity capital. However, the growth of the business (which the bank loan facilitated) meant that by 1913, the proportion of debt attributable to the bank had dropped to barely 5 per cent of equity capital.[116]

Claims on the firm's revenue arising from the transfer of ownership from Burroughs to Wellcome did not affect the company's ability to continue to finance business expansion from reinvested profits. Net profits were positive in every year except 1893, a year of financial crisis in the City, though as a substantial net profit of £21,687 was declared for the previous year a purely accounting factor may be the explanation. A short-term liquidity problem was accommodated by the City Bank in the form of two months promissory notes. Purchases at Dartford were cut back to a 'hand to mouth' basis.[117] Thereafter, long-term debt (figures for which can be calculated from 1897), was roughly one-third of equity capital. They fell to around one-fifth by 1901, falling further to between one-sixth and one-seventh in the period up to the First World War. Although it is necessary to rely on net profit figures only, it is clear that the fluctuations around a relatively stable profit level in the 1880s (when the maximum reached £6,648 in 1886) were left behind after 1893. In only six of the 11 years between 1895 and 1905, did net profits fall below £20,000. Profits fell below £40,000 in only one year between 1906 and 1913, though the rise is overstated because of price inflation.

Throughout the period of rapid expansion, the balancing of quality and profit through an application of scientific method and scientific knowledge to industrial production was achieved with occasional difficulty but without experiencing major crises. Rates of return on capital were below 10 per cent in only four of the 15 years for which figures are available; the average figure was 13.4 per cent. Net profit as a percentage on sales reveals similar chronological fluctuations; the average was 12.1 per cent. These levels indicate a sound but not unusually high rate of return by contemporary standards.[118] They were maintained, moreover, while the company undertook investment in the foundation of pioneering laboratory facilities, the recruitment of highly qualified scientific staff, and the commencement of innovative pure research. Table 3.6 shows that this activity was to be unprofitable for several years after 1894, when the first Wellcome research laboratory was established, and of minimal profitability before the First World War.

The company's financial history between 1889 and 1914 highlights an essential dilemma posed by the pursuit of a long- or medium-term public interest that involved the sacrifice of short-term private financial gain. The problem was inherent in Wellcome's aspiration to advance and harness science and industry and to ensure quality to the point of perfection in, and profit from, the company's products. The questions how, to what extent, and with what success this dilemma was resolved provide a continuing counterpoint to the narrative history of the company.

Table 3.6 *Aggregated commission, trading and other profits, 1898*

	Gross profit (£)	Fairchild commission	Lanoline profit	WCRL profit	WPRL profit	Aggregate profit
1898	85,282	2,236	2,166			
1899	93,879	2,758				
1900	88,058	2,916	2,864	163		94,001
1901	102,631	2,196	2,938	68		107,833
1902	78,044	2,283	2,939	124	124	83,514
1903	101,958	2,283	2,769	1,269	1,527	109,806
1904	105,066	2,627	1,562	4,212	870	114,337
1905	114,168	3,273	774	1,873	1,352	121,440
1906	105,066	3,253	2,369	907	1,843	113,438
1907	142,086	3,980	1,829	5,132	2,471	155,498
1908	139,819	4,001	2,135	6,301	2,914	155,170
1909	154,507	4,505	1,928	10,670	3,246	174,856
1910	176,404	4,580	1,850	2,452	4,257	189,543
1911*	240,282*	5,254	2,819		4,016	252,380
1912	274,483	5,407	2,972		5,030	287,892
1913	300,316	5,247	2,601		5,199	313,363
1914	325,765	5,178	2,699		1,161	334,803

* Hereafter, gross trading profits appear in the annual amalgamated trading and profit and loss accounts incorporating the trading activities of the overseas branches. WFA, F/FA/328, WFL trading and profit and loss accounts which show profits from agency profit and commission and profits attributable to the laboratories in addition to gross trading profits.

CHAPTER FOUR

'Friend and brother' in dysfunctional partnership: Burroughs versus Wellcome

The partnership in the 1880s; early disagreements

Relocation to the much more extensive Dartford site in 1889 and the expansion in the scale of operations that then became possible occurred a year after an article appeared in the *Chemist & Druggist* entitled 'Progress in pharmacy' which referred to the firm having successfully established a world-wide reputation as a pioneering pharmaceutical company.[1] The American *Pharmaceutical Era* carried a similarly warm recognition of the partners' achievements, describing the new factory as an important step towards the fulfilment of the partners' ambitions.[2] In fact, the acquisition of the Mills was a matter of dispute between the two men while its grand opening was an occasion that led to mutual recriminations.[3] This was symptomatic of a deteriorating personal relationship originating shortly after the partnership was formed. In some respects the commercial success between 1880 and 1895, when Burroughs died unexpectedly at the age of 49, was achieved despite, rather than because of, the business alliance. Although Burroughs' obituarist writing in the *Pharmaceutical Era* expressed the view that 'No partnership could have been more ideal in its constitution', he also noted:

> The influence of Henry Wellcome in cementing and organising the business of the firm cannot be lost sight of in commenting upon the brilliance of the senior partner. While Burroughs was a man of intense mental, physical and commercial energy, of buoyant individuality and brilliant initiative, he lacked that steady persistence, capacity for directing others, shrewder judgement, love of executive work, and a care for detail that distinguished his partner. Burroughs threw off multitudes of red-hot ideas. Wellcome, brimming over with energy and originality himself, had sometimes to work out Burroughs' as well as his own ideas before they could be given to the world as definite artistic entities.[4]

The postcard's handwritten message reads in part:

Villingen
Aug 14. 94

Dear old Boy I left Triberg after lunch today & have had a plen... did Cycle ride through the beautiful black forest. We expect to reach the Ladies daily at Schaffhausen...

FIGURE 4.1
Back of a
postcard
from Silas
Burroughs to
his wife Olive,
from the
Black Forest,
on his way
to St Moritz,
post-marked
14 August
1894.

The degree of complementarities in their skills, inclinations, and approaches to business was potentially an advantage in setting up and developing the firm. However, the absence of trust between the partners almost from the beginning was an outcome as much of some similarities in temperament as of differences in personalities and undermined the possibility of a mutually supportive, co-operative management.

At the outset, the Wyeth brothers had expressed reservations regarding Burroughs as a suitable partner, though were confident of Wellcome's ability to restrain Burroughs' extravagant tendencies. Wellcome was warned that he would need to 'exert an influence and keep in check ... unnecessary expenditures' on advertising, to restrain Burroughs' inclination to establish too many agencies, and to prevail upon him 'not to accept business that paid ... too small a profit'. The Wyeths conveyed these concerns to Wellcome in person, probably during his visit to the US in December 1880.[5] It was, perhaps, inevitable (or at least understandable), however, that because of seniority in age, his preponderant share in the partnership, experience of the English market, familiarity with the culture of its medical profession and the trading customs among chemists and druggists, that Burroughs should regard his own ambition for the business, his priorities, and his opinion on how to achieve them, as over-riding those of the younger, less experienced Wellcome. Wellcome, however, proved to possess comparable ambition and a self confidence based on his own achievements, which led to continuing open disagreements over business strategy and management practices specifically manifest in trading policy, partnership finance, and staff appointments. Wellcome was convinced that Burroughs constantly undervalued his partner's contribution to the business.[6] Geographical distance between the two partners was a contributory factor. Beginning with Burroughs' world tour that lasted from October 1881 until February 1884, the partners spent much of the time apart, travelling either on business or to visit family in the US. Not surprisingly, during the first long spell of separation Wellcome felt isolated, inexperienced as he was in managing production. He was also unfamiliar with British institutions and culture and unable, except through correspondence, to discuss the considerable problems encountered by the infant enterprise with his more experienced partner.

Soon after Burroughs embarked on his travels he proceeded (without consulting Wellcome) to appoint agents and representatives in Lisbon, Constantinople, India, and Ceylon. This, together with heavy sampling and expenditure on circulars for the medical profession and inserts for the trade press of the countries he visited, confirmed Wellcome's conviction that the Wyeths'

FIGURE 4.2
'Tabloid' Forced March, c.1890, a mixture of cocaine and caffeine intended to 'prolong the power of endurance'. The 'Poison' stamp was added at an unknown later date.

criticisms of their erstwhile employee were justified. While Burroughs was in India early in 1882, Wellcome wrote to him, not for the first time it seems, repeating those criticisms as more agents were appointed in various parts of the country. Conceding that Burroughs' approach to marketing was 'enthusiastic', Wellcome proceeded to deplore wasteful expenditure, the failure to record fully tabulated lists of doctors and chemists in the cities and towns he visited, and spending insufficient time visiting physicians in the major cities. Wellcome told Burroughs that although they had both agreed that the trip would take perhaps two years, Wellcome 'had not favoured a superficial jaunt, and less so now. It is no good appointing sub-agents ... and then moving on leaving them to do all the important work. If that is what happens, it will bear an enormous expense for very little'.[7] While Burroughs accepted the justice of Wellcome's rebuke, at the same time he countered with the accusation that Wellcome had ignored requests to dispatch further samples to Indian wholesalers, 'slipshod conduct' which threatened to undermine his overseas campaign.[8]

Exchanges of allegations and counter allegations were punctuated by expressions of regret, remorse, and mutual assurances of respect (though Wellcome was the more prolific, and Burroughs a rarer correspondent).[9] Criticisms are delivered in unrestrained language and apologies offered with intense protestations of enduring friendship. Mutual recrimination ended temporarily in 1883 with an apology from Burroughs: '... I should have first proceeded to cast out the beam in my eye before calling attention to the apparent mote in yours.'[10] Emollient sentiments from Wellcome reaffirmed a wholehearted brotherhood with Burroughs whom he described as 'no truer friend.' Wellcome wrote: '... we have had different opinions but have always compared, noted, and settled differences as friends should.' The first crisis concerned trading and credit policy that Burroughs agreed to change. After assuring his 'dearest and best and always true friend' that his criticisms of Wellcome's management of the business were thoughtless and attributable to his own impulsive nature, Burroughs acceded to Wellcome's insistence that credit sales must be strictly limited in number and duration, the 'only safe policy, especially as our business is increasing faster, I suppose, than our capital.'[11] Later, he returned to his regret for his 'unkind and ungenerous' responses to Wellcome's constructive criticism: '... this disturbance, caused by my own stupidity, carelessness, and obstinacy is over. I think we shall have smooth sailing together the rest of our lives ... You will get no more ugly words from me, and you, dear patient kind-hearted old fellow, have never given me any at all ...' He ended the letter: 'In sorrow, affliction, loneliness, but yet in faith and hope, ever your friend and brother'.[12]

The second important issue arose when Burroughs attempted to perpetuate his financial dominance in the partnership by proposing that Wellcome should waive the right to increase his shareholding in the company to equal that of Burroughs. The 1880 deed of partnership envisaged equality by September 1882, but Burroughs wanted to postpone this until September 1884, a year before the partnership deed was due for renewal. A *quid pro quo* was another proposal relating to share transactions involving the purchase of the KMEC. The verbal agreement had been that once the partners had purchased the shares of remaining holders, each partner should transfer his shares to BW&Co. for the average price paid to other shareholders. Wellcome had prepared the paperwork but Burroughs prevaricated, introducing a condition for the transfer of the shares in his name. He proposed to implement transfer, though at twice the cost; he also proposed that he should forego interest in royalties and commissions accruing to him as a result of acquiring the shares held by Lockwood, the original patent holder on whose

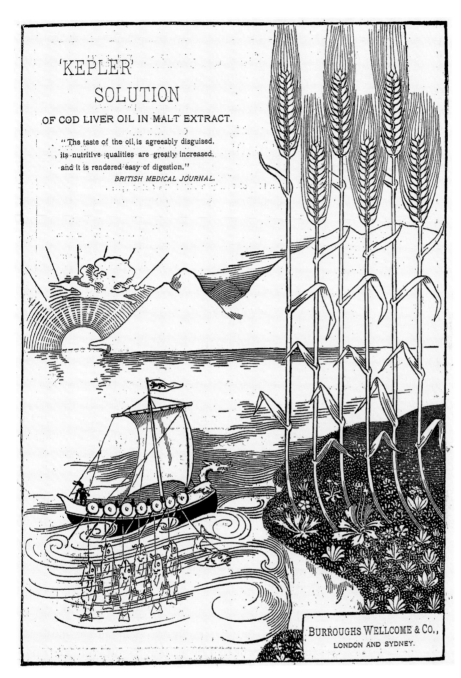

FIGURE 4.3
An eye-catching advertisement for Kepler solution of cod liver oil in malt extract (*British & Colonial Druggist*, 14 Jan. 1898).

patent KMEC had been formed. However, the proposal depended on a prior undertaking from Wellcome not to request parity in the partnership until 1884.[13] With regard to the KMEC shares, Wellcome, whom Burroughs had left to negotiate details of the acquisition while he was abroad, pointed out that the payment to Burroughs of 5 per cent royalties plus commission received by agreement through SMB&Co. in 1879, was due to cease in one week's time. This was in accordance with the agreement with Lockwood on the date due for final legal transfer of KMEC to part-ownership by BW&Co. However, Wellcome also drew attention to the dubious basis of the royalty income Burroughs had received in the past. Wellcome had discovered that it rested on an agreement between KMEC and Burroughs which had not only expired but which had never been signed. 'I do not bring these things up to taunt you with your mistakes, but simply to remind you that the burden of correcting the implications which you had brought upon us has fallen mainly on my shoulders.'[14] The advice from a QC was that the agreement was invalidated and that therefore Burroughs had no right of claim under its provisions.

Expressing 'very serious regret and chagrin' at the proposal that he should waive his right under the partnership agreement to become an equal partner in 1884, Wellcome emphasised the burdens he had continued to carry since Burroughs' departure overseas and the achievements in building a successful business: '... the management and success of a business does not depend upon sales alone. There is a <u>necessary care which you have never known</u> – the thinking and judgement which are <u>essential</u> do not come in hasty flashes of impulse. Careful judgement in the government of a business is the result of hard brain work.' He described Burroughs' proposal as 'a most <u>stinging reflection upon me</u> – and one which I <u>most positively resent</u>. Every man who knows anything about our business knows that the value of my services has been as great as yours, and I claim the <u>full right</u> under the partnership agreement to an equal partnership on the first of Sept. 1882.'[15] He described the move by Burroughs as 'a very unhandsome one, and one that you should feel very heartily ashamed of.'[16] None the less, in the hope of avoiding deterioration in their relations Wellcome offered a compromise, postponing his rights for a year on condition that Burroughs signed an agreement confirming Wellcome's full rights to a half share.[17] Burroughs replied, apologising for being too inconsiderate, too quick to take offence, and

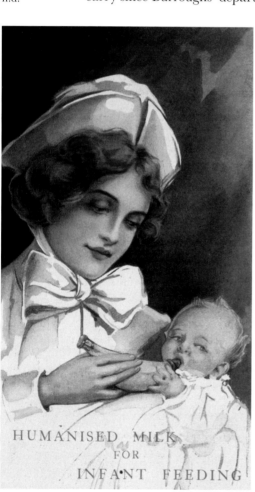

HUMANISED MILK
FOR
INFANT FEEDING

guilty of 'ugly words', promising in future to be 'as a brother'.[18] Wellcome's response was equally emollient, and – not for the first time – contained a character analysis:

My dear Burroughs,

No truer friend has any right to get offended at such criticism as you have written – particularly not until there had been explanations made if they were thought to be offensive. I know very well your impulsive and often too hasty disposition and although you have written some very severe and cutting criticisms I have made allowance for <u>impulse</u> and not allowed them to annoy or anger me. You ought to be well enough acquainted with me to <u>know</u> that if I had been angered I should have <u>told you</u> of it in frankly the very plainest English that I could command ... You know I am not a fellow to harbour ill feeling and that I can hold strongly different opinions from my friends and yet not lose my most sincere feeling of hearty friendship'.[19]

Issues of ownership, control and management; the renewed partnership agreement of 1885

However, there are further indications of Burroughs' continuing intention to alter the nature of the partnership. In September 1882, Burroughs wrote to Wellcome from the US to propose that Dr Smith, an American he had met, should be introduced into the partnership as a substitute for himself receiving a salary of $1,000 paid from Burroughs' own pocket. After ascertaining that the proposed new partner lacked business experience of any kind, Wellcome dismissed the idea completely.[20] A month later, Wellcome received an announcement (described by Burroughs as a 'surprise') that he had offered H. John van Schaack, another American acquaintance, a share in the partnership. The agreement gave van Schaack responsibility for trade with Europe. Wellcome expressed dismay that Burroughs appeared to regard the partnership so lightly whereas he personally 'look[ed] upon partnership as next to matrimony ... and there are very few men in this world I would associate myself with as a partner'. He accused Burroughs of 'dashing off hasty and unthought documents' exemplified by the 'indiscreet clauses, most unbusinesslike and compromising – entangling BW&Co. without any obligation on van Schaack.' Fearful of the company's legal liability (as well as his own reputation with the American family), Wellcome none the less insisted on cancellation of the agreement and payment of six months salary. He opposed engaging van Schaack even as a traveller, let alone admitting him as a partner, not only because he lacked credibility but because Wellcome regarded the prospects for profitable trade with the Continent to be poor.[21] However, when Wellcome met van Schaack on his arrival in

England in January 1884, he was so relieved to find van Schaack willing to cancel the agreement without compensation that he felt morally obliged to offer him an appointment as a Continental representative. Predictably, Van Schaack proved to be a failure and resigned within months.[22]

In September 1884, Burroughs informed Wellcome that Sudlow needed £2,000 to expand the business which could not be found within the company because of existing capital commitments.[23] Burroughs proposed three possible solutions. The first was that Wellcome should increase his equity in the partnership by £4,500 to be linked not to the capital growth of the business but to the *withdrawal* of the same amount by Burroughs (who also mentioned the possibility of setting up on his own in the US). He suggested that should Wellcome find difficulties in raising this amount a second possibility was that perhaps McKesson and Robbins, long-time friends who knew and trusted Wellcome, might fund this investment.[24] Should neither solution prove feasible, Burroughs envisaged adding a third partner or of converting the partnership into a joint stock limited liability company funded by shares to be issued only to firms which sold BW&Co.'s goods, and to employees.[25] Wellcome refused to entertain any of these proposals. Burroughs, meanwhile, enlisted his solicitors in pursuit of a real investment from Wellcome to bring his share equal with that of Burroughs. After accusing Wellcome of having drawn up the accounts of the firm in a manner prejudicial to his interests, the solicitor's letter continued: 'Mr Burroughs considers the present state of affairs unsatisfactory and strongly suggests that you should without delay contribute to the business a capital proportionate to your two-fifths share of the profits.'[26] The new partnership indenture drawn up in 1885 did not alter the existing capital structure. The partnership agreement was extended from 1885 to 1895, terminable in 1890 by either partner in writing to give six months notice. Should such notice be given the remaining partner was entitled to have first option to buy the former partner's shares. Unless with the consent of the other partner, both undertook not to engage in business other than of BW&Co.[27] Through the purchase of shares from Wellcome, Burroughs increased his share in the partnership to 70 per cent and a proportionate entitlement to profits.[28]

Under the terms of the new partnership agreement in May 1885, the notion of equality that had existed in the past was abandoned. In strict accounting terms, Wellcome appeared to have been contributing more to the finances of the partnership than was the reality, for the figures represented only a guarantee towards equality. The May 1885 agreement showed that £10,500 of the company's capital was attributed to Burroughs and £4,500 to Wellcome.[29] There is no surviving correspondence to reveal why the partners agreed to an entirely different arrangement from any of those which Burroughs had presented to Wellcome or why Wellcome had accepted. There was no provision for Wellcome to increase his share.

Any additional capital invested in the business was to be treated as a loan at 5 per cent interest. Moreover, the case for the injection of further capital into the business was well founded. The business needed capital to grow; Wellcome could not raise the capital and would not approach his American friends; Burroughs possessed personal wealth to fund expansion. The business benefited. Equity capital doubled between 1885 and 1887 and trebled by 1890, a surge in sales accompanying capital growth.[30] Subsequent events, however, suggest that Burroughs' ulterior motive was an increase in his financial control over the partnership and that he manoeuvred Wellcome into a position from which there were no alternatives unless *he* left the partnership. However, the inclusion of the new clause that provided for a written termination ensured that Wellcome could not be forced out of the partnership, whereas if Burroughs left, Wellcome would have the opportunity to become the sole owner.

A year after the new agreement was implemented, Wellcome visited the US (on his partner's suggestion) to recover from cumulative exhaustion. He was diagnosed later as having ulcerative colitis, which his heroic rescue of a woman from the River Thames had aggravated.[31] From the beginning of the onset of serious illness in late autumn 1885, Wellcome was away from London and the business for eighteen months. During his absence and

FIGURE 4.5
Henry
Wellcome
c. 1887, taken
in Bangor,
Maine on one
of his trips to
the US.

without his knowledge, Burroughs began to investigate the possibility of acquiring premises in the US for the purpose of manufacturing malt extract and malt milk, and considered the possibility of discontinuing malt production in England should comparative costs favour relocation. Together with Witte, the Works Manager responsible for malt production, they travelled to the US to seek a suitable location. In April 1887, Burroughs telegraphed Wellcome from Newburgh, Maine to inform him of their arrival and the purpose of their visit.[32] Wellcome replied: 'Re the factory in America. I have given this matter very careful consideration ever since my arrival and taken advice on the subject. I am not fully satisfied that it is wise to take such a step yet.' He insisted that no action should be taken until after thorough discussion of advantages and disadvantages.[33] Less than a month later, Burroughs informed Wellcome that he had made an offer on a factory, completion to follow in June.[34] On Wellcome's return to London he wrote to Burroughs, reassuring him of his recovery and of his determination on returning to business to exert himself even more to promote their mutual business interests: 'I trust that with united feelings and united strength we may realize our best hopes.'[35] Burroughs, also back in London, replied, expressing a long held suspicion that Wellcome was failing to fulfil his

obligations to the partnership, that dissolution could no longer be avoided, and that his solicitors would initiate the process.[36] Termination under the terms of the 1885 partnership agreement could not occur until 1890, though a notice to terminate before that time would necessarily hand Wellcome the option to buy the business. The allegations were threefold. The first was a charge of dereliction through his absence from the business for roughly 12 months while he was in America when his neglect of the firm was alleged to have been 'entire and continued'. The second was that without consent and contrary to the agreement, he had engaged in business with the publishing firm of Saxon & Co. The third was that Wellcome had drawn a larger share of the profits than that to which his capital in the business entitled him. Dissolution by mutual consent was proposed as the preferred solution. Failure to agree would be followed by an application to the Chancery Division to obtain a decree of dissolution.[37] It transpired that Burroughs was proposing to pay Wellcome the net value of his capital invested in the business, his share of profits to the date of dissolution, and a quarter of the cost,

FIGURE 4.6
Another distinctive advertisement for Kepler solution of cod liver oil in malt extract (*British & Colonial Druggist*, 4 Nov. 1898).

rather than current value of the firm's trade marks, patents, and contracts. No goodwill appeared in the balance sheets and Burroughs did not intend to offer any payment in consideration. Wellcome wrote to Ben and Ann Fairchild in August 1887 (requesting that they burn his letter) telling them that '... in all probability Mr Burroughs and I will separate ere long'. He emphasized his own 'keenest attachment' to a business which had succeeded 'despite efforts of my partner to introduce erratic and wild projects.' None the less, should he decide to sell his share, he possessed sufficient 'to make a good strong start.' He made it clear that his criterion for choosing between pressing for a sale or a purchase would be purely a matter of which would be financially most advantageous.[38] In the event, Wellcome rejected the proposals, refusing either to sell, vary the terms surrounding the termination clause, or to agree to a conversion of the partnership into a limited liability company.[39] Burroughs decided to force the issue. His solicitors served Wellcome with a writ intended to secure dissolution by the Court. A confident Burroughs informed some of the firm's representatives abroad that he was about to dissolve the partnership and that Wellcome was to retire from the business; others were told of plans to form a limited company.[40] Solicitors preparing the case for Burroughs against his partner noted privately that 'Mutual confidence does not subsist between them'.[41] Their relations, however, were yet to reach the nadir.

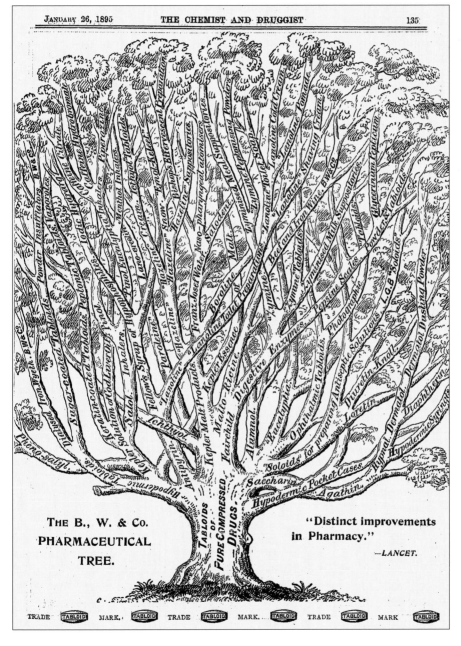

FIGURE 4.7 'The BW&Co. pharmaceutical tree', illustrating the range of products available from the company (*Chemist & Druggist*, 26 Jan. 1895).

The case of Burroughs *versus* Wellcome, 1887–1889

Mutual distrust produced marked differences between the partners' behaviour. At the same time that Burroughs was informing others of an impending dissolution of the partnership and of his intention to form a new enterprise, he believed that Wellcome was conducting his own propaganda by offering reassurances to employees that *he* was about to take over the business and that the jobs of those who would stand by him in the impending litigation would be safe. In a confidential memorandum a member of the office staff reported a conversation with Burroughs in which he had rehearsed the many ways in which he believed Wellcome to have failed to honour his obligations to the partnership and to have been disloyal to Burroughs personally. Wellcome was accused of deceit, ruthless exploitation, and neglecting correspondence. An inability to communicate other than in a dictatorial manner or with insolence was also unacceptable to Burroughs. He alleged misconduct in Wellcome's personal life, referring to womanising and association with 'gay women', the circulation of 'lustful books', and keeping late nights and late mornings, all of which Burroughs claimed had adversely affected the business. Since Wellcome's return from a lengthy convalescence, the justification for which Burroughs expressed doubts (though had actually advised) he was accused of having given the business little attention. Revealing the basic flaw in the relationship between the partners from the beginning, he described Wellcome as 'a first rate man as a servant but not at all as a manager [being] incompetent to manage a business of this distinction',[42] a verdict completely at odds with historical reality. Wellcome described his own approach to the dispute in a confidential letter to the Fairchilds to leave 'aggression entirely to the adversary', to take matters as 'calmly and placidly as possible … with quietness and firmness I shall stand by my rights'.[43]

Wellcome's confidence in the outcome of the case was fully vindicated for charges set out in the affidavit were shown to be baseless. Wellcome's illness was well documented and had been a matter of personal concern to Burroughs. William Kirby, assistant manager, confirmed that Wellcome's lengthy period of rest and travel in the US had been in response to his partner's suggestion.[44] Placed in context, Wellcome's intermittent poor health originated during a period of extraordinarily heavy pressure when establishing the business, adding manufacture to trading operations, and coping with continuing concern for financial liquidity for much of the time in his partner's absence. The sheer volume of correspondence from Wellcome to all connected with the business, exceptional in its scale during those years and thereafter, is testament to the commitment and energy he invested in the firm. Commenting upon Wellcome's contribution, Kirby's statement denied Burroughs had ever asked him to monitor the condition of Wellcome's accounts. Likewise he maintained that he had not overheard Burroughs protest to Wellcome about overdrawn accounts.[45] Finally, Kirby maintained that Burroughs had given Wellcome written permission to be involved in the publishing venture with Saxon & Co.[46]

Privately, the solicitors acting for Burroughs were advised by counsel: 'Court will probably say "mere squabbles between partners are not sufficient grounds for dissolution", although if partners' mutual confidence is totally destroyed court might order dissolution.'[47] The case was heard in the Chancery Division of the High Court on 24 and 25 June 1889 by Mr Justice Kekewich. The number and status of the witnesses appearing for each of the partners is indicative. Only Prevost, a clerk in the accounts department, appeared for Burroughs, whereas Wellcome's witnesses included Sudlow (the general manager), Kirby (the accountant and assistant manager), Spratlin (assistant accountant), and Collett Smith (corresponding clerk in the partners' office). It is significant that both Sudlow and Kirby had been recruited by Burroughs before the partnership was formed. In the event, none of Wellcome's witnesses were called. Only Prevost, the single witness for Burroughs, was asked to give evidence, though it amounted to little more than an assertion that since returning from the US Wellcome's custom had been to be at the office between about 11am and until some time in the afternoon. Burroughs contradicted his own deposition, admitting that Wellcome had received his written consent to take an interest in Saxon & Co., that at times he had accepted Wellcome's advice arising from business correspondence, and that he was still on friendly terms with his partner, often taking lunch together. He conceded that the firm's well-established prosperity continued. None the less, in response to a direct question, Burroughs stated categorically that he could not continue conducting business in partnership with Wellcome.[48] Because Burroughs' replies were sufficient to prove Wellcome's case, the cross examination of Wellcome was brief, cut short by the judge who concluded that there was no ground for dissolution.[49] The judgement of the court was that no such order should be issued, that Wellcome should end his association with Saxon & Co., and that costs should be borne by both parties.[50]

Immediately after the hearing, Wellcome telegraphed his mother with the message 'Victory'. He also told his mother that just as he had been courteous to Burroughs throughout the two years leading up to the court case, since the victory he had also treated Burroughs 'as though nothing had happened … offered him my hand and requested that the hatchet should be buried and forgotten … but he has not ceased to intrigue behind my back.' Burroughs responded by refusing even to speak to Wellcome,[51] thereby introducing a longstanding practice of written communication rather than face to face meetings between managers and directors at Snow Hill, Dartford, and later the Wellcome laboratories.

Towards dissolution of the partnership

Silence from Burroughs, however, did not presage peace but concealed his initiative in mounting a carefully planned event that could only lead to a further deterioration in relations with Wellcome. This occurred on the occasion of the grand official opening of the Dartford factory in July 1889, barely two weeks after Burroughs' defeat in court. The event was intended to be a major publicity exercise witnessed by an invited audience comprising two thousand workers and their families and friends, leading figures in the medical profession friendly to the firm, representatives from county politics, the trade, and the trade press. Burroughs, active in local politics and an ardent supporter of Henry George, the leading American socialist and advocate of land reform, secretly invited him as the guest of honour, an invitation of which Wellcome was apprised only after George had accepted. An assurance was given that George's speech would be strictly non-political. Inside a packed building, Burroughs addressed the audience as 'Friends and fellow citizens' before George's denunciation of property rights and advocacy of the abolition of all taxes except those on land. This received enthusiastic applause. Burroughs followed, his own harangue directed at those outside the building, reiterating George's message which was later printed and subsequently (without Wellcome's knowledge) circulated to the company's customers. As coverage by newspapers and the trade press did not distinguish between the tumultuous event constructed around George and the official ceremony to celebrate the opening of the Dartford factory that preceded it, Wellcome's exasperation is not surprising. He was furious both because of the deception perpetrated by Burroughs and the damage to the company's image among customers, indicated by the complaints received.[52] In a lengthy, surprisingly restrained letter to Burroughs several months later, Wellcome rehearsed a list of actions taken by Burroughs in the past that he considered to have been contrary to the partnership agreement. He complained that by ordering the erection of new buildings at Dartford Burroughs had acted without agreement,[53] had given the works manager authority to open a banking account in the name of the firm,[54] and had arranged for political meetings to take place in the factory grounds.[55] In the following month, Wellcome took the initiative. In November 1891, his solicitors drew up terms of an agreement designed as an alternative to dissolution. He offered to sell his interest to Burroughs for £40,000 on the condition that Wellcome's name disappeared from that of the company within one year. In the proposed division of assets, which presumably reflected Wellcome's perception of the partners' respective contributions to the business, Wellcome would take stock, plant and machinery, and trademarks related to compressed drugs, Fairchild preparations, and 25 per cent of the remaining unspecified assets. In addition to all property and premises in London and Dartford, Burroughs would retain Kepler products, beef wine, Fellows' hypophosphites, lanoline, all other articles designated pharmaceutical stock, and other such assets as were to be agreed upon as representing 75 per cent of such assets. Both partners would be permitted to manufacture or sell only those products assigned to them under the agreement and neither should use the partner's name in advertising.[56] Burroughs did not reply.

Wellcome adopted a more aggressive stance. Under the terms of the 1890 partnership agreement, any capital over and above the partners' equity capital remaining as an investment in the company's balance sheets was to be credited with 5 per cent interest. This was a matter of concern to Wellcome for two reasons. The first related to Burroughs' existing loan to the company amounting to £13,178, a debt that Wellcome considered the firm no longer required. He asked Burroughs to accept payment to eliminate the debt and terminate interest paid from the business. After prevarication, Burroughs complied in May 1892.[57] The second reason for concern was the company's continued exposure to unnecessarily heavy liability because of the method of financing the acquisition of the Phoenix Mills. Purchased personally by Burroughs, an agreement was made whereby the premises should be leased to the company at a rental of £250 per annum. The £5,000 investment was treated as a loan from Burroughs at 5 per cent. However, the agreement gave the firm the option of liquidating the loan at any time within the seven-year lease.[58] Wellcome attempted to effect the transfer of the Dartford factory to the company in 1891 by depositing £5,000 at the bank in their joint names, leaving a cheque with his solicitors signed for the same amount to be passed to Burroughs; this was because so long as the £5,000 was on deposit, the interest was credited to the company. Acting for Wellcome when Burroughs refused to co-operate, Markby Stewart & Co. drew his attention to the heavy liability for interest this arrangement imposed on the company. Not until after a solicitor's reminder, however, was the transfer eventually completed in 1893.[59] The resolution of the Phoenix Mills debt revealed continuing mistrust shared by the solicitors. Wellcome's solicitors advised that the deeds should be deposited with the company's bankers. Radford and Frankland, Burroughs' solicitors, warned him that Wellcome might use the deeds to obtain an overdraft on behalf of the firm to which Burroughs might object.[60] He was advised not to deposit the deeds of the Phoenix Mills to the joint order of the two partners but instead to place them in a safe deposit to which each partner should hold a key. Shortly before Burroughs left for the US in January 1893, Wellcome's solicitors issued a formal warning to Burroughs insisting that 'no contract shall be entered into, and no liability in expense incurred on behalf of the firm, for any exceptional or material amount without his [Wellcome's] express and antecedent approval in writing ... Mr Wellcome regrets to be obliged to

give you a notice in this nature, but past experience has shewn him that it is necessary in his own and the firm's interest that he should do so.'[61] Burroughs was specifically instructed not to recruit travellers in the US.[62] The explanation is to be found in a letter Wellcome wrote to Burroughs in March 1893 in which he referred to the current improvement in business as having occurred 'despite extravagance on needless expenditure' incurred by Burroughs. This involved between £5,000 and £6,000 on price list covers sufficient for five or six years' supply, excessive numbers of show cards, and the hiring at an annual cost of several thousand pounds of four travellers for the Continent where Burroughs himself had failed to make much progress despite repeated and prolonged visits. Such actions had been taken either without consultation and 'contrary to our plan' or despite Wellcome's view of the senseless waste of money such activity involved.[63] Wellcome also prevented Burroughs from introducing bonus payments to travellers which depended upon the number of medical practitioners or chemists they visited. Wellcome pointed out that this practice was completely opposite to the system adopted hitherto and that should it be introduced, the firm would be put 'at the mercy of the representatives'.[64]

Three other different criticisms were made. One was the expenditure of $700 to $800 on advertising in the *New York Journal*, which he described as 'an extremist political journal'. This financial expenditure was small and wasteful, but Wellcome considered that the effect had been to expose the firm to ridicule among members of the wholesale trade.[65] He also continued to oppose the employees' bonus system introduced by Burroughs in 1891. He favoured the award of fixed and secure increases in salaries where merited. Conscious of the sensitivity of this matter, Wellcome objected to the unseemliness of Burroughs' writing to him on scraps of paper (postal orders were mentioned) and of breaching confidence by leaving correspondence open for employees to read; he referred specifically to those containing 'remarks asserting or implying that you are anxious the firm should offer the employees benefits which I will not consent to do.'[66] Because of such improprieties, Wellcome informed Burroughs that he would no longer receive any letters of a private nature that had been dictated and passed through the hands of the office staff.[67] He was critical of Burroughs' absence in the US in August 1893, ostensibly on a business trip that Wellcome had considered to be unnecessary. Once again he forbade Burroughs to enter into contracts: 'I regret that your hostile and erratic course renders it necessary for me to take ... steps for the protection of the firm's interests and for the protection of my own personal interests and rights. I trust that you will recognise that a more reasonable and peaceable method of procedure will best serve our firm's interests as well as your own'.[68] Burroughs did not desist. While in Chicago for the World Fair Exhibition in September 1893, Wellcome questioned the authorisation of a large showcard he discovered had been sent from Snow Hill that described and advocated the company's profit-sharing scheme and the eight-hour day introduced in 1889.[69] He also discovered 'political pamphlets' on the tariff question distributed from the firm's exhibit that he found unacceptable and had confiscated. Wellcome wrote to Burroughs: 'You must not forget that I am a member of the firm and that as such I have equal command and controll [sic] of the firm's business and the firm's exhibit ...'[70]

Frustrated by the Court and faced by an increasingly bullish Wellcome, in 1894, Burroughs revived an earlier idea for resolving the partnership problem by forming a limited liability joint stock company. Wellcome revealed agreement in principle to explore such a possibility but was anxious that any proposal that Burroughs might make should be 'full, clear, explicit, definite', explaining to his solicitors that he would not (and they should not) accept any scheme Burroughs or his solicitors might propose as in good faith. He felt unable 'to rely on them to be capable of the usual honour between solicitor and solicitor'.[71]

The next step, which may have been initiated by the solicitors seeking a resolution to the relentless and increasingly acrimonious dispute, was the appointment by each of the partners of a friend as representative. The brief was to assist in the negotiation of an agreement to convert the partnership into a joint stock company in which both would be major shareholders. Burroughs chose Liberal MP, Dr Clark FRCS (a land reform advocate). Wellcome chose Dr Alfred Chune Fletcher, whom he had known since 1881 when he set up in practice and from which time they remained the closest of friends until Fletcher's death in 1913. He was medical officer of the Charterhouse and the Sutton Foundation, serving in a similar capacity for insurance and other firms in the City. A.W.J. Haggis, an employee of the Wellcome Historical Museum and author of an unpublished biography of Wellcome shortly after his death, described him as a medico-legal expert. Both partners undertook to accept terms of settlement judged by both of their representatives as fair.[72] The consideration of proposals for conversion and the details of separation and division of assets and goodwill were on the agenda set for a conference at which the four were present in December 1894. It seems likely that the Burroughs' proposal, the only one of which details were recorded, formed the basis for discussion. This envisaged a capital of £120,000. Burroughs would sell one third of his 75 per cent holding while Wellcome would sell one third of his share. Wellcome's refusal to sell any of his shareholding so enraged Burroughs that he vowed that he would not renew the present partnership contract or make or enter into a fresh agreement 'on any terms', even if this meant recourse again to the Court. He concluded that it would 'be best not to include him in the formation of any company and that we will be better off without his presence or name. Burroughs & Co. or The Burroughs Co. Ltd will go just as well.'[73] The standoff remained unresolved when, on doctor's advice, Burroughs was in Monte Carlo for recuperation from a persistent cold and bronchitis. He died suddenly from pneumonia on 6 February 1895.

Under the terms of the 1890 partnership agreement Wellcome now had the option of becoming the sole proprietor of BW&Co., a prospect that he relished. In a letter to the Fairchilds in March, Wellcome wrote: 'I regard the business as quite in its infancy … I intend to put redoubled energy into the work of propagating and extending …'[74]

The death of Burroughs; consequences and his role and impact on the pharmaceutical industry in Britain

The death of Burroughs presented Wellcome with an immediate financial problem. Olive Burroughs disliked Wellcome intensely (probably as a consequence of Wellcome having advised Burroughs against the marriage).[75] Through the executors and lawyers she created maximum difficulty despite Wellcome's legal right, under the deed of partnership, to acquire the share of the business owned by her deceased husband. Both the settlement sum and the date for payment were contested strongly in a protracted process that culminated in legal action against Wellcome. The dispute was resolved only after a court order was issued in July 1898. This gave Wellcome sole ownership of all partnership assets. Conveyance of the Phoenix Mills property to Wellcome was formally completed in April 1899. In addition to repaying on demand the sum of £33,558 credited to Burroughs' drawing account, the cost to Wellcome in acquiring his erstwhile partner's assets was £97,906.[76] Wellcome paid £97,444 for his deceased partner's interest in the firm, partly by withdrawing £38,512 from the partnership between 1895 and 1897 when cumulative profits amounted to £47,629, and partly through a loan of £40,000 advanced on security by the City Bank. In 1897 this was equivalent to roughly one-third of the equity capital of the business. By 1913, when the loan stood at £39,059, the proportion had fallen to barely 5 per cent, a result of the growth in asset value of the business.[77]

Burroughs died when the company's history was at a turning point. His contributions to its achievements were acknowledged by suppliers, customers, and observers in the trade. These contributions were vital though erratic to the end; a fact not completely ignored but nevertheless seriously undervalued by Wellcome's biographers. Even before he had taken Wellcome into partnership, the innovations introduced by SMB&Co. had laid a foundation for the subsequent success of BW&Co. While Burroughs may have been a year or possibly two years later than Allen and Hanbury's in introducing American compressed medicines into Britain, he was the first to introduce American methods of marketing drugs to the trade by 'detailing physicians'. He promoted his vision of a company possessing extensive overseas markets through energetic travelling, though shortcomings in his style and a tendency to misjudge those with whom he came into contact probably

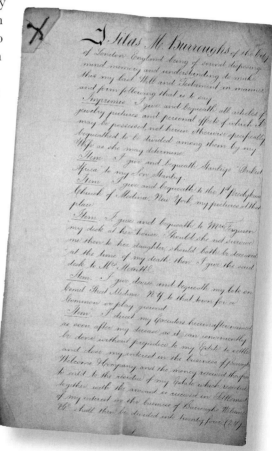

FIGURE 4.9 The last will and testament of Silas Burroughs, February 1893. He directs his executors to 'settle and close my interest in the business of Burroughs Welcome [sic] & Company'.

explain in part the limited success (apart from the Australian agency) achieved before his death. After launching the initial partnership, he twice demonstrated a greater willingness to risk heavier fixed investment in order to expand the business than did a reluctant Wellcome. In the case of the Dartford factory, Burroughs acted independently, committing personal resources from outside the business. He was responsible for bringing into the business the first commercially successful and highly profitable product in Kepler brand goods. The strong revenue stream which Kepler products generated was to underpin the development by Wellcome of increasingly science-based products following the establishment of the research laboratories by Wellcome, beginning in 1894.[78]

This marked another important turning point in the company's history, for in the long run, the establishment of a growing research function was to transform the product range, structure, and organisation of the firm. The contribution of Burroughs to the long-term success of the business is incontestable, though his vision was accompanied by neither an inclination nor a capacity for the exercise of executive and organisational skills in the conduct of business. Wellcome explained to his mother that Burroughs '... has never had the comprehensive grasp of the management.'[79] This flair was possessed by Wellcome who applied himself so assiduously to remedy the omissions and errors made by his partner that he seriously undermined his own health. The introduction of manufacturing and the organisation of two major relocations of factory and warehouse contributed to the heavy burdens leading eventually to the temporary but prolonged breakdown in his health. His invention of the firm's powerful brand name, Tabloid, and the systematic policy to ensure its legal protection proved to be of comparable importance to sales and profits as were Kepler products. Paradoxically, potentially perfectly complementary in partnership, however, Burroughs and Wellcome proved to be temperamentally incompatible in their seriously dysfunctional alliance. The company's success also depended heavily upon Sudlow, the general manager recruited by Burroughs in 1879, the man in the middle, who proved equal to the task of providing a level-headed senior management contribution and (important, given the frequent absences of one or other partner) an equable managerial presence and continuity. After the death of Burroughs, Wellcome was unhindered in directing his administrative and management capacities towards achieving his own aspirations for the company. These would combine advanced scientific research with commercial success, the accomplishment of which would depend on a problematical congruency between the pursuit of knowledge and reputation with profit.

Biographers of Wellcome have tended to emphasise the failings of Burroughs' record before (though especially after) his partnership with Wellcome. In describing the origins of their partnership, Haggis remarked that 'vision in business was a quality with which Wellcome was perhaps better endowed than his partner', that 'Wellcome was even more aware than his partner that in the world of pharmacy great progress was bound to ensue …' and, 'Again it was Wellcome more than Burroughs who realised that BW&Co. could only progress by research and a determination to keep ahead of all competition'.[80] However, Burroughs' letters to Wellcome when he was persuading him to come to Britain are full of references to the huge potential for such an alliance. 'Think there is a big show for manufacturing Pharmaceutical Preparations and if we go into it, it will be about the first in the field. Our house is the only one in the kingdom calling on doctors with samples of new things'.[81] This is the first explicit evidence of Burroughs' intention of embarking upon the manufacture of drugs in addition to KME, a policy that in time would reduce his dependency on the Wyeth agreement. Burroughs was also sanguine with respect to the financial prospects: 'You are the man I want to pull with' he wrote to Wellcome 'and we have confidence in each other's ability … Don't fail to come. I'm sure if you do and see the prospects here and look over our books you will stay …'[82] As for Haggis' reference to Wellcome's perception of the need to progress by research, there is no evidence that Wellcome had this in mind at the time of joining the partnership. His acquisition of the agency for Young, Ladd, and Coffin's perfumes in Burroughs' absence in 1882 with the aim of selling to the London elite is indicative of an opportunism which has been more associated with his partner's approach to business.[83] So, too, is his enthusiasm for Nubian Blacking, which, in the same year, Wellcome urged Burroughs to push on his travels in India, Ceylon, and Australia where he thought selling prospects would be strong.[84] By contrast, Wellcome rejected Burroughs' proposal that they should pursue the development of vaccine with a view to production; this followed his survey of the state of research and development of vaccine on the Continent in the early 1880s.[85] Wellcome's rejection of this proposal was based on criticism of the quality of the resulting products that prompted caution, and the importance of exercising control over any such production. Financial requirements for such a venture depended on the commercial success of general dietetic goods and Tabloids. Profitability was central to Wellcome's business philosophy in these early years, and as Burroughs continued to widen the range of products to be supplied by the firm, he expressed doubts to Burroughs.[86] Wellcome questioned whether it was worth bothering with marketing any product unless it produced 'a very large and liberal profit, & such as will allow … a good margin for advertising … Our business is sufficiently well established that we should begin to make some money out of it.'[87]

Even by the summer of 1879 Burroughs had signalled his inclination to commence the manufacture of pharmaceutical preparations once he had recruited a partner.[88] We may also assume that his anxiety to recruit a partner whom he believed could take responsibility for managing the business in London was evidence of his ambition to build a truly international business. The first step of establishing contacts and identifying potential markets was an objective that, after barely a year of the partnership, was to involve him for two and a half years of travelling across the globe.

While appreciating his dynamism, Rhodes James's assessment of Burroughs' business activities stressed his shortcomings, accepting without question the pithy condemnations delivered by the Wyeths.[89] Yet they were familiar with neither the culture nor customary practices of the British trade. Specifically, they were unaware of the attitude of medical men and of chemists and druggists to American pills and proprietaries which they tended to associate with patent medicines, or of their dependence on professional journals for information on new drugs which required advertising costs higher than in the US, or the system of long credit which was the norm.[90] Rhodes James drew attention to the 'severe limitations' of the BW&Co.'s Goods List of 1881, accurately describing them as primarily cosmetic rather than curative. 'Hazeline … was entirely cosmetic, the value of Kepler Oil and Malt was debatable, and 'Ergotin' was a totally unknown and untested element. On these very slender foundations was their business to be created.'[91] Also included in the List were the American McKesson & Robbins pills brought into the business by an agreement made by Wellcome following encouragement by Burroughs. Haggis described the McKesson & Robbins products (63 items, the largest category in the Price List by far) as an important asset to the partners which met with immediate success. This judgement probably rests on the favourable report the pills received in the *British Medical Journal* following the exhibition presented at the annual meeting of the British Medical Association in 1881.[92] Rhodes James described the personal arrangement reached by Wellcome with his former employers, whereby Wellcome retained the sole rights to the McKesson & Robbins agency, as a 'trump card' and 'a powerful weapon with which to negotiate with Burroughs'. This implies that McKesson & Robbins's pills contributed to the swiftness with which the attention of other pharmacists and the medical profession was drawn to comment on the quality of the firm's products and led to a rapid increase in business.[93] It is not clear, however, whether the favourable analysis in the *Lancet* in 1881 referred to by Rhodes James was applied specifically to the pills made by McKesson & Robbins or to Wyeth's 'Tablets' or both.[94] In any case, two years later, McKesson & Robbins's pills were condemned by a reputable analysis conducted in the US, whereas Wyeth's pills were not.[95] In the light of this evidence, the claim that Wellcome's introduction of McKesson & Robbins's pills into BW&Co.'s product portfolio was important to the success of the partnership, is not convincing. The response of customers reported by sales representatives[96] and the absence of profit from sales provide further evidence which explains why the agency was terminated in 1886 after even Wellcome admitted that five profitless years could not justify extending the agreement with his former employers.[97] Another, more successful, product innovation claimed to be the brainchild of Wellcome was the medical chest, though the initial idea we have shown to have originated with Burroughs.[98]

Both Wellcome and Burroughs brought knowledge, marketing skills, experience, connections, and personality to the partnership. However, it is Wellcome alone who has been given the credit for introducing the detailing system into Britain. Liebenau's history of marketing pharmaceuticals claimed that 'The "detail man" was introduced by Henry Wellcome ...', placing its introduction in the mid-1890s. The history of SMB&Co. demonstrates the inaccuracy of the claim; Burroughs was the first to innovate; Wellcome built on those foundations.[99] Burroughs also brought capital (and with it control) which, though vital to the business, soon became a de-stabilising factor in a partnership which none the less made an immediate impact in the British pharmaceutical trade, and which, within a decade, was acknowledged to be the leader in the British industry.[100]

CHAPTER FIVE

The 'new crusade':
Burroughs Wellcome & Co.
versus the retail trade

Introducing resale price maintenance

Just as apothecaries had lost their monopolistic control of the preparation and dispensing of drugs from pharmacies, growing numbers of retailing chemists and druggists trading from fixed shop premises found their dominance under pressure from newer forms of trading. In response to the mounting intensity of competition from the 1880s, BW&Co. adopted two initiatives. One devised by Burroughs and introduced in April 1890 was intended to secure voluntary arrangements with chemists and druggists aimed at countering price-cutting.[1] In effect this was a form of retail price maintenance applied to all BW&Co. products. The other innovation was a shift in emphasis in an existing policy, the introduction of a more aggressive approach to the prevention of substitution or passing off by undertaking legal action in defence of the Tabloid brand compressed medicines under the trademark dating from 1884.

The trigger which led the company to introduce retail price maintenance was the increasing practice among the large retailers, such as Boots, Day's Drug Store, Lewis & Burroughs, and Taylor's, to sell BW&Co. products as loss leaders; they allowed customers 5 per cent from the company's price list, and at times even charged cost price. The price protection policy was the first of its kind in the pharmacy trade.[2] In return for strict observance of BW&Co.'s price list, the scheme offered retailers 20 per cent at least on the sale of the company's goods, protection against cutters, exchange of unsaleable goods, and supplies of printed materials containing chemists' own names free of charge.[3] Through a series of agreements, annually renewed, chemists in all parts of the country voluntarily undertook not to sell the company's products at prices below those appearing in the company's printed list and to inform on chemists discovered to be in breach of the agreement. Excluded from the printed lists were discounts and any other terms (volume discount for example), which left either the office or representatives to communicate directly to individual chemists.[4] According to the company's 1903 report on price-cutting and substitution, the system was met at the time with general approval in the trade, though those who showed reluctance to agree were 'brought into line' by interviews and/or pressure through wholesalers.[5] Otherwise, the agreement was enforced in two ways. One was assiduous attention paid by travellers to the activities of chemists who had signed up. The other was through rapid reaction to any chemist suspected of price-cutting by sending a traveller to investigate wherever it had occurred regardless of whether the culprit was a large store or a small cash chemist.[6] Culprits would be supplied henceforward only at full price and application for an injunction would be made to restrain him for breach of contract and action to secure damages and costs. Steps taken against the large stores which led the initial loss-leading policy appear to have had some success; Wellcome maintained that in many places the products of BW&Co. were sold at prices of up to 50 per cent *above* the list price. Small chemists, however, were difficult to control.[7] Although the policy was less than completely effective, Wellcome regarded success to have been sufficient to settle the trading climate in which price maintenance was no longer an issue.[8] This remained the case until the late 1890s when deterioration in relations between the company and the trade advanced rapidly. In 1903 an internal report produced at Snow Hill referred to large numbers of chemists displaying an unfriendly attitude and having led to 'trade warfare'.[9]

Defending brands from substitution

The first battle in the war was fought not, however, over price mainte-nance but over substitution which, in the most extreme form, involved 'passing off' the products supplied by other producers (or chemists' own preparations) as Tabloids. Successful action had been undertaken in the past against a Manchester firm for an infringement of Hazeline, putting up a similar product sold as 'Haseline'.[10] In 1883 legal action was taken against Fred Lewis & Co. of Dublin for imitating the label on Lundberg's perfumes. Action against Cleaver & Sons for infringing the 'Edenia' trade mark for Young, Ladd & Coffin's perfumes by putting up 'Edenica' resulted in a public apology in the trade press, the award of costs and damages, a signed undertaking from the infringers to transfer the profits made on the product, delivery of all labels and plates, and communication to buyers, and the redirection of any orders to BW&Co. The 'great victory', as Wellcome described it, however, cost the partnership £200 in legal expenses to overcome the resistance of the wealthy London firm.[11] Whether for reasons of cost or the deterrence effect of the Edenia case, legal action appears to have ceased until 1897 when Tabloids, one of the company's most important brands, came under a series of attacks.

The first originated in Milan and involved Dompe, a chemist whom Wellcome discovered to have been substituting his own products for similar goods he was supposed to be selling for the Wyeths, and subsequently also for Tabloids.[12] In 1901 Dompe was convicted of unlawful competition, usurpation of name, and the misuse of the Tabloid trade mark.[13] A positive outcome for the British company, however, and undoubtedly of greater importance than punishing Dompe financially, was the widespread publication in the Italian medical professional and trade journals of the judgement of the Milan Court in full. Equally helpful was the ability to use the judgement and its coverage in publicity in other countries, not least during the more important case brought against British chemists in 1903.

This was the culmination of BW&Co.'s attempt to check the practice of substitution that had intensified in Britain in the late 1890s. In 1899 a similar process for detecting price-cutting or substitution applied in Milan was adopted to restrain chemists in England. The method was to arrange for a sympathetic doctor or chemist to issue a prescription or order, which would be presented to the suspect by a trusted friend of the local traveller. To ensure complete secrecy, testing in a large city was conducted by a 'district messenger' acting under an assumed name.[14] In accordance with Wellcome's instructions, travellers kept him apprised of the increasing trend towards substitution. In 1900, clearly contemplating legal measures, Wellcome wrote to Sir Thomas Beecham, manufacturer of the popular Beecham's pills and powders, requesting printed records or reports on the 60 injunctions that he had obtained since 1891 against retailers who had been found selling bogus 'Beecham's pills'.[15]

Wellcome perceived the problems of substitution and price cutting as local phenomena. He described the dynamics of the process at local level where one or two men began cutting, others followed 'and the whole place got afire'[16] To prevent such a sequence local monitoring was seen to be vital and the company's travellers provided the key to implementing the policy. The country was divided into regions – London, the south east, the north west, the east and west midlands, the north east and north west, Wales, Scotland, and Ireland – within which each traveller was allocated a territory for which he became responsible. Travellers' connections with traders were crucial for maintaining a flow of intelligence that provided the basis for analysis by managers at Snow Hill, the formulation of policies, and their local application.

Hitherto, Wellcome's approach in the home market had allowed for three stages; first, to arrange for a test for substitution to be applied to chemists whom a traveller might suspect of selling anything but the company's Tabloids when that name appeared on a customer's prescription or on a written order; second, to dissuade culprits and try to avoid further action; and third, if necessary, to threaten prosecution against those who refused to comply. Warnings against substitution of Tabloids appeared in medical journals and the trade press. Letters were addressed to medical men assuring them that the warnings aimed only at the suppression of substitution and did not refer to the action or properties of the company's products. As an additional safeguard, it was suggested that when placing orders for the company's products doctors should specify that they should be dispensed only in original bottles.[17]

Travellers were asked to report on chemists' reactions to the circulars and advertisements and specifically, to a pamphlet entitled 'Substitution Question' produced by the company, in which Beecham's original description of culprits as 'trade pirates',[18] was deployed in raising the stakes, as was an accusation that the retail pharmacy was guilty of a 'morality and business aptitude ... lower than that of the oyster-seller'.[19] Travellers were advised that:

> whenever a question of prices, margin of profit, etc. arise, point the chemist or dealer to paragraph one in which a well-known chemist refers to Burroughs Wellcome and substantial profits afforded on our products and remind him that our goods yield better profits than any other really staple and popular goods – that we create a demand and that we have done more than any in the Kingdom to prevent the cutting of prices and have been most successful, that our direction has cost us vast sums of money and most enterprising chemists really appreciate it.[20]

Alarmed by the terms used by travellers in their reports to describe offending chemists, they were urged not to be too explicit: 'We want to get this information gentlemen but we do not want you to write it. Such phrases as 'this man is a bounder of the very worst type' or 'this man is a very bad egg' were to be avoided, while 'rank substitutor' should be substituted for 'rank subs'[21] Tactics for isolating substituting or price-cutting chemists were explained in a memo to Burnett, the traveller in Lancashire; copies were sent to all representatives. Headed 'Re – principle to be followed with unfriendly chemists', it advised:

> Doubtless you will from time to time find chemists who take up an antagonistic position towards us and our products. In any such instance we think a very excellent plan for you to follow will be to get all chemists' neighbours to display our show cards and signs and, as far as possible, to induce them to make a display of our products. In this way you will probably make an unfriendly chemist feel his position, and the neighbouring chemists will as a matter of course profit by the transaction because of the unfriendly chemist declining business by not stocking our goods.[22]

Further advice was for travellers to make arrangements with the neighbouring chemists to send out a circular (at the company's expense) to medical men reassuring them that they and their patients could be supplied with genuine BW&Co. preparations. Meanwhile, travellers were urged to negate the hostility of disaffected chemists by cultivating the goodwill of all other chemists located in their neighbourhoods by offering the use of showcases and other suitable advertising media to be supplied from Snow Hill.[23] Representatives were requested to supply Snow Hill with the names of two or three responsible persons in each town and city in their territory whom the company could approach should it be necessary to obtain intelligence locally. Such potential witnesses need not be chemists, but must be people of the 'utmost reliance' to whom the company could write in confidence.[24] Travellers were advised to approach medical men 'with tact, caution and diplomacy', particularly if questions were raised regarding confidential correspondence (of which the traveller would, of course, be ignorant) between Snow Hill and the doctor. Under such circumstances, the traveller should avoid expressing an opinion but obtain all information possible for reporting back to the office.[25] George Pearson, formerly the company's senior salesman who had succeeded Sudlow as General Manager in 1905, explained that even when doctors or chemists spoke to them privately they should remember that they were speaking to them as the firm's representatives; anything they heard must be reported to the office under private cover. Reassurance was given any such intelligence would be treated with confidence in the office.[26]

The Tabloid case: Burroughs Wellcome & Co. *versus* Thomas & Capper

The publicity campaign against substitution did not prevent sporadic attempts to challenge the company's trademark though typically defendants had withdrawn after being issued with an injunction. Thomas & Capper, owners of multiple chemist shops in Liverpool and Manchester, ignored three warnings, even though the partners were aware that infringement of the trademark had been detected and evidence obtained. The initial response to legal action commenced in 1902 was the defendants' consent to an injunction.[27] On receipt of the injunction, however, Thomas & Capper decided to fight the case. Wellcome called on the services of Fletcher Moulton QC, an outstanding lawyer and scientist who was on a retainer from the company, as well as those of Sir Edward Clarke, formerly a Conservative Solicitor General and also regarded as a formidable courtroom lawyer.[28] Wellcome mobilised expert legal resources with which to take the case of Burroughs Wellcome versus Thompson & Capper to the High Court if necessary. Three King's Counsel served in Moulton's team for

Wellcome, for whom Markby Stewart & Co., the firm's solicitors organised 72 witnesses. The list, bristling with knights and professors, consisted of the most prominent members of the medical profession and included the president of the Pharmaceutical Association and the editor of the *British Pharmacopoeia*.[29] The 14 defence witnesses consisted of ten professional men, principally from Liverpool, among whom six were homeopathic doctors and chemists.[30]

Although Wellcome had ascertained informally and anonymously that the firm of Thomas & Capper was practising substitution, the case would depend on unquestionable evidence from reliable witnesses. Such evidence was to be accumulated with the assistance of Chune Fletcher.[31] As part of the process of gathering evidence, he was asked to send four prescriptions in duplicate to two provincial medical friends, each of whom should be asked to produce three copies. The prescriptions were neither signed nor did they contain addresses, though they were initialled. He was also provided with a list of names to be used in addressing the prescriptions. Fletcher was reassured that the names of his medical friends would not be used in legal proceedings.[32] Giving evidence in the High Court in 1903, Wellcome responded to an accusation of having set a trap for the defendants by denying any knowledge of the tests conducted in Manchester through Slater, Heelis & Co.[33] In fact, the solicitor's instructions came directly from Snow Hill. They specified which products and how to order them; when to seal containers which the tester should initial and date; when a witness to the transaction was necessary; and directions to avoid using people who had already made tests in the area.[34] In total, 13 witnesses who made 12 purchases (three made on verbal and nine on written orders and prescriptions) supported the charges of passing off at the defendants' shops.[35] The outcome of the case depended on whether Tabloid was a 'fancy' word, devoid of meaning except as applied to certain products manufactured by BW&Co., or a descriptive term applicable to other goods. Not only did the witnesses for the prosecution support the first contention, but Wellcome gave evidence that, after he had made clear that the word was meaningless except as a trade mark invented by himself, the editor of the *Century Dictionary* (the first to include 'Tabloid') had amended the revised edition to define the word as a trade mark belonging to BW&Co. Wellcome also revealed that other dictionary editors had also agreed to remove 'Tabloid'.[36] Counsel for the defence referred to the word 'Tabloid' being used by editors of the *Daily Mirror, Daily Mail, Nature* and *Tatler,* and their contributors. The inclusion of 'Tabloid' as part of a joke in the humorous magazine, *Punch* was interpreted by Wellcome as a tribute to the effectiveness of his company's advertising, and the same, he argued, was true of its appearance in the contemporary novel, *They Call it Love*.[37] Once the validity of the trademark was established, the evidence of witnesses regarding the passing off of other products as Tabloids clinched the case. Mr Justice Byrne ruled completely in favour of BW&Co. An appeal was defeated.

The case was important to the company, not only because of the decision and its legal implication but because of the huge publicity generated in the medical and trade press in Britain and overseas. All leading journals carried extensive detailed coverage, none more so than the *Medical Times and Gazette* which published a 49-page special number in which much of the case was reported almost verbatim. Travellers were urged to refer to the article when interviewing chemists and medical men: '... some specific incitement to read the article in the *Medical Times* is what we want.'[38] Also recommended for propaganda purposes was a strong *Lancet* editorial in support of the decision, underlining the unanimity of the cream of the medical profession in support of the company's reputation for high-quality medicines, a message the company reckoned disaffected chemists could not ignore.[39] The outcome of the case was also of vital importance because, unlike a patent, a trade mark did not have a finite duration.

After the verdict, Wellcome was sensitive to the problem of dealing with the alienation of chemists, particularly those in the north-west who were known to have supported the defendants. One such chemist was J. Rymer Young, whom T. H. Moore, the traveller in Lancashire, was advised to visit. He was told to adopt an 'attitude of politeness and courtesy, just as it would be in the case of any other chemist; avoid entering into any controversy and know nothing in reference to the Tabloid case. These instructions will cover your calls upon all witnesses who appeared on the other side in the Tabloid case.' He was instructed to provide full reports on reactions to the Tabloid case in the towns where Thomas & Capper owned branches, but to avoid their shops.[40]

Emollient engagement was the firm's policy. Aware of the need to mend fences with the trade as a whole, a representative's proposal that prices of products should appear on advertisements was rejected because to do so would compromise the flexibility enjoyed by wholesalers and retailers.[41] Nevertheless, problems remained during a period when intensifying competition prompted many chemists to resist the advance of branded products, especially when a medicine hitherto available only on prescription was made available over the counter when they might compete with the chemist's own preparations.[42] Relations with the trade deteriorated rapidly.

The challenge to resale price maintenance

Dissatisfaction among retailers crystallised around the company's vigorous implementation of its resale price maintenance policy that threatened to undermine the hitherto loyal network of chemists carefully built up since 1880. Retailers' efforts to sell BW&Co. products had received support from the company's expenditure on advertising, local sampling campaigns, and the provision of trade cards, circulars and displays for trade promotion. Representatives had been instructed to identify 'the leading man' in the trade in every town and to report on his business. His firm was then designated as a depot where stocks of BW&Co.'s products were held in volume sufficient to supply local demand from other retailers.[43] The exclusive status accorded to the local depots did not, however, extend to a monopoly on the sale of the company's goods. The basic organisation of the work of travellers remained essentially unaltered from the beginning of the partnership in 1880, though the growth in the numbers employed (about 16 by the mid-1890s),[44] led to the setting up of a sales department under an administrative head in 1895. The sales office was responsible for correspondence with customers, particularly over accounts, returns, complaints, dispatching orders, and notification of forthcoming visits by travellers. It was also the communications centre for the reports of travellers and therefore of strategic importance when the company's policies were challenged by the trade. This occurred in a context of increasing competition as territorial colonisation spread from town to town, sometimes involving an intensive campaign to capture towns hitherto the strongholds of competitors. For example, Parke Davis & Co. almost exclusively dominated the pharmacy trade in Colchester, Chelmsford, and Braintree until in 1903, BW&Co. mounted a concerted attempt in which travellers sought to convert chemists in these towns to stock the company's goods. Medical men in the district were visited to persuade them to prescribe the company's medicines, a pre-condition for patients passing on prescriptions to those local chemists who stocked the company's goods.[45] The defection of one of the company's travellers to a competitor, as in the case of the popular J.W. Hull who had defected to Parke Davis & Co., was perceived to pose a problem because of his connections and his knowledge of the company's business. His replacement was urged to 'be extremely alert and in every way on your guard'.[46]

To competition from other manufacturers was added a movement initiated by local retail trade organisations in pursuit of better terms from BW&Co. The first indication of this was a communication to the Sales Department in March 1899 from J. Burnard, the company's representative in Ireland. He reported a motion to be tabled at a forthcoming meeting of the Dublin Chemists' Federation: 'Burroughs Wellcome having neglected to secure any adequate profit to chemists who are faced by competition to retail even poisons and dangerous drugs of their manufacture at a profit of from 10 per cent to 15 per cent, it becomes the duty of the Dublin Chemists' Federation to discourage the sales of these specialities by every legitimate means'.[47] The response from Snow Hill was to instruct the traveller to make discreet inquiries to ascertain whether the motion reflected a widely held view, was limited to militant members of the federation, or only to

Dr MacWalter who proposed the motion.[48] Identified as a persistent agitator for higher discount, in December 1902, MacWalter succeeded in gaining a concession from Snow Hill in the form of a 20 per cent instead of 15 per cent discount. However, in agreeing to that, D. L. Kirkpatrick, then the Dublin representative was instructed that he must avoid giving the impression that this was a concession: 'We should like him to APPLY for these terms rather than they be offered to him as we think the effect will be greater. We should like you as far as possible to cultivate Dr McW. Make a friend of him without in any way losing your dignity and get him when writing to us to asking for best terms to undertake to push our products in preference to others.'[49] Snow Hill suggested to Kirkpatrick that he should steer the doctor to include in his letter to London an outline of his plans for pushing the company's goods once he had received best wholesale terms.[50] The concession to MacWalter, therefore, was a response to an individual who was regarded in some sense as of strategic importance to the Dublin trade; the decision was not part of a general retreat.

That the company was the focus of an orchestrated campaign among retailers emerged later in 1899 when several local federations of chemists passed resolutions critical of the firm. For the next two years, resolutions and letters urging the company to join the Proprietary Articles Trading Association (PATA) flooded in from across the country. The purpose of the campaign in support of the PATA was described in a letter from the Barnsley Federation as that of assisting chemists in 'endeavouring to secure a living profit on proprietary articles.'[51] This was part of a new policy of the PATA to recruit drug manufacturers as well as traders and for this purpose a conference was called to take place in November 1902. In addition to manufacturers interested in becoming members, representatives from all chemists' local associations were invited to attend with a view to discussing the implications of the change in membership and agreeing future policy. Wellcome appears to have been involved in preliminary meetings with other manufacturers but resigned before the conference took place. The company was not represented at the conference, though intelligence relayed by senior sales representatives described the event (attended by retailers, whole-salers, and a few 'unimportant manufacturers') as 'a fizzle' and a 'fiasco'.[52] Wellcome was advised to affect ignorance of the proceedings and not to be drawn into discussion on the subject. In view of the congruency between the PATA's aim to tackle price cutting and BW&Co.'s well-established policy to police prices charged for the company's products, it seems likely that Wellcome's reluctance to become involved with the PATA is attributable partly to scepticism as regards the effectiveness of the methods which the PATA proposed to adopt. These consisted of the drawing up of a 'stop list' including products which, under the rules of PATA membership manufac-turers would be obliged not to supply to chemists who sold below list price.

While Wellcome acknowledged that his own anti-price-cutting policy had not achieved complete compliance, he was still satisfied with the extent of its success. He regarded substitution to be a greater threat to the company and had been disappointed with the failure of the PATA to tackle that problem. Indeed, his vigorous campaign against substitution earlier in 1902 had provoked outrage among local associations, another factor contributing to Wellcome's reluctance to identify with the PATA.

Substitution and 'trade pirates'; Wellcome *versus* the retail traders' association

Wellcome had turned his attention to substitution which he suspected was connected to profit margins rather than prices per se: 'agitators appear to have convinced many of the trade that substitution is justifiable unless a certain liberal percentage of profit is guaranteed to them'.[53] Headed 'Special Caution', the company issued circulars to all chemists. Anyone practising substitution was referred to as an 'imp of darkness'. Robust advertisements that appeared in the trade press under the banner 'Pirates' referred to the behaviour of 'trade pirates and trade jackasses' against which (implying guilt by association) the Federations of Local Trade Associations took strong exception.[54] The company also produced a seven-page pamphlet entitled 'The Substitution Question' which quoted from the *Pharmaceutical Journal* and the *Anti-Cutting Record*, defining and condemning substitution. It also included articles from the *National Druggist*, an American journal. One referred to the first instance when the criminal law was invoked to punish tampering with physician's prescriptions. The conviction in a New York court that involved Fairchild's Essence of Pepsin is indicative of the initiative undertaken by Wellcome's longstanding friend and business associate, Sam Fairchild, and was perhaps a further influence on Wellcome's forceful campaign. Another article described resolutions passed by the American Pharmaceutical Association and the National Association of Retail Druggists denouncing substitution and demonstrating a preparedness to initiate prosecution against offenders in the trade.[55]

The Federation of Local Pharmaceutical Associations was outraged by the contents of the 'Special Caution' circulars, described as containing 'sweeping … charges made upon the honesty of the general drug trade'.[56] Some chemists refused to exhibit the company's showcards. The correspondence pages of the *Chemist & Druggist* were for a time filled with letters hostile to the company. Wellcome alerted his travellers to the importance of presenting their visits to chemists as routine: '… do not actually raise the matter of correspondence in the *Chemist and Druggist* re the 'Special Caution' circular but attempt to establish any views which may be volunteered on that subject. Talk as little as possible yourself and listen with all your intelligence and duly transmit what you hear.'[57] The firm continued to be deluged with more resolutions and letters (more or less abusive) complaining of inadequate profit margins. From this correspondence it is clear that one of the most fundamental causes of the problems faced by traditional chemists and druggists derived from the effects of the expansion of the multiple retailers, notably the cash chemists, Boots, Taylors, and other relatively large local chemists attempting to compete with them. Wellcome's response was selective, concentrating either on localities that appeared to be suffering greater competitive pressure than others or where the company's business seemed more vulnerable. For example, Wellcome instructed Sixsmith, a senior traveller, to visit Blackpool where the Blackpool and Fylde Chemists' Association had been particularly critical of the company, noting that several other large proprietors had complied, and that as a result there was 'much more pleasure and satisfaction in handling their goods'.[58] Armed with the list of names, status of each retailer, and the terms received from BW&Co., Sixsmith's assignment was to avoid giving any impression that the visit was a response to criticism, and 'to bring them as well into line as it is possible … to show them that we can co-operate with them to mutual advantage.'[59] Once in Blackpool, he discovered that Boots and W. C. Richardson gave 20 per cent discounts compared with BW&Co.'s 15 per cent for account customers.[60] A different source revealed that managers of Boots shops received salary and commission to stimulate pushing, the amount determined by the volume of Boots specialities sold at their branch.[61] Wellcome recognised Boots as a problem. When, in response to requests from Glasgow, it was decided to raise the prices of BW&Co.'s goods containing poisons, Boots' agreement to the rise was sought before implementation. The traveller was instructed to answer chemists' queries regarding the attitude of Boots to the rise by saying that it reflected the Nottingham company's recognition of the greater trouble and care required in selling scheduled poisons (limited to qualified pharmacists) than the more usual preparations sold by chemists.[62]

The pressure to join the PATA and place the company's products on the stop list, however, continued. In January 1906, the London Chemists' Association (LCA) conveyed a resolution expressing its disapproval of BW&Co. for refusing to join the PATA, a copy of which was sent to the Local Pharmaceutical Association's secretary, James Reid.[63] On receipt, he wrote to the company: 'So long as you adopt a system of threats and prosecutions in place of introducing a system of conciliation and consideration, the feeling among chemists will be bitter against you as I know it is at present. You mark my words. You will join the PATA before three years are up and you will be sorry you didn't do it sooner.'[64] Doubtless intended as an insult to Wellcome, coercion, he concluded, was 'not according to the British spirit. There is less of anxiety to pile up the Almighty Dollar in this country and more inclination towards justice and fair play than is the case in 'the land of freedom'.[65] Distribution to the local associations resulted in the same resolution being passed by several, some registering stronger disapproval.[66]

Wellcome's response was both local and general. As in other instances, he asked the area traveller for the identities of the aggressive Glasgow chemists, an assessment of their professional positions and of influence in the trade. In answer to complaints from Eastbourne concerning price maintenance there, Wellcome's response was that if the local association wished to increase the minimum rates on the company's products, the assistance would be given 'in every way practicable'.[67] He told his managers: 'Our policy must be to temporise – avoid towns where the fever is burning and avoid controversy. Representatives should be warned to tread with care.'[68] At the same time, he asked for information on the 'new crusade' in England, Scotland, and elsewhere, its effect on depots in various towns, on the attitudes of leading chemists, and on sales. 'Our adversaries and would-be competitors again combined forces. The resolution passed by the LCA and circulated to all provincial associations is a declaration of war. We must stand firm … Our intelligence department should provide us with clear information. Above all, the representatives should keep their nerves.'[69] Critical of Weld, head of the Sales Department, for applying insufficient energy to the campaign, Wellcome told his general manager:

> … we want him to carry an olive branch but not with trembling hand. The introduction to our price list sets out our policy for Friendly, Cordial and Fair but NO nonsense! Urge Weld to gird on his armour with more courage.'[70]

Armageddon arrived in 1906 when, at the request of the provincial associations, the LCA invited Wellcome to receive a small deputation, to which he agreed. The resulting 'conferences' took place on 21 June, 28 June, and 2 August 1906 at the Holburn Viaduct Hotel. The deputation consisted of five senior members of the LCA, including the three London officers (chairman, deputy and honorary secretary, and the president) and the secretary of the Eastbourne Chemists' Association (originators of the idea to hold a conference). Wellcome represented the company accompanied by Pearson and Collett Smith, though they contributed little to the proceedings. Wellcome presented the company's case and answered criticisms and questions. The central issue embodied in the resolution was Wellcome's refusal to join the PATA. However, the deputation's approach to the conference also revealed an underlying dissatisfaction with the company's 15 per cent discount policy. This was regarded as insufficient, particularly on low-priced items and especially for the small chemist.[71] Wellcome rejected this complaint, as he did the deputation's insistence that national rather than local systems of price protection were the most effective methods of countering price-cutting (which, it was agreed, both sides opposed). Wellcome's defence was that manufacturing products required research, control, and precision, which the deputation members separately endorsed as having resulted in the company's production of goods of the very highest quality. His second line of defence was that his company also invested heavily in creating a demand for products, a costly process that was to the mutual benefit of chemists and his company. He argued that small, independent chemists, as well as co-operative stores and multiple cash chemists, rendered the policing of price maintenance much more difficult, if not impossible, on a national basis. He drew attention to the relative success of his company since 1890 in implementing a price maintenance policy that might vary between localities but took account of the practicality of exercising discipline on retailers. The market was still local and regional, rather than national. Wellcome also maintained that many chemists continued to charge above the privately circulated price list in several towns and districts. He argued that the resolutions condemning the company had been based upon a misrepresentation of the facts and succeeded in persuading at least some of the deputation that, contrary to the resolution, the company's price protection was efficient.[72] He sought to balance the resolutions as evidence of associational irritation and individual dissatisfaction against the many letters of support that the firm had received.[73] Wellcome's initial approach, therefore, was measured and reflective in tone. As the discussion proceeded, however, he adopted two further tactics. First, he expressed his disappointment that the Association's campaign against the company had coincided with a plan he had prepared the previous year for a 'modification of terms' for the trade to mark the beginning of the company's second quarter century. The result, he declared, would have been mutually beneficial to the firm and to traders but, because the company would not yield to coercion, the plan was held in abeyance. Second, in commenting on some of the more extreme threats of direct action, notably of boycotting, advocated by some of the local associations and some individuals, he chose not to separate these from the London Association's decision to circulate a resolution critical of his company's policies (though not advocating direct action). Wellcome insisted that by circulating the resolution to the Local Association the London chemists had thereby raised the level of agitation against the company and by implication against himself.

Wellcome wrong-footed the deputation whose members had anticipated that discussion would turn into an issue of personal integrity and had not expected that Wellcome might improve trading terms. Faced with the prospect of the withdrawal of a plan before it had even been introduced, the deputation expressed dismay that what they had intended as a 'persuasive motion' could be interpreted as a vote of censure. Wellcome continued to insist that disapproval was equivalent to a censure, unprecedented in its kind in the history of the trade: 'You are all gentlemen of such minds and comprehension, that you cannot fail to realise what an expression of this kind means to any firm or individual who has any sense of self-respect and honour ...'[74] After several spoke to dissociate themselves from the resolution interpreted thus, Wellcome returned to the more extreme positions adopted by the provincial motions for which he held the LCA indirectly responsible. He demanded that the vote of censure should be revoked as a condition for introducing the planned revision of terms because otherwise they could be interpreted as a result of coercion and censure, an outcome that no company could countenance.[75] The meeting adjourned, to be reconvened for the third time a month later when the deputation presented Wellcome with the following unanimous resolution that: 'the Association regrets that Mr Wellcome regards the resolution passed by this Association on Jan. 3rd 1906, as a vote of censure; that it was, as it purported to be, an intimation that the members were not satisfied with the present trade terms of Messrs Burroughs Wellcome.'[76]

At the final meeting, Wellcome dealt skilfully with the pressure, politely exerted by the Association, to reveal his plans to reform terms. He ended with a question: 'I take it gentlemen, from the assurances which you have already given me, that as a response to whatever I do in this way that I should have very liberal support from the trade?'[77] He received an affirmative answer. The assumption underlying it implied that in subsequent exchanges prices would be raised. The meeting ended with mutual expressions of respect, goodwill, and friendship. Wellcome concluded with an affirmation of the company's policy to offer chemists 'fair play ... I want to approach this matter from a perfectly equitable point of view, and, on the other hand, I hope an equitable spirit will be exercised by those who judge what I am doing.'[78] The entire proceedings were printed and a marginal index added by the company. Bound copies were issued for distribution – to among others, the editor of the *Chemist & Druggist*. The journal gave full coverage, a distillation of the essence of the meeting appearing in verse under the heading '*Apologia Pro?*'

> They met, the valiant foemen, at the Viaduct Hotel,
> They met to fight for profits and the naked truth to tell;
> But the bland and cordial Wellcome (for a Wellcome never rails)
> And the sympathetic manner, took the wind out of their sails;
> Soon that awful resolution they regard with pained surprise.
> 'I am deeply hurt', said Henry, 'so you must apologise'.
>
> So they called a hurried meeting, and another motion penned,
> And on bended knees protested that they never would offend:
> They were shocked to think they ever had given any pain,
> For they yearned to retail 'tabloids' at the maximum of gain;

And at hint of surrogation they were properly surprised.
'I will think of it', said Henry, 'now that you've apologised.'[79]

Writing on behalf of 'lowly chemists' and 'pill-punchers', an anonymous correspondent also versified the event, ending with an appeal:

Oh Mr Wellcome! Pity us poor chemists and relent
And grant us, we beseech you, sir, that little five per cent.[80]

The restructuring of terms occurred in the form of higher discounts, varying from between 20 per cent and 25 per cent on Kepler and Hazeline products and on most Tabloids. However, these were accompanied by a 10 per cent price increase.[81] Numerous chemists conveyed their views on the change introduced on 1 October 1906. Thornber of Accrington regarded the discount as 'a heater to the trade',[82] whereas Poingdestre of Greenwich concluded his letter: 'What is the use of granting extra discounts if you raise prices?'[83] Kemsey-Bourne of West Bromwich thought the terms still insufficient and dismissed the publication of the conference proceedings as a waste of money that could have been better spent by giving it to Tabloid dealers.[84] Editorial comment in the *Chemist & Druggist* drew attention to the so-called 'mutual advantage' that Wellcome (described as 'the top dog') had promised at the conference. Of the 10 per cent increase in prices for some products the retailer would keep only half. The retailer might well ask 'why not all?'.[85]

Positioned between the multiple retail cash chemists and the small price-cutting retailer (the most vulnerable to the company's strategy of providing higher rewards based on sales volume) was the average retailer who was inclined to avoid patent medicines and did not cut prices – though he might be compelled to do so through competition. Without prompting by senior managers, some of the company's travellers showed an awareness of the need to retain and cultivate the goodwill of small retailers, several having taken the initiative to encourage combined ordering. By enabling them to benefit from a higher discount for volume orders, it was expected that sales would increase. However, it was also seen as a method of circumventing those wholesalers who were not passing on the higher discount introduced by the company in 1906.[86] McBride described the success he had achieved in Birmingham, where all but six 'of the utterly superior class' were now co-operating and receiving 25 per cent discount, had led to increased sales in the district.[87] There is no evidence that this success was indicative of a widespread growth of cooperative buying as a long-term development. Clark underlined the problem in his district by appointing a 'consignee' who would organise the distribution of goods to local chemists belonging to a combine and be responsible for paying the company regardless of whether he received payment from the other retailers. A further problem was presented by the £100 gross minimum value of an order regarded as economic under these circumstances. Carmichael, who claimed to have arranged ten such combines, reported that a combine's order tended to be around £20.00.[88] It seems likely, however, that these experiments were translated into no more than local, short-lived arrangements. They are, however, evidence of representatives' awareness of retailers' problems and a willingness to innovate in order to expand trade.

It is difficult to exaggerate the importance to the company of Wellcome's success in enforcing resale price maintenance and in defending the Tabloid brand. The significance of Wellcome's remarkable victory extends beyond the company's history. Historians of retailing in Britain characterised the 1890s and early 1900s as a period of price wars generated by the price-cutting multiples[89] among which Boots and Day were the most prominent exponents.[90] A movement to stop price cutting was initiated by independent retailers who in 1896 recruited wholesalers and manufacturers to form the PATA.[91] Most manufacturers (including BW&Co.), either declined or (in the case of Boots and Day's Drug Store) campaigned vigorously against membership, a position which Yamey interprets as a failure to appreciate the advantages of price control, particularly with respect to advertising on a national scale.[92] Ten years passed before membership included more than one-third of the country's retail chemists, most wholesalers, and 200 manufacturers.[93] The weakness in the organisation before 1906 was adduced by Yamey to explain why it was not until shortly before the First World War that reasonably effective price control was achieved.[94] Holloway refers to the major difficulty hampering the PATA's progress which was the impossibility of wholesalers conducting their business on the basis of numerous separate price agreements with manufacturers.[95] The success of BW&Co., therefore, provides an important exception requiring explanation.[96] Hitherto completely overlooked by historians of retailing, the company's effective independent action rested on the strength of its brands, the measures of support provided for retailers, and a carefully orchestrated policing and implementation of policy both in and outside the courts designed to end substitution and establish price control. The implementation of this overall marketing strategy depended much on the company's travellers.

Selling medicine; the role and management of travelling representatives

The company's travelling sales representatives were well aware of their importance to the success of the business. Addressing his fellow representatives in 1907, one of the most experienced travellers described them as 'the eyes of the firm'. As such they were able to support implementation and monitoring of the price and substitution campaigns, but Rogers noted that travellers were also 'constantly seeing the work and ideas of others as we move about. Let us study the methods of others and report from time to time on all new ideas and even the success of old ones.'[97] Curry, another experienced representative, was appreciative of the benefits they enjoyed through the support they received from Snow Hill which he believed afforded them a significant advantage compared with their counterparts employed by other firms. He described the typically passive role of drug house representatives in Britain 'wandering around every three months in the ordinary way and having the orders handed to them'. He contrasted this approach with the pro-active engagement of travellers working for BW&Co. who were adequately prepared through regular briefings to discuss with chemists the links between the company's products, the chemists' trade, and local dispensary practices, as well as to interview medical practitioners.[98] The office issued 'push lists' of products from time to time, indicating those on which travellers should concentrate their efforts. A confidential Monthly Letter, Points for Propaganda, circulated to all representatives also set out 'selling points' to assist in introducing new products or re-launching those already established.[99]

These were additions to the long established practice of careful attention to recruitment and close attention to monitoring and advice. Desirable personal attributes were paramount. When references were requested from Dr Parkin for Creasley Holland in 1904, the referee was asked to provide information on the length of his acquaintance with the applicant and '... whether during the whole of this period you have been in intimate touch with him, whether you think him to be a man of unimpeachable honour and integrity, scrupulously and rigidly conscientious and just, and someone in whom we may safely place the most implicit reliance.'[100] The company also

FIGURE 5.1
BW&Co.'s
sales repre-
sentatives
and Head
Office staff at
BMA annual
meeting,
Carlisle 1896.

B. W. & Co. medical representatives and Head Office staff at the Carlisle B.M.A. Congress in 1896. Standing (left to right): Messrs. W. D. Howison, J. W. Rollings, G. E. Davis, W. E. Taylor, H. W. Lane, J. H. Harris, J. Dowdeswell, F. Ashley Rogers, Dr. Peter Short. Sitting: Messrs. Geo. E. Pearson, E. F. Linstead, W. R. Mealing, T. W. Davies, J. H. Francis, M. C. P. Irish, J. F. Burnett required each candidate to undergo a medical examination before his application was considered.[101] The long-established system of detailed monitoring of representatives' activities by the partners had been reformed in 1894 as part of a reorganisation of the business into functional departments located in designated rooms and offices where employees were supervised by heads possessing specialist knowledge.[102] The responsibility for sales management was separated from advertising (which transferred to a new department headed by Linstead) and delegated to Weld, the senior salesman. Accorded the status of management staff but without the title, henceforward he was the person through whom the travelling representatives communicated to the general manager. Territorial clerks were appointed, charged with the task of drawing up monthly reports on their respective territories based on detailed correspondence received from representatives on the road. These territorial reports were passed to the head of the Home Sales Department for comment, then to two 'supervising representatives' who produced reports for the general manager, (Sudlow until his retirement in 1905, thereafter Pearson). The general manager's further comments were passed to Wellcome himself. Pearson described the company's approach: '... the firm has no use for a man who stands still – he blocks the way for a better and more competent man who is ambitious to succeed and it is kinder to him and to the mutual interest of his fellow workers that he should be promptly removed.'[103] Wellcome, the ultimate arbiter, subjected the reports to a final scrutiny that resulted in travellers receiving encouragement, advice, reprimand, salary increase (or decrease), promotion, or dismissal.[104]

The earliest examples of such reports to survive are those for February 1898. It is not clear whose comments have been recorded, nonetheless they provide sufficient indication of the degree of control exercised by Snow Hill. While the letters may have been written by Collett Smith, Sudlow, or later Pearson, the prevailing authorial voice, displaying attention to the minutest detail, use of military metaphor, and robust didacticism is, when compared with early correspondence, characteristic of Wellcome himself. Full reports containing valuable information on the London territory by Pearson and Rogers was described as excellent. In the provinces, McBride received particular praise for sending 'well phrased letters' presumed to have been the reason why he had secured interviews with several medical men on his first visit to a long under-worked territory. His strategy of focussing first on the medical men, followed by chemists (many of whom were correctly described in 1898 as antagonistic[105]), was regarded as the most effective approach. Burnett's first trip to Ireland drew praise for the energy he had applied to the task, the report accepting distances between outlying parts as justifying an otherwise disappointingly 'small weekly average of 29 effective calls on doctors and chemists'.[106] Criticised for spending up to an hour with some medical men, Tingle was advised to limit both the number of products detailed and conversation to no more than 20 minutes, an approach designed to focus the doctor's mind.[107] To another traveller accused of making too few visits, it was suggested that he had found Christmas Eve 'too near to Christmas to work.'[108] Blanchflower was rebuked for the lack of directness in his approach to selling: '... the friendly remarks and the little pleasantries which pass between you and the doctors and chemists regarding our products are of no value whatever'.[109] Letters also reveal detailed advice on the selling of medicines, especially when a new product was introduced. The response to McBride's reported difficulty in persuading Ipswich chemists to stock Salodent was that opposition among chemists was to be expected when a medicine hitherto available only on prescription was made available over the counter. His task was to counter the opposition: 'That is the principal object we have in sending our repre-sentatives: viz. to create a demand for our preparations, and we are quite confident that you will no way be deterred from pushing and creating a sale for Salodent by these pessimistic remarks of grasping chemists'.[110] Sixsmith was criticised for writing letters that fell below the company's standards for grammar, spelling, relevance, and meaning. Particular exception was taken to his use of the term 'stuff' to refer to the company's products: 'We had supposed that your own personal vanity would have pointed out to you that a representative selling "stuff" was not so much to be desired as a position where the goods being pushed were of the very highest quality and the greatest excellence possible'.[111] He was also criticised for excluding small retailers who should be 'regularly and consistently cultivated'.[112] Hull, whose territory was Yorkshire, was accused of complacency regarding the towns in his territory: 'The chemists of Bridlington are apparently very courteous and pleasant to you but immediately your back is turned they do everything they can to persuade customers who desire our goods to purchase others ... there is no excuse at all for thinking or feeling that it is not necessary to exert yourself in a town you do not do so.'[113] In his territory in the south of England, Blanchflower was accused of naivete in dealing with competition from Parke Davis & Co. His report had attributed the pushing of Parke Davis' hypodermics by Worthing chemists to the American company's provision of a display unit. Snow Hill suggested that a more likely expla-nation was the offer of larger discounts: 'Any chemist and many doctors will soon get into the habit of saying these nice little things to you if the effect is that you rest satisfied and raise no protest'.[114] Blanchflower was instructed to visit Worthing at least every six months, possibly every four: 'You have not yet succeeded in exterminating the enemy. Let us know which products we should send to the medical men in Worthing – and suggest any other plan which will assist in capturing this town completely'.[115] The unfortunate Blanchflower was denied an increase in salary in 1904 because his letters were described as much alike as peas in a pod and that 'parrot-like reiteration suggests ... your work is of too superficial a character to have the results we would like and which we expect ... take hold of yourself and make your territory what it should be.'[116]

Travellers in conference and on the road; promotion and publicity

Coinciding with the nadir in relations between BW&Co. and the formal bodies of chemists and druggists and the PATA, it was probably in 1905 that the company introduced annual training conventions. Lasting for two days, they were attended by all home representatives, office sales staff, and managers. They provided a forum for the exchange of accumulated information and experience between managers and travellers.[117] This innovation also coincided with an increase in the recruitment of representatives, a further justification for attempting to diffuse marketing knowledge in a more systematic method. Of 21 present at the 1907 home sales convention, four had been recruited since the 1906 event.[118] Only the 1907 and 1908 convention reports have survived, but the verbatim accounts reveal a mixture of sophistication and practicality in developing a systematic approach to marketing strategy connected with the various parts of the organisation.

In addition to exchanging information and ideas about products and various aspects of marketing, the conventions provided a forum for education

FIGURE 5.2 BW&Co.'s sales representatives, Dartford, 1905.

Kept.

and discussion focused on the company's new biologicals, first introduced in the mid-1890s, and Wellcome Brand Chemicals introduced into the market in 1902. Information and advice from the office on the science underlying the products and their therapeutical applications introduced a new element in the training of travellers that was to grow as the science and applications became more complex. The introduction of diphtheria antitoxin and other biologicals marked a conceptual shift because of the difference from all other known therapeutic methods, a change which presented a challenge to companies to educate practitioners. However, first, the representatives needed education, to which end at the conference in 1906, Dr Pyman lectured on ergot, and in 1907, Dr Henry Dale delivered a wide-ranging lecture on modern therapeutics; cascara was the subject of Dr Pyman in 1907. These developments aimed at educating representatives are evidence of an increasingly difficult problem for medically unqualified salesmen in selling the new science-based products. However, they do not support the assertion that scientific advances resulted in the marketing innovations spearheaded by BW&Co. These innovations were introduced by Burroughs for SMB&Co. before 1880, long before the company produced medicines that originated in scientific research.[119]

The established professionalism of the detail man in the American pharmaceutical industry, exemplified by the education, accomplishments, and early careers of the two partners, meant that the leading American companies were well equipped to mount such a campaign of educational propaganda.[120] In Britain, however, since its formation in 1880 BW&Co. was the first and remained the exception, recruiting representatives for the purpose of detailing physicians and chemists in the American style. The reputation achieved by the company and dramatically endorsed by the medical profession in the course of the Tabloid case of 1903, must have made it easier to attract candidates possessing the desired skills. None the less, evidence from the home sales representatives' conventions in 1907 and 1908 suggests that qualifications and experience in pharmacies, rather than in doctors' surgeries, comprised the typical background of those present.[121] This may account for the division of opinion regarding the best approach to selling the new products. The problem encountered in selling Wellcome Brand Chemicals was straightforward and resulted from the reluctance of retail chemists accustomed to purchasing supplies from well-established fine chemicals manufacturers to try a new source. Travellers were urged to emphasise to potential buyers the scientific research that ensured products were of the highest quality for dispensing.[122] Weld's insistence that 'quality will sell no matter what the price', was not a widely held view.[123] Ample acknowledgement was made of the high quality of Wellcome Brand Chemicals; however, Curry insisted that the most effective way to introduce them was to offer them almost as an afterthought:

The best way to go to work in selling these is to take your order for regular lines, e.g. 6 dozen Hazeline Snow, 3 gross small size pastilles, 2 gross Tabloid Tea, and then say 'And what about drugs?' Sometimes the chemist will say: 'I didn't know you made drugs.' 'Yes, we do.' 'I thought you only made alkaloids.' 'How about Extract of Cascara Liquid?' Get right down to business rather than speak about the beautiful crystals and the latest developments in scientific research.[124]

In Curry's opinion the ability of scientific understanding to sell had its limits, especially among conservative doctors. For doctors who expressed their disbelief in drugs (preferring electrotherapy, massage, breathing exercise, hypnotism, or homeopathy), they should be asked if they sometimes had the need for laxatives, external applications, ophthalmic preparations, or 'General Goods'.[125] Clark listed the obstacles encountered in propagation and the effective methods of overcoming them. The introduction of Wellcome Brand Chemicals meant that those doctors who never used proprietary medicines could be told that they did not have to. An objection to 'fancy names' should be countered by indicating that they were the guarantee to the patient of being certain of receiving the same prescription. Overton was sceptical regarding the effectiveness of a science-oriented selling approach, at least so far as chemists were concerned. He wanted the office to produce a pamphlet containing selling points for the whole list of products, 'something readable from the chemist's point of view in a chatty style which would make the ground far more ready for tilling when a representative visited'.[126]

Curry emphasised the importance, when approaching the physician, of first gaining a complete understanding of the new science-based products. He gave Ernutin, which representatives were experiencing particular difficulty in promoting successfully, as an example. He suggested that giving a 'determined and authoritative introduction of the product' (even to the extent of hinting at possible liability to damages by not using it), could produce results.[127] Educating the representatives to educate medical practitioners was a process hampered by the conflicting interests of the representatives themselves as their salaries were affected by sales volume rather than by the particular products they sold. Reviewing the pattern of sales, Curry concluded that while sales had continued to increase more rapidly between 1905 and 1907, expansion was not the result of a growth in sales of the 'new generation of products', but of 'regular lines which have been long established' – 'General Goods', notably Kepler Cod Liver Oil and Malt and Tabloids.[128] Related to this finding, in 1908 he expressed the concern that the ratio of visits to medical practitioners to calls on chemists had fallen.

The highest proportion of conference time was spent on presentations and discussions concerning the marketing of 'General Goods' which dominated the 1908 push list: Tabloid laxative fruit pastilles and Alaxa, a new laxative, Xaxa, a preparation of salicylic acid identical with aspirin, though half the price, Opa, an antiseptic mouthwash, and menthol snuff. The only scientific pharmaceutical on the push list was Ernutin.[129] Curry's concern was the variability in sales between districts which in some were extremely low. He maintained that greater efforts should be directed towards gaining access to the surgeries of general practitioners in places where sales were below expectations as well as towards penetrating the conservatism of small chemists, with most of whom the company conducted no business at all.[130]

Kirkpatrick attributed his own success to a loss leader strategy. His tactic was first to draw the chemist's attention to tincture of hyoscyamus, a preparation rarely used but which could be shown to be substantially cheaper than the tinctures normally used. 'He looks up the price list and discovers it is true and thinks if that is cheap some others must be too.'[131] However, Curry was convinced that sales could be increased further through 'propagation' (not to be confused, representatives were told, with selling), an approach common in the US, which had been introduced by one or two competitors to Britain. 'Propagation', which he defined as 'enlightened demonstration work' was the subject of Curry's lecture at the 1908 convention. His thesis was that in the past the sheer novelty of the company's products, especially Tabloids, could impress doctors. To be successful, a traveller required no more than a good appearance, an average knowledge of the goods he sold, and an opportunity to show and describe them.[132] He urged all representatives to adopt similar tactics, devising 'spectacular and picturesque' demonstrations of selected products, which could be carried in the traveller's bag,[133] a necessary accompaniment whose neglect by travelling staff Curry criticised.[134]

Detailing doctors and chemists; the travellers' art of 'propagation'

The allocation of time for practical demonstrations was in part an acknowledgement that incorrect demonstrations could be counter-productive at a time when representatives were expected to sell increasingly complicated products requiring expert presentation. Thus in 1904, a traveller in the Midlands was discovered to have been demonstrating all-glass aseptic hypodermic syringes to medical men in an incorrect manner, the effect of which implied that the Tabloid product was practically insoluble. He was provided with written instructions on the procedure to be used and told: '... take hold of yourself that your work will from now on show more uniform results and a more thorough and complete grasp of the situation.'[135]

Curry was the representative chosen to lead the session on demonstrations. He recommended all representatives to carry concentrated tinctures in their bags, ready opened to demonstrate. He invariably carried a rack containing tubes of tinctures, some Wellcome Brand Chemicals and others of competitors. He took pains to ensure that each tube represented the same value of tincture showing that Wellcome Brand Chemicals concentrated tinctures produced much more for the same price.[136] Visual aids and a script were used to demonstrate the virtues of Alaxa, a highly purified, potent cascara extract for the treatment of habitual constipation. Curry adopted a connoisseur's approach: 'Hold the glass in your hand the same as you would test cognac and then inhale the bouquet. "Now taste it, doctor". Refer to the warming sensation as it runs down the throat … You induce him to smell it, and then dipping your tasting rod into the product, approach the doctor with a confident air, and he has licked it before he knows where he is.' Grieg was similarly enthusiastic about selling Alaxa, declaring: 'I have swallowed much, but I have poured whole bottle-fulls (in proper doses) down the throats of open-mouthed doctors … ¼ oz of Tabloid grows in a glass of water like a tree of an Indian conjuror. I have had a doctor stand open-mouthed in astonishment.'[137] Tabloid Laxative Pastilles received a similar approach when introduced to doctors. Curry's tactic was to '… have one apiece to show there is no hard feeling. The flavour and bouquet is [sic] commented on as of some rare vintage …'[138]

Securing a testing or tasting required less imagination compared with the psycho-dramas created by some of the representatives. Both Blanchflower and Rogers were enthusiastic about the dramatic potential for propagating Vaporole Aromatic Ammonia. Rogers described how on entering the doctor's consulting room he would look around, asking if smelling salts were available. He would ask the doctor to open the stopper of the bottle which, in his experience, almost invariably stuck. That afforded a basis for comparison between administrations using the Vaporole. Even when sticking did not occur he would observe that the salts lost strength through imperfect stoppering. The doctor was invited to break the capsule before smelling, the cue for remarking that Vaporole ensured continued strength and utility.[139] Another example of a carefully choreographed presentation is offered by a demonstration of Soloid Corrosive Sublimate, a preparation that varied in solubility. In order to conceal this, the demonstrator was advised first to drop one product into a little water to which dye was added and shake

FIGURE 5.4
Carved
panelling in
main show
room at Snow
Hill, n.d,
*c.*1900.

('there is a little art to this'); the spectator's attention was then directed to a small tube containing the product which allowed the demonstrator to compare the two and remark on how little dilutant was used. Holding the spectator in conversation, attention was then to be drawn to the dye. This was of no significance to the process but presented as a great feature which would turn the solution blue and remain that colour for a week. In the meantime, the solution was transferred from tube to bottle and filled with water in which the Soloid would be seen to dissolve rapidly. Demonstrating Tabloid Quinine Bisulphate similarly employed an element of illusion in order to persuade sceptics of its disintegrative capacity. In this instance, the demonstrator was advised to allow a small portion of water to remain at the bottom of the tube before demonstrating, 'the doctor does not attach impor-

FIGURE 5.5
BW&Co.
exhibit,
St Louis
Exposition,
1904.

tance to it.' While the representative talked about the product's unvarying quality and portability he was advised to say: '"Bless my soul, I have put scarcely any water into it and yet it has gone – it is anxious to disintegrate." The solution is very rapid.'[140] McBride demonstrated compound menthol snuff, explaining that the incorporation of camphor with menthol prevents

FIGURE 5.6
BW&Co.
exhibit at
the Turin
International
Exhibition,
1911, demon-
strating
chemical
extraction
procedures.

volatilisation and that even should that occur, the crystals would be so fine that irritation in the nostrils typical of cheap snuffs would be avoided.

> You say 'I should like to take a pinch of this. I have had a bit of a cold myself recently and find it of great value'. I usually take a tooth pick and use the flat end ... Of course, I do not always take a pinch ... I merely pretend, and the chemist is not sufficiently observant to notice ... he tries it and likes it, but says his customers would not pay 6d. for a box ... I put it to him that 6d. is a very small sum for having a cold relieved. I go on with the usual arguments which were elaborated in the 'Monthly Letter.'[141]

Even greater scope for propagation was provided by exhibitions. Since 1881, the company had exhibited at national and international shows and exhibitions within the terms and conditions laid down by organisers. However, in 1907 the company began to organise its own exhibitions in selected towns. The intention was not only to attract the attention of doctors and chemists, as in the case of conventional exhibitions, but to engage their interest through practical demonstrations. Technology and ingenuity had been enlisted for the campaign. A 'cascarometer' was devised for the purpose of revealing the difference between the disintegrating properties of Tabloid Cascara and that of other brands; a 'polariscope' showed the difference between atropine sulphate purchased on the open market and the Wellcome Brand; the 'bismuth barometer' had been designed to make similar comparisons, while an insufflator facilitated the application of snuff to the interested visitor.[142] At the exhibitions, Curry used an insufflator with which to 'blow a little snuff up the doctor's nose', observing that 'by the time he has had a pinch of Menthol Snuff, tasted Alaxa, Tabloid Pastilles, cascara in different forms, Vana etc., he goes away with a good working knowledge of some of our products'.[143]

As an essential part of the process of introducing new travellers to the difficulties they could expect to encounter was the discussion of some of the differences between promoting products to doctors and to chemists and highlighting some of the objections to the company's products. Curry contrasted the dominance that representatives tended to concede to the doctor in an interview with the 'conquering spirit' more in evidence when they called on chemists. He thought that in past times doctors had been approached no differently than chemists and told the travellers: 'You can be as insistent with the doctor as with the chemist, but in a different way'. This applied to securing an interview as well as to the demonstration once inside the consulting room. When a doctor refused an interview pleading pressure of business, travellers were advised to show politeness in asking for a more convenient time.[144] Blanchflower's habit of never asking a doctor for more than three minutes of his time appears to have been effective, persuading even the most reluctant medical men to agree to an interview.[145] Clark also revealed that in order to reassure medical practitioners of the company's ethical standing, an 'eliminating list' was being drawn up in the office which would exclude unqualified practitioners, so as to avoid appearing to cultivate business with quacks.[146]

Anticipating objections to ordering BW&Co.'s products, Curry pointed out that an aversion to other than liquid medicine among some doctors could now be met from a long list, samples of which, in vulcanite glass-stoppered bottles, should be carried. A reply to the assertion of a greater risk of abuse resulting from over the counter medicines was that misuse could occur regardless of the nature of the medicine. The objection that prescribing the company's medicine would be financially injurious to his practice ('a pithy rejoinder rather than a slashing one' was suggested) should be countered by asserting that this belied the experience of other medical men. Any questioning of the quality of the company's drugs should be met with a list of those included in the *Pharmocopaeia* and reference to the drugs' appearance in virtually every wholesaler's list. Claims of excessive cost could be countered by showing that an apparent high price concealed a lower per capita cost in use and reiterating quality and controlled dosage.

Viewing the trade from a completely different perspective, Wellcome himself regarded the cultivation of business with doctors to be as much a responsibility of office staff as of travellers. The reason for this was their position in a credit network in which practice, patient, and drug suppliers were interdependent. In advice to office staff, he observed:

> We know from long experience that as a rule medical men are not well versed in business methods and usages, especially in regard to accounts, credits and collections. Eminent medical men almost invariably receive their fees 'on the spot' but by far the greater number of medical men find that their patients usually pay every other financial obligation before they pay their doctor, although in many cases he has saved their lives. In a large percentage of cases patients reluctantly settle their medical accounts but once a year, or at best once in six months. Sometimes the 'medico' is obliged to wait for his patient's executors to settle his fees. According to long established ethics, Fellows and Members of the RCP and RCS are not permitted to take legal action to collect medical fees from their patients.[147]

FIGURE 5.7
Tradecard
for Kepler
malt extract,
c. 1910.

For this reason Wellcome urged that consideration should be shown in composing letters to practitioners. 'In our dealings with professional men we should be "as wise as the serpent and as harmless as the dove" ... we must be forbearing, courteous, and diplomatic, and exercise the greatest possible care in correspondence to avoid provocative expressions or implications', though politeness did not mean that the letter should be ambiguous.[148]

'KEPLER'
MALT
EXTRACT

The concentrated digestive nutriment of the finest Barley Malt

'The chemist as a propagator' was the title of Johnson's address to the convention. He began with the supposition that the representatives were 'smarter salesmen' than the chemist. Many chemists, he believed, were keen but many were of the older type of pharmacist: 'those guardians of ancestral flydirts who regard innovations and methods with keen intolerance', and who manifested 'too much passion for selling their own stuff'.[149] It was in the interests of representatives to help them develop a more active approach to selling. Displays of every kind should be encouraged in order to draw the attention of nurses to pastilles and Alaxa for their recommendation to patients, while chemists should send circulars to nurses listing compressed dressings, Hazeline Snow, Lanoline, and Soloid products; the same with respect to midwives who should recommend Soloid antiseptics, Enule Glycerine, Borofax, Hazeline Snow Cream, and Kepler goods.[150] He advocated encouragement of exhibitions of goods suitable for specialists (Opa, for example, the new antiseptic liquid dentifrice), which could be mounted at the premises of a progressive chemist who should be asked to circulate dentists to notify them.

Extending the market to include a neglected niche was the subject of Turnbull's address at the 1907 conference entitled 'Propagation with veterinary surgeons'. He began by remarking that hitherto the vets had not been regarded as among the company's targets, but that even so, when in agricultural towns he had always made calls on them. However, while veterinary surgeons used gallons of tinctures and also hypodermic products (described by Hill as 'cheap and nasty' of a quality not produced by the company), Rogers admitted to having been at a disadvantage on his visits when unable to answer the question: 'what is the dose for a cow or a horse?' This information had been hidden away in Burroughs Wellcome's Chemist's Diary, whereas Compark, a competitor who enjoyed a large trade in fluid extracts, had issued vets with cards showing tinctures for application to specified animals directly from the package.[151]

Advertising medicine

The company's policy towards the content of advertising was that it should be directed only at medical professionals and the trade, that it should be truthful and avoid projecting an image of the company and its products that might be associated with the pill and potion manufacturers who advertised direct to the public. For this reason, the principal vehicles for the firm's advertising were the leading professional and trade journals, though this caused some difficulty when presented to an editor possessing a different perception of the difference between information and advertising.[152] Publicity and promotion embodied these principles, to which after 1898 was added an historical dimension when Wellcome appointed Dr C. J. S. Thompson. He was an expert in medical history hitherto privately employed by Wellcome to seek and purchase medical manuscripts and objects of historical, medical interest. On Wellcome's instructions, Thompson began to assemble information on various historical themes. for use in a new series of finely illustrated 'antique advertisements' for Tabloids focused on the history of medicine. They complemented the science-oriented image of modernity that Wellcome sought to project. The first appeared in 1900 and featured the zodiac. Similar series followed, those featuring Assyrian and Egyptian designs in 1901 revealed the considerable investment of time and effort to ensure complete authenticity of the advertisements, the details of which absorbed Wellcome who exercised a veto on the final image and text.[153]

The introduction of the new biological products and therapies during the

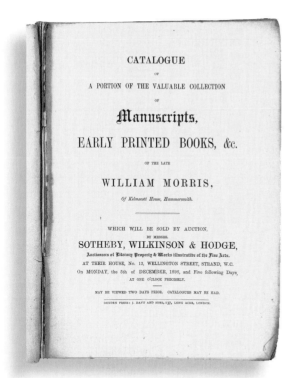

CATALOGUE

OF

A PORTION OF THE VALUABLE COLLECTION

OF

Manuscripts,

EARLY PRINTED BOOKS, &c.

OF THE LATE

WILLIAM MORRIS,

Of Kelmscott House, Hammersmith.

WHICH WILL BE SOLD BY AUCTION,
BY MESSRS.

SOTHEBY, WILKINSON & HODGE,

Auctioneers of Literary Property & Works Illustrative of the Fine Arts,

AT THEIR HOUSE, No. 13, WELLINGTON STREET, STRAND, W.C.

On MONDAY, the 5th of DECEMBER, 1898, and Five following Days,

AT ONE O'CLOCK PRECISELY.

MAY BE VIEWED TWO DAYS PRIOR. CATALOGUES MAY BE HAD.

DRYDEN PRESS: J. DAVY AND SONS, 137, LONG ACRE, LONDON.

FIGURE 5.8 Title page of catalogue 'of a portion of the valuable collection of manuscripts, early printed books etc. of the late William Morris' 1898.

mid-1890s and the production of Wellcome Brand Chemicals from 1902 was accompanied by increased attention to the delivery of educational propaganda informed by scientific knowledge and understanding in a style of presentation intended to render the innovations comprehensible during the course of a one to one interview.[154] Some sales representatives were critical of the company's advertising policy, which made no provision for their own input into the advertising department in the preparation of new schemes.[155] Holland felt there was not enough medical advertising, though he conceded that it possessed dignity. And while he acknowledged the need for educative literature to promote Wellcome Brand Chemicals, he pleaded that it should not be too scientific, but simply that it should stress the purity and activity of the products. Another complaint was that products had been introduced without adequate advertising at the outset. Ernutin, a product for emergency use and obstetric surgery, was offered as an example.[156] Linstead, head of the advertising department, explained that the competitive rush to bring new products to market allowed the advertising department too little time to compose text for labels and other printed matter that had to be absolutely reliable in describing the contents accurately and avoiding false claims. With respect to Ernutin, he observed that 'the firm's own medical men, the Institute best calculated to know all about it, and the firm's medical referee ... agree nothing more must be said about Ernutin for the present'.[157]

Scientists at the WPRL produced a series of illustrated pamphlets describing the laboratories and the products developed therein. Issued to all doctors, chemists and medical officers in the Empire, Wellcome regarded these as 'doing vastly more good in impressing the medical profession and trade than any amount of ordinary advertising'.[158] In 1906, following a pamphlet issued on hemisine, he called for a new one dealing with Ernutin 'to be carefully written, scientific yet possessing special human interest', and asked to see a draft.[159]

For Wellcome 'human interest' meant history; this explains why the characteristic content of a series of pamphlets beginning in 1907 was a combination of medical science and its historical origins. These were chosen in order to provide an historical account of an area of medical interest

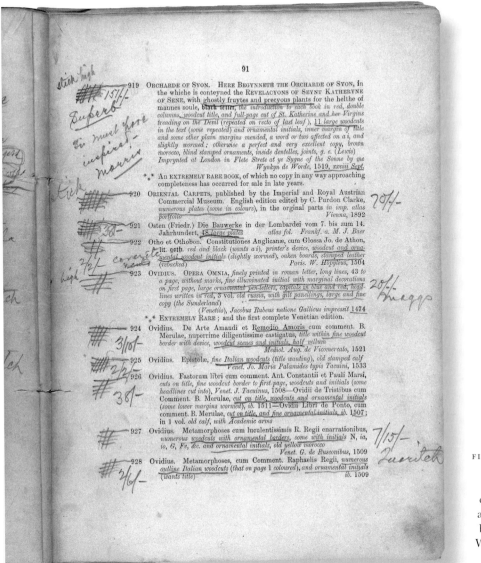

relevant to a particular category of the company's products. Explanation of recent scientific developments associated with them required contributions from the scientists. Usually timed to appear coincident with an international medical congress or meetings of the American Medical Association, between 1907 and 1914 these pocket-sized volumes, handsomely bound, illustrated, and exceeding 200 pages, dealt in turn with anaesthetics, antiseptic surgery, urine analysis, inoculation and vaccination, 'dental art' and leechcraft. A section dealing with the history of medical equipment was preceded by an illustrated commentary and price list for the company's medical chests and cases.[160] Each included sections describing the *materia medica* farm, the research laboratories, and other activities of the firm.[161] The series was supplemented by pamphlets specific to Burroughs Wellcome products, such as *Tabloids: A Brief Medical Guide* and *Quinine as a Weapon Against Malaria*. The production of relevant educational literature, however, did not guarantee informed responses. The difficulty encountered by representatives in selling the new science-based products was a subject that surfaced during the 1907 convention of home sales representatives. A widespread ignorance was reported to exist among physicians, many of whom professed to know a great deal but who displayed a lack of understanding of pharmacy of even the crudest kind. However, when visiting medical men, travellers were advised to ensure that they did not reveal that ignorance when introducing new products.[162] Chemists were described as uneducated but eager to learn.[163]

FIGURE 5.10
Booklet
on *The Age
of Risks*,
front cover,
BW&Co.
c. 1914.

While broadly in harmony with such an approach, the author of an address at the 1907 conference entitled 'The firm's advertising from a representative's point of view' clearly favoured a more forceful style of advertising, such as had been introduced to promote Hazeline Snow, Kepler goods, and Tabloid Rytol for photographers. Unlike medicines, these products were advertised to the public (though not in newspapers) through window displays (fitted by dressers sent out by the company's advertising department), counter displays, showcases, dummies, and circulars which the firm issued to chemists. The speaker interpreted this approach as a recognition that '... the days of passive persuasion have gone; activity is the keynote of modern advertising'.[164] He favoured the introduction of more products in the toiletry line that were attractive to chemists as sources of supplementary income and which could be advertised effectively as a group. Another expressed similar views, urging greater efforts in the direction of public advertising, notably in support of the new laxative fruit pastilles (described as 'a good field for laudatory language').[165]

Several advertisements for 'General Goods' displayed these characteristics. A series of advertisements entitled 'The economy of first aid' and 'The age of risks' highlighted the utility of Tabloid medical cases for car drivers, cyclists, campers, boy scouts, and sports-men and -women.

Photographic, food supplement, and toiletry products were also advertised in groups in pamphlets with such titles as 'The simplicity of success in photography'. Hazeline products were featured in a pamphlet entitled 'The Book of Beauty Culture' which included price lists and a photograph of Lady Barrow. The advertisements for Hazeline Snow claimed to impart 'fascination to the complexion' and 'radiant beauty to the skin'.

It was also described as 'soothing after shaving'. Hazeline Cream was advertised as preserving 'natural silkiness and elasticity of the skin' and Ozozo for 'bringing rosiness to the cheeks'. Opa was described as 'preserving natural whiteness to the teeth ... and fragrance to the breath'. Kepler goods were recommended for bodybuilding 'to full round form'.[166] The contents of these advertisements were similar to those for competitors' proprietary goods and showed attractive young women to promote toiletries; fish and fishermen and mothers and babies to support Kepler goods.

Authenticity and ingenuity were also characteristic of Wellcome's approach to national and international exhibitions that played an important part in the company's advertising policy from the beginning. An example of the extraordinary lengths he was prepared to go to create a spectacle unrivalled by competitors is the display at the 1896 annual conference of the BMA in Carlisle. To illustrate the natural purity and principal sources of lanoline products, live sheep inhabited the BW&Co. stand, while Kepler products were represented by four live cod swimming in a tank of deep sea water into which was pumped a continuous supply of air to keep the fish alive during the return journey by sea and rail. To obtain this, Pearson (at that time the London West End representative in charge of the arrangements for the display) chartered a tug to travel 20 miles out to sea. Haggis recorded Wellcome's pleasure at the considerable interest stimulated by the exhibit that received prominent coverage in press reports.[167]

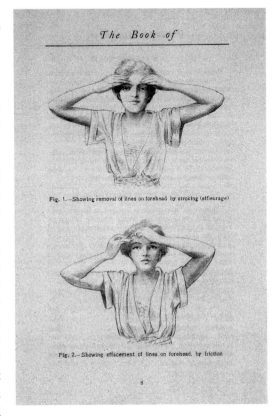

The Book of

Fig. 1.—Showing removal of lines on forehead by stroking (effleurage)

Fig. 2.—Showing effacement of lines on forehead, by friction

8

FIGURE 5.11
Beauty culture,
BW&Co.,
1914.

How far the spectacle stimulated sales we do not know. Lack of evidence makes it impossible to measure precisely the composition of sales product by product to establish which were the most successful. A contemporary observation and estimated output figures provide clues. When manufacturing commenced at Dartford, a reporter for the American *Pharmaceutical Era* wrote

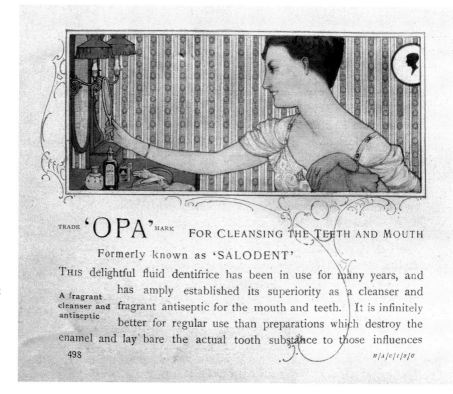

TRADE 'OPA' MARK   FOR CLEANSING THE TEETH AND MOUTH

Formerly known as 'SALODENT'

THIS delightful fluid dentifrice has been in use for many years, and
A fragrant   has amply established its superiority as a cleanser and
cleanser and fragrant antiseptic for the mouth and teeth. It is infinitely
antiseptic
              better for regular use than preparations which destroy the
enamel and lay bare the actual tooth substance to those influences

498   H/A/C/T/S/U

FIGURE 5.12
BW&Co.
advertisement
for 'Opa'
dentifrice,
formerly
known as
Salodent,
c. 1910.

a three-page account of the company, listing the most important product
categories. These were Tabloids (particularly those incorporating alkaloids),
cocaine, saccharine, borax, cascara sagrada, rhubarb and soda. Valoid fluid
extracts were for the preparation of tinctures, syrups and infusions, and
lanoline preparations, ointments, cold creams, and soaps were sold under
the Hazeline trade mark. The reporter described Kepler Extract of Malt as
'the one great speciality of the House of Burroughs Wellcome', noting that
it was manufactured in 'vast quantities'. He also listed various combinations
of malt extract with beef and iron, cascara sagrada, pancreatin, pepsin, and
cod liver oil, the latter was given special praise.[168] This was confirmed by
an interviewer's report of a visit to the Dartford factory in 1893 as part of
Charles Booth's survey of London trades and industries. The products of the
firm were described as consisting 'largely in malt preparation for which they
have large vacuum pans, and in the making of almost all kinds of medicines
by a patent process into Tabloids ...'[169] Not until 1909 is it possible to
construct a crude estimate of the relative importance of Kepler sales to the
firm. Output in 1909/10 was 147,088 dozen bottles and 164,465 in 1910/11.
Depending upon the relative sales of Kepler products at 33 shillings or 36
shillings per dozen lb bottles, roughly £250,000 might have been the value
of sales in 1909/10, and £280,000 in 1910/11. In the company's sales, system-

atically recorded from 1904, Kepler goods were included within the category 'General Goods' or 'General Stock'. However, that also included other staple products such as Tabloids, Soloids and Valoids, lanolin, and the Hazeline line; it excluded Wellcome Brand Chemicals, serum, and Fairchild goods. Our estimates for Kepler sales suggest that they might have represented between 56 per cent and 77 per cent of this category in home and overseas trade in 1909/10; between 55 per cent and 80 per cent in 1910/11. However, the malt manufactured in Australia has to be subtracted from these figures. Total sales of 'General Goods' there in those years amounted to £43,969 and £49,609. It is also likely that sales estimates are inflated because of the heavy discounts on Kepler received by hospitals. Nonetheless, there is good reason for supposing that Kepler goods accounted for over half of the total sales of 'General Goods' and was the largest category by far. It is also plausible to regard Kepler goods as contributing a high proportion to the company's profits. In 1896 the manufacturing cost of Kepler Malt Extract and Kepler Solution of Cod Liver Oil Extract of Malt was 5*d.* per lb, including the cost of containers.[170] This compared with the current list price cost of 3*s.* per 16 oz bottle and 1*s.* 8*d.* for a 12 oz bottle. The

ratio of 1 to 7 exaggerates the profit margin as discounts from list prices to retailers, wholesalers, and to institutions varied between 20 and 40 per cent. This nonetheless leaves a possible profit margin of perhaps 5 times manufacturing cost. Prices had been reduced twice; by roughly 10 per cent in 1884 and again by about 5 per cent in 1892, but discounts remained unaltered between 1892 and 1906. However, the size of bottles was reduced from 24 oz to 16oz and from 12oz to 8oz. In effect, this represented a price increase by one-third.[171] There is no indication that the price increase seriously adversely affected sales.

FIGURE 5.13
BW&Co.
advertisement
for Hazeline
cream,
c. 1913.

The profit and loss accounts record profits generated by sales of Fairchild products Lanoline (separately from general goods), Sera, and Wellcome Brand Chemicals.

Table 5.1 *Profit on selected products, 1898–1914 (£)*

	Net profit of BW&Co.	Fairchild Bros & Foster agency	Lanoline	Sera	Wellcome Brand chemicals
1898	28,976	2,236	2,166		
1899	25,637	2,758			
1900	24,219	2,916	2,815		163
1901	18,589	2,196	2,938		68
1902	11,195	2,283	2,769	124	
1903	21,909	2,627	1,295	1,527	1,269
1904	13,359	3,263	1,562	870	4,212
1905	11,506	3,373	774	1,352	1,873
1906	43,460	3,253	1,562	1,843	907
1907	56,183	3,980	1,829	2,471	5,152
1908	50,411	4,001	2,135	2,914	6,301
1909	43,416	4,505	1,928	3,246	10,670
1910	31,140	4,580	1,849	4,257	2,452
1911	42,109	5,253	2,819	4,016	
1912	65,573	5,407	2,972	5,030	
1913	85,321	5,247	2,602	5,199	
1914	83,265	5,178	2,699	1,161	

WFA, F/FA/328, WFL trading accounts and profit and loss.

Profits from sera were slow to be achieved and did not reach levels similar to Fairchild products until 1910, a discovery consistent with the company's claim that sera was sold at below cost during the early years of its development. Profits from Wellcome Brand Chemicals were erratic, in some years high but below the average figures recorded for the other products during the years when data is available. Profits from Kepler goods and Tabloids in the general goods category were not entered separately; it is not possible, therefore, to quantify the relative importance of these general goods which sales figures show to have been the largest category by far. When the profit figures for the selected products are aggregated and expressed as a percentage of the company's net profits, the high profitability from the sales of general goods is revealed. The average percentage between 1900 and 1914 was 75 per cent. The dominance of 'General Goods' is even greater when measured by sales. As a percentage of total sales, general goods exceeded 80 per cent in 1906–8, falling to 78 per cent thereafter. The explanation for the fall was the growth in sales of Wellcome Brand Chemicals from £11,127 in 1906 to £68,639 in 1914. During the same period, serum sales rose from £9,483 to £41,768.[172]

Part of this growth is explained by an expansion of exports. Total sales of BW&Co.'s products supplied directly from London (which included 'foreign' orders from overseas agents and wholesalers made directly to Snow Hill) began to surge from the mid-1890s. They reached £175,701 in 1899, almost doubled between 1899 and 1910 and increased by another 20 per cent by 1913 at £417,312. These figures are exclusive of overseas sales sold through branches and depots, including those goods put up or manufactured locally. By 1913 overseas sales of £681,849 represented almost 50 per cent of aggregate home and overseas sales. This compared with 30 per cent in 1904/05 (of a total of £369,907), the first year when such a breakdown exists.[173] This reflects the efforts directed to developing overseas sales examined in chapter 8.

CHAPTER SIX

Creating products, producing knowledge, and gaining respect: research laboratories, 1894–1914

Within BW&Co. scientific work had many functions. Analytical and synthetic chemistry became part of the factory's routine quality control procedures, whilst innovative experimental work, usually in laboratories away from the factory, led to product development and to academic renown. Both of these contributed to the success and reputation of the company.[1]

From the outset, the Wandsworth factory included some sort of laboratory for quantitative and qualitative chemical analyses of products, including those of competitors; work of immediate commercial relevance. What, if anything, was done in the way of innovation or development is difficult to ascertain, and contemporary distinctions between these activities may not be so apparent as they are today.[2]

Of less obvious or immediate relevance to BW&Co.'s commercial objective were research laboratories physically apart from the Works. Wellcome proclaimed these as completely independent, although operationally and administratively they were integral parts of BW&Co. The first, established in 1894, became known as the Wellcome Physiological Research Laboratories (WPRL) after the death of Burroughs in 1895. They were created to produce the new wonder medicines, the serum anti-toxins, which required biological rather than chemical expertise, and were thus a completely new departure for the company.

The creation and management of this and later research laboratories (in chemistry, and in tropical research), their relationships with the company and with each other, and their standing in the external worlds of science, medicine and commerce, all had to be negotiated and defined. The Wellcome research laboratories brought to the fore several issues and problems associated with conducting scientific research in association with a pharmaceutical company, and whether such research was acceptable, or at least tolerable, to the scientific and medical professions. It may well be that their academic sounding titles were deliberately chosen to suggest professional scientific authority, and Wellcome always insisted that these were private laboratories, pursuing research objectives quite independent of his business. That distinction, however, was neither recognised nor accepted, especially by the medical profession. Despite Wellcome's protestations to the contrary the laboratories were all, to differing degrees at different times, patently components of BW&Co., and ultimately contributed both scientific prestige and innovative products to the company.

Each laboratory fitted into a different research tradition. The Wellcome Chemical Research Laboratories (WCRL, founded in 1896) were analogous to laboratories within other manufacturing companies, although more extensive and far-ranging in their research brief. As such, they were neither unusual nor controversial. The Wellcome Tropical Research Laboratories (WTRL, founded in 1902) were closely similar to tropical laboratories established in London and Liverpool and initially were clearly distinct from the company both in their objectives (to aid tropical medicine and health) and in their location (The Sudan, until 1913).[3] The Wellcome Bureau of Scientific Research (WBSR, 1913) was effectively the successor body to the Tropical Laboratories but based in London. The WPRL, however, created problems because they encroached directly on medical territory and challenged medical authority. They raised unique questions about research conduct and professional etiquette in what was then an entirely novel setting. These issues included, inter alia: the employment and service conditions of medically qualified staff (at a time when the medical profession was trying to enhance its professional standing and to distance its members from 'trade'); the right to publish scientific papers unfettered by business constraints or editorial prejudice; the propriety of a manufacturer having the same rights as medical practitioners, for example under animal experimentation legislation; and the relationship of financial and legal restrictions, such as those about trade names applied to scientific work. How some of these difficulties were resolved within the Wellcome organisation, and how they affected the development of the pharmaceutical industry in Britain warrant detailed consideration.

The Wellcome Research Laboratories, 1894–99

BW&Co. was extremely perspicacious in recognising the potential of the new therapeutic development of serum anti-toxins, but as pioneers faced many of the early production difficulties alone. The laboratories initially occupied rooms at 10 Devonshire Street, Central London, belonging to Dr Thomas Bokenham who was also their Director. Like Witte and Smith in the factory, Bokenham was to prove another unreliable employee: his work was frequently unsatisfactory and he was hot-tempered.

The Home Office and animal experimentation, 1896[4]

The first serious challenge to Wellcome's scientific intentions occurred in 1896. The laboratory moved to larger premises in Charlotte Street, and simultaneously the Home Office realised, from company publicity, that experimental animals were being used. Wellcome was invited to apply to register the premises under the 1876 Cruelty to Animals Act, which governed such work in the United Kingdom.[5] This Act applied to 'experiments calculated to cause pain', using vertebrate animals.[6] Scientists working under it were licensed and their place of work registered with the Home Office and subject to random inspection. With respect to work on therapeutic sera, Wellcome's application provoked two important questions. Did producing anti-toxin by injecting toxins into horses require a licence? Did the subsequent toxicity testing and quantification of the anti-toxins, using guinea pigs, need a licence? If the answer to either question was yes, then the WPRL had to be registered. By 1896 the operational consensus at the Home Office was that raising anti-toxins in horses was not an experiment, because the procedure was not painful and the outcome was known. The subsequent testing of anti-toxins was, however, considered to come under the terms of the Act. None of these assumptions had been tested in a Court of Law. The three other British institutes then producing anti-toxins, the British Institute for Preventive Medicine, the Leicester Bacteriological Institute and the Brown Animal Sanatory Institute in London, were already registered because of other experimental work, and such questions did not apply to them. In May 1896 Wellcome applied to register the WPRL. His was the first application solely to produce serum anti-toxins, and that he was a commercial manufacturer asking for facilities that might benefit his business added complications: should the Home Office register 'private' laboratories, especially those associated with commerce? Officials sought legal advice about taking such a radical step, and enquired about the consequences to the WPRL if registration was withheld. This indicates that to some extent the Home Office was concerned not to hamper or prevent the laboratories' work unnecessarily. On being reassured that the work could be done elsewhere the Home Office refused Wellcome's application. Bokenham was furious, denouncing the Home Office's request for registration 'quite unjustifiable and a deliberate attempt to mislead us and to give us unnecessary trouble'.[7] Wellcome's views are unknown, although given his robust approach to the same problem four years later (see below) it's likely that he would have protested vigorously. But he had more immediate problems to deal with.

In August 1896 a very public humiliation occurred when the *Lancet* criticised BW&Co.'s sera. Bokenham's complete failure to resolve the problems resulted in his dismissal.[8] External experts re-organised the laboratories and Dr Walter Dowson, became the new Director. A former general practitioner, Dowson had used a small inheritance to study the new science of bacteriology at Cambridge, before moving to the WPRL. He was therefore comparatively inexperienced in research work when compared with the renowned chemist Fred Power who became Director of the WCRL in 1896 (see below).

The Wellcome Physiological Research Laboratories, 1899–1914

The bacteriological laboratories moved from Central London to a larger site at Brockwell Park in Herne Hill at the end of 1899, just as the chemical laboratories also moved. This was when they became clearly identified as the Wellcome <u>Physiological</u> Research Laboratories. The expansion allowed Dowson to recruit staff at every level to develop and extend their work and in particular, he engaged local schoolboys to train in laboratory methods. Two of these, Arthur Ewins and Alexander Glenny, became exceptionally successful scientists, elected to Fellowship of the Royal Society in the early 1940s, when another former Wellcome scientist, Sir Henry Dale, was President. Technical laboratory training was unknown at the time, and Dowson adopted an industrial model of apprenticeship, assigning them to different sections of the WPRL to learn specific techniques and methods. They also studied for University of London external degrees: Ewins in chemistry, whilst Glenny studied mathematics and chemistry.[9] Additionally,

FIGURE 6.1 Staff of the WPRL, *c.* 1900. The Director, Walter Dowson is seated in the middle.

FIGURE 6.2
Laboratory
assistants in
the WPRL,
c. early
1900s. Front
row, from
left to right,
A. T. Glenny
and Arthur
Ewins.

the WPRL staff comprised the bacteriologist H. J. Sudmersen, the chemist Dr Stanislaus Pinkus, a general laboratory assistant, a boy who prepared the nutritive media, numerous ancillary workers, including stablemen and grooms to look after the horses, and women packers and labellers who issued the sera. The move to larger premises and the provision of enhanced facilities for routine production and experimental research focussed attention once again on the legal question of the WPRL's status with regard animal experimentation.

Home Office application, 1900–01

At the beginning of 1900 Wellcome applied again for the WPRL's registration under the 1876 Cruelty to Animals Act. He provoked negotiations that lasted for over 20 months, and his eventual success was critically important for the development of a research-based pharmaceutical industry in Great Britain. Wellcome detailed a range of innovative research to be carried out, in addition to the routine anti-toxin work. These included research on 'biological' preparations such as sera and hormones; improving toxicity and efficacy tests for the Company's products; and promoting basic research that might lead to new therapies. It was, Wellcome maintained, in the national economic interest to improve British goods, but the lack of physiological work severely handicapped the pharmaceutical industry, 'with all it involves in loss of trade, loss of employment to the citizens of this country in a field where they could excel, and loss of prestige is all the more serious because it is unnecessary.'[10] He stressed that most products sold in Britain as standardised on animals were imported, and that some foreign companies (meaning the American Parke Davis & Co.) made financial arrangements with academic laboratories in Britain for the requisite work to be done.

Wellcome also sought explicit sponsorship from members of the medical profession. Professors of physiology, including Ernest Starling of UCL, Sir Michael Foster of Cambridge, Edward Schäfer of Edinburgh and Francis Gotch of Liverpool; distinguished practitioners, including the surgeon Victor Horsley of UCH, Lord Lister, the Queen's surgeon, the Presidents of the Royal Colleges of Physicians of London, Ireland, and the editors of both the *Lancet* and the *British Medical Journal*, all supported Wellcome's objectives.

His formal application was finally submitted to the Home Secretary on 15 February 1900.[11]

Concerned that licensing one firm might confer considerable commercial advantages, the Home Office turned to the medical Royal Colleges of Physicians and of Surgeons and the Pharmaceutical Society for advice. All counselled against the application. Their objections were not unbiased: all were then involved, or were negotiating to become involved, in either producing their own, or testing other manufacturers', serum. They suggested that BW&Co. should make similar arrangements, but Wellcome believed it neither possible nor desirable to come to such an agreement with a body that was essentially a rival. Privately, he learned that there <u>was</u> concern at the Home Office that it might be a mistake not to register the WPRL. Officials were not prepared, however, to go against the advice of the Royal Colleges. As the Home Secretary noted,

> the work will certainly be carried out by the Firm in France or Germany if not done here, and if they [the testing experiments] are impossible an important and lucrative branch of trade will have been driven from our country, the results of which are most useful in saving life and alleviating suffering.[12]

His lawyers sternly reminded him that legally he had to be convinced that the proposed experiments were useful and necessary, and were to be performed by qualified persons. They continued, '<u>If this is so,</u> it settles this case, <u>when once we are satisfied</u> of the nature of the arrangements made' [underlined in the original]. The Home Office decided to offer Wellcome a lifeline: he could supplement his original application.

A full year later, Wellcome submitted a further document to the then Home

FIGURE 6.3
Drawing of physiological laboratory, WPRL, Brockwell Park, c. 1906.

Secretary.[13] He emphasised that the WPRL was entirely separate from the business, and that the WRCL played a complementary role in developing new drugs. Appendices listed several possible therapies from the WCRL that were awaiting physiological testing, including Jaborandi alkaloids, Strophanthus, willow bark, and new synthetic varieties of morphine. Wellcome also played a strong commercial card,

> at present Germany has the monopoly... The petitioner, in his capacity as the principal of the firm of Burroughs Wellcome and Co. is a purchaser of hundreds of thousands of pounds worth of chemicals which are not, but ought to be, made in this country... the value of the British imports of chemicals and dyestuffs for the year ending 1899 was £5,768,890.[14]

He stressed the professionalism of his staff, 'guided by the same spirit and by the same aims as actuate all research workers,' and argued that it was invidious to infer that a scientist would work in a 'proper' spirit in a University but not in any other laboratory.[15] Sir Michael Foster, Professor of Physiology at Cambridge, prepared a list of proposed experiments for the laboratories, including raising new anti-sera; standardisation work on digitalis, ergot and lobelia; and purely experimental work on supra-renal gland extracts. On receiving this information, the Home Secretary 'reluctantly' concluded that he must register the WPRL,

FIGURE 6.4 Drawing of the buildings and grounds of the WPRL, c. 1906.

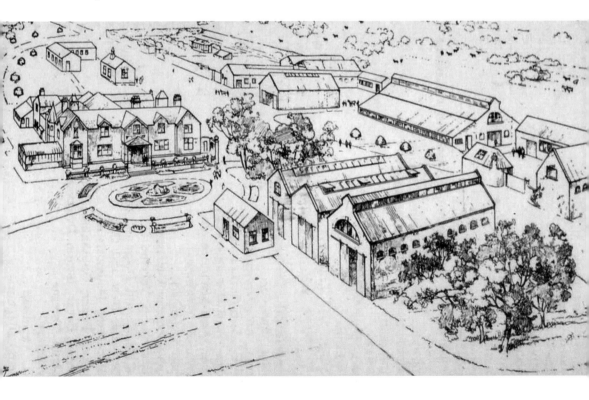

I say 'reluctantly' because I think that besides the outcry which will no doubt be raised by the anti-vivisectionists, the Home Office will be taking a new departure, which will lead to some difficulties, but which in my view is inevitable.[16]

Having made the decision, the Home Office ignored the 'rather awkward task' of telling the Royal Colleges or the Pharmaceutical Society and left them to find out for themselves.[17]

On 6 September 1901, the WPRL finally received registration.[18] There was little public outcry or comment at the decision. Ironically the *Chemist & Druggist* of the following day praised Parke Davis & Co's standardisation work, and suggested that the 'Anti-Vivisection Act [sic]', prevented British firms conducting such work themselves.[19] That was about to change. Wellcome had successfully convinced the Home Office and much of the medical profession that research on 'commercial' premises was not necessarily tainted or substandard. It was an important victory. It prevented Wellcome from moving his laboratories abroad, and it encouraged the development, albeit slow, of a research-based pharmaceutical industry in Britain. Before the Second World War, the WPRL pioneered pharmaceutical standardisation work and was a major manufacturer of therapeutic sera for nearly four decades; the programmes of experimental research work led to at least one Nobel Prize, and brought much credit and distinction to Wellcome and his company.

'I want him to develop my ideals'[20] – *Henry Dale's influence on the WPRL, 1904–14*

In 1904 Wellcome started to search for a professional physiologist to develop the laboratories in the ways that had been so enthusiastically and vigorously detailed to the Home Office. A letter to Ernest Starling, Professor of Physiology at University College London, indicates the qualities he was looking for,

A man who is capable of broad and deep thinking, who has fertility of mind, originality and alertness, and patient persistence; a man who will concentrate his whole mind and energies on this work. I want the work in these laboratories to be done on the highest scientific lines and with such a thoroughness and precision that it will stand the test of time and the keenest criticism.[21]

Henry Dale, trained in the Physiological Laboratory Cambridge and then working with Starling and his brother-in-law William Bayliss, was recommended for the position. Colleagues warned him that, 'I should be selling my scientific birthright … for a mess of commercial pottage'. His concerns, however, were with his salary, and the security of unorthodox laboratories that apparently existed on the personal whim of a rich man, then in his early fifties.[22] He was offered £400 per annum with a promise of £600 after two years (he was then earning £150 at University College) and, he recalled, 'I never had to mention the matter again'.[23] Dowson was then receiving £1,000 a year, which Dale too was earning when he left the WPRL in 1914.[24] On the second point Dale had to accept Wellcome's reassurances that despite the fact that he was the father of a small son, his Will would put his business and private concerns in the hands of a board of Trustees.[25]

Dale's arrival at the WPRL heralded a major shift towards innovative physiological research, and Wellcome acquired a very different kind of scientist from those he had previously employed. Dale was equipped with all the up-to-date investigative techniques of an experimental physiologist, and he prospered from the direct daily contact with chemists and access to the superb resources at the WPRL, the WCRL, and the Wellcome Chemical Works, all of which were readily available to him and were vital to his success at the WPRL. It is unlikely, had he remained in a university laboratory, that he would have had anything comparable. Wellcome had also appointed the chemist, George Barger, to the WPRL shortly before Dale's arrival, and urged the two men to work together to discover, analyse and develop new biologically active compounds. Neither had any burning scientific problems they wished to pursue and readily agreed to Wellcome's suggestion that they study the pharmacology of ergot of rye, then used in obstetric preparations.

FIGURE 6.5 Scientific staff of the WPRL. From left to right: C. J. Symons, H. H. Dale, W. Dowson, H. J. Sudmersen. G. Barger, c. 1906.

FIGURE 6.6
Pharma-
cological
laboratory,
WPRL.
Henry Dale
(second from
left) doing an
experiment,
c. 1908.

Thus Dale and Barger started work that was to bring them both scientific glory and lead Dale to the 1936 Nobel Prize. Barger's expertise and the generous facilities of the WPRL in terms of time and resources provided Dale with superb and incomparable research support. The interactions between analysis and synthesis in the chemical laboratory and subsequent physiological experiment were rapid and synergistic; biologically active fractions were identified, and specific chemicals produced, with an immediacy unavailable elsewhere. Just a few months after Dale's arrival, Dowson wrote to Wellcome:

> You were quite right about our new physiologist ... His energies are all in the right direction and you will be glad to hear that he is doing <u>epoch making</u> work at ergot ... There is no doubt he is going to make a fine pharmacologist and this ergot work will give the new departure a splendid kick off. Dr Barger is also doing fine work in separating the active principles for Dr Dale to test. Curiously the latter has quite turned the tables on him. Previously, Dr Barger could not get his things tested. Now with such a brilliant operator as Dr Dale to help him, he cannot get out things fast enough for the physiological laboratory.[26]

Wellcome's response, 'How about Dr Power's products of research [from the WCRL] to keep him busy', indicates his determination that the different parts of his 'empire' be functionally integrated. It had also occurred to Dowson 'I particularly desire to raise the question of the relation between the physiological laboratories and the Works at our next interview. It seems to me that this relation might with advantage to all concerned be more direct than it is at present.'[27] From 1905 onwards, joint papers from the WPRL, the WCRL, and the Works became a common feature, which owed much to the industry of Henry Dale. More importantly for the company, new products also emerged from these collaborations.

In addition to work on ergot, Dale and Barger examined the chemical properties and physiological activities of numerous therapeutically interesting compounds. They discovered that some drugs with closely related chemical constitutions had similar pharmacological effects, which was of enormous importance to a pharmaceutical manufacturer.[28] Such discoveries did not come to commercial fruition until after the Second World War, when rational drug design became a recognised way of pharmaceutical development, in contrast to the empiric techniques used in the first half of the century by Wellcome's scientists. But the possibility was recognised in the WPRL before the First World War.

Contracts and conditions

Research scientists were an entirely new class of employee for BW&Co. and the routine contracts offered to their manufacturing and managerial staff seemed somewhat inappropriate,

> It is understood that you are to treat as strictly confidential, and respect as my property, all my manufacturing processes, formulae, apparatus, etc. and all improvements therein, and also any inventions or new discoveries which may be made by you or anyone else in my employment; on the understanding that I shall not extract from you with respect to any discovery a confidence which is contrary to the ethics of your profession.
>
> It is also understood that before publishing any communications upon physiological matters or upon any work connected with the Laboratories you are first to submit same to and obtain the approval of the Director.
>
> The two clauses just written refer to work done at any time either in or out of the Laboratories.[29]

Opposition to these 'workmen's' contracts was first raised by Alfred Chune Fletcher, Wellcome's close personal friend and frequent adviser, whom Dale considered 'knew [Wellcome] better than anybody else'.[30] Fletcher pronounced such contracts totally unsuitable for the staff Wellcome wished, and needed, to attract. He bluntly reminded his friend that recruiting suitable staff with appropriate experience and qualifications in physiology, pharmacology or bacteriology was vital.[31]

> ... so that they [the WPRL] can make a thoroughly good start now that they are registered [with the Home Office], every consistent concession should be made. The trouble and anxiety which we have had to secure men for these laboratories, has been exceedingly great, and one must not forget that the proportion of men sufficiently broad-minded to be associated with your laboratories is very small ... we think there is a great opportunity for creditable work to be done at the laboratories, but they must have every encouragement and stimulant possible.[32]

Wellcome did make some concessions about holidays and allowed that attendance at meetings was permissible at the discretion of the Director. Despite this, contracts and terms of conditions for research staff troubled the company for years. At the beginning of 1902, Wellcome decided that all such contracts would be with him personally, rather than with the company.[33] Perhaps he expected this to alleviate the problem. Somewhat contrarily he also emphasised that his scientists had responsibilities for testing and validating company products.[34] As Wellcome had reminded Dowson when appointing Dale,

> [It] should be thoroughly understood that if any literature upon scientific subjects is to be corrected he [Dale] is to do this, although it may be a business matter of my firm. You know the kind of literature which is sent down to you from time to time for correction, and Dr Dale will probably be required to go through some of it and make notes etc. In conversation, therefore, with Dr Dale it must be made perfectly clear that this may be a portion of his work.[35]

Ironically, it was routine activities that gave rise to some of the major scientific discoveries emanating from the WPRL before the First World War. In another attempt to emphasise their separateness from the company, Wellcome insisted in early 1901 that all correspondence to and about the laboratories should be signed on his personal behalf, rather than that of BW&Co. The significance of this, on letters written on BW&Co. headed paper and often by Snow Hill staff, seems to have been lost on most recipients. At the same time, on Wellcome's personal instructions, advertisements referred to BW&Co. as 'distributing agents' for the WPRL's sera, emulating the terminology employed by both Parke Davis & Co. and Allen & Hanburys, in selling the sera of St Mary's Inoculation Dept and the Lister Institute, respectively.[36]

Some irksome conditions for staff remained. Dowson, as Director, had to approve all papers before submission for publication, and was expected to keep confidential reports on WPRL staff, which was standard practice throughout the company. His refusal to provide the requisite details brought a sharp reprimand from Sudlow,

> I may say I am very sorry the report does not include these particulars, because experience shows that they are extremely useful to the management and I know they would have been useful to you personally. I invite you to reconsider the matter. I need hardly say that the record is absolutely private <u>to the firm</u>[37] (our underlining).

Publishing and publications

Many medical and pharmaceutical organisations were suspicious of, and even downright hostile towards, what were seen as commercial laboratories. The Pharmaceutical Society refused to elect Power, the Director of the WCRL and an internationally renowned pharmaceutical chemist, to its Fellowship in 1900.[38] Four years later it refused to publish scientific papers from the Wellcome laboratories, classifying them as advertisements.[39] Wellcome immediately threatened to withdraw all advertising from the *Pharmaceutical Journal*. The dispute continued for almost three years until the Society reluctantly and under some pressure agreed to accept again papers from the WPRL and the WCRL.[40] The Society's attitude, unlike that of the medical Royal Colleges that saw Wellcome's laboratories as threatening interlopers into medical territory, is difficult to understand. It was an association primarily of manufacturing and retail chemists, with no apparent reason to penalize a company for undertaking innovative research. It is tempting to speculate that the scale and success of Wellcome's research laboratories engendered hostility and jealousy among fellow pharmaceutical manufacturers, which gains more credence when the Society's decided opposition to his application to undertake animal experimentation is remembered.

This was not the only example of such attitudes. In 1900 BW&Co. had been involved in a similar battle with the *British Medical Journal*, when their business manager declared that scientific papers bearing the name 'Wellcome' would be considered as advertisements. Wellcome complained, in letters written on company notepaper, to every member of Council. Eventually, on Chune Fletcher's advice, he agreed to the publication of papers without an address being included. BW&Co. decided that it was a simple matter to print a separate cover bearing the laboratories' address, a solution subsequently adopted for every paper from all the Wellcome laboratories.[41] Ironically therefore work that the *British Medical Journal* was determined to display as anonymous and insignificant became easily identifiable as part of a distinctive, uniform series. It is hardly surprising, however, that confusion and objections were expressed about the 'independence' of the laboratories and the work done therein, when it was the company, not the laboratories, which fought such issues and used its commercial muscle in seeking resolution.

From animal substances to hormone preparations

BW&Co. had been associated with animal gland preparations since the mid-1890s. The discovery of adrenaline in 1894 prompted considerable interest in using it therapeutically. George Oliver, one of its co-discoverers, suggested it as a treatment for Addison's disease, a disorder of the supra-renal (adrenal) glands. Although the disease is now known to be caused by a hormone deficiency from a different part of the glands, it seemed a reasonable suggestion to make in 1895.[42] Wellcome sent Oliver's article to Bokenham,

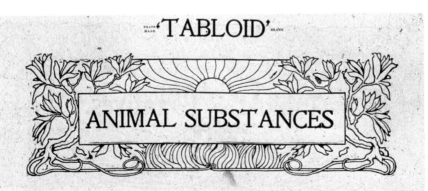

'TABLOID'

ANIMAL SUBSTANCES

WHILST the therapeutic values of many of the animal substances, which have been made the subjects of physiological and clinical research, still remain undecided, there can be no doubt that certain of the 'Tabloid' Animal Substances have proved most useful in the treatment of disease.

'Tabloid' Thyroid Gland Substance

has been, from the first, most closely associated with successful Thyroid-Therapy, and reports conclusively demonstrating its value are repeatedly appearing in the British and Foreign Medical Journals.

'Tabloid' Supra-renal Gland Substance

has also been the subject of clinical investigation and favourable report. It causes contraction of the arteries, and consequently increases the blood pressure. Reprints of articles will be gladly forwarded to medical men on request. For Therapeutic Notes see *Wellcome's Medical Diary,* page 130.

'Tabloid' Thyroid Gland Substance is supplied in two strengths, gr. 1-1/2 and gr. 5, in bottles of 100, at 10d. and 2s. per bottle.

'Tabloid' Supra-renal Gland Substance is supplied in bottles of 100, at 4s. 6d. per bottle.

Burroughs Wellcome and Co., LONDON and SYDNEY.

Telegrams—"BURCOME, LONDON."

[COPYRIGHT]

H 124

FIGURE 6.7 Advertisement for 'Animal substances' stressing that although the therapeutic claims for many animal substances remain unproved, 'Tabloid' thyroid and adrenal gland preparations 'have proved most useful in the treatment of disease' (*BMJ* 1 April 1899).

the then director of the WPRL, to encourage work in the field. Unfortunately, the problems of serum contamination, so well-publicised by the *Lancet* in 1896, diverted research interest for some years and the matter was not pursued (see Chapter 7, pp. 207–10). From 1895, however, the company did manufacture Tabloids of both supra-renal and thyroid glands. These were produced at the Dartford Works under the supervision of Lloyd Williams.[43] One apparently satisfied customer was the Prince of Wales (later King Edward VII) who, according to a gossip column had rapidly shed two stones in weight because of a 'marvellous remedy', that is, thyroid tabloids from BW&Co. The anonymous columnist hinted that it might also be appropriate for the rather corpulent Queen Victoria to avail herself of such 'elegant and invaluable preparations'.[44] Whether she did remains unknown.

These Tabloids also met with medical approval.[45] To deal with the demand for animal substances a separate department was created at Dartford in January 1896.[46] Six months later eight 'animal remedies' were delivered to the *Chemist and Druggist* for appraisal, including extracts of salivary glands for dyspepsia, pineal gland tabloids to treat 'softening of the brain', and Fallopian tube samples for neurotic afflictions.[47] Two years later, further diversification was evident when the Snow Hill management asked the Dartford factory to make preparations of 16 organs or tissues, including bone, spinal cord, prostate, testes, ovary, pancreas, pineal, pituitary, spleen, thymus and thyroid.[48] Some of these were made at the specific request of individual practitioners and not widely marketed. For example, an extract of agminate glands (these appear to be what are now known as Peyer's patches in the intestine) was made for Dr Thomas Maclagan of Cadogan Place. He had approached both Allen & Hanburys, and Oppenheimer, Son & Co. for assistance, but neither had the resources to help. To emphasise the scientific abilities of its staff it was important for BW&Co. to succeed where others had failed. After considerable difficulties it finally produced the agminate Tabloids and encouraged by medical approval it included the preparation in Tabloid Compound Gland, which was successfully marketed for many years.[49] What, if any, efficacy or toxicology testing was done on these Tabloids is unknown, although as with other products, they were distributed *gratis* to practitioners for trial, with the hope that satisfactory results would lead to publication to their mutual advantage.[50]

After the WPRL was registered for animal experimentation in 1901 Wellcome again raised the matter of animal products with Walter Dowson, the Director of the WPRL. He was influenced by the success that Parke Davis &Co. was then enjoying with such products. Having acquired the rights to the name 'adrenaline' from Jokichi Takamine, Parke Davis & Co. pushed the product so successfully that BW&Co. went to considerable trouble to acquire surreptitiously the company's promotional material to aid in the preparation of its own.[51] '[T]he supra-renal matter' Wellcome wrote to Dowson, 'is exceedingly important and we ought not to be behind anybody'.[52] Dowson appears not to have responded; certainly no publications on the subject appeared. He was also asked to test BW&Co.'s preparations of the substance, but again there is no record that he did so.[53]

It was the arrival of Dale at the WPRL in 1904 that initiated a serious programme of endocrine research. Initially adrenaline was used as a tool in Dale's ergot investigations, not as the subject of study itself. However, whilst doing a routine analysis of ergot Dale accidentally discovered the oxytocic (stimulation of uterine contractility) properties of the posterior pituitary gland.[54] As he commented later, 'by chance, I observed the potent stimulating action ... which led to a new and probably the most frequent application in practical medicine of such a pituitary extract, which had, till then, been little more than a reagent of academic interest in the physiological laboratory.'[55] This opened up an entirely new line of hormone research at the laboratories.[56] Coincidentally, William Blair Bell, later the first president of the (Royal) College of Obstetricians and Gynaecologists, wanted to test such a pituitary extract on his patients. As he explained, '[I] wrote to Messrs. Burroughs Wellcome & Co. for a supply and they very courteously put me in communication with Mr H. H. Dale who made for me a large quantity for intravenous injection'.[57] BW&Co.'s usual policy of assisting practitioners proved to be synergistic. Bell's work also suggested the extract had therapeutic possibilities, and he obligingly added a note in his paper that 'Messrs. Burroughs and Wellcome will shortly put [it] upon the market'.[58] Simultaneously BW&Co.'s Tabloid pituitary gland was proudly heralded in adverts as 'Products of Research'. It was not, however, until after the First World War that sustained endocrine research was undertaken by BW&Co.

The use of the word 'adrenaline'[59]

At the beginning of 1906 a problem arose when Dale wanted to use the word 'adrenaline' in a scientific paper. The word was a registered trade-name of Parke Davis & Co. Coming from any other physiological laboratory, Dale would have had no problem: the word was commonly accepted in the British scientific community. But coming from laboratories associated with a pharmaceutical company raised fresh issues

FIGURE 6.8 'Products of Research', stressing the role of 'the laboratories of BW&Co.' in bringing new products to market (*Chemist & Druggist*, 12 February 1910).

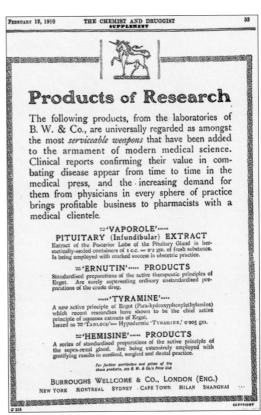

about their relationships, and those within and between the different Wellcome laboratories. Two sets of problems needed resolving. On one hand were legal and commercial issues if laboratories associated with one company flagrantly used the tradename of another. On the other hand, there was internal dissension about scientific authority within the Wellcome organisation, between chemists and physiologists, and between physiologists and the company managers. During February and March 1906, scientists from the WPRL and the WCRL, managers from Snow Hill, external advisers, and Wellcome himself became deeply engaged in a flurry of correspondence. Wellcome initially refused to allow Dale to use the word: Dale responded that if he could not use the terminology of fellow professional physiologists, his position at the WPRL was 'untenable'. He was supported by Professor John Langley, the editor of the *Journal of Physiology*, and Wellcome immediately recognised that inordinate damage would be done if Dale resigned under such circumstances. The laboratories' reputation for independent scientific research, already ambivalent, would be severely compromised. He allowed the manuscript to be submitted.[60]

Less than 24 hours later he changed his mind.[61] Staff from the WCRL and Snow Hill had convinced him that the physiologists should use the word 'epinephrine', which was used then by chemists. Dale refused to accept the imposition of an inaccurate word (at that time 'epinephrine' was a physiologically inactive preparation, although confusingly the same word was later used in the US as a synonym for adrenaline). His letter must have given Wellcome pause for thought:

> The position is one of far more difficulty than you, probably, can conceive. There is among English medical men and particularly among physiologists, a strongly marked prejudice against any connection with commerce. That prejudice I am earnestly and constantly trying to break down on my own behalf, and on that of any pharmacological workers in your laboratories. I have great hope of success: but the position I am striving for, on your behalf as well as my own, would be seriously imperilled by a breath of suspicion that the publication of my work was hampered or modified by other than scientific considerations.[62]

Chune Fletcher was consulted and confidently reported, 'as a physiologist he cannot describe the substance with which he has been working as 'Epinephrine' – the substance Dr Dale has been working with is known to physiologists as 'adrenaline' [underlined in red in the original].[63] Faced with this, Wellcome again agreed that Dale could submit his paper.[64] In reply Dale frankly acknowledged the situation, 'I hope that the vigour with which I have urged the difficulties in the way of changing the attitudes of the physiological world has not given you the impression that I viewed at all lightly the difficulties of the commercial position'.[65]

Was there a legal problem with infringement of Parke Davis & Co.'s trade-name? There is a hint, but nothing more, in company correspondence that Parke Davis & Co. *had* threatened legal action.[66] It is not even clear if Parke Davis & Co. held trade-name protection in the UK.[67] The 'adrenaline' controversy and its resolution challenged the aspirations to achieve scientific respectability and acceptability for his laboratories that Wellcome so actively proclaimed. Torn between commercial propriety and scientific credibility, ultimately, the claims for scientific reputation won. The episode also established the scientific independence of the WPRL, Dale's authority within the laboratories and within the company. Wellcome's contemporary notes are revealing:

> Dr Dale is a very able man and has will and a way of his own that needs very diplomatic handling & he has <u>very strong ideas</u> about professional ethics and, I think he probably knows & has thought more about this side which it is necessary for us to keep in view – I am sure Dr Dale will not <u>intentionally</u> do anything not strictly loyal … I consider him the best man in his work I have ever met – for a young man, and he is developing well & I want him to develop my ideals in this Physiological work – in which we are far ahead of others.[68]

Over 50 years later, Dale reflected, 'I am not nearly so sure now, as I was then, that I was completely justified to the merits of the case. I am very sure however, that I won an important victory for the staff of the Laboratories'.[69] The debate was certainly pivotal in emphasising within BW&Co. the scientific autonomy of the WPRL and its staff, and established the base for scientific excellence that distinguished research within the Wellcome organisation for many decades. The fostering of innovative scientific research in the environment of a pharmaceutical company had created novel problems, but by addressing these difficulties Wellcome and his managers developed policies to accommodate pure scientific research alongside commercial interests, policies and practices that were later emulated by other companies.

Ergot research at the WPRL
Initially Wellcome maintained a close personal interest in the ergot research, regularly offering encouragement and support to Dale and Barger.[70] At the conclusion of one early experiment, a 'fortunate accident' occurred. A batch of suprarenal gland extract (later called adrenaline, the word that will be used here) was sent by the Dartford Works to the WPRL for routine analysis of its efficacy and toxicity. Dale injected the solution into an anaesthetised cat he had just used for an ergot experiment.[71] Much to his surprise, the usual pressor (raising of the arterial blood pressure) effect did not occur – the animal's blood pressure fell dramatically. Dale, 'with the confidence of

inexperience', condemned the entire batch. Two days later a further sample was sent from the Works, and in later life, Dale speculated that it may have been from the same batch as a test of his abilities.[72] His suspicions were absolutely correct. Samples from the original consignment and from freshly made extracts were indeed dispatched to check his verdict.[73] Fortuitously, the situation was exactly as before. Dale had done an ergot experiment and using the same test animal to analyse the adrenaline, obtained the same startling result. At this point he 'put on his thinking cap', not believing that the regular output of a reliable factory could be faulty twice in one week.[74] Testing the extract again, on a fresh animal uncontaminated by any ergot, he found it was entirely normal. This satisfied BW&Co., confirming both the potency of the chemical *and* the accuracy of their new pharmacologist. It also started Dale speculating about the abnormal response he had observed, and he realised that somehow the ergot had blocked the normal response of the suprarenal extract. This observation was to lead him eventually to the Nobel Prize for Physiology or Medicine in 1936.[75] Further work by Francis Carr at the Dartford Works and George Barger at the WPRL, isolated and identified the extract concerned which they called ergotoxine.[76] This, the company rapidly marketed under the trade-name of Ernutin as a new ergot fraction.[77] Securing adequate supplies of the raw materials to manufacture the new extract because a recurring problem and in 1905, in an attempt to improve ergot availability and quality the company created the Wellcome Materia Medica Farm at Dartford.[78]

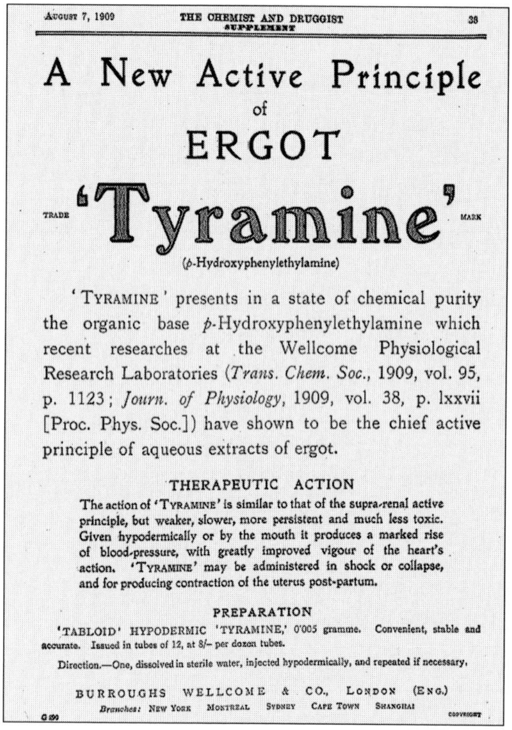

As detailed above, Dale's first publication on ergot caused problems because of the word 'adrenaline'.[79] He also proposed using the word 'ergotoxine', although company managers wanted him to use 'Ernutin', their trade-name. Dale stoutly declared that nothing he wrote from the WPRL would ever deal with anything protected by a commercial secret or trade-name. Coming immediately after the 'adrenaline', debate the company accepted his decision without any further discussion, an important acknowledgement of the WPRL's scientific autonomy. However, Dale was not insensitive to the commercial needs of BW&Co. In 1906, for example, German pharmacologists claimed to have isolated a new ergot alkaloid named 'Hydroergotonin', which appeared to be an impure preparation of

FIGURE 6.9 'A new active principle of ergot – Tyramine', a product and advertisement that appeared just weeks after the original scientific publication of the discovery (*Chemist & Druggist*, 7 August 1909).

August 7, 1909   THE CHEMIST AND DRUGGIST   35
SUPPLEMENT

A New Active Principle
of
ERGOT
TRADE '**Tyramine**' MARK
(*p*-Hydroxyphenylethylamine)

'TYRAMINE' presents in a state of chemical purity the organic base *p*-Hydroxyphenylethylamine which recent researches at the Wellcome Physiological Research Laboratories (*Trans. Chem. Soc.*, 1909, vol. 95, p. 1123; *Journ. of Physiology*, 1909, vol. 38, p. lxxvii [Proc. Phys. Soc.]) have shown to be the chief active principle of aqueous extracts of ergot.

THERAPEUTIC ACTION
The action of 'TYRAMINE' is similar to that of the supra-renal active principle, but weaker, slower, more persistent and much less toxic. Given hypodermically or by the mouth it produces a marked rise of blood-pressure, with greatly improved vigour of the heart's action. 'TYRAMINE' may be administered in shock or collapse, and for producing contraction of the uterus post-partum.

PREPARATION
'TABLOID' HYPODERMIC 'TYRAMINE,' 0'005 gramme. Convenient, stable and accurate. Issued in tubes of 12, at 8/- per dozen tubes.
Direction.—One, dissolved in sterile water, injected hypodermically, and repeated if necessary.

BURROUGHS WELLCOME & CO., LONDON (ENG.)
Branches: NEW YORK   MONTREAL   SYDNEY   CAPE TOWN   SHANGHAI
COPYRIGHT

ergotoxine.[80] Noting 'the opportunity afforded of bringing our results thus directly before the continental scientific world may in the end be much to our advantage and that of the laboratories', Dale and Barger engaged in a spirited and protracted exchange with the Germans.[81] Agreement was eventually reached that 'Hydroergotonin' was indeed a form of the ergotoxine originally isolated and characterised by the Wellcome scientists, and sold by the company.

Dale and Barger's ergot work was further stimulated when Francis Carr from Dartford reported that during commercial production of ergot there was a strong, unpleasant putrefactive odour. Investigation revealed two entirely new physiologically active chemicals, iso-amylamine and tyramine.[82] Shortly after this discovery tyramine was marketed as yet another new ergot extract, the company proudly quoting the scientific publication in its advertisements. This neatly illustrates the rapid translation of laboratory research into a marketable product, based on the close collaboration and interaction of Wellcome staff.

It might appear therefore that Wellcome's initial request to Dale and Barger to produce the obstetrically active principle of ergot had reached a satisfactory conclusion. This was not so. Despite these early discoveries it was to be nearly three decades before the problem of isolating *the* obstetrically active principle of ergot was eventually solved.[83]

Dale as Director of the WPRL, 1906–14

In 1906 Dowson resigned unexpectedly when the export of BW&Co. sera to the US was banned because of contamination. Dale was appointed Director in his place, and over the next eight years created a first-class research institute. He also assumed managerial responsibilities to BW&Co. that were unknown to his professional colleagues in universities or medical schools. For example, he supervised all therapeutic sera and vaccine production and routinely tested company products. He wrote publicity material for the company about the laboratories and their work, and was on call to provide technical information for use by the company representatives.[84] He also lectured at the firm's annual training conference for its travellers, although he admitted that 'old fashioned clinicians' might regard the scientific details he provided as 'unnecessary bother'.[85] His determination to make the WPRL a highly professional research establishment staffed with dedicated staff at every level was demonstrated early when he advised several of the young men employed by Dowson towards other careers, retaining only Ewins and Glenny.[86] Surviving correspondence suggests that the working relationship between Dale and Wellcome was not as close as those between Wellcome and the directors of his other laboratories, Power of the WCRL, and Balfour of the WTRL (and later the WBSR). Many years later, after Wellcome's death, Dale's fellow Wellcome Trustee T. R. Elliott found reports

FIGURE 6.10
Arthur Ewins
in chemistry
laboratory at
the WPRL,
c. 1902.

and correspondence between Wellcome and his other laboratory Directors but almost nothing from Dale. 'Evidently', he wrote to Dale, 'you ran your own show and did not waste time in detailed reports to keep him in touch with all your plans and to encourage him to make suggestions to you for new lines of work. That may have been a reason why your department prospered so well'.[87] Whether that is true or not, Dale was never confident that he knew Wellcome, 'The real trouble is, of course, that Wellcome took elaborate pains to 'present' to his staff and to others, the conception of himself which he wished them to receive; so that hardly anybody, and certainly nobody in the more recent years, had any notion of what he was really like'.[88]

By 1910 Dale succinctly and confidently summarised the relationship between the WPRL and the company:

> In addition to the drugs which have thus been investigated from all points of view in the Wellcome Physiological Research Laboratories, many others have there been physiologically examined which owe their production or chemical investigation to the Wellcome Chemical Research Laboratories or the experimental department of the Burroughs Wellcome Chemical Works. Incidental to this pharmacological work has been research on the purely physiological problems which it suggests

and involves. Methods have also been originated and developed for controlling and standardising by physiological experiment the activity of those potent drugs to which chemical methods of assay are not appropriate.

Whilst devoted primarily to original research, the results of which appear from time to time through the ordinary channels of scientific publication, the laboratories have, therefore, also performed much work of a nature more directly applicable to the needs of Mr Wellcome's firm.[89]

The Wellcome Chemical Research Laboratories, 1896–1914

The Chemical Research Laboratories were established just eight days after Burroughs' death in February 1895. Wellcome wrote to his old college contemporary in America, Dr Frederick Belding Power, telling him of Burroughs, and making a proposal:

> Now Fred by the rule of fates I have become sole proprietor of this great business into which I have put my heart and the best years of my life ... My first thought is to desire you to come to London. I feel that I could aid you in your progress and I know that you can greatly aid me. What I suggest is that you come and let me fit up for you a most thorough and complete experimental laboratory near my offices, ... I

FIGURE 6.11 Staff of the WPRL, 1914. Standing in the doorway under the ivy, from left to right, are J. B. Buxton, R. A. O'Brien, Henry Dale, H. J. Sudmersen, George Barger, Arthur Ewins, G. H. K. MacAlister.

want you for constant consultation as I propose to enter much more into scientific medical chemical products ... I should not ask you to take up any business cares or actual manufacturing drudgery but only experimental and strictly scientific work etc such as I know is most congenial to you.[90]

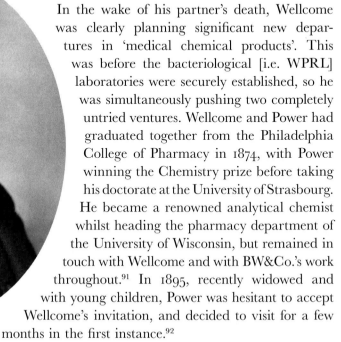

In the wake of his partner's death, Wellcome was clearly planning significant new departures in 'medical chemical products'. This was before the bacteriological [i.e. WPRL] laboratories were securely established, so he was simultaneously pushing two completely untried ventures. Wellcome and Power had graduated together from the Philadelphia College of Pharmacy in 1874, with Power winning the Chemistry prize before taking his doctorate at the University of Strasbourg. He became a renowned analytical chemist whilst heading the pharmacy department of the University of Wisconsin, but remained in touch with Wellcome and with BW&Co.'s work throughout.[91] In 1895, recently widowed and with young children, Power was hesitant to accept Wellcome's invitation, and decided to visit for a few months in the first instance.[92]

FIGURE 6.12
Frederick
Belding
Power, *c.* 1890.

As soon as Power decided to leave Wisconsin, Wellcome asked him to visit Squibbs' factory to inspect their 'ingenious' drying rooms and method of grinding glass stoppers; to buy cork cutting machines in New York; and to see Dr Genese at Johns Hopkins University who produced suppositories based on a design of Wellcome's.[93] Power also started a major revision of BW&Co.'s 1897 *Medical Diary* and developed a specialised *Chemist's Diary*. His contributions to both attracted considerable professional praise when they appeared the following year.[94] His arrival and the opening of the new 'Wellcome Research Laboratories' was celebrated on 21 July 1896 at a flamboyant London dinner. Wellcome announced that these special laboratories were to be quite different from those of his business, intended for 'work ... controlled and dictated with the highest regard for science.'[95] Dr Hooper Jowett, former assistant to Professor W. Dunstan at the Pharmaceutical Society was hired as Power's assistant and together they established a laboratory at 42 Snow Hill, close to BW&Co. Despite expansion in early 1898, shortly after Dr Samuel Schryver's arrival, these premises rapidly became inadequate for the type and quantity of analytical and experimental work being undertaken, much of it for the company. In May 1899, as the serum producing laboratory moved from Central to South

London, the chemists transferred to 6 King Street, Snow Hill, 'a handsome modern building of Venetian style and architecture'.[96] The laboratories on the upper three floors were all provided with gas, electricity, telephones, and the most sophisticated, up to date equipment available for chemical analysis. The building served the WCRL until the completion of the Wellcome Research Institution on Euston Road in 1932 (see Chapter 14 below). These moves meant that the extant research laboratories became known respectively as the 'Wellcome Physiological Research Laboratories' and 'Wellcome Chemical Research Laboratories'.[97] The national, local and medical press were invited to the opening of the new WCRL and a determined effort was made to emphasise their 'scientific work' as being distinct from BW&Co.[98] This was whilst Wellcome was petitioning the Home Office for the WPRL's registration and promoting the WCRL in this way was a deliberate strategy to advertise the independence of both from the company.

Although Wellcome had promised that Power would not be engaged in 'actual manufacturing drudgery', what he meant is unclear. What did become clear, however, is that rather than being devoted to pure experimental research, Power became deeply involved in practically every aspect of Wellcome's business empire. Early memoranda and correspondence refer to Power's work on the 'improvement of processes for the manufacture of new articles as approved by Mr Wellcome and requested by him to be officially communicated to the factory', and 'formulae and directions for hypodermic tabloids suggested by Dr Jowett and approved by Mr Wellcome'.[99] Serious problems for the WCRL arose in 1897 when German authorities alleged both impurities and inaccuracies in BW&Co.'s imported Tabloids. In Wellcome's absence abroad Sudlow, Smith, Weld and Power managed the crisis, and Power performed all the requisite analytical work needed to counter the damaging charges. Every chemical used to manufacture every Tabloid sold on the German market was analysed to the standards of the *German Pharmacopeia*. All were found to be satisfactory.[100] Every Tabloid sold in Germany was then analysed for accuracy of weight and dosage and some justification was found for the German complaints, which were largely believed to be a protectionist move against imported pharmaceuticals. Power discovered discrepancies in the weight of over 20 varieties of Tabloids, ranging from 1 to 24.5 per cent.[101]

FIGURE 6.13
WCRL on
King Street,
London,
c. 1900.

To try to rectify the problems Power also investigated several weighing machines to replace those at the Dartford factory. BW&Co. became increasingly confident that their products could be adequately defended, but allegations continued to appear against the improved Tabloids.[102] Again, Power painstakingly examined each disputed product, finding a slight variation in the composition of one. This precipitated a major research project, the formula and composition of *every* Tabloid sold in Germany was re-examined as were all German Pharmacopeia standards and every German preparation of the same chemicals, against which no complaints had been recorded.[103] Power found that the German goods were even more variable in weight and composition than were BW&Co.'s Tabloids. His results, confirmed by German consultants employed by Wellcome, made little impression on the German authorities, and the disputes over imported Tabloids continued intermittently for some years. However, the occasional deficits in Tabloids that Power had discovered came as a severe shock to the company and Wellcome was recommended to employ an analyst solely to examine Tabloids. Although based in Dartford, the analyst was supervised by Power and Jowett of the WCRL and his tests were devised by the WCRL. Simultaneously, and for the same reasons, a complete re-organisation of the factory was planned.[104]

WCRL staff were routinely and regularly involved with 'business' activities. They drew up products; on the suitability of new plant; on formulae; and on factory layout.[105] Power drew up a petition presented to the Chancellor of the Exchequer to reduce tax on alcohol in medicinal preparations,[106] and in 1902 spent several months analysing further preparations, when claims were made that a vial of mercuric potassium iodide had been mis-labelled as quinine bisulphate.[107] These activities all blurred whatever distinction there was between the independent WCRL and the company, although gradually as more scientific and technical staff were appointed to the former, research gained ascendancy over routine tasks. The research objectives of the WCRL were proclaimed as 'the complete chemical examination of a large number of plants or plant products which, on account of reputed medicinal value or other properties have been considered of special interest', and between 1897 and 1940 staff published almost 270 research papers.[108] The first of these was by Jowett on new preparations of hyoscine, hyoscyamine and atropine, in the *Journal of the Chemical Society* the premier journal of British chemistry. WCRL staff contributed to the *Journal* every year until 1940.[109] Their publications report extensive qualitative and quantitative analyses of commercially available compounds and new synthetic pathways for pharmaceutically important extracts.[110] Power, however, saw commercial production, not knowledge production alone, as his desired end point. Writing to Wellcome at the beginning of 1900, he admitted 'We are not yet making any chemicals for the market as was anticipated … and under present conditions it seems very doubtful whether this will be realised in the near future'.[111] He elaborated: the 'present conditions' included high labour costs, inefficient methods of working and poor supervision and administration in the Dartford laboratories. His criticisms had some effect, and in 1902 the 'Wellcome Brand' of fine chemicals was launched, 'a class of medicinal chemicals of unsurpassed and, in many cases, of exceptional purity'. Their production involved close collaboration between the WCRL and the Works, many of the initial investigations and syntheses of the former being taken up for commercial production by the latter.[112] An early example of such translation of research was the production of aloin (an extract of aloes) devised at the WCRL, and then worked up by Lloyd Williams and Carr at Dartford to produce 'a good yield of handsome product by a very economical method'.[113] Not all such collaborations were successful. An over-enthusiastic Works analyst rejected consignments of bismuth and gold salts claiming they did not meet new quality requirements. Re-testing at the WCRL declared them all acceptable;[114] an extensive WCRL research project on manganese salts resulted in the sale of only four bottles.[115] Before the First World War the 'Wellcome Brand' range of chemicals included entirely new preparations of, *inter alia*, pilocarpine, strophanthus, salicin and cascara. The powerful antiseptic hexamine was first synthesised in Dartford; glycerophosphates, used as general tonics and to increase the appetite, were advertised as the outcome of a 'successful collaboration of the firm's research and technical staff'; and high-quality cocaine for local anaesthesia was first produced in Britain by BW&Co. in 1914.[116]

Chemical research in the factory and the WCRL, 1897–1914

Chemical research was not confined to the WCRL. An Analytical Department was formally established at the Dartford factory in 1897 to ensure product purity, although prior to that analytical and some experimental work had been carried out by Lloyd Williams and others.[117] Of especial importance were refinements and modifications to the malt production procedures, because Kepler Malt was of overwhelming importance.[118] In August 1897 Francis Carr, another protégé of Professor Dunstan like Jowett, was hired to run the new department.[119] Chemical work was re-organised in the wake of the German Tabloid problems when he arrived, and 'making himself useful' he soon took charge of all chemical work, analytical and synthetic, at the Works.[120] An early responsibility was to ensure that the Wellcome laboratories could be self-sufficient in quinine salts, and to ensure the quality of the final product as external supplies were frequently below the desired standard.[121] During his first few months Carr concentrated on manufacturing quinine, ipececuanha, and bismuth salts, and agreed with Lloyd Williams to make several other chemicals solely for the company's use. Making chemicals this way was not always the cheapest option, and despite Carr's success, Snow Hill managers sometimes had to accept that large-scale manufacturers and suppliers could undercut their in-house chemists.[122] The death of Lloyd Williams at the end of 1899, a loss to Wellcome of a colleague and valued friend, instigated a rationalisation of the exchange of information between the WCRL and the Works.[123] Power at the WCRL and Carr in the Chemical Department held identical, locked copies of company formulae, copies being formally exchanged and updated whenever new practices or procedures were agreed.[124] That the WCRL had been established to do 'strictly scientific work' seems to have become ever more obscured.

Two initiatives of this early period deserve brief mention. One was by Samuel Schryver of the WCRL, whose analytical work on the constituents of morphine resulted in the successful isolation, and subsequent synthesis, of codeine a significant breakthrough in morphine chemistry.[125] Recognising the commercial significance, Wellcome immediately deposited details of the process with his solicitors, although Schryver was allowed to publish his work. When the manufacturing process was modified by Carr for transfer into the factory, particular care was taken that no one individual knew the full formula or sequence of preparation.[126] Also of note was Power's investigation of the Burmese chaulmoogra plant, from which he isolated 'chaulmoogric' and 'hydnocarpic' acids as leprosy treatments.[127] His experimental work was rapidly transferred, via the newly established Experimental Department at the Works, into manufacture. Soon BW&Co. was producing 'Moogrol,' upon which, according to Power's obituarist, 'the whole of the modern treatment of leprosy is based.'[128] Chaulmoogra oil and its derivatives were important constituents of BW&Co.'s tropical medicine catalogue until the Second World War, and considerable work was done in this area during the interwar period.[129]

Important work in plant chemistry was also done by Paul Pérrèdes of the WCRL in the early 1900s.[130] In 1902 Pérrèdes was sent to the US West Coast to investigate plants with possible medicinal effects and to find new sources of cascara bark. He was instructed to behave discreetly and not to mention his association with the firm. Elaborate mechanisms were devised for him to send samples to the company via several intermediaries so that he need never use the word 'Wellcome'. Unfortunately the commercial need for secrecy was lost on Pérrèdes, who gave a candid interview to a Californian journalist, which subsequently appeared in *Chemist and Druggist*. Staff at Snow Hill were apoplectic with fury, Power 'deeply shocked', and Pérrèdes sternly admonished for his breach of confidence.[131] Despite its anger, BW&Co. instructed Pérrèdes to continue his investigations and he not only acquired a variety of cascara bark samples, but also learned details of its growth, harvesting and storage.[132] Somewhat contrarily the company then encouraged him to publish an account of his trip.[133] By 1907 his principal responsibilities were to maintain the materia medica collection in WCRL's 'Museum', and to help scientists identify the plant and seed samples sent to BW&Co. by its representatives from around the world.[134] From these he and Power compiled regular lists of 'drugs available for investigation' for analysis by either Dartford or WCRL staff.[135] When the specimen collection was moved from the WCRL to Dartford, Pérrèdes' time was formally split between the two sites, giving weekly materia medica classes to teach Wellcome employees plant identification and basic pharmacognosy.[136]

In 1905, a new Experimental Department was established at Dartford to devise and improve existing processes. This intermediate laboratory enabled the WCRL to be devoted to more purely academic work while the Chemical Department of the Works concentrated on developing manufacturing processes, and analytical work became a routine part of all production processes. The first head of the Experimental Department was Dr Jowett from the WCRL, who a year later became Manager of the Works where he remained until he died, shortly after Wellcome, in 1936. Jowett was the first of many to transfer between the WCRL and the factory, and it was largely his influence that enabled staff at the Wellcome Chemical Works to research and publish, often in collaboration with colleagues from the WPRL and WCRL. Principally chemists moved across the organisation, including Pyman, who travelled from the Works to the WCRL to replace Power in 1914; Goodson from the WTRL, who moved to the WCRL in 1914, King, who transferred from the works to the WCRL in 1915, and Bacharach from the WCRL to the Works in 1916. As this movement suggests, chemical interests united the varied components of the Wellcome empire. The analytical and experimental laboratories at the Works collaborated with the WCRL to a great extent, 'in synthetic chemistry a number of new organic compounds have been produced and among inorganic salts several have been brought into new forms of combination whereby they have been rendered more suitable for medicinal use.'[137] In turn new chemical products were sent for biological test to the WPRL, and the BW&Co. 1912 price list of over 160 items advertised several preparations as validated by the WPRL.[138] Chemical work was also important to the newest of Wellcome's research initiatives, the tropical laboratories he founded in The Sudan.

Wellcome Tropical Research Laboratories, 1902–1913

By the final decades of the nineteenth century, searches for the causative organisms of tropical diseases and for therapeutic drugs to treat them were of considerable importance for European colonial ambitions. Wellcome personally had a life-long fascination with exploration and the lives and welfare of native peoples, which started with the Indians of his mid-West

Mrs. FRENCH SHELDON'S PALANQUIN.

This palanquin was made at Whiteley's for Mrs. French Sheldon, the "Lady Stanley" who is bound for Central Africa, from designs by Mr. Henry S. Welcome (of Messrs. Burroughs & Wellcome, Snow Hill). It is a unique specimen of strong, light, and artistic cane and bamboo work, and Mr. Wellcome must be congratulated on his excellent taste. The palanquin will be carried by four of Mrs. Sheldon's Zanzibari porters.

FIGURE 6.14
Mrs French
Sheldon's
palanquin
'from designs
by Mr Henry
S. Wellcome'
(*The Mirror*, 2
March 1891).

American home.[139] By the final decades of the nineteenth century, as European nations fought each other and native populations, the 'scramble for Africa' was well under way.[140] Newspapers and books were full of accounts and stories of African adventures. In London, Wellcome mixed socially with Henry Stanley, Mounteney Jephson, and Eli Sheldon and his wife May, all known for travelling in, and writing on, Africa. A particular British preoccupation was with the Sudan, where General Gordon had been murdered in Khartoum in 1885.[141] In September 1898, the Sudan was finally re-taken. Two months later, Lord Kitchener launched an appeal to establish a college in Khartoum in Gordon's memory, to which Wellcome immediately contributed 100 guineas and offered to equip the College's dispensary.[142] In the winter of 1900/01 he travelled in Egypt, and was one of the first civilians to visit Sudan after Kitchener's success.[143] The medical conditions there made a powerful impact, 'One thing that impressed me greatly when I was at Khartoum was the possibility of making that city as healthy as New York, London, or any other place. With its central location, it occurred to me that one could reach out in various directions from Khartoum, as a base, and collect materials and specimens for scientific investigation'.[144] Sir Reginald Wingate, the Governor General, and James Currie, the country's Director of Education, showed Wellcome the plans for the Gordon Memorial College. These had been somewhat expanded since Kitchener's appeal because of the public's generous response, and Wellcome offered to provide additional bacteriological and analytical chemical laboratories with the <u>proviso</u> that the authorities contribute to their upkeep.[145]

The offer was enormously generous. The British High Commissioner of Egypt estimated that it was equivalent to about £15,000, and that the annual running costs of about £820 could be shared by the College authorities and the Government.[146] Wellcome suggested six main lines of investigation:

a) tropical hygiene and tropical disorders, of man and animals;
b) plant diseases;
c) cases of poisoning;
d) chemical and bacteriological tests of water etc and other sanitary matters;
e) analytical work on soils, minerals, ores etc;
f) agricultural and forest products and any material of economic importance to the development of the Sudan.[147]

There was no suggestion that these laboratories were associated with, or contributed to, the company. Unlike his other laboratories, these were not Wellcome's property. They had no dealings with other parts of his organisation, although all correspondence to do with them passed through the Snow Hill headquarters of BW&Co. Wellcome only employed the Director, and '... that the work of the laboratories may be thorough and efficient it is very desirable that the director be skilled and resourceful and be prepared

FIGURE 6.15
Gordon
Memorial
College,
Khartoum,
site of the
WTRL
c. 1908.

to direct and carry out with zeal and energy all branches of work for which the laboratories are equipped, and a man who is willing to devote his life to the work of the Institution'.[148] Back in Britain he rapidly selected Andrew Balfour, a Rugby-playing Edinburgh medical graduate, a published novelist, a protégé of Sir Patrick Manson, with some tropical experience, a private income and a modicum of Arabic. Writing to Currie in August 1902, Wellcome stressed these 'exceptional qualities', and Balfour duly became the first Director of what were called the Wellcome Research Laboratories, until the word 'Tropical' was added in 1911.[149]

In London, Wellcome organised a farewell dinner for Balfour in December 1902. All the senior management of Snow Hill, the Directors of the WPRL and the WCRL, and eminent medical figures, including the editor of the *Lancet*, Sir Patrick Manson, Sir Dyce Duckworth, and the leaders of several other research institutes, were invited. Sir Henry Stanley, making his last public appearance, spoke optimistically that laboratories such as Wellcome's would soon banish the 'deadly plagues' that tortured Africa. The dinner, with its glittering array of eminent medical and scientific men, the widespread medical publicity and the absence of trade associations, was a concerted effort to situate these latest Wellcome laboratories firmly within the British medical establishment.[150]

The work of the WTRL quickly confirmed their scientific validity and medical utility.[151] Some advances were simply the result of consistent and regular applications of stringent hygiene, as Balfour recruited sanitary inspectors and engineers, many from his native Scotland, and established an efficient waste-disposal system and clean water supply for the city. He focussed attention on the eradication of insect vectors, and by 1910 Khartoum was declared mosquito-free. Camel caravans travelled across the country to study diseases and collect specimens for analysis and classification back in Khartoum, and in 1907 a floating laboratory that could travel to the upper reaches of the White Nile was built and paid for by Wellcome. The pathological services were rapidly utilised by civil, military and private medical practitioners across the Sudan. One medical officer before the First World War emphasised, 'it is not possible to speak too highly of the work of the Wellcome Tropical Research Laboratories'.[152]

The most direct association with the company was through chemistry. A chemical laboratory under Dr William Beam, an American, tackled a range of Sudanese agricultural problems, including the treatment of the economically important acacia trees, which produced gum Arabic and which had been damaged during the military skirmishes. Beam's examination of plant materials and native remedies, similar to Perrédès' work for the WCRL, was probably of most interest to BW&Co. To quote an oft-used phrase of Wellcome's these laboratories were governed by 'scientific high-mindedness'. Medical visitors interested in tropical medicine were accommodated in the laboratory, and helped with their research.[153] The very title of the laboratories, however, by including the name Wellcome, provided extensive free publicity for BW&Co. Papers from Balfour and his colleagues appeared in the same journals as those from his other laboratories, and in which BW&Co. advertised. They were, in a way that eluded the WPRL and the WCRL, independent of direct commercial association. Their activities publicised the name 'Wellcome' to RAMC and colonial staff in Egypt and Britain at a time when BW&Co. was bidding for lucrative overseas contracts.[154] *Reports from the Khartoum Laboratories* were also produced detailing their biological studies on insect vectors of disease.[155] Four exquisite volumes appeared between 1904 and 1911, describing the work of the laboratories, illustrated by specially prepared art-work, commissioned and supervised by Wellcome himself.[156] Wellcome imposed one pre-publication condition: the phrase 'under the auspices of Mr. Wellcome' had to be removed, so

FIGURE 6.16
Wellcome
Bureau of
Scientific
Research,
10 Henrietta
Street, *c.* 1914.

that no explicit link with the commercial company could be misrepresented or criti- cised.[157] During his years at the WTRL Balfour was plagued by bouts of malaria, and added to the pressure of work and the hostile climate, his health was undermined. In 1913 he decided to return to Britain, a move of consequence for all Wellcome's research laboratories.[158]

Wellcome Bureau of Scientific Research

Wellcome took the opportunity of Balfour's move to establish a new venture, a centre of research and teaching in tropical medicine and hygiene. By then he had spent frequent periods in the Sudan, got to know Balfour well, and been impressed with his energy and successes. The proposed new institute, the Wellcome Bureau of Scientific Research (WBSR) of which Balfour was to be head, was clearly analogous to the Liverpool and London Schools of Tropical Medicine. Premises were found in Henrietta Street in Central London, close to the Wellcome Historical Medical Museum and BW&Co.'s main London showroom, and Charles Wenyon, who had been in charge of the floating laboratory on the Nile, re-joined Balfour. Among other staff the chemist J. A. Goodson from Khartoum was employed, as had Perrédès before him, to analyse native remedies sent from around the world by Wellcome's commercial agents, and to work in the WCRL on plant chemistry. Once more, chemistry extended and consolidated links between different parts of Wellcome's research enterprise.

In establishing the WBSR, Wellcome decided that Balfour's position was to be that of 'Director-in-Chief' of all his Laboratories and have 'general control of the research work of the WCRL and the WPRL – though such institutions may continue to be conducted separately under the present Directors or their successors – also of any other Research Laboratories, either at home or abroad, I may found.'[159] His decision appears to have been made without wider consultation. It clearly offended Power, the Director of the WCRL, and Dale, the Director of the WPRL, who suddenly found Balfour, a man well known to Wellcome but not to them, effectively placed above them. Within months, they both resigned. Henry Dale left in June

1914 to join the newly created Medical Research Committee, taking Barger and Ewins with him. Power resigned 'for family reasons' at the beginning of the First World War and returned to America in November 1914. Whatever the veracity of the excuse (and his motherless daughters were growing up in America without him), it provided a face-saver for Wellcome, who had thoughtlessly lost his old friend and trusted adviser. In recommending Power to the Bureau of Chemistry at the Department of Agriculture in Washington, Wellcome admitted he 'deeply regret[ted] parting with him'.[160] Power was replaced by Dr Frank Pyman, who had been head of the Experimental Department at the Chemical Works at Dartford since 1906. Dale was succeeded by the bacteriologist R.A.O'Brien who had been at the WPRL since 1908.

Under Power and Dale both laboratories had established themselves as research institutions producing work of high quality as assessed by publications in respectable scientific journals (see Table 6.1) and by providing products for BW&Co.

Table 6.1 *Publications from the Wellcome laboratories, 1897–1914* [161]

	WCRL	WPRL	WCW	WBSR	Total
1897	1				1
1898	2				2
1899	3				3
1900	10				10
1901	9				9
1902	6				6
1903	9	1			10
1904	8	2			10
1905	10	4			14
1906	8	2	2		12
1907	12	2	4		18
1908	10	6	4		20
1909	11	1	5		17
1910	21	21	4		46
1911	15	9	8		32
1912	11	7	8		26
1913	14	14	7	3	38
1914	8	19	6	6	39

An additional 'product' of BW&Co. was scientific manpower. Shortly before his departure from the WPRL, Dale was elected to Fellowship of the Royal Society, the highest scientific honour in Britain. He was the first scientist associated with a pharmaceutical manufacturer to achieve this distinction. Dale had almost single-handedly removed, or prevented, the explicit prejudice against 'commerce' pertaining in the US where commercial scientists were banned from the professional pharmacological society. As a British supporter of Dale's explained to an American at the time,

> He is of course with Burroughs W. & Co., but incurs no restrictions on that account here as he has done such admirable work and does nothing whatever to aid the commercial side ... I merely want to point out that he is not quite in the same class as P.D.'s [Parke Davis] men, as he has never represented the firm and never 'writes up' their products &c. except in the way that you or I might do.[162]

Replying to Wellcome's congratulations on his honour, Dale emphasised the importance of the unique situation he had enjoyed at the WPRL,

> When I entered your laboratories I had no thought that the opportunities, there afforded me, would lead to such an advance in my scientific position that a position elsewhere would be offered to me, which I should feel obliged to accept. You may be assured that I shall spare no effort, during the remainder of my tenure of the directorship of the WPRL, to leave things in going order & to give to my successor, whoever he may be, under Dr. Balfour, the best chance of holding the post with as much advantage & satisfaction to himself as has been given to me. I feel, at least, that I am leaving the Laboratories an institution of established scientific reputation, which I am sure my present colleagues will worthily uphold. I shall hope to see you before my resignation takes effect, & to have the opportunity once more of assuring you of my whole-hearted gratitude for the opportunities which the past 10 years have given me.[163]

Those 'opportunities' not only provided Wellcome and BW&Co. with the unique and pioneering accolades of scientific reputation, they also produced new goods and services that captured the rapidly changing pharmaceutical marketplace of late nineteenth century Britain.

CHAPTER SEVEN

Products and prestige: sera and vaccines before the First World War

Serum production – the beginnings and early problems, 1894–1896

Bacteriological research within BW&Co. was stimulated by the discovery in Germany and France in the early 1890s that experimental animals could be effectively immunized against diphtheria or tetanus. If the appropriate bacterial toxin was injected into horses, a therapeutic serum could be prepared from their blood and used to protect other animals and humans from these diseases.[1] The medical possibilities of this new approach were quickly recognised in Western Europe and North America, and as successful reports of diphtheria treatment began to appear, private and University laboratories rushed to produce the new 'miracle drug' as the scientific and commercial implications were recognised by many. In Britain, the British Institute for Preventive Medicine (BIPM, later the Jenner, later the Lister, Institute) set up a Serum Department as early as August 1894 under the direction of Armand Ruffer, a protégé of Louis Pasteur.

These developments came to BW&Co.'s attention. In September 1894, BW&Co. approached the BIPM to buy an inoculated horse for £50. The Honorary Treasurer of the Institute, Sir Henry Roscoe refused, announcing 'we must not let people like B. & W. run off with all the profit'. Although a chemist, Roscoe was well aware that medical practitioners had a living to make, and had a clear view of the financial possibilities of the new therapy. He proposed that the serum be sold at ten shillings a dose in private practice, with a lower price for hospitals. He suggested it might be useful to give BW&Co. 'a few tubes to get their custom', and then negotiate a price with the profits being split 2:1 in the Institute's favour.[2] Two months later, BW&Co. wrote to the BIPM's Governing Council offering to be agents for their sera, and 'any other products you may discover'. A provisional price of 1s. 6d. per 20mls (between 1 and 3 doses), was offered and the BIPM was asked to provide BW&Co. with full instructions for serum usage. The company undertook to distribute and advertise the product, and provide doctors with appropriate information.[3] This suggestion was discussed by the BIPM's Council on 8 October, but it was decided 'That Messrs. Burroughs and Welcome's [sic] offer be declined with thanks'.[4] A request three weeks later from Allen & Hanburys received the same response. There was growing interest in serotherapy. Shortly after, the Conjoint Laboratories also started producing serum in London, and the BIPM made rapid moves to develop production further. To pay for the work, Sir Joseph Lister, the Chairman of the BIPM, appealed in *The Times* for donations to the 'Anti-toxin Fund', modelled on a similar scheme started by *Le Figaro* in France, which in turn was based on appeals in Germany for funds.[5] As competition increased, the BIPM re-considered their earlier decisions about agents, but by then BW&Co. had made other arrangements and were no longer interested (see below). Thus the BIPM entered into a commercial relationship with Allen & Hanburys, an association that would cause disquiet and irritation to BW&Co. for several decades.

Undeterred by the BIPM's initial rejection, BW&Co. began to manufacture its own serum. No records survive of how this decision was made. Burroughs was still alive, and as he and Wellcome were then engaged in legal action to dissolve their partnership, it is difficult to believe that either would have taken a major decision independently at such a critical time.[6] From the Central London premises of Dr Thomas Bokenham the first successful product was announced in November 1894.[7]

There was little co-ordinated or concerted public health response in Britain to this new therapy. Elsewhere, notably along the Eastern seaboard of the US, public health bodies took up the challenge of producing and using serum.[8] In Britain it was the producers themselves who prepared, tested, promoted and advocated the therapy. For several decades BW&Co. continue to argued for the diagnosis and treatment of, and later prophylaxis and susceptibility testing for, several infectious diseases. British health authorities showed far less interest in the dissemination and evaluation of these new therapies than did the company.

No records survive of the costs to BW&Co. of setting up this new venture. Beginning serotherapy production was not a cheap decision, nor was it unique. The BIPM's records show that from September to December 1894 expenditure for animals, land, buildings, equipment and staff amounted to almost £1600, whilst serum sales for the same period were a little under £80. The Anti-toxin Fund provided a substantial subsidy of £1250.[9] BW&Co.'s immediate expenditure may not have been as great but neither did the company benefit from the financial support of the Anti-toxin Fund. At the same time the market price of sera was dropping as companies from Germany and France exported to the UK.

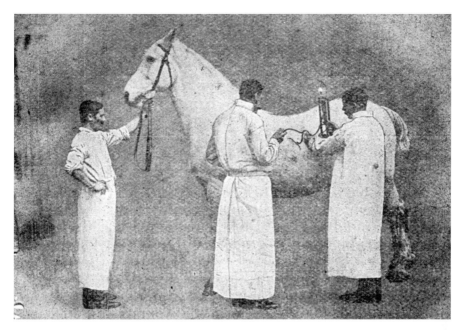

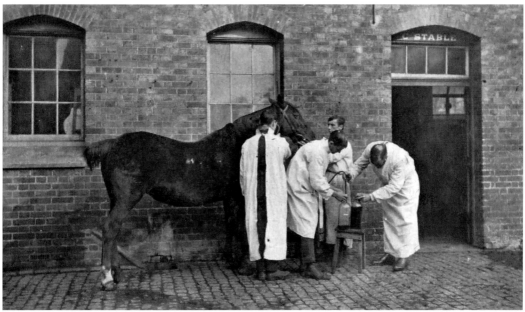

In 1895 Burroughs died, which left the direction of these bacterio-logical, and all subsequent, research laboratories to Wellcome. It also gave Wellcome the financial security and operational independence to indulge his widespread interests, including archaeology, the collecting of books and artefacts related to the history of medicine, and creating exhibitions and museums.[10] Few of these were explicitly related to his business. He also established further scientific institutions: the WCRL, the WTRL, and the WBSR. As will be demonstrated Wellcome took a keen personal interest in all the laboratories, and as demonstrated in Chapter 6, he was at pains to promote them as independent of the company. Work at the WPRL on producing serum anti-toxins was, however, closely related to the commercial interests and activities of BW&Co. From the very earliest days of the WPRL, Wellcome constantly encouraged Bokenham to improve the diphtheria anti-toxins and to experiment on producing anti-toxins against other infectious diseases. Initially, every stage of serum production was hit-and-miss. The bacterial toxin had to be extracted, maintained in culture, and 'measured' by checking its lethality in guinea-pigs. The toxin was injected into a horse, and at unspecified periods, blood samples taken from which the therapeutic serum was prepared. The serum was tested for pathogenic micro-organisms, and its strength titrated against the original toxin by injecting known amounts of both into guinea-pigs and determining the dose of anti-toxin that effectively neutralised a known dose of toxin. Bokenham encountered problems with all these steps, as did other producers. Doctors administering the serum also had difficulties, and BW&Co.'s earliest adverts contain detailed instructions for the use of the new therapy. Dismissive of the syringes already available, the company also marketed a new aluminium serum syringe that could easily be re-sterilised, an early example of its 'added-value' approach to product development and marketing.[11]

Wellcome's personal involvement is illustrated by his correspondence with Bokenham in April 1895 that 'we should be in the forefront with this', and suggested experiments to develop anti-toxins for consumption, erysipelsas and puerperal fever.[12] Some of his ideas were taken up, although Bokenham principally worked on the diphtheria and, to a lesser extent tetanus, anti-toxins. By the beginning of 1896 more space was needed and the laboratories moved to larger premises in Charlotte Street, still in Central London, with stabling in Lisson Grove. Small amounts of new of anti-toxins were produced in line with Wellcome's wishes, and in 1896 Bokenham published an account of an anti-streptococcus serum 'prepared by myself, and supplied to the profession through the firm of Burroughs, Wellcome and Co.'[13] Serious problems that retarded the serum production in the short term were on the horizon however. The first was a letter in May from the Home Office advising Wellcome that the laboratories should be registered under the 1876 Cruelty to Animals Act. Two months later, the *Lancet* produced a damning report on the poor quality of commercially available anti-toxins, including those of BW&Co.[14] Both caused immediate, but different, anxieties for the company. The Home Office matter, which raised fundamental questions about the propriety of a commercial organisation engaging in medical research, was discussed in Chapter 6. The *Lancet*'s investigation had more immediate, commercial implications for the company.

The *Lancet*'s report on serum anti-toxins, 1896

The weekly medical journal the *Lancet* instigated several 'Special Enquiries' into medical matters, frequently evaluating new therapies and equipment. In July 1896 it investigated the potency and efficacy of anti-toxic sera and condemned all British products, from the BIPM, the Bacteriological Institute of Leicester, and BW&Co., for being well below their claimed strength. This contrasted with the German, Swiss, Belgian and French products evaluated. This public castigation by a well respected and widely read medical journal was a serious blow to the company. Serum production represented an important new departure at the cutting edge of contemporary scientific medicine. It was of critical importance that the sound reputation BW&Co. had patiently and methodically built up for the quality, efficacy and reliability of its goods should not only carry over to this new venture, but also should not jeopardize that good name. Wellcome took the lead in dealing with the crisis, and Fletcher Moulton QC (later Lord Moulton) was retained for legal advice. Wellcome analysed every stage of the serum production and 'determined that the source of error shall be discovered whether it be on the side of the *Lancet* or ourselves', he invited Dr Alfred Kanthack, Director of the Pathological Department at St Bartholomew's Hospital, to supervise an internal enquiry.[15] Bokenham was far from pleased at this development. He rejected any procedural review, failed to provide serum for independent testing, and refused to allow Kanthack and his colleagues into the laboratory.[16]

A further blow struck on 21 December when Dr J.W. Washbourn wrote to BW&Co.,

FIGURE 7.3
The *Lancet*'s Special Commission on diphtheria antitoxins, August 1896.

> Dr. Lucas of Burnwell, Cambridge sent me an unopened bottle of your Anti-diphtherical Serum today for examination. I am sorry to inform you that it is full of bacteria, and consequently unfit for use. I thought

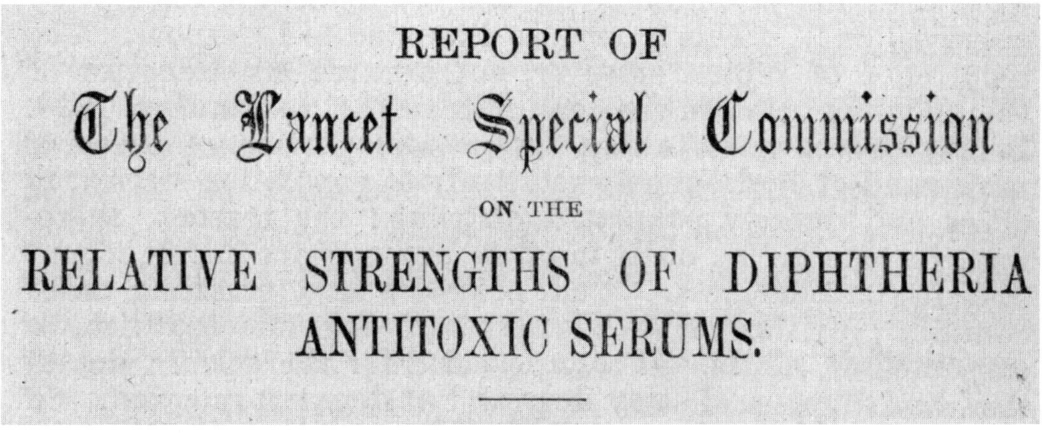

REPORT OF

𝕿𝖍𝖊 𝕷𝖆𝖓𝖈𝖊𝖙 𝕾𝖕𝖊𝖈𝖎𝖆𝖑 𝕮𝖔𝖒𝖒𝖎𝖘𝖘𝖎𝖔𝖓

ON THE

RELATIVE STRENGTHS OF DIPHTHERIA ANTITOXIC SERUMS.

it wise to let you know at once because Dr. Lucas has had two deaths from vomiting and diarrhoea occurring shortly after injection with Serum obtained from your firm.[17]

Washbourn, a Physician at the London Fever Hospital, had conducted the BIPM's first trial of diphtheria anti-toxins and advised it on the development of new sera.[18] Recognising the danger, Snow Hill staff immediately wrote to him and to Lucas promising that 'certainly no trouble must be spared to investigate this matter' although shrewdly adding 'we note that you used part of the same supply of serum with good results'.[19] Bokenham was becoming increasingly difficult, as Sudlow reported to Wellcome,

> Fearing that Dr. Bokenham did not appreciate to the fullest extent the position as regards possible publication by Dr. Washbourn, I had a special interview with the former. I was able to convince him thoroughly that at all costs publication was to be avoided. I also gathered from Dr. Bokenham the manner in which he proposed to approach Dr. Washbourn, and made certain suggestions by which the end in view I thought might be secured.[20]

The company realised the serious and enormously damaging effect that these fresh allegations against their product would have if they became public, especially in the wake of the *Lancet*'s report. Bokenham was instructed to write to Lucas, copying a draft prepared by Snow Hill staff.[21] Yet again, Sudlow had to step in to modify Bokenham's hot-headedness, as he reported to Wellcome, 'The communication that Dr Bokenham proposed to send to Dr Lucas was an impossible one, and I had no hesitation in at once condemning it. I hope you will approve the final draft.'[22] Fortunately for BW&Co., Lucas decided 'for many reasons' not to publish his adverse experiences, even though he was strongly encouraged to do so by Washbourn.[23] Although publicity would undoubtedly have damaged BW&Co., the newness of the therapy, the problems associated with it, and the inexperience of practitioners administering it, might well have reflected even more badly on Lucas himself, who had a practice to maintain.

The company waited anxiously to learn of further problems with serum from the same batch that Washbourn had used but no other complaints arose. This culmination of errors, which Bokenham arrogantly dismissed, led to a showdown with Wellcome. He offered a generous financial settlement to secure the silent resignation of yet another unsatisfactory employee, who, like Dr Witte and Dr Smith, had failed to live up to the expectations and achievements required of him. Sweeping changes were instigated in the laboratory. Over the next two and a half years the procedures, staff, and premises underwent major changes. Wellcome was determined that this innovation was going to have the best possible chance of success, and when his external advisor Dr Alfred Kanthack from Cambridge finally considered the anti-diphtheria serum production to be satisfactory in late 1897, one of his protégés, Walter Dowson, became the new Director of the WPRL.

The first anti-toxins to be re-introduced were against diphtheria and tetanus, and other experimental sera were gradually produced. Any phial of suspect serum, returned for whatever reason, was sent immediately to Dowson for bacteriological examination and an individual report sent to each customer.[24] The success of the WPRL meant that by late 1898 their central London facilities were no longer adequate for the increased workload. Wellcome leased Brockwell Hall in Herne Hill, South London, for conversion into laboratories.[25] The new establishment, now publicly identified as the 'Wellcome Physiological Research Laboratories', attracted lavish reviews in the pharmaceutical and medical press, and featured extensively in the company's advertising and marketing material.[26] The premises included specialised facilities for the culture of bacterial toxins, incubation rooms for nutritive media, and serum preparation and packing rooms, in addition to extensive stabling, 'which in equipment reminds us somewhat of the Queen's stables', according to one correspondent.[27] Experimental laboratories for bacteriological, chemical and physiological research were also provided, as were secretarial offices, a dark room and a small library.

These new facilities indicate another direction in which Wellcome saw the

FIGURE 7.4
Drawing of
bacteriological
laboratory,
WPRL,
c. 1906.

INTERIOR OF ONE OF THE STABLES

FIGURE 7.5
Drawing
of stables,
WPRL
c. 1902.

laboratories developing, although WPRL's principal purpose remained the development and production of therapeutic sera for BW&Co. Inspired by the success of the sera, and influenced by developments abroad, especially in his native United States, Wellcome wanted to promote therapeutic innovation, to develop biological substances such as animal glandular products, and to standardise, with physiological methods, preparations that could not be tested chemically. However, the scale of Wellcome's investment in new facilities and staff pales besides those of Parke, Davis & Co. in Detroit. There, according to their General Manager in 1899, 30 medical graduates were employed in research laboratories, over 150 horses were kept for serum work, and 'thousands of guinea-pigs, goats and other animals to work upon, for we make a point of testing physiologically those things which we cannot assay chemically'.[28] At that time the WPRL employed three graduate staff, about half a dozen technical staff and kept 30–40 horses.

Diphtheria diagnosis service

In an attempt 'to make the laboratories indispensable to medical men in this country', the company provided a bacteriological diagnostic service, whereby doctors could send samples to the WPRL for testing – initially throat swabs from suspected diphtheria patients for microscopic examination.[29] This was not novel. Pasteur had established a rabies testing service in France, upon which Victor Horsley had modelled a scheme at the Brown Animal Sanatory Institute in London.[30] The BIPM had started a diphtheria diagnostic service in late 1894, contemporaneously with their first serum production. In 1896 what became the Clinical Research Association (CRA) was established at Guy's Hospital by John Wade and Frederick Gowland Hopkins, for the purposes of carrying out laboratory tests and examinations on a wide range of materials.[31]

BW&Co.'s service was widely used. Between late October 1900 and March 1901 there was heavy usage from doctors, medical officers of health and infirmary matrons from London and Southern England, infected material was also sent for diagnosis from the rest of England, Scotland, Wales and Ireland, and occasionally from overseas.[32] Several doctors used the service frequently, the majority coming from London or the South East. A single diagnosis fee was 2s. 6d, or 3s. to include a telegraphic response. A set of test tubes and stoppers, in which the swabs could be dispatched, was available for 6d., and users of the diagnostic service were supplied with price lists of therapeutic sera. Testing was done by the WPRL, but BW&Co. issued invoices and received payment. Details of the service were advertised in the medical press, and a telegraphic code was devised for practitioners to order the right sera without mentioning the word 'diphtheria' in front of patient or family. Approximately 195 samples per month were tested, from which the annual income for the laboratories was approximately £314.[33] However, patchy information from company records indicates that the income from the diagnostic service *and* the sale of sera was approximately £450–600 per month, giving an annual income generated by the WPRL of between £5,400 and £7,200.

The costs of raising sera and running the diagnostic service can be estimated from the sparse details available. Between October 1900 and March 1901, the WPRL bought 12 horses at an average price of £5 6s. 8d. Over the same period they obtained £3 12s. 4¼d. for a used horse.[34] The annual maintenance costs were between £1 and £1 5s. per horse per month. Guinea-pigs cost about 1s. 1d. each, and approximately 150 were used each month.[35] Assuming that the laboratories housed 30 horses at a time, replacing 50 per cent annually, then the animal costs alone (purchase and maintenance) would be nearly £700. Annual salary costs would include Dowson and professional colleagues, although they were not dedicated totally to serum work, and stablemen, glass-washers, laboratory assistants and packers. Even estimating £3,000 for such costs, and £1,000 for routine materials and consumables, the serum and diagnosis work was still profitable for BW&Co.

Once Home Office registration for animal experimentation was granted in 1901, expansion of the laboratories was agreed by Snow Hill. A. T. Glenny, who spent his entire working life in the WPRL, compiled a detailed report on the necessity and feasibility of extending the stabling and acquiring more land. These estimates caused concern at Snow Hill. Quotes for new stables at £650 to be erected by company staff were considered exorbitant; an outside estimate was still too expensive at £250; the purchase of new horses at £200 was queried; and the whole scheme was reconsidered.[36] A new guinea-pig room was rejected, and the company insisted on economies in scale and building materials.[37] Over several years the requisite new facilities were gradually installed, although increasing demands for sera and vaccines necessitated several further expansions on the site, especially during the First World War, until the WPRL moved to Beckenham in 1922.[38]

In September 1901 the diagnostic service expanded and in December Dr Vernon Shaw, from the Pathology Department at St Mary's Hospital, London, was appointed to run it at an annual salary of £350, raised to £400 six months later.[39] The costs of providing an 'all hours' service for serum orders and diagnostic samples increasingly worried the company's managers. After normal working hours, orders arriving at Snow Hill were diverted to the warehouse where three men were employed to stay until 11 p.m. each night, and until 6 p.m. on Sundays. The cost was more than £310 per annum, and as an average of only one cable per night was received, the company decided, despite initial objections from Wellcome, to cancel these arrangements at the end of 1901.[40]

At the beginning of 1902 company managers expressed concern that the diagnostic service was losing its competitive edge to the CRA, which charged 2s. 6d. per telegraphed report, making the WPRL's charges higher. As Collett Smith of Snow Hill emphasised to Dowson, 'The diagnosis work of the Wellcome Physiological Laboratories is to aid the medical profession'.[41] It was company policy that the service should be indispensable to medical practitioners, to generate good will and trust, not profit, and the laboratory's charges were scaled down to those of the CRA. The possibility of expanding the service to include blood tests for anaemia, post-mortem examinations, and of making the WPRL's expertise available nationwide were considered. The company's enthusiastic draft advert offering tests for clients 'in any part of England, Scotland or Wales' was quashed by Dowson who pointed out that Shaw might spend weeks away from the laboratory, if he was on country-wide call.[42] By December 1903 additional arrangements were made with Dr Edward Bousfield, Bacteriologist for Camberwell, and a regular correspondent with the company, to assist with the diagnostic work.[43] By then there was sufficient work to warrant an extra pair of hands although Snow Hill staff had originally been cynical of Bousfield's advice and suggestions for new sera, believing that he wanted the WPRL to do work for which he would accumulate glory and royalties.[44] Wellcome insisted that Dowson should continue to do diagnostic work and ensure that his assistants got relevant training and experience – it was important that the expertise remained firmly within the WPRL.[45] In appointing Bousfield, Wellcome yet again stressed his view that the laboratories were independent, 'Please note that all communications to do with the WPRL are dealt with in my name and not that of my firm, as the laboratories are distinct from the company.'[46] Although this seems to have been clear only to Wellcome, he continued, throughout his life, to proclaim that his research laboratories were 'independent' and run on 'high-minded scientific principles', but it is far from clear what he meant.[47] In a period that valued 'amateurs and gentlemen' was this a safe-guard in the face of prejudice against commercialism? Was it a genuine conviction that laboratories with their own 'Directors' were somehow separate from the man and company that created and paid for them? Whatever Wellcome's complicated views, it is quite clear that the WPRL, the WCRL and later the WBSR, were to all intents and purposes part of the Wellcome empire.

The diagnostic service was offered by the company for many years and became a routine function of the WPRL. Representatives were reminded from time to time to push the fact that BW&Co., 'have arranged with the Wellcome Physiological Research Laboratories for the testing of diphtheria cultures for virulence'. By the 1920s these were no longer throat swab tests for the presence or absence of the diphtheria bacillus, but more sophisticated bacteriological assays to identify patients, carriers and contacts who had already tested positive for the organism. By 1923 the cost of such a test was 10s. 6d., payable to the company, which was advertised as 'distributing agents for the laboratories'.[48] All users of the service were also provided with price lists of sera and other medications, and usually offered a discount.

Serum production before the First World War

Whilst Wellcome's application for registration under the 1876 Cruelty to Animals Act was considered by the Home Office, serum production had continued and expanded at the WPRL. One American visitor favourably compared the laboratories' organisation and products with both those of Parke, Davis & Co. in Detroit, and Behrings at Marburg.[49] In 1900 Glenny, in charge of the serum producing activities, rationalised the existing random and grossly inefficient manner adopted for raising anti-sera, by devising a 'horse-card' for each animal on which the time and date of all injections and bleedings were recorded, as was its daily temperature as a guide to the infective process. This allowed full bleedings to be taken when the highest anti-toxic levels were achieved, and greatly increased the production of usable, saleable serum. It was rapidly adopted by other serum-raising organisations. Initially the cards were carried as if on a ward round in a hospital, but as the numbers of horses and the variety of types of sera increased, each

FIGURE 7.6
A.T. Glenny,
c. 1920s.

stable had its own duplicate set.[50] Glenny prided himself that the system allowed all the salient facts about any horse ever housed in the stables to be retrieved within 90 seconds. The model was replicated in, and adopted by, other departments, such as the testing and production laboratories; during the Second World War, Glenny controlled over 1500 horses used in sera production employing the same system.[51]

Serum production continued to have problems. Contamination still occurred, and the keeping properties of the serum were poor. Considerable research effort was put into perfecting a dried serum that would not deteriorate quickly, which was of considerable commercial importance when the company hoped to gain large export markets.[52] By early 1902, Dowson reported optimistic results. Samples of dried sera had been prepared and re-hydrated, which gave him confidence that the company would soon have a marketable commodity.[53] The dried serum had another important advantage – it allowed BW&Co. to utilise low strength serum that would otherwise have been discarded, because the resultant dried product could be made into a higher strength solution.[54] Developing new sera and new markets were increasingly important for BW&Co. The initial drive came directly from Wellcome, who sent reports and papers in the scientific press of new developments and competitors' products to his laboratory staff. Competition continued to increase at the beginning of 1902, the Lister Institute was rumoured to be investing a further £10,000 on new facilities at Elstree, and several town councils were setting up their own production laboratories. Despite this enthusiasm, serum therapy was not universally accepted.[55] There were problems with the quality and availability of reliable sera, and difficulties with storing the ampules were compounded by the awkwardness of administering the therapy at a time when giving any injection was an elaborate and rare procedure. An additional difficulty was 'serum sickness', an adverse reaction now known to be caused by anaphylaxis to foreign proteins in the serum. Added to these problems were those of misdiagnosis and inappropriate use of serotherapy, and it is not surprising that many doctors expressed caution or hostility to this troublesome new medicine. As early as 1901, BW&Co. proposed issuing a booklet written to push serum specially for practitioners, but Dowson cautioned against this as too blatant, suggesting that commercial travellers should be coached to introduce the subject naturally in their conversations with medical men, and to mention all successful treatments and case studies.[56] BW&Co. also encouraged medical men to undertake trials of their sera, with a view to subsequent publication, a subtle form of free and targeted advertising that seems not to have caused problems with the medical journals concerned.

An urgent project was to increase the strength of the anti-diphtheria serum whilst decreasing the volume that had to be injected. Diphtheria anti-toxins were measured in Ehrlich units, and by 1901 were issued in 5ml phials of 800 units. By December 1904, the WPRL confidently reported to the company that they could routinely produce 2,000 units in less than 3.0 mls, with a single treatment dose consisting of 1,000–2,000 units. This news was rapidly transmitted to the company's travellers, who made a special effort to promote the product to Medical Officers of Health. Just a month later Dowson urgently appealed for this to stop, as unexpected problems had arisen with its production at the WPRL. Immediately the home sales team was urged to push all other available strengths and volumes of sera.[57]

In his annual review to Wellcome in January 1905, Dowson confidently

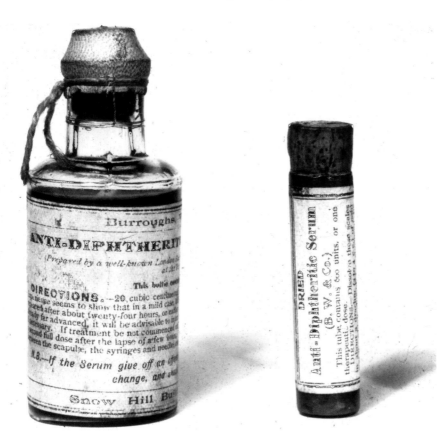

FIGURE 7.7
Vials of anti-diphtheria sera, *c.* 1900.

reported that the maximum production now possible from the laboratories was equivalent to 800–1200 phials of 2000 units each per 100 horses. There were a few problems, one of which was the variability of horses' responses to injected toxin. Might, Dowson wondered, it be worthwhile the laboratories breeding their own horses from good responding stock? Wellcome's annotation was 'Try it', although there are no records of attempts to establish such a stud. The cost in manpower and time, because young horses did not tolerate immunisation well which meant a delay of eight or nine years before a return on investment, might have persuaded Wellcome against such expansion. His immediate enthusiasm for such an expensive course is, however, noteworthy. Dowson also emphasised the importance of acquiring reliable toxins, upon which the whole process depended. Most of the source material used came from hospitals and it was vital that staff from the WPRL and the company maintained good relationships with relevant medical staff.[58]

As serotherapy began to be used in more closely defined circumstances and the quality improved, demand for anti-diphtheria and anti-streptococcus serum began to increase dramatically, and further experimental work on new products was anticipated. A number of issues for forward planning in the laboratories had to be addressed. Yet again the number of horses was increased and larger reserves of sera were built up. These had immediate implications: more stables, including isolation facilities, and exercise paddocks were required, as were specialised laboratory and storage space, and further rooms for packers and labellers.[59] In addition to securing a large proportion of the home market, BW&Co. was keen to promote and supply sera throughout the world, and the problem of preserving serum to be transported long distances had to be addressed. The Royal Army Medical Corps, as a major overseas user of sera shared BW&Co.'s concerns and in 1902 they collaborated on a series of experiments. Samples of BW&Co.'s anti-diphtheria sera were kept for more than a year in a military hospital in the UK, whilst others were put on ships travelling to and from India for either one or two voyages. All samples were then analysed by either the Lister Institute, the Conjoint laboratories, or the WPRL itself.[60] All proved that the serum kept well, which was of considerable importance to both users and BW&Co. By this time the Lister Institute (via Allen & Hanburys) was also supplying sera overseas, to colonies including Fiji, Honduras, Australia, and to Crown Agents around the world.[61] In 1906, the year after unsuccessfully trying to infiltrate the Canadian market (see below), the Lister Institute arranged to supply the Bombay Bacteriological Laboratory with sera, and to undertake some limited production in India in Kasauli. Such a move was never imitated by BW&Co., which retained all serum and vaccine production facilities within the WPRL and under its own control.[62]

At the end of 1904 BW&Co. pushed sera strongly at the Cape Town Industrial Exhibition, and in the following year made a concerted effort to capture the North American market.[63] This infuriated Allen & Hanburys, which was beginning to introduce the Lister Institute's sera into Canada in the face of much opposition from American companies.[64] American serum, whatever its source, was all the same price, and despite being more expensive than British imports, sold very well.[65] Lloyd Wood, the Managing Director of Allen & Hanburys in Canada, attributed the American manufacturers' success to their aggressive advertising and promotion tactics.[66] There was little understanding in North America, more familiar with pharmaceutical companies, of the work of the Lister Institute, and in this market it was no handicap for the WPRL to be recognized as part of a commercial enterprise.[67] Lister Institute staff believed that once their sera became better known, physicians would quickly learn that their sera were reliable and cheaper, and sales would subsequently improve.[68] By the end of January 1905, Allen & Hanburys in Toronto was confident that a demand could be created in Canada and the United States, and mailing and advertising campaigns to individual doctors and hospitals were optimistically begun.[69] A few months later, when BW&Co. entered the market, the situation changed drastically.

Allen & Hanburys' Canadian Manager complained bitterly that the BW&Co. representative was detailing Canadian physicians across the country in the style of American travellers.[70] BW&Co. was successfully selling cheaper anti-toxin than the Lister sera, 'consequently', he added, 'since their product has come into Canada we have not had any demand for ours'.[71] Cost was a particular problem. BW&Co. sold at lower prices and with larger discounts than Allen & Hanburys in Canada could afford, as its sera was supplied by Allen & Hanburys in London, who in turn had to buy from the Lister Institute, whereas BW&Co. employed no such agents or middlemen.[72] The lower prices, active campaigning and targeted detailing of BW&Co. meant that the company rapidly captured much of the Canadian market. Allen & Hanburys in London had two proposals: to re-negotiate a lower price with the Lister Institute to enable them to pass on savings to their Canadian partners; and to suggest that Lister staff ask BW&Co. to raise their prices in Canada and the United States. Dr Macfadyen of the Lister Institute undertook this uncomfortable duty, but not surprisingly Wellcome refused to increase BW&Co.'s prices.[73] By October 1905 Allen & Hanburys in London reluctantly decided that the only sensible way forward was for them to relinquish their agency for Lister Institute products in North America, and to advise the Lister Institute to employ Allan & Hanburys in Canada directly, thus eliminating all the attendant problems of the British company acting as intermediaries. In handing over the business, the British company offered important advice to their North American colleagues on how, as a commercial organisation, to deal with the medical establishment of the Lister Institute. The advice emphasises difficulties and problems that also faced BW&Co.,

> ... you are dealing with the elite of the medical profession in this country and with some important titled people, many of whom will have little sympathy with ordinary trade methods. You must be careful therefore in the tone you adopt and the nature of the suggestions you put before them for approval.[74]

The increasing importance also of the Australian market can be gauged by the company's response to a contamination problem in early 1906. When the Fairfield Park Hospital in Melbourne banned BW&Co.'s sera because of one faulty phial, the company immediately employed University of Melbourne scientists to test its products, shipped Australian sera back to the WPRL for examination, and launched a major publicity campaign to re-assure its Australian customers of the safety and efficacy of its goods.[75]

Development of new anti-sera

By the middle of 1900 the company was advertising five different varieties of serum (against diphtheria, streptococcus, tetanus, typhoid and venom, although these did not all appear in the regular price lists) and a range of diagnostic tests, for diphtheria, gonococcus, tuberculosis and typhoid.[76] These were all widely promoted. Advertisements in the medical and pharmaceutical press were serious and informative, providing scientific information to modern minded practitioners, rather than the more eye-catching material used for staple lines such as Kepler products. BW&Co. was not alone in pushing antitoxins strongly. By 1903 six firms in Britain were supplying sera and vaccines: Parke, Davis & Co.; the Royal Veterinary College; Allen & Hanburys; Meister, Lucius & Bruning and the Jenner Institute (formerly the BIPM) all doing so, in addition to BW&Co.[77] Allen & Hanburys spent about £250 on serum adverts in 1905, incorporating the additional strategy of sending samples to all registered practitioners.[78] BW&Co.'s travellers were trained to discuss

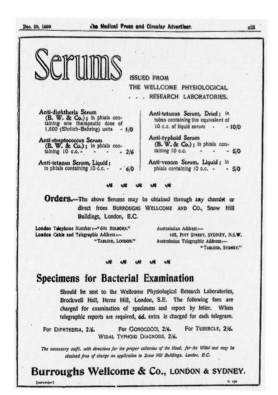

FIGURE 7.9
Girls packing
serum vials,
WPRL,
c. 1900.

serotherapy, based on regular circulars sent to medical men to remind them of the efficacy, and availability, of sera.

Initially, successful production of a new line of serum at the WPRL did not ensure continuing good results. At the beginning of 1905 there were a number of promising lines in development at the WPRL (see Table 7.1), although Dowson admitted to Wellcome that the anti-typhoid serum was 'still useless, in spite of many experiments and much expense'; that the anti-streptococcus puerperal fever serum was still not consistent after three years; and the anti-streptococcus polyvalent would probably remain an experimental line for many years.[79]

Table 7.1 *Horses at the WPRL, 1905*

No. of horses	Anti-serum	purpose
40	Diphtheria	production
10	Streptococcus	production
4	Puerperal	experimental
3	Venom	production
2	Diphtheria mixed	production
1	Staphylococcus	experimental
1	Colon	experimental
1	Typhoid	experimental
1	Thyroid	experimental
1	Normal	production

In 1906 Dowson resigned unexpectedly because of problems exporting serum to the United States. The considerable success of BW&Co. sera in Canada had encouraged the company to sell in the US, where all

imported material had to be licensed by the US Public Health Service. The American authorities banned the importation of Wellcome sera because of bacterial contamination, even though the isolated organism was non-pathogenic. In a scenario reminiscent of Bokenham's problems ten years earlier after the *Lancet*'s investigation of deficient anti-diphtheria serum, Dowson queried their findings. Wellcome referred the matter to external investigators and when they confirmed contamination, Dowson resigned.[80] His successor, Henry Dale had worked completely in experimental physiology and pharmacology at the WPRL, and had had no contact with, or knowledge of, the serum-producing side of the laboratories' activities. He had to learn rapidly. The immediate issue facing him was to deal with the problem that had precipitated Dowson's departure. He ordered all existing serum processing and packaging rooms to be moved from Brockwell Hall into a specially constructed building fitted with a one-way ventilation system supplying sterile air. Within a few months the problems were resolved, and BW&Co. serum was allowed back into the United States.

Suggestions for new sera products were often made to the company or its representatives directly by practitioners, and all were passed to the WPRL for evaluation. Such was the expectation and optimism of anti-toxins as 'wonder drugs' that therapeutic sera were proposed for numerous conditions, including cancer. Some suggestions were made directly to Wellcome by people who would lay what Dale cynically called 'the train of flattering enticement'.[81] Occasionally bespoke sera were manufactured at the specific request of a medical practitioner, and then if successful, modified for regular production. No charge was made for such experimental serum, although all recipients were expected to report to the WPRL and encouraged to publish their work in the medical press, as a form of payment.[82] Production figures from shortly before and during the First World War indicate that over 200 litres of experimental sera were produced although none was converted into commercial production. Some experiments were also undertaken to produce types of sera already available from competitors.[83]

In the years before the First World War an increasing number of new sera products appeared commercially: against dysentery, endocarditis, gonococcus, tetanus and several anti-streptococcal preparations against rheumatic fever, scarlatina and a polyvalent serum.[84] 'Wellcome' Brand Sera and Vaccines prepared at the WPRL 'under the immediate supervision of a skilled staff of highly qualified experts', covered four pages of the Company's 1913 Price List.[85] They included not only the diphtheria anti-toxins with which the laboratories originated, but also 16 other anti-toxic sera and 17 vaccines against diseases such as cholera, influenza, and typhoid. All sera and vaccines issued by the company were produced only by the WPRL, and although they would pass on orders to other companies for anti-sera they did not manufacture themselves, BW&Co. refused to act as agents for other manufacturers.[86] In contrast, Allen & Hanburys, whilst acting principally as the distributors of the Lister Institute's biological products, also marketed others' sera, and in 1908 for example, were advertising six products, including anthrax and thyroid anti-sera, from continental laboratories, such as Sclavo, Merck and Calmette.[87] BW&Co.'s insistence on issuing only its own sera may well have been a handicap in penetrating foreign markets, but it ensured the company's total control over production.[88]

Vaccines

Like many serum producers, BW&Co. investigated the production of vaccines. The practice of vaccination had been known for decades since the introduction of smallpox vaccination by Edward Jenner at the end of the eighteenth century, but it was Pasteur and others in the late nineteenth century who started scientific investigations into, and use of, vaccines against a number of infectious diseases. As early as 1884, on a trip to Geneva, Burroughs sent samples of an unknown vaccine to a sceptical Wellcome in London, who was 'strongly opposed to taking up vaccine matter of any manufacturer'.[89] Although this might indicate an early reluctance to act as an agency, BW&Co. was then distributing other manufacturers' goods, and in 1894 had been eager to act for the BIPM in such a capacity. In Britain, Almroth Wright, first at Netley, and later at St Mary's Hospital, London, spearheaded vaccine therapy as a treatment for acute infections, work later denounced as a 'lamentable project'.[90] Wright, like many of his colleagues, had an ambivalent attitude towards BW&Co. For example, in 1901, a request to BW&Co. for anti-typhoid vaccine was passed straight to Wright. He refused outright to deal with the company as that would introduce a 'commercial element' into the matter.[91] Wright's definition of commerce clearly underwent modification, because his Inoculation Department at St Mary's was supported for many years by the profits of its vaccines and sera that were marketed by Parke, Davis & Co.; one historian calculated that this arrangement paid for all the routine and capital expenditure, staff salaries and maintenance expenses for 38 years.[92] Despite this, Wright's Department, like the Lister Institute that benefited economically from Allen & Hanburys, was always regarded as 'academic' by government authorities when it came to co-operation in national research schemes such as Foot and Mouth Disease or Tuberculosis work (see Chapter 11), unlike the WPRL which were constantly denigrated as 'commercial'.

BW&Co. was producing some vaccines by 1910, as were Allen & Hanburys (marketing the Lister Institute's products), W. Martindale (Wimpole Vaccines), the Roborat Company, Parke, Davis & Co. (marketing those from the Inoculation Department, St Mary's Hospital), and the CRA; all offered products for both therapy and prophylaxis.[93] Vaccines were, however, a minor part of a sales list and research effort dominated by anti-toxin serum production.

Veterinary research and products

During the first decade of the twentieth century, the WPRL's increasing experience with serum production encouraged the raising of anti-toxins against specific veterinary diseases. As early as 1898, the company had developed a limited range of Tabloid Hypodermics for veterinary use.[94] The 1901 price list included 16 specialised veterinary products, many made especially for the Army Veterinary Department.[95] At the same time, the company was alerted to the problems and economic impact of infectious avian diseases, and investigated the possibility of using the anti-diphtheria serum as a treatment for bird roup.[96] Although initially successful, tests of the serum on infected birds were not continued.[97] A specialised veterinary department at the WPRL was created just before the First World War, and from the 1920s, the laboratories developed an extensive programme of veterinary research, including the successful development of prophylactics against a number of fatal livestock diseases that were of considerable economic significance.

The increasing success of sera for human use encouraged further veterinary experiments. The first specific veterinary 'biological' to be marketed was an anti-tetanus serum in 1912, a further six were added to the company's portfolio the following year. A range of diagnostic products including tuberculin and mallein was also developed specifically for veterinarians, which other companies, including Allen & Hanburys (on behalf of the BIPM, later the Lister Institute) also supplied.[98]

As the First World War approached, serum production by the WPRL was well-organised and commercially successful. It included an extensive range of well known and trusted products for human and veterinary use supported by an active research programme investigating new sera and improving existing lines. Sera were actively pushed by BW&Co.'s representatives at home and overseas, and some military contracts had already been fulfilled. The laboratories and the company were well situated to fulfil the enormous demand for serum and vaccine therapy that was about to be created by wartime demands.

CHAPTER EIGHT

In search of overseas markets; agencies, depots, branches, and multinational enterprise

Problems and policies

The establishment and growth of overseas trade had been one of the partners' objectives from the beginning; Burroughs was especially enthusiastic to secure export sales. Between 1880 and 1883, the partners invested more than £2,200 in developing trade with Europe (equivalent to roughly 2 per cent of gross sales) but the extent and complexity of tariffs and regulations undermined their attempt.[1] Burroughs' worldwide tour between October 1881 and February 1884 was part of this campaign, during which he promoted the company's goods in more than twenty towns in India and in Ceylon, in the major towns in Australasia, in Italy, Spain, Portugal, Gibraltar, Greece, Turkey, Malta, Egypt, China, and Japan.[2] The problems he encountered fall into two broad categories: political and cultural, characteristic of those presented in Continental Europe, to which in Asia and the Far East were added distance, transport, and climate.

Undoubtedly Burroughs shaped the foundation of the company's enduring presence in so many countries, especially in the colonies. However, Wellcome did not regard his contribution an unmitigated success. From the outset, the approach adopted by Burroughs was the cause of mutual recrimination. In addition to their differing attitudes to long versus short-term credit (a difference settled in Wellcome's favour who insisted on short-term credit in 1882), two other points of disagreement were connected to the appointment of agents and relationships with them.[3] Wellcome acknowledged Burroughs' success in securing orders; however, he was especially critical of his partner's propensity to appoint agents and travellers without inquiring into their experience and consulting him.[4] His own acquaintance with trading in tropical countries led Wellcome to believe that, as a rule, agents neglected business; they consumed finance, and when they went bankrupt did not pay for stock.[5] With some justification,[6] he was also concerned that some of the agreements to which Burroughs had committed the company would result in complications in its relations with other suppliers and wholesalers.[7]

Despite the shortcomings to which Wellcome drew attention, Burroughs was responsible for constructing the network of agencies and depots overseas which remained until his death in 1895. Some of those recruited were individuals acting mostly as independent salesmen who contracted to handle the goods of a single company. Some agencies consisted of wholesalers, though several substantial retail chemists were also appointed as agents in return for undertaking to add BW&Co's goods to an existing range of products supplied by other producers. Some of these traders, either at the invitation of the partners or after application by an indigenous trading enterprise, evolved into depots. Indeed, the differences between 'agency' and 'depot' (and between 'depot' and 'special depot') cannot be strictly defined, just as it is not always possible to distinguish between a 'depot' and a 'branch'. The terms used are not always consistent, partly because the precise nature of contractual relationships depended upon particular local market environments and partly because each change in status was the outcome of secret negotiations between company and trader, contractual arrangements being confidential between the two parties. Normally a depot signified the holding of substantial stocks of goods that the agent undertook to advertise and promote in return for special discounts. A branch was a depot holding stocks exclusively of the company's products and possessing the option of taking orders directly from local retailers rather than indirectly from London. More advanced branch status involved the preparation of products supplied from London before sale; the most advanced status included local manufacture.

Trading in Europe

Burroughs first visited Continental Europe in 1878, after the French authorities had refused to allow drug imports of Wyeth's drugs he sought to introduce.[8] A representative for BW&Co. resident in France was appointed in 1883 and the company's sales literature translated into French in preparation for stocking Robert & Cie, a pharmacy in Paris.[9] However, continuing trade restrictions led to the abandonment of this venture, as unprofitable and unpromising, in 1885.[10] Through the efforts of another French retail chemist, in 1891 BW&Co. succeeded in securing the list of selected products permitted to enter under the tariff; but the values attached to the goods were set so high that the duties payable were virtually prohibitive. Efforts to secure revision through the relevant Ministry failed and the market remained closed.[11]

German, Spanish, and Italian ventures proved to be no less problematical with respect to profitability. In 1897, within a year of the appointment of

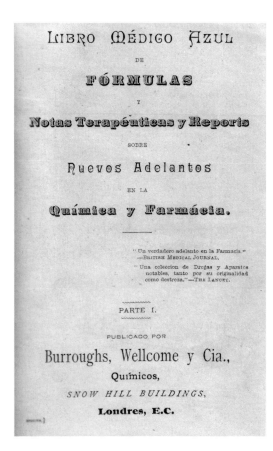

LIBRO MÉDIGO AZUL

DE

FÓRMULAS

Y

Notas Terapéuticas y Reports

SOBRE

Nuevos Adelantos

EN LA

Química y Farmácia.

"Un verdadero adelanto en la Farmacia."
—BRITISH MEDICAL JOURNAL.

"Una coleccion de Drogas y Aparatos
notables, tanto por su originalidad
como destreza."—THE LANCET.

PARTE I.

PUBLICADO POR

Burroughs, Wellcome y Cia.,

Químicos,

SNOW HILL BUILDINGS,

Londres, E.C.

FIGURE 8.1
Title page
of Spanish
translation
of BW&Co's
formulary,
therapeutic
notes and
medical
recommenda-
tions, 1884.

Linkenheil & Co. of Berlin as an agent, the Medical Council of the Duchy of Brunswick issued a decree, one effect of which was to outlaw the sale of BW&Co's goods hitherto sold by the local chemist who ran the depot in Brunswick. The decree was published in the German trade journals, arousing Wellcome's concern that other states or duchies might issue similar decrees (Hamburg and Schleswig Holstein were mentioned).[12] Detecting commercial protectionism, Wellcome proceeded to mobilise eminent medical men in Germany (whose enthusiastic support was forthcoming) and some in England known to be highly respected by German doctors to challenge the charges that Tabloids contained impure drugs and incorrect dosages. The situation deteriorated in December 1898 when the German government banned all 'compressed compound medicines prepared in factories, the dosage of which chemists cannot examine and therefore cannot guarantee.' It was decreed that such preparations were in every instance to be prepared by chemists upon medical prescription.[13] A year later, a new decree issued by the Kingdom of Prussia seems to have allowed imports of some compressed medicines, though the picture was unclear even to Wellcome and his advisers.[14]

No such problems existed in Spain. Grounds for optimism with respect to sales and profitability were confirmed by a series of reports initiated by a Medical Commission and based on tests carried out on Kepler Malt Extract by the Royal Academies of Medicine in 1884; it concluded that the product was invaluable, one of the best preparations of its kind and to be thoroughly recommended to all Spanish doctors.[15] However, exploiting this endorsement was checked by a serious cholera outbreak in 1885 when the company's resident representative in Spain returned to England. In 1885 the accumulated loss recorded on the Spanish business was £4,000 on sales of £3,000.[16]

An agency agreement in Italy negotiated by Burroughs in 1894 was concluded despite Wellcome's concern that control and management would be problematic and that Milan, rather than Genoa, where the negotiations for an agency arrangement began initially with de Giovanni, would be a preferable base from which to penetrate the Italian market.[17] In

1896 an agreement was reached with Raffo Dalmazzo, and Dompe & Co., a self-styled Anglo-American agency in which Dompe was agent for BW&Co. in Genoa; Dalmazzo was sub-agent in Milan.[18] Relations with Dompe disintegrated when he became the subject of legal proceedings for substitution affecting the compressed medicines of Wyeth and of BW&Co.[19] A subsequent agency agreement included a partnership between Dalmazzo and Signor Giongo, President of the Italian National and International Pharmaceutical Society. This, too, proved unsatisfactory. Records of travellers in 1901 revealed only four visits daily to chemists and no visits at all to doctors. Giongo was accused of spending too much of his time on his association commitments to the detriment of the business, his incentive to promote the company's interests having been blunted after inheriting a legacy; he was also distrusted.[20] When the agency went into liquidation in 1905 it was not possible to discover whether the financial balance was in the red or the black. Wellcome proceeded to open a depot in Milan. The Austrian market was supplied by Kris, an agent based in Vienna who held stocks and pushed the company's goods in return for a favourable (confidential) discount. From 1899 Kris employed a representative to introduce the company's goods into Romania and Hungary.[21] By 1906 wholesalers also designated as special depots were located in Amsterdam, Barcelona, Berlin, Brussels, Copenhagen, Geneva, Zurich, Lisbon, Nice, Paris, and Stockholm.[22]

FIGURE 8.2
Front cover of Russian price list, 1909 (from private collection).

Expansion beyond Europe

Though geographically more distant, in the long term overseas markets outside Europe, especially those within the British Empire, proved to be more receptive to the company's efforts to develop an export trade. These presented different kinds of problems to those encountered in Continental Europe, as Burroughs discovered on his travels: the effects of shipping and climate on the condition of goods on arrival (particularly of heat and humidity in the tropical areas within the Empire), and on their shelf lives.

Burroughs was also impressed by the implications of cultural factors for the potential to develop a trade in pharmaceuticals. Although the size of the population of India was large, Burroughs reckoned the numbers of potential consumers of the company's products was small because:

> the majority of the natives ... send for a native doctor or priest when sick for incantations and administration of bugs, reptiles, and native roots enough to frighten or kill any but the natives who have got used to such things.[23]

Affordability also presented a problem among an impoverished population. The potential market for drugs was limited to the European populations, of whom Burroughs reckoned nine-tenths were government employees or missionaries. The medical civil service and the British Indian Army, including the hospitals associated with them, were supplied through medical storekeepers. Through this channel to the civil and military markets, the government in India sent large quantities of drugs. Burroughs described the government as the world's largest wholesaler. Free hospitals and dispensaries in almost every town tended to undermine the local dispensing trade because medicine was free for civil servants and the military. Burroughs' target was formal recognition of the company's products by the Indian government. He wrote 'We would hardly need any more business if the

FIGURE 8.3
Pages of
Russian
price list,
advertising
different types
of medicine
cases, 1909
(from private
collection).

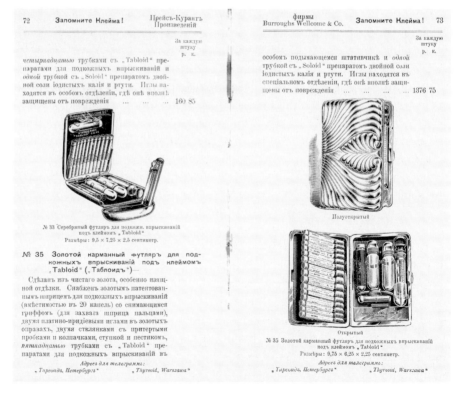

Indian Medical Department would take them up'.[24] Having learned that the government usually purchased whatever the doctors ordered from the medical store, Burroughs visited all doctors on the army and navy register. This iniative marked the beginning of a flourishing trade which in 1901 was perceived from the London office to offer an 'almost unlimited possibility of business'.[25] Demand was for Kepler goods, Beef & Iron Wine, Tabloids, and Fellows' Syrup Hypophosphites.[26] The Bombay depot became a branch in 1912.

Burroughs had also expressed scepticism with regard to the market potential in the Far East during the early 1880s:

> China is no good; no educated doctors, no medical schools, plenty of quacks, much prejudice against foreign medicine. Japan is very uncertain. Much depends on the whim of the council (Nimsho) who have the power to provide the stamp of approval or otherwise to permit medicines to be sold. Few English-speaking doctors, therefore a problem. In Batavia, the Dutch are a lot of lazy Europeans.[27]

Not until 1905 did the company appoint a permanent traveller located in Shanghai where an advertising campaign concentrated on Kepler goods.[28] The Shanghai depot became a branch in 1908. Special depots had been established in Cairo, Alexandria, Port Said, Calcutta, Mexico City, and Pernambuco.[29]

Increasingly, BW&Co.'s renewed efforts to expand exports following Burroughs' death were directed towards Europe and countries where substantial British and European populations lived. Responsibility for leading this policy was George E. Pearson who was to play a major role in managing the company during the twentieth century. He was born in Bradford in 1868, educated at Bradford Grammar School, and served an apprenticeship in a Northallerton pharmacy. This was followed by employment at the counter of John Bell & Co., a leading London pharmacy which he left in 1885 to join BW&Co. as a traveller covering the London West End territory. The export campaign that he led in 1897 marked the introduction of metricated products for Europe. After visits to South Africa in 1899 and Australia in 1901, he was appointed Head of a new Foreign and Colonial Department.[30] When the Boer War ended, Pearson produced a report on the prospects for a peacetime demand. He predicted a boom, a view shared by Weld, head of the Sales Department in London, who also supported Pearson's recommendation that the depot should be replaced by a branch. Referring to the company's experience in Australia, Pearson drew attention to the transport and communication difficulties that had produced delays in meeting orders. It was only after a well-stocked branch was opened that sampling with the support of visiting travellers achieved success. Pearson's optimism rested partly on the interest stimulated among doctors and retailers by the firm's

FIGURE 8.4
Line drawing
of BW&Co.'s
office, Cape
Town, South
Africa, c. 1911.

products, but it was also encouraged, he thought, by the local perception of BW&Co. as a 'white firm, perfectly honourable and fair-dealing'. He also predicted that after the war there would be an influx of Europeans who would enlarge the market for the firm's products.[31] Pearson's assessment was based on the assumption that such a population would be a proportionately larger consumer of drugs than it would have been had it remained in Europe, enjoying the advantages of superior sanitation and a temperate climate. His view was that the advantage of a branch over a depot was the elimination of the company's dependence on indigenous wholesalers. In South Africa most of these wholesalers, regardless of inducements, showed a marked reluctance to hold an adequate range of BW&Co.'s stock, giving priority to their own goods which they sold through tied retailers. A branch could supply orders direct both to other wholesalers and retailers (a distinguishing difference between a branch and a depot). A branch also facilitated the introduction of new products. Another advantage was greater control from London through delegation directly to local managers recruited by head office (a lesson learned in Italy). Such an arrangement also facilitated action against substitution and encouraged direct negotiation for business with mining and exploration companies, government, and the army.[32]

Initially, Wellcome was reluctant to follow Pearson's advice, probably because of the costs of such a policy (estimated to exceed that of opening the Melbourne branch) and of the difficulty Pearson predicted in recruiting effective staff, particularly at managerial level.[33] An emergency depot was opened in Cape Town in 1902 under the management of one of the company's former travellers. Thereafter, letters from London sometimes referred to 'our Cape Town branch'. That there was a contradictory policy regarding the South African business is clear from London's declared preference for large wholesalers to order direct from London. This inevitably limited the sales potential of the Cape Town office that was nonetheless required to maintain high stock levels to meet any sudden demand. However, the decision not to raise Cape Town prices (already 13.5 per cent higher than London prices) for 1902, when the London List was revised upwards by 12.5 per cent, was a discouragement to direct ordering.[34] Competition began to intensify after the Boer war as newly established local wholesalers challenged the major established firms. Compressed goods consigned in bulk to local firms paid a lower duty than Tabloids which were imported in bulk for putting up, then issued under a brand name as proprietary goods. As in the past in dealing with Somerset House, the London office had difficulty in explaining to the Cape government the difference between patent and proprietary medicines.[35]

The prospects for increasing the sale of Beef & Iron Wine, however, suffered a setback because of an amendment to the tariff in 1906 which introduced a new maximum proof spirit content fixed at 20 per cent. The proof spirit content in the company's product at that time was 32.4 per cent. In the hope of circumventing the regulation, no percentage figure at all was shown on the label; a statement of the total *quantity* contained avoided the declaration of either an excessive percentage or a false one.[36]

Table 8.1 *BW&Co., home and overseas sales, 1881–1914 (£)*

Year ending August	Home sales	Home and foreign sales from London	Foreign sales from London	Sales from overseas branches and depots	Aggregate sales
1881		17,811			
1882		33,158			
1883		57,165			
1884					
1885		52,184			
1886		55,724			
1887		72,147			
1888		81,846			
1889		99,339			
. . .					
1899		175,701		13,356	189,057
1900		187,282		13,733	201,015
1901		204,690		17,869	222,559
1902		211,616		20,985	232,601
1903		220,439		21,774	242,213
1904		233,000		n/a	
1905	218,625	290,336	71,711	n/a	
1906	221,320	310,025	88,705	59,882	369,907
1907	225,524	320,758	95,234	81,636	402,394
1908	227,365	321,381	94,016	96,034	417,410
1909	233,104	347,863	114,761	117,890	465,754
1910	233,276	360,996	127,721	147,550	508,546
1911	244,428	388,462	144,034	187,294	575,756
1912	250,694	409,660	158,967	224,286	630,715
1913	258,345	424,967	166,625	254,791	681,849
1914	277,633	454,836	177,203	286,347	740,710

Rhodes James, *Henry Wellcome*, p. 141; WFA, Acc. 82/1, sales and profits; WFA, Acc. 96/45, sales book 2, 1905–44. Discrepancies in figures for aggregate sales may be explained by adjustments for returns.

Sales levels achieved during and immediately after the Boer War were not repeated until 1913. Sales of £25,000 in 1902/03 fell back to £20,000 in 1903/04; even at these levels, however, losses were recorded of £291 and £1,518.[37] A continuous series of sales beginning in 1905/06 shows a substantially lower turnover following local management problems. After a prolonged period of general trade depression in the Cape beginning in 1902, a turnover of £11,689 in 1905/06 rose to £19,863 by 1910/11 and reached a pre-war peak of £26,450 in 1912/13. The figures above may be compared with Australian sales of £42,127 in 1905/06 and £102,753 in 1912/13. A breakdown of South African sales shows general goods (mainly Tabloids, Kepler goods, Hazeline, and Beef & Iron Wine) accounting for the overwhelming proportion of sales in the South African market. From less than 1 per cent in 1905/06, by 1908/09, Wellcome Brand Chemical products, the next largest category, had reached 13.7 per cent. By 1912/13 the figure was 12.3 per cent of a sales figure almost double that of 1908/09. Serum, the next largest, accounted for 3.4 per cent in 1908/09 rising to 8.8 per cent by 1912/13. Lanoline and Fairchild goods remained at insignificant levels.[38] Insufficient evidence has survived to continue the history of the depot, until then staffed by only two people, beyond this period.

The Australasian market; the first overseas branch

The most promising of all potential markets for BW&Co.'s products visited by Burroughs in 1883 were those in Australasia, where the numbers of chemists and druggists was rising rapidly during the late nineteenth century.[39] His reports also convinced Wellcome that Australasia offered a large growth potential.[40] Agency agreements were entered into with wholesalers in Melbourne, Sydney, Brisbane, and Christchurch. Elsewhere, leading chemists and druggists were appointed as agents for the company's products, primarily Kepler oil and malt extract, Beef and Iron Wine, and Hazeline.[41] Bearing samples and advertising blotters, and supported by a heavy advertising campaign in the Australasian medical and trade press,[42] Burroughs visited doctors and chemists. The *Australian Chemist & Druggist* carried editorial commentary praising the modernity of the business and its products.[43] A resident representative to co-ordinate activity was appointed in Melbourne in 1883 to such good effect that the company's first branch was opened in 1886. When Shepperson, a successful salesman in England who was appointed manager, returned to London in 1889, he described the business as 'going very steadily' but that continued success required a close understanding of the markets in Australasia.[44] In the late nineteenth century, 70 per cent of all prescriptions in Australia consisted of liquid preparations, a consequence of increasing use of tinctures. Pills accounted for only 9 per cent,[45] therefore representing a challenge to the sale of

Tabloids introduced into the market in 1884.[46] Shepperson's successor was J.C. Langley, an Australian wholesale pharmacist, who during an enduring trade recession when the Melbourne branch sustained losses, was blamed for overstocking.[47]

Following a review of the branch conducted by Weld, head of the Sales Department sent from London in 1896, he recommended the termination of Langley's contract and the relocation of the business to Sydney.[48] In 1898 Alec B. Hector, formerly a Scottish pharmacist who became a traveller for BW&Co.,[49] was sent to manage the Sydney branch at a time when the optimism expressed by Burroughs and Wellcome in the mid-1880s began to be revised as local economic conditions deteriorated. Haines' history of pharmacy in New South Wales claims that one effect of the 1890s depression was that people turned to chemists instead of consulting doctors as a cheaper alternative source of health advice.[50] This is consistent with London's perception of the Australian market, which was that 'self medication is rife'.[51]

Evidence suggests that after a review of marketing policy in 1902 circulars were distributed to chemists showing the name of the chemist, which it was believed, 'in a mild way' might appeal directly to the self-medicating public.[52] Items appropriate for self-medication figured largely in BW&Co. price lists at that time: sal volatile, saccharine, toilet lanoline, digitalis, quinine, bicarbonate of soda, Compound Menthol Snuff, Tea Tabloids, and such tonics and laxatives as Forced March and the Livingstone Rouser, a compound consisting of julap, rhubarb, and quinine, labelled as 'tonic, cathartic and antimalarial.'[53]

A serious setback to the branch operations occurred in 1901 when the Commonwealth Parliament introduced a tariff, the effect of which was a 25 per cent *ad valorem* duty applied to Tabloids and Soloids, 20 per cent on Toilet Lanoline, and 15 per cent on Hazeline; sera entered free. Following Pearson's review of the situation while he was in Australia for a year temporarily replacing Hector (who was ill in London)[54] it was decided to manufacture Tabloids locally and also Kepler goods and Beef & Iron Wine.[55] The production of saccharine as Saxin was another priority, as was the re-bottling of Hazeline Cream and Snow, delivered directly from Fairchild in New York to Sydney.[56] Within a year, the company acquired the lease of Waterloo Mills, a former paper mill.[57] In order to enable the company to pack goods in bond to meet inter-state orders, which as a consequence of the new legislation became subject to different levels of duty, the company also acquired premises to be used as a bonded warehouse in the charge of a private customs officer.[58]

The criteria for choosing which products to manufacture in Sydney were: the level of demand; the least difficulties in manufacture and packing; and the potential for scale economies from volume production more than offsetting the higher costs resulting from duties, freight costs and dock dues.[59] Inter-state customs presented further problems, not least because of their complexity.[60] The lowest duty which BW&Co.'s products imported into Australia paid was 15 per cent. When sending goods from Sydney to other states outside New South Wales they were invoiced at the price in force in Sydney prior to the introduction of the Commonwealth tariff. In the case of those goods issued in Australia, the company recovered the duty paid by forwarding them under inter-state certificates showing the amount of duty paid upon the original imported value. Customers were then sent a debit note for the amount of duty actually shown on the certificate to have been paid by the company. In that way the company avoided paying the duty on the higher net value at which the goods were invoiced to the customer by the company. This presented a problem in issuing the price list for Australia. If only New South Wales prices were quoted (10 per cent higher than the London price list), customers outside New South Wales would believe that a general price increase of 10 per cent had taken place and that in future goods would be invoiced to them at those rather than the prevailing London prices.[61] Exactly how this problem was resolved remains unclear, but separate price lists for Australia and for New Zealand were being issued by 1907.[62] During the early years, the most successful staple lines sold in Australasia were Kepler and Hazeline products, Beef & Iron Wine, Tabloid cascara, and Lanoline, none of which caused problems arising from inter-state orders because no private bond arrangements were necessary.[63]

Under detailed instructions from London, before Pearson left Sydney in May 1902, he briefed Hector on how he should manage the branch. This involved criticisms of past practice and an outline of future policy. Secrecy was central: 'No exception is to be made to the rule that no one is to be shown over our works in Sydney', the methods of ensuring this to be secured by implementing the rules for the Dartford factory. Except for 'very trusted members of staff', workers in one department were prohibited from visiting another, the work in each to be secret from other departments. 'Restriction as to non-admittance of outsiders applies not only to members of trade and profession but to anyone, whether adversaries, neutrals or friends, no matter of what position or profession'.[64] All formula books were to be kept under lock and key and accessible only to the branch manager and his deputy.[65] (An instruction issued from Dartford in 1903 later emphasised the vital importance of securing the Sydney Formulary Books in a small strong safe rather than a japanned iron box).[66]

The problems associated with the commencement of production were acknowledged at the outset. Wellcome's managers warned him that the project would '... need vast amount of detail thought out ... will need to decide what machines can be spared and also the men, which is more difficult'.[67] A. T. Hill, Works Manager at Dartford, was put in control of the operation becoming responsible for ordering machinery and its dispatch to Sydney. He was instructed that 'none of the essential and private features of our compressing machines shall be divulged or discovered by others'.[68] As was the practice in Dartford, the work was to be divided 'in such a manner to absolutely prevent anything like a clue being obtained by the various firms'.[69] Five skilled men employed at Dartford were selected for short-term contracts to staff the new manufacturing facility under Hector's management. James French was sent from the compressing department to work with Hector and Hill. Other office and factory workers were to be recruited locally as were salesmen.[70]

Drugs for manufacturing purposes were shipped in the form of granules in as pure a form as possible. As they consisted mostly of vegetable matter, they travelled well. In the case of granules containing chemicals such as phenacetin, sulphenol, and antipyrin, that was not the case, consequently pure drugs were shipped to Sydney. Because shipping companies regarded acetone, chloroform, and potassium chlorate as dangerous, the policy was to find local sources. Three other problems affecting local manufacturing policy were the untested effects of tropical heat on shipments, the loss associated with the use of re-granulated materials in the process of production, and the higher labour costs incurred through re-working of spoiled product.[71]

The production of Tabloids commenced shortly after Hector's return in May 1902 when he became responsible for implementing the transfer of the systematic, highly controlled process of manufacturing and putting up to meet Dartford's standards. These were conveyed to him in a series of instructions already in place at Dartford. The objectives were the same: accuracy in formulae and manufacture, purity in content, cleanliness and safety in preparation and processing. To this was added a system of control and a transparent system of multiple checking, recording, and initialling to ensure identification of each single item in every batch of every product line and of the person responsible for it.[72] Employees were subject to strict control, both by Hector and by London managers. Regular reports on staff were compiled by Hector, his comments and recommendations regarding wages and salaries subsequently conveyed to London for decision.

Other managerial problems relating to London's concern over capital expenditure and local factors affecting production were considerable, notably those affecting KME, Hazeline, and Beef & Iron Wine that dominated sales. Heavy expenditure on constructing a malt tower far exceeded the anticipated costs discussed in London with Hector.[73] Once in production, however, the unsatisfactory quality of local barley supplies contributed to a failure to meet Dartford's manufacturing standards.[74] Production cost was inflated because the price of barley was one-third higher than English prices, though this was assumed to be abnormal and due to drought.[75] Once the plant was in operation, labour productivity in brewing malt was half that at Dartford, while additional costs rendered Kepler goods manufactured in Sydney barely profitable.[76] London was also critical of the high cost of unmechanised production of Hazeline Cream, asking for particulars of production costs before beginning, and subsequently criticising the presence of dust particles, unsatisfactory labelling, and badly pasted tubes.[77] Hazeline Snow costs were badly affected by the cost of shipping bottles and pots from London that incurred heavy freight costs and import duties. For this reason, local sources, notably the Melbourne Glass Bottle Company, were explored, though the quality of their products were not initially considered to be satisfactory.[78]

Because of higher costs resulting from local manufacture, Hector was instructed to raise prices in New South Wales by 10 per cent, though Kepler and Hazeline which faced a more competitive market were excluded.[79] London insisted that Sydney should be able to compete with Elliotts, a wholesaler in Sydney which had been offering hospitals malt and cod liver oil in large tins at 1s. 6d. per pound; that a cost level that allowed competition at 1s. 3d. for KME, a fair profit margin, should be possible and would enable larger sales and output yielding further cost reduction and higher profitability.[80] A further problem arose from the difference between local tastes and those of consumers in England. Preference for a lighter, thinner extract than KME had already been established by the American company selling Maltine, which required variation of the BW&Co. formula introduced initially in New Zealand.[81] Beef & Iron Wine in Australia was initially made with Madeira, replaced by sherry. It was only after reversing the view that Australian wine was 'unfit'and by reducing the iron content that consumers became more receptive.[82]

The financial consequences of such problems were cumulative losses recorded in Sydney's accounts. Annual turnover between 1900 to 1902 was £25,590.[83] Annual average losses between 1897 and 1902 were recorded of £1,190, amounting in total to £7,137.[84] Once again, Hector was told: 'further expenditure must be rigorously kept down ... at Sydney where for a time at any rate we can look for no immediate return upon the money we have sunk there.'[85] These figures are extremely misleading, however, for the losses did not refer to actual losses of the Sydney enterprise but losses incurred on the basis of charging Sydney with products manufactured in London 'at certain fixed rates'.[86] These bore no relationship to the prices charged to Sydney's customers; prices were determined in London in relation to London prices. Hector was told: 'The Sydney Works are merely to be looked upon as in competition with London, and they are in no case to be credited with a lesser sum than that which London is prepared to invoice at Kent Street [Sydney] plus freight and duty'.[87] In other words, Sydney was actually treated as a large customer, rather than as a branch, to whom London granted special terms yet at a discount (list prices less 20 per cent and 20 per cent rather than the manufacturing cost of the goods landed to the ship's side in London) that enabled London to take a share of the profits that might otherwise have been attributed to Sydney. Furthermore, the Sydney sales figures included neither Fairchild's digestive ferments, including pepsin and Pepule brand products, nor lanoline imported from Germany. Profits resulting from orders from Australian wholesalers supplied direct from London are also excluded from profit attributed to Sydney, though these particular omissions were rectified from 1902/03. It is impossible, therefore, to gain an accurate measure of Sydney's financial performance in this period. The picture becomes clearer following the reforms to the Australian business initiated in London and implemented in 1904, from which time the success of the Sydney branch in terms of sales began to add substantially to the income stream in London.

The growth in sales thereafter, which outran those of other overseas depots and branches by an increasingly wide margin, was the outcome of greater control over costs and of the quality of local inputs, and the adoption of London's approach to defence of the company's brands in 1903/04.[88] Evidence on the activities of the Sydney branch end in 1906; however, sales and profit figures are available between 1905/06 and 1907/08. These show

FIGURE 8.5
BW&Co.'s
exhibition
rooms in
Montreal.

the 'losses' of the earlier period until 1904/05 turn into rising profits on increasing sales in successive years.[89] The ratios of profits to sales were 14 per cent in 1905/06, 15 per cent in 1906/07, and 18 per cent in 1907/08. It is not possible to attribute this turnaround entirely to the revised accounting procedures introduced. Sharply rising sales, to which the introduction of serum and Wellcome Brand Chemicals into the product range contributed little though caused considerable trouble, were fundamental to the profits trend. The composition of sales in Australia changed little. Throughout the period between 1905/06 and 1913/14, 'General Goods' accounted for roughly 70 per cent of sales. These consisted of Kepler Malt Extract, Tabloids, and Hazeline products. Wellcome Brand Chemicals comprised the second largest, though still small, product category. Sales rose from less than 10 per cent of Sydney's sales in 1905/06 to nearly 20 per cent in 1913/14. Serum accounted for barely 5 per cent throughout this period. 'General Goods' continued to dominate sales between the wars, fluctuating between 77 and 82 per cent. Wellcome Brand Chemicals also remained between the 15 to 20 percent levels. Other than sales data, beginning in 1906, virtually no evidence of the history of the Sydney business after 1906 (which until that time rests entirely on Wellcome's correspondence) has survived.[90]

Table 8.2 *BW&Co. sales by origin, 1906–1914 (£000)*

	London	Sydney	South Africa	Milan	Montreal	New York	Shanghai	Buenos Aires	Sales: overseas depots and branches
1906	310.0	42.1	11.7	6.1					59.9
1907	320.8	52.0	13.0	8.5	4.4	3.7			81.6
1908	321.4	55.1	14.0	10.2	8.3	8.5			96.0
1909	347.9	60.4	14.6	13.2	13.3	12.2	4.2		117.9
1910	361.0	70.6	16.8	15.8	18.7	16.9	8.8		147.6
1911	388.5	84.4	19.9	17.0	26.6	25.1	12.4	1.8	187.3
1912	409.7	92.8	23.6	18.3	33.9	34.8	12.7	5.0	221.1
1913	425.0	102.8	26.5	20.4	36.7	44.8	17.6	6.2	256.9
1914	454.4	111.5	25.8	23.3	38.0	55.7	21.9	5.6	286.3

WFA, Acc. 96/45, BW&Co. sales book 2.

The annual sales recorded in 1905/06, £42,127, amounted to nearly four times the volume sold by the company's next largest branch in South Africa. The Australian figure doubled in five years to £84,436, and by 1913/14 had risen to £111,509 representing 15 per cent of the total sales of BW&Co. and its branches. This was twice the level of sales from the Montreal and New York branches established in 1906. Table 8.2 shows the erosion of Australia's lead, culminating during the First World War with the reversal of the relative importance compared with the North American branches.[91]

Initiatives in North America

Little evidence has survived of the history of the Canadian branch which, when it opened as a depot in Montreal in October 1906, preceded the formation of its American counterpart by two months. With a typical sense of timing, two months before opening the branch, Wellcome arranged for a display of the full line of BW&Co.'s products intended for introduction into the Canadian market to coincide with the British Medical Association's meeting in Toronto.[92] The person appointed to spearhead the first sales offensive was D. L. Kirkpatrick, a pharmacist formerly working in a Belfast dispensary, who was recruited to be a traveller in 1902. After working the Irish market briefly, he was sent to Ontario.[93] In 1904 Kirkpatrick received an application to become an assistant representative from Thomas Nevin, another young Irishman who at that time was employed by Nicholl & Co., Belfast chemists. Without consulting head office, Kirkpatrick took Nevin on, though when the appointment was discovered London withheld confirmation until references and satisfactory reports on his progress during a probationary period could be submitted.[94] Six weeks later Kirkpatrick dismissed Nevin, again without consulting London and once more contrary to procedure. Kirkpatrick was given the option of retrieving the position but London made it clear that, subject to satisfactory references from outside the firm, Nevin would be welcome in London to attend the required coaching in the duties he would undertake as a new representative.[95] The references received in London from four doctors in Ireland and England and from a firm in Toronto, evidently contained affirmative responses to the request from head office regarding the candidate's 'reliance, integrity, irreproachable honour', whether he was 'scrupulously and rigidly conscientious', and whether he was a person in whom the firm could place 'the most implicit trust.'[96] Kirkpatrick's dismissal was set aside. Furthermore, within months of returning to Toronto, Kirkpatrick was sent to Philadelphia to introduce goods there and Nevin assumed command of the Canadian branch.[97] Evidently impressed by Nevin while on his training visit to London in 1904, a prescient Wellcome expressed his personal conviction that 'If Nevin works

PRICE LIST OF

FINE PRODUCTS

❦ U.S.A. Edition ❦

1904-5

Burroughs Wellcome
and Co., London, Eng.,
Sydney and Cape Town

The 'Wellcome' Chemical Works and Laboratories, Dartford, near London, England

5

with enthusiasm and vigour and British pluck he will capture the region'.[98] Seven years later he was to manage the New York branch. On Nevin's recommendation, his own replacement as the second traveller in Canada was J. S. Lang from Toronto. After a slow beginning, within four years sales in Canada exceeded those in South Africa, when for the last time they were also to exceed those of the American branch: Canadian sales in 1910 reached £26,621 compared with £25,079 of American sales. The future, however, lay with the American branch. By 1913/14 sales in Canada were valued at £37,969, compared with £55,678 in the US.

Origins and development of the New York branch

Until the American branch opened in New York in December 1906, the products of BW&Co. had been sold through Fairchild Brothers, the Philadelphia-based manufacturer of digestive ferment preparations for which, since 1885, BW&Co. had been the sole agent in Britain, Continental Europe, and the British Empire. As the American firm began to concentrate increasingly on enzyme products, the brothers felt unable to devote sufficient time to the promotion of the products of BW&Co.[99] Another factor leading to the setting up of a branch may have been the Tabloid trademark infringements in the US. These led to preparations for legal action, in which the London office relied heavily on the advice and active support of Sam Fairchild. In 1904 Wellcome's attention was drawn to advertisements for Dr Conway's Bust Tabloids. It was difficult to believe that they were more than a parody of BW&Co.'s claims for Tabloids to meet every possible need: 'Enlarge your bust ladies, 4 to 10 inches ... at trifling cost'. Fairchild arranged for a private enquiry agent to research the owners, managers, financial standing, and reputation of the Conway Specific Company and of Conway's determination to fight.[100] Threat of legal action ended Conway's advertisements.[101] Neither this nor other efforts to spoil the market deterred Wellcome.[102] In preparation for an 'unusually important' campaign to expand trade in the US, in 1904 Wellcome engaged Martin K. Kallman of St Louis Missouri on a temporary basis for the purpose of advising how the company's interests in the US might be advanced.[103] His review produced a comprehensive report on compressed goods production in the US, on machinery used in production and packaging of all kinds, corking and capsuling, office machinery, systems of internal communication, card systems for keeping advertising accounts and for compiling and maintaining cost and employees' records. Kallman was also expected to arrange for Hill, works manager at Dartford, to visit Edison's laboratories, the Winchester Small Arms factory, the Arkansas brewery, and Pulman's model town.[104] Intended to apprise managers in England of best practice with respect to advanced business organisation and manufacturing systems in America, the report has not survived. Meanwhile, Kirkpatrick, formerly head of the Canadian depot, left his assignment in Philadelphia to begin his new role as leader of the sales campaign that began during the winter of 1905/06. When Kirkpatrick resigned in March for personal reasons: Wellcome advised his replacement, hitherto a traveller in Scotland, that when selling to Americans he should mention the American origins of BW&Co. and when to Germans (as he would in St Louis) he should mention the popularity of the company's goods among Germans.[105]

One priority set in London for the manager in New York was to push Kepler, especially Kepler Solution: '... there is a large field for it – already got a footing in the south. Kepler is vastly superior to any cod liver oil product they have in America'.[106] The solution was available with beef and iron, haemoglobin, iron and quinine extracts, pepsin, phosphorous, or cascara sagrada. The promotion of Tabloid products was equally important. An advertisement for Tabloid cascara sagrada ran: 'It has been remarked that constipation is the bane of modern civilisation'.[107] This product and sodium salicylate also spearheaded the company's assault from New York.[108] Another priority (much more difficult to achieve) was to keep the company's scientific products to the fore. Wellcome Brand Chemicals were limited to chloroform and quinine, priced keenly in order to compete with those supplied by Squibb and Merck. Both the introduction of Wellcome Brand Chemicals and sera brought BW&Co. into competition with Parke Davis in America. In 1898 Parke Davis employed one thousand people plus 126 travellers (compared with BW&Co.'s 721 plus fewer than 20 travellers) to sell the company's pills (for which the firm possessed a manufacturing capacity of more than six million daily), liquid extract of cascara (described as one of its famous lines), and sera.[109] Competing in the American market presented another problem because it was necessary to ensure that products placed on the market met the standards laid down in the US Food and Drugs Act of June 1906. From the beginning, the company's guarantee that 'all products are ... strictly in accordance with all the requirements of the Food and Drugs Act' was a feature in American advertising literature.[110]

Limited expansion of trading and manufacturing capacity during the early years was the outcome of careful preparation. This began in February 1907 when Thomas Henry Moore, the local manager who formerly managed the Cape Town branch, met a deputation representing New York jobbers and wholesalers, and the Proprietary Goods National Wholesale Druggists' Association to discuss the level of discounts that BW&Co. might offer. The outcome was 25 per cent and 15 per cent off retail list prices, though head office in London advised a further 5 per cent, conditional on an initial minimum purchase of $500. The same terms were offered to the company's depots regardless of whether the associations recognised them as jobbers.[111]

As in the company's other overseas offices, recruitment of reliable local staff presented difficulties. These were not eased by London's reluctance to lose travellers from Britain. Moore was advised to concentrate on recruiting 'energetic young Canadians possessing the kind of qualifications required … we are reliably informed that many large American firms prefer to have Canadians on their staff as they have been found to possess better ability and business qualities than the average American'.[112] Philadelphia was another recommended source of representatives, particularly among 'enterprising men from other states working their own way in life who have moved there to study pharmacy at the Philadelphia College and have taken temporary positions to pay their way through college … The greater number of them are set free in the Spring immediately after graduation … training added to the push and enterprise of enthusiastic western boys makes for success'.[113] The resemblance of this ideal type to Wellcome's own experience suggests that he might have been the author of this advice and of the initiative taken at the outset to warn travellers against the temptation to succumb to alcohol. Moore was sent 20 copies of a booklet entitled 'Alcohol. Its effects on the human system from the medical point of view' by Sir Frederick Treves, to be distributed to all members of staff. It was also suggested that Mr Merkley should be handed a copy personally, providing the opportunity for a few timely words of caution 'based on extended knowledge of his habits'. Merkley was one of two recently appointed representatives regarded as failures and ripe for dismissal.[114]

A three-year lease of 310–14 Hudson Street beginning on 30 December 1907 offered a convenient location for boat dock facilities and freight terminals. Wellcome appointed Pearson to assume day-to-day responsibility for the American business from London through the local manager, T. H. Moore was assisted by Gibb from the London office in setting up and organising the new enterprise.[115] Central control from the branch office was planned to supersede management of distribution from Montreal. The plan was to establish wholesaling, jobbing, and retailing firms to be designated as depots for the company's products. In the spring of 1910, the office staff moved up-town to a more prestigious location at West 33rd Street, near Fifth Avenue,[116] and an additional five-year lease was acquired on larger premises situated at 340–42 Hudson Street.[117]

Close and critical auditing in London of the trading accounts drawn up by the New York staff was the subject of detailed scrutiny and annual commentary presented for the attention of Pearson and Wellcome. These reports conveyed frustration and at times disbelief at the incompetence of those responsible for presenting the accounts in New York. After auditing the first annual balance struck in 1908, G. Leslie Moore, the firm's senior accountant in London, described the stock sheets as disgraceful and the accounts unreliable. On arrival in New York, a luckless yet highly regarded bookkeeper recruited from the Montreal office found the books to be badly in arrears. Unable to call on sufficient staff to catch up, his desperate solution led to his dismissal for 'cooking a trial balance'.[118] In addition to methods of presentation, Moore was critical of the payment of excessive expense claims made by travellers and expressed incredulity at the manager's defensive response; this was to the effect that as the expense sheets supplied from London had included columns for 'gratuities and entertainment', the average representative had believed these to be legitimate expenses and had claimed accordingly. The sheets supplied were discovered to be outdated, the offending columns having already been deleted in the replacement sheets issued in London.[119]

The persistent criticisms levelled at management by the London accountant may have contributed to the manager's decision to resign in 1911 and to return to England with his family.[120] Reviewing the progress of all the company's foreign and colonial houses from their foundation until 1910, the London accountant praised the efforts of staff to carry out instructions issued from London and to 'attend carefully to all our requirements'. New York, however, was excluded from this benign judgement, the office staff was criticised as inefficient and showing a lack of adequate control. This was attributed to an uncooperative attitude: '... the local atmosphere is one if not of hostility to the Head Office's instructions, then of barely restrained resentment at London's requirements.'[121] He complained that the chief bookkeeper ignored the importance of detail and failed to organise and control his clerks. Accusing the manager of complacency, the London accountant suggested that:

> ... the manager of the New York House would do better to look upon the auditors as allies and make it clear to them that he regards them as such, and that he will willingly adopt any useful hints they can give him ... We are still very largely in a state of ignorance so far as the profit earning capacity of the New Works is concerned ... Figures relating to costs and stocks are not such as to instil confidence because of mistakes in pricing, mistakes in calculations and in every possible direction.

Pearson was urged to instigate a 'searching investigation' to be conducted by the local manager into the American business's entire accounts.[122]

Nevin succeeded T. H. Moore as the New York manager in 1911, but he too was criticised by the London accountant two years later in a report which described the New York House appearing '... to aim at giving us the barest minimum of information that will satisfy us instead of giving us all that is available'.[123] Speculating that perhaps the omission was explained by the absence of more information (reprehensible in itself) and therefore not reportable, Moore concluded that the lesson that accounts were vital to efficient management had still not been learned. Wellcome's marginal comment instructed Pearson to write to Nevin requesting that immediate attention should be given to Moore's critique.[124] By 1914 arrangements had been made to have the accounts audited in the US before being submitted to Moore and Pearson in London. While Moore considered this change to have improved the quality of the presentation of the accounts, he considered it to fall short of the standards reached by the Sydney office.[125]

Moore's negative view of the financial management of the American business did not end with the accounts. It was symptomatic of a fundamental philosophy hostile to the transformation of the company's overseas trading enterprises into local manufacturing businesses. He articulated this philosophy in 1909, after the introduction of American tariffs affecting BW&Co. triggered a review of activities. Hitherto, production in New York had been limited to putting up goods imported from London. The tariff raised the question whether in future, manufacture would be more economic. Moore opposed a policy of establishing local manufacture because of the increased costs due to the duplication of plant, higher labour costs resulting from higher wages, difficulties in recruiting experienced labour, greater costs incurred by Dartford because of the diversion of production to local factories, and the additional costs incurred in England in supplying raw materials, information, and supporting activity. He concluded: '... the tendency must always be for local works to be at best ineffective producers of profit and possibly producers of loss.'[126]

The precedent for a transition to local manufacture, which attracted Moore's disapproval as a general policy, had been set in Australia in 1900, before Moore joined the company. At that time, the introduction of post Federation duties of 16.5 per cent on Tabloids and 27.5 per cent on Hazeline Snow appear to have tipped the balance in favour of local production. In terms of sales and profits (and in the presentation of accounts), by 1906, the Sydney House was regarded as a success. Comparative tariffs prevailing in the US were 25 per cent on Tabloid products (the rate for medicinal products), 40 per cent on Kepler goods, and 50 per cent on Hazeline Snow. However, the cost of raw materials and labour were higher in the US than in Australia, complicating comparative transaction costs. Moore specified the conditions that he regarded as necessary to justify manufacture: products were subject to a high rate of duty; products could be manufactured locally in high volume and find a demand; sales could yield high profit margins. The volume sales/profit ratio applied favourably to Tabloids, but Moore regarded the duty rate on imports as sufficiently low to offset any advantage of local manufacture compared with imports from London. With respect to Hazeline and Kepler goods, however, his criteria were met to a degree and provided financial justification for local manufacture.[127] This began in 1907/08.

While Nevin favoured local manufacture and Moore did not, both agreed that the key to profit was the scale of output of the firm's specialities (branded goods). Moore continued to be pessimistic concerning the prospects for the New York business. Nevin's optimism, based on his managerial experience, capacity, and energy, underlay his vision of the American business as a major manufacturing competitor in the American market. In retrospect, Nevin described the machinery installed for manufacturing when he joined the company in 1911 to have been unsatisfactory, continually causing problems until it was replaced. Despite this, Nevin remained confident that an expansion of sales, primarily of Tabloids, Kepler, and Hazeline products, was possible and would lay the foundation for a successful profit-making business.[128] His predecessor's record had been to increase sales from £8,785 in 1908 to £24,312 in 1911. Nevin built upon this expansion by increasing the number of sales representatives employed from roughly a half dozen in 1910 to 37 in 1912, equivalent to a ratio of roughly one for every £1,000 sales.[129]

FIGURE 8.7 Illustration emphasising the use of 'Tabloid' at both the North Pole and 'as near the South Pole as man has gone', from BW&Co. *A Brief History of Missionary Enterprise*, a booklet prepared for the World Missionary Conference, Edinburgh, 1910.

Before 1914, the American enterprise was primarily a marketing organisation; roughly one-third of the 103 employees (excluding office staff) were sales representatives, the others employed in putting up and packing products shipped from London.[130] The reminiscences of Henry C. Rasmusen, a pharmacist who joined the business in 1904 as a detail man described his activities. He was trained for a month by a chemist and an 'advertising man', before he set off from his base in Dallas to begin his three monthly cycle of visits to doctors and pharmacists. Later, he recalled that the alligator bag he carried contained Kepler Malt Extract, Tabloid Forced March 'for hunger, physical and mental well-being, and fatigue', a mixed gland product, and the Tabloid photographic outfit. After working Dallas for a month, typically his tour continued for a week each in Fort Worth and Waco, a month in Houston, three days each in Galveston, Hot Springs, and a week in Little Rock, Arkansas, before returning to Dallas.[131]

Expenditure on travellers' salaries and expenses increased by 20 per cent and advertising by 16 per cent between 1912 and 1914. Sales more than doubled to £52,316 (comparable with Sydney's record).[132] The enlarged sales volumes consisted almost entirely of 'General Goods' (as distinct from Wellcome

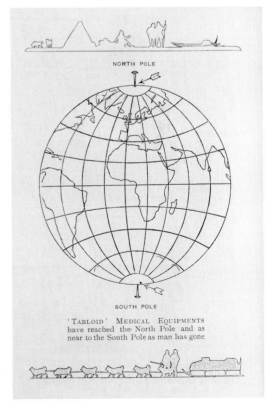

NORTH POLE

SOUTH POLE

'TABLOID' MEDICAL EQUIPMENTS have reached the North Pole and as near to the South Pole as man has gone

Brand Chemicals and Sera). Between 1911 and 1914, they consisted of Kepler and Hazeline products and Tabloids, which together comprised 98 per cent of the total (though disaggregation is impossible).

The American branch on the eve of the First World War

By the time the war began, roughly one half of sales from the New York house consisted of goods manufactured by the branch; London supplied roughly 28 per cent, the remainder supplied from American sources.[133] Two-thirds of raw materials were supplied from London because costs were lower than those in the US.[134] In response to Moore's comment on the 1913 accounts noting a falling *rate* of sales expansion, Wellcome's marginal note was: 'I am not discouraged in the least but we must spur on the manager'.[135] When Moore proposed that Kepler prices should be raised in order to bring the rate of profit on sales to a similar level to that achieved in Sydney, Wellcome remarked that prices for the American market were already very high and that it would be desirable to lower them if possible. This suggests that Wellcome was concerned with establishing a larger sales and output base in the short to medium term regardless of profitability, the strategy favoured by Nevin with whom Wellcome was developing a supportive relationship in spite of Moore's persistent critiques. Moore, however, continued to put profitability before sales expansion, even though it was acknowledged that at the level of current sales the two were incompatible. He was critical of the rising expenditure on advertising, travellers' salaries, and travel and accommodation expenses which he calculated at between two-thirds to one-half as large as total manufacturing costs. He also drew attention to the additional costs borne by London because of cash remittances to New York of £14,000 in 1910/11, £9,000 in 1911/12, and £5,000 in 1912/13, a falling but still a substantial, financial drain (see Table 8.3).

FIGURE 8.8
Cover of
*Tabloid
First Aid for
the Mother
Out Back*,
a booklet
prepared for
'the Mothers
of the Empire
who toiled
bravely in
the loneliness
and solitudes
of the Back
o'Beyond',
BW&Co.,
1924.

Table 8.3 *The New York branch; sales, investment, and profit*
1907–1918

Year ending	Sales ($)	Capital ($)	Trading profit (loss) ($)	Trading profit (loss) (£)
1907 (6 mths)	33,654	66,953	(2,271)	(528)
1908	42,755	105,045	(52,079)	(12,702)
1909	62,955	118,721	(88,759)	(19,724)
1910	79,807	139,451	(116,337)	(25,290)
1911	118,327	151,712	(150,766)	(32,775)
1912	162,258	160,450	(160,612)	(34,138)
1913	211,836	168,353	(149,341)	(32,465)
1914	254,624	171,660	(152,890)	(44,968)
1915	331,529	181,627	(97,232)	(19,843)
1916	331222	259,778	(31,516)	(6,565)
1917	421,296	286,844	(72,322)	(15,067)
1918	479,410	382,668	(15,573)	(3,244)

GWHC, coll. 107, 'Brief analysis', a paper presented by W. N. Creasy, President of BW&Co. (USA) Inc., to a Wellcome Foundation Board Meeting, London, 6 Jan. 1959.

Moore's view was that a major explanation for the trading losses incurred year by year by the New York House (in effect, the sales department of the American business) was excessive marketing costs. When substantial 'losses' were recorded in 1912, Nevin was instructed that he must cable London each time a remittance was needed in order to moderate marketing expenditure. This had some effect.[136] After buying goods based on the London list price less 20 per cent plus 20 per cent (equivalent to a full wholesale price), to which freight costs and duty were added, the New York House was unable to sell them at a price to cover cost. The New York Works (in effect, the production department of the business), on the other hand, was allowed to record the value of output manufactured there as the equivalent landed cost of goods shipped from London (the same amount that London would have invoiced the goods to the New York House). Selling its output to the New York House at London list price less 20 per cent, plus 20 per cent, plus freight and duty from London placed the New York Works on a level playing field as a seller. As long as it was able to cover more than the costs of freight and duty by achieving lower local manufacturing costs, profits were possible.[137] In effect, therefore, London treated the New York House as little more than a wholesaler, crediting the revenue difference between production cost and wholesale price as profit. It is hardly surprising that profits proved impossible to achieve, even though an increasingly protectionist American policy, culminating in a consolidating tariff in 1909 resulting in a 30 per cent addition to the cost of products imported into the New York branch from London.[138] The consequent alteration of transaction costs changed the balance of advantage in favour of local manufacture, especially under the prevailing pricing policy for the New York business dictated by the London office. Nevin's attempt to remove the discriminating effects of that policy in 1914 elicited a classic statement from Pearson that revealed his perception of the role of the New York business. Nevin told Pearson: '... we cannot accept your decision ... without explaining further why, in our opinion, you are in error'. Pearson replied: 'I am afraid ... you have allowed your zeal to outrun your discretion', reiterating that control over management decisions lay with England. 'Such discretionary powers given to staff in charge of overseas houses are <u>always</u> subject to any amendment, modification, or alteration the firm may think fit'.[139]

Details of capital expenditure other than its volume have not survived. The initial capital investment of $66,953 during the first six months of 1907 and $105,045 in the first full year in 1907/08 rose gradually to $171,660 in 1914. Net profit was equal to trading profit (no dividends were paid), and during the period under consideration all investment transfers were directed from London to New York. Together, the sales and production activities of the New York business recorded mounting losses in every year, a trend that only began to reverse during the First World War. By that time, the numbers employed had reached 66 plus 39 sales representatives in addition to office staff.[140]

Nevin received no encouragement from Moore's annual reports containing a sustained attack on the American business as a misguided investment doomed never to be profitable. Moore justified this position by introducing to his annual commentary on the current balance sheets and profit and loss accounts a figure for opportunity cost, i.e. the revenue which the London business would have generated had the investment in the US branch been invested in securities. The formula consisted of *accumulated* losses to which he applied a 5 per cent imputed notional interest that could be assumed to have accrued to London had the amount lost been invested in the US (see Table 8.4). For example, in 1914, he recorded the total accumulated profit since the formation of the business as a loss of £225,687 on distribution plus a profit of £37,988 from the works, giving a net accumulated loss of £187,699. He estimated the gross profit made by London on shipments to New York at roughly 25 per cent of the value of the shipments (£18,462) which, when deducted from the overall loss figure, produced a deficit of £169,237. 'This amount may be said to represent the amount sunk for the goodwill of the existing USA business and represents an annual charge upon the profits of that House when they begin to accrue of £8,462, this representing 5 per cent upon net losses to date'.[141] He calculated the cost of selling goods (per £1 value) during the previous five years to have been £1 3s. 4d., though the trend was downward and had fallen to 17s. 8d. for 1913/14. 'The above figures, if they represent an attempt to do a profitable business in the US are not encouraging.' Sales were rising, though not at an increasing rate; 'It is easy to see that unless the rate of increase is very largely increased there is no prospect of converting the USA business, while run on present lines, into a profitable undertaking'.[142] However, there was no comment on the continuing practice whereby goods and raw materials had to be purchased from London at the same prices at which they were exported (hitherto through Fairchild) *directly* from London – to ensure a level playing field. The same formula (including the imposition of a cost equivalent to the high American customs duties) was applied to purchases by the New York House from the New York Works which, as a result, did make profits. The New York House was simply unable to sell such goods at prices that would cover selling costs, prices which Wellcome considered too high.[143] Moore concluded: '... it is difficult to find any indication whatever that the New York business can be placed upon a profitable basis. There may be of course, conditions of which I know nothing which entirely justify the continuance of the present policy, but the fact remains that a very large sum has already been expended in the building up of the business and it appears likely that a further large sum will be required in the immediate future to maintain the business.'[144] Wellcome made no comment on Moore's calculations, merely noting in the margin the figure for actual average annual losses shown in the balance sheets as £25,026.

Table 8.4 *BW&Co. New York Branch, 1908–14: investment, sales, and profit/loss (£)*

Year ending	Capital invested	Sales	Profit/loss
1908	21,583	8,785	−10,700
1909	24,393	12,935	−18,237
1910	28,652	16,398	−23,903
1911	37,172	24,312	−30,977
1912	32,967	33,338	−33,000
1913	34,591	43,525	−30,684
1914	35,270	52,316	−31,414

GWHC., coll 107, Public affairs, 'Brief analysis'.

The evident disagreement between Moore (pressing the case at least to review the financial logic of continuing to invest in the American business), supported by Pearson on one hand, and the optimistic Wellcome and Nevin was the subject of a highly illuminating letter written later by Wellcome in 1927 in which he explained his earlier policy towards overseas branches. A large volume of sales was necessary as a basis for volume production and low costs in the home market:

In pioneering new territories I adopted the same principle by expending freely but with deliberately considered methods of effectual propaganda for a term of years – and at a loss when necessary – until we established a favourable reputation and created a volume of business that covered expenses and finally yielded substantial profit ... We did not attempt to capture the whole Universe at one stroke, but selected one field at a time for thorough treatment, until we had won secure footing and substantial returns ... In each case we continued our propaganda in regions already covered, and used funds from the income derived from the already successfully developed countries for cultivating the new and untilled field.[145]

In the special case of the American branch, he attributed the delay in the commencement of manufacturing to mismanagement of the business, which implies criticism of Thomas Moore and the staff he employed, though he was not referred to by name:

> When we took over the consignment stock of the firm's products from our American agents and organised our own establishment in New York, for a time we were unfortunate in being represented by men who were inexperienced in the customs, methods and usages of the medical profession and trade in America. Furthermore, these men held narrow and prejudiced views which lessened their influence and usefulness.[146]

Yet this begs the question regarding the locus of responsibility for the pricing policy of the American branch. It seems surprising that Wellcome, who was familiar with the American market, appears not to have been involved in the formulation of the policy from the outset, even though he may have delegated the detailed implementation to Moore. After he returned to London, it also seems unlikely that Nevin, his successor as manager who was already acquainted with North American practices from his spell as representative in Canada and the US, would have committed such a blunder. It is conceivable that the responsibility for establishing the company's financial system involving overseas activities was given to Moore, or that Pearson as general manager, to whom Moore was responsible, either supported or merely accepted the perverse pricing policy put in place. In a thinly veiled criticism of Moore, Wellcome noted:

> In all business undertakings it is a sound principle and always an essential practice for the sake of security, to keep under close observation and continuous check the question of profit and loss as well as the account of sales, expenses, taxes, etc. <u>However, an accountant's view that immediate profits are the all-essential points for consideration in promoting the development and best interests of the business, may not prove to be the most practical policy in building up a successful business, especially in pioneer fields</u> ... Under-experienced and more efficient management of the American business, better selected and trained staff and representatives, together with moderated prices for the products, improved methods of propaganda and finally by the estab-

lishment of works for manufacturing in New York, the firm's business has now for a considerable period been developed into a healthy and prosperous condition and is continuing to make steady progress.[147]

The First World War was the *deus ex machina* which precipitated this transformation.

PART TWO

1914–1940

The impact of war: innovation and transformation from laboratory research to factory production

The suspension of German trade marks and the drive for synthetic substitute drugs

The onset of war led to an immediate government ban on the export of fine chemicals, notably alcohol, alkaloids and bismuth compounds, and bromides. While Britain was not dependent on Germany for the supply of any natural substances, she was dependent on German imports of numerous commonly used drugs and fine chemicals.[1] When war began, therefore, fine chemicals from Germany were unobtainable. For a time, BW&Co. continued to import some drugs from European countries outside Germany, packing and selling them under the Wellcome Brand.[2] Prices rose rapidly due to initial speculation, particularly affecting bromides, salicylates, and potassium salts. The NHI commissioners reported a sixfold increase in the price of bromides during the war.[3] Simultaneously, a newly appointed government Advisory Committee on Drug Supply, composed of representatives of the Pharmaceutical Society and civil servants, began to monitor the situation. Where necessary, the committee suggested methods of alleviating shortages, either by tapping new sources of supply or the use of substitutes.[4] In the case of more complex drugs the manufacture of substitutes required detailed knowledge of the structure of known products in order to replicate or to incorporate some aspect of design into other products already in the process of development.

Patent protection of German medicines presented a further problem. Both the exploitation of an established research capability to develop drugs and a suspension of German trade marks were important factors explaining the history of BW&Co. during the war. It was, however, sexual behaviour rather than armed conflict that presented BW&Co. with the most important opportunity, for venereal disease and syphillis could be treated successfully only with Salvarsan in 1914, after the first major therapeutic agent had been developed by Ehrlich in 1909, protected by and manufactured under licence by Hoechst since 1910. Venereal disease had long been associated with war; the First World War was to prove no exception. The 1916 Royal Commission report suggested that one in five of the armed forces was afflicted.[5] Once imported stocks of Salvarsan ran out and hostilities prevented further imports, the only available alternative was the less effective anti-gonococcus serum. BW&Co.'s annual production tripled, reaching 65 litres in 1915.

The danger of the spread of syphilis increased as action to prevent an outbreak was delayed. In September 1914, Wellcome seized the initiative and applied to the Commissioner for the suspension of three patents protecting Salvarsan and Neosalvarsan, and for permission for his laboratories to develop a substitute drug. Applications by manufacturers for a suspension of trade marks were initially refused by the Commissioner for the Suspension of Trade Marks. His concern was that as long as German manufacturers continued to hold significant stocks of the drugs in question the predicted short duration of the war posed the prospect of commercial anarchy should trade marks be suspended. Wellcome persisted. At the hearing to consider the submission, Jowett expressed confidence in the chemical and physiological testing capacity of the laboratories to replicate the highly toxic drug, stressing that a small quantity for experimental purposes had already been prepared. His confidence was based on Frank Pyman's work on arsenic derivatives at Dartford which had already resulted in Soamin as an anti-syphilitic agent.[6] His work had attracted prescient comment:

> ... the great bulk of chemical research in this country [compared with Germany] is of an academic nature [and] it rarely happens that the outcomes of it are directly applied industrially ... The arylarsonates [Pyman's compounds] are an instance of a valuable product educed in a British laboratory of that kind, and are notable in this regard.[7]

When the Commissioner raised the question of price and the level of royalty that might be acceptable, Pearson declared that the company was even prepared to risk losing money in the public interest. Pearson offered to accept the conditions laid down by the Board of Trade, but entered the caveat that should several firms be granted licences it might not be worthwhile for any single applicant to proceed to manufacture.[8] Even though the Commissioner referred to BW&Co. as one of Britain's best-known manufacturer of drugs and chemicals, he was not prepared to sanction monopoly. Responsibility for co-ordinating the process by which a few selected companies should be set the task of developing a substitute was passed to the MRC, to which Henry Dale had been appointed as head of the Department of Biochemistry and Pharmacology of a new Central Research

Institute. He was familiar with the company's well-equipped research facilities, its reputation for quality control, and its proven record of research and production in the field of organic arsenicals. Given Jowett's intimation to the Commissioner that the company had already experimented successfully with a substitute preparation, it is not surprising that BW&Co. quickly established a monopolistic advantage. War broke out in August 1914. After a 'laborious investigation', Kharsivan, the company's substitute for Salvarsan, was reported to the Board of Trade in September by which time Power had informed Balfour that all research had stopped and the entire staff of the WCRL directed to 'investigations of such special problems as have been suggested by the Ministry of Works'.[9] The directions for making Salvarsan were fairly complete in the patent specifications. The challenge to Wellcome scientists was to devise techniques that would produce a uniform product corresponding in chemical composition and biological properties. Neosalvarsan was more difficult to produce as the patent specifications were less adequate and the relationship between the chemical formula and therapeutic efficacy unclear. In the light of such uncertainty, the MRC felt that the German practice of issuing Neosalvarsan untested could not be followed and must be toxicity-tested.[10] Early in 1915, the Board of Trade asked the MRC to supervise the biological testing of every batch of both Kharsivan and Neokharsivan to be offered for sale in Britain, work that was directed by Dale.[11] Staff at the WCRL and WPRL collaborated in the production and testing of all the products, many of which had toxicity problems.[12] In October, three independent senior scientists reported to Dale that Kharsivan was toxicologically and clinically 'practically equal to Salvarsan'.[13] The first issue received MRC approval in January 1915.[14] Although problems of toxicity continued to present difficulties for Wellcome scientists involved in production and testing,[15] both products were placed on the market as Kharsivan and Neokharsivan.[16] A rapidly expanding demand resulted in the construction of a new specially equipped building from which the first commercial batch was issued in January 1917.[17] Once Salvarsan substitutes became readily available, BW&Co.'s production of the anti-gonococcus serum dropped to less than 5 litres in the final years of the War.[18] The company also met the demand generated by the army's concerted hygiene campaigns to prevent VD, producing, *inter alia*, potassium permanganate and Calomel cream for large-scale disinfections and personal use.

The early success in producing the Salvarsan substitutes prompted Pearson to persuade the Commissioner to suspend the enemy trade marks protecting Aspirin and Utropine as an appropriate reward for the company's costly research in developing a British Salvarsan.[19] Neither drugs were difficult to produce (the former was already manufactured but necessarily sold as acetyl-salicylic acid). The manufacture of other synthetic substitutions of hitherto imported German chemicals followed: benzamine, emetine bismuthous

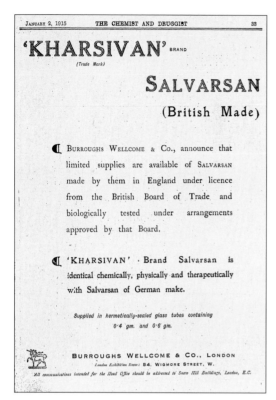

JANUARY 2, 1915   THE CHEMIST AND DRUGGIST   33

'KHARSIVAN' BRAND
(Trade Mark)

SALVARSAN

(British Made)

❡ BURROUGHS WELLCOME & Co., announce that
limited supplies are available of SALVARSAN
made by them in England under licence
from the British Board of Trade and
biologically tested under arrangements
approved by that Board.

❡ 'KHARSIVAN' · Brand Salvarsan is
identical chemically, physically and therapeutically
with Salvarsan of German make.

Supplied in hermetically-sealed glass tubes containing
0·4 gm. and 0·6 gm.

BURROUGHS WELLCOME & CO., LONDON
London Exhibition Room: 54, WIGMORE STREET, W.
All communications intended for the Head Office should be addressed to Snow Hill Buildings, London, E.C.

FIGURE 9.1
Advertisement for Kharsivan, BW&Co.'s replacement for Salvarsan (*Chemist & Druggist*, 2 January 1915).

iodide, flavine, glycerophosphates of calcium, magnesium and potassium, hydroqinone, lanoline, phenacetin, pyramidon, and salicylic acid. Quinine was in particular demand as the war extended into malarial regions; during 1916 alone over 21 tons (nearly 65 million doses) were issued. All, however, were in short supply and required for immediate military use. The official war record reported that 'the number of tablets of compressed drugs issued during the war amounted to 1,080 millions, in addition to a very large number of tubes of hypodermic and ophthalmic tablets'.[20] Undoubtedly, most were Tabloids.

Other German products replaced in manufacturing processes included several hundredweight of benzoyl chloride, large quantities of salol, lysidine and cholesterol, and a specialised immersion oil for microscopes. Not all were for use by BW&Co. which supplied other pharmacists and manufacturers. Boots alone was purchasing more than 80 products in 1914, including antipyrin, aspirin, phenacetin, and saccharine, all of which BW&Co. continued to manufacture throughout hostilities.[21] Products for widespread use in military and domestic hospitals included the powerful antiseptics chlorine and flavine, and the local anaesthetic cocaine was produced by a newly developed synthetic process for which a licence to manufacture at Dartford was obtained in 1917.[22] Responding to government requirements, scientists at the WCRL investigated chemical methods to remove poisons from water and research leading to the production of a soluble plug for submarine mines.[23]

The haemorrhage of knowledge and skills; the challenge from Jesse Boot

Whereas the shortage of skilled workers was a direct consequence of war demands, the most dramatic loss of personnel occurred as an indirect result of war. Before the War, Boots was primarily a multiple retailing enterprise, Britain's biggest company chemist which claimed to be 'the largest chemists in the world'.[24] In 1900 Jesse Boot's sales revenue, generated by his retail shops, amounted to £600,724, compared with £319,439 received from the sale of manufactured goods. Among these, 'pharmacy and patent medicines' accounted for roughly 75 per cent. Before the First World War, however, the items in this category resembled some of the proprietary preparations which had been sold by BW&Co. thirty years before: bicarbonate of soda lozenges, sulphur tablets, liquorice pellets, glycerine pastilles, cough emulsions, voice jujubes and foot powders.[25] Boots' retail sales approached £3 million in 1914 and exceeded £5 million in 1918. In accordance with Boot's strict secrecy policy, even towards his shareholders, there are no further data giving a breakdown between manufactured products, no information on sales, and no reliable financial record.[26] An analytical department set up in 1908 was limited to monitoring the quality of consignments of raw materials used in the manufacture of perfumery, soap, buying samples, and developing new toiletry products.[27] This policy of diversification

appears to explain why in 1911, a BW&Co. employee named J. A. Hogg became the first of the company's workers to be poached by Boot, in this case for the purpose of experimenting with the production of compressed bandages and surgical dressings that took place in an expanded analytical laboratory. Hogg also developed the first aromatic tube, a small friable glass ampoule containing smelling salts from which Boots later developed ampoules for amyl nitrate and iodine.[28]

When war began, Boot seized the opportunity created by the demand for pharmaceuticals. Within two years, possibly fifteen former employees of BW&Co. had been lured to Boots.[29] The most damaging loss of all was the departure of F. H. Carr, chief manufacturing chemist and head of the Chemical Department of BW&Co. since its formation in 1898. His special value to the company had lain in his ability to manage the process whereby new preparations from the WCRL were converted into products manufactured on a commercial scale at Dartford. He joined Boots towards the end of 1914 at the time when Boot was extending the existing laboratory and constructing plant for the manufacture of chemicals in a new department. Carr was appointed head and commenced production in 1915. He was also admitted to the company's Board of Directors.[30]

There is some uncertainty surrounding Carr's decision to leave Wellcome. Whether Carr was approached by Boot or whether Carr made the first move is unclear. According to Carr's account, on the outbreak of war he had submitted a proposal to Wellcome for a £10,000 investment at Dartford to expand production capacity.[31] Wellcome's failure to reply annoyed Carr. Whether Boot's decision to invest heavily in the production of fine chemicals was influenced by his meeting with Carr also remains unknown. There is another connection (albeit somewhat tenuous) between Boot and Carr. A cousin of Pyman, Carr's colleague at BW&Co., became engaged to Boot's son at the same time. Carr later referred to this as having played a part in his decision to defect to Boots in November 1914.[32] Pyman's house was the location where Boot and Carr first met.[33] Whatever the precise circumstances, the departure of Carr, who combined a scientific knowledge of drugs with a capacity for effective production management, dealt a grave blow to BW&Co.

Barrowcliff, another research chemist and colleague of Carr, who had experience of both Experimental and Analytical Departments of BW&Co. followed him into the new department at Boots, proceeding to assembling a staff of four or five former BW&Co. staff to form a research division.[34] This included Wilson, who knew about the manufacture of quinine salts, glycerophosphates, and chloroform, and Thompson, another chemist who possessed detailed practical knowledge of the manufacture of alkaloids. Both were key recruits. Others included Belthle, a plant engineer who set up an engineering department; Spencer, described as an 'experimentalist' who had carried out 'some very private work' for BW&Co. several years before; and one unnamed plant foreman.[35] From the same source, in 1916, Boot recruited three more, including Nutter Smith, an expert on tablet manufacture, and Bull, an authority on pharmaceutical products.[36]

The exodus of those described above was not a chance migration but the outcome of a carefully planned scheme initiated by Boot to enter the ethical pharmaceutical industry. Carr's role was pivotal for the future of Boots. He led the recruitment of others at BW&Co. whom he knew to possess practical experience and knowledge of the more secret processes worked out in his own and other departments, a matter which Wellcome's remaining managers acknowledged to be of serious concern.[37] In November 1915, an internal review conducted by Jowett of the events leading up to Carr's defection and of the effects of subsequent departures revealed the detailed planning behind the recruitment programme. Carr had invited his staff to dinner, among whom was Fidler, a machine engineer, who followed up Carr's offer that if at any time he wanted a job at Boots he should get in touch. Shortly after, Fidler agreed terms at a meeting with Boot at the St Pancras Hotel. Once Carr had left Dartford, he sounded out possible candidates by letter before Boot met interested parties to decide terms which invariably included removal expenses. Fidler, however, returned regularly to Dartford to approach people directly, a tactic that earned him the title of 'the recruiting sergeant'. Barrowcliff, too, was an active recruiter for Boot.

In October 1915, he arranged a rendezvous with Lees, BW&Co.'s senior analyst at the Strand Palace where Barrowcliff intimated that Carr wished to replace Boot's analyst whom he described as 'one of the old set and quite unsystematic'.[38] When Lees showed no interest in such a move, Barrowcliff inquired about Norgrove, another member of the analytical department at Dartford, and Pyman of the WCRL. Supplementing the personal approach was the targeting of individual BW&Co. employees who were sent copies of advertisements for chemical workers appearing in Nottingham newspapers. A box number concealed the name of the advertiser, but a Nottingham postmark was interpreted as sufficient evidence of its origin. Other evidence corroborating Jowett's suspicions of an orchestrated campaign was the use of identical vocabulary in resignation letters which referred to 'concern for their future dependants' as the reason for leaving.[39] Jowett's attempt to stem the flow by offering substantial pay increases to those who had been approached failed, perhaps because the base from which the increase would take place was low (one defector referred to the poor reputation of BW&Co. regarding remuneration levels).

An assessment of the migration to Boots formed part of Jowett's review. It revealed that antiseptics, including Lysol, Formamints, and the tonic, Sanatogen (the initial basis of chemical production), had been transformed by former employees of BW&Co. In addition to three Fidler machines and a chloroform plant similar to that at Dartford, Boots had acquired a small company manufacturing sodium sulphate in preparation for the commencement of sulphuric acid production.[40] A £200,000 investment in 1917 followed the receipt of government licences to manufacture aspirin, phenacetin, and atropine, in direct competition with BW&Co. Carr explored alternative ways of making Bayer's patent Adelin and Casella's patent Flavine, both in demand for treating wounds. Burnol acriflavine cream was produced in large quantities under contract with the British Fire Prevention Committee, while Boot claimed that his company was producing almost enough phenacetin to supply 'the entire normal British demand'.[41] Former employees of BW&Co. were central to these developments; Wilson was turning out two tons of aspirin weekly while Thompson worked with atropine and other alkaloids, including painkilling belladonna alkaloids (much in demand), atrophine sulphate, and saccharine.[42] From 1917 Boots was one of five companies (including BW&Co.) chosen by the MRC to produce local anaesthetics to which were added antipyretics. In a full page advertisement in the *Daily Mail* Boot boasted: 'German science has no secrets from our analysts'.[43] Between 1914 and 1918, the company's capacity as a manufacturer of pharmaceuticals was transformed.[44]

Describing Carr's campaign as 'treachery',[45] Jowett had accused him of preaching loyalty to Jesse Boot whom he dismissed as merely 'a cabinet maker by trade', unqualified in pharmacy but who deviously took advantage

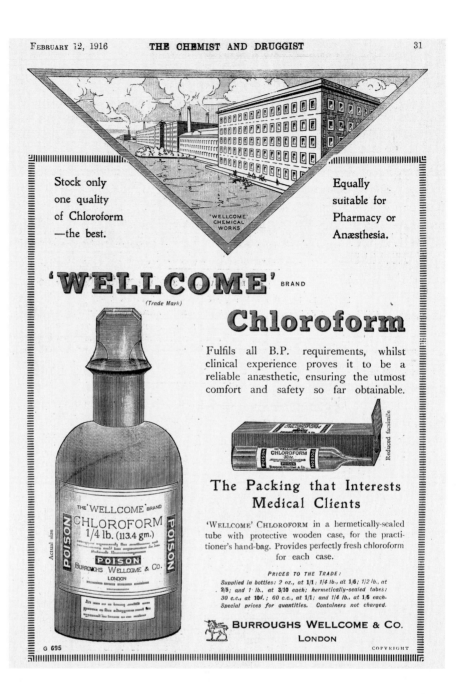

Stock only one quality of Chloroform —the best.

Equally suitable for Pharmacy or Anæsthesia.

'WELLCOME' BRAND
(Trade Mark)

Chloroform

Fulfils all B.P. requirements, whilst clinical experience proves it to be a reliable anæsthetic, ensuring the utmost comfort and safety so far obtainable.

The Packing that Interests Medical Clients

'WELLCOME' CHLOROFORM in a hermetically-sealed tube with protective wooden case, for the practitioner's hand-bag. Provides perfectly fresh chloroform for each case.

PRICES TO THE TRADE:
Supplied in bottles: 2 oz., at 1/1; 1/4 lb., at 1/6; 1/2 lb., at 2/5; and 1 lb., at 3/10 each; hermetically-sealed tubes: 30 c.c., at 10d.; 60 c.c., at 1/1; and 1/4 lb., at 1/6 each. Special prices for quantities. Containers not charged.

BURROUGHS WELLCOME & CO.
LONDON

FIGURE 9.3
Advertising for Wellcome Brand Chloroform (*Chemist & Druggist*, 12 February 1916).

of the 'widow's clause' in the Poisons and Pharmacy Acts of 1852 and 1868 to justify ownership of several chemists' shops'.[46] By 1918, however, Jesse Boot's background and lack of professional training had become irrelevant. His company's transition from multiple retail chemist to one of Britain's largest producers of fine chemicals supported by extensive research laboratories implied a threat to the pre-eminence of BW&Co. after the war.

Wellcome, BW&Co. and the wider war effort

Behind the successful record of innovation in the research laboratories and at Dartford, however, lay problems of production and management. The management of the company during wartime fell mainly upon the shoulders of Pearson, Wellcome's deputy, who since 1905 had become increasingly responsible for the business during Wellcome's frequent and prolonged absences from England. Wellcome spent several months in Africa in 1900/01, several more in Europe in 1901/02 and in North America in 1904/05; from 1907 onwards he was often abroad indulging his newly found enthusiasm for motoring, undertaking lengthy tours across Europe. He became increasingly absorbed in pursuing his personal interests: his extensive Jebel Moya archaeological project,[47] the accumulation of large numbers of items to add to his collection in the Wellcome Museum, and simply in travelling.[48] As early as 1900, Wellcome's frequent absences prompted a caricature of Wellcome that appeared in the *Chemist & Druggist* where he was depicted as an exotic bird, rarely sighted in London.[49] Poor health took him to America again in 1915, where, for nearly two years, he invested time, energy, and money in the New Metlakahtla settlement for native Indians,[50] leaving Pearson and Jowett, as general manager at Dartford, to manage the business.

When war broke out, Wellcome placed the Wellcome Bureau of Scientific Research at the government's disposal as part of the war effort, a 'generous and patriotic offer', gratefully accepted by the Army. From December

FIGURE 9.4 Henry Wellcome with native workers at Jebel Moya, Sudan, *c.* 1915.

The Pharmaceutical Aviary.

The Welcome Bird.

FIGURE 9.5

'The Wellcome bird' as depicted by Fred Reynolds in 'The Pharmaceutical Aviary', taken from *Chemist & Druggist*, 2 June 1900. The accompanying legend reads 'This is a very compact and fascinating bird. It lives on tabloids. It is not often seen in London, as it prefers the warmer climate of the Canaries. In fact, if it stays in England late on into the year, a beautiful ruffle appears round its neck. It may be easily distinguished by its handsome appearance, and particularly by its slightly striped wings and starred breast. It warbles in low, soft tones, is dainty in its banquets, and is reputed to be very fond of large pumpkins. It has never mated.' (Reproduced with permission.)

1915 the Bureau's resources and personnel were used by the MRC, the Royal Society, and the War Office's Medical Advisory Committee to train protozoologists to undertake diagnostic work overseas. The MRC initiated laboratory, clinical, and field studies of a wide range of protozoan infections. Staff from all the Wellcome laboratories collaborated in the first major investigations into amoebic dysentery which was a problem throughout the war period associated particularly in the Middle East and East Africa. Unlike bacterial dysentery, amoebic dysentery could not be treated with serum anti-toxins. BW&Co.'s production of anti-dysentery serum increased sevenfold between 1914 and 1917, contributing to a decline in the bacterial disease on the Western front from four per thousand to below 0.8 in 1918.[51] However, amoebic dysentery presented particular difficulties, diagnostically and therapeutically, and training at the WBSR introduced non-medical biologists to the requisite diagnostic techniques under the supervision of Clifford Dobell, working with Balfour and Wenyon. At the same time, Dale from the MRC studied the therapeutic effectiveness against amoebic dysentery of combinations of emetine and bismuth iodide and alkaloids of ipecacuanha. WCRL staff provided all the chemical samples for his physiological tests, from which preparations of emetine rapidly became accepted as the standard remedy.[52]

The staff's war services outside the WBSR included equipping a mobile bacteriological laboratory that Wellcome presented to the government and regular lectures to military and civilian workers on problems of public health: anti-typhoid inoculation, malaria, dysentery, and sanitation.[53] Several

FIGURE 9.6 'The enemy scientifically bombed' (*Lancet*, 17 November 1917), announcing that 'Direct hits have been obtained on the enemy's important chemical interests ... the raid is still in progress'.

served overseas, notably Balfour and Wenyon as lieutenant-colonels on the Medical Advisory Committee for the Prevention of Disease. Balfour was chairman when the committee inspected the Mediterranean Expeditionary Force, Salonika, Egypt, Mesopotamia and East Africa, which earned the title in some quarters as 'Balfour's Travelling Circus'. He advised on, and

organised, sanitary reform in all theatres of war and was sent by General Allenby to examine anti-malarial procedures in Palestine.[54] Subsequently Balfour was heavily involved in writing two volumes of the official medical history of the war.[55]

From laboratory research to factory production; manufacturing and management

Success in the laboratories which provided a basis for meeting the expanding demand for the company's products presented management with a major problem as to how the company could 'keep the men together'.[56] Fearing

opposite

FIGURE 9.7 'BW&Co.'s resourcefulness defeats enemy activities' (*Lancet*, 23 February 1918). All the planes, boats and submarines are named after BW&Co.'s chemicals.

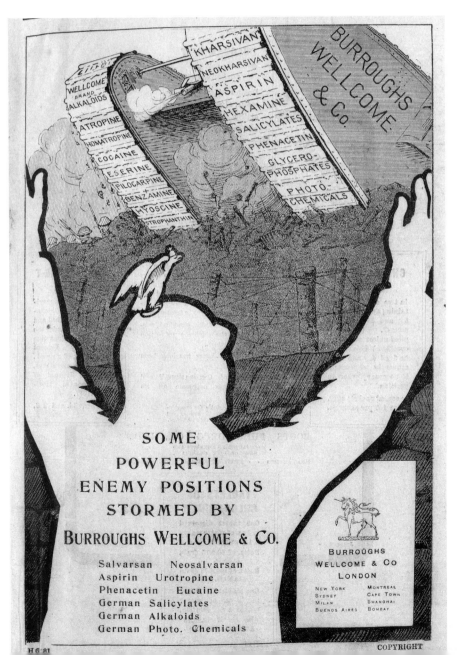

SOME
POWERFUL
ENEMY POSITIONS
STORMED BY
BURROUGHS WELLCOME & CO.

Salvarsan   Neosalvarsan
Aspirin   Urotropine
Phenacetin   Eucaine
German   Salicylates
German   Alkaloids
German   Photo. Chemicals

BURROUGHS
WELLCOME & Co
LONDON

NEW YORK   MONTREAL
SYDNEY   CAPE TOWN
MILAN   SHANGHAI
BUENOS AIRES   BOMBAY

COPYRIGHT

FIGURE 9.8 'Some powerful enemy positions stormed by BW&Co.' (*Lancet* 23 March 1918). The tank tracks list the chemicals and pharmaceuticals made by the company to replace items formerly imported from Germany.

267

Scientific Bombardment

by Burroughs Wellcome & Co.'s

Long-range Gun

❡ Before the outbreak of war, the British fine chemical industry was harassed by the attacks of enemy competitors.

Burroughs Wellcome & Co.'s scientific batteries were actively engaged in repulsing those attacks for many years. Since August, 1914, they have proved increasingly efficient and have secured many direct hits on selected targets.

BURROUGHS WELLCOME & CO., LONDON   COPYRIGHT

FIGURE 9.9 'Scientific bombardment' (*Lancet*, 22 June 1918) emphasising that BW&Co.'s 'scientific batteries were actively engaged' since August 1914.

that active service or munitions work might exercise a stronger appeal to those of patriotic sentiment, in December 1914, heads of department were instructed to reassure male workers that they were doing their duty by remaining at the factory because they were assisting in supplying medical goods for military and civil use.[57] Hourly rates for all workers began to rise early in 1915, favouring males but including females. Supplementary war allocations and special rates for night work were additional.[58] In October 1917 Wellcome endorsed Pearson's policy of increasing wages to retain and recruit the most skilled, highly trained employees: '... feel perfectly free in making such increases in salaries and wages as you deem desirable having regard both to present and future'.[59] Overtime working was permitted to assist workers in meeting higher living costs, while the practice of requiring medical examination before hiring men and boys was abandoned, as was compulsory vaccination.[60] With a view to creating a more flexible internal labour market through reallocation of jobs, responsibility was given to a named individual to whom all heads of department were to report slackness or a shortage of workers.[61]

The pressures of work during the early months of the war were exacerbated by the loss of key staff through enlistment, resignation, and illness and created difficulties for the WCRL. Pyman succeeded Power as Director when he returned to the US in November 1914 and some replacement research chemists were finally appointed in 1915. Because of the calibre of staff who left BW&Co. to work for Boot, the losses were particularly serious.[62] Despite the wartime pressures some primary research continued at the WCRL, particularly into tropical remedies and chaulmoogra, one of Power's original research interests as a treatment for leprosy; this reached the stage of clinical testing by Sir Leonard Rogers in 1916.[63] Anti-malarial preparations reached a similar stage after the war.[64]

Sera and vaccines

No research activity was possible at the WPRL, which on the outbreak of war became practically a full-time serum factory developing and producing large volumes of anti-toxic sera, principally for military use.[65] Not until 1921 did WPRL staff retrieve their position in the research field, explained partly by staff losses and illness but essentially because the scale of serum production imposed immense demands on staff, the whole of which O'Brien noted rather plaintively, by May 1915 was 'suffering somewhat from stress and will require "nursing".'[66] The production of sera (excluding diphtheria and tetanus sera) during the 40 months from the outbreak of war until December 1917 amounted to nearly 3,000 litres.[67] In 1910 the WPRL prepared and dispatched 239,000 packages, whereas in 1915 the figure rose to 627,000; this increased to 1,554,000 in 1918.[68] Not surprisingly, the monthly reports issued by the WPRL throughout the war repeated the same message: that producing large amounts of serum absorbed the entire attention, time, and energy of staff.[69] Experimental and development work in physiology and bacteriology ceased and was replaced by the development of vaccines and laboratory diagnostic materials for military requirements. Research by the small veterinary department created in 1914, headed by J. B. Buxton, into spontaneous abortion in cattle and distemper in carnivores had barely started when war broke out.[70] These too were halted as the staff assumed responsibility for expanding the rapidly growing horse population required for serum production. Competition with the heavy military demand for horses created a serious problem in sustaining the enlarged stud as 'bled-out' horses had to be replaced by fresh horses.[71]

The burden of supervising the production of vast amounts of anti-toxic sera fell almost entirely on the shoulders of Alexander Glenny under the newly appointed director, R.A.O'Brien. At least 17 different sera were produced by the WPRL during the war, although not all were marketed. In addition, an array of vaccines, tuberculins, and other laboratory diagnostic materials for both human and veterinary use were produced in greater quantities than before. Some sera continued to be produced at pre-war levels: coli, erysipelas, puerperal, staphylococcus and the anti-staphylococcal pyogenes, rheumatica and scarlatina anti-sera. Much of the demand for these was probably domestic, as the laboratories continued to supply home and overseas doctors and chemists dealing with routine illnesses. A surprising inclusion in this category, however, is typhoid anti-sera, which was certainly required by troops but the annual production of which dropped from almost 40 litres in 1914 and 1915 to below 5 litres in 1916 and 1917. By this time laboratories may have switched almost entirely to anti-typhoid vaccine production, for which military demand was considerable and which BW&Co. began to market in 1916. Production figures have not survived either for these or for anti-diphtheria serum for military and domestic use. An unexpected military usage occurred in 1917, however, when diphtheria anti-serum was recommended by the Royal Army Medical Corps (RAMC) as a treatment for 'desert sore', which first appeared during the Africa campaign.[72] BW&Co. became one of the companies under contract to supply the sera to the Army Vaccine department responsible for issuing all military sera. The possibility of developing a large market as a result of compulsory vaccination (as required in the German forces) vanished when an alliance of anti-vaccinationists and anti-vivisectionists successfully targetted public health and military authorities as well as pharmaceutical companies in opposition.[73]

Tetanus

The market for sera and biological products was not entirely limited to therapeutic use. Many sera were used by military doctors in agglutination tests for diagnosis for which BW&Co. supplied an extended range of materials during the war.[74] For some diseases, especially tetanus, sera and vaccines were not only used as treatments for confirmed infections but also prophylactically to prevent infection, developments which greatly increased the usage of, and demand for, the products with immediate effects on the market. Throughout the war on the Western Front, tetanus was the infection which generated substantial demands for BW&Co.'s sera and vaccines. This was because troops were fighting on, and in, highly manured soil and because most wounds resulted from shellfire. No such problem had been encountered during the Boer War, first because fighting took place over the veld rather than in trenches and second, because bullet fire produced cleaner wounds.[75] Widespread tetanus infection became apparent shortly after the beginning of hostilities in 1914 when anti-tetanus serum was used by the RAMC for treatment, although 'there was no great quantity of it'.[76] With the exception of a few hundred doses purchased in Paris when the war commenced, all serum used subsequently by the British Expeditionary Force (BEF) for treatment and prevention was from British or American sources.[77] The official war history reports the issue of over 12 million doses of anti-toxic sera during hostilities, of which more than 11 million were anti-tetanus.[78] Two major developments emerged from the extensive experience gained in serum use. It began to be administered prophylactically and it was routinely administered in base and some home hospitals as well as in the field. Two months after war began, the RAMC changed standing orders to require all wounded to receive 500 units of anti-tetanus serum. The scale of demand and the speed with which the decision was made by the RAMC presented initial difficulties for BW&Co. for the Lister Institute and the army's own Vaccine Laboratory. By November, adequate supplies were again available as all laboratories increased output; the incidence of the disease dropped from 8 per 1,000 wounded men to 1.4. Henceforward, according to the official historian, 'the almost constant use of anti-tetanic serum eliminates any satisfactory non-inoculated control group with which to draw comparisons'.[79] Production of anti-tetanus serum at the WPRL more than doubled in 1914 compared with 1913 to more than 200 litres, rising to almost 350 litres in 1915. This increase was to continue, given a further boost in June 1917 when the RAMC again altered standing orders to ensure all wounded would receive four injections of 500 units weekly. While the clinical efficiency of this approach was not clear, it was good news for serum manufacturers. In December, tetanus cases brought by accidental cuts, scratches, abrasions, and trench foot were also treated thus. In June 1918, the primary prophylactic dose was increased further from 500 to 1,500 units. However, the larger volume of serum needed to contain 1500 units (usually nine millilitres) caused considerable irritation and adverse reactions. In practice, therefore, the 500 unit dose (in three millilitres) continued to be popular. BW&Co. responded to the RAMC's adjustments by increasing production of the 1500 unit phials but also experimented with the production of even higher value phials for medical and veterinary use. The introduction of BW&Co.'s 'tetanus toxoid', a more potent but less reactive anti-serum, significantly reduced irritation.[80] The amounts of material produced both in routine

(500 and 1500 unit phials) and higher strengths were considerable. Although largely for human use, for a time serum was also routinely used to inoculate the mules, camels, and horses (numbering one million in 1917) employed by the army.[81] However, the cost to the Army Veterinary Services proved to be comparatively high because, unlike wounded men, horses suffering serious sickness were shot. The routine use of veterinary serum, therefore, was abandoned.[82] A small but consistent veterinary market for anti-tetanus serum (and later vaccine) remained in serum-producing establishments, as it was critically important that horses used for raising therapeutic sera did not accidentally contract tetanus through cut or injury which would contaminate its serum with tetanus-causing bacilli. Since 1912, all horses used for serum production by the WPRL had been immunised routinely, a practice that other manufacturers soon followed.

Gas gangrene and other sera and vaccines

During the closing months of the war, the company received another boost in demand for serum for the treatment of gas gangrene, the second most important infectious cause of mortality and morbidity among the BEF. Until the early months of 1918, treatment was essentially surgical. BW&Co. provided the RAMC with experimental serum containing anti-toxins to the two organisms then thought to be causative agents for gas gangrene, *Bacillus welchii* and *Vibrion septique*.[83] Extremely difficult to prepare, the titre (strength) of the serum was not high, though it was used none the less. The disappointingly low titre, however, led to experimentation and trials of a dual serum in which gas gangrene anti-toxins were introduced into anti-tetanus serum. Initial trials of this combined serum were extremely promising, prompting the planning of a massive programme of anti-gas-gangrene serum production at Brockwell Park. In the event, the plan was curtailed as demand fell away when the war ended. This research, however, did provide the foundation for several new veterinary product developments after the war.

Other sera and vaccines produced in greater quantities for military use included the polyvalent anti-streptococcus serum which was administered routinely for all streptococcal infections in the field. Production rose from roughly 90 litres in 1914 to almost 300 litres in succeeding years. Anti-meningococcus serum to treat cerebrospinal fever proved to be of limited success in reducing mortality but none the less received official recommendation in 1917. The company's production rose more than fivefold in 1915. No records of the WPRL's vaccine production has survived, though it seems inconceivable that BW&Co. and the Lister Institute were not substantial suppliers, supplementing the 24 kinds of vaccine issued by the Vaccine Department of the Royal Naval College and contributing to more than 34,000 litres issued by the Army Vaccine Department between 1914 and 1919.[84]

Between 1914 and 1919, the resources of the Wellcome research laboratories were mobilised almost entirely to meet military requirements, satisfying demands involving experimental serotherapy and supplying vital chemicals no longer available in Britain. Behind the successful record of innovation in the laboratories lay the pressures which production expansion on an unprecedented scale was hampered by the loss of staff and the pressure of work on staff retained. Parallel innovation and resourcing difficulties were experienced in the Dartford factory where – in the absence of Wellcome – problems of production and management fell upon others' shoulders, adding to difficulties affecting the company during the war.

In 1914, managers drew attention to the need for scrupulous attention to checking products, processes and packaging so vital for the maintenance of quality at the same time when special efforts were being made to increase output. Emergency instructions issued to department heads noted: 'Rigid economy compatible with <u>efficiency</u> is to be encouraged, every precaution to prevent waste and leakage of expense must be followed by immediate action to transfer employees to other departments or to work short time'.[85] Emphasis, therefore, was on the optimal use of scarce resources. In 1917 additional rules and instructions issued to employees re-emphasised the company's continued demand for efficiency, precision, punctuality, and exemplary behaviour. Notification of absence through illness must be by telegram to the head of department; infectious disease at an employee's residence was to be reported in writing. Borrowing or lending money, gambling, or betting were banned. Unless related to the job in hand, talking during business hours and discussion of the firm's business to outsiders were banned. 'Bad language' rendered employees liable to instant dismissal.[86] Control to this degree was an adjunct to measures to ensure high quality combined with efficiency.

Further losses in a competitive market for human resources

The loss of senior scientists produced a manpower shortage and presented a threat to research and development in the company in an increasingly competitive market environment. Some staff were replaced by worthy, some eminent, successors; however, internal problems in the laboratories were exacerbated over the longer term because of the destinations of some of those who left the company. Carr's contribution to the transformation of Boots into a competitive force has been described above. Arthur Ewins (who between 1899 and 1914 had been one of the scientists at the WPRL investigating ergot) was to make a comparable contribution to the challenge from May & Baker. In 1914 he followed Dale to the Department of Biochemistry and Pharmacology of the MRC's newly established Central Research

Institute. Three years later, however, he was recruited to become chief chemist at May & Baker where he established a research and development department at its Wandsworth factory.[87] The significance of this relocation is that as British agents for Poulenc Frères, May & Baker benefited from the Board of Trade's agreement to issue the French company a licence to sell its products through May & Baker on a profit-sharing basis. Their products included Arsenobenzol-billon and Novarsenobenzol-billon, drugs which were chemically identical to Ehrlich's original Salvarsan and Neosalvarsan. Ewins' appointment was important because of his experience of BW&Co.'s developments in this field of research before 1914 and his position at the MRC, the body responsible for testing the toxicity of such drugs. Established connections with Poulenc Frères and Ewins' research leadership proved a powerful combination not only for the manufacture of the two drugs but also for future developments in chemotherapy.[88]

From 1918, a third competitor was to benefit from the experience of BW&Co.'s history of scientific research and production. After joining Boots in November 1914, Carr added to his reputation as a successful chemist that of research manager and company director. The publication in 1918 of his paper entitled 'Synthetic organic chemicals: their manufacture as affected by the war' received extensive coverage in the *Chemist & Druggist*.[89] In 1918, after a dispute with Boot concerning an aspect of his private life, Carr resigned, taking with him a research team to British Drug Houses (BDH), where he was appointed company director in charge of chemical production.[90] Formed in 1908, BDH was the result of an amalgamation of five businesses, each established in the eighteenth century and bringing wholesaling, retailing, and production experience together into the new company which by 1911 employed roughly 500 people.[91] Under a dynamic managing director, C. A. Hill, formerly managing director of Davy, Hill, and Hodgkinson Ltd, a process of consolidation, integration, and investment in the production of fine chemicals began in 1914. Between 1914 and 1918 production capacity doubled as a result of the construction of modern plant and the introduction of laboratory equipment comparable, according to the *Chemist & Druggist*, to that to be found in university laboratories. The company was aggressive in establishing high standards of purity of the drugs produced. Signified by the letters AR, the standards were recognised by the Institute of Chemistry.[92] Like Boots and May & Baker, BDH was to become one of BW&Co.'s research-based competitors after the war. Conditions in the labour market, however, had changed fundamentally for BW&Co., for the wartime emergence and growth of three research-based pharmaceutical companies provided expanding opportunities for the employment of science graduates and skilled researchers in the industry after the war ended. The erosion of the company's human capital continued after the war. By 1920, according to Thomas Henry, then Director of the WCRL, the laboratory had 'lost nearly all its staff' which it would take two years to replace and train, which temporarily halted research.[93] Meanwhile BW&Co.'s former scientists appointed to recently established research-based laboratories of competitors contributed to the emergence of a modern pharmaceutical industry in Britain.

The dramatic implications of this development are evident in the ability of Boots by the end of the war to cease relying on BW&Co. for many of the 80 products supplied hitherto, including atropine, aspirin, saccharine, and phenacetin, in such volume.[94] Eight years after the war ended, Jowett continued to brood over Carr's 'treachery', and was convinced that, unfairly, Carr had secured much of the credit for Boots for replacing German specialities with British substitutes.[95] Jowett accused Carr of assisting Boot's opportunistic exploitation of wartime conditions in setting up a cosy business in Aspirin and exploiting publicity from high profile, though 'gimmicky', products such as chemicals used in gas masks. Jowett contrasted the lack of recognition or kudos extended to BW&Co. for developing the complex process of preparing a British Salvarsan.[96] Jowett was aggrieved by a similar episode after the war, when he perceived that Carr had outsmarted BW&Co., by joining with Allen & Hanburys to be the first (albeit by only weeks) to market a British insulin under the A. & B. Brand.[97] Robson has interpreted Jowett's 1926 memo as indicative of BW&Co. falling behind BDH and Boots. However, an invitation issued by Dale in 1927 to the WPRL and to BDH to collaborate with the MRC in an inquiry into the use of liver extract in the treatment of pernicious anaemia suggests that both were considered to be the leading research-based companies at that time.[98] During the early post-war years, Jowett advocated increased investment and a reorganisation to improve communications between the laboratories, factory, and office as vital if the company's position was to be maintained *vis à vis* its competitors.[99]

Measuring the impact of war

The impact of war on the principal pharmaceutical manufacturers is only partly susceptible to measurement, but within serious limitations. Discursive accounts of Boots indicate its transformation into a manufacturer of fine chemicals. Sales data, however, are not available. The same is true of BDH. No sales data exist that are distinguishable from retail data. Sales figures are available, however, for BW&Co., Allen & Hanburys, and May & Baker. The absolute sales increase of goods produced by BW&Co. in England comprising war-related products exceeded those of Allen & Hanburys; the same is true of the rate of increase. The product range of Allen & Hanburys overlapped with that of BW&Co., though wartime demand for surgical instruments, appliances, and aseptic hospital furniture was generated by hospitals at home and the provision of operating theatres in the field.[100] The war did not, however, immediately shift Allen & Hanburys towards a more scientific approach to medicine. Its analytical laboratory, strictly for testing materials and drugs, was the only concession to modernity and was congruent with the opinion expressed by Cornelius Hanbury in 1916 that synthetic drugs were no more than 'a passing phase'.[101] Both companies experienced growth in sales and profits during the war, however, the scale of the expansion of May & Baker's sales was substantially greater. The reason is to be found in the company's product range. In addition to Salvarsan substitutes, the company supplied tungstic acid (manufactured on exclusive licence and sold to steel producers), nitric acid (used by dyestuff and explosive manufacturers), and cyanide.[102]

Table 9.1 Sales of BW&Co., Allen & Hanburys, and May & Baker, 1914–1918 (£)

Year ending	Total BW&Co.	BW&Co. (Home and foreign)	BW&Co. (overseas)	Allen & Hanburys	May & Baker
1914	740,710	454,363	288,347	508,000	301,557
1915	733,882	461,093	272,789	544,000	714,577
1916	881,895	594,008	287,887	597,000	836,496
1917	984,102	658,712	325,390	650,000	850,612
1918	1,070,994	720,790	350,024	766,700	1,136,250

Tweedale, *At the Sign of the Plough*, p. 118. Slinn, *History of May & Baker*, pp. 38, 57, 66, 79; WFA, Acc. 96/45, BW&Co. sales book 2.

Only net profit figures are available for these companies (profits before withdrawals). Because they exclude distributions to shareholders (and in the case of BW&Co., Wellcome's withdrawals) they are of limited value other than to indicate minimum profit levels.

Table 9.2 Net profits of BW&Co., Allen & Hanburys and May & Baker (£)

Year ending	BW&Co.	Allen & Hanburys	May & Baker
1914	83,265		6,490
1915	175,341		15,116
1916	177,842		28,917
1917	94,140		56,864
1918	151,414	87,054	29,773

Tweedale, *At the Sign of the Plough*, p. 118; Slinn, *History of May & Baker*, pp. 38, 57, 66. WFA, Acc. 90/1 Box 149, account ledger BW&Co.

BW&Co.'s sales figures suggest that while the wartime ban on chemical exports may have affected adversely the company's sales outside Europe, from the standpoint of the company viewed as a multinational, the export ban was no more than a minor setback for BW&Co.'s trade. Although the

Australian branch sales dropped by roughly ten per cent, South African sales increased by 50 per cent and Canadian sales by roughly ten per cent; sales by the US branch almost doubled, by far the most significant change which more than outweighed others' losses. Part of the explanation lies in the ability of the branches to supply overseas depots, though the resilience of the overseas sales figures also underlines the dominance of general goods in overseas markets.[103]

Table 9.3 shows that the modest growth in aggregate sales by the overseas branches conceals an increase from the New York branch to almost double the level of 1914. This rate of growth in 1917 led Nevin, manager of the American branch, to inform Wellcome (then on a visit to New York) that congestion at the works was hampering production levels and efficiency.[104] American sales doubled again between 1918 and 1920, replacing Australasia as the largest market. New York also superseded Sydney as the biggest branch.

Table 9.3 *Overseas branch sales, 1914–1918 (£)*

Year ending	Sydney	New York	Montreal	Cape Town	Milan	Shanghai
1914	111,509	55,678	37,969	25,832	23,334	21,900
1915	99,401	59,517	33,495	25,433	20,294	21,991
1916	93,156	68,324	38,529	23,899	22,635	23,973
1917	94,404	87,070	45,396	31,978	23,648	24,292
1918	110,938	99,091	41,062	32,132	22,303	23,250

WFA, Acc. 96/45, BW&Co. sales book 2.

The overall effects of the war on BW&Co. were both positive and negative. Sales and profits grew faster than inflation. Rapid sales from the New York branch resulted in lower overall unit costs. This enabled the branch (even under the continuing handicap of the price formula imposed on it from London) to approach the break-even point and profitability. The superiority of the research basis of BW&Co. when the war began also gave the company the opportunity to benefit from the demand for substitutes for German synthetic medicines and the waiving of patent protection. Development to meet the demand for Kharsivan included a new building and production plant equipped for the purpose.[105]

The purchase in 1919 of the Temple Hill Estate, a site of 250 acres adjacent to the Dartford works, and a further 37 acres in 1920 implied optimism regarding the long-term future of the business.[106] Writing to Pearson in 1917, Wellcome agreed with his prediction that the company would face 'many great problems' after the war, but expressed the view that higher wages and salaries and material costs then being experienced would be offset by continuing high prices which might even increase.[107] Overseas depots established in the Dutch East Indies in 1920 and in Sweden in 1921, are indicative of a similar optimism. The lease from the LCC of

Brockwell Park, Herne Hill, expired in 1919 but was extended until 1922 to accommodate the continued production of serum by the WPRL. In that year, these laboratories moved to Langley Court, in Beckenham, a large mansion possessing a private park consisting of more than 100 acres which had been purchased in 1921.[108] The capital developments coincided with a sharp economic downturn which from 1919 to 1921 saw Wellcome turn to the bank for support in the form of a loan of £150,000.[109]

Table 9.4 *BW&Co. sales, financial structure, and profit, 1914–1923*

Year ending August	Home and foreign sales (£)	Total home, foreign and overseas sales (£)	Net profit (£)	Equity capital (£)	Long-term debt (£)	Profit/ capital (%)	Profit/home and foreign sales (%)	Profit/ total sales (%)
1914	454,363	740,710	83,265	466,074	23,023	17.9	18.3	11.2
1915	461,093	733,881	175,341	628,965	6,441	27.9	38.0	23.9
1916	594,007	881,895	177,842	790,328	5,899	22.5	29.9	20.2
1917	658,712	884,102	94,140	875,928	8,362	10.8	14.3	9.6
1918	720,969	1,070,994	151,414	1,018,134	10,920	14.9	21.0	14.1
1919	693,928	1,109,994	31,430	1,030,446	41,214	3.1	4.5	2.8
1920	766,964	1,304,257	84,352	982,258	280,480	8.6	11.0	6.5
1921	646,516	1,187,483	104,554	846,931	237,812	12.4	16.2	8.8
1922	615,823	1,218,167	177,882	1,005,438	142,222	17.7	28.9	14.6
1923	604,014	1,245,169	200,204	921,912	142,533	21.7	33.2	16.1

WFA, Acc. 90/1, Box 149, account ledger BW&Co.

The success in replacing German drugs did not induce complacency with respect to future competition from leading German companies after the war. In 1921 Pearson wrote to *The Times*, drawing attention to the pre-war conditions. Then British companies had been in the 'ignominious' position of being no more than brokers selling imported drugs, a function which he predicted they would resume unless the industry received protection by an import duty of 50 per cent.[110] In 1921 the company was included among the 19 fine chemical manufacturers who were signatories to a petition seeking to extend protection of the industry.[111] Under the Safeguarding of Industries Act of 1924, limited protection was forthcoming for fine chemicals, defined so as to include hormones, though inexplicably the duty was removed from insulin.[112] The industry was, however, denied DSIR funding to promote research. One of the Department's few refusals of such financial support, it was, in part, a consequence of the reluctance of the pharmaceutical manufacturers themselves to collaborate in developing the industry with a view to improving international competitiveness. This contrasted with the willingness of manufacturers in some other industries to seek solutions to common problems through the formation of recognised research associations.[113]

The impact of war on pharmaceutical manufacturers' profits is revealed by comparing pre-war with wartime profits. This also provides a basis for judging whether BW&Co. was guilty of profiteering, a general question prompted by the deliberations of the Royal Commission on Venereal Disease published in 1916.[114] The Commissioners inquired whether the extraordinarily high price of Salvarsan was justified by production costs. Manufacturers who gave evidence (among whom BW&Co. was not represented) sought to provide assurance that cost did justify price which ruled out profiteering. However, no cost data were presented to support their view.

Attitudes to pharmaceutical manufacturers after the war were influenced by the Royal Commission's accusation that they profiteered from the production and sales of Salvarsan, an accusation which they rejected.[115] Whether BW&Co. was guilty of profiteering depends upon definition, which, in any case, cannot be tested with confidence for neither sales nor profit data relating to Kharsivan and Neokharsivan exist. Estimates based on production figures and current price lists indicate an output value of perhaps £75,000 in 1916, rising to £280,000 in 1918.[116] The expansion in sales of sera from £149,168 in 1917 to £174,231 in 1918 was attributed to 'large war contracts for tetanus'.[117] Comparing sera sales and profits as a whole is none the less instructive. Between 1910 and 1913, serum sales averaged roughly £15,000; between 1914 and 1919 (the last inflated figure), the comparable figure was £105,655.[118]

With respect to profit, because profit data are missing for 1915 and 1918, two sets of calculations have been made. The first assumes that the extra large gross profit relating to sera sales for 1919 (£60,000 compared with sales of £113,883) represents profits for both 1918 and 1919, a possible consequence of delayed receipts for contracts from government departments and, or, accounting problems.[119] The second calculation applies the 53 per cent profit-to-sales figure for 1916 (when sales were nearly twice those of 1915) to the sales figure for 1918. On the basis of the first calculation of profit, the annual average rate of profit on sera sales between 1914 and 1919 was 14 per cent. On the basis of the second calculation of profit the figure was 32 per cent. Whether this constitutes profiteering depends on definition. Sales dropped by 58 per cent in 1920.[120] What is certain, however, is that profitability as well as sales increased during the war.

The company's average net profit/sales ratios for the years 1910–1913 were 9.3 per cent compared with 13.6 per cent between 1914 and 1918. This represents an increase of net profits by roughly one half whereas average sales revenue increased by about one quarter. Such comparisons, however, must be understood in the context of the exclusion of profits from sera sales by the amounts withdrawn from gross profits by Wellcome. It is not possible to measure the whole of Wellcome's expenditure; however it is possible, at least for most years after 1895, to calculate his withdrawals from the business. After 1924, a continuous series of fee and dividend income can be calculated.

Table 9.5 *Withdrawals by Wellcome 1905–1923 (£)*

1905	8,504	1911	20,212	1917	8,540
1906	14,458	1912	31,572	1918	9,208
1907	18,949	1913	37,042	1919	19,118
1908	17,869	1914	46,843	1920	22,374
1909	15,502	1915	12,450	1921	19,459
1910	14,863	1916	16,479	1922	17,903
				1923	24,393

WFA, F/FA/328, WFL profit and loss accounts.

Withdrawals between 1895 and 1897 amounted to £68,867 at the time when Wellcome was in the process of purchasing Burroughs' share of the partnership. Following a gap in the data until 1905, Wellcome's withdrawal of £8,504 in 1905 represented 74 per cent of net profit, though the reduced levels of withdrawal during the rest of the decade show a one to three ratio, a total of £15,056 in 1905–09, £30,034 in 1910–14, and £13,159 in 1915–19. Significantly, perhaps, between 1910 and 1914, the ratio increased to one to two (a total of £150,172). Wellcome was heavily involved and financially committed to the major Jebel Moya archaeological expedition during this period. Begun in 1910, at its peak in 1914, the project employed 3,000 workers.[121] His financial support for the development of the Settlement for the Metlakahtla Indians was another drain on Wellcome's resources, though it has not proved possible to calculate the actual cost of these projects. During the First World War, his annual withdrawals as a percentage of net profits fell to single figures. After the war until the formation of the Wellcome Foundation in 1924, they averaged £20,649, roughly 20 per cent. These levels were sustainable because they coincided with years of rapid growth in sales and levels of profitability of the business which allowed both substantial withdrawals and increased investment. Thereafter, as sole owner and Governing Director of the Foundation, Wellcome received an annual fee of £24,000 plus annual dividend. From £76,048 in 1925, the first full year of trading, dividend payments rose annually to a peak of £136,000 in 1930.

When the war ended, the company possessed an expanded production capacity and a broader product range than had existed in 1914. However, the balance between the major categories of products (as defined by the company's sales statistics), general goods (mainly Kepler, Tabloid, and Hazeline products), Fairchild products, Lanoline, Wellcome Brand Chemicals, and sera, had altered dramatically. While remaining the largest category, sales of general goods fell from 81 per cent of total sales from London in 1913 to roughly two thirds during the war. It is reasonable to assume that compressed and hypodermic medicines accounted for an increasing proportion of sales within this category. Lanoline sales, which depended on the German source and were already declining before the war, came to an end. Fairchild products fell from an average of roughly £33,000 between 1910 and 1913 (8.3 per cent) to £24,000 between 1915 and 1917, and to an all time low of £11,000 in 1918. Wellcome Brand Chemicals showed a marked increase in sales from an average of £20,000 between 1910 and 1913 to roughly £44,000. The peak of £57,251 occurred in 1917.

Serum sales dropped from the wartime and immediately postwar high levels in 1920, almost by one half to £62,677, and reached a nadir in 1924 at £44,651.[122] Price deflation contributed to this trend, Stone and Rowe's drug price index showed a steady decline from 158.7 in 1920 to 110.7 in 1924.[123] However, the higher profit rates from sera achieved during the war were maintained during the 1920s: 45 per cent in 1920–24 and 40 per cent in 1925–29. It seems likely that the trends applied to each of the major categories to some extent, but more to some than to others. Because 'General Goods' combined several different products, and especially because they ranged from toiletries to compressed medicines, it is only possible to speculate that the products of the WPRL and Wellcome Brand Chemicals (for example those derived from ergot, from chaulmoogra and hydnocarpus oils, and strophanthus), were more likely than general goods to have been subject to similar influences as implied by Stone and Rowe's indexes. 'General Goods' sales did not experience the sharp downturn affecting serum sales. They continued to rise until 1920 when they reached £649,068, though by 1924, they had fallen to £560,217 (a decline of 13.7 per cent); this, however, compared well with the 48 point drop in the drug price index. Fairchild products resumed their pre-war levels. The sale of Wellcome Brand Chemicals remained at levels twice as high as those shortly before the war. A post war peak of £47,826 in 1920 (the wartime peak was £57,251) fell to an average of £37,675 between 1921 and 1924. As a proportion of sales from London, by 1924 general goods once more accounted for 84 per cent. This confirms the persistence in peacetime of the pre-war dominance of compressed medicines, Kepler goods, and to a much lesser extent, Hazeline. While the volume of production rose dramatically, only for a brief period did the war radically alter the company's product range in such a way as to change substantially sales patterns immediately after the war.

The formation of The Wellcome Foundation Ltd

A more enduring change affecting the company was a restructuring of the company's activities, through the formation in January 1924 of the Wellcome Foundation Ltd. The new organisation was unusual inasmuch that it consisted of the wholly privately owned firm of BW&Co. together with nine overseas

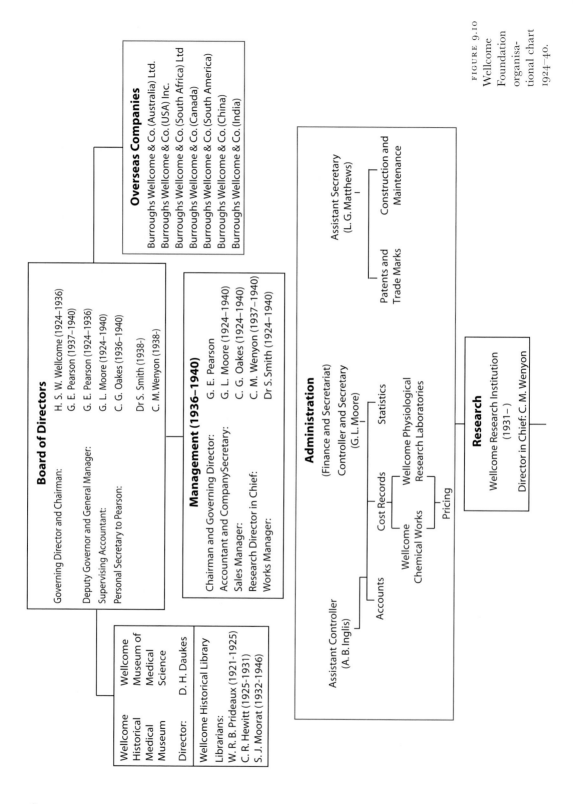

Board of Directors

Governing Director and Chairman:	H. S. W. Wellcome (1924–1936)
	G. E. Pearson (1937–1940)
Deputy Governor and General Manager:	G. E. Pearson (1924–1936)
Supervising Accountant:	G. L. Moore (1924–1940)
Personal Secretary to Pearson:	C. G. Oakes (1936–1940)
	Dr S. Smith (1938-)
	C. M. Wenyon (1938-)

Overseas Companies

Burroughs Wellcome & Co. (Australia) Ltd.
Burroughs Wellcome & Co. (USA) Inc.
Burroughs Wellcome & Co. (South Africa) Ltd
Burroughs Wellcome & Co. (Canada)
Burroughs Wellcome & Co. (South America)
Burroughs Wellcome & Co. (China)
Burroughs Wellcome & Co. (India)

Management (1936–1940)

Chairman and Governing Director:	G. E. Pearson
Accountant and CompanySecretary:	G. L. Moore (1924–1940)
Sales Manager:	C. G. Oakes (1924–1940)
Research Director in Chief:	C. M. Wenyon (1937–1940)
Works Manager:	Dr S. Smith (1924–1940)

Wellcome Historical Medical Museum

Director: D. H. Daukes

Wellcome Historical Library
Librarians:
W. R. B. Prideaux (1921-1925)
C. R. Hewitt (1925-1931)
S. J. Moorat (1932-1946)

Wellcome Museum of Medical Science

Administration
(Finance and Secretariat)
Controller and Secretary
(G. L. Moore)

Assistant Controller
(A. B. Inglis)

Accounts
Cost Records
Statistics

Wellcome Chemical Works
Wellcome Physiological Research Laboratories

Pricing

Assistant Secretary
(L. G. Matthews)

Patents and Trade Marks
Construction and Maintenance

Research

Wellcome Research Institution (1931–)

Director in Chief: C. M. Wenyon

FIGURE 9.10
Wellcome Foundation organisational chart 1924–40.

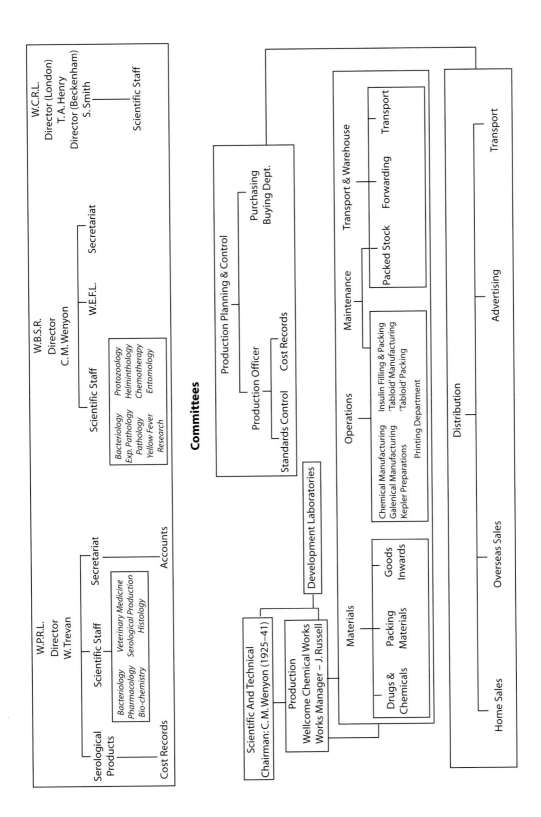

W.C.R.L.
Director (London)
T. A. Henry
Director (Beckenham)
S. Smith

Scientific Staff

W.B.S.R.
Director
C. M. Wenyon

Scientific Staff   W.E.F.L.   Secretariat

Bacteriology   Protozoology
Exp. Pathology   Helminthology
Pathology   Chemotherapy
Yellow Fever   Entomology
Research

Committees

W.P.R.L.
Director
W. Trevan

Scientific Staff   Secretariat

Bacteriology   Veterinary Medicine
Pharmacology   Serological Production
Bio-chemistry   Histology

Serological
Products   Accounts

Cost Records

Production Planning & Control

Production Officer   Purchasing
                            Buying Dept.

Standards Control   Cost Records

Operations   Maintenance   Transport & Warehouse

Chemical Manufacturing   Insulin Filling & Packing   Packed Stock   Forwarding   Transport
Galenical Manufacturing   'Tabloid' Manufacturing
Kepler Preparations   'Tabloid' Packing
Printing Department

Development Laboratories

Scientific And Technical
Chairman: C. M. Wenyon (1925–41)

Production
Wellcome Chemical Works
Works Manager – J. Russell

Materials

Drugs &   Packing   Goods
Chemicals   Materials   Inwards

Distribution

Home Sales   Overseas Sales   Advertising   Transport

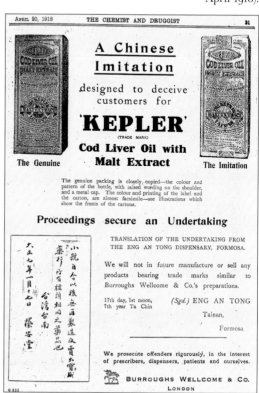

FIGURE 9.11

Apologies, used in an advertisement, from two British companies that infringed BW&Co.'s 'Tabloid' trademark (*Chemist & Druggist*, 21 April 1917). The text emphasises that 'We prosecute offenders rigorously, in the interests of prescribers, dispensers, patients and ourselves'.

houses, each of which was reconstituted as a separate indigenous subsidiary company. The Foundation also included not only the research laboratories, which continued to possess a high degree of independence from the business, but also the museums and library. Haggis explained this 'consolidation' of Wellcome's business and scientific interests as having been motivated by unspecified 'private reasons'.[124] Rhodes James refers to the Mayo Foundation as the source of Wellcome's novel creation, though he concedes that unlike Mayo the Foundation lacked charitable status, a financial flaw which was to prove an Achilles heel.[125] In fact, preparatory documentation associated with the formation of the Foundation (in particular of BW&Co. (USA) Inc.) reveals other factors to have been influential. Expansion of the business in the US during the War under Nevin's effective management convinced Wellcome of the immense potential for growth in the American market after the War and that investment in manufacturing should begin. Operations on this larger scale undoubtedly led to a consideration of the structural arrangements affecting the relations between not only the American business but other overseas activities. Planning the restructuring began with arrangements between London and New York, in relation to which tax avoidance was an important initial consideration. In April 1923, the New York office

A Japanese Imitation
of one of Burroughs Wellcome & Co.'s Packings

The Genuine

The facsimile illustrations on the left and right show the genuine package of "'HAZELINE' SNOW" and a Japanese imitation which was sold in China.

So great was the danger of the public being deceived that the Chinese authorities issued the proclamation of which a translation is printed below.

The Imitation

The colour and design of the genuine package are reproduced almost exactly in the imitation. The only difference is that the words "Nippon Toilet & Co. made in Japan" appear instead of "Burroughs Wellcome & Co., London (Eng.)." The fronts of the cartons are here shown. On the back are the Chinese labels printed in red ink on yellow paper, and here also the imitation matches the genuine package.

THE PROCLAMATION
BY THE SPECIAL COMMISSIONER FOR FOREIGN AFFAIRS IN SHANTUNG

WHEREAS in accordance with instructions issued by the Board of Commerce and by the Governor several proclamations have been issued prohibiting Chinese from engaging in such malpractices as the sale of goods with fraudulent trade marks, the imitation of foreign trade marks, and the imitations of the wrappings of foreign goods;

AND WHEREAS I have received a despatch from the British Consul at Tsinan stating that the British firm of Burroughs Wellcome & Co., of Shanghai, accuse four Tsinan shops (Yu Yuan Ho, Lu Wan Chu, Chu Shong Ho and Chih Hsiang Lou), of selling imitations of their Company's "'Hazeline' Snow"; the trade mark of which article has for long been registered at the Shanghai Custom House;

AND WHEREAS I summoned to this Bureau and carefully examined the proprietors of these four shops, all of whom bore witness that they had bought the imitation products in other ports and had no intention of imitating foreign trade marks with a view to deceive their customers;

AND WHEREAS I gave judgment that they must not sell any more such imitation products, and solemnly warned them against continuing in their evil ways;

NOW recently there have been several cases where the trade mark on foreign goods has been imitated with a view to deceive in order that the imitators may gain an illicit profit, and the Chinese tradesman not noticing whether the article is genuine or imitation has also been deceived and ordered a stock of such goods for sale, thereby not only injuring the genuine article to a great degree, but also bringing discredit on Chinese trade. I must accordingly take action in the interests of trade and therefore ssue this Proclamation that all tradesmen both inside and outside the City may know that if hereafter they sell Burroughs Wellcome & Co.'s "'Hazeline' Snow," they must be careful to examine carefully the trade mark and to distinguish between the genuine and the imitation, and not to confuse them, nor to sell any imitation "'Hazeline' Snow," or they will be summoned to the Courts for trial.

Fear and obey. Let none disregard these commands.

Urgent: A Special Proclamation:

(*Signed*) TANG K'O SAN,

Concurrently appointed by the Wai Chino Pu as Special Commissioner for Foreign Affairs in Shantung.

7th. Year of Chinese Republic (1918), 3rd month, 21st day.

We prosecute offenders rigorously, in the interest of prescribers, dispensers, patients and ourselves

BURROUGHS WELLCOME & CO., LONDON

G. 841

of Price Waterhouse confirmed that an individual was not liable to surtax where the stock of a US corporation was owned by a British company. The question of corporate liability, however, did present a problem. In May, the same source regretted being unable to give Wellcome official advice on tax avoidance as Price Waterhouse also worked for the US Treasury. None the less, the source conveyed to Wellcome an 'unofficial view' that by incorporating the American business as a resident enterprise, the effective rate of tax on profits would fall from 40 per cent (to which foreign companies were liable) to 12 per cent for a resident business.[126] The actual saving was small on the company's current gross profit of £47,380 in 1923, though the expansion expected to follow when manufacturing commenced at larger premises, then being contemplated, was perceived to offer scope for significant savings by changing the company's status, a prediction that proved to be amply justified.[127]

Capitalised in 1924 at £1 million, the Wellcome Foundation's sole share-holder was Wellcome himself, the self-styled 'Governing Director', who was described in the articles of association as commanding 'complete authority', as did his deputy in his absence. In addition to Wellcome, the board of directors consisted of two others, Pearson, the 'Deputy Governor', and G. Leslie Moore, hitherto the company's accountant, as Company Secretary. The board met annually to receive the financial report; otherwise, until after Wellcome's death in 1936 board meetings did not take place.[128] As in the past, Wellcome's complete control was mediated through Pearson who was responsible for the day to day management of the business from the London office. It seems likely that Wellcome was consulted by Pearson on policy issues at informal meetings between the two or more likely, through correspondence, none of which (if it existed) survived. With the singular important exceptions affecting the North American companies during the late 1920s and early 1930s when he became personally involved in the details of policy and development, Wellcome rarely exercised personal intervention in the management of the business. Pearson's successor as managing director from 1940, T.R. Bennett, described the structure and organisation of the company at that time as having tended to 'perpetuate the proprietorial form of management.'[129] This was to be tested severely during the 1920s and 1930s.

CHAPTER TEN

Policy formation, research and development

Postwar problems in the research laboratories

As the company emerged from the war it faced two urgent problems. In every department, staff were exhausted and their numbers depleted. Of more long-term consequence, the company was rapidly losing its pre-eminence. German, Swiss and American companies such as Bayer, Roche, and Eli Lilly expanded and diversified. Although British companies had been slow to follow Wellcome's lead in developing in-house research laboratories, and registering them with the Home Office for animal experimentation. By the beginning of the 1920s, Boots, Allen & Hanburys, May & Baker, Nathan & Sons, and BDH were expanding their existing facilities and supporting laboratories and research programmes, which allowed them to develop the new biological therapies that appeared during the inter-war period, including vitamins, hormones, and new sera. They also began to provide BW&Co. with serious competition. More damagingly they heavily recruited Wellcome staff to manage their programmes, as did the newly created Medical Research Council. BW&Co. and their research laboratories were the main supply of qualified scientists and staff to undertake research, to develop that research into commercial production, and to advise on the marketing and advertising of the products of that research.

The laboratories slowly began to resume limited publication of innovative research. Table 10.1 illustrates the effect of the war on publications from the Wellcome laboratories compared with the output from Parke, Davis & Co.'s Chicago laboratories, which had not been disrupted by the demands of the war. It was not until June 1920 that the WPRL appointed the pharmacologist, John Trevan, to undertake new experimental projects. O'Brien immediately directed him to work on 'hot' research topics previously undeveloped in the laboratories: accessory food factors, pancreatic extracts, and pituitary preparations.[1] Promising beginnings were entirely destroyed in March 1921 when virulent disease wiped out all the experimental animals. Research effort in the laboratories was entirely diverted for some weeks, as the investigation of their own pathological problems became critical: new work was once again hindered.

Table 10.1 *Numbers of papers published by the Wellcome Laboratories and the Research Laboratory of Parke, Davis & Co., Detroit*[2]

	WPRL	WCRL	WBSR	WCW	Total Wellcome	P.D. & Co.
1910	21	21	n/a	4	46	n/a
1911	9	15	n/a	8	32	14
1912	8	11	n/a	8	27	16
1913	14	14	3	7	38	21
1914	19	8	6	6	39	22
1915	5	1	11	2	19	22
1916		1	9		10	18
1917		2	6	1	9	30
1918		1	4		5	49
1919		9	7	2	18	46
1920		7	13		20	29
1921	13	6	17		36	n/a

Finance was an additional problem. In 1919 the WPRL's stables contained three times as many horses as in 1914, and it was estimated that each one cost two to three times as much to maintain.[3] Fodder and glassware were more expensive and the production cost per phial of issued serum multiplied many times. The loss of military contracts meant that the demand for sera returned to pre-war levels, and required economies. The stud was rapidly reduced and the gas-gangrene programme, no longer so attractive in peacetime, was suspended. Wellcome sternly reminded O'Brien that he wished his firm 'to be used as the purchasing agents for his scientific institutions' to take advantage of their experience and discounts.[4] Purchasing arrangements throughout the Wellcome organization began to be rationalised and centralised.[5]

In 1921, Wellcome acquired 105 acres of land, including Langley Court, in Beckenham, Kent, to replace Brockwell Park as the lease there expired. To the £30,000 purchase price was added considerably more investment in laboratories and stables, which in 1922 prompted renewed questioning of the company regarding the purpose and conduct of activities therein.[6] One MP claimed in the House of Commons that the cultivation of germs would be hazardous to local residents.[7] A public enquiry was held, at which Wellcome's Counsel, Sir Albion Richardson, spoke of the laboratories' 'highest national utility', and reminded members that 'during the war the Army was mainly dependent upon it for its supplies of serum'.[8] Pearson stressed that the laboratories were not commercial, and O'Brien elaborated the important therapeutic sera that would be prepared, without any danger to nearby householders.[9] The enquiry went in Wellcome's favour.[10]

FIGURE 10.1
'The last
photograph
of the senior
staff BW&Co.
Brockwell
Hall 1919'.
Standing in
the second
row, from
left right, are
J. W. Trevan,
R. A. O'Brien,
H. J. Sud-
mersen.
Standing
immediately
behind
Sudmersen is
A. T. Glenny.

A similar post war exhaustion and depletion of staff also affected the WCRL. Further resignations of key scientific staff occurred during 1919 and 1920.[11] Harold King followed former Wellcome colleagues, Henry Dale, Arthur Ewins and George Barger, to the department of Biochemistry and Pharmacology at the National Institute for Medical Research; Robert Fargher left to head the chemical section of a new institute being organised by the Cotton Research Association.[12] Alfred Bacharach, oscillating between the Works and the WCRL became frustrated and left to join Nathan & Sons. There, he became a member of their baby food division, Glaxo, and pioneered vitamin research that greatly facilitated the transformation of that brand into a major pharmaceutical company in its own right.

In common with the other research laboratories, the major problems for the WCRL were the limitations of space and facilities. Until 1932, when they moved with the WBSR into new accommodation on Euston Road in Central London, the WCRL occupied the same premises on King Street to which they had moved in 1899. Praised for its equipment and location in 1899 by the end of the First World War the site was 'crowded and inadequate'. A chemist from that period, Humphrey Paget, later recorded with particular

FIGURE 10.2
A chemist
in WCRL,
c. 1920s.

horror the narrow, varnished wooden staircase that was the only connection between the four floors, in a building where the extraction techniques involved enormous quantities of petrol, alcohol and ether, and there was no fire escape.[13] The facilities for chemical work attracted particular concern at a meeting of the newly created Scientific and Technical Committee (STC) in December 1926. A circulated report reads 'At almost every meeting of the Scientific and Technical Committee so far held, it has been necessary to postpone or actually give up investigations, because the facilities at the disposal of the Foundation are inadequate'.[14] Several deficiencies were identified: in particular a lack of suitable men in both the Experimental Department at Dartford and the WCRL meant that work on, *inter alia*, thyroxine, adrenaline, anti-helmintics and antiseptics was held up. The reputation and importance of the WCRL notwithstanding, frequent appeals for refurbishment, renovation, and extensions to the company managers at Snow Hill remained largely unanswered.

Contrasting with economies enforced at the WPRL and WCRL, Wellcome simultaneously invested in accommodation and staff for the WBSR. In 1920 they moved to new premises in Endsleigh Gardens, central London. For the purposes of breeding insects, premises were rented from the Royal Horticultural Society at Wisley, known as the Wellcome Entomological Research Laboratories or simply 'the field laboratories'. The WBSR remained in Endsleigh Gardens until late 1929, when the building was demolished to make way for the Wellcome Research Institution (WRI),

FIGURE 10.3
Scientific staff
of the WCRL
1923. Back
row, from
left to right,
Humphrey
Paget, J. A.
Gordon;
front row,
W. H. Gray,
T. A. Henry
and T. M.
Sharp.

of which it became a constituent part. Several scientific and technical staff and a librarian were recruited, and in 1923 Charles Wenyon succeeded Balfour as Director, when the latter became the Director of the London School of Hygiene and Tropical Medicine (LSHTM). Wenyon also assumed Balfour's 'Director in Chief' role in relation to the other Wellcome research laboratories. It was in this capacity, when the STC was formed in 1925, that Wenyon became chairman.

Several research projects were undertaken at the WBSR. Wenyon's own research was in protozoology, in collaboration with Cecil Hoare publishing widely on human intestinal infections such as amoebiasis and leishma-niasis, and disease transmission between humans and animals.[15] Other staff

FIGURE 10.4
Staff at the
Wellcome
Bureau for
Scientific
Research.
The Director,
Dr (later
Sir) Andrew
Balfour is
seated in the
centre, with
his successor
Dr Charles
Wenyon on
his left, 1923.

focussed on basic problems in helminthology, bacteriology and virology. Research programmes on leprosy and yellow fever combined in particular the skills of the WCRL and WBSR, often with additional overseas clinical input to test the resulting compounds in field trials. At the same time, collaborations between the Wellcome laboratories continued in the treatments of several tropical diseases, including malaria, kala-azar, amoebic dysentery and leishmaniasis.[16] Some projects were targeted directly at producing drugs. An early project was on hookworm, an infestation of men and animals in which parasitic worms attach to the intestinal wall and feed on the host's blood, thus causing considerable blood loss and anaemia. At the beginning of 1919, Pyman of the WCRL confidently reported considerable progress to Balfour investigating native hookworm remedies from Brazil, especially the tropical plant Epazote. By December of that year a number of experimental compounds isolated from the plant, including chenopodiun oil, were distributed for trial, including tests by Dr Thomas Dalling, newly appointed to lead veterinary research at the WPRL.[17] By August 1920, after encouraging reports from the earlier tests, and further chemical and pharmacological modifications, a number of biologically active compounds were dispatched to doctors and clinics in Brazil for widespread trial and treatment.[18] The following year a chenopodiun oil preparation was included in the company's price list for the first time.[19]

Other tropical diseases also warranted attention. Amoebic dysentery was a problem that had attracted considerable research effort during the First World War, and it remained an active project well into the 1920s.[20] Additionally, the laboratories, and subsequently the company, produced a range of antimony compounds for patients with sleeping sickness, and especially for leishmaniasis. Confirmatory reports of their success encouraged the investigation of improved, more effective, compounds.[21] By 1925 the STC authorised 'Neostam' (stibaine glucoside) for commercial production. Originating in the WCRL, under W. H. Gray, this mixture of compounds required very close supervision during its manufacture and careful toxicity and efficacy testing, and was also successfully trialled for the treatment of kala-azar and bilharzia.[22]

Formation of the Scientific and Technical Committee

Potentially, the most significant organisational change affecting the management of the business was the formation of the STC, a management forum the purpose of which was 'to consider questions of fundamental research, utilitarian research such as is involved in the practical development of chemotherapy, or scientific and technical advice relating to new drugs'.[23] The lack of effective communication within the organization, and especially between the Works and the WPRL with regard to the manufacture of insulin, plus Wellcome's plans for co-ordinated chemotherapy research had stimulated its establishment. This body met quarterly beginning in February 1925. Membership comprised the heads of laboratories plus Jowett, the Works Manager, though each could, and did, co-opt others possessing special knowledge of any item listed on a quarterly agenda. New reporting arrangements were introduced which troubled O'Brien. Hitherto, the laboratories had been managed largely through informal links between the research directors of the WCRL and WPRL. Since the formation of the WBSR, each had submitted monthly reports to its Director (Balfour until 1923 when he was replaced by Wenyon) who reported to Snow Hill and Wellcome. Even under this system, O'Brien had sometimes found it difficult to resolve the dilemma which he perceived to arise from his simultaneous status as both a professional scientist and as a company employee. He believed that some scientific information suitable for communication to fellow scientists should not be forwarded to the commercial departments of the organisation. He had frequently resolved this problem by preparing one report for scientists and an edited version for submission to Snow Hill.[24] Under the new system introduced by the STC, reports sent to Pearson and Wellcome consisted of minutes of the meetings. This ended O'Brien's selective reporting practice, though his anxieties remained.[25]

The STC's activities were significant in two ways. One was through the impact on the company's commercial policy towards innovation, cost, and profit; the other was its effect on research and development. The origins of the Committee were in part a response to the crisis that followed when the company became one of a controlled number of licensed producers of insulin in Britain in 1922. The difficulties encountered in effecting the transition from laboratory production to manufacturing on a commercial scale revealed the need to improve lines of communication between the laboratories, the Dartford factory, and the Snow Hill office if the problems were to be resolved. Even O'Brien, sometimes averse to frank and open exchanges, acknowledged that poor communication had led the company to underestimating the problems of transition. The result, in his view, was that the firm had been premature in placing insulin on the market before having adequately explored and resolved the problems of the translation from laboratory development to production on a commercial scale. Jowett, too, considered that without improved communications between different parts of the Foundation, its resources could not be 'used to their fullest advantage'.[26] O'Brien and Trevan shared Jowett's frustration with the laboratories' difficulties, which arose from problems with new production facilities at Dartford, where buildings and plant had been rapidly constructed and commissioned, before teething problems had been resolved. The formation of the STC offered a structure within which regular face-to-face communication would begin to take place. Jowett, and to some extent Pearson, also seized the opportunity to use the new system to attempt to harness the research conducted in the laboratories to the company's need to develop a commercial product.[27] Discussion and communication affecting priorities and policies, however, addressed only one layer of the problem affecting relations between office, factory, and laboratories, as O'Brien's perception of divided loyalties reveals. The context of his work as a scientist in the Wellcome laboratories was one in which Wellcome had insisted privately and in public that the laboratories pursued independent scientific research and were only marginally involved with the business. Experience had taught Wellcome that the medical establishment and relevant government departments in the UK were deeply suspicious of connections between scientific research and business. Writing to Balfour in 1915, Wellcome referred to the successful effect of the strict rules he had introduced regarding correspondence conducted by the various departments and laboratories with external bodies, the effect of which was to project an image in which firm and laboratories were distinct and separate entities.[28] That separation was a fiction; the financial accounts of the laboratories appeared in the trading and profit and loss accounts of BW&Co. However, a less tangible diversion in attitudes among staff grew out of Wellcome's rhetoric. The language employed in memoranda among and between laboratory and other staff reveals that almost invariably the Snow Hill office and the Dartford factory were referred to either as 'BW&Co.' or 'the firm', a linguistic distancing which also reflected differences between the interests and concerns of scientists and business staff. From 1921 the isolation of the largest group of scientists of the WPRL at Langley Court, Beckenham, intensified the division.

An illustration that tensions between the two groups had developed shortly after the establishment of the laboratories is the outcome of a dispute between Dale and Wellcome over the use of the term 'adrenaline' in 1906. The disagreement showed Dale anxious to maintain scholarly, scientific integrity, whereas Wellcome's objection to use of the term stemmed from a concern over the commercial repercussions in the event of litigation over a trademark.[29] An important decision affecting the history of the organisation, Wellcome's reluctant concurrence on this occasion underlined a growing independence secured by scientists and an increasing influence of the scientific ethic in the laboratories, even though their activities rested on the commercial success of the company. As the laboratories became increasingly involved in the production of marketable products, notably sera, vaccines, insulin and other hormones, the historical fiction of separate spheres began to assume an increasing degree of substance over the years, exposing two distinctive cultures within a single organisation,

FIGURE 10.5 Dr Hooper Jowett, from an obituary notice (*Foundation News*, October 1952).

Professional research staff and the commercial company

The considerable scientific reputation that the Wellcome laboratories established before and during the war was enhanced after 1918, resulting especially from the WPRL's work on an increasing range of sera, vaccines, insulin and other hormones for human and veterinary medicine. Prestige also grew as a result of the efforts of staff of the WCRL, the WBSR, and the Works to produce chemical treatments for infectious diseases, and innovative pharmaceutical compounds for other medical conditions. Laboratory staff were invited to sit on official committees and commissions; they published in peer-reviewed journals; and contributed to professional scientific and medical societies. Increasingly, though with some notable exceptions, Wellcome scientists received recognition as professionals, as if they were working in an academic rather than a commercial institution.[30]

Questions of professional identity still arose. In 1928, as part of a review of medical employment, the BMA questioned the status of the medically qualified staff employed by Wellcome. Was their work, the BMA asked,

'in any part devoted to work incidental to the organisation and preparation of the therapeutic products manufactured by Messrs Burroughs &
Wellcome?'[31] Admitting that the question was 'a little difficult to answer',
O'Brien suggested that the best analogy was with the Lister Institute,
pointing out that medical personnel there devoted time to the production of
therapies marketed by Allen & Hanburys, while WPRL staff also performed
research, for example, on the scarlet fever toxin 'as many people of pure
academic standing are doing'. The WPRL staff were neither working in a
purely academic environment nor in an entirely commercial organisation.[32]
The company allowed scientific staff to travel to conferences, to maintain
or initiate contacts with fellow researchers in other laboratories, and to
exchange information with them and other scientists, all of which O'Brien
strongly encouraged though pressure of work allowed him little time for
such activities himself and he frequently refused invitations to visit and
lecture abroad.[33] However, problems did arise from the duality of their
position concerning pay levels, tenure, and annual leave for scientific staff
employed in the laboratories. Similar questions had occurred, and been
resolved, in the early days of the research laboratories. In 1923, faced with
a haemorrhage of staff, O'Brien informed Wellcome that conditions at the
WPRL were no longer good enough to attract and retain good men. He
described the maximum leave allowance of four weeks as paltry compared
with the seven weeks allowed for staff at the Lister Institute and nine for
heads of department, which was comparable with conditions at the NIMR
and in universities. The one month's notice contract for Wellcome scientists
(except for the Director) was similarly inferior to the tenure granted in
other institutions. O'Brien regarded the remuneration of senior staff to be
just about adequate but thought it poor for junior staff; and was critical of
the practice whereby even a modest increase required a formal recommendation by the Director and was subject to ratification by BW&Co.[34] Pearson
resisted O'Brien's appeal for reform, insisting that no commercial organisation would provide tenure for its employees comparable to that prevailing
at research institutes. The decision, however, rested with Wellcome, whose
response has not survived, and leaves the outcome of O'Brien's attempt to
improve the working conditions of scientific staff unknown. However, there
is no further correspondence from O'Brien on the matter, and these issues
appear never to have been discussed at a later STC meeting. It seems likely
that Wellcome was prepared, as he had been 20 years earlier, to make
concessions to his scientific staff.

Further tension, between the laboratory staff concerned about overstretched resources, and their Snow Hill managers anxious to advance
public relations, is illustrated by contrasting attitudes towards visitors to the
laboratories. Visits by sympathetic individuals and organisations had, since
the WPRL moved to Herne Hill in 1900, been encouraged by Snow Hill

as opportunities to exploit the laboratories as a showcase for research and to engender both goodwill and favourable publicity. Wellcome staff were willing to entertain visitors who were genuinely interested in the laboratories, often regarding it as payment for hospitality they themselves received elsewhere, but there were strong objections to becoming an exhibition piece for the Wellcome Foundation. Their resentment of the time and resources increasingly absorbed by such visits was expressed in 1924 by O'Brien, who criticised the use of the WPRL as 'a bait to enlist interest ... not in accord with the professional dignity or the tradition of [the] laboratory'.[35] This sentiment was prompted by Snow Hill's desire to invite Dr E.W. Fairfax, an Australian known to be indifferent to the company's work, to visit the laboratories. Although O'Brien acknowledged that should Pearson or Wellcome insist on the visit, it would take place, he indicated that no invitation would 'come spontaneously from the laboratories'.[36] Fewer requests followed this exchange. As long as Wellcome's presence loomed large in the organisation, he succeeded in reconciling the potentially competing objectives of reputation for research scientists and profits from the business. However, his increasingly arms-length approach to management, even before the restructuring of 1924, did little to improve internal relations which experienced increasing pressure in an environment of increased competition and falling prices.

Research strategy and innovation under the STC

In part, the fall in prices during the early 1920s was a correction to the immediate post-war inflation, though an additional contributory factor was the further implementation of the National Health Insurance scheme. One consequence of the increased expenditure by government was a reduction in expenditure on drugs by consumers, a response which probably affected proprietary drugs most as they tended to be more expensive.[37] Competition, however, was also an important factor, a combined consequence of war-induced expansion and the emergence of more competitors. The creation of an enlarged and modernised capacity in the fine chemical industry during the war presented the expanded company with a peacetime problem. The drugs developed by the company as substitutes for German products had been successful, but other British manufacturers had achieved similar success by transforming themselves into research-active pharmaceutical producers on the Wellcome model, a process aided by former BW&Co. employees.

After the war, therefore, the competition in the home market created the need to develop new products. During the war, the priorities had been set by government and the objectives for the scientists had been specified. When the war ended, a drift occurred into a 'me-too' approach to product innovation which O'Brien attributed to the company's overall policy of not attempting to match the huge resources and numbers of scientists mobilised by German pharmaceutical companies. He acknowledged that an inevitable consequence was to rule out the possibility of BW&Co. being able to match organisations in which costs were viewed within a long-term planning horizon. This was his explanation for the Germans' considerable lead in synthetic chemotherapy (an area of research which Wellcome wished to develop). O'Brien explained BW&Co.'s alternative strategy: 'In the meantime, there is a natural temptation to investigate compounds made by other firms and try by substitution to improve on them. Probably it will be impossible to avoid following this course to a certain extent, but it is questionable whether it will be wise to direct the main effort thus'.[38]

Abandoning the 'me too' approach to innovation implied a necessity to invest scientists' time and company resources into one or more lines of research. Selection implied the need to formulate criteria with respect to outcome and required a method of implementation. This was the problem addressed by Jowett in a proposal drafted in May 1925 and adopted by the STC six months later.[39] Jowett was anxious to avoid the undertaking of costly research and development on new or improved products which might prove to be of little or no 'direct commercial value'. He focused on the transfer of procedures from the laboratories to the Works. Hitherto, the supply sources, cost estimates of raw materials, and investigation of patents on intermediate or manufactured inputs had been undertaken *after* a decision to proceed from research and clinical testing to manufacture. Jowett's reform established a formal procedure by which investigation would *precede* transfer from the laboratories to the Works.

In the new system, laboratory heads would submit research proposals considered to be potentially profitable to the STC before being presented to Pearson and Wellcome for approval, rejection, or recommendation. The new procedure required reports on raw material, geographical sources, physical availability, and price; the same was required for manufactured inputs. Further requirements included lists of patents held and by whom they were worked. An assessment of likely demand was to be explored. Estimates were also required of the cost of the finished product 'whether cost prohibitive except for a few rich sufferers, or whether product could be made cheaply to supply a large demand'.[40] Implying the laxity of the preceding procedures, Pearson insisted that 'It should also be decided as a matter of principle that before any new substance is sent out for extended trials it should be prepared in the Experimental Department of the works at Dartford with some approximation to manufacturing conditions'.[41] The intention, therefore, was to establish economic and financial criteria as the prime determinants of research strategy, a stern message to scientists which Pearson appears to have softened by offering an assurance (hardly consistent with the new criteria) that the degree of independence they had enjoyed in the past would continue. The new procedures were not, he explained, intended to apply to 'work of academic interest undertaken by the various research institutions.'[42] Both Henry and O'Brien expressed reservations regarding the ability of the laboratories to transform research into 'usable direct commercial product'. Henry described the premises as 'inadequate for modern chemical research' and maintained that a continuing shortage of trained chemists and technical assistants to carry out literature searches had led to the abandonment or postponement of work on the synthesis of several drugs.[43]

Insulin

Early production problems

The first major therapeutic breakthrough of the post-war period was the discovery of insulin in late 1921, by Frederick Banting and Charles Best at the University of Toronto. Insulin was a specific treatment for diabetes mellitus, then a fatal condition for which there was no known treatment.[44] The problems of translating experimental research into a commercial product, and developing and improving insulin production were to occupy the STC and the company's laboratories throughout the years before the Second World War.[45] The University of Toronto entered into a commercial production agreement with Eli Lilly & Co., and the Toronto Insulin Committee, which held the patent rights, was established to approve all subsequent licensing agreements. In July 1922 the Committee invited the MRC to accept the British patent rights, and Henry Dale and Harold Dudley of the National Institute for Medical Research visited Canada to investigate.[46] They reported enthusiastically on the new therapy, and although reluctant to see a beneficial medicine the subject of a commercial arrangement, recognised the market realities of the situation. In recommending that the MRC accept the rights, they argued that it would enable the Council 'to exercise a moral control over the manufacturers, and would induce the latter to submit to a system of supervision, as regards this product, which the law does not enable the Council at present to enforce'.[47]

Possessing a long history and vast experience of dealing with glandular extracts, the Wellcome laboratories immediately sought permission to become a licensed producer. Within the MRC there was considerable support for the company: 'the position of such a firm as Burroughs Wellcome is so outstanding from the scientific aspect'.[48] The MRC considered having a regional distribution of licences, and it was clear that if only one London firm was to be allowed to manufacture, it would be BW&Co. whose laboratory research facilities and scientific staff were highly regarded.[49] They were not, however, alone, as Allen & Hanburys and British Drug Houses (BDH) pooled their research and production resources and successfully applied to be licensed. Shortly afterwards, licences were allocated to Boots and

Evans Medical Co. Several companies, including Sumner & Co., Oxo, the Association of Clinical and Analytical Laboratories, and Duncan Flockhart, also expressed initial interest but did not proceed.[50] Others, including May & Baker, Martindale, and Oppenheimer, Son & Co., approached the MRC for permission to distribute and market insulin but not to manufacture.[51] The conditions imposed by the MRC on manufacturers included: a maximum selling price that took costs into consideration; a testing and certification scheme for every batch of insulin conducted by staff at the National Institute for Medical Research; every company to use the name 'insulin' for their product; and nominal royalties to be paid by manufacturers.[52]

The MRC's strict criteria for insulin production necessitated crucial experimental work and clinical trials to ensure that only reliable preparations were produced. As one contemporary practitioner pointed out 'were it not for the measures taken by the Medical Research Council it is probable that the country would now be flooded with useless preparations, and an excellent remedy might have fallen into disrepute'.[53] Wellcome, his senior management, and his scientific staff agreed that it was essential for the company in the face of UK and overseas competition, to produce consistent batches of high-quality insulin as soon as possible. That urgency may well have encouraged undue haste rather than a more measured approach based on careful research. Widespread publicity of the new drug had provoked a desperate clamour from patients and their relatives, at a time when it was estimated that at least ten diabetics died every day in the UK. Over the winter months of 1922–23, fewer than 50 British diabetics received insulin treatment. Several laboratories, not only those involved in insulin manufacture, and most notably Dale's department at the NIMR, worked hard to improve extraction procedures.[54] Any technical advances were communicated to all the manufacturing companies, but enormous problems remained. In Britain, these were worsened by difficulties obtaining animal pancreases, the raw material necessary for production. A strike in abattoirs, plus an embargo on the export of live cattle from Canada exacerbated a supply situation already poor compared with the cattle-rich states and provinces and great slaughterhouse areas of North America. A contemporary analysis showed that sheep and pig organs could be used to extract insulin, and for some time fish pancreases were also investigated by the MRC, although there is no evidence that BW&Co. considered using this source.[55]

By October 1922, Trevan at the WPRL had started work on 'Bunting's [sic] method' and just two months later the first batch of insulin was produced by the Experimental Department at Dartford.[56] Soon insulin was being prepared with an activity greater than the experimental batches produced by the WPRL.[57] However, that success was short-lived. The transfer from laboratory extraction to large-scale commercial production was not smooth, although BW&Co. were not the only firm having trouble. After confirmation of the potency and therapeutic possibilities of insulin, a flood of publications appeared from laboratories and companies in Europe and North America, announcing new and improved methods of extracting and purifying the hormone. There was no general agreement about the best techniques, and consequently manufacturers around the world, as well as academic scientists in university laboratories, kept experimenting. Even Eli Lilly who were in advance of all other producers were constantly modifying their own processes. Details of their changes were passed to the MRC, which in turn sent out regular *Insulin Memoranda* to all their licensed companies. During 1923 alone, at least ten such documents were produced, each with new variations and developments in production techniques and testing procedures.[58] One particular problem was how to measure the biological activity of insulin, which was essential information from which to work out dosages for patients. By March 1923, the MRC accepted three units of measurement. The original Toronto Unit was defined as the smallest amount of insulin that would reduce the blood sugar of a 2kg rabbit to the level at which hypoglycaemic convulsions occurred. This was known as 'a rabbit unit', although a 'new rabbit unit', which was one quarter the value of the old unit, became widely used in North America. Translated into treatment terms, the average dose for a patient was 10 new units, instead of 2.5 old units. The third, 'mouse unit', was physiologically similar, assessing the dose required to induce hypoglycaemic convulsions in mice, and being 1/5,000th of the old rabbit unit, and 1/1,200th of the new.[59] This was confusing enough. The manufacturers were also struggling with erratic supplies of raw materials, capricious extraction techniques and sterility problems. But the units kept changing and in April 1923 the manufacturing firms were told that Eli Lilly had raised the value of a 'new rabbit unit' by 25 per cent, making what was 10 units now 12.5 units. The MRC considered it had no option but to accept such measures, so as to retain uniformity with US production.[60] In July of that year the Standardisation Committee of the League of Health Nations met in Edinburgh and agreed that the 'old rabbit unit' should be universally used, although increasing experience revealed the variability of rabbits' responses, which introduced further discrepancies into insulin assays. To ensure uniformity, the Conference report suggested that a stable, dry form of insulin should be prepared.

Before being able to produce such a sample, manufacturers had to overcome other difficulties. In early 1923, the Allen & Hanburys/BDH consortium, eager to get a headstart in the UK before Eli Lilly started importing their insulin, marketed its first batch of 'A & B' insulin.[61] A few weeks later, BW&Co. advertised its first samples. However, all three companies (initially both BDH and Allen & Hanburys produced insulin at their separate sites but pooled their expertise and their results) experienced inconsistent production until mid-1923, when consecutive batches of insulin began to pass the MRC's tests. In May 1923, BW&Co.'s travellers were urged to push their success and emphasise to doctors and chemists the pre-eminence of the firm in supporting research and developing new products. An explanatory leaflet was hastily produced for distribution and the company reps were given detailed training about treatment protocols, rival therapies, and the scientific rationale of the new product.[62] As is the way so often with new therapies, insulin was not initially confined to the treatment of diabetes, and BW&Co.'s South American agents reported enthusiastically to Snow Hill that doctors in Argentina were finding insulin effective in treating paediatric digestive problems, eczema and thyroid problems, all of which opened up potential new markets, although these remained unexplored.[63]

During the week ending 10 September 1923, a total of over 24,500 units of insulin from all sources were sold in the UK, compared with fewer than 2,000 in the week ending 23 April. Supplies were still poor, however, an official at the Ministry of Health reckoning that the producers' entire stocks would last less than one week.[64] In October, Evans, Lescher & Webb finally managed to produce a small batch of satisfactory insulin, and in March 1924 so did Boots. However, Evans very quickly stopped regular production, leaving the field to BW&Co., BDH and Allen & Hanburys, and Boots.[65] By the end of 1923, the Director of the WPRL, O'Brien estimated that about 200 insulin-testing experiments were still being done in his laboratories every day because Dartford staff could not cope with the work. The pressure on the physiologists was intense, O'Brien's desperate attempt to draft in temporary workers, often women, to help, achieving little success.[66] Pure research in the WPRL was at an almost complete stop because of continuing problems with the insulin production. The *ad hoc* arrangements then in place meant that, to the irritation of the physiologists, samples were sent from the Works for testing by the WPRL without any description of the method of preparation used or the objective in view.[67] The cumbersome method of postal communication that existed in the Wellcome organisation, whereby all correspondence was channelled via Wenyon of the WBSR (i.e. O'Brien could not write directly to Pyman or Jowett, let alone an external correspondent, without a copy and a separate explanatory letter going to Wenyon, who in turn, forwarded correspondence to Snow Hill) did not assist the development of easy or synergistic relationships between the laboratories. By the latter half of 1923, it was becoming clear that new techniques devised in the WPRL had not transferred well into the Works.[68] Although the initial extraction was satisfactory, the next stages became more troublesome and the resultant insulin was considerably weaker than expected. Production was 'disheartening': the average yield was low, only about 20 human doses per kilo of animal pancreas, and it was well known that some commercial rivals had overcome these and similar problems. O'Brien and Trevan considered that the difficulties were entirely because a new building and plant for insulin production had been hastily erected at Dartford without proper consultation or preparation. In the WPRL, experiments on extraction and purification from different raw materials continued to be successful, and O'Brien proposed to the company that while examination of the flawed large-scale process at Dartford continued, the WPRL could produce small batches for the company. Simultaneously he appealed to his former colleague, Henry Dale, for help from the MRC. By now the responsibility for sorting out the firm's problems rested firmly on the shoulders of the physiologists. Staff from the WPRL, especially Trevan, spent the next few months at the Works, checking every procedure, analysing each production stage, and testing all the insulin produced. Samples were also sent to the MRC, the final arbiters of the strength and efficacy of the insulin. Batch after batch of Dartford produced insulin was rejected. Then a new problem emerged. Some of the first satisfactory batches had lost potency when re-tested, although Eli Lilly's insulin kept in the same conditions did not. Further work was urgently needed. However, unlike other manufacturers, BW&Co.'s scientists did little original research themselves into insulin preparation (as opposed to biological effects of insulin) and this undoubtedly handicapped efforts to resolve their difficulties. Eli Lilly's scientists were the first to publish their early investigations into preparative techniques, while in Britain former Wellcome employees Carr and Underhill, then working in the 'A-B Insulin Physiological Laboratories' of BDH, spearheaded research examining the problems.[69] Of over 160 publications from the WPRL from 1922 to 1929 only three were on insulin, and none was on methods of extraction. This lack of innovative work in an organisation that had been strongly dependent on its own research initiatives was largely a matter of manpower availability. The major physiological and chemical research workers, Dale, Barger and Ewins, had all left the WPRL in 1914, and not been replaced. O'Brien and Glenny, both outstanding scientists in bacteriological and immunological studies, did not have the time, let alone the relevant expertise, to initiate appropriate research in this area. The appointment of John Trevan in 1920 as staff pharmacologist to the WPRL had only partly addressed this deficiency of expertise.

In December 1923, O'Brien wrote separately and somewhat irritably to both Jowett and Wenyon. He was exasperated with the insulin situation and insisted that the company had rushed into commercial production before all the problems had been identified and resolved. Considering the apparently smooth and successful insulin production of Eli Lilly, he added 'one may be forgiven for breaking the tenth commandment'.[70] Allen & Hanburys and BDH were also doing well. Between April and October 1923 they sold 2,525 thousand units of insulin, whereas BW&Co. sold only 490 thousand units. By the end of that year 95% of the market went to the 'A-B' brand, a success that did much to establish BDH as a major pharamaceutical manufacturer.[71] In the Wellcome organisation, relationships between Jowett and O'Brien, and between the Works and the WPRL, were far from happy. Finally, during the first few months of 1924 Jowett visited the WPRL several times to discuss the insulin problem. O'Brien believed these personal visits advanced matters far more than had the previous lengthy correspondence. Part of O'Brien's irritation was due to the fact that this was not the first time such issues had arisen between the WPRL and Dartford. Since the end of the war production difficulties at Dartford with both dried diphtheria serum and Infundin, BW&Co.'s pituitary extract, had also necessitated the WPRL taking over production.[72] The latter had been particularly

frustrating as experiments had shown that BW&Co.'s Infundin was twice as strong as pituitary preparations marketed by Mulfords and Parke Davis & Co., and the company had been eager to push the extract.[73] Coping with such commercial emergencies diverted staff, especially Trevan, away from the laboratory where they were still trying desperately to recover from their wartime existence as a serum factory. Frustrated by the resulting difficulties in developing new research programmes, staff greatly resented the imposition of further engagement in manufacturing.

By 1924, the production problems experienced earlier at Dartford had been largely resolved, principally through the efforts of Trevan, although staff from the WPRL continued to stay closely involved and to work on new refinements in insulin production and development. Boots, too, had difficulties, having devoted considerable space and money to the project. A report to the MRC stated that the company had invested in a 'huge establishment and a factory site covering 14 acres', especially for the work.[74] Boots, however, was completely new to the field of hormone preparations and, being unable to resolve technical problems themselves, established a series of regular staff visits to Charles Best's Toronto laboratory to learn about improving the preparation and standardisation of insulin.[75]

As insulin production became more

reliable and extensive, commercial competition between the three UK producers gradually forced the prices down, as shown in Table 10.2.

Table 10.2 *British insulin prices in the UK: retail prices of 5 ml (20 units per ml), 1923–1924* [76]

Date		A&H/BDH	BW&Co.	Boots
1923	(Apr.)	25s. 0d.	25s. 0d.	25s. 0d.
	(July)	17s. 6d.	–	12s. 6d.
1924	(Jan.)	12s. 6d.	12s. 6d.	–
	(Feb.)	–	6s. 8d.	6s. 8d.
	(Apr.)	6s. 8d.	–	–
	(May)	–	4s. 8d.	4s. 8d.
	(June)	–	–	3s. 0d.
	(July)	–	2s. 8d.	2s. 8d.
	(Oct.)	2s. 8d.	–	–
1929	(May)	2s. 0d.	1s. 8d.	–
1934	(Jan.)	1s. 10d.	1s. 10d.	1s. 5d.

Over the next few years the major commercial push was to produce increasingly pure material. In 1925 an International Standards Conference was convened in Geneva to discuss the measurement of the activity of insulin preparations. By this time, confident of the standard of BW&Co.'s production, Henry Dale requested the assistance of Trevan and the WPRL to create a standard for insulin. Acting on behalf of the MRC, he subsequently presented the conference with an ampule of dried insulin powder that was immediately adopted as the international standard.[77]

While this was indicative of BW&Co.'s continuing high reputation among scientists, the significance of the company's involvement in the development of insulin needs to be placed in a wider perspective. First, the company secured a small market share, second, the rapid price fall of insulin implies low profitability, which in any case was regulated by the MRC. The combination of limited supply and low profitability suggests that judged by commercial criteria, had the company not obtained an insulin licence, it would have been in a position to apply resources to one of the other promising lines of research identified by Wellcome scientists. This was frustrated to a considerable extent because of the difficulties the company encountered in the early stages of the development of insulin, which absorbed staff and resources at a time when they were in short supply. The forgone lines of research and development and their potentially higher profitability were the opportunity costs of creating an international standard for insulin.

Science versus commerce: advertising claims for insulin

Of the three research papers on insulin published from the WPRL, one in particular caused problems about the use or misuse of scientific information by the commercial managers of BW&Co. Authorship was by a consortium of scientists led by Charles Harington from University College London. It comprised two parts, one section containing chemical observations on insulin, and another comparing the available physiological assays. This latter study consisted of three sets of observations: by Kathleen Culhane of the Allen & Hanbury/BDH insulin laboratories; D. A. Scott and H. P. Marks of the NIMR; and Trevan from the WPRL.[78] BDH, BW&Co. and the Connaught Laboratories of Toronto had provided the insulin samples for the study. One finding was that the mouse method of insulin standardisation, pioneered in the UK by Trevan, was the most reliable of all the techniques examined, a point of some gratification to BW&Co. The Tabloid insulin was also shown to be far more potent than that from BDH or the Connaught laboratories. BW&Co. immediately seized upon this fact, and advertising material rapidly appeared in medical and pharmaceutical journals lauding the Tabloid preparation as 'the purest insulin ever obtained by research workers'. The claim was subsequently repeated in the Monthly Memoranda prepared for BW&Co.'s representatives to push to their customers.

Staff at the WPRL objected strongly to this interpretation. O'Brien complained to Wenyon that using a scientific paper in this way was a 'regrettable ... serious mistake' that could severely damage their relationships with scientists outside the company. For the joint experimental work the Company had made a gift of insulin, with no conditions attached. It was a betrayal of the scientists' trust, O'Brien protested, to use their results for commercial advantage. Although mistaken in believing that scientific papers had never been used before in company adverts (see for example the publicity for tyramine, Fig 6.9) O'Brien was particularly angry that the data was being used in a very obvious marketing battle with BDH. He emphasised that it would not look good to the MRC who still controlled insulin licences, and that 'without doubt, this lapse at Snow Hill will be pointed out to Dale by Carr'.[79] Trevan had been placed in a particularly invidious position with his professional colleagues;

FIGURE 10.7 BW&Co. advertisement for 'the purest insulin ever obtained even by research workers' (*BMJ* 26 October 1929), with a citation to the research paper in the *Biochemical Journal* written by scientists working for several companies and organisations.

O'Brien considered that the company had scored an astonishing commercial own-goal. The Tabloid insulin in the study had assayed at a strength of 21 units/mg.; that of BDH at 13 units/mg. The inference that the Company's advertising staff had put on this, that all Tabloid insulin was purer, was entirely fallacious. O'Brien believed, correctly, that Jowett had sent one of BW&Co.'s best batches. BDH, however, may well have supplied a lower

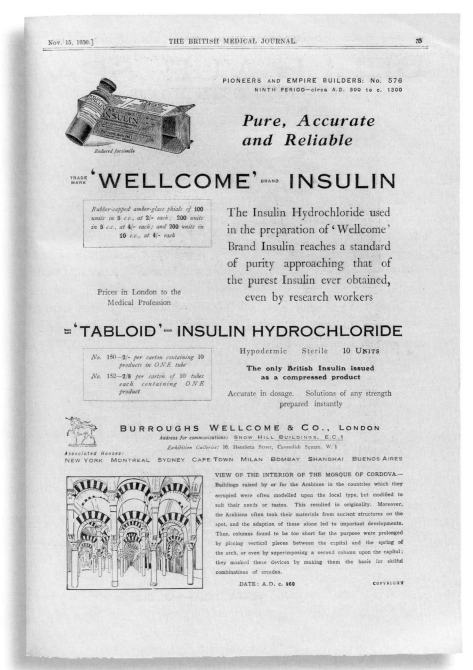

FIGURE 10.8 BW&Co advertisement for insulin (*BMJ*, 15 November 1930) still claiming it to be 'the purest insulin ever obtained even by research workers', but without the journal citation. Note the inclusion of a non-related image and historical text, relating to the mosque at Cordoba as number 576 in a series of 'Pioneers and Empire Builders'.

strength insulin, because the experiment was not to test the strength of the insulin, but to test the assay methods. The matter needed careful handling – the purpose and value of the scientific work done in the WPRL might be seriously questioned by both scientific colleagues and prospective customers.[80] Wenyon immediately took up the matter with Pearson, reminding him how vital it was for the WPRL, and the company, that the scientists be protected against any charge of bias towards Wellcome products, otherwise they would lose the respect and collaboration of other researchers. Pearson's reply has not survived, and although the claim that BW&Co.'s insulin was the 'purest available' continued to appear, the controversial reference to the scientific publication was removed. Despite the scientists' concerns, exchanges and collaborations with colleagues outside the laboratories were not irreparably damaged and continued in a number of research projects, including the development of canine distemper vaccine, and the testing and manufacture of ergometrine.[81]

Industrial collaboration: British Insulin Manufacturers

By the latter half of the 1920s, all the earlier problems of inconsistent samples and low quality batches of insulin had largely been eradicated. United by their common technical problems, and their licensing agreements with the MRC, the four manufacturing companies, BW&Co., Allen & Hanburys, BDH, and Boots, formed an alliance, later formalised as the British Insulin Manufacturers. In 1933 the Manufacturers challenged a decision by the Board of Trade to exclude foreign insulin from import tax, and during the legal proceedings F.H.Carr estimated that almost 90 per cent of the insulin sold in Britain at that time was supplied by BDH and BW&Co.[82] As preparations became purer, two problems emerged. The first was with the units of measurement, as insulin standardised on mice consistently registered as weaker than insulin calibrated in rabbit units. BW&Co. was the only British firm to use the mouse unit which was also used by the Leo company of Denmark. Henry Dale discussed this with each company, and reported to the MRC that Leo had agreed to assign an appropriate strength value to their products so as to eliminate confusion between their products and others'. BW&Co. on the other hand 'showed their usual attitude of short-sighted resistance' to calls to increase the strength of their insulin, then estimated by MRC scientists to be 25 per cent weaker than other preparations. BW&Co. argued, with some justification, that suddenly increasing the strength of their insulin could be dangerous to patients accustomed to the product. Dale however, was dismissive, suggesting that they sold weaker insulin because 'their real trouble is not concern with danger, but for profits'.[83] Gradually however, BW&Co. did bring the strength of their insulin into line with that of other producers, clearly concerned that acquiring a reputation for weaker insulin would damage their product in the market place.

The second and surprising problem was that the purer forms of insulin produced by BW&Co. and other manufacturers seemed less able to control diabetes than did the earlier material. This indicated some unknown contaminant had actually improved its efficacy. Experiments in Toronto demonstrated that the addition of zinc, and work in Copenhagen (that was patented) showed that the inclusion of protamine, a small protein molecule, stabilised and increased the insulin's activity.[84] The British manufacturers watched the proceedings with interest, and met together to discuss the situation. Pyman, formerly of the WCRL, then of Boots, suggested that they work together in deciding whether to manufacture under the Danish licence. All present agreed.[85] Francis Carr wrote to Henry Dale, then in Stockholm to receive his Nobel Prize, suggesting that the firms acting

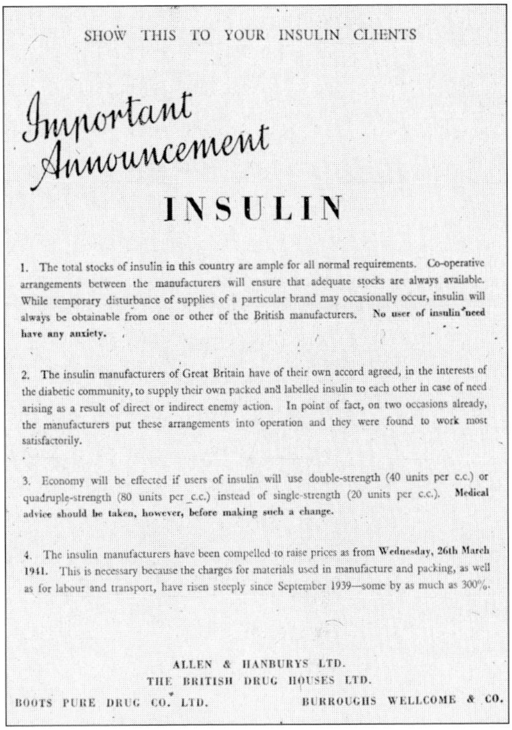

SHOW THIS TO YOUR INSULIN CLIENTS

Important Announcement

INSULIN

1. The total stocks of insulin in this country are ample for all normal requirements. Co-operative arrangements between the manufacturers will ensure that adequate stocks are always available. While temporary disturbance of supplies of a particular brand may occasionally occur, insulin will always be obtainable from one or other of the British manufacturers. No user of insulin need have any anxiety.

2. The insulin manufacturers of Great Britain have of their own accord agreed, in the interests of the diabetic community, to supply their own packed and labelled insulin to each other in case of need arising as a result of direct or indirect enemy action. In point of fact, on two occasions already, the manufacturers put these arrangements into operation and they were found to work most satisfactorily.

3. Economy will be effected if users of insulin will use double-strength (40 units per c.c.) or quadruple-strength (80 units per c.c.) instead of single-strength (20 units per c.c.). Medical advice should be taken, however, before making such a change.

4. The insulin manufacturers have been compelled to raise prices as from Wednesday, 26th March 1941. This is necessary because the charges for materials used in manufacture and packing, as well as for labour and transport, have risen steeply since September 1939—some by as much as 300%.

ALLEN & HANBURYS LTD.
THE BRITISH DRUG HOUSES LTD.
BOOTS PURE DRUG CO. LTD.   BURROUGHS WELLCOME & CO.

'in complete unison', could meet with him to discuss the Danish patent.[86] A striking marker of the influence of Wellcome's research laboratories is that of the seven people at that initial meeting, five (Dale of the MRC, Carr of BDH, and Pyman of Boots, plus Pearson and Smith) had been or were employed by Wellcome. Amongst themselves, they agreed to manufacture Protamine Insulin Zinc under licence to Nordisk Insulinlaboratorium, and to collaborate with each other and the MRC to produce reliable standards of the new product.[87]

The links and collaborations forced upon insulin manufacturers during the early years of its commercial preparation fostered some degree of working together, though co-operation did not extend beyond insulin production.[88] Prompted by BW&Co., during the Second World War the four British producers agreed to supply insulin to each other in case of shortfalls brought about by that emergency, and all four companies became founder members of the Therapeutic Research Corporation in 1942.

FIGURE 10.9 Display card for chemists, announcing that the 'Insulin manufacturers of Great Britain' (Allen & Hanburys, BDH, Boots and BW&Co.) have arranged to collaborate to supply insulin in the event of disrupted supply. March 1941.

Other drugs and developments

The (eventual) resolution of the ergot problem

A report in early 1925 that a collaboration between former Wellcome staff Barger and Carr might result in BDH putting out an improved ergotoxine preparation stimulated BW&Co. to re-activate research that had lain dormant since before the First World War.[89] There were local factors that also explain the resumption of the research. The company had recently issued one of its regular information booklets, *Rational Obstetrics*, on the US market, which reported a considerable amount of scientific work undertaken by the laboratories. Staff at the WPRL were unhappy with the pamphlet. The question at heart related to the product sold by BW&Co. under the name 'ernutin' which was a mixture of two ergot extracts, ergamine and ergotoxine. By the mid-1920s ergot supplies from Russia, Poland and Spain had all failed, partly because of post-war and post-revolution difficulties. The company's materia medica farm in Kent was unable to produce sufficient quantities and ergotoxine production halted for want of ergot. In these circumstances, but without consulting its scientific staff, the company started to produce and promote 'new ernutin', a preparation that did not contain ergotoxine. However, *Rational Obstetrics* promoted 'new ernutin', but used scientific information relating to old ernutin, the effects of which were undoubtedly due to the presence of ergotoxine.[90] This 'oversight' as O'Brien diplomatically referred to it, needed immediate correction, although he accepted that as a member of the scientific staff, he could merely advise the company. A further problem arose when the company's American promotional material also claimed that the new ernutin possessed 'the therapeutic efficiency of [the American] fluid extract of ergot'. This, O'Brien pointed out, was completely untrue. 'May I suggest', he wrote, 'the advisability of making a fairly complete pronouncement on the situation? This announcement would state that from the point of view of scientific medicine and practical therapeutics, the position in connection with ergot preparations is unsatisfactory'.[91]

Once more, profound differences arose between the scientists and managers of the Wellcome Foundation. O'Brien pointed out that if 'Mr Wellcome's organisation' issued such an inaccurate and misleading booklet it would rightly forfeit its position as a respected scientific company.[92] His letter threw BW&Co. into confusion. The senior management had apparently been unaware of the scientific significance of their decision, and were shocked at the confusion they had created. Considerable efforts were made to secure ergot supplies at any price, and by August 1925 Dartford was able to manufacture limited amounts of ergotoxine. By the following year large-scale commercial production had resumed, and ernutin again contained both ergotoxine and ergamine.[93] The decision to re-introduce ergotoxine, was timely and of commercial significance. Reports to the STC indicated that clinicians using the 'new' ernutin in the USA were, not surprisingly, becoming dissatisfied with it and sales were dropping. The New York branch of BW&Co. began demanding the original formula so as to re-capture the 'excellent sales and big reputation' of the original product.[94]

One research problem raised by these events was a push to produce a purer form of ergotoxine. By 1927 the WPRL and the WCW produced a purified chemical, ergotoxine ethanesulphate, which first appeared in the 'Wellcome' Brand Chemicals list in 1928. It was rapidly accepted as *the* standard preparation.[95] By this time BW&Co., as did other manufacturers, marketed a number of preparations and extracts of ergot, all of which displayed some biological activities as obstetric preparations.[96] On

FIGURE 10.10 BW&Co. advertisement for their ergot preparation, Ernutin (*BMJ*, 17 August 1929), number 524 in the 'Pioneer and Empire Building' series.

BW&Co's list alone were ergotamine, ernutine, tyramine, the original old fashioned extract of ergot, ergotoxine and ergamine.[97] In 1929 the marketing department returned once more to the question of ernutin and suggested to O'Brien that because ergamine (later shown to be a form of histamine) acted more quickly on uterine tissues than did ergotoxine, this should be made a 'selling point by advertisement and propaganda' and the proportion of ergamine be correspondingly increased in ernutin preparations. O'Brien immediately reminded them of the recent problems that such tinkering had produced, and suggested that not only should clinical trials be undertaken on a new formulation, but that in future the marketing department take on the serious responsibility of informing the medical profession, by labelling and adverts, if they changed the formulation.[98]

Increasingly scientists and practitioners inside and outside the company regarded the position of ergot and all its extracts as 'anomalous' and unsatisfactory.[99] By the beginning of the 1930s, the Therapeutic Trials Committee of the MRC commissioned an investigation by Dr Chassar Moir, an obstetrician at University College Hospital, London, to resolve the situation. Using extracts made for him by BW&Co., Moir quickly showed that neither ergotoxine nor ergotamine, which were clinically indistinguishable, was responsible for the traditional fast effect of ergot.[100] Moir's clinical and lab work finally revealed yet another extract of ergot, one that did have the traditional rapid effect.[101] In collaboration with scientists under Dale's direction at the NIMR, he successfully isolated and chemically identified the new alkaloid in 1935, which was named ergometrine.[102] At this point, professional rivalries and competition for precedence enter the picture, as rival groups from the US and Switzerland, representing a variety of university and commercial interests, all claimed to have isolated the extract and all used their own names.[103] Anxious that the pharmaceutical world could be flooded with preparations of the same chemical under several names, Dale offered, on behalf of the MRC, to provide British companies with all the necessary technical data to allow them to start production, on the understanding they would not apply a proprietary name.[104] BW&Co., along with Boots, BDH, Allen & Hanburys, May & Baker and Duncan Flockhart, immediately accepted the MRC's conditions and started to manufacture ergometrine.[105]

Chaulmoogra and derivitives

As with the early laboratory investigations of ergot by Dale and Barger, chaulmoogra oil and its derivatives, especially hydnocarpus oil, had been examined by Power as leprosy treatments, during the earliest years of the WCRL's existence. BW&Co. continued to be interested in chaulmoogra, manufacturing and promoting Moogrol, a mixture of derivatives of chaulmoogra oil, after the First World War. Strong links existed between the company and the British Empire Leprosy Relief Association (BELRA), fostered largely by Wellcome's personal membership of organisations such as the Royal Society of Tropical Medicine where he associated with tropical experts and government advisers. BELRA was enormously important to BW&Co. in providing initial access to patients world-wide on whom experimental compounds could be tested, and then subsequently also as a major purchaser of effective medication.[106] After extensive experience of its use, BELRA pronounced Moogrol 'excellent', but noted it was 'somewhat expensive', especially as most sufferers lived in comparatively impoverished parts of the world.[107] Additional problems with the administration of the preparation persisted, absorbing the efforts of the researchers in the Experimental Department at Dartford and the WCRL who were constantly trying to improve its formulation and production.[108] Neither oral nor injectable forms were acceptable to the patient, because of its very oily consistency. In 1926 a new hydnocarpate preparation was being manufactured and tested, based on a formula devised by Professor Chuni Lal Bose in Calcutta. This appeared to be particularly effective, and relatively painless, whether injected subcutaneously or intra-muscularly, thus eliminating the problem of blocked veins. It was enthusiastically tested by Rogers who encouraged BW&Co. to manufacture the compound commercially.[109] Known as Alepol, worldwide trials confirmed its efficacy, at an annual treatment cost of about five shillings per head (compared with £5 previously).[110] BELRA distributed almost 10 kilograms of the drug around the world.[111] At the end of 1929 Rogers could again report with some satisfaction that Alepol had been successful in many thousands of cases.[112] Two years later, at the International Leprosy Conference, he spoke with almost possessive pride of the drug 'made for me by Burroughs, Wellcome & Co., over a million doses of which were used with good results intramuscularly and subcutaneously in British African colonies alone last year'.[113]

Throughout the 1930s similar experiments to modify formulations of Moogrol were constantly in progress.[114] Prolonged use of hydnocarpus preparations induced pain and irritation, which prompted analysis to identify the noxious components. Henry worked methodically to reduce the acidity of the preparations, which had been increased to make the hydnocarpic salts more soluble and easily injectable.[115] In 1932 an iodised Moogrol preparation finally produced encouraging test results and was rapidly marketed by the company.[116] Efforts were made to make an oil, paste or cream which could be absorbed through the skin, but the oily nature of the hydnocarpic oil made such a preparation difficult.[117] The sodium salts of hydnocarpus were not successful in all cases, and the WCRL continued to investigate promising reports of other remedies, often guided by Sir Leonard Rogers, who quickly arranged clinical trials of potential new compounds.[118] The WCRL and the Dartford works also collaborated to produce a preparation of mercury dissolved in hydnocarpus oil, to treat leprosy complicated by syphilis. After successful field trials Avenyl entered large-scale production in 1926, followed by the manufacture of a combined Avenyl-Moogrol product. Although much of the leprosy work was 'pure' research, it did result in several well-selling compounds which did much to alleviate the misery of a disease for which little treatment was available.

Other chemotherapy plans

Once the immediate post-war problems at the laboratories had been resolved as best as possible, Wellcome began to think about future directions of work. He was keenly interested in developing chemotherapy research thoroughly and systematically, and asked O'Brien to consider how all the research laboratories and the Dartford Works might collaborate more effectively to realise these ambitions.[119] O'Brien regarded the infrastructure and scale of research in synthetic chemotherapy conducted by German companies to be beyond the resources at the disposal of BW&Co. He proposed that physiological chemotherapy, research into how drugs act, would probably be more feasible and fruitful. However, recruiting qualified scientists presented a problem, as O'Brien's lack of success in appointing a senior physiologist to assist Trevan had demonstrated. Former Wellcome staff who would have been able to contribute were now working with Dale at the NIMR, the leading group in the field. Moreover, attention to solving problems associated with insulin production had required all the pharmacological resources of the WPRL, leaving no opportunity for innovative research. Given these constraints, O'Brien favoured continuing research on lines already established: endocrinology and alkaloid chemistry and physiology. This also required an immediate increase in pharmacological staff to develop work in physiological chemotherapy to achieve a long-term aim of supporting work in synthetic chemotherapy.

In response to Wellcome, O'Brien suggested that the research team assembled at the pre-war WPRL offered the ideal template.[120] Then, the physiologists Dale and Laidlaw had worked closely with the chemists Barger and Ewins and collaborated with Carr, Pyman, and King at Dartford. O'Brien believed that regular contact and constant presence in each other's laboratories had facilitated the scientists' ability 'to carry on suggestions and translate the result of any researches into production on the commercial scale'.[121] He recommended a re-creation of the conditions that had allowed such synergy. By then, however, the laboratories had become even more physically separated. The Wellcome Chemical Works was at Dartford, the WPRL at Beckenham, the WBSR at Endsleigh Gardens, and the WCRL at King Street in London. Although the formation of the STC in 1924 was intended to improve communications between the laboratories and between Snow Hill, Dartford and the laboratories, the close contact of the pre-war model was virtually impossible.

O'Brien proposed two schemes to rectify this separation. The first was for the WCRL to join the WBSR at Endsleigh Gardens, which would then become the centre of chemotherapy research, whilst the WPRL would be mainly responsible for developing organo-therapy, continuing hormone, sera and vitamin work. Plan B was to amalgamate the WCRL with the WPRL at Beckenham, although he realised the chemists would resent what they would interpret as a take-over by the physiologists. Neither scheme was ideal, and the management issues were particularly acute. O'Brien also urged, along with the re-organisation of the research laboratories, the closer involvement of the Dartford Experimental Department, emphasising '[w]ithout this possibility the full usefulness to the Foundation of a big chemotherapeutical research organisation would not be obtained'. Any development would be costly. There were no suitable senior scientists available to be brought into a new department and BW&Co. would have to invest in people, buildings and resources for some time before any results would be forthcoming. O'Brien estimated that expenditure of between £20,000 and £40,000 per year for up to ten years might be necessary.[122] The financial and administrative considerations were enormous and the organizational difficulties that O'Brien recognised were not adequately resolved until well after Wellcome's death in 1936. This perpetuated a fragmented research and development framework which proved to be increasingly unsatisfactory during the 1930s. This was a period when competition from other companies, often possessing their own more recent and more integrated research and development capacities, began to undermine BW&Co.'s historic pre-eminence in pharmaceutical research and in the market for ethical medicines.

In 1932 the 'Wellcome Research Institution', WRI, was opened on Euston Road, central London. This housed the WSBR, the WCRL and Wellcome's historical and medical museums. The WPRL remained at Beckenham, and Dartford continued to have its own experimental section. After the bombing of Snow Hill in 1941 during the Second World War, the WRI became the 'temporary' headquarters of the company until 1986. New Chemical Research Laboratories (CRL) were established at Beckenham in 1940, and shortly after the retirement of Thomas Henry as Director of the WCRL, all the laboratories at Euston Road were re-named the Wellcome Laboratories of Tropical Medicine. In 1965 these laboratories too were moved to Beckenham, finally uniting most of the original research laboratories established by Wellcome under one roof.

Communication between the laboratories

Effective communication between different parts of the organization was a frequent problem. Uncertainty about the future directions of research, and the prospect of possible integration of all laboratories on one or two sites delayed decisive decision making and compounded the immediate difficulties. Pressure on existing space was especially acute at the WPRL and O'Brien frequently requested relatively modest additional funds to allow ad hoc expansion to meet critical needs. In November 1927, for example, he requested alterations to the bleeding rooms in the stables; a new storage shed; and new breeding sheds for rodents, at a cost of nearly £2,500.[123] The following year a request for further expansion revealed that the WPRL employed between 190 and 200 staff, including 22 scientists, and had annual salary costs of over £20,000. O'Brien stressed, the growth of the laboratories was almost entirely due to advances in basic research and that the output of 'sera, etc, [which] we send to Burroughs Wellcome and Co. and which they sell' was only a little more than when the laboratories arrived at Beckenham seven years earlier.[124] This observation underlines the extent to which he was out of touch with the business. Sales of sera in 1921 amounted to £58,285; in 1928 the figure was £74,223.[125]

In 1930 O'Brien reiterated the pressing need for expansion, advancing as evidence the increases shown in the number of staff employed, litres of serum, tuberculins, and vaccines produced, numbers of experimental animals used for testing, and the number of 'horse weeks' during the previous decade. He drew attention to the increase by 50 per cent in the operating cost of the laboratories between 1924 and 1930.[126] An encouraging response from Snow Hill prompted O'Brien to prepare plans for a major development scheme for submission to Beckenham Council in March 1931. He argued that the independent academic standing of the laboratories and the importance of their collaborative work with the Ministry of Health, the MRC, the Ministry of Agriculture, as well as with professional and regulatory bodies around the world fully justified expansion of the research facilities.[127] He drew attention to the Wellcome laboratories' contribution to the enormous increase in medical knowledge, specifically resulting from work on scarlet fever, veterinary diseases, diabetes, and pernicious anaemia, all of which made heavy demands on limited resources, which overstretched accommodation and resulted in working conditions less than desirable from the standpoint of convenience and safety.[128] O'Brien's rough estimates for essential work came to £11,000, which he calculated would be totally re-paid if insulin production was improved by just 5–10 per cent.[129] The timing of his submission, however, was critical, unfortunately coinciding with the slump in the economy and a concomitant search for widespread economies within the organisation. The company rejected his proposals. O'Brien's comments referring to overcrowding and safety were prescient, as later events in Ireland leading to the so-called 'Ring case', were to prove.[130]

The difficulties of communication resulting from the continuing physical separation of office, factory, and the laboratories are evident in the demarcation disputes that arose even after the formation of the STC. In 1928, for example, Jowett was keen to investigate a new liver extract, Heparmone, produced by Eli Lilly & Co., then being trialled for arterial hypertension. Jowett insisted that the Works facilities were unsuitable and asked O'Brien to undertake the relevant investigations at the WPRL. Already understaffed on the biochemical side, O'Brien suggested that a 'rough distinction' should be drawn between responsibilities; attempts to manufacture or improve 'on what one might crudely call "rival productions",' should be made in Dartford, while the WPRL should work on entirely novel lines.[131] In suggesting such a division, he was imitating, doubtless unknowingly, the arrangements between the Experimental Department and the WCRL at the beginning of the century. With regard to the liver extract, after discussion with Henry Dale who considered it to be a mixture of choline and histamine and therefore nothing new, O'Brien decided that further investigation should not proceed.

Research choices, product development and commercial interests: tropical medicine

Not only did the formation of the STC not mark the end of demarcation disputes, the new commercial criteria adopted by the STC when deciding on research options proved more difficult to apply than Jowett had initially envisaged. The problems raised by the new criteria are revealed in extreme form in the field of tropical medicine. Here, the potential conflict between patients' need for treatment and the economic imperative of securing scale economies was crucial to decision-making. Thus, when in 1931 representatives from the British Empire Leprosy Relief Association and the Culio Leper Colony in the Philippines showed interest in Moogrol being developed by the WBSR, Henry explained that 'the difficulty with Moogrol is that BW&Co. could not be expected to be interested in the sale of a litre here and there'. What was required was 'the prospect of a good market.'[132] The visitors' response was to outline a method of centralising demand by contacting governments and leper institutions throughout the Empire to underline the advantages of securing supplies centrally. This proved sufficient to convince Jowett and Henry that 1500ccs of iodised Moogrol should be produced. Another example of the importance of orchestrating markets for tropical medicines is provided by the connection with the Bilharzia Committee in South Africa. The committee included members drawn from the Public Health and Educational Departments and the South African Red Cross which established camps in territories infested by bilharzia. Dr Murray, the Secretary for Public Health, assured the company that he would do his best to establish the BW&Co.'s Antimony Tartrate Soloid as standard in the treatment for the disease. The only competitive product was Bayer Antimosan which faced the disadvantage that all medical supplies were ordered by Dr Murray's Public Health Department; hence the confidence in the British company that its Soloid would succeed. In 1933 the STC considered the production of tryparsamide, a sleeping sickness therapy patented by the Rockefeller Institute for which the firm of May & Baker was the sole licensee in the UK. Wellcome and Wenyon were in favour of analysing the Bayer product in order to prepare to enter the field once the patent expired in October 1933. Wenyon described the product as 'not a fancy remedy which may or not be used according to the ... inclinations of physicians'.[133] He felt that the company's reputation would be enhanced by adding sleeping sickness to the Burroughs Wellcome 'index of diseases' contained in the medical diaries. Even though Pearson initially objected on cost grounds, manufacture commenced in 1935.[134] Discussions with sleeping sickness officers in Northern Nigeria produced estimates of the size of the market and the probable value of projected sales but Pearson regarded these as insufficient to support a level of production at a cost and a price that would be profitable.[135] Research for the purpose of developing a yellow fever vaccine on a large scale during the 1920s by Dr Hindle, a Beit Research Fellow working in the WPRL, produced 'discordant results' which prompted a pencilled marginal note, possibly by Wellcome but probably by Pearson: 'This work has involved considerable expenditure'.[136]

The aspiration to accord financial criteria a central consideration in determining the direction of research and development remained little more than that. A search for a new anti-dysentery drug to improve on Emetine was undertaken without attention to either cost, price, or profit. Demand depended principally on orders from medical missionaries who were admitted always to be 'short of money'.[137] An exception was also made with respect to Hirudin, a preparation used in small amounts by physiologists for experimental purposes. In 1927 the STC agreed that, while the 'total demand would always be small' and the supply of Hirudin would be for 'little or no profit', it was desirable to make it available because of the contribution to reputation among the medical profession.[138]

Another consideration when choosing directions for research was that of innovative potential. O'Brien favoured research in physiological chemotherapy. While not dissenting from his general analysis, Jowett drew attention to the important pre-war research into arsenicals which had provided the scientists with expertise in handling Atoxyl and subsequently facilitated the production of Salvarsan. Jowett therefore proposed an investigation of Bayer 205 (and Fornea 309) because of the unusual physiological properties. Jowett's view was that 'even from the commercial standpoint it would be advantageous to have some staff familiar with every aspect of this substance'.[139] Such an approach rested on the probability that research into a protected compound might open up a completely new class of drugs. Jowett also favoured a policy which envisaged research for discovery in a field rather than replicating a specific product for modification or 'improvement'. How far economic and financial criteria were adhered to or whether the laboratories responded to external pressures, for example, from local health authorities and 'enthusiastic medical officers of health', superintendents of hospitals, and educational institutions is an important question.[140] Dr H.J. Parish, research scientist at the WPRL between 1923 and 1962, asserted that the major area of clinical research conducted during the 1920s which concentrated on vaccines was a result of 'pressing invitations to control diphtheria outbreaks.'[141]

Choices that affected the direction of research in the laboratories were made within a context of constraints on space and personnel. Annual research expenditure at the WPRL remained broadly static for most of the interwar period, averaging £26,698 between 1920 and 1933. Figures for 1935 and 1938 were £30,547 and £25,665. Comparison with advertising expenditure is instructive. Between 1920 and 1927, after which an upward trend began, the annual average expenditure on advertising was £49,956, almost twice the level of research expenditure. Between 1928 and 1933 (after which the series is discontinuous but suggests stability), the comparable figure was £76,276, an even higher ratio to sales revenue than was research expenditure.[142]

Patents, publications and research

Choice affecting product development was also limited because of patent protection and the difficulties encountered in obtaining licences for products developed by other companies. The company's policy with respect to patenting products developed within the laboratories represented an attempt to preserve the reputation of the laboratories established by scholarly publications, yet at the same time securing the commercial advantage that patents might offer.[143] Views expressed in the medical press reflected the opposition of the medical profession in Britain to the patenting of proprietary medicines, further evidence of which is the exclusion of patented medicines from the *British Pharmacopoeia*.[144] In 1932 the company relinquished patent rights to ergotoxine supplied under the trademark Ernutin in order to make it available for inclusion in the new *Pharmacopoeia*.[145] This indicated the company's high regard for approval from the medical profession. Parish emphasized the importance of the separation of research from commercial activities in enabling the company to attract dedicated research workers who otherwise would not have joined a commercial organisation: '... they had a freedom not possible in a commercial organisation which was a most important incentive in pursuing really worthwhile research'.[146]

After the hiatus of the First World War, all the laboratories associated with BW&Co. returned to scientific productivity, as illustrated by Table 10.3.

Table 10.3 *BW&Co. publications by laboratory, 1920–1940* [147]

	WCRL	WPRL	WCW	WBSR	*Total*
1920	7			13	20
1921	6	13		17	36
1922	2	14		23	39
1923	3	15	1	31	50
1924	3	18		22	43
1925	4	25		14	43
1926	3	26		11	40
1927	5	29	1	16	51
1928	7	21	1	15	44
1929		17		17	34
1930	4	18	3	18	43
1931	5	22	2	13	42
1932	5	31	4	27	67
1933		14		24	38
1934	5	11	1	20	37
1935	2	12	4	21	39
1936	2	13	7	30	52
1937	4	14	2	26	46
1938	10	20	2	22	54
1939	5	15	1	25	46
1940	1	12		22	35

The only quantitative data available on patenting refer to the limited period between 1936 and 1941.[148] They reveal BW&Co. to have filed only 6 patents compared with 40 by May & Baker, 13 by Glaxo, 12 by Boots, and 7 by BDH. There was a marked contrast between the numbers of articles published by scientists in these five companies: 233 authored by scientists at BW&Co., 34 at Glaxo, 32 at BDH, 11 at M&B, and ten at Boots.[149]

While these figures may be accepted as a crude proxy, an indicator of differences between the respective companies' propensities for commercial development and pure research (D compared with R), the data do not reflect the quality or scientific importance of either patents or publications. However, they do confirm the extent to which the heavy emphasis on independent academic research in the laboratories of BW&Co. was unique among British pharmaceutical companies. In 1945 T.R.G. Bennett referred to the WPRL as having contributed to the revenues of the Foundation through the preparation of therapeutical products, but he maintained that primarily 'they are a research organisation whose policy is neither to patent nor to conceal the methods of production'. He cited the case of Glenny and Pope's discovery of alum precipitated diphtheria toxoid and Pope's method of purifying anti-toxin, both of which were patentable but which were freely published and used by competing organisations: 'This policy can succeed only if research work is kept at the highest level of quality and quantity'.[150]

The culture which preferred publication to patenting became increasingly disadvantageous as the practice by other pharmaceutical companies of filing blocking patents reduced the company's room for innovation. While prepared to produce on licence from other patent holders, the company's opportunities were circumscribed by decisions beyond its control. This applied especially to the development of the rapidly growing field of hormone therapy in which the company had been a pioneer.[151] By the early 1920s, other companies led the way in the research and development of ovarian hormone therapy in which the Swiss firm CIBA of Basle, Schering-Kahlbaum, and IG Farben had taken out patents. In 1927 negotiations with CIBA to obtain a licence for ovarian extract failed.[152] Henry, of the WCRL, expressed the opinion that because advances in glandular therapy had depended on teamwork involving hospitals and medical laboratories, the company should establish close links with St Thomas' Hospital whose clinic, he thought, was 'likely to hit upon something, or at all events set the fashion in glandular therapy'.[153] He suggested that the company should approach St Thomas' and point out that BW&Co. possessed the manufacturing facilities and would be prepared to prepare sufficient material of whatever kind they required for clinical research, conditional on the company's receiving proper recognition.[154] Trevan and Smith scrutinised the pre-patent literature while Jowett reported optimistically on the prospects for large-scale manufacture and Trevan was left to arrange clinical trials. However, the initiative lost momentum. Between 1926 and 1934, the subject of sex hormones was on the agenda of the STC twenty times. Objections to proceeding included the patent position, the number of researchers in the field, and the uncertainty regarding the therapeutic value of ovarian hormone treatment, the latter being probably the most influential factor.[155] In 1934 the STC arranged for the preparation and maintenance of a list of patented products in which the company was likely to be interested 'in order that some system might be devised for taking action when patents are about to lapse'.[156] A limited measure, it reflected the frustration caused by existing patents. Impressed by recent important publications and a conviction that biomedical research offered 'huge potential' to yield 'something of real clinical value to medicine' and to result in 'commercial output',[157] O'Brien and Trevan reopened the argument in favour of proceeding with investigations into pituitary and sex hormones. Acknowledging the difficulties in securing licences (which it was believed had not been secured by other British companies who were suspected of merely importing hormone products), they proposed that, should it prove impossible to negotiate licences, the company should proceed with research into ovarian hormones without consulting the patentees. O'Brien proposed that licences should be disregarded until an infringement charge was brought against the company by a patent owner. This approach, which probably reflected the difficulty of securing valid patents in the biological field, was endorsed by the STC and became general company policy until 1944.[158]

In 1933, Jowett requested the STC to return to the question of whether to proceed with research into sex hormone research in the light of the appearance of a preparation of the ovarian hormone oestrin on the market.[159] Quoting Jowett's support, in February 1934, Henry expressed exasperation to Wenyon regarding the lack of progress in this direction, referring to the 'voluminous but so far barren discussions of ovarian hormones during the last nine years'. He suggested that a separate organisation for biomedical research located within Beckenham might be desirable.[160] O'Brien also argued strongly in favour of action. He reckoned that it would require expenditure of between £2,000 and £5,000 over two years to test clinical and financial justification for a major investment in this direction. Fearing that unless research commenced forthwith, the field would be developed and planted with patents by others, he also drew attention to the large sales of oestrin in Britain and predicted that innumerable similar substances would be offered to the public. He expressed the view that only a few would be useful clinically but that it would not be 'fantastic to predict that within a few years synthetic hormones and the carcinogenic elements in the substances would lead to progress in the cancer field.' He considered the case presented was so compelling that a conference was set up. It included Wenyon, Oakes, Thompson, Jowett, and Pearson, a composition which privately O'Brien believed could not fail to approve the expenditure.[161] Pearson, however, remained the obstacle. In November 1935 (eleven years after O'Brien's similar bid had been rejected[162]), plans for Henry's proposed 'Biological products at Beckenham' section were 'postponed'.[163] Pearson drew attention to O'Brien's own complaints of inadequate accommodation and staff for the research already being carried out, telling him to solve those problems first before seeking to assume additional responsibilities.[164] However, it is probable that cost was the major consideration, for the proposed initiative resembled the chemotherapeutical research organisation envisaged by Wellcome in 1924 when O'Brien had estimated the total cost of investment in buildings, plant, equipment, and human and other resources over perhaps ten years as being between £200,000 and £400,000.[165] This prediction was made at a time when actual research expenditure in 1924 amounted to £22,358. Over the next ten years, total expenditure on existing research in the laboratories was £274,461.[166]

Patents clearly contributed to the company's delay in developing sex hormones. It is more difficult to judge how important patents and the anti-patent culture affected the company's record of product innovation. An item appearing in the Monthly Memoranda in 1932 reported a hospital pathologist's view that the company was always behind in issuing new therapeutic remedies, citing insulin, liver extract, and anti-pneumococcus serum as examples. The company's representative to whom this observation had been made concurred. Far from intending to criticise the company's policy which the pathologist supposed 'cost the company dearly financially', he explained that this was the reason why he purchased the company's products in preference to any others.[167] This was the precise objective of the policy with respect to vitamins, vitamin concentrates, and animal substances which was clearly set out in the Monthly Memoranda ten years before. Regarding vitamin products: 'The manufacturers who thoughtlessly rushed into the market place with these preparations have injured their reputations with all thoughtful conscientious people'.[168] As for animal substances (of which the company claimed to sell more worldwide than any other firm), the issue of a booklet so named was consistent with past policy: 'We have been in the forefront from the dawn of the modern movement, but never in the forefront in making therapeutic claims … We never consciously make a false or exaggerated statement and that is why doctors tell our representatives they can depend on anything published by the firm.' The 'conservative' way in which the company issued therapeutic information was reckoned to be appreciated by the profession, for the literature contained not 'a maze of hypotheses and wild claims', but presented the subject 'wholly and fairly giving contra-indications and disadvantages as well as indications and advantages.'[169]

The company's literature on gland preparations issued during the early 1920s revealed a distinction between two categories. Medical knowledge supported a universal acknowledgement that the administration of thyroid and similar gland preparations would alleviate or cure certain symptoms or diseases. The second category included such preparations as mammary, ovarian, and thymus glands which, while many among the medical profession believed their use obtained favourable results, was not supported by scientific evidence to explain how or why they offered effective therapy. However, in response to demand, the company made these available to general practitioners, ensuring that the preparations were the best possible.[170] By drawing attention to the two categories, the company's promotional literature contrasted favourably with the sweeping claims (so deplored by the medical press) made by manufacturers generally with respect to extracts of virtually every organ of the body. A leading article appearing in the *British Medical Journal* accused physicians of displaying impatience with the slow pace of scientific advance in the field of glandular therapy at a time when, in pursuit of commercial interests, others were making 'bold raids into the unknown far in advance of consolidated positions'. Commercial interests were accused of exacerbating the problem of misinformation, lured by a 'rich and easily exploited field … modern medicine is, indeed, threatened with a reversion to medieval magic disguised under a pseudo-scientific terminology.'[171] The same concern was contained in a letter written by a Dr Altounyan to *The*

Lancet in 1933, in which he complained of a 'flood of pseudo-scientific preparations' appearing during the early 1930s. He urged his fellow medical men to accept only products of which the therapeutic worth had been established beyond doubt through extensive clinical trials.[172] A similar message in the Monthly Memoranda was conveyed to the company's representatives in 1938 in a review of methods of introducing medicinal agents to the medical profession. The author asserted that many companies failed to conduct adequate clinical trials or to await definite scientific proof of the therapeutic activity of a product from independent and authentic sources. They gave them a brand with a 'coined name' and claimed to have been the first to introduce them. If they were subsequently proved to have therapeutic value, a monopoly might be ensured. This premature promotion of new products contrasted with the company's declared policy. This had long been to secure supplies, or to manufacture experimental batches of new drugs which held out any prospects of real therapeutic value and to submit them to a long course of chemical as well as clinical research, until their stability, reliability, and clinical value were established beyond doubt.[173] One consequence of this approach to innovation is suggested by an analysis of production and sales of general goods. Sales and production data reveal that general goods (mostly compressed medicines and Kepler goods) continued to form the company's major product lines between the wars.

CHAPTER ELEVEN

Academic reputation counters commercial stigma: sera and vaccines 1918–1940

Sera and vaccines

During the inter-war period the staff of the WPRL established and maintained an unrivalled reputation for the study of human and veterinary infectious diseases and for producing high-quality therapeutic sera. Research was conducted on practically every aspect of the transmission, diagnosis, treatment and prevention of several infectious diseases. Sera remained the mainstay of the laboratories' therapeutic output during this period, and vaccine production continued, although debates raged throughout the period about their respective therapeutic and prophylactic value.[1] Although increasingly recognised as a high calibre scientific institute by colleagues around the world, the laboratories continued to be regarded as 'commercial' by medical authorities, especially those involved in public health. During the 1930s, the advent of antibiotics and other effective chemotherapeutic measures against infections effectively ended the demand for serotherapy. Shifts towards preventive strategies stimulated vaccine research and development, although both occurred more markedly after the Second World War.

Diphtheria anti-toxins: the beginning of the inter-war period

Immediately after the end of the war Percival Hartley, soon to move to the National Institute for Medical Research (NIMR) as the Head of the Department of Biological Standards, re-evaluated the methods used to produce diphtheria anti-toxin, the mainstay of the lab. He designed a toxin concentration method that raised the titre of the resultant anti-sera and reduced the production of low titre anti-toxic sera. This eliminated wastage and allowed the number of horses to be reduced, all much needed economies welcomed by Snow Hill. The laboratories also laid the scientific foundations of numerous public health immunisation measures. They devised all the technical methods by which BW&Co., and the other firms who later

325

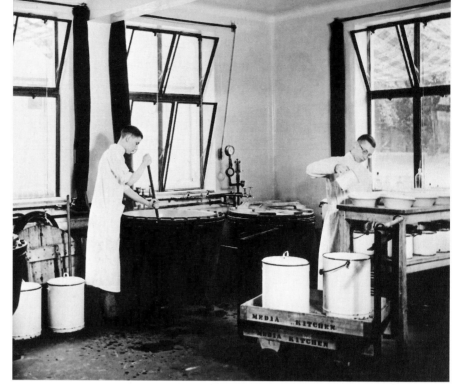

copied them, produced material for such programmes. A major advance made by Glenny and Sudmersen revolutionised both the theory and practice of immunisation: they had already noted that a *mixture* of diphtheria toxin and anti-toxin was particularly effective in raising further anti-toxins with fewer side effects of local irritation or adverse reactions.[2] Subsequent experiments giving two such injections confirmed the known response and also revealed a faster, secondary response, which raised yet more antitoxins.[3] This was reliably repeated in animals and man, and researchers around the world rushed to repeat and extend this work to determine the procedures that induced the maximal response. The WPRL's work became the basis for world-wide immunisation programmes, and scientists and public health authorities. Abraham Zingler in New York City, and Claude Dolman and John Fitzgerald in Toronto, Canada, all adopted, adapted, and refined their discoveries.[4]

Wellcome scientists also worked closely with MRC staff, often their former colleagues, in standardising diphtheria toxin, anti-toxin and mixtures of the two, to create national and internationally agreed standards.[5] O'Brien, the Director of the WPRL, was happy to prepare experimental batches of sera, vaccines, hormones and other pharmaceuticals for the MRC, which benefited from a ready supply of new compounds prepared by a reliable company. BW&Co. also benefited. Such work added to the scientific experience and authority of the laboratories, and by assisting in the creation of national standardisation criteria, the company's products were at an advantage in meeting such requirements when they subsequently became mandatory.[6]

Another discovery of scientific and commercial importance was made accidentally as a consequence of Hartley's more efficient production of toxin. This resulted in the build up of excess toxin stocks that were stored in earthenware containers too large to be autoclaved. They were washed with formalin prior to use, and during routine testing Glenny discovered that the stored toxin had became less, even non-, toxic, although retaining its ability to raise anti-toxins when injected into horses.[7] He showed that this attenuated toxin, or toxoid as it was called, also induced immunity when injected directly into patients. This was a significant innovation that gave the company a virtual commercial monopoly for many years after its introduction.[8]

In the laboratory, Glenny was a difficult man to work with, yet not only did he survive the unique environment of the WPRL, he flourished. Henry Parish, who became Head of Bacteriology in 1930, was first aware of tensions caused by Glenny when he joined the WPRL in 1923.[9] One problem was Glenny's resentment of medically qualified colleagues, especially those whose work overlapped his own. The hostility was particularly directed towards O'Brien, a medically qualified bacteriologist, who was also the Director. To this academic antagonism was added a physical separation that

exacerbated Glenny's feelings of isolation and sense of disregard. Since the move in 1922 of the WPRL from Brockwell Park to Beckenham, which the ever-efficient Glenny organised, O'Brien had occupied a large office next door to the main bacteriological laboratory in the mansion house that was at the heart of the estate. Glenny's own office and laboratory was in a 'temporary' corrugated iron, four-room hut that he openly referred to as 'the slum'. He was not given up-to-date accommodation until 1936.[10]

Within an organisation where the Director communicated only with individual heads of department, and cautioned each not to speak to the others, Glenny's acerbic personality and style did little to help him get on with his colleagues. Apart from female assistants whom he divided into those who could do no wrong, and 'nit-wits', Glenny had no close associate throughout his years at the WPRL. Parish recalled that C. G. Pope, later Head of Biochemistry, was summarily told to leave in 1925. He remained, but out of Glenny's way. Harry Proom, Parish's successor as Head of Bacteriology, 'waged war' with Glenny for years; F. V. Linggood, unhappy working with Glenny, flourished in the Biochemistry Department; C. L. Oakley, who succeeded Glenny as Head of Immunology, 'survived a long period of insult and lack of appreciation'. Parish himself would seek statistical help from the pharmacologist Trevan, rather than brave the scorn and disdain that Glenny directed at those of lesser mathematical ability than himself.[11] Astonishingly, despite his astringent personality and pungent sarcasm, the enormous contributions to bacteriology, immunology and preventive medicine made by the WPRL would not have been possible without him.[12]

In contrast to Glenny, O'Brien cultivated academic contacts around the world, thereby benefitting the scientific work of the laboratories and reflecting well upon the company. For example, a short trip to a standardisation conference in Geneva in October 1926 prompted visits to institutes in Switzerland and France to investigate, *inter alia*, diphtheria prophylaxis, tuberculosis prevention, and gas gangrene work in association with lamb dysentery.[13] He readily associated with British medical men, including the Chief Medical Officer, Sir George Newman, and Surgeon Commander S. F. Dudley who organised Schick test (for diphtheria susceptibility) trials at the Royal Naval School, Greenwich, largely supported by BW&Co. Later, as Surgeon Vice-Admiral Sir Sheldon Dudley, he was Medical Director General of the Navy during the Second World War, and remained a keen proponent of immunisation and a collaborator with WPRL scientists throughout his career.[14] O'Brien invited local Medical Officers of Health to visit the WPRL, consult its staff, use its products in clinical trials, and to publish their results.[15] Likewise O'Brien encouraged his staff to engage with local and national medical and veterinary practitioners. Parish, for one, spent his annual break touring England and Scotland, frequently dropping in on local Medical Officers of Health as he passed.[16] Another important association was with Dr Guy Bousfield, whose father, E. C. Bousfield, had worked for the WPRL's diagnosis service at the beginning of the twentieth century.[17] Bousfield, a 'most enthusiastic

pupil' in the Wellcome laboratories, published a popular practical guide to diphtheria testing techniques which included numerous references to BW&Co. products, a useful form of 'advertising' direct to practitioners.[18] He was one of the first to promote giving two consecutive injections of toxoid for enhanced immunity, a scientific advance which was clearly commercially advantageous to BW&Co.[19] The technique was rapidly followed by Parke, Davis & Co., Sharp & Dohme Ltd, and Eli Lilly & Co. Bousfield devised ingenious drug-delivery systems, including an aerosol toxoid spray that he tried on himself and his family, until they all fell ill with allergic respiratory reactions.[20] Another scheme was to promote oral immunisation with gelatine lozenges produced by the Dartford Works. The resultant antibody responses were very variable, and the project was abandoned, although Bousfield continued the experiments with Parke, Davis & Co.[21] 'Few men' Parish declared 'have done more for the popularisation of immunisation than Guy Bousfield'.[22] Directly and indirectly, he also did a great deal for BW&Co. in his development, utilisation and promotion of their products.

Occasionally, O'Brien's intellectual generosity worked against the company's commercial objectives. In April 1928, Snow Hill sent him a curt memo received from the South African office. A Dr. J. Pratt Johnson, of Clinsearch Laboratories, Johannesburg, was apparently issuing Schick testing kits and therapeutic toxin/anti-toxin mixtures, claiming O'Brien's

FIGURE 11.5
Girls packing
medicines,
WPRL,
Beckenham,
c. 1925.

support and assistance. This had come to the astonished attention of Dr
Dunn who promoted BW&Co.'s Schick test in South Africa. As BW&Co.
(South Africa) commented, 'Presumably in the absence of help from the
Wellcome Laboratories local competition in Schick products and Diphtheria
anti-toxin might still be in the background.'[23] The tart conclusion was
that 'It is no business of ours to comment on the policy of the Wellcome
Physiological Research Laboratories and we do not presume to criticise
their policy in any way, but we may be permitted to say that it must be an
extremely difficult matter to arrange that the altruistic policy of the laboratories shall always be in complete harmony with the material interests of
BW&Co.'[24]

In addition to the Toxoid preparation first marketed by BW&Co. in
1924, the laboratories developed and the company promoted two major
new prophylactic measures against diphtheria: toxoid anti-toxin floccules
(TAF) in 1926, and alum-precipitated toxoid (APT) in 1930.[25] Despite the
ready availability of such increasingly effective prophylactics and intermittent campaigns in the medical press, there was considerable reluctance to
promote large-scale public health immunisation in Great Britain.[26] This was
accompanied by an official disinterest in mass screening programmes using
the Schick test. It was left to the staff of the WPRL to spearhead the earliest
work in Britain on diphtheria prevention. At the beginning of 1939 the

lamentable British situation was contrasted with that in Canada, where the decline of the disease following large-scale public health initiatives, 'shows indubitably that diphtheria is a preventable disease'.[27] By the outbreak of the Second World War only four other British companies or institutes held manufacturing licences for anti-diphtheria preparations: St Mary's Hospital (agents: Parke, Davis & Co.), the Lister Institute (agents: Allen & Hanburys), British Drug Houses, and Evans, Sons, Lescher and Webb, although the vast majority of sera came from the Wellcome Foundation.[28]

Diphtheria susceptibility testing

A major problem in preventive medicine was that of identifying the susceptible population, and then offering appropriate prophylaxis. In 1900 the WPRL had started a diphtheria diagnostic service for general practitioners. Twenty years later they were continuing the tradition by promoting the diagnostic test devised by the Austrian physician, Bela Schick, to evaluate diphtheria susceptibility in asymptomatic individuals.[29] For the WPRL scientists there was a clear public health imperative, independent of the commercial interests of BW&Co., to promote a test that identified susceptible individuals which enabled them be offered protection. For the Company, there were two commercial outcomes that could arise from the successful introduction of the test: the first was that standardised toxin would be required to perform the test; the second was the possibility of subsequent

FIGURE 11.6
Drawing of
the WPRL,
Beckenham,
1926.

large-scale, inoculation of susceptible populations with serum. Either would create considerable demand for BW&Co. products.

Official support for this sort of work from the government and much of the medical profession was lacklustre and Wellcome staff were lonely pioneers. After several attempts to get Schick tests done in London at Metropolitan Asylums Boards hospitals, O'Brien finally managed to get a trial organised at the City Hospital in Edinburgh. The WPRL's report for November 1919 is emphatic '[It] seems lamentable that in connection with this aspect of control of diphtheria we are 6–8 years behind NY'.[30] Public health responses in the United States had been much more robust than in Britain, and Schick testing had been extensively trialled in New York by Park and Zingher before the Great War, a telling indication of different national attitudes to therapeutic innovation and implementation.[31] The very first paper on the subject in Britain was from the WPRL in 1921, which strongly advocated the test and the subsequent immunisation of the vulnerable. The authors concluded somewhat cynically, however, that 'English physicians … have apparently been too busy to investigate the tests', and stressed that well-known laboratory investigations should be supported and extended by clinical experience.[32] Despite the apathy of much of the medical profession, the WPRL promoted and explored the utility and reliability of the tests in several populations: medical students, nurses, children previously exposed to the disease, children from non-infected schools etc.[33] Experimental work was also done refining test materials to make them readily and easily usable by general practitioners, and the WPRL issued regular reports and papers on advances in products, techniques and analysis for the medical profession and the company's representatives.[34] In March 1924 O'Brien wrote formally to Sir George Newman, the Chief Medical Officer, emphasising the significance of the test and the importance of immunisation. He calculated that the WPRL staff had performed thousands of tests and immunised hundreds of children. This was a serious drain on the financial and personnel resources of the laboratories, yet without official sanction and support, they would always be open to the accusation of pushing BW&Co.'s products.[35] A public health campaign was desperately overdue in Britain, especially considering that Park and colleagues in New York had greatly reduced the death rate there from diphtheria. O'Brien emphasised the statistics: in London alone diphtheria was caught by approximately 10,000 a year, of whom 1,000 died. Yet who, he asked, was to undertake the necessary testing and immunisation work? There were few experienced personnel available in the country apart from BW&Co. staff. Newman, a trained bacteriologist (who ironically had applied for a position at the WPRL as a young man) was cautiously sympathetic to the suggestion that widespread testing was desirable.[36] Despite such apparent sympathy, nothing was done, and Government recommendations and advice remained just that: recommendations and advice.[37]

In late 1925, the Ministry of Health suggested that a 'pronouncement' about testing in the medical press would be valuable, and invited O'Brien to write the piece, because, as he somewhat scathingly remarked, 'Newman funked it'.[38] O'Brien was uneasy that this would open him to the charge of producing 'a defence of a BW product masquerading as a scientific article', and he turned to Henry Dale for counsel.[39] Dale believed that such was inevitable given the circumstances, but that it was perfectly acceptable because nothing was kept secret or protected by trade name. He advised his successor, 'I do not think the fact that BW&Co. may, and probably will, make more profit than other people out of the work which they have financed, and supported, ought to deter you from telling the Medical Profession what they ought to know in the interests of public health'.[40] O'Brien took his advice.[41]

Several individual practitioners and Medical Officers of Health did introduce Schick testing on their own initiatives, and in 1928 alone BW&Co. sold more than 1200 test kits, an increase of nearly 400 per cent since 1923.[42] Compared with successful large-scale immunisation campaigns in the United States, France, Canada, Belgium and Germany, however, Britain continued to lag seriously behind in dealing with diphtheria.[43] A leading article just before the Second World War in *Medical Officer*, a journal for those 'in government and municipal services', was particularly blunt about the British position. The author thundered 'For these deaths [3–5000 per year] there is no valid excuse; they occur because we have not done what we know we should have done'.[44] It was only during the Second World War that the Ministry of Health finally issued revised guidelines that encouraged diphtheria prophylaxis.[45]

FIGURE 11.8
Chemical
laboratory,
WPRL,
Beckenham,
1926.

Scarlet fever (scarlatina)

Scarlet fever testing presented similar problems to BW&Co., compounded
by licensing disputes. A test for scarlet fever susceptibility, analogous to
the Schick test for diphtheria, was first introduced in the USA in 1924 by
George and Gladys Dick. Subsequently known as the 'Dick test' it involved
the subcutaneous injection of dilute scarlet fever toxin, and the visual
assessment of the subsequent skin reaction.[46] Given their experience with
diagnostic testing, and in the treatment and control of infectious diseases,
this new technique was of much interest to the WPRL. The very first tests
in Britain were done by O'Brien, Okell and Parish, on each other.[47] These
were not without hazards. Further tests on themselves and a group of
human volunteers in Birmingham City Hospital, led to Parish developing
whooping-cough for the second time; all three developing general allergic
reactions.[48] Continuing research work in the WPRL, however, made a
connection of both scientific and commercial significance. The haemolytic
streptococci derived from a number of what were considered to be different
diseases, including scarlet fever, erysipelas, and puerperal septicaemia, all
produced the same, rather than different, toxins. Up until that time, all had
been treated separately, but now all could be neutralised by just one: the so-

called 'scarlet fever' anti-toxin.[49] The commercial implications of producing one effective serum against a range of diseases were immediately obvious to BW&Co., who began to gear up laboratory production, and to promote the susceptibility test.

There was, however, a problem for BW&Co., as for all organisations using the Dick Test. In what the *British Medical Journal* described as an 'objectionable practice', the Dicks had patented their procedure and materials, the patents being held by a 'Scarlet Fever Committee of the United States'.[50] Objectionable or not, BW&Co. could not ignore the legal implications that the test and serum they wished to push was 'owned' by another organisation. Several American companies, including Parke, Davis & Co. accepted the licensing agreements, and according to the Dicks they offered 'one of the largest manufacturers in England' a licence.[51] Although this probably refers to BW&Co., no confirmation of their offer, if it was made, has been located. The Wellcome staff did, however, seriously have to consider their position with regard to patent infringements and the possibility of paying licence fees to the Scarlet Fever Committee. In February 1927, the

FIGURE II.9
Autoclave and sterilising room, WPRL, Beckenham, 1926.

FIGURE 11.10
Guinea pigs
in animal
house,
WPRL,
Beckenham,
1926.

Scientific and Technical Committee convened to discuss the situation, the first of several such discussions.[52] Demand for serum was increasing, and in a series of internal memos, O'Brien, Wenyon, and Pearson discussed whether the Scarlet Fever Committee would defend their patents if BW&Co. decided to ignore them.[53] The two scientists, Wenyon and O'Brien, firmly believed that although the Committee had some rights to the actual test procedure, they had none whatsoever to the anti-toxic serum. O'Brien emphasised that the mass of British medical opinion was in agreement, and that Professor Charles Martin, Director of the Lister Institute which also produced the anti-toxic serum, was not applying for a licence but seeking legal opinion on the whole matter.[54] The fact that the attitude of the Lister Institute was identical to that of the Wellcome organisation, was of some importance. O'Brien confided to Pearson that publicly it would be to the advantage of BW&Co. to be seen following the same course, and for the same reasons, as the Lister Institute.[55] With Pearson's permission, O'Brien came to an agreement with Martin that the two organisations should act together, their legal Counsel being H. Fletcher Moulton, the son of Henry Wellcome's old legal adviser.[56]

The issue brought to the fore yet another difference of opinion between the scientific and managerial staff of the company. The staff of the Wellcome and Lister laboratories were united in believing on scientific grounds they should fight the Dick patent.[57] Pearson, as a businessman, cautioned that, if they infringed the Dick patent, legally the chances of either laboratory successfully defending an action were slim. Counsel's opinion agreed with Pearson.[58] After considering that opinion, the Lister Institute decided to neither infringe the patent, nor apply for a manufacturing licence. Likewise, the Wellcome Foundation decided not to infringe the patent, but to apply for a manufacturing licence under the Americans' patent. Retrospectively, Henry Parish of the WPRL considered that having their products tested for compliance by the Scarlet Fever Committee had been 'all rather irksome although there were no failures in these tests'.[59]

But whilst there had not been a 'failure', there had been a problem that had caused the company and the laboratories considerable difficulty. The Dicks insisted on their rights to dictate precisely what serum strengths and dosages should be used.[60] By this time, the WPRL had considerable independent experience of susceptibility testing and toxin/anti-toxin manufacture. O'Brien wrote to the Scarlet Fever Committee asking for samples of approved material so that a comparison could be made with their own products. Despite scientific reservations about the standardisation and quality of the material they were now expected to produce, the Licence Agreement was signed.[61] The following year, the Dicks visited Beckenham during which Gladys Dick, regarded as 'an imposing personality who dominated our discussion', took some of the WPRL's toxin and anti-toxin for testing in Chicago.[62] Unhappy with the results, she complained to O'Brien that their toxin was too strong, which could result in immune people reacting positively, i.e. exhibiting signs of non-immunity. Conversely, she reported the Wellcome anti-toxin as too weak. She believed the WPRL's testing techniques were faulty and offered to arrange, presumably at some cost to BW&Co., to standardise the WPRL's toxin and serum for them.[63] Not surprisingly, this caused immense irritation. But BW&Co. was contracted to manufacture serum and anti-toxin according to her standards. The matter could be neither ignored, nor easily dismissed.[64] O'Brien wrote to Warren, the Wellcome Foundation's in-house lawyer: 'This is the first communication since the signature of the licence contract, and it clearly indicates the little chance there is of any prospect of agreement between Dr Gladys Dick's views and our own'.[65] The serious scientific differences could have equally serious commercial implications. O'Brien reported to Warren that the WPRL routinely tested Parke, Davis & Co.'s materials (also produced under licence to the Scarlet Fever Committee), and were well aware of the differences pointed out by Gladys Dick. They were confident that the Wellcome material was better. Three-quarters of English hospitals were then using

'Wellcome' brand anti-toxin, although three years earlier Parke, Davis had had the market entirely to themselves. O'Brien continued,

> I should imagine that if our anti-toxin were, as Mrs Dick concludes from this one instance, one-third of the strength of Parke, Davis' serum, the majority of English clinicians in fever hospitals would not have been willing to replace Parke, Davis' serum in three years by 'Wellcome' brand.[66]

O'Brien hinted that it was to Parke, Davis & Co.'s considerable commercial benefit if BW&Co.'s material was not so clearly distinguishable from their own. He warned Warren, 'Dr. Dick's connection with this firm [i.e. Parke, Davis & Co.] may be close. In making appointments while in London the telephone number she gave to medical men was that of Parke, Davis & Co.'[67] WPRL material had also been rigorously tested by Henry Dale's staff at the NIMR, and Wellcome scientists had recently presented data at a standards conference in Germany.[68] No expert had challenged the Wellcome results nor their interpretations. O'Brien emphasised to Warren '… the error of the method used by Mrs. Dick, in the hands of the most competent dozen men in England, working in conjunction with us and with Dr. Dale, is much greater than Mrs. Dick will admit'.[69]

It was quite clear that BW&Co. was not carrying out the conditions of the licensing agreement, and O'Brien could not see how it would be possible to do so. If the Scarlet Fever Committee insisted on its rights, then one course of action would be for the Wellcome Foundation to appeal to the Comptroller of Patents for a modification of the licence to exclude the standardisation requirements. O'Brien suggested that the Foundation would be in a strong moral position if it voluntarily resigned from its licensing contract and applied to the Comptroller for a compulsory licence that would continue to pay royalties to the Scarlet Fever Committee but released them from its testing standards.[70] BW&Co. was not alone in having problems. In the USA too, the Dicks' actions received condemnation and challenges, and for many years, Gladys Dick 'waged war' against the Lederle Laboratories for what she considered 'improper toxin manufacture'.[71] BW&Co., however, adopted a simple solution to the problem, continuing to produce its own anti-toxic serum, but marketed it, as in

FIGURE II.II Advertisement for scarlet fever prophylactics, including Wellcome Brand products for the Dick test (*Chemist & Druggist*, 1 December 1928).

previous years as 'Anti-streptococcus (scarlatina) serum' with no reference to the Dicks' test or material.

TB testing and treatment

During the First World War, tuberculin testing for tuberculosis had been completely dropped from the WPRL's diagnostic service, but was rapidly re-instated after the end of hostilities. By the early 1920s, the subject was again attracting much attention. O'Brien's regular policy of encouraging practitioners to use the company's products resulted in tuberculin being increasingly used for a number of conditions.[72] At the same time the WPRL staff devoted a considerable amount of research effort on standardising the test and its constituent materials.[73] It was during these experiments that A.J. Eagleton developed a particularly sensitive intracutaneous tuberculin assay, which was rigorously investigated by other members of the laboratories.[74] This led to an astonishing scientific discovery, with immediate commercial significance. By the late 1920s there were over a hundred different kinds of tuberculin on the market, many of which were produced by BW&Co. Using Eagleton's more sensitive assay, the Wellcome scientists produced convincing evidence that the biological activity of *all* tuberculins was due to a single protein constituent.[75] This became known as the purified protein derivative (PPD) of tuberculin and was first isolated by the American scientist Florence Seibert.

In the WPRL, F.V. Linggood prepared a PPD which was first used in human diagnosis in 1938, and in animals in 1939.[76] Unfortunately the uptake of large-scale TB testing was slow in Britain. As with scarlet fever and diphtheria, an intradermal assay, the Mantoux test, was devised to assess natural or acquired immunity to TB.[77] But like other public health surveillance techniques at the time, there was widespread distrust surrounding the introduction of anti-tuberculosis measures in Britain.[78] In the United States, Mulford & Co., and Parke, Davis & Co. produced large quantities of tubercle bacillus for the testing programmes being set up by the National Tuberculosis Association, and by the end of the 1930s, Sharp and Dohme were producing PPD for widespread testing and evaluation.[79] These were profitable markets that were not replicated in Britain until after the Second World War.

Influenza, common cold and pneumonia

The major human disease of concern immediately after the Great War was the influenza pandemic that devastated the world and attracted much research effort in the USA and Britain. Given their vast experience in infectious disease therapy, the WPRL also studied influenza, particularly therapeutic and preventive strategies. The work was technically difficult, as a stable toxin, the starting point for any successful serotherapy, had never been successfully isolated.[80] BW&Co. had produced an anti-influenza vaccine during the final years of the First World War which was a mixture of *Bacterium influenzae*, streptococci and pneumococci, in proportions recommended at a conference convened at the War Office by the RAMC in 1918.[81] After the war, the company continued to tinker with the constituents and their proportions, on the basis of very little evidence as to their effectiveness or otherwise. Although an official report in 1920 concluded that results with the vaccine were 'encouraging' and that a moderate degree of protection might be achieved, it was hardly a ringing endorsement.[82]

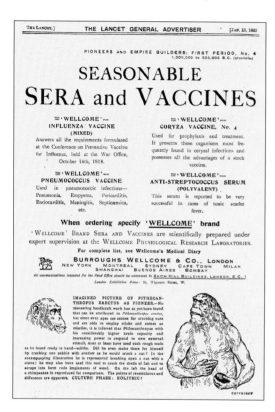

FIGURE 11.13 'Seasonable sera and vaccines' (*Lancet*, 10 January 1920) against influenza and other wintry ailments. Number 4 in 'Pioneers and Empire builders' this features *Pithecanthropus erectus* as a pioneer.

There were similar concerns about the common cold. W.W.C.Topley, Professor of Bacteriology at Manchester University who always gave himself a 'good blunderbuss anti-cold vaccine', a home-made shot of haemolytic streptococci and a variety of pneuomococci vaccines, approached the WPRL to make such a preparation commercially.[83] Admitting that the common cold was 'a bit of an obsession' of his own, O'Brien described BW&Co.'s available products: several bacteriological cocktails of varying strengths and composition. Unfortunately, the company had never been able to organise a large-scale test of any of their vaccines.[84] Topley immediately offered to organise such a trial if BW&Co. made a vaccine to his specifications.[85] A trial in the winter of 1924–25, using staff and students from Manchester University, provided disappointing results for all concerned. This caused an immediate dilemma for BW&Co. Should the source of the 'failed' vaccine be acknowledged in Topley's resultant publication? As O'Brien put it to Wenyon, there were several points both in favour, and against. The principal argument against acknowledging the source of the vaccine was a business case. Publishing details of the ineffectiveness of one of their products created an enormous difficulty; could the company still market it? Would sales plummet? It would be a marketing gift to Parke, Davis & Co., which was about to market a vaccine, produced by St. Mary's Hospital, that had been shown to be effective in a limited trial. But by publicly acknowledging the source of Topley's vaccine, O'Brien argued, the company would enhance its reputation for 'rigid honesty in vital matters'. He emphasised, 'It is such a rare thing in the business world for a firm to announce that a product required by its clients, is, in the opinion of the firm, not effective, that the reputation for uncalculating honesty to be gained from the incident may well be worthwhile from the point of view of eventual financial return'.[86]

O'Brien argued that the reputation of the laboratories was a valuable asset to the company, and they should not misrepresent or suppress what they believed to be the truth based on scientific considerations, for commercial interests. He reminded Wenyon that Topley could have simply bought BW&Co.'s vaccine and published his results without notifying anyone at the laboratories or the company. Additionally, O'Brien suspected that the source of the vaccine would be identified eventually, and that any attempt at secrecy would re-bound to the discredit of BW&Co. Wenyon agreed, and advised Pearson, 'I think it would be a great mistake to withhold the information'.[87] What Pearson considered doing is not known, because fortunately, at this point O'Brien recalled that Topley's vaccine had been a bespoke preparation, not a regular commercial vaccine issue. Acknowledging the WPRL for making a special vaccine would cast no slur on current Wellcome products. Scientific honour and commercial advantage were both preserved.

Throughout the 1920s and 1930s BW&Co. continued to produce pneumococcal vaccines, although their inconclusive remedial efficacy and prophylactic effect did not encourage their use by medical practitioners and research effort was directed more towards other products. Until the end of the Second World War, many organisations, including the Rockefeller Foundation in the USA and several American boards of health and federal and state bodies, continued to advocate and develop serum therapy.[88] The situation was broadly similar in Britain. With the advent of antibiotics the majority of such work became redundant in the short term.[89]

Other products
Throughout the inter war years, the WPRL produced and developed a very wide variety of sera and vaccines for therapy and prophylaxis, and also biological reagents for diagnostic work. Some products were devised solely for veterinary use.[90] By the end of the 1920s, other companies were also increasing their serotherapy commitments, and in 1929, O'Brien noted specifically that Parke, Davis & Co. and BDH (which sold serum from the State Serum Institute, Copenhagen) had notably increased their competitive pressure that year.[91] From 1923 until 1928, a period for which detailed figures

are available, output increased for several sera, and O'Brien, Glenny and their colleagues developed several improved products and immunisation procedures.[92] As war loomed in 1938 the army expressed considerable interest in BW&Co.'s tetanus work. Lieutenant-Colonel John Boyd (later Sir John 1958, Director of the Wellcome Tropical Research Laboratories 1946–1963, and a Wellcome Trustee 1955–1966) was then in charge of the Army Vaccine Department at Millbank, London, and was well aware that manufacture of an adequate supply of tetanus prophylactics was well beyond the Department's resources.[93] He turned to O'Brien and Glenny at the WPRL, and their successful collaborative results persuaded the British Army to adopt tetanus immunisation as its official policy just in time for the start of the Second World War.[94] The bulk of British forces that went to France in 1939 were thus protected, and by 1944, when the Normandy landings were planned, Boyd was in a position of such authority that he could order all immunised soldiers to receive a 'booster' shot. During the subsequent campaign only six cases of tetanus, with one fatality, were recorded.[95]

Tropical diseases: yellow fever vaccine

Work in the field of vaccines for tropical diseases also produced marketable goods for the company but, more importantly, provided considerable scientific kudos for the laboratories. The work was heralded by the arrival of Edward Hindle at the WBSR in 1928, which in itself marked an important professional recognition of the laboratories. Hindle had been awarded a prestigious 5-year Beit Memorial Fellowship, the rules of which were strict about the scientific standing of the laboratories where they could be held. Hindle's award, the first to be held in commercial laboratories, provides a clear measure of the academic regard and reputation of the Wellcome laboratories that time. His work at the WBSR focussed on viral diseases, especially yellow fever, and the development of a successful prophylactic vaccine. Specialised facilities were also prepared for him at the WPRL, which was experienced in dealing with dangerous pathogens, although some work was undertaken at the WBSR in Central London, a decision that was to have unfortunate consequences.[96] Initially, his work went well. He first announced a successful prophylactic at a meeting of the Royal Society of Tropical Medicine in January 1929, at which Wellcome himself was present.[97] Small-scale field trials in Brazil soon confirmed the vaccine's utility.[98] Based on this, the Colonial Office requested large volumes of the vaccine for trial in British West Africa which the company readily, and freely, supplied. Unfortunately this proved unsuccessful. Wellcome's personal disappointment, compounded by a keen sense of the expense of the project, immediately closed the vaccine development work.[99]

Hindle's associated work on yellow fever transmission was equally, if not more, troubled. In July 1930, he and a colleague caught the disease and were admitted to the Hospital for Tropical Diseases in London. Although they both recovered, a hospital technician became infected and died. It became clear that a droplet of infected blood had transmitted the disease.[100] The incident was not widely known until journalists from the *Evening News* investigated. The presence in central London of a laboratory working on dangerous pathogens caused widespread alarm, and at the WBSR work on the virus was immediately halted.[101] The official Adviser on Tropical Medicine to the Ministry of Health, Sydney James FRS, suggested that such work be moved out of London.[102] The experience was not without its scientific value. Hindle realised that his illness and recovery indicated that mild, non-fatal, cases of the disease existed. The fatal disease that was known up to that time was only part of a broader clinical picture, in which large animal and human reservoirs of the disease could, he believed, go undetected.[103] Although Hindle himself could not immediately translate these insights into diagnostic procedures to identify occult cases, the sera of the two Wellcome staff who had recovered from the diseases, including Hindle himself, eventually became the basis of a diagnostic test for the virus. There was to be one further indirect, but tragic, consequence of this accident. The former director of the WBSR, by now Sir Andrew Balfour and Director of the LSHTM (which included the Hospital for Tropical Diseases) committed suicide whilst suffering from depression, worried that he would be blamed for the fatality.[104]

After the suspension of vaccine development at the WBSR, work on yellow fever continued elsewhere, notably and with some success at the Rockefeller Institute in New York. In 1932 interest at the WBSR was renewed when the virologist G. Marshall Findlay went to New York, and returned with a new, less virulent strain of the causative virus. From this strain, he and Hindle prepared several vaccines that were consistently successful in successive trials.[105] Five years later, BW&Co. were manufacturing a reliable prophylactic and prepared thousands of doses to immunise Royal Air Force crews and British Colonial service staff going abroad during the Second World War. As Hindle's obituarist noted in 1974, '[The vaccine] is now probably one of the most successful vaccines in existence, both in protective value and duration of effect'.[106]

Veterinary products

Veterinary research attracted many of the same professional problems that occurred in the development of human therapeutics. In late 1923, O'Brien cautioned that if BW&Co. hoped to benefit from veterinary therapies, they had to develop a commercial infrastructure and relationships with the profession similar to those so carefully built up with medical practitioners.

FIGURE 11.14
Veterinary
laboratory,
WPRL,
Beckenham,
1926.

Admitting that he was straying from his proper concerns into business territory, O'Brien suggested that as a service to practitioners a separate 'veterinary' price list of chemicals be prepared, including compounds not already in production. Both British Drug Houses (BDH) and Parke, Davis had been producing such lists for some time, and O'Brien considered such a list would gain the profession's attention and custom, making it easier to sell them new biological therapies, the sera and vaccines.[107]

Lamb dysentery and related diseases

In 1922 the veterinarian Thomas Dalling joined the laboratories, attracted by the scientific reputation, facilities and opportunities available there. An early priority was to study lamb dysentery, stimulated by an epidemic in the Borders and Yorkshire Dales. With Glenny, Dalling identified a previously unknown strain of the gas-gangrene-causing bacterium as the cause of the disease, and devised an ingenious method of protecting newborn lambs. Pregnant ewes were inoculated with a sub-lethal dose of the bacterial toxin, to which their immune systems generated anti-toxins, then passed in colostrum to their newborn lambs, who thus acquired protection over the relatively short danger period of about one week.[108] Dalling showed that less than 2 per cent of lambs from inoculated ewes died compared with over 24 per cent of the offspring of uninoculated animals. Immediately, a familiar question arose – should he publish the results that would facilitate manufacture by others, or should he produce a short note to establish his priority without revealing technical details that could then be patented to confirm commercial advantage? O'Brien advised that full publication was always best, not least in this instance to help the farmers who suffered huge livestock losses each year, and the vets who assisted the WPRL scientists so much.[109] The veterinary department relied greatly on local farmers and veterinary practitioners to inoculate and monitor huge numbers of animals when undertaking large-scale field-testing of vaccines, despite the fact that Wellcome veterinary researchers frequently spent long periods in sheep rearing districts around the country.[110] Conscious of promoting loyalty and respect within both veterinary and farming constituencies, Dalling was allowed to publish. As O'Brien commented to his predecessor, Dale, '[He is] doing such a remarkable lot of good work in the last year that I am very anxious indeed to push on with the veterinary side of the work here.'[111]

Although lamb dysentery took a major share of the laboratories' veterinary research in the early 1920s, other diseases were investigated and other effective prophylactics developed. Dalling's research and its practical application attracted widespread attention, and he and his colleagues frequently addressed meetings of farmers and vets, which not only spread information about their work, but also promoted interest and trust in the company's products.[112] By 1927 the veterinary research team had produced reliable prophylactic vaccines against lamb dysentery, braxy and blackleg.

The benefits of Dalling's work to the company were two-fold. At one level, the research in what one Scottish farmer called BW&Co.'s 'great laboratory' attracted respect and reputation. Vets were happy to meet the company's representatives and scientists and assist in field-work. Secondly, that regard spilled over into commercial loyalty, even when the price of the serum was considered to be 'stiffish', at 1s. 6d. per inoculation. As one farmer pointed out, when considering a flock of 1,000 lambs, this was a 'staggering' amount, but preferable to the loss of over 20 per cent of the flock.[113] Others quickly imitated BW&Co., and by the dawn of the Second World War in 1939, several companies urged farmers to inoculate their ewes and lambs to protect the country's food supply. The pioneer in the field had been BW&Co., through the extraordinarily productive scientific work of Thomas Dalling and his colleagues. Mortality from lamb dysentery alone dropped from between 10 and 60 per cent to less than 1 per cent. Such was their

FIGURE 11.15
Dr (later Sir) Thomas Dalling.

regard that a group of Northumbrian farmers proposed inscribing a golden statue in Dalling's honour.[114]

Dalling's research extended far beyond these diseases. Experimental prophylactic immunisation was tried, with varying degrees of success, for the control of sheep diseases including Struck (a toxaemia), Pulpy Kidney Disease (affecting young lambs), infectious enterotoxaemia (affecting older lambs), grass ill (intestinal inflammation of young lambs), and black disease (infectious hepatitis). Individual and mixed vaccines were all tested, many of the latter proving particularly successful and correspondingly popular.[115] Dalling also investigated the prevention and control of swine erysipelas; some preliminary work on canine distemper; experiments on the avian distemper, roup, and a particularly virulent fowl disease, bacillary white diarrhoea of chickens.[116]

Veterinary research and commerce

In 1928, tensions developed between the veterinary scientists and BW&Co. because of the latter's decision to adopt the practice of other companies, including Parke, Davis & Co., to sell veterinary sera via chemists as a method of increasing the availability of products to the key users, the farmers.[117] Dalling and his colleagues were disquieted by the arrangement, which meant that farmers need not employ a veterinary surgeon. The *Veterinary Record* voiced its opposition and O'Brien requested BW&Co. as a 'matter of urgent importance' to respond to the critical article with a clear statement of the company's policy. In particular, he wanted to disassociate WPRL staff 'from a policy which is apparently considered by the general veterinary profession to be in opposition to the interests of the profession and the public interest'.[118] The company argued that the policy was identical to that pertaining to medical products.[119] O'Brien, however, reminded Snow Hill that diphtheria antitoxin or typhoid vaccine was administered by a doctor, not by the patients themselves. In this case, he argued

'the veterinary patient, (or his owner, the farmer) will buy directly and will himself inject without the intervention of the veterinary doctor'.[120] There was a strong feeling at the WPRL that cutting out the veterinary surgeon was a poor reward for all the help they had been given during the extensive trials necessary to produce safe therapeutic vaccines, and they strongly disapproved of the business decision. Paradoxically, Pearson permitted O'Brien to respond directly to the *Veterinary Record* to stress that the WPRL scientists 'regretted the necessity' of the company's decision. It was a curious ambivalence. On the one hand, BW&Co. allowed its scientists to express dissatisfaction with the company in a public scientific forum, but was not prepared to allow that dissatisfaction to influence commercial policy.[121] As a small concession, however, the company agreed not to implement the policy for 'another year or two'. Just a few months later, matters came to an unexpected head. O'Brien had confided his views to Fred Bulloch, the Secretary of the Royal College of Veterinary Surgeons. In a mistaken gesture of loyalty to the staff of the WPRL, Bulloch raised the matter at a College Council Meeting, who agreed to censure BW&Co. and wrote a stiff letter to Snow Hill threatening to boycott their products. It was regarded there as a 'bombshell'. Discussing the situation with Pearson, O'Brien explained that if the Royal College, which exerted legal control over the profession, disapproved of BW&Co. or considered any action ethically unacceptable, any veterinary surgeon on the Wellcome staff could be placed in a difficult position. This might be so great, O'Brien suggested, 'as to imperil our future'.[122] Like Dowson 30 years earlier, O'Brien and Dalling embarked on a series of explanatory visits to their professional colleagues, and to soothe ruffled feathers at Snow Hill. Equilibrium seems to have been rapidly restored for the company soon instigated a policy of selling via both chemists and veterinary surgeons. No further complaints were recorded in the veterinary press.

Foot and mouth disease, and tuberculosis: the commercial taint continued

Despite their enormous and unique contributions to the production of effective chemical and biological drugs during the First World War, or perhaps because of jealousy and resentment engendered by that success, blatant prejudices against the Wellcome laboratories as part of a commercial organisation surfaced again after the war. These were particularly evident when it came to their participation in national efforts against foot and mouth disease, and veterinary tuberculosis.

In 1924, in the wake of the second outbreak of the disease in two years, a Foot and Mouth Disease Committee was established to investigate the disease and the development of therapeutic strategies against it.[123] Laboratories wishing to work on the disease had to be authorised by this Committee to which O'Brien duly applied for registration in July.[124] In November he was interviewed by the Committee as there had been some discussion about vetoing the WPRL's application.[125] O'Brien was confident that he could clarify any misunderstandings and secure approval, but his optimism was misplaced. A month later, the Committee refused the WPRL's application entirely because of its association with the commercial company. Despite that, the Committee asked O'Brien to provide them with a report on his recent visit, funded by Wellcome, to several European laboratories working on foot and mouth disease, and also to provide the Committee with samples of all the viral strains then being studied by the WPRL.[126] Astonishingly, and with considerable scientific and commercial generosity, O'Brien provided a five-page report of his contacts, and all the research activities he and Dalling had inspected. He concluded with a series of suggestions of experimental protocols and trials that might be carried out.[127]

It was an iniquitous situation: the WPRL was considered unsuitable to undertake such work because of its commercial associations, but on the other hand the scientific contacts and ideas of its staff, many of which resulted from precisely such associations, *were* acceptable and deeply valued. In contrast to its attitude towards the WPRL, the Foot and Mouth Disease Committee readily accepted the facilities offered by the Lister Institute, and even paid for staff salaries and costs, conveniently ignoring the Lister's commercial relationship with Allen & Hanburys.[128] The only immediate consolation for BW&Co. was that if the Lister Institute did succeed, which O'Brien thought possible, a considerable demand for serum would be created, and they might then be able to enter a profitable field.[129]

Less than a year later, almost identical circumstances arose when the Ministry of Agriculture and Fisheries refused the WPRL permission to become a registered pathological institute, responsible for the bacteriological examination of milk under the Tuberculosis Act of 1925. This Act resulted from the National Tuberculosis Conference of 1924, which had called for the eradication of all tuberculous milk.[130] In that year alone 28 per cent of the cows in just one abattoir of the City of London were found to be tuberculous, a figure acknowledged to be lower than the rest of the country. This indicated a serious health problem.[131] Registration under the Act would have given the laboratories a nationally recognised scientific status, yet the WPRL's application was rejected once more because 'laboratories conducted by private firms are not being approved'.[132] O'Brien immediately challenged the decision, as did several local agricultural committees concerned that it indicated a sign of official disapproval of the laboratories and their work.[133] This was a serious problem for the WPRL when they depended so much on the goodwill and support of local farmers and vets, and after they had so assiduously nurtured their scientific reputation within that constituency. O'Brien was considerably annoyed that, yet again, the Lister Institute was registered. In a letter to the Chief Veterinary Officer he emphasised that the Lister Institute carried out research and raised sera for sale in exactly the same way as did the WPRL. Indeed, he added somewhat peevishly, 'it was at the [Lister] Institute that I myself for a considerable period carried out examination of samples of milk for the London County Council'.[134]

Further correspondence to the Ministry stressed that the laboratories carried out research with, or on behalf of, the Ministry of Health and the Medical Research Council, and had already received 20 requests from veterinary surgeons and local authorities for assistance under the Tuberculosis Act.[135] Sir Stewart Stockman, the CVO, readily acknowledged that the decision was in no way a judgement on the quality of the laboratories' work. Somewhat pompously, he reported it was a consequence of the Committee's decision not 'to agree to private individuals or Laboratories in the ownership of commercial firms being admitted into undertakings in connection with administrative government'.[136] The prejudices against the Wellcome laboratories, so pronounced during their earliest years, and so readily forgotten during the First World War, had been quickly resurrected.

Canine distemper vaccine

On the whole, the WPRL's veterinary research effort was focussed on animals of economic importance, sheep, cattle, poultry and pigs, and to a lesser extent, horses. However, domestic animals were not entirely ignored. In 1925 an investigation of leptospirosis in dogs, often known as 'yellows' to veterinary surgeons and kennel men because it caused jaundice, was started.[137] Work along the lines they adapted for all such studies, i.e. identifying and culturing the causative organism, developing a prophylactic vaccine; and then undertaking selective field trials; led to the large-scale production and marketing of therapeutically successful and commercially viable vaccine products.[138]

BW&Co.'s development of a protective vaccine against canine distemper was somewhat different. Much of the initial research and trial work was done outside the Wellcome organisation, and the firm became involved later, principally to translate laboratory results and experience into commercial production. This was to become a model for a number of future drug developments although in this instance it was to prove troublesome.[139]

After the First World War, the Medical Research Committee supported a research programme at the National Institute for Medical Research to investigate diseases caused by 'filterable viruses'.[140] This was a response to the worldwide pandemic of influenza, and distemper, an acute infectious disease of carnivorous animals, particularly common in puppies and causing a high canine mortality, seemed to be a suitable subject to study. In late 1922 the country magazine *The Field* added its support to the research work.[141] By early 1926, members of the MRC team had some initial success with a trial vaccine, and the following year test immunisations of foxhounds encouraged them to believe they had found a suitable prophylactic.[142] Lacking facilities for developing commercial production of the vaccine, the MRC approached

O'Brien for assistance. With Pearson's approval, the WPRL eagerly accepted the challenge of providing a reliable vaccine, building on the NIMR's basic research.[143]

Initially, BW&Co. issued experimental batches of prophylactics, before concentrating on marketing only NIMR's most successful preparation. The procedure they advocated was an injection of vaccine, followed a week later by an injection of virus to 'test' the effect of the vaccine. No response at this stage was taken to indicate a successful vaccine. It was a critical mistake: no one realised that the absence of a response could equally well indicate inadequate virus, and thus give a false positive result suggesting immunity where none existed.

A few months after the first vaccination of dogs, BW&Co.'s material was found not to provide reliable long-term protection. Over the next two years, numerous adverse reports appeared. Several factors contributed. Some veterinary surgeons did not follow the instructions properly and dogs were incompletely or inappropriately immunised; and dogs that developed any post-inoculation illness were often misdiagnosed as suffering from distemper. At the end of 1929 the Distemper Research Committee, reviewing BW&Co.'s supply of vaccine and virus for over nine months, noted that although 99 per cent of inoculations were satisfactory, the remaining 1 per cent gave concern. Dalling noted in a lecture to the Dog Owners' Club in December of that year that if *every* possible adverse report was counted, they still amounted to less than 2 per cent of all inoculations.[144] But it was these cases that attracted adverse publicity against BW&Co., the sole suppliers of the vaccine. Charged with investigating the disaster, O'Brien immediately wrote to every veterinary surgeon in England seeking reliable confirmation of deaths from distemper.[145]

Experiments revealed that both the virus and the vaccine were unstable, and in many cases dead virus had been sent to veterinary surgeons. By the beginning of 1930, O'Brien expressed his concern to Wenyon that 'we [i.e. WPRL staff] took too much for granted ... It was clear in the light of what has happened', he admitted, 'I have tried to organise the work on lines that were too economical'.[146] A report from the Distemper Committee also pointed to failures of both vaccine and virus, which O'Brien did his best to amend. He was concerned that to 'the ordinary veterinary reader or dog owner' the company would appear not to have tested the vaccine. This, he argued, would be an inaccurate but obvious interpretation, because the company had tested *batches*, but not every phial, in accordance with the MRC methods.[147]

Immediately after the report was published, BW&Co. advised that a maximum of 48 hours should be allowed between receipt and use of virus.[148] The WPRL also began experiments with a frozen virus preparation, which gave encouraging results and was rapidly issued by the company. This, too, had distressing effects. This now more potent virus immediately caused problems, and reports followed of severe reactions and deaths.[149] By the middle of 1930, O'Brien was convinced the product must be withdrawn.[150] A letter from the company for publication in *The Field* emphasised that 'It is clear that the balance that should exist between issues of vaccine and virus ... has been disarranged'.[151] The public and professional humiliation of withdrawing the product was a bitter blow for BW&Co. The fact that it had effectively 'taken over' MRC research and not controlled every stage was an additional hurt, especially when press reports drew invidious comparisons between the MRC's early successful trials with the company's later experiences.[152] As O'Brien put it rather bluntly to Wenyon, 'There is no point in my commenting here on our obvious failure to do all this work a year ago. As I told you, we took too many things for granted – the original research not being our own'.[153]

After these two serious problems, initially with dead virus, and then with highly potent frozen virus, take-up of the vaccine dropped dramatically. Concern that many vulnerable animals were not being immunised because of the prevailing confusion prompted O'Brien to ask Pearson to allow the WPRL to issue vaccine and virus free of charge for a period. He alerted Pearson to an additional reason for the wider publication of the laboratories' continuing concerns with the problem. An American preparation, Cutter's vaccine, was being pushed very strongly on the British market in the absence of the BW&Co. product. In O'Brien's opinion, Cutter's vaccine was just as good as their own, and, once more stepping over the line that divided scientific from commercial territory, he stressed to Pearson, 'I am naturally not desirous that people should be driven into using it – and so perhaps discovering its merit.'[154] Not surprisingly, Pearson readily gave permission for the WPRL to provide free material.[155] To resolve the technical difficulties the WPRL staff worked closely with their colleagues from the NIMR, who were equally bewildered as to what had gone wrong with the preparation.[156] By the beginning of 1931, work on improved virus and vaccine production and testing convinced Dalling and O'Brien to phase out the free issue and to restore commercial supplies.[157] The success, therapeutically and commercially, of these new preparations did not halt research. Canine distemper prophylactics continued to be an area of active research within the Wellcome organisation until the 1970s.

By the beginning of the Second World War, BW&Co. had achieved a commanding position in the supply of veterinary drugs, especially biological preparations. The WPRL's scientists had identified the causative organisms of an enormous number of animal diseases; produced, refined and field-tested numerous sera and vaccines; and developed novel production methods. The diseases they helped conquer included some of considerable economic importance in horses, cattle, sheep, pigs and poultry, work that assumed

FIGURE 11.17
Group
portrait
of senior
WPRL staff,
Beckenham,
c. 1930. Seated
at the far
right of the
front row is
the Director,
R. A.
O'Brien; on
the window
sill at the
back left is
J. Trevan;
and seated
directly in
front of him is
A. T. Glenny.
Thomas
Dalling is
standing third
from the right
in front of the
window on
the right.

national significance as war loomed and food supplies had to be protected. BW&Co. were not alone however. One author has estimated that more than 30 firms were providing veterinary medicines in the UK in 1937, in a market worth over £600,000 annually.[158] The Lister Institute developed a line of sera and vaccines, marketed by Allen & Hanburys without them ever being accused of commercial association; BDH advertised a range of appropriate products; Willows, Francis, Butler & Thompson acted as agents for a number of European and American laboratories.[159] The beginning of the antibiotic era was as enthusiastically embraced by the veterinarians as by the medical profession. May & Baker's first sulphonamide M&B 693 was rapidly made available for animal use, and in 1943, the year after curing the wartime Prime Minister Winston Churchill of pneumonia, it also cured Nero, the lion of Harry Benet's Majestic Circus, of the same disease.[160]

Diphtheria immunisation: problems and the end of an era

Throughout the interwar period, research and development work continued on BW&Co.'s original serotherapeutic product, anti-diphtheria serum. In 1928 a much-publicised disaster with diphtheria immunisation (although not BW&Co.'s product) occurred in Bundaberg, Queensland, Australia. Twenty-one children had been inoculated from the same bottle of toxin/anti-toxin mixture. Twelve of them died within 48 hours; only three were completely unaffected. After a previous report of deaths (in Concord, Massachusetts) caused by chemical deterioration of the preservatives, the Australian producers (never named, but suspected by O'Brien to be the Commonwealth Serum Laboratories) had deliberately not added preservative to the batch used in Bundaberg. The tragedy caused world-wide alarm.[161] The *British Medical Journal* sought to reassure the medical profession. It stressed that the toxoid–anti-toxin material most commonly used in Britain was produced by the WPRL, whose continuous monitoring of production procedures and experimental work meant that doctors could proceed with confidence.[162] The article had actually been written by O'Brien at the request of the *British Medical Journal's* editor, who was concerned that adverse publicity of distressing, but statistically rare, events seriously hampered the progress of immunisation campaigns. O'Brien admitted that parts of his article read as 'an unblushing advertisement for the Wellcome Laboratories', but as they were the major supplier of such material in Britain, there was little alternative.[163] The Royal Commission appointed to investigate the Bundaberg tragedy made recommendations about the production, packaging, testing, storage and use, all of which resembled the procedures already in place at the WPRL.[164]

The Ring Case

Disaster with diphtheria immunisation directly related to BW&Co. occurred in 1936. It was a recurrence of complaints that reached back to the very beginning of BW&Co.'s anti-toxin production in 1896, a claim that material was lethally contaminated. At the end of 1936, 38 children at Ring Irish College in County Waterford, Ireland, were inoculated with diphtheria vaccine from a single bottle of BW&Co.'s TAF. Five months later, one of the children died from miliary tuberculosis and 23 came down with the disease in varying forms, but recovered. The inquest in the following June was attended by O'Brien and Parish on behalf of the Wellcome Foundation. The school medical officer, Dr D.T. McCarthy, was exonerated of all culpability by the jury, who declared that the vaccine bottle must have contained tubercle bacilli. This was a most damaging verdict for the Wellcome Foundation, but its response was muted. Reports in the British medical press focused on Mr J.J. Horgan, BW&Co.'s counsel, who declared that the tragedy was a 'mystery [that] has definitely not been cleared up'. Horgan emphasised that contamination during manufacture would have affected hundreds of bottles, not just one, and stressed that Ireland's high diphtheria mortality rate had been significantly reduced because of BW&Co.'s immunisation campaigns and prophylactic products.[165]

After the inquest, the obvious question was that of damages. The girl's father sued both Dr McCarthy and the Wellcome Foundation, with the expectation that the rich English firm would provide adequate compensation.[166] Several sets of solicitors urged BW&Co. to settle out of court. By this time Henry Wellcome was dead, but following his tradition, Pearson opted to contest all claims. Preparing for the legal case, O'Brien supervised numerous experiments designed to provide sound evidence for the defence.[167] The choice of expert witnesses was critical. The two external consultants chosen, Joseph Bigger, Professor of Bacteriology and Preventive Medicine, Trinity College, Dublin, and Jack Blacklock, St. Mungo Professor of Pathology, Glasgow, were clearly Celts, not Englishmen. Parish himself, when the case came to Court, was advised by the Wellcome Foundation's legal team to draw attention to his own cultural heritage. This he did by apologising for his Scottish accent. In February 1939 the case for damages was heard in Dublin, where the jury was asked to decide, 'Did the defendants, the Wellcome Foundation Ltd, negligently issue a bottle containing live tubercle bacilli in suspension for use instead of a bottle of TAF?'[168] The Wellcome Foundation mounted a vigorous defence, and its witnesses gave evidence for over two weeks. The technical and scientific evidence for the WPRL was principally given by Henry Parish, the Head of Bacteriology at Beckenham who dealt with issues of potency, sterility and toxicity, and was responsible for the quality of all products issued for human use. As the chief witness for the defence, his role was absolutely critical as he was the one person who could lose the case for the Wellcome Foundation.

The key problem was: what had caused the disaster? Blacklock and Bigger both pointed to several deficiencies at the hospital; the sterilisation procedures used for syringes and needles, a faulty autoclave, and regular re-use of soiled dressings. 'No one' Bigger pronounced, 'could honestly hold that the so-called sterilisation in the hospital was adequate or sufficient for any surgical or medical purpose, including injection.'[169] At that time most doctors re-used syringes and needles (this was decades before the ready availability of disposable equipment), as exemplified by a letter in the contemporary medical press from a Medical Officer of Health who suggested that an entire school could be immunised by using just three BW&Co. glass syringes and 50 needles.[170] As a consequence of the Ring case, Blacklock, Bigger and Parish recommended, years ahead of their time, that after being emptied every syringe and its needle should be re-sterilised before re-use.[171] Accidental substitution of a bottle of living tubercle organisms for thera-peutic serum was rapidly dismissed because the two products were prepared in completely separate facilities at the WPRL, the bottles were of different sizes and shapes, and labelling and packing were carried out in distinctly separate rooms. Summing-up, the Judge concluded, 'It is difficult to say how the methods [adopted at Beckenham] could be improved upon'.[172] On the final day the jury took less than half an hour to return to respond to the original question, 'Did the defendants, the Wellcome Foundation Ltd, negligently issue a bottle containing live tubercle bacilli in suspension for use instead of a bottle of TAF?' with a resounding, 'No'. The Wellcome Foundation was vindicated.

The whole event had been a considerable worry to the Wellcome Foundation and to the newly created Wellcome Trust. Sir Henry Dale, former Director of the WPRL and by then Chairman of the Wellcome Trust, had been in contact with O'Brien throughout the pre-trial experiments at Beckenham. He had attended the daily meetings between the lawyers and witnesses in Dublin, offering support and advice where possible, such was his concern over the situation.[173] The case attracted considerable attention throughout the Republic. Bets were placed on the outcome. Walter Webb, the company's Dublin representative, reported the odds daily. Irish interest was further demonstrated by a dinner menu for the Wellcome team that included: 'Huitres à la Wellcome Foundation, Grapefruit immunisé, Consommé Tuberculine, and Galette Jalousie à l'autoclave.' Port was available in '25c.c. phials'.[174]

Once the case had been successfully defended, the WPRL came in for internal review and subsequent criticism. During the inter-war period there had been a considerable increase in the volume of products issued by the laboratories, where shortages of space, equipment and manpower had required 'making-do'. O'Brien's request in 1928 for replacement of the serum building, which he had been told in 1921 was a 'temporary arrangement', was refused by BW&Co. as a matter of economics. A further appeal for additional facilities in 1930 was also dismissed by the company.[175] A former assistant bacteriologist at Beckenham, R. A. Q. O'Meara, then working with Bigger in Dublin, compiled a report on the shortcomings of the WPRL, which he sent to Sir Henry Dale. He suggested that had *he* been called to give evidence at the trial, the company would have lost the case, and consequently have suffered enormous, probably irremediable, damage to its scientific reputation and commercial markets.[176] Whatever the truth of his belief, his criticisms were taken seriously. O'Brien, increasingly distracted and indecisive, came in for much criticism and was advised to take an extended break in his native Australia. The outbreak of war increased pressure for O'Brien to be retired, which was a difficult decision for Dale. He and O'Brien had been professional colleagues and personal friends for over 30 years, their close relationship had facilitated many formal and informal interactions between the WPRL and the MRC.[177] Eventually Dale agreed to demands for O'Brien's removal. Trevan became the Director from 1 January 1941.[178] Writing with the benefit of 20 years' hindsight, Parish admitted that his conscience worried him at the time because O'Brien, again a close personal friend, had 'achieved wonders for the Wellcome Research Laboratories'.[179] That is undoubtedly true. During the stresses and strains of the First World War, under O'Brien's leadership, the WPRL had made major contributions to British military and civilian health by its production of vast quantities of therapeutic sera and vaccines. During the inter-war period, the laboratories had achieved an unrivalled reputation and unique experience in developing, promoting, and utilising, preventive and therapeutic strategies against infectious diseases, advances often initiated, frequently performed, and certainly supervised, by O'Brien.

Sulphonamides

The final years of the 1930s heralded an even more drastic change for the WPRL. In 1935 Gerhard Domagk of the Bayer laboratories in Germany announced that Prontosil red dye could successfully treat streptococcal infections. Later that year scientists at the Pasteur Institute discovered that the effective component of Prontosil was a molecule called sulpho-nalimide, a well known non-patentable compound.[180] These events did not go unnoticed at BW&Co. Buttle at the WPRL immediately examined the new drug's potency against several strains of streptococci. He shared his results with Leonard Colebrook, then running an MRC trial of the therapy against puerperal fever at Queen Charlotte's Maternity Hospital London. Colebrook's work reinforced the reports of the clinical efficacy of sulpha-nilamide, and pharmaceutical companies raced to produce the new drugs, collectively known as sulphonamides.[181] It was to be May & Baker, under former Wellcome employee Arthur Ewins, that achieved most success and fame in the field, especially with M & B 693, which was particularly active against pneumococcus and used by the British Prime Minister, Winston Churchill, in 1942.

At the end of 1936 all the Wellcome research laboratories were working on a unique compound, sulphonamide P, which was first marketed in March 1937.[182] By then there was increasing evidence that these new drugs, regarded by one doctor as 'an outstanding event in medical history', were effective against a wide variety of infectious diseases.[183] BW&Co.'s Monthly Memoranda urged representatives to push the drug, *inter alia*, for gonorrhoea, puerperal fever, pneumonia, and meningitis.[184] This was made temporarily difficult in the USA when an 'Elixir of Sulphanamide' manufactured by Massengill caused nearly 100 deaths because of contamination with diethylene glycol, although very quickly the sulphonamides began to achieve wide recognition and correspondingly increased sales.[185]

But what of serotherapy? Over the preceding two decades, the Wellcome laboratories had vigorously campaigned for local and national schemes of testing and immunisation. It could be argued that it was not surprising that they adopted such a strategy, which would reap enormous financial rewards if large-scale schemes were effected. That argument not only ignores the cost to the laboratories and ultimately the company, of supporting their own production, testing and clinical trials, but also discounts the readiness with which other companies, such as Allen & Hanburys (marketing the Lister Institute's serum) and Parke, Davis & Co. (as agents for St. Mary's Hospital), would have geared up their own production and sales efforts, once a captive market was established. Other companies may well have been content to let BW&Co. pioneer new treatments and techniques, and fight for their recognition, secure in the knowledge they would quickly be able to share in the benefits of any success.

The undoubted importance of BW&Co.'s scientific advances in serotherapy should be set in the context of the relative financial significance of sera sales and profits. Table 11.1 shows sera sales as a low percentage of the company's sales until the First World War, followed by a reversion to pre-war levels until 1930. Steadily rising sales beginning in 1928 carried them above the 10 percent figure during the mid-1930s, rising sharply to 14 per cent under wartime conditions in 1940. Profits were minimal until the First World War, but remained well above thereafter, even during the immediate postwar drop collapse. After a gradual increase during the 1920s, profits were stable until the mid-1930s, when a discontinuous series suggests that they fell. Profits as a percentage of sera sales reveal a similar chronological course. The inflated profitability during the First World War was followed by a fall, but to a level well above the pre-war ratios. The fall during the 1930s, the result of increasing competition, cut profit margins by roughly one half compared with those shown for the 1920s. Except during wartime, sera sales and profits continued to be small compared with General Goods. However, because General Goods sales declined, particularly in the home market, and almost certainly profits and profit margins too, the relative importance of sera sales and profits grew during the inter-war period.

By the end of the 1930s, the sulphonamides had begun to render therapeutic sera redundant, and the postwar development of antibiotics confirmed their demise. The Wellcome laboratories continued to produce anti-toxins for research purposes, biological products for diagnosis, and an extensive range of vaccines, but large-scale sera production effectively stopped in the late 1930s. In December 1966, all serum work ceased at Beckenham after 43 years, during which over 27,000 horses had been immunised.[186] The golden age of serotherapy was over, and with it, the original work of the WPRL, which had been created in 1894 to provide just such treatments.

Table 11.1 *Total BW&Co. sales, sera sales, sera profits and ratios, 1901–1940*

	Total sales (£)	Sera sales (£)	Profits (£)	Sera sales/ total sales	Profits/ sera sales
1901	222,959	7,565		3	
1902	232,601	7,226	124	3	
1903	242,213		1,527		
1904			870		
1905			1,352		
1906	369,907	9,483	1,843	3	19
1907	402,394	11,831	2,472	3	21
1908	417,409	13,715	2,914	3	21
1909	465,704	18,521	3,245	4	18
1910	508,546	22,747	4,257	4	19
1911	575,756	28,210	4,017	5	14
1912	630,715	32,861	5,030	5	15
1913	681,849	37,361	5,199	5	14
1914	740,710	41,768	1,161	6	3
1915	733,882	54,361		7	
1916	881,895	100,522	3,353	11	3
1917	984,102	149,168	14,158	15	10
1918	1,070,994	174,231		16	
1919	1,109,994	113,883	60,040	10	53
1920	1,304,257	62,677	33,183	5	53
1921	1,187,483	58,285	23,730	5	41
1922	1,218,168	53,510	20,338	4	38
1923	1,245,170	48,197	19,735	4	41
1924	1,368,474	44,651	22,358	3	50
1925	1,441,292	54,033	24,903	4	46
1926	1,501,843	59,973	22,840	4	38
1927	1,539,995	58,240	26,820	4	46
1928	1,612,741	74,223	26,560	5	36
1929	1,713,974	83,716	28,411	5	34
1930	1,632,496	107,800	29,838	7	28
1931	1,549,563	104,027	31,241	7	30
1932	1,462,459	110,306	30,937	8	28
1933	1,416,203	124,190		9	
1934	1,461,908	158,494		11	
1935	1,499,064	186,890	30,547	12	16
1936	1,515,775	163,959		11	
1937	1,579,378	161,390		10	
1938	1,523,635	157,765	28,665	10	18
1939	1,639,013	186,745	18,808	11	10
1940	2,205,842	313,175		14	

WFA, F/FA/328, WFL trading and profit and loss accounts.

CHAPTER TWELVE

Competition and product development between the wars: Tabloids, Kepler, and other 'General Goods'

The postwar Tabloid range

Once the exceptionally high wartime demand for sera had disappeared, the composition of the company's sales divided between general goods and sera, and Wellcome Brand Chemicals, returned to a distribution similar to that prevailing before 1914. While sera and Wellcome Brand Chemicals accounted for consistently higher proportions within the overall total, sales revenue from general goods remained overwhelm-ingly the largest. The relative success of sera and Wellcome Brand Chemicals is attrib-utable to a considerable degree to the high standards of quality control introduced, not only in the factory but in the laboratories. Behind the company's product purity lay the work of scientists possessing chemical and physiological research expertise whose professional training enabled them to exercise routine control of the highest order.

Within the general goods category, compressed medicines were the major items, both before and after the war. Before 1914 an upward trend in annual output reached 470 million tablets in 1912, when the production series ends. Estimates of sales revenue based on production and price data suggest that this represented more than 50 per cent of general sales.

FIGURE 12.1
Advertisement for 'Tabloid' products 'all over the world'. *c.* 1920s.

Table 12.1 *BW&Co. Home, foreign and overseas sales by product category 1920–1940 (£)*

Year ending	General goods	Sera	Wellcome Brand Chemicals
1920	1,122,094	62,677	93,316
1921	1,019,105	58,285	78,338
1922	1,049,681	53,510	78,915
1923	1,092,906	48,196	77,060
1924	1,204,778	44,650	89,466
1925	1,274,173	54,033	83,323
1926	1,322,638	59,972	91,877
1927	1,369,329	58,239	87,538
1928	1,432,569	74,223	82,475
1929	1,520,067	83,716	86,046
1930	1,417,015	107,800	85,839
1931	1,347,011	104,027	76,663
1932	1,247,644	110,306	84,909
1933	1,196,339	124,189	78,555
1934	1,206,646	158,494	80,504
1935	1,212,956	186,887	83,395
1936	1,250,461	163,959	86,239
1937	1,326,186	161,389	77,709
1938	1,269,258	157,765	83,188
1939	1,345,298	186,784	94,187
1940	1,674,651	313,175	205,047

WFA, Acc 96/45, sales book 2.

Production reached a peak of 506.5 million tablets in 1917 followed by a reversal when the war ended, production falling below 400 million from 1920, stabilising at around 340 millions during the late 1920s. Between 1930 and 1935, when the production series ends, the annual average was 284 million: about 45 per cent of general sales. This declining trend partly reflects an increasing proportion of general goods hitherto manufactured at Dartford being produced in Sydney, and especially after 1925 in the new factory at Tuckahoe, New York. It is possible to estimate the proportion which sales of compressed medicines manufactured at Dartford represented of general sales sold in the home market and *directly* overseas, i.e. excluding the Sydney and New York manufacturing branches.

In 1924 Jowett referred to the company as manufacturing and stocking thousands of different products.[1] Yet within the Tabloid range it is possible to identify no more than a half dozen being produced in bulk. The principal chemicals manufactured at Dartford from which Tabloids were made remained essentially the same before and following the war, at least until after 1925, the only period for which reliable figures have survived. These were cascara sagrada, quinine, sodium salicylate, bismuth, and ergot.[2]

Table 12.2 *Estimated sales of compressed medicines, 1908–1923*

	General goods sales (£)	Production of compressed medicines (million tablets)	Estimated sales of compressed medicines (£)	Sales of compressed medicines as a percentage of general goods
1908	334,863	318.0	195,000	58
1909	364,057	328.8	207,000	57
1910	397,482	354.0	223,000	56
1911	452,015	360.0	227,000	50
1912	499,819	470.0	296,000	59
1913	538,154			
1914	580,583			
1915	572,876			
1916	667,990	481.4	505,000	
1917	705,656	506.5	602,000	
1918	788,927	410.9	518,000	
1919	896,872	401.2	533,000	
1920	1,122,994	390.4	519,000	46
1921	1,019,105	356.7	475,000	47
1922	1,049,651	342.5	456,000	43
1923	1,092,906	301.0	379,000	35

WFA, Acc 96/40:1 Dartford works production journal; Acc 99/6/14, Wellcome Chemical Works production record; Acc 96/45, Sales book 2; WFA, PB 111, BW&Co. annual price lists. Compressed medicine sales were estimated by constructing a wholesale price series by applying a 30 per cent discount to the BW&Co. price lists and applying the result to production figures.

In 1920 representatives were given the 'Tabloid ten' selling points with which to remind and convince doctors of their superiority compared with other branded and unbranded compressed medicines. These were purity, reliability in therapeutic action, accuracy of dosage, portability, preservability, convenience, taste, compatibility, no weighing or measuring, and no waste.[3]

The expiration of the patent on Aspirin during 1915 encouraged the company to mount a major campaign to expand sales of Tabloid Aspirin after the war. Long before 1915, the company had included Tabloid acetyl salicylic in its price list, a scientifically accurate description which, however, lacked the more popular appeal and reputation of the world renowned brand even though the price had been substantially lower. By 1924 Jowett could refer to this as one of only a few products made by the company 'handled by the ton'. A ton of aspirin contained roughly 1.5 million doses, equal to the production of the number of Tabloid Aspirins.[4] Tabloid Empirin, essentially identical in content and degree of purity to Tabloid Aspirin, also appeared, sometimes creating difficulties for representatives when they introduced it to medical practitioners.[5] The rationale for introducing Tabloid Empirin was that concealing the aspirin content from the patient would deter self-

SOUVENIR
BRITISH EMPIRE
EXHIBITION, 1924

WELLCOME & Cº

FIGURE 12.2
Souvenir
booklet
produced for
the British
Empire
Exhibition,
1924.

Table 12.3 Estimated sales of compressed medicines 1924–1935

	General goods sales (£) excluding Australia and USA	Output of compressed medicines produced by BW&Co. in Britain (million tablets)	Estimated sales of compressed medicines (£)	Estimated sales of as percentage of general goods produced by BW&Co. in Britain
1924	774,325	333.0	420,000	54
1925	792,127	345.7	436,000	55
1926	781,385	349.0	440,000	56
1927	802,594	345.8	436,000	54
1928	829,281	362.8	457,000	55
1929	874,512	363.1	407,000	47
1930	808,790	338.5	380,000	47
1931	761,931	310.0	347,000	46
1932	707,573	286.4	320,000	45
1933	682,239	282.3	316,000	46
1934	675,521	272.2	285,000	42
1935	651,125	270.4	284,000	44

Because production figures for Australia and the US have not survived, the figures presented here show sales generated from London after assuming that all general goods sold in the US and Australia were also produced by the two overseas subsidiary companies. Although this probably results in underestimates, the discrepancy is likely to have been relatively small and diminishing over time. WFA, Acc 96/40/1 Dartford works production journal; WFA, Acc. 99/6/14, Wellcome Chemical Works production record; WFA, Acc 96/45, Sales book 2; WFA, PB 111, BW&Co. annual price lists. Compressed medicine sales were estimated by constructing a wholesale price series by applying a 30 per cent discount to the BW&Co. price lists and applying the result to production figures.

medication and reduce the likelihood of substitution. In the US, where Empirin was to prove a great success, Compbayer's Aspirin continued to be protected by patent until 1917.[6]

The possibility of exploiting a potentially large demand was communicated to the company's representatives in 1919.[7] The context for the sales campaign was that of competition from other companies (including Boots under Carr's direction) which similarly had taken advantage of the suspension of patent protection. A feature of this expansion, first in the US and subsequently in Britain, was the proliferation of unbranded makes of aspirin which varied in quality. This resulted from the use of inferior chemicals in manufacture, either not conforming to the BP requirements or meeting only the minimum standard. The *Chemist & Druggist* reported instances where aspirin was claimed to contain 5-grains of salicylic acid BP, but had been discovered to contain 3.5 grains, the product being made up with French chalk, reducing sugar, and other diluents.[8] The confiscation of 400,000 tablets, which was reported in the *American Druggist & Pharmaceutical Record* in 1919, resulted from the discovery that they contained mainly talc and starch with a little salicylic acid.[9] The representatives were reminded that the brand names Tabloid Aspirin or Tabloid Empirin guaranteed weight, instant solubility, absolute purity, freedom from salycilic acid and metallic impurities, occasioned no gastric irritation, and conformed to a standard higher than that of the BP.[10] A series of advertisements in the medical press provided authenticated evidence of frauds being perpetrated by manufacturing chemists who relied on price to promote sales of aspirin.[11] Representatives were advised to use the 'Tabloid ten' points when meeting doctors and retailers who were perceived to be more vulnerable to the appeal of low prices. This involved the presentation of Tabloids, not as drugs to purchase, but as a service in the form of a dose of high-quality medicine at low cost. Thus, at current Tabloid prices the cost of removing a headache was estimated at about 0.3d., a cost similar to that of a dose of Tabloid Easton Syrup prescribed to replace depression with a feeling of well-being. Tabloid Easton Syrup was compared with the cost of a bottle of champagne as an alternative tonic. One hundred nights free from acidity, reckoned to be a major cause of sleeplessness, cost one third of a penny which was similar to the cost of a voice Tabloid (chlorate of potash): 'a silvery voice ought to be worth a small fraction of a penny to a barrister, a singer or lover. It may make the difference between failure and, as the case may be, a favourable verdict, an artistic success, and or happiness'.[12]

Of all the claims for Tabloid Aspirin and Empirin, purity was increasingly emphasised during a period when adulteration by price-cutting producers elicited the strongest criticism from the medical and trade press. One of the company's advertisements introduced in 1920 showed a diagram indicating the percentage of talc found in the *Lancet*'s analysis of many brands of compressed tablets.[13] Tabloid products had been found to be entirely free from talc, whereas all other 11 tablets were found to contain percentages of talc, the highest two revealing 14.8 and 18.6 per cent talc.[14] Another advertisement using similar data published in British and American journals, compared aspirin tablets from six suppliers with Tabloid aspirin. Whereas the Tabloid product contained 5 grains of pure acetyl salicylic acid, the weight in others varied between 4.25 grains to zero.[15] The superiority of Tabloids was also reported in the *Chemist & Druggist* in 1926, based on tests by the City of Birmingham analyst in which 1,700 tablets of sodium salicylate were examined. Representatives were urged to use the report as a weapon with which to combat the sale of some of the cheap and nasty compressed medicines.

Aspirin was one of the analgesic medicines most threatening to the traditional chemist and druggist because it encouraged self-medication and the expansion of over-the-counter sales outside the pharmacy trade.[16] A proliferation of outlets for the sale of such products, combined with other compressed medicines 'of dubious composition in imitation of Tabloids flooding the market' increased the possibilities for misinterpretation of prescriptions.[17] One resulted from those in which the imprecise 'Tab' instead of Tabloid indicated the item prescribed. Representatives were reminded to rehearse the distinctive features which gave Tabloids qualitative superiority as 'weapons of precision': they were 'scientifically designed, prepared, and adjusted to meet the ever-advancing requirements of medical science'.[18]

In 1936, the company began to push Tabloid Empirin compound. This probably reflected the increasing competition from other lower-priced proprietary and unbranded aspirins, aggressively advertised to the public and widely available outside pharmacies from grocers and general stores. Successfully marketed by BW&Co. (USA) Inc., Empirin had received less attention from British representatives. They were now urged to make an 'extra push' to approach doctors and pharmacists to explain its advantages in the treatment of neuralgias and pain in general, especially when associated with rheumatism, sciatica, or dysmenorrhoea. In addition to reducing cold fever it was effective when administered for dental pains and headaches. Another advantage to those prescribing or recommending the use of Empirin was that the patient would not be aware of the aspirin content which therefore removed, or at least reduced, the possibility of the patient opting to take a substitute. This was important because the price-protected profit margin for the retailer was high compared with that for cut-price aspirin.[19] To reinforce this, representatives were advised to adopt the 'personal experience' approach to introducing Empirin, firstly by dosing themselves to justify authoritative accounts of effects, and secondly by persuading doctors and chemists themselves to try the medicament.[20] In 1938 Tabloid Empirin Compound with Codeine, an analgesic offering a wider range of applications, was added to the home list. Successfully marketed by the American company for several years, this appears to have been the product intended to re-establish the strong position the company had occupied in the British market during the 1920s.[21]

Just as the company experienced intensifying competition in the market for analgesics after the war, Tabloid quinine came under pressure from firms entering the market for the first time. A booklet entitled 'Good health all the year round', first issued in 1912, was intended for Europeans in the Far East and showed statistics and charts indicating the capacity of quinine to reduce the incidence of malaria. The use of quinine in that part of the world was described by Wenyon:

> ... individuals who take their own prophylactic quinine in the tropics may frequently have the BW&Co. bottle of Tabloids placed on the dinner table. They take a Tabloid 5-gr, before the soup.[22]

Again in 1924, attention was drawn in Monthly Memoranda to this growing market, especially in the British Empire, which the company was well placed to meet. However, as in the aspirin trade, inferior products destabilised the market. Whereas BW&Co. invariably used only sugar in coating compressed medicines to ensure perfect solubility, many manufacturers were using talc as a substitute, reducing solubility but cutting the price of the products.[23]

Tabloid alkaline compound effervescent, a product prepared to relieve acidosis was also considered to command a large commercial potential when it was launched in 1929. To avoid the risk of lowering the scientific standard of the company's booklet, 'Acidosis – notes on causes and treatment', which the company claimed to have been written by a distinguished (though unnamed) physiologist, the product received the briefest notice.[24] This was because the product was used for a much wider range of conditions than acidosis. Described as 'a sparkling draught', possessing 'pleasant features', it was prescribed by general practitioners for patients for whom a simple prescription of an alkali in the form of sodium bicarbonate might otherwise have been given. The company's intention in launching the new alternative Tabloid compound effervescent was to provide doctors with an appropriate medication that appeared to be novel and which patients might regard more seriously.[25]

The single most scientifically and commercially important addition to the Tabloid range between the wars, however, was Digoxin, the last major pre-war drug to be discovered and developed completely in-house. After nine years of research into digitalis culminating in clinical testing completed successfully in 1934, Digoxin appears to have been the major new product to help compensate for the decline in General Goods.[26]

From digitalis to Digoxin

First introduced into medical practice by the English physician William Withering in 1785, digitalis was extracted from the foxglove Digitalis purpurea, and was widely used for congestive heart failure. It was included in the very first British Pharmacopeia that appeared in 1864. As early as June 1878 Evans, Lescher & Evans had offered to supply Burroughs, newly arrived in London, with digitalis and belladonna, two popular remedies of the day.[27] Since the 1890s BW&Co. were buying their digitalis from Messrs. Gehe & Co. of Dresden, after analysis at the Dartford factory had identified theirs as one of the purest products available. Increasingly however, the company became dissatisfied with the preparation, which was not soluble enough to be made into a hypodermic Soloid.

In 1903 George Barger and Vernon Shaw of the WPRL undertook an extensive investigation of the tincture of digitalis marketed by the company, and rival preparations. They quickly realised that the physiological effects of digitalis were due not to any of its then known constituents (digitoxin, digitonin, digitalin and digitalein), but to another, entirely new, physiologi-

FIGURE 12.3
Harvesting
foxgloves at
BW&Co.'s
materia medica
farm, for
manufac-
turing
digitalis
products
including
digoxin,
c. 1930s.

cally active principle. This emphasised that the chemical assay of digitoxin then used to measure digitalis' activities was not a reliable guide to its biological activities, and they began to develop a physiological assay, based on the drug causing permanent ventricular asystole (i.e. killing a frog by causing the heart to stop beating). This rapidly became a widely used, standard test for digitalis.[28] However, driven by the League of Nations worldwide concerns to achieve standardization of pharmaceutical preparations, BW&Co. entered into competition with Parke, Davis & Co., which in 1922 had produced a preparation called Digifortis, which was heavily advertised as being 'physiologically standardised'.[29] Dr Sydney Smith of the Experimental Department at Dartford was instructed to begin extraction experiments, the progress of which were regularly reported back to the STC.[30]

A key 'push' in this ultimately successful research came from the eminent cardiologist Sir Thomas Lewis, arising from a timely, if unusual encounter. In late June 1925, one of the company's sales representatives called on Lewis, attempting to interest the physician in the company's latest preparation of digitalis leaves. Lewis, 'often brusque to the point of rudeness' disliked pharmaceutical company representatives, although he was occasionally prepared to see those from BW&Co., of whose work and products

FIGURE 12.4
Dr Sydney
Smith.

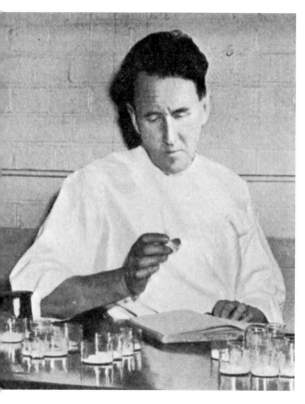

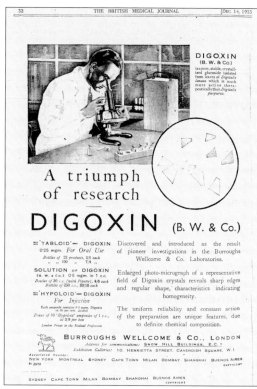

FIGURE 12.5
Mr Fox, one
of Sydney
Smith's
research
team at the
Wellcome
Chemical
Works,
demonstrating
how samples
of digoxin
were sorted
(*Foundation
News*,
February
1951).

FIGURE 12.6
Advertisement
for Digoxin
(*BMJ*, 14
December
1935).

he approved.[31] This was one of those occasions. Lewis not only heard out the representative, but added his own views on digitalis preparations, and suggested that rather than prepare a purified preparation of digitalis leaf, they should try to isolate its therapeutically active components. Further, he offered, should the company be successful, to supervise a clinical trial himself. The rep's report was immediately forwarded by Snow Hill to Wenyon at the WBSR, who rapidly passed it to O'Brien at the WPRL and Jowett at the Works.[32]

The STC decided to concentrate research efforts solely on digitalis and not to investigate other heart drugs.[33] Such researches were enthusiastically directed by Sydney Smith whose work proceeded along the classical lines already used so successfully in the Wellcome laboratories. Alerted to these new developments the Advertising Department produced a new booklet, *Digitalis in Cardiology* which was widely distributed to doctors to inform them of the company's latest research in 'digitialisation'.[34]

By October 1928 Smith had isolated a cardio-active glucoside that could be issued for limited clinical trial.[35] An advertising campaign was planned, a patent applied for, and Digoxin was launched in November 1929.[36] Unfortunately, the strength of the commercial preparation regularly failed to meet the standards achieved in the laboratories, necessitating further collaborative work between the WPRL and the Chemical Works to stabilise a consistent formulation.[37] Trials continued around the country, and published and verbal reports sent back to the STC increasingly attested to its efficacy.[38] By the early 1930s reports issued by the Theraputic Trials Committee of the Medical Research Council, confirmed the advantages of Digoxin over other digitalis preparations.[39] In 1934 the STC finally agreed that Digoxin could be recommended as a substitute for digitalis and that no further clinical trials were needed.[40] Under the trade name 'Lanoxin', the product continues to be used at the beginning of the twenty-first century.

Kepler cod liver oil and malt extract and the infant health food market

The production and sales revenue estimated for compressed medicines imply that Kepler goods accounted for less than one half of all sales of products in the general goods category. The relative volume of advertising and sales effort devoted to the Kepler line reported in Monthly Memoranda and in the pages of the trade and medical journals, however, suggest that Kepler products continued to secure a substantial share of general goods sales, though these, too, probably declined during the 1930s.

FIGURE 12.7
BW&Co.
advertisement
for cod liver
oil, *c.* 1926–27.

When the war ended, sales representatives were urged:

> Keep hammering away to drive home your old good points on Kepler products. Emphasise their value as galactagogues, for which purpose (as well as the plain Malt Extract and the Malt and Oil) remember Kepler Malt Extract with Haemoglobin. Its blood-enriching and milk-forming properties make a good combination. Every nursing mother who takes this combination benefits her child by the improved quality and quantity of her milk and lessens the strain which lactation imposes on herself... new methods of demonstration are particularly valuable for Kepler products because there is always a danger of getting stale when making old points in the old way.[41]

One such recommended method of demonstration which claimed to offer

FIGURE 12.8
A display of
packaging
and promo-
tional
material for
Kepler malt
extract. No
date.

'psychic value' was that practised by an American representative reported in Monthly Memoranda. This involved placing a sample of Kepler Malt Extract with Haemoglobin onto a spatula 'allowing light to strike the material as it thins out. The effect is to show up the characteristic blood red colour, and it seems to make quite an impression on the doctor … since the product is prescribed for its *blood*-enriching and tonic properties'.[42]

'Propagation' became increasingly important in the context of competition which in the postwar period was based to a considerable extent on product development and diversification by rival firms taking advantage of a burgeoning market for infant health foods. In an environment of increasing concern among the medical profession, nutritionists, and medical officers for infant health, a growing body of medical opinion linked rickets and tubercular conditions in children with a food fat deficiency for which dried milk could compensate.[43] Two firms were particularly attuned to these developments. Allen & Hanburys had produced Mother's Milk Food since 1893. Under the Allenburys brand, malted foods for infants and Allenburys Milk Foods for babies aged below six months became increasingly important to Allen & Hanburys' sales revenue; milk and malted food products accounted for 59 per cent of sales and 60 per cent of net profit in 1920.[44]

Another significant entrant into this market was the New Zealand merchanting firm of Joseph Nathan & Co. which, by introducing Glaxo dried milk into the market in 1908, began to challenge the established dried milk manufacturers in Britain whose products included Cow & Gate and Trumilk as well as Allenburys Milk Foods.

After Glaxo dried milk failed in the general household market, effort was re-directed towards the infant and childcare market, notably through advertising and educative publicity aimed at medical and welfare professionals and mothers. Louis Nathan, in charge of the Glaxo department, was not constrained by any perceived need to adhere to ethical principles in advertising his company's products. A vigorous marketing policy included direct appeals through newspaper and poster advertising to consumers.[45] The result was a growing demand for Sunshine Glaxo – the food to 'build bonnie babies'. Dried milk sales received a further boost from government contracts during the war which continued after 1918. In 1921 sales of Glaxo dried milk reached £1.5 million, roughly three times those of Allen & Hanburys whose sales of malt products were £94,700 and of cod liver oil, £44,500.[46] In contrast, Kepler

FIGURE 12.9
Advertisement for Kepler cod liver oil with malt extract (*Chemist & Druggist*, 6 January 1923).

malted products were increasingly promoted as 'humanised milk' in an attempt to share the rapidly growing infant and baby food market and to withstand competition from the dried milk manufacturers.

The challenge of vitamins to Kepler goods

The transformation of the market resulting from advances in nutritional science and the subsequent 'vitamania'[47] which began to sweep across the US and, albeit to a less extent, Britain in the 1920s added to the increasing competition faced by Kepler health foods. This followed the identification of 'Vitamines' in 1911 by the Polish scientist, Casimir Funk, who was working in England. Shortly after the First World War Dr Frederick Gowland Hopkins announced his discovery of 'accessory food factors', soon renamed 'vitamins' (the 'e' was dropped on discovering that not all vitamins were amines, i.e. nitrogen-containing compounds). These first achieved popular as well as scientific prominence in the early 1920s. To a very large extent, BW&Co.'s labs were unable to exploit the new development because of the absence of appropriately qualified research staff. The WCRL was suffering a shortage of chemists able to undertake and develop synthetic chemical work in addition to work then under way in tropical therapeutics. The loss of Carr (previously Director of the Experimental Department) who had joined Boots in 1915 and BDH two years later was damaging because Carr took charge of BDH's product development strategy in which vitamin research and production formed a major part. Alfred Bacharach had joined the WCRL in 1915, subsequently working in the Analytical Department at Dartford. His loss in 1920 to Nathan & Co. (later Glaxo) where he led vitamin research was an equally serious blow to BW&Co. The WPRL was recovering from large-scale wartime serum production and was ill equipped to undertake detailed chemical analysis. It was left to the newly appointed John Trevan to supervise WPRL staff in carrying out such little vitamin research as was possible. He was, however, already dealing with problems of poor insulin production at a time when several lines of new scientific inquiry were appearing and when the laboratory was in the midst of moving to new premises (see chapter 10).

An immediate question was to determine the vitamin content of the company's food products. The discovery that the therapeutic value of cod liver oil in the treatment of rickets was comparable with that of dried milk, according to an article published in a medical journal in 1921, offered the company an opportunity to reactivate interest in Kepler goods. Representatives were urged to speak to medical men about the therapeutic properties of cod liver oil and malt, and to use the journal article.[48] Another study predicted the disappearance of rickets by administering cod liver oil, an opinion prompting more advice to salesmen to mention this angle.[49] Advances made in nutritional research and its wider dissemination increased the commercial importance of communicating to consumers a new scientific credibility of the claims made in promoting the advantages of health foods.[50] Such communications in the form of extravagant claims by advertisers attracted condemnation among the scientific and medical communities underlined by an investigation carried out by the Council on Pharmacy and Chemistry of the American Medical Association in 1922 which concluded that claims being made by commercial producers concerning vitamin B could not be supported by 'adequate, acceptable evidence'.[51] Similar disapproval was expressed in Monthly Memoranda which reported the American study: 'It is only by prolonged scientific investigation in a well-equipped physiological laboratory that dependable information can be gained'.[52] Although BW&Co. began to test oil for the presence of vitamins in 1923, company scientists remained sceptical of the results because they considered current known methods of testing for vitamins using rats to be too crude a form of scientific method to produce accurate results; they opposed their use in labelling or advertising.[53]

Vitamin concentrates were also subjected to critical scrutiny in Britain.

Researchers at University College London tested the preparations of vitamin concentrates advertised in Britain by six American companies. These included Metagen, made by Compark (Parke Davis); Virol, made by Oppenheimer (which also produced Roboleine, advertised as 'very rich in vitamins A, B, and C ... supersedes cod liver oil'); Maltine, made by the Maltine Manufacturing Company; and Mellin's Food, made by Mellin. The researchers' conclusion was that none of these manufacturers had succeeded in securing concentrated vitamins on a commercial scale.[54] Similar tests carried out on twenty such preparations showed the same result. Such reports were summarised in Monthly Memoranda as justification of BW&Co.'s cautious approach to vitamin concentrates:

> ... in the present state of knowledge, it cannot be done on the commercial scale. The repeated exposure of preparations of other firms and the claims made for them now leaves no doubt of the wisdom of the course we adopted.[55]

Probably intended to answer representatives' concerns that profitable opportunities were being ignored, reassurance was offered that 'If and when such products can be offered honestly on a scientific basis the firm will be first in the field'.[56]

The company's reputation among the medical profession had been established in part on the basis of the successful preparation of the active principle of numerous drugs. In the case of cod liver oil, however, vitamins were so easily affected by heat and other influences, and so little was known about their constitution that Wellcome scientists considered that production of concentrated preparations on a commercial scale would be unsafe.[57] Entitled 'The destruction of vitamins', an editorial in the *BMJ* pointed out that one implication arising from this difficulty was that all preserved foods were liable to be deficient in vitamins by comparison with fresh foods, notably cod liver oil.[58]

This argument was confirmed by J.C. Drummond, Professor of Biochemistry at University College London, who, in 1925, analysed cod liver oils for medical use. His conclusions, reported in the *Lancet*, were summarised in Monthly Memoranda. Representatives were urged to read the summary reproduced for the purpose, paying close attention because 'Every point goes to establish a reason for the superiority which Kepler Cod Liver Oil and Malt Extract has established clinically'.[59] This superiority was confirmed in 1925 by the Canadian government analyst who tested 152 samples of malt extract purchased in the normal manner. Among only ten that met the government's standard criteria in every respect, seven were Kepler Malt Extracts. As a result, these findings were adopted as the standard for comparison in subsequent official investigations.[60]

As nutrition research increased and vitamin concentrates proliferated, the commercial pressure on BW&Co. to respond finally persuaded the scientists to agree to emphasise vitamin content in the company's literature. A special review of selling points appeared in Monthly Memoranda, reminding representatives that Kepler goods had 'done as much as any group of preparations to establish our reputation for quality of production' and that they were a considerable factor in the company's commercial success. Three or four unique selling points were listed for each of the categories. These were: Kepler malt products (perceived as reliable by independent examination, relatively highly priced, well-packed, and satisfactory 'profit yielders'); Kepler Malt Extract (B.P.) containing active vitamin B, an excellent vehicle for many drugs, masking taste and preventing decomposition; and Kepler Cod Liver Oil (best preparation of the best oil, containing vitamins A and B in active condition, palatable and digestible).[61]

From 1927 all cod liver oil used in producing Kepler goods was subjected to physiological testing in the company's laboratories.[62] Scientists insisted that it was still not possible to indicate the precise vitamin level on labels and advertisements. However, by advertising the comprehensive testing process, the company sought to reassure medical men, chemists and druggists, and other purchasers of a satisfactory (though unquantified) vitamin content in the final products.[63] Claims made by other producers for *levels* of concentration contained in their products were condemned as 'thoroughly dishonest'.[64] Travellers were advised that while they should continue to adopt a conservative attitude in promoting the company's own products by adhering strictly to claims supportable by scientific evidence, they should also be alert to the possibility that clients interviewed might be misled by the rash claims made by competitors. The critical authoritative sources quoted in Monthly Memoranda were supplied to assist representatives' rebuttals.

Sensitive to the commercial potential of the development of vitamins, in 1925 Jowett had raised the subject at a meeting of the STC which agreed to explore the possibility of producing a vitamin concentrate, beginning with an investigation into the value of Drummond's techniques of irradiated cholesterol. Dr Henry of the WCRL was asked to supply a concentrated preparation of vitamin A from the WCRL. Combined research by the WCRL, the WPRL, and the Works began.[65] The Glaxo department of J. E. Nathan & Co. had been producing and marketing vitamin A since 1924. This was the culmination of the efforts of Harry Jephcott, the company's young chemist, who had assembled a small scientific group which was intended, initially, to end the uncertainty over the effect of heat on the vitamin content of the dried milk produced by the company. The other leading nutritional researcher in the laboratory was Alfred Louis Bacharach, whom Jephcott had recruited from BW&Co. in 1920 when the research began.[66] A prolific researcher who possessed an energetic, entrepreneurial approach to business, Jephcott travelled to the US in 1923 and met the leading nutritional researchers, Prof. Elmer V. McCollum and Dr Theodor Zucker. In the early 1920s, McCollum had identified the growth-inducing vitamin A as distinct from the antirachitic vitamin D. Zucker was the patent owner of a process of extraction from fish liver oil which produced extremely high levels of concentration of vitamin D. On Jephcott's advice, the Nathans secured the British licence and, in 1924, commenced the production of Ostelin vitamin D, the earliest standardised vitamin concentrate from cod liver oil to be marketed in Britain.[67] The *Lancet* described Ostelin as 'a reliable and concentrated preparation';[68] advertisements referred to the 'sunlight vitamin' and 'bottled sunshine'.[69] The gross profit margin of Ostelin was reckoned at 70 per cent.[70] Although admitting to initial production and marketing problems, Jephcott expressed satisfaction in 1926 that the company was well ahead of competitors, but asserted that only sustained focused investigation of production and product, requiring a specific allocation for funding research, would enable it to retain that lead.[71]

BDH, already established in the infant food market, was the first to follow the Nathan firm into the market for vitamin concentrates. This began with the development of Herogen, an infant health food consisting of meat, milk, eggs, cereals, and water. First produced and marketed in 1912, this later became 'improved' by vitamin enhancement.

This development occurred under Carr's direction and involved heavy investment in the establishment of a physiological laboratory for biological and physiological testing together with manufacturing plant. These facilities were placed at the disposal of Drummond for the purpose of studying the chemical nature of cod liver oil with a view to producing vitamin-tested cod liver oil and vitamin concentrates, initially A and D, 'on a semi-manufacturing scale' intended to achieve 'reasonably large yields'. By 1926 the company was producing vitamins in cod liver oil extracts and marketing vitamin concentrates A and D.[72] The *Chemist & Druggist* reported that the BDH laboratories

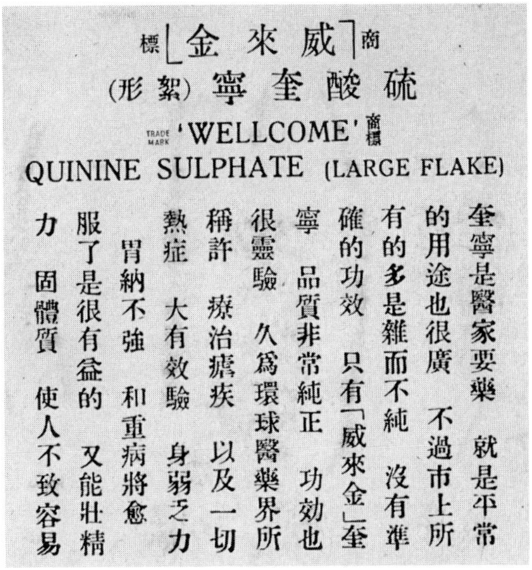

FIGURE 12.10
Label for quinine sulphate in Chinese, c. 1926.

enabled the company to meet a sudden increase in the demand for 'chemical foods' which the plant was producing at a rate of 1,000 gallons a month.[73] In 1928 Allen & Hanburys began to add vitamins to its Allenburys foods by using the American Steenbock method of irradiating ergosterol.[74] However, the company's hold on the milk food market began to weaken, as the Nathan firm, trading as Glaxo Laboratories from 1932, expanded rapidly during the 1930s.[75]

Vitamin research and marketing policies

Developments at Glaxo and BDH put pressure on BW&Co. to reconsider policy regarding the newly emerging market for vitamin concentrates. Hitherto, given other existing priorities in serotherapy and tropical medicine and the handicaps caused by lack of scientific staff and of facilities, the company had adopted a policy of 'wait and see'. Wellcome scientists continued to be sceptical towards claims for vitamin content made by competitors based on testing either raw materials or finished products. This explains why the STC strongly advised Pearson (who was anxious to respond to competitors' advertisements) that BW&Co. should not adopt similar tactics in advertising Kepler goods. O'Brien insisted that the methods of testing available were 'so fallacious' as to be seriously misleading and that only a long-term growth study in rats could provide a reliable test.[76] However, in 1925, the year when McCollum identified the antirachitic factor in cod liver oil (subsequently known as vitamin D), WPRL scientists carried out a series of experiments to examine the therapeutic efficacy of Kepler Extract, specifically in the treatment of rickets. The results were claimed as convincing proof of the therapeutic as well as the dietetic properties of Kepler.[77]

FIGURE 12.11 'The smallest medicine chest in the world'. A replica of a Tabloid chest made in 18-carat gold, for a doll's house, presented to Queen Mary 1934.

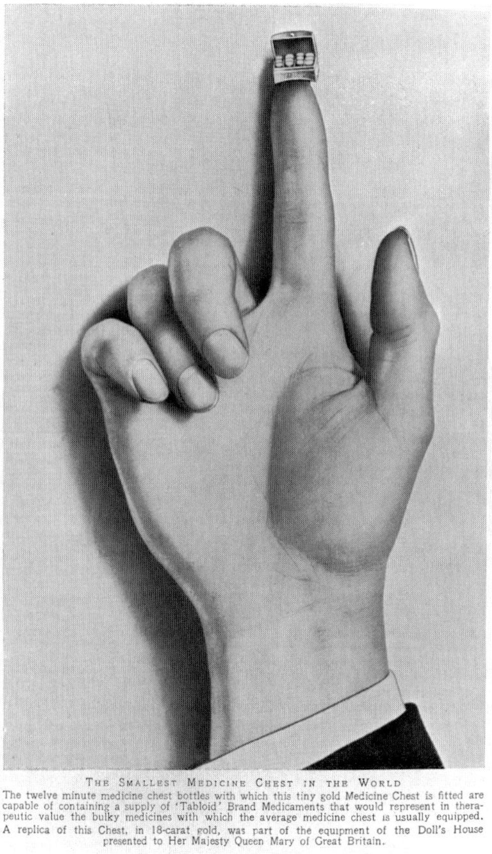

O'Brien, however, reminded Wenyon that the clinical benefit of cod liver oil might depend on factors other than its vitamin content, a possibility remaining because of the uncertainties surrounding testing.[78] The STC even suggested that BW&Co. might issue a statement expressing the worthlessness of current testing methods, though this was rejected because it risked alienating the MRC, the *United States Pharmacopoeia*, and other authorities working to standardise chemical tests. The fear that such a blanket condemnation might encourage competitors to analyse Kepler products with a view to finding shortcomings was a further consideration. Although the scientists expressed confidence in the consistent quality of Kepler, they acknowledged that unavoidable variation between oil samples and the vagaries of testing might result in a sample being discovered to be deficient. O'Brien regarded such an eventuality as undesirable from a scientific standpoint; Pearson agreed

THE SMALLEST MEDICINE CHEST IN THE WORLD
The twelve minute medicine chest bottles with which this tiny gold Medicine Chest is fitted are capable of containing a supply of 'Tabloid' Brand Medicaments that would represent in therapeutic value the bulky medicines with which the average medicine chest is usually equipped. A replica of this Chest, in 18-carat gold, was part of the equipment of the Doll's House presented to Her Majesty Queen Mary of Great Britain.

on commercial grounds.[79] However, acknowledging that an insistence on complete scientific accuracy in publicity was 'handicapping BW&Co.', O'Brien proposed that the company should advertise oil as certified by 'tests accepted by biochemists at the present time'. This formula, which satisfied scientific honour and extended parity to commercial considerations, was incorporated in the 'Points for Propaganda' for March 1927.[80] Nevertheless, the STC continued to be critical of the company's 'authorised statements' (then in use by the Advertising Department at Snow Hill) with respect to vitamins and cod liver oil. The claim that 'Kepler cod liver oil has been specially selected for its vitamin content since the year 1923' was dismissed as inaccurate. O'Brien conceded that *batches* of oil had been tested by Jowett using a crude colour-reaction test, but O'Brien insisted that vitamin content had led neither to selection nor rejection of oil. Exasperated that inaccurate advertisements continued to appear from Snow Hill, O'Brien addressed Edgar Linstead, Advertising Manager, with the question: 'Would it not equally meet your point to say that samples from various oils purchased by the [Wellcome] Foundation have been tested at intervals during the past few years by colour and animal test and that on every occasion when those tests were carried out the evidence pointed to a high content of the vitamin it was tested for?'[81] Regular testing for the presence of vitamin D (though not A) was adopted as routine from 1927.[82]

At a key meeting of the STC in February 1928, it was agreed that BW&Co. should respond to the demand for vitamins despite expert opinion that the advertising claims which had led to consumer demand were unsupported by reliable scientific evidence. Collaborating with Professor Rudolph Peters at Oxford and with Sir Charles Martin of the Lister Institute, the WPRL and the Experimental Department at Dartford reviewed suitable sources of vitamins B, C, and D. The STC regarded the tests to assay vitamins as untrustworthy but proposed, as a way forward, the issue of standardised products without specifying the measurement techniques employed. The phrase suggested to appear on labels and publicity was 'methods quoted with official approval'.[83]

The company's cautious approach to marketing Kepler products was once again vindicated by the 1929 report on the medical status of vitamins which had been produced by an Advisory Committee on the Definition of Drugs for the Purpose of Medical Benefit, appointed by the Minister of Health. The Committee agreed on three definitions: 'never a drug'; 'sometimes a drug'; and 'always a drug'. The Kepler line, like Scott's emulsion, the malt and oil products of Allen & Hanburys, and similar products, was placed in the 'sometimes a drug' category, its status depending on the circumstances, therapeutic rather than alimentary, in which it was prescribed.[84]

Purely for research purposes and as a matter of scientific interest, the company exhibited a specimen of vitamin A concentrate at the British

Industries Fair of 1928.[85] However, Jowett's attempt to take the company into the vitamin concentrates market on a commercial scale did not find favour with the members of the STC who 'felt that BW&Co. could not, with the knowledge at their disposal, take part in the extravagant claims for concentrated preparations now being made in various quarters.'[86] Bearing in mind the importance of supporting the company's claims for the quality of the Kepler line, it was agreed that cod liver oil should be subjected to rigorous testing for vitamin content. Seeking to compensate for their own biochemical deficiencies, WPRL staff collaborated with a number of external scientists. Professor Peters examined a range of vitamin preparations made by the company and reported that BW&Co.'s vitamins were as good as the best samples he had prepared.[87] He encouraged the STC to advise further development of several vitamin preparations, suggesting, for example, that the company's travellers might ascertain the demand for a pure vitamin B preparation for the treatment of beriberi,[88] a potential market unlikely to have survived Snow Hill's commercial tests to show profitability.

Although behind other companies in the commercial development of vitamin preparations, BW&Co.'s laboratories sustained their scientific standing with respect to vitamin research. In 1925 BW&Co. supplied pure Ergosterol for the original research into irradiation by Rosenheim and Webster at the NIMR.[89] In 1926, irradiated ergosterol was prepared in the form of Tabloids for the British Industries Fair in 1927, where it was displayed albeit strictly as an exhibit 'without any special attention being directed to it'. The Monthly Memoranda explained that the product would not go into commercial production until the completion of investigations into the efficiency of the new product, 'in preference to attempting a commercial "stunt". We have done the pioneer work and it is our custom never to utilise new discoveries in medical science until exhaustive researches have established their value beyond doubt'.[90]

Following a positive report on irradiated Ergosterol produced by the MRC in 1927, Tabloid Ergosterol (each dose equivalent to one tablespoon of cod liver oil) was placed on the market. Ever cautious, the company's claims regarding antirachitic properties were limited to promotion as reinforcement, emphatically not as a replacement of the vitamin content of cod liver oil intended for severe and resistant cases of rickets.[91] This was consistent with Drummond's continuing scepticism regarding vitamin concentrates in general and with his view, prominently referred to in Monthly Memoranda in September 1929, that cod liver oil was a fundamental food whereas substitutes, irradiated ergosterol for example, were supplementary.[92] By providing an adequate supply of other vitamins, A and B, the administration of Kepler Cod Liver Oil and Malt avoided the risk of a hypovitaminosis developing in rickets patients treated only with vitamin D.[93] Consistent with Drummond's analysis, the emphasis in advertising Kepler goods was as 'natural food products containing the vitamins natural to them in their natural form and association'.[94]

Vitamin research took an important step forward when in 1929, employing different methods, researchers at the NIMR and at Göttingen succeeded in isolating a substance from irradiated Ergosterol, to be known in England as Calciferol (vitamin D2). Free from contaminants, research at Glaxo revealed that the purity of Calciferol resulted in a 40,000-fold effect on the experimental rickets of Bacharach's albino rats compared with the existing International Standard Preparation. In 1930 BW&Co.'s travellers were told that they were expected 'by judicious endeavour' to stimulate the prescription of a pure crystalline Tabloid Irradiated Ergosterol (later known as Tabloid Calciferol) of definite strengths for use 'scientifically alone or as an adjunct', in the treatment of rickets and to supplement antenatal diet.[95] This development brought BW&Co. directly into competition with Glaxo, where in 1932, following the isolation of pure crystalline Calciferol, Jephcott switched from the Steenbock irradiated Ergosterol process to Calciferol GL (Calciferol GL was the name of the pure crystalline vitamin D from which Ostelin was made) as the basis of Ostermilk production.[96] BDH had also diversified into health foods specifically directed at infants, including. syrup of figs and malt extract (1,000 tons combined volume annually), vitamins in cod liver oil extracts, and Lysol.[97] In January 1927, a new product was launched which, although resembling a malt extract, contained irradiated oils in place of cod liver oil. Described in the *Chemist & Druggist* as 'the latest development in the administration of vitamins A and D',[98] marketed under the Radio Malt trademark and appealing to nursing mothers, the scientific community was less than impressed with the new product.[99] The chairman of the Radium Commission expressed the view that such products were either harmless or fraudulent because they contained no radium or a negligible trace; or if they did contain radium were 'potentially deadly' because of the poisonous content.[100] An article in the *British Medical Journal* also deplored the 'exploitation of the mystery of vitamins and radium' and the 'pseudo-scientific literature adorned by fantastic chemical nomenclature'.[101]

FIGURE 12.12 'Blossom and the Kepler twins'. Illustration by C.W. Hesling (Hez) for a children's booklet promoting Kepler cod liver oil and malt extract, 1924.

Nonetheless, Radio Malt proved popular with the public and the trade[102] to whom it was promoted by the issue of a free booklet on 'Vitamin Therapy' distributed with the *Chemist & Druggist*.[103] Radiostol (crystalline vitamin D) was launched in 1932 for use in ordinary medical practice.[104]

In complete contrast, BW&Co.'s ethical approach to advertising meant that promotional literature for Kepler goods continued to emphasize elements of *natural* value. While vitamin concentrates were accepted as suitable for the intensive treatment of rickets (for which Tabloid Calciferol should be used as a supplement to Kepler), the company's position was that in prophylaxis against rickets the Kepler extract was preferable because of the presence of *other* nutrients.[105] In 1930 representatives' attention was drawn to the view of the renowned nutritionist expert on vitamins and rickets, Dr Edward Mellanby, that 'cod liver oil is still the main source of vitamins A and D'.[106] His was one of two reports on clinical studies of the treatment of rickets favouring oil as a preventative.[107] Representatives were also informed that a chemist stocking the company's goods supplied Kepler Cod Liver Oil and Malt to the owner of a well-known racing greyhound to keep it in condition.[108] Thus, both authoritative and anecdotal advice was given to travellers to support their propaganda 'to drive home the superiority' of the product.[109] A revised 'Vitamins booklet' issued for the use of the company's sales staff and pharmacists explained the characteristics and properties of vitamins generally and Kepler products in particular. Revised versions and advertising copy incorporated research advances. Beginning with vitamin A, promoted for antirachitic and anti-infective qualities, vitamin D followed, the claim for which was linked also to bone and muscle building properties and specifically to the effective treatment of rickets. Vitamin B1 and vitamin B2 were respectively the anti-neuritic and pellagra-preventing constituents. However, neither these specific properties nor the possible presence of a third growth-promoting factor was alluded to in the company's literature, though representatives were advised that, if questioned, they were permitted to volunteer this information.[110] While vitamin content was mentioned on product labels, vitamins were not designated by letters. The reason for this was to avoid further alteration of

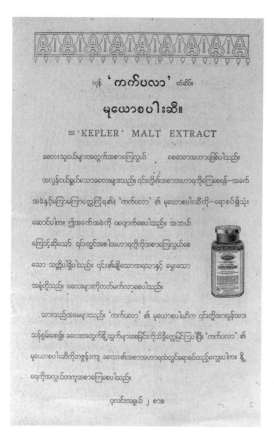

labels as scientific opinion developed.[111] In 1930 a new advertisement referred to every batch being tested for vitamins A and D as having been checked 'by parallel biological tests and accuracy tested from time to time by biomethods'.[112] In 1931 dextrin was added to the malt used in the production of Kepler Cod Liver Oil and Malt Extract.[113] At the same time, a major re-packaging included a shallower bottle with a wider neck and improved cap. A ten per cent increase in content at existing prices was a concession to competition.[114]

Vitamin concentrates, natural foods, and Kepler goods

Throughout the 1930s representatives were updated on developments in the 'battle of the vitamins' through the pages of Monthly Memoranda. Based on the American Food and Drug Administration's investigation of the vitamin value of commercial cod liver oil products, a report in 1932 revealed a wide variation in the vitamin content of their large sample of preparations. Tablets and capsules made a particularly poor showing. Liquid preparations, usually sold as 'tonics', were blended with alcohol (as much, in some cases, as 20 per cent), hypophosphates, various plant extracts, and aromatic compounds. They were described by the FDA as 'wholly fraudulent. Not one of the twenty-eight samples contained the vitamins of cod liver oil in reasonable proportions'.[115]

Vitamin concentrates continued to receive criticism from nutritionists. In 1933 Sir Frederick Gowland Hopkins warned of the danger presented by excessive consumption of vitamin concentrates and emphasized the benefits offered by natural foods such as cod liver oil. Containing vitamins A, B, and D as well as other essential foods (carbohydrates and assimilable fats) they were necessary to supplement food lacking in vitamin concentrates.[116] In the same year, Professor Burn, Dean of the College of Pharmacy, Head of the Pharmaceutical Society's Research Laboratories (and a former employee at the WPRL), developed a similar theme which was also reported in Monthly Memoranda. Not surprisingly, his assertion that 'It is difficult to overestimate the importance of giving cod liver oil to infants', and that 'there is no true substitute for cod liver oil, however expensive it may be', was recommended as quotable for propaganda purposes.[117] Likewise, the 1934 report of the Nutrition Committee, appointed by the BMA, endorsed a preference for natural foodstuffs as a source of vitamins necessary for a satisfactory diet and specifically mentioned cod liver oil of certified vitamin content in its advice to consumers.[118]

However, the advent of the new vitamin concentrate, Calciferol, posed a serious threat to cod liver oil as a treatment for rickets because the MRC clinical trials concluded in favour of its therapeutic value. This development, added to ease of administration and greater acceptability

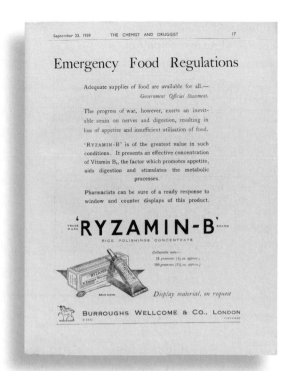

September 23, 1939   THE CHEMIST AND DRUGGIST   17

Emergency Food Regulations

Adequate supplies of food are available for all.—
Government Official Statement.

The progress of war, however, exerts an inevitable strain on nerves and digestion, resulting in
loss of appetite and insufficient utilisation of food.

'RYZAMIN-B' is of the greatest value in such
conditions. It presents an effective concentration
of Vitamin B₁, the factor which promotes appetite,
aids digestion and stimulates the metabolic
processes.

Pharmacists can be sure of a ready response to
window and counter displays of this product.

'RYZAMIN-B'
RICE POLISHINGS CONCENTRATE

Display material, on request

BURROUGHS WELLCOME & CO., LONDON

FIGURE 12.14
Advertisement
for Ryzamin–
B a vitamin
B supplement
(*Chemist &
Druggist*, 23
September
1939).
Appearing
in the first
months of
the Second
World War, it
suggests that
'the progress
of war exerts
an inevitable
strain on
nerves and
digestion,
resulting
in loss of
appetite and
insufficient
utilisation of
food'.

to patients than Kepler preparations, prompted BW&Co. to introduce Tabloid Calcium Gluconate with Calciferol in September 1933.[119] Kepler products also experienced increasing competition from Allen & Hanburys' liquid Haliborange 'the nicest way of taking halibut liver oil'.[120] In capsule form, Crookes' Halibut Liver Oil and Seven Seas Cod Liver Oil, and Vinatol, a synthetic vitamin sold by Wanders were other major competitors.[121]

In 1936 BW&Co. added two new vitamin concentrates to the list. These were Tabloid Ascorbic Acid containing vitamin C, and Ryzamin-B Rice Polishings Concentrate, an anti-neuritic preparation containing vitamin B₁.[122] Developed in the Tuckahoe research laboratories, Ryzamin-B was launched as a dietary supplement. In the introductory campaign, representatives were advised that although no specific disease might be attached to a condition for which the product would offer relief or remedy, they should refer to its suitability for treating 'below par feeling – off colour, off food' which often afflicted adults, and the lack of 'proper vitality' and physical development widespread among infants and children. It was packed in a nozzled tube from which the exudation of:

> a golden viscous fluid creates a distinct impression. The small size of the tube and its delivery of its content into the small measuring spoon suggest that it is 'precious', as in fact, it is. The impression of condensed power is conveyed at once to the doctor's mind ... Here is the psychological approach making the mind ready for and receptive to your detail concerning the established vitamin B₁ content ... [123]

Portability was the selling point: 'convenient for the weary city man to carry and take at intervals during the day. You know, from cases reported to you personally or described in these pages, how enthusiastic physicians and patients can be about improvement in the whole outlook of a patient after a short course of Ryzamin-B'.[124] Representatives were to introduce the product 'diplomatically' not only to doctors and chemists but also into health clinics and centres, schools, and other institutions through interviews with officials, nursing sisters, headmasters, and others in positions of authority.[125] Veterinary practices also became targets for the product already widely used in the treatment of small animals for loss of appetite, listlessness and debility, and for canine hysteria.[126] In 1938 two preparations of crystalline synthetic Vitamin B1 were introduced: Hypoloid Vitamin B1 Hydrochloride and a Tabloid product for oral administration.[127]

The decline of Kepler goods and the search for new products

The remaining General Goods category changed little during the interwar period. Hazeline Snow and Cream were advertised as soothing irritation caused by sun and wind, particularly after sea-bathing or 'reckless skin exposure'.[128] They continued as a minor line which appears to have achieved most success overseas, particularly in Asia. Lubafax, a sterile surgical lubricant, soluble in water and non-greasy, was a new product introduced in 1919 and accompanied by heavy advertising.[129] So too, in 1921, was Menthofax, a compound of methyl salicylate, menthol, eucaplyptol, and oil of cajuput in ointment form. Considerable efforts were made through adver- tising to promote this combination of an analgaesic and local anaesthetic as suitable for rheumatic and neuralgic conditions.[130] Sketofax, described as an insectifuge, was first issued in 1920. It was advertised as different from others by having been scientifically tested by entomologists. The Monthly

Memoranda reported a good reception among the medical profession: 'So many doctors are keen anglers and golfers that for personal reasons they are only too glad to learn of a deterrent to flies, gnats, and mosquitoes, while the use of a product as a preventative of malaria and other insect-borne infection appeals to their professional interest'.[131] Borofax, 'a general emollient and sedative application ... useful for the eyes when motoring', completed the range of products, newly introduced and packed in collapsible tubes.[132] Tubes of Borofax and Sketofax, together with tea Tabloids, Tabloid cascara, soda mint, and aspirin were offered as ideal for holidaymakers and necessary for a 'holiday outfit'.[133]

The leisure market was also a target for advertising the firm's photographic goods, widely regarded as of the highest quality. Like the Tabloid medical cases, the photographic goods accompanied leading practitioners over land, sea, and air thus

FIGURE 12.17
Front page of product information booklet for
Tannafex, a tannic acid jelly for the treatment of
burns and scalds, *c.* 1936.

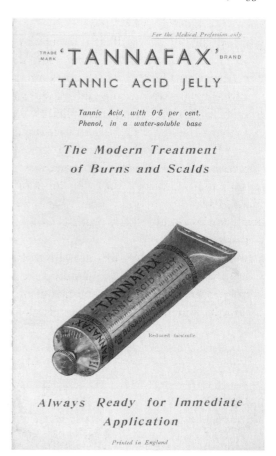

MARCH 24, 1928   THE CHEMIST AND DRUGGIST   83

FIGURE 12.16
Advertisement for Tabloid photographic chemicals
(*Chemist & Druggist*, 24 March 1928) aimed at
chemists. The success of Tabloid chemicals
'encourages users and makes good customers all the
year round'.

providing suitable advertising copy. However, the sale of photographic
products appears to have fallen for several years before 1932. This was
attributed to a decline in home developing. To counter this trend, representatives were encouraged to seek out and infiltrate amateur photographic
societies in their territories. Meanwhile, in addition to the trade and photographic journals, advertisements were placed in *Boys' Own* and *Meccano
Magazine*.[134] None of these products seems successfully to have offset the
stagnation and decline in the sale of General Goods overall. There is no
evidence either that tannic acid for the treatment of burns, introduced
under the trade name 'Tannafax' in 1934, was an exception, though it seems
likely that it was not until the Second World War that substantial sales were
possible. This product was developed following the publication of a brochure
by the MRC in 1929 on the subject of tannic acid in the treatment of burns.
In direct response to this, the company produced a special burn-dressing

case in anticipation of a potential demand from factories and workshops. Hopes were dashed immediately by a statement in the House of Commons by the Under Secretary of State for the Home Office in 1930, to the effect that tannic acid was unsuitable for first-aid treatment except in premises where a properly equipped first-aid room existed, attended by a suitably qualified member of staff. Tannafax did, however, receive a favourable response in Canada following the initiative taken by the chief medical officer employed by the Canadian National Railways. He approached the Montreal House with a suggestion that tannic acid jelly would be a useful product. Following a sample supplied by Dartford, orders were received in 1931. Suggesting the trade name of Tannafax, the Montreal House requested this addition to its price list which subsequently proved successful in the North American market for industrial first aid.[135] In Britain, the product was directed more towards leisure consumption in accordance with the general policy referred to in 1922, which was to expand 'additive business'[136] for retailers who could sell the product either as a preventative for sunburn or as an emollient.[137]

It is possible to discern a strategy, though it may not have been articulated within the organisation, of expanding the range of General Goods. These included refining the long-established health food Kepler line, attempting to sustain the equally well-established Tabloid line, and increasing the range

FIGURE 12.18
Illustration of treatment of burns from product information booklet for Tannafax, c. 1936.

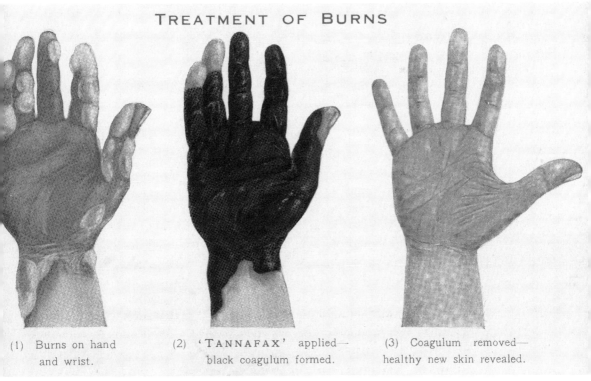

TREATMENT OF BURNS

(1) Burns on hand and wrist.

(2) 'TANNAFAX' applied— black coagulum formed.

(3) Coagulum removed— healthy new skin revealed.

of products which would address low level chronic medical conditions or perceived ailments. It also included the development of products which would provide retailers with additional business either from toiletries or leisure-related preventative or palliative items and photographic chemicals. This was in tune with trends in the composition of the trade conducted by retail chemists. However, as the company's policy continued to be to avoid producing goods already popularly advertised in the market because of the large expenditure required to support direct advertising, the scope for stemming the long-term downward trend in the sale of General Goods was severely limited. Innovations in science-based medicines and the growth of the market became increasingly crucial to the company's long-term performance and survival.

Following the deaths of both Wellcome and Jowett in 1936, the company's record of innovation, marketing and sales of both general and science-based product markets was subjected to unprecedented external scrutiny by the newly appointed Wellcome Trustees. Appointed in accordance with Wellcome's will, their first task was to conduct an assessment of the financial position of the business necessary in order to comply with his philanthropic directives and to formulate a strategy to satisfy his aspirations for the promotion of medical research and the material and cultural history of medicine. The commercial and financial success of BW&Co. was a precondition for the achievement of these aims.

CHAPTER THIRTEEN

Wellcome's American agenda: tariffs, war and the transition to manufacturing and research at the New York branch

Protection, war and policy

The transition from trading to manufacturing at the New York branch was partly a consequence of developments in American commercial policy which protected the drug industry. War added to this protection. It is not surprising, therefore, that the shift in the balance of advantage towards local manufacturing should have attracted Wellcome's interest. In 1917 Wellcome asked Pearson 'to carefully consider the question of further development of BW&Co. (USA)'s manufacture in America and on the extension of productive propaganda in such a way that the firm will share in whatever commercial prosperity is before us in the USA during and after the war'. He predicted that America would become the most productive and profitable field of operations:

> We have laid a good foundation with our reputation being at the top. Our expenditures have not been wasted here if we, when practicable, extend our operations in a suitable and efficient manner.[1]

Pearson's response, based on the accounting methodology employed by Moore at Snow Hill (whose views Pearson also echoed) was to draw attention to the unprofitable investment in the American business, referring to deficits calculated from the cumulative aggregated balance of capital and current account plus an imputed foregone interest. Annual trading accounts showed losses since trading as a branch had begun in 1906, though adjustments to take into account profits accruing to London on its wholesale sales to New York suggest that the business was probably profitable by 1915.[2] Pearson wanted to postpone any decision about manufacture until after the presidential election when it was anticipated a boom would follow a Coolidge victory.[3]

Wellcome's initiative occurred in a context in which because of the difficulty of securing continuing supplies of any goods from London, the balance between distribution and manufacture had begun to change. In 1915 local supplies of malted barley were used to produce Kepler malt extract,[4] which accounted for 20 per cent of sales. Tabloids manufactured on second-hand tabletting machines[5] accounted for 50 per cent. The third largest (though representing only 5 per cent) was Three Bromides Effervescent. It was promoted as a therapeutically valuable sedative in a readily acceptable form possessing 'calming qualities', diminishing a tendency to worry, decreasing 'subjective fatigue', and 'suitable for all conceivable uses.'[6] Claims were also made that the drug was more palatable than those supplied by competitors and was free from any tendency to cause gastric irritation (a claim that encouraged the public to infer that similar drugs offered by competitors might be harmful.) Other products were Hazeline and Rytol photographic goods.[7] Sales from the New York branch had risen from $0.25 million (£53,340) in 1914 to $1.3 million (c.£350,000) in 1923, when Kepler goods remained one of the three products that sold in volume accounting for 27 per cent of sales in 1923; sales of Three Bromides Effervescent accounted for 24 per cent. The proportion of sales these two represented in 1930 fell to roughly one-third though sales revenue was larger by 50 per cent.[8] The declining relative importance of Kepler and Three Bromides Effervescent was a result of the rapid growth in sales of Tabloid Empirin which originated from Tabloid Aspirin introduced in England when the German patent was suspended. Following the suspension of the German patent, BW&Co.'s Empirin was introduced, achieved a breakthrough in the market during the flu epidemic in the US in 1918, and remained a market leader in the US throughout the inter-war period.[9] One contributory factor to this was the hostility generated in the medical profession and among editors of medical journals towards Compbayer's aggressive advertising campaigns to the general public.

Nevin considered that his success in taking advantage of the business opportunities resulting from war were achieved despite the managers at Snow Hill. He was critical of the reduction in New York's advertising budget which fell from levels between 30 and 40 per cent of sales during the period between 1910 and 1914 to below 3 percent during the early 1920s. The number of salesmen remained relatively static. This decline in the marketing budget is evidence of the strict controls imposed by London, both on account of limits and the management of the budget. Nevin complained that the effects of Pearson's restrictive policy were worsened by delaying supplies of advertising material from London and in not allowing unspent balances to be carried over. Nevin suspected that this represented a deliberate method of reducing expenditure below even the allocated annual budget.[10]

Nevin believed Pearson's policy was frustrating the ambition, which Wellcome and Nevin shared, for the future of the New York branch. The condition of war had demonstrated to Nevin the possibility of successfully transforming the business into a manufacturing enterprise and expressed confidence in the feasibility of developing manufacturing operations 'of a much more technical and scientific character', for which he envisaged appointing staff experienced in the pharmaceutical business and a chemist. Meanwhile Nevin planned to reorganize the New York works while assuring Pearson that the standards, rules, and restrictions in force applying to Dartford would also pertain in New York.[11]

The persistent tension between Pearson and Nevin became a head-on clash over policy and managerial power. The trigger was the resignation, in 1920, of Nevin's Works Superintendent for whom Pearson sent a replacement from London, a young man named Atkins, described by Pearson as sound technically but lacking administrative experience.[12] Nevin regarded him as too inexperienced to manage the reorganisation of the works, moreover Atkins soon antagonised local workers. Despite Pearson's disapproval, Nevin proceeded to appoint Blain, one of the American representatives, to act as Works Superintendant whereupon Atkins asked Jowett to arrange for Blain's dismissal.[13] Wellcome's intervention temporarily resolved the tension between Pearson and Nevin. He suggested that Nevin should seek a suitable local replacement and that Atkins should return to England. Blain was transferred to the Works staff on a permanent basis as Acting Superintendent.[14] When Pearson objected, Nevin wrote directly to Wellcome, drawing his attention to the improvement in cost control and in morale among the staff since Blain had been in charge: 'Blain has shown marked ability to absorb the finer points in regard to the manufacturing end of the business [notably Tabloid production] and he has also shown special ability in handling the staff. We would be strongly opposed to his transfer [to the representative staff]'.[15]

With a satisfactory supervisory team in place, in 1923 Nevin signalled to Pearson not only that further sales expansion was possible but on a scale of production which would generate higher profits, though would require substantial investment to expand capacity. He pressed for a decision before the end of 1924 (coinciding with the restructuring of Wellcome's entire business interests) and suggested to Pearson that the proposition should be discussed with Wellcome.[16]

The formation of the Wellcome Foundation, Burroughs Wellcome (USA) Inc. and the drive for manufacturing at Tuckahoe

Restructuring in the form of the Wellcome Foundation took precedence. The principal overseas operations became companies, though owned and controlled by a newly created board of directors. The board of BW&Co. (USA)

Inc. consisted of Wellcome, as president, Pearson as deputy, and Nevin (who was also general manager) as vice-president. This did not fulfill the legal requirement in New York State that two-thirds of the board members of any company must be American citizens, but did meet the alternative condition that at least one-third of the directors were resident in the State.[17] This enabled the company to be registered also in each State where business was conducted. Quoracy consisted of a single board member, consequently Nevin continued to have day to day control over the business within guidelines laid down by Snow Hill. In practice, through his increasingly close personal rapport with Wellcome, even the guidelines became subject to Nevin's influence.

Under the restructuring, BW&Co. (USA) Inc. was required to pay the Foundation 3 per cent on net sales of goods manufactured or prepared or got up by the American corporation. London was to provide information on formulae and processes to enable the BW&Co. (USA) to extend manufacture, though (in theory) London would determine which of the products hitherto manufactured in London should be produced locally. All proprietary rights would remain with the Foundation in all existing and future trade names. BW&Co. (USA) was required to adhere strictly to the formulae, recipes, and methods prescribed by London which BW&Co.'s representatives had the right to inspect, sample, and test. The American business was also required to communicate any proposals for patenting or trade marking inventions and improvements developed in-house.[18] In practice these requirements did little more than codify existing arrangements which, in the past, had produced tensions between London and New York.

Nevin's immediate concern in 1924 was the limitation imposed on production by working in cramped conditions and the use of obsolescent tabletting machines, which caused delays and hampered efficiency. Referring to London's previous refusal to replace machinery, Nevin emphasised the significance of the disparity between labour/capital cost ratios in Britain and the US. The Dartford Works Superintendent's preferred option (for

FIGURE 13.2
Thomas
Nevin (left).

policy both in London and New York), was based on British experience: slow capital depreciation and higher expenditure on the skilled labour of maintenance engineers, a formula which was uneconomic in the American context.[19] More important in the long term, however, was Wellcome's decision in 1925 to invest in the acquisition and equipment of a substantially larger plant, a project in which he became personally involved, spending considerable time in New York to select production and office sites, negotiate prices, contribute to planning the works, and designing the facades of the newly acquired prestigious offices, a 12-storey building on East 41st Street in Manhattan.[20] The premises acquired for manufacturing were owned formerly by the Hodgman Rubber Company at Tuckahoe in New York State. Located on the Hudson River on a 3.5 acre site, the factory could accommodate more than 1200 workers,[21] whereas it seems unlikely that more than perhaps 300 were employed at Hudson Street.[22] Pearson's reaction to Wellcome's purchase of the Hodgman plant was that it was 'a great surprise ... I can only hope Mr Wellcome's optimistic prophecy that the entire buildings will be occupied in 5 years will be realised.' He favoured selling-off substantial parts of the land and buildings,[23] whereas Wellcome declared his intention to acquire more property should contiguous plots become available: 'I have no doubt whatsoever that if we adopt the vigorous ethical policy in propagating and extending our medical business, within five years, or perhaps within three years, ... these new buildings will be found inadequate for our requirements'.[24] After visiting Tuckahoe in October 1926, Wellcome reported that he was impressed with the progress of reorganisation of production ... and well satisfied that systems were working smoothly and efficiently 'discipline was excellent and ... the mood of staff and workers at all levels positive'.[25]

Such harmony was absent from the relations between Pearson and Nevin, evidence for which are the guidelines formulated by Pearson governing the management of the American company as part of the Wellcome Foundation. After discussion with Jowett, Pearson informed Nevin that new lines would continue to be initiated by the London office, as would any improvements or alterations in manufacturing processes, even regarding those lines peculiar to the American market.[26] This prescription for continuing London's dominance in all respects, however, soon provoked Wellcome's dissent manifested in his intervention in support of Nevin who favoured an Americanisation of the business. The investment in Tuckahoe may be interpreted as evidence of Wellcome's sense that his ambition for the business in America when he embarked on the project in 1906, was about to be realised. Then he had declared: 'The American mission is unusually important and no man is too good for it.'[27] On Nevin's appointment as branch manager Wellcome confidently predicted that he could 'capture the region'.[28] Nearly twenty years later, Nevin received Wellcome's full support in releasing the American company from the constraints imposed by Pearson, Moore, and Jowett. In 1926 Wellcome explained the need for a new commercial policy for the American company:

> This is the psychological moment for us to put faith in our utmost endeavours to greatly extend the value of our business by practical ethical propaganda most favourable for our particular work, [and] ... materially increase our list of products for this market by adding items likely to command large and steady demand, suited to the views, usages, and fancies of the medical profession in this country. This would include distancing the company's products sold in the US from association with Britain by removing references to English origin from advertising and labels ... I believe that this is the opportune moment to reconsider the whole question of policy in respect of our American business by adapting more to the requirements of American ideas without lessening our ethical standards.[29]

He adduced two specific reasons for this policy shift. The first was expressed to him by American medical men impressed by the quality and range of chemical products available from the London firm which they acknowledged to be highly regarded in Britain and Europe. This suggested the need for a wider range supplied by the American business. The second was the suspicion of anti-British sentiment among influential German medical practitioners and among 'Sinn Fein elements throughout the country', referring to the militant Irish separatist movement.[30] These were personal perceptions, whereas a difference of opinion between Pearson and Nevin a few months before was the probable trigger for the change in policy to introduce more product lines in accordance with American preferences. The issue was whether to manufacture and introduce a new Tabloid alkaline effervescent into the range.

Three Bromides Effervescent was a product which, for nearly forty years after its introduction, competitors had matched neither quality nor sales.[31] Fears for the company's trade in bromides were aroused in 1923 by the FDA's investigation of such drugs, though in the absence of proof that they were addictive the prospect of a ban disappeared.[32] Perhaps encouraged by this verdict, two years later, Sharpe & Dohme advertised Solmide compounds consisting of sodium, potassium, and ammonium bromides with an effervescent base. Added to similar remedial claims to those made by BW&Co. for Three Bromides Effervescent, Solmides were described as possessing a capacity to lessen the onset of 'cerebral excitement' and to 'subdue over-excitement of the genital apparatus'[33]

In 1926, Nevin submitted a proposal to Pearson to expand the bromide range by introducing a new Tabloid alkaline effervescent to meet the demand for a type of product frequently prescribed by American doctors as a remedy for dyspepsia, believed to be unusually prevalent in the US because Americans habitually ate at irregular intervals. The particular formula, combining several alkalines with carbonated water, was regarded as suitable for treating all forms of nausea. As a compressed product, it would compete with bottled mineral and alkaline waters.[34] Pearson expressed his personal reservation about the proposal but left the decision to Nevin who, for reasons unknown, decided not to proceed. When Wellcome learned of these exchanges he was critical of Nevin's timidity. Nevin then wrote to Pearson recounting Wellcome's insistence that he (Nevin) 'should show more initiative and carry these suggestions through when I know that I am right and further that I am to take his instruction to have the Tabloid Alkaline Effervescent product completed and put on the market'.[35] The outcome was an immediate success comparable with that of the launch of Three Bromides Effervescent.[36]

In accordance with Wellcome's wishes, Nevin began to exercise greater independence which again brought him into direct conflict with Pearson. Nevin's plan was to replace local supplies of liquid malt extract used in the production of Kepler goods at Hudson Street with barley. To manufacture malt products from raw material at Tuckahoe he planned to install conveyors and vacuum plant.[37] Wellcome blamed Pearson for a year's unacceptable delay before this transfer of production occurred as a source of damage to the business. Pearson's explanation why the New York order for plant from London was put on hold was that complaints had been received from customers supplied with malt and oil which had fermented,[38] a possible consequence, he believed, of American USP regulations which required the use only of diastatic malt for Kepler products which increased the risk of fermentation.[39] Pearson also rejected the charge of damaging delay. He urged Wellcome to show caution with respect to the plans for malt and oil production at Tuckahoe, both on cost and quality grounds.[40]

The response from New York was to accuse London of showing no sense of urgency. Nevin rejected the complaints regarding fermentation. He emphasised that, while inferior to the quality of barley used at Dartford, local supplies had not prevented the production of malt and oil of the standard laid down by London and that fermentation had actually declined since using local supplies. The New York house was currently paying $2.30 per gallon for imported diastatic malt, whereas the new Tuckahoe plant was predicted to produce at less than $2 per gallon. Wellcome's attention was also drawn to the risk the company ran if manufacture at Tuckahoe was delayed any further:

> ... recent experience indicates that the US government intends to keep a very close watch on pharmacy houses in the future and if inspection at our works should result in them becoming aware that the malt extract we use is made by a firm not generally employed in pharmaceutical manufacturing, it would create a very unfavourable impression.[41]

No doubt trying to exercise tactful criticism, Nevin ascribed the lengthy correspondence over the matter to efforts by the London office 'to help us to a greater extent than was really possible' (i.e.prevaricating by requesting excessively detailed information and hence causing delay).[42] The manufacture of malt extract commenced at Tuckahoe in August 1927.

The potential for large-scale production opened up the prospects for expanding sales, though these continued to depend on effective marketing. This was another area for dispute between Nevin and Pearson. Hitherto, Pearson had restricted the marketing budget of the American business (limiting the possibility of employing more representatives), and controlled all advertising. Because all advertising matter originated from the London office, Nevin was prevented from loosening London's grip on advertising. However, the cash flow from increasing sales enabled Nevin to recruit more salesmen without seeking Pearson's permission. Numbering 40 in 1922, they rose to 62 by 1929, of whom 13 were appointed in 1928 and 1929.[43]

The continuing tension between Nevin and Pearson is not in doubt, though an explanation must be speculative. One possibility is that Pearson saw the American business as competing with the London enterprise and for that reason was anxious to restrain growth and development. Moore's annual reports on the American accounts prepared from a London perspective undoubtedly gave Pearson a statistical basis on which to sustain a sceptical if not hostile attitude to Nevin and the policies he favoured. Alternatively, Pearson may have been convinced by Moore's reports and adopted the accountant's analysis of the costs and benefits of the American business, consistently conveying the deepest scepticism regarding the American enterprise.

After the First World War, however, neither Moore nor Pearson could

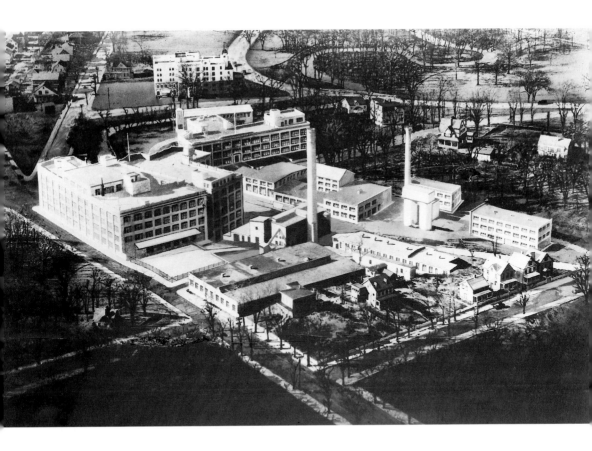

FIGURE 13.3
BW&Co.'s
'Chemical
and Galenical
Works'
Tuckahoe,
New York. No
date.

convince Wellcome either of the wisdom of the pricing policy imposed by London since the formation of the American company, or of the criteria they employed in evaluating the performance of that business. Moore continued to present the company's history of profitability in a downbeat long-term historical context emphasizing deficits though even he could not conceal the diminution of the 'accumulated deficit' on current and capital accounts beginning with the first dividend distributed in 1926/27.[44] This coincided with Wellcome's final agreement, under pressure for so long from Nevin, to reform Moore's accounting system.[45]

It is true that the investment in premises during 1925 and 1926 was financed by large balances transferred from London to New York, though these began to be partly offset in 1926/27 when the American company paid out its first dividend of $400,000 (£82,475). The upward trajectory of sales and profitability, however, was temporarily reversed after the Wall Street crash of 1929 and the ensuing slump until 1933, when sales reached their lowest point since 1924/25. One effect of the downturn was to increase the overhead costs of the considerably under-employed Tuckahoe premises; another was failure to find tenants or buyers for the East 41st Street buildings which imposed a continuing limitation on cash flow. Pearson's grave

reservations appeared to have been justified, but despite these continuing difficulties Nevin's ambitions did not flag and Wellcome's support did not diminish. Diversification was implicit in the development of an experimental laboratory which had its origins in 1928 when Nevin appointed an analyst named Engstrom, a recent graduate of the Philadelphia College of Pharmacy (Wellcome's former college) and regarded as the outstanding student.[46] It was not, however, until 1929 that expenditure in connection with 'research laboratories' at the New York works appeared in the accounts submitted to Moore in London. An expenditure amounting to £3,850 rose to £11,222 in 1930 which was equal to roughly two thirds of the annual cost of the WBSR. Research expenditure at Tuckahoe doubled between 1930 and 1938 to $117,782 (£25,602 compared with the WBSR total of £35,850). Pearson was critical of this development, his discouraging attitude providing a difficult environment at Tuckahoe, where resignations of heads and senior staff were frequent.[47] The effect was to frustrate an attempt by Nevin, supported by Wellcome, to begin to transform the company from a producer primarily of general goods developed in England to one able to generate its own new science-research-based products which would compete in the US market with those supplied by American pharmaceutical companies.

Marketing and product development

Nevin's determination to expand sales to secure scale economies in production relied heavily on marketing strategy, the subject of a report by Oakes on tour of the US and Canada to review the overseas subsidiaries in 1926/27 and report back to Pearson. Oakes was especially struck by the recruitment of high-quality representatives and the superior training programme each was required to undertake in the US. The most important difference between the distribution policy of the company in the US and that in Britain was the wider range of channels through which products were sold. The marketing policy set in London focused salesmen's efforts exclusively on physicians and independent chemists and druggists. London did not regard multiple retailers as bone fide wholesalers, whereas Nevin's policy in the US was to encourage depots to supply chain stores by allowing them discounts similar to those enjoyed by wholesalers.[48] When a new type of dealer, the surgical supply house, emerged, the American company sold through these too, for such enterprises usually employed several outside men specially trained to talk intelligently regarding surgical instruments and a highly diversified range of pharmaceutical products. Other organisations approached directly by BW&Co. (USA)'s representatives included government bodies and large business corporations. One result of this diversity in the distribution channels was that the competitive commercial environment of the pharmaceutical trade in the US was even more intensive than in Britain.

Responding to an instruction from Pearson, Oakes' review of distribution and sales paid special attention to the training and supervision of the US representatives. For despite Pearson's overall negative attitude towards the American company, he acknowledged the excellent performance of its sales force which had exceeded by far the results achieved by other BW&Co. overseas houses. One factor to which Pearson attributed this success was the tendency for physicians' rooms to be located together within the same building, which facilitated access by representatives. A second factor was the good relationship the representatives had established with jobbers who allowed access to their stock rooms and for whom the salesmen had introduced a simplified method of up-dating stocks.[49] In this respect, BW&Co. was among the few pharmaceutical companies exercising best practice. In a book entitled *Detailing the Physician*, published in 1940, the author Thomas Jones, an American graduate pharmacist and pharmaceutical sales representative, observed that by that time only some of the larger manufacturers conducted training schools for new representatives and required proper qualification before allowing the salesmen to call on doctors. These were the considerably larger companies of Parke Davis, Eli Lilly, E. R. Squibb, but also included BW&Co. (USA).[50]

Expansion of the sales force during the 1920s was accompanied by careful selection followed by systematic training along lines laid down at Dartford before 1914. Applicants were required to have had several years of practical work in the drug field as well as a theoretical course of study prior to undergoing training in the company.[51] Induction was followed by work in the field under the supervision of a senior representative.[52] Only unmarried men were hired to cover the remote areas where no headquarters existed.

Each representative was equipped with a wardrobe trunk, Gladstone bag, detail bag, and a typewriter. A laundry allowance ensured that shirts were washed and starched while the salesmen were on the road.[53]

Coinciding with the commencement of manufacture at Tuckahoe, an enlarged sales force received a Monthly Memoranda, Points for Propaganda produced in London. The earliest issues were filled mainly with reproductions of features printed in the London version, essentially those describing the company's products sold in the US, detailing their properties and applications, and with summaries of reports and articles from the London and international medical press. Soon, articles began to appear by American doctors, dentists, drug store owners, and the public, each reporting instances of therapeutic usage and experiences printed in the letters under the heading 'Therapeutic notes'.[54] Methods of selling specific products were the subject of comment. An account in the Monthly Letter defined the tasks of the representative:

> to sell the jobber and druggist, to detail the druggist, both chain store
> and regular, to sell the surgical supply house, the photographic dealer,
> the hospital, and the physician.[55]

Each representative was expected to cover his territory three times a year.[56]

The American Monthly Letter, frequently advised in detail on expected standards of personal presentation, mental approach, conversation, and the need to be self critical: 'Get busy and take an inventory of yourself not only for the firm's sake, but for your own'.[57] A regular, final column was headed 'Thoughts on life and business'. The May 1926 issue listed numerous injunctions:

> Promise yourself …
>
> • To look at the sunny side of things, to wear a cheerful
>   countenance, to make your optimism come true.
> • To think only of the best, to work only for the best, and to expect
>   the best.
> • To be just as enthusiastic about the success of others as you are
>   about your own.
> • To forget the mistakes of the past and press on to greater
>   achievements in the future.
> • To give so much time to the improvement of yourself that you
>   have no time to criticise others.[58]

In a campaign to stimulate sales in 1926, representatives were urged to explain to retailers the mutual advantages to the company, the patient, and to the retailer of large size containers. The retailers stood to gain 'additive business' because patients tended to administer larger and more regular dosages from large size containers. Representatives were advised to suggest to retail managers that they should pay a percentage of their commission to retail sales assistants and were encouraged to cultivate small retailers and advise them on how to grow.[59] When a monthly survey report of one representative drew attention to his success in placing large orders for Wellcome Brand Toilet Lanoline by emphasising the slightly perfumed character of the product, the advice was conveyed to all in the Monthly Letter.[60]

The company's marketing effort was focused on cities and towns of at least 5,000 inhabitants, in which prescribing doctors were the principal targets. A distinction was drawn between the perfunctory call, the routine visit, and the productive interview. After two, or three perfunctory visits it would be possible to determine whether the doctor would develop into 'a useful supporter' or be dropped from the list. The routine call could degenerate into the perfunctory classification but should be taken as an opportunity for some initiative. For a successful and productive interview, the representative should be equipped with data regarding the physician, his speciality and prescribing record, and should present knowledge of the products and supporting literature. Representatives advised that interviews with physicians should take 15 minutes. They should bear in mind the cost of the call and the need to ensure that it should be fully justified by the outcome. Each salesman was reminded that he was 'pitting his knowledge and training against a brief few minutes of the doctor's time and to be successful must make every minute count in his favour.' They were also were told that 'To keep the calling list at highest efficiency, it is equally as important to drop the older doctors who are not productive as it is to add the young active physicians.'[61] In 1926 sales of Kepler goods and Tabloid Empirin achieved their highest levels so far, as did Three Bromides Effervescent and Tabloid Sodium Salicylate Effervescent, the latter being a new product reported to have sold well because of having been introduced to doctors simultaneously with the well-established bromide.[62]

Because of the greater difficulty in explaining gland products compared with general goods, representatives were expected to memorise 'meaty proportions of the therapeutic information prepared for the benefit of the practising physician ... The most successful men are those who are known to the house as "readers".' Selling by instinct was regarded as inferior to well-informed presentation, which itself could fire a latent spark of sales initiative: 'Study the Price List from cover to cover thereby preparing yourself for a higher state of salesmanship.'[63] Representatives were also required to pay close attention to physicians as prescribers of the company's medicines. The slips returned to the office provided the evidence from which each physician was classified into one of two 'calling list' categories. In class 1 were those superior physicians enjoying a large practice. Class 2 included the type of physician 'who has apparently outlived his value as a prescriber of our products', and was required, according to recorded policy, to be replaced by a younger man who would develop a practice of sufficient importance to belong to class 1. Such a man should become an especial target for detailing. As a similarly long-term policy, representatives were also expected to 'spread propaganda' among young hospital interns and recent medical school graduates, most of whom would be future practitioners in locations remote from their current placements. A gift of BW&Co.'s *Excerpta Therapeutica* was regarded as an essential support in this policy of enlisting a favourable mental attitude among interns towards the company's products.[64] *Excerpta Therapeutica* was described as 'a silent representative' because of its intended use as a handy reference book for physicians. It was also a constant reminder of the firm's products and the trade names under with the products were issued, thus constituting a subtle form of advertising.[65]

The slips used in monitoring the active calling list of physicians provided a record of the products appropriate to their particular specialisms. At the same time, while the representative's main objective in visiting physicians was to create a prescription demand for the products, 'the power of observation should be exercised during your interview for the purpose of determining whether or not he is a prospective buyer of our Hypoloid and Tabloid hypodermic lines'.[66] Several representatives had already advanced to this stage and elicited orders for these products when this advice was disseminated to all representatives in 1927.[67] Notes recorded in their daily call sheets provided the office with information which resulted in the dispatch of appropriate literature to potential customers describing particular products and their characteristics in greater detail.[68] The diversification of lines sold in hospitals was also regarded as providing an entry into the prescription activity in the private practices of doctors on the hospital visiting staff. A former company representative for BW&Co. (USA), Stuart Jacobs, recalled that the representatives were taught how to cultivate the doctors' secretaries who typically controlled access to the clients. Gifts to both secretaries and doctors in the form of blotters bearing the name of BW&Co.'s products appear to have provided the key wherewith to unlock doors and the opportunity to present the company's literature.[69] In selling to jobbers, representatives were advised to establish friendly relations with employees holding subordinate positions who were more or less responsible for the care of the various numbers of BW&Co. lines in stock. They were advised to pay particular attention to new employees whom they should suitably educate to appreciate the company's products. 'Never overlook the fact that propaganda in the stock room is of inestimable value to all concerned'. They were also instructed to ensure that stocks of the company's products were kept in an orderly arrangement.[70] In dealing with the buyer himself, representatives were advised to vary their selling approach to induce favourable anticipation before each visit. The representative's bag should contain a mix of fast-selling lines together with 'trailer products' which possessed the potential to become fast-selling. A display of items and an explanation of methods of detailing physicians and retail druggists were expected to encourage the jobber to purchase more 'push items' in anticipation of a share in the bigger volume of sales. It was also suggested that representatives visit jobbing company presidents and vice presidents occasionally to consolidate BW&Co.'s high ethical standing in the pharmaceutical field.[71] In 'Selling the retailer', representatives were advised that it was not sufficient merely to place orders for the most popular, fast-selling lines, notably Three Bromides Effervescent, Empirin, Mixed Glands, and Thyroid, '... and last but not least, the various Kepler combinations in season'. It was also expected that the representatives should conduct regular 'educational campaigns'. They should explain in detail to the physician and to the retailer the therapeutic value of the company's scientific products for prescription, and make him aware of the research that lay behind such specialities as Wellcome Brand Tincture Digitalis, Ernutin, Epinine, Infundin, and Ethidol.[72]

An illustration of the complications of entering the US market is the company's attempt to introduce Hypoloid Infundin, a pituitary extract which was among the first of the company's products to be introduced as an 'entering wedge' into hospitals.[73] The company's initial policy was to concede the lowest possible price (but covering costs) to institutions of a charitable nature, though in this case other suppliers quoted much lower prices. From this weaker position, the company emphasised its reputation for ethical transactions and product quality. Meanwhile, representatives were advised to seek information from hospital physicians of the *dosage* required when substantially cheaper competing products were used. Armed with this information, the representative could apply 'quick thinking', legitimately apply a multiple to its cost, and secure a comparison which revealed the BW&Co.'s product as 'cheap' or cheaper in real terms.[74] Under the heading 'Superiority of product wins', representatives were reminded: 'An article is dear if the customer thinks it is. Consequently, before mentioning price, you must get him into a mood of desire. You must prepare his mind before you give him the price'.[75] Where hospital orders went through a jobber because so many directors of hospitals had business links with the wholesale drug industry, the possibility of diversified stocking benefited the sales of other lines.[76]

Products such as Borofax, Menthofax, and Sketofax (sold as necessary additions to the domestic medicine chest) and Wellcome Toilet Brand Lanoline, and Tabloid Tea (described as 'front shop' items) were regarded as particularly suitable for advertising through counter and window space. Because, unlike prescription medicines, these could be presented attractively at the point of purchase, they were regarded as particularly valuable 'push items' securing name recognition for the company among prospective purchasers of other BW&Co. products. Persuading the retailer to display counter items, therefore, was reckoned to deserve special attention. Observing that 'the clerk of today is the proprietor tomorrow', representatives were advised to give him, and the prescription man, a 'cheery "hello".'[77] They were warned that the type of high-pressure salesmanship practised by the contemporary 'go-getter' and 'super-salesman' was to be avoided. In an article entitled 'Meeting competition through co-operation with the buyer', representatives were advised to approach the buyer as a collaborator rather than as an opponent. In interview, 'the sense of haste or tendency to "crowd" must be avoided. Better a few well-chosen phrases that create a definite impression than a rapid-fire patter ... No wise salesman today resorts to back-slapping and hand-crushing methods.'[78]

Competition and development in the American market

No competition was fiercer than that which faced Kepler products. From the commencement of their manufacture at Tuckahoe, they were at the forefront of the company's annual 'cooperative effort' to persuade the medical profession of their efficacy in treating coughs, colds, and influenza. Through '... steady detailing, by campaign letters, and by a gentle hint here and there from our friend the druggist', each year the company sought to exploit the period of inclement weather to the maximum.[79] The winter of 1928/29 was chosen to commence a major campaign to double Kepler sales. Sanctioned by London, every physician on representatives' calling lists received advance literature followed by a regular-sized container of Kepler Cod Liver Oil and Malt Extract (55,000 in total), as did numerous physicians in territories too remote for visiting. The representatives were to report this campaign to the jobbers to prepare them for greater stocking. The provision of statistical reports of the progress of the campaign in representatives' respective territories enabled them to maximise results.[80] Though unsupported by the intensive sampling that was a feature of the 1928/29 campaign, a Kepler exhortation campaign became an annual project.[81]

The 1928/29 campaign was successful, the unprecedented peak in sales being in part the consequence of a combination of a booming economy and an influenza epidemic. However, the subsequent stock market crash and its immediate consequences formed a less favourable economic environment. It intensified competition, particularly from products resulting from vitamin research introduced in the mid-1920s. In 1928 Parke Davis & Co., a leader in vitamin research at that time, advertised Compmalt, a standardised cod liver oil,

> so rich in vitamin that it contains as much vitamin A as 1 lb of best creamery butter, or 11 pints of whole milk, or 9 eggs and as much vitamin D as 7.5 eggs.[82]

The novelty of the product was to some extent overshadowed by the response of the pharmacy profession to Parke Davis & Co.'s announcement of its proposed departure from an ethical advertising policy. In addition to the *American Druggist*, advertisements were to appear in the popular *Saturday Evening Post, Women's Home Companion, Collier's, Time Magazine, Hygeia, The Literary Digest*, and *The National Geographic Magazine*. An editorial in the *Pharmaceutical Era* entitled 'Moral obligation' suggested that such an action qualified the company to join the ranks of the 'commercial pirates' in the industry who lacked all integrity.[83] BW&Co. repudiated the policy as unethical and in any case probably counterproductive because of the predicted adverse effects on the trade arising from prescriptions that reputable physicians and other prescription writers would re-direct to other companies.[84]

Moral indignation did not check the trend. Squibb's Viosterol (the official name in the US for irradiated ergosterol) was widely advertised in 1929 as 'available in plain or mint flavours'.[85] Described as 'vitamin tested and vitamin protected, the complete substitute for cod liver oil',[86] Squibb's Viosterol was advertised, not only in the *American Druggist* but also in a range of popular women's magazines, and in the newspapers of 20 leading cities.[87] The impact of this competition on Kepler sales was acknowledged in the October 1930 issue of the Monthly Letter.[88] In 1929 the company received intelligence to the effect that Squibb had been advising jobbers to 'go light' when ordering cod liver oil preparations because that item would be largely replaced by vitamin D concentrates (i.e. Voisterol). BW&Co. (USA)'s representatives were instructed to combat this marketing ploy by intensive detailing, referring customers to the alternative and negative interpretation of reports on vitamin preparations; they were also instructed to spend more time with retailers to convince them of Kepler's superiority.[89] As a matter of policy, throughout this attempt at counter-attack the names of the competitors who were perceived to be falsely advertising and passing off were not mentioned.[90]

The Monthly Letter drew attention to the appearance of seemingly ethical announcements by competitors who described their products in restrained language in the medical journals, but which contrasted with the same advertisers' direct appeals to patients in the pages of the daily and weekly press. Claims were made for cures for advancing age, for serious derangement of the circulatory system, and for other conditions which it was only safe for a qualified practitioner to treat. Items featured in such advertisements were purgatives, painkillers, and vitamin concentrates. To counteract this publicity, representatives were urged to reiterate the company's longstanding policy of ethical advertising which avoided general claims that preparations offered cures and restricted promotion to the medical profession to items on prescription.[91]

Added to the threat to Kepler sales by vitamin concentrates was the proliferation of other competitors' own label preparations bearing a strong resemblance to Three Bromides Effervescent and Tabloid Alkaline Compound Effervescent, with respect both to ingredients and packing.[92] This was a trend which emphasised the need not only for an effective marketing response through advertising and selling, but also to introduce new products or create new markets for existing ones. Part of the product diversification policy pursued by the company after the move to Tuckahoe included the creation of new markets for boxed medical kits. Whereas London had a long history of supplying medical chests and cases to explorers of various kinds, advertisements for which had appeared in price lists in the US since 1910, promotion of first aid kits was first taken up with vigour in 1927, when the American company set up a first aid department. Aviation offered the first market following the action of the US Department of Commerce when it required all airports and aeroplanes to be equipped with first aid kits.[93] The nationwide network of gasoline stations, most of which were owned by a few large organisations which, in turn, controlled numerous subsidiary companies, was another target for sales of first aid kits, as were fire and police departments, hotels, and schools. Some states required first aid equipment to be available in all such institutions.[94] The potential demand for Tabloid first aid kits in industry at large, but especially those establishments open to government regulation (utilities and transportation, in which the increasing technological complexity also resulted in accidents producing wounds, burns, and suffocation), was the subject of a series of articles printed in the Monthly Letter beginning in 1928. 'First aid items' became a regular feature along with 'Therapeutic notes' and 'Photographic corner'. Representatives' attention was drawn to the fact that many large corporations employed physicians on a full time basis, though many other physicians devoted up to half their time to public service organisations and the remainder to their private practices. For this reason, visits to dispensary, clinic, or consulting room also offered potential access to a market for first aid kits. The observance of a nation-wide 'First Aid and Safety Week' (which became an annual campaigning event) underlined the potential offered by increasingly widespread concern in the industrial field and at home.[95] The company focused on key products to push for this purpose: Tabloid compressed bandages and dressings, Tabloid Empirin, calomel, rhubarb and colocynth, Phenofax, and Menthofax. In 1929 the company introduced a pocket first aid kit for the home which sold well in a year when unprecedented and widespread publicity was given across the national radio network in co-operation with the National Safety Council.[96] From 1930 these kits included the newly introduced Tabloid Adhesive Boric Compress, an early form of the later ubiquitous band-aid, marketed widely in hospitals, clinics, and first aid departments in industrial plants and public service organisations. Representatives were instructed to push kits appropriate to the organisation: '... everybody is a Potential Buyer of our first aid units'.[97] A special version of the kit, the Snake-Bite Outfit, proved to be popular among such major employers as Western Electric, AT&T, Shell Petroleum, Pure Oil, Gulf, and the US Army and Navy which ordered lots of 1,000 for distribution to their men in the field.[98] The company's strategy, which underpinned efforts to develop a potential market for the sale of first aid kits, offered two opportunities. One was to expand sales by concentrating initially on organisations and others for whom orders possessed 'advertising value'. An example of this was the successful placement of a Tabloid First Aid kit in the Yankee Stadium in 1929 that triggered a campaign to capture other baseball stadia.[99] Whereas eye-catching association with the Yankees might assist the company to sign up other sports organisations as customers, it was the very large organisations (the second opportunity) which offered the potential for volume sales. Selling to such organisations was perceived as offering indirect methods of publicising the company's products. First, physicians' use of the preparations contained also in the workplace kits would familiarise them with BW&Co.'s products. Second, application of such preparations under these circumstances was also expected to teach those treated to discriminate between products and encourage the public to ask chemists, drug store, and other retail store staff for the various items contained in the kits by the trade name.[100] The principal targets in the initial campaign begun in 1927 were the large railroad companies, several of which had placed contracts for Tabloid First Aid equipment by March 1928. With the intention of 'forming a basis for permanent business, repeat orders, and refills', the plan was to visit heads of first aid work in these and similar organisations, whether nurses, superintendents, purchasing agents, safety engineers, or physicians in charge of corporate dispensaries.[101]

The campaign to promote first aid kits relied on the success of repositioning existing products (the contents) into newly defined market segments. Nevin also perceived that the company's heavy reliance on two or three products in an increasingly competitive market for pharmaceutical, healthcare goods and toiletries was excessive and that product diversification was essential if the business was to expand to fill Tuckahoe's large manufacturing capacity. He regarded the establishment of research laboratories on the English model to be necessary for the implementation of such a diversification strategy aimed at the American market.[102] This introduction of such a policy, however, produced another crisis in the relations between owner and managers. Because this development throws light on the relations between Wellcome, Nevin, and Pearson and illuminates contrasting organisational cultures of the American and British companies they are described in greater detail in chapter 15.

Prosperity and depression; Tuckahoe manufacturing and the Tuckahoe Research Laboratory

The establishment of a well-equipped Tuckahoe Research Laboratory (initially known as the Experimental Research Laboratory) began in 1928. It resulted from a combination of Nevin's aspirations and his application of energy and managerial skills with Wellcome's enthusiasm, commitment of resources, and personal involvement in the project. Wellcome insisted that the laboratories should be the most up-to-date and that the atmosphere in the laboratories should be 'thoroughly scientific and ethical but at the same time thoroughly practical'.[103] Equipment was purchased after visiting leading American laboratories while core staff were recruited from American academe.

Nevin was soon to engage the 'practical' dimension of the laboratory in order to develop new products in the 'fast moving' category in a response to sliding sales during the Great Depression. Tabloid Alvesen, was a new variant effervescent.[104] Tannafax was a superior tannic acid jelly applied to prevent absorption of the toxin produced by burns. Medical professionals, especially those employed in, or were advisers to, hospitals, industrial plants, fire departments, and public utilities, were quick to adopt the product because unlike other treatments it was readily applicable on the spot.[105] However, the most important new product expected to meet the criteria for fast moving goods developed in the laboratory at Tuckahoe was Dexin. This milk-water-carbohydrate mixture differed from other breast milk substitutes in containing maltose as a source of energy and a high dextrin content to facilitate digestion. Launched into the market in 1932, Dexin took the company into a growing segment of the market and into competition with Parke Davis & Co's Compmead. Although the initial target market was that of food for infants, this widened following the first published clinical report on Dexin conducted in 1935 by Earl May, Head of the Paediatric Department of a Detroit Hospital. The report gave such an unqualified assertion of the superiority of Dexin over other carbohydrates that May's opinion was immediately incorporated in the company's promotional literature.[106] This was used in detailing hospital dieticians and specialists in infant and maternal care, the purpose of which was to create a market for Dexin among convalescents and pregnant women.[107] Copies of the report were circulated to representatives and to a range of medical societies.[108]

The attraction of the product from both the standpoint of representatives and of the company was that Dexin could be sold as a repeat item. Representatives were advised that when used throughout the bottle feeding period, the average mother could be expected to purchase between 35 and 40 tins, offering therefore 'infinite sales possibilities.'[109] This was considered particularly true because the product introduced a new brand name and new talking points to enable salesmen to persuade retailers as well as specialists of the quality and value of Dexin.[110] Anticipating scepticism among representatives who were well aware of the existing competition in the market, the tactic adopted was to promote the product to physicians, mainly paediatricians in important institutions in every territory (many of whom would be familiar with the company's ethical medicines and aware of its reputation). The product was to be offered for use with infants who were 'hard to feed', who had diarrhoea or persistent vomiting, or were markedly under weight. The assumption (which proved justified) was that if Dexin could be demonstrably successful in circumstances when other products had failed, recommendation would follow and hospitals would be the first to order. Representatives were advised to pay attention to paediatric nurses, hospital dieticians, hospital superintendents, buyers, and pharmacists, as well as to paediatricians.[111] Medical institutions of this kind were employing increasing numbers of physicians as regular, consulting, or courtesy staff who from the company's standpoint represented a growing contact base through which to expand hospital orders in bulk, both new and repeats.[112]

The company's scientists were also involved in the quality control of Diginutin, a new product which had been introduced first in London in 1933 as an advance on the Wellcome Brand Tincture Digitalis and Tabloid Digitalis Leaf as a treatment for heart failure.[113] Although an important development from a clinical standpoint, it did not meet the criterion that fast moving products (such as Dexin was expected to be) were needed to halt the slide in sales. Neither did Globin Insulin, a new product developed in the Tuckahoe laboratory during the 1930s. Work on various derivatives of insulin carried out by Reiner, Searle, and Lang culminated in 1938 in the production of a therapeutic agent which slowed the rate of absorption of insulin. As a consequence, dosage intervals for diabetic patients could be lengthened and daily requirements reduced to a single dose. Globin Insulin first became available from Tuckahoe in 1939. Therapeutically significant, the manner in which Globin Insulin was developed at Tuckahoe (completely independently from the Wellcome laboratories in London) is indicative of a lack of co-ordination of research across the organisation. This weakness in corporate control of R&D was afterwards admitted by Wheeler, later managing director in London, who declared it was a historical fact which he believed contrasted with arrangements in other pharmaceutical companies.[114] A difference in attitudes between Tuckahoe and Beckenham towards patenting also divided the two companies, as is shown by the patenting of Globin Insulin by Grant, the American research director, contrary to a decision of the Board taken in London.[115] Even within the Tuckahoe business, however, a perception of conflicting priorities between the need for commercial product development and the management of scientific research presented problems. Differences among managerial and scientific staff (and between Wellcome, Nevin, and Pearson) contributed to a continuing uncertainty in research strategy which had been discernible ever since the Tuckahoe laboratories were established.[116]

Competition and marketing during the Great Depression

When the Great Depression began to bite in 1930, Nevin appointed six additional representatives (having recruited 12 in the previous year), six more in 1931, three more in 1932 and again three in 1933.[117] Among these was Ted Holmes, a PhD in pharmaceutical chemistry who agreed to move from the Tuckahoe laboratory in 1931 when depression caused retrenchment in research expenditure. After completing marketing courses at New York University, he became one of the senior representatives, co-ordinating new product development.[118] An even more significant appointment was that of W (Bill) N Creasy then aged 22, born in England and raised and educated in Ontario, who graduated from the University of Toronto College of Pharmacy in 1929 and joined the company in 1930 after working for a short time in a pharmacy in Ottawa.[119] His initial application to join the company as a representative was rejected because Nevin considered him to be too young to go on the road. However, Nevin did offer Creasy a temporary position, checking and pricing orders. Weeks later, after persistent pressure by Creasy, Nevin agreed to give him a trial on the road, beginning with a full territory in Brooklyn, close to home, subsequently replaced by another full territory in San Francisco. His success in securing sales in hospitals and to veterans' organisations attracted attention in the New York office to which he soon returned as assistant sales manager. In that capacity during the rest of the 1930s, Creasy handled advertising, wrote copy, and carried out market research. Beginning in 1934, he became involved in analysis for the newly established business research and statistics department. He revised the company's price list to facilitate alphabetical ordering of products (a system later adopted throughout all BW&Co. companies), and trained representatives. He became the General Manager of the Canadian company in 1943, promoted in 1945 to President and General Manager of BW&Co. (USA) Inc.[120]

In 1930, the products referred to as the

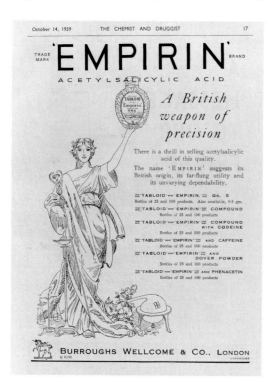

FIGURE 13.5 Advertisement for Empirin 'a British weapon of precision' (*Chemist & Druggist*, 14 October 1939).

'super-highways' of the business, produced in volume, and comprising a high proportion of the heavy shipments from Tuckahoe, were Tabloid Empirin, Tabloid effervescent products, and Kepler extracts.[121] The company's trade in Empirin benefited from the policy of strictly ethical promotion, in part because the main competitor was subjected to persistent criticism from the American medical establishment. The Council of the American Medical Association denounced Compbayer's claim that its product was unique as completely unsubstantiated, describing it as 'merely a commercial proprietary name for the U.S.P. acetylsalicylate' and for which a fictional difference was sustained only through extensive advertising to the laity. The Council's verdict was that, contrary to Compbayer's claim, aspirin could only alleviate symptoms but was in no sense a cure for the common cold. It rejected the company's statement that according to medical opinion aspirin was not harmful, did not depress the heart and could be taken freely, observing that '*when taken indiscriminately, as may happen when members of the public dose themselves with it*' aspirin had been shown repeatedly to be potentially harmful.[122] The response of the London office of BW&Co. was to contrast the often grossly exaggerated claims made by other manufacturers to induce the public to dose themselves, with the 'sane and reserved statements' made for Empirin advertised exclusively to the medical profession. The company's claim for Empirin with respect to the common cold was limited to those of reducing fever; relieving headache and malaise.[123]

The Tabloid alkaline effervescent products sold into a similarly highly competitive market.

In the market for Kepler goods the emergence of dietetic science and a rapidly growing popularity of vitamin products revealed the dilemma of the company's ethical promotion and advertising policy in its most extreme form.[124] In order to counter these competitive pressures intensified by the Depression, Nevin recruited an increasing number of representatives of high calibre and raised the number and frequency of visits to physicians, retailers, and jobbers. Representatives were advised to reject the general gloom communicated by buyers and to redouble effort: 'Mental depression is worse than business depression'.[125]

In addition to greater effort invested in selling the company's staple products, others were promoted to the push list. 'Cascara-the

ideal evacuent' was the title of a column in the Monthly Letter which urged representatives to revive demand for the Tabloid as an over-the-counter product. It was suggested that a new booklet – 'Some Disorders of the Large Intestine', supplied by London might help in this drive.[126] Representatives were also urged to push products during the summer of 1931, Tabloid Tea, Sketofax, Carofax, and Hazeline, each of which was supported in an advertising campaign. The science-based products were also presented as an opportunity to increase sales through hospital business, notably through the sales of Wellcome Brand products.[127] The representatives were encouraged to be assertive, to display 'self-assurance, gumption – call it what you will ...'[128]

However, because of the ethical strategy intended to sustain the confidence of the medical profession and the emphasis on the scientific research which lay behind the company's products, distribution policy presented a problem. Sales depended increasingly on over-the-counter transactions through retailers pursuing aggressive pricing policies, notably 'drugless drug stores', chain drug stores, department store drug counters, modern cut-rate drug stores, and neighbourhood drug stores. Diverse in the character of the competition they generated, their common characteristic was the virtual absence of experienced, qualified pharmacists.[129] Representatives were reminded that the hospital pharmacist was the most important figure in securing volume orders, and that these were primarily for the firm's staple products.[130] Advice to representatives was that if they found sales diminishing it was because they had 'confused the art of visiting with the science of selling: "Always try for a sale",'[131] a harsher approach to the sales philosophy than that which had been articulated before the Depression. 'More calls' was now the slogan.[132] The task of reversing the downward trend in sales was made more difficult in 1933, when reduction in government expenditure restricted funds available to federal institutions which had hitherto formed an important market for the American company's products. Also affecting federal institutions was the government's 'Patronising USA Industries' policy. This required companies to purchase only American-made products. By 1933 most of the company's products passed this test, nonetheless the policy was received with slight apprehension because of the company's historic roots and close connections with Britain alluded to by the representatives of some competitors in their 'Buy American' appeals.[133]

Developing new OTC products was seen to be vital in reviving sales, not only by Nevin at BW&Co. (USA) but also by his competitors. This was the conclusion of a report on the American pharmaceutical market issued by the J. Walter Thompson advertising agency in 1932. The pharmaceutical business in the US was described as offering a large but not a growing market; the greatest opportunities for expansion and profit were in the 'growing market for common specialities', both on and off prescription, i.e. branded medicines, preparations, and food supplements.[134] Wholesale production values based on the US Census of Manufacturing reveal that the largest category of druggists' preparations in 1929 were tinctures, fluid extracts, medical syrups, and synthetic preparations ($47,385,821) followed by pills, tablets, and powders ($42,135,632). Biological products ($15,966,143) accounted for less than one third of these as did alkaloids, derivatives, and pharmaceutical metals and their salts ($ 14,369,111). The total value ($119,856,707) was dwarfed by the value of total patent and proprietary medicines ($205,082,759). This included ethical specialities sold through physician's prescription ($55,902,046). OTC goods, however, amounted to almost three times that figure ($149,180,718) and this was the market which Thompson's report considered to possess the greatest potential for growth. Antiseptics, disinfectants, germicides, deodorants, and insecticides ($93,370,954) offered another field overlapping with fine chemical production, though manufacturers from outside the pharmaceutical industry also inhabited this market. The same was true of the market for perfumes, cosmetics, and toilet preparations ($25,964,915 in 1914 rising to $207,461,838 by 1929), among which creams and dentifrices formed the largest categories, accounting for roughly one third of the value of production at wholesale prices.[135]

Nevin's product diversification policy was consistent with these findings. Carofax was introduced as a superior substitute for Carron Oil (linseed oil and lime water), a traditional and widely used treatment for burns. Carofax incorporated Carron Oil in which the addition of 2 per cent phenol ensured sterility and imparted a local anaesthetic action to relieve pain. Packed in a collapsible metal tube with screw cap instead of the glass bottle in which Carron Oil was sold, the product became conveniently portable. Other ointments for burns were considered disadvantageous because of their non-absorbable petroleum bases, some of which contained irritants. The market for this product was perceived to be unlimited among industrial workers, sportsmen, and housewives. The retail chemist would provide the channel for distribution, though with or without the first aid kits, the commercial as well as the medical organisations and practices offered a direct route to a large potential market. Under the heading 'New avenues for business' in the Monthly Letter, representatives were alerted to the need to search for more ideas to supplement the staples of Tabloids and Kepler goods and to create new markets for existing products. Representatives were reminded of the importance of hospitals and other institutions as large purchasers of Kepler and other goods. Those listed were the US army, navy and marine hospitals (whose demand was primarily for products for the consumption of veterans), general and children's hospitals, T.B. sanitaria, insane asylums, homes for the aged, boards of health and visiting nurses, medical schools, and industrial clinics.[136] A trend towards an increase in the numbers of patients in large public institutions, especially in maternity hospitals and maternity departments of general hospitals, favoured the company which had established outlets for Hypoloid Ernutin and Hypoloid Infundin.[137] Among other new applications sought for Kepler goods were those in the veterinary field. In 1933 it was suggested that the attention of veterinary surgeons should be drawn to Kepler goods which were described as suitable for rearing young pedigree animals and later to Laxamel, a preparation containing malt which was recommended for breaking down hair balls in cats.[138]

Casting around for even less obvious markets, representatives were asked to push Vaporole Aromatic Ammonia (a Burroughs product with a history of 50 years), hitherto stocked mainly by high-class drug and department stores. Cinemas were believed to offer potential markets, where supplies were made available to treat emotionally overwrought patrons.[139] It was suggested that each representative should visit funeral parlours and mortuaries and request an interview with staff. Familiarity with the tendency among mourners to faint or feel indisposed during the funeral service might predispose undertakers to stock a supply. Bismuth and mercury products were the means of opening up new accounts with the growing numbers of private, commercial, 'small fee' V-D clinics.[140] Carofax was promoted as a relief for sunburn.[141] Another new avenue for business was identified among the owners of the ever-increasing fox ranches. Tabloid Worm Capsules for Foxes were advertised in the publications of the National Fox Breeders' Association.[142] In May 1930, representatives were advised that in answer to a medical man's frequent interrogation: 'What's new?', they might refer, as had some already, to Tabloid Pig Bile.[143]

Vitamin wars in the USA

A priority for Nevin from the mid-1920s was to find new products to compensate for the sharp drop in the sales of Kepler goods following the introduction of Viosterol Squibb.[144] A further threat came from the introduction of Vitamin D drops in 1932 and Thiamin in 1935.[145] Scientists at Tuckahoe worked extensively on methods of assay for the various vitamins, especially the B complex from which they developed useful concentrates to produce an improved Kepler line of fast-moving products. With the intention of extending the Kepler season to spring and summer, Tabloid Special Formula No. N.Y. 101 (a preparation derived from brewers' yeast containing vitamin B in concentrated form) was added to Kepler Malt Extract with haemoglobin.[146] Dispensed as Kepler HMOV, the introduction of Kepler Haemoglobin with Malt Extract and Cod Liver Oil (B vitamins fortified) in 1932 was regarded as an important event.[147] Containing vitamins, A, B, and D, plus flavouring to increase palatability as the novel selling point, Kepler HMOV (Haemoglobin Malt Oil and Vitamin) was intended to replace the widely used Kepler iron iodide combination and specifically to retrieve a market share from single vitamin concentrates, notably Viosterol Squibb.[148] Squibb's advertisements appealed directly to druggists: 'Strengthen your professional background with a vitamin department. Vitamin products are profitable and account for 18 per cent of the total business done in drug departments. They are the third largest selling group'.[149] By 1936 Squibb offered 25 vitamin preparations covering A, B, C, D, E and G (B2), claiming them to be essential to the medical and dental professions.[150] Like Parke Davis, Lilly, Abbott, and Upjohn, Squibb introduced multi-vitamin capsules aggressively advertised and extensively sampling. Although this adversely affected Kepler sales,[151] the American company's profits held up well.[152] The same was true for Three Bromides Effervescent which, like other bromides, competed with the new barbiturates. The promotion of Phenobarital and Three Bromides Effervescent (to which was added the revival of another old combination, Butyl Chloral Hydrate and Gelsemine) was also unsuccessful. During the 1920s, the company had tried to develop a trade in oral glandular products such as ovarian and orchitic substances, mixed glands, and various pituitary preparations supplied from England. However, in the 1930s sales of these were hit by the potent hormone products introduced by competitors another major factor enabling Lilly, Upjohn, Squibb, and Abbott to grow sufficiently rapidly to join Parke Davis as leaders of the American industry.[153]

BW&Co. (USA) also advertised heavily, notably in a campaign launched in 1934, but the claims made for the new vitamin and endocrine products were tempered by an insistence from London that scientific staff remained to be convinced of the therapeutic value of the new preparations the medical claims for which had yet to be substantiated.[154] The Monthly Letter for American salesmen printed in 1936 contained an internal review of the literature on vitamin therapy which concluded that medical opinion was swinging back in favour of cod liver oil as a source of vitamins A and D.[155] Representatives were encouraged to emphasize the importance of diet and nutrition in relation to physiological development and disease and to detail Kepler goods as dietary adjuncts rather than as medicines.[156]

Like Kepler and other products, sales of Empirin had fallen since the all-time peak of 1928/29. However, a nation-wide influenza epidemic in January 1933 resulted in a sharp increase in the output of Tabloid Empirin Compound with Codeine Phosphate (issued at increased strengths at the request of representatives). The previous peak level was surpassed and had the effect of establishing a steady non-seasonal prescription demand.[157] A concerted campaign in 1934, which exceeded even the previous year's sales inflated by the influenza outbreak, was attributed mainly to an increased number of calls on retailers. By 1935 Empirin Compound had become the company's largest single selling Tabloid.[158] This was an indication that whereas in the past Empirin had been one of the company's products sold on prescription, a growing over the counter (OTC) trade was being developed.[159] In 1930 the attention of representatives was drawn to the implications for selling OTC drugs: '... two separate, individual policies should govern and be maintained independently of each other at all times, everywhere'.[160] In detailing the physician, a direct and honest approach 'with no camouflage' was recommended, whereas selling genuine compounds and preparations without prescription over the counter were described as 'something else again ... These may be featured with the consumer in mind, without effecting harm or injustice to anyone concerned.'[161]

Product planning and policy; reputation building and marketing

A further sign of growing independence from London, in 1934 Nevin set up a business research and statistics department under the direction of Bill Creasy for the purpose of developing the company's own intelligence-gathering exercise for product planning. The department was part of a reformed organisation of the sales staff, four of whom had been chosen to act as supervisory representatives in each of the four sections into which the entire US market had been divided. The intention was that the supervisors would be responsible for co-operating with the representatives in each sector, monitoring and co-ordinating their individual efforts to secure uniformly best practice in detailing every product throughout all territories. Dexin and Kepler HMOV were presented as examples of uneven market penetration by two new products anticipated to become fast-moving volume items.[162] Tabloid Emocin, a medicated throat lozenge issued in 1937, was another product expected to achieve comparable popularity.[163] Representatives were also reminded of long established products which were likely to achieve fast moving status, and were urged to bring these to the attention of wholesalers to acquaint them with BW&Co.'s smaller-selling OTC products. These included Hazeline Snow and Wellcome Brand Toilet Lanoline, historically popular which were regarded as possessing further potential for growth in response to an increasing national interest in beauty preparations for women.[164]

However, Nevin and Creasy were also mindful of the value of associating the company with the science-based medicines that fell outside the OTC category. Nevin explained the overall marketing strategy at a meeting of departmental heads and 24 of the company's representatives from the New York metropolitan area and adjacent territories in 1934. A sales recovery was seen to depend on the success of fast moving as well as proprietary goods on prescription. The company's other products, however, were also important to successful recovery. Many of these preparations were intended for a limited, though steady market, which was unable to compensate in the event of a drop in the sale of one of the company's few staple items, the mainstays of the business. Of the roughly one thousand items included in the company's price list, 900 were worked only 'sporadically' and sold in small quantities. Their value to the firm was in maintaining the company's reputation as a manufacturer of the highest quality pharmaceutical preparations. Keeping these items on the list and sporadically advertising and detailing them was a method of adding interest to an interview and brought the attention of the medical profession, retail druggist, and wholesale distributor to the firm's name and reputation. This underlay the marketing logic of bringing such items to the attention of physicians and others responsible for purchasing preparations for medical institutions, even though it was acknowledged that the products would neither generate a high level of demand nor become fast moving goods.[165]

This marketing philosophy was also the foundation on which the company's exhibit at the major 'Century of Progress' Exposition held in Chicago in 1933 was constructed. It seems unlikely that the immediate prospects of the American business received a large boost by Wellcome's decision that BW&Co. should mount its largest exhibition, coinciding, as it did, with an upturn barely discernible in the economy at the time. Located in the Hall of Science, one of the most spectacular buildings in the exposition, Wellcome personally played a major role in determining the composition of the display. Opposed by Pearson and Moore in London as an unjustified expenditure in view of the slump, the exhibition was nevertheless financed from the London accounts which, as Moore pointedly noted in retrospect, bore the whole of 'the very heavy charges'.[166] Taking two months to assemble and occupying over 3,000 square feet, the firm's pioneering work in scientific research and production of medicines of the highest quality was illustrated with hundreds of fine chemical and pharmaceutical products sent from London for display. Chemical and pharmacological material demonstrated the work of the Tuckahoe Experimental Research Laboratories. The official journal of the exposition described the exhibit as 'one of the most thrilling displays we have ever seen'.[167]

Although the exhibition may not have had an immediate impact on business, the involvement of salesmen in the enterprise seems likely to have affected their attitude to the company. With the intention of improving the efficiency and morale of representatives by becoming personally engaged with the display, almost everyone was involved for a period in staffing the exhibit, meeting visitors, and 'making contact with brother representatives'.[168]

> Each man who had the opportunity of attending the exhibit had the ethical standing of the House, the excellence of its products, and the high esteem in which the medical profession holds those products brought strikingly to his attention ... It is natural for us, in view of the inspiration created by the firm's exhibits, to expect a pronounced improvement in each man's work for the 1933/34 fiscal year.[169]

This policy of re-invigorating an already impressive sales record from the mid-1920s was accompanied by an increase in the number of representatives from 62 in 1929 to 82 by 1936, and 91 in 1940. This maintained a ratio of representatives to the number of other employees at around 1 to 6. Their efforts were supported by a rising ratio of advertising expenditure to the numbers and costs of employing an increasing number of representatives. Not until 1927 did expenditure on advertising surpass by roughly 10 per cent the figure for 1913, a low figure of 2.5 per cent of sales. The number of representatives employed, however, had increased by 25 per cent., a policy pursued by Nevin to counter the effects of the limited budget he was allowed for advertising. Expenditure on marketing overall rose to unprecedented levels in 1929, reduced by 30 per cent during 1930 and 1931, but exceeded the 1929 figure during the next two years. This was clearly a policy of spending out of the depression; the added expenditure on the Chicago Exhibition in the following year (though funded by London) underlined the confidence of both Nevin and Wellcome in the company's future. Sales had dropped by one-fifth between 1930 and 1933, but they had completely recovered the 1929 peak in 1936. During the post depression period until 1940, the ratio of advertising expenditure to sales was roughly 6 per cent, a figure which in retrospect was regarded as low and the result of Pearson's continuing control over the advertising budget following Wellcome's death. This was the period when Pearson re-iterated that general expenses, particularly those relating to advertising, should be kept to a minimum.[170]

The company's success in expanding sales beginning in the mid-1930s is explicable by several factors. The research and marketing philosophy underlying both the Chicago Exposition in 1933 and articulated on the introduction of the marketing strategy and reforms of 1934 required reputation to underpin trade in fast moving consumer pharmaceuticals and food supplements. The Chicago exhibit could project the company's scientific reputation in the US by referring to the recent incorporation of the company's ergot preparation in the USP and the immediate issuance into the American market of two marketable products: Tabloid Ergometrine and Wellcome Brand Solution of Ergometrine. Representatives were told that although they should not expect fast-moving sales in volume the products offered the opportunity to raise the company's profile.[171] This principle also applied as a rationale for the development of Globin Insulin at Tuckahoe.

Reputation, the object of the exhibit in Chicago, proved in retrospect to be timely and was considered to be especially important in dealing with government departments from which volume contracts were the prize. A new opportunity for securing these opened up in 1934, in part a consequence of a reform in the procedures for Federal contracting. This enabled the company to secure preferred price listing through inclusion in the General Price List of the US Treasury Department of Supply. The significance of this achievement was that in the majority of cases personnel in government institutions could place direct orders for the company's products up to the value of $100 without submitting requisitions to the Departments of Purchases in Washington DC. The company's business with government institutions had been increasing, but a degree of decentralisation of decision-making offered greater opportunity to exert pressure on the various separate departments and institutions rather than having to deal with a monolithic Washington bureaucracy. The company took the initiative immediately. Before the end of 1934, literature on certain Tabloid and Hypoloid products in the list was sent to the medical officer at leading hospitals.[172] An advertising campaign to promote Stipolac, a dye used in diagnosis, saw direct mailing to every US administrative facility, regional office, and supply depot. All surgeons in the US Public Health Service received literature promoting Tabloid Empirin Compound whereas leading officers in the Service were sent material relating to Wellcome Bismuth Salicylate in Oil (for the treatment of syphilis) and Ryzamin-B.[173]

By 1936 the company had secured contracts with numerous departments. One of the most valuable was a bulk order for Empirin Compound from the central buying department of the Post Office in Washington through which supplies were made available nationally. Through the General Supply Schedule of the State Procurement Office of the US Treasury, tens of thousands of unit-type Tabloid First Aid Pac Kits had been sold and distributed throughout every state, thus contributing to the company's claim to be the national leading supplier.[174] The requirement introduced by the Bureau of Motor Carriers under the Interstate Commerce Commission in 1937 that all passenger buses involved in interstate commerce must carry first aid equipment resulted in immediate orders for the company's kits.[175] As the only other suppliers issuing first aid kits of the type approved by the Bureau were a 'large surgical house and a few manufacturers of safety devices', the company view was that no 'missionary work' appeared to be necessary.[176]

The company also benefited from a national campaign, introduced by the new Surgeon General in 1937, which was intended to combat and control venereal disease. Syphilis was thought to affect 10 per cent of the population; an unknown proportion was afflicted by gonorrhoea.[177] The US Treasury's initial allocation to the campaign begun in 1937 was $10 million, expected to rise to $25 million once the campaign was under way. BW&Co. (USA) was already in receipt of a US contract to supply Marine Hospitals and Public Health Service Stations throughout the country. The VD initiative, however, offered a new opportunity for the company whose salesmen were each instructed to contact the Department of Health representative in his state with a view to securing further orders for bismuth and allied products.[178] The State of Pennsylvania was quick off the mark, arranging to supply Wellcome Bismuth Salicylate in Oil free of charge to all

State hospitals.[179] Other states followed this example, though in many cases limiting the free distribution to indigent and part-pay patients. The Federal campaign thus helped to enlarge the promotion of business with federal, state, and municipal authorities.[180] In 1938 over 0.5 million doses for the treatment of syphilis were distributed free, though 80 per cent of the drugs, notably Wellcome Bismuth Salicylate in Oil, went to private physicians.[181] When in March 1937, the company issued Tabloid Sulponamide-P following favourable, though only preliminary, clinical trials of sulfanilamide therapy in the treatment of gonorrhoeal infections, representatives were advised to be cautious in the claims made when detailing physicians.[182] By June 1937, however, some American physicians had already become sufficiently confident to use the preparation. In the light of this vote of confidence, it was decided to approach government hospitals and state institutions to establish first mover advantage in view of the existence of several potential competitors who might enter the market. An immediate setback for the Tabloid, however, followed publicity surrounding a fatality resulting from the administration of a competitor's 'Elixir of Sulfanilimide'.[183]

Hospitals, including those for veterans, figured prominently among bulk purchasers.[184] In concentrating resources on hospital visits the company was responding to a trend which between 1930 and 1935 saw the number of physicians connected with hospitals rise by 35 per cent.[185] The company regarded hospitals as 'the graduate school' for hospital staff as well as for the intern, where they first became acquainted with the best medical procedures, apparatus, material, and products essential in the care of the sick. Establishing close relations with hospitals and securing regular use of the company's products was a priority which had knock-on effects for prescriptions issued in private practices.[186] These, however, were thought to be declining because growing numbers of patients were receiving drugs during their stay in hospital.[187] Hence the injunction to representatives: 'Make the hospital the pivotal point for sales before detail work'. This involved first visiting the hospital pharmacist through whom knowledge of new preparations could be diffused among medical staff. By 1935 getting stocks into the hospital pharmacy was regarded as important for sales as distribution through the large retail prescription pharmacies.[188] Beginning in 1937 the report by the American Medical Association of Hospital Statistics showed types of service, ownership and control, bed capacity, the numbers of staff and patients and their distribution between individual hospitals, and the number of babies born therein. The company's business statistics department regarded the data sufficiently robust to estimate the purchasing power of each hospital from which to plan a campaign to maximise hospital sales.[189] Historically the number of patient days in hospitals in 1927 was 2.5 million compared with 3.4 million in 1937, an increase of 41 per cent. Hospital births had increased by more than 50 per cent. A review of the findings of the

American Hospital Association's report concluded that this upward trend would not only continue but intensify, fully confirming the wisdom of the company's policy of concentrating marketing effort on hospitals.[190]

The increasing importance of hospital demand for medicines was only one justification for further intensive marketing in that direction. The other was the growing challenge from competitors seeking to establish a foothold in the market for certain specialities in which BW&Co. held the lead. One such product was Ernutin, widely used in obstetrics, especially in the form of Wellcome Brand Hypoloid Ernutin. Many hospitals had used this product for at least 20 years. However, during the early 1930s competing firms which had developed ergot preparations of their own, such as the price-cutting Ergone, began to detail hospitals, supplying them with donations of ampoules. BW&Co. (USA)'s representatives were advised to counter propaganda and to sell the product to institutions in large sizes at bulk price so as to maximize the period until the next decision to order. They should concentrate on young physicians who were thought to be more easily influenced than older physicians used to Ernutin over many years. The concern to cultivate younger physicians was a more general policy based on the observation that the frequency of prescriptions issued declined with the age of practitioners.[191] In 1938 it was suggested that representatives should meet interns in groups, issue them each with a copy of Wellcome's *Excerpta Therapeutica* which would be valuable in their studies, detail them on the company's outstanding products, and instil in them an appreciation of the high quality of Tabloid and other preparations supplied by the company. To facilitate reinforcement and follow-up, representatives were also alerted to obtain pertinent information regarding interns, including their future placements, appointments, and addresses.[192] Evidence of the success of the aggressive marketing strategies pursued by the American managers is presented in Table 13.1.

FIGURE 13.7 Sir Henry Wellcome (seated) in the US in 1935, with Thomas Nevin (left) and George Pearson (right).

After a rapid growth in sales following the commencement of manufacturing at Tuckahoe, the fall during the Great Depression was limited and brief before an upward trend resumed. The profit history was more erratic. A single loss in 1931 was followed by a period of profitability, though at considerably lower levels throughout the remainder of the decade, which reflected pressure on margins. Underlying this, however, was product developmental research in the experimental laboratory thanks to substantial investment by Wellcome during the 1920s. To what extent this investment and sales in relation to profits affected the relationship between London and New York, especially after Wellcome's death in 1936, and with what effect on both businesses, is examined in chapter 15.

Table 13.1 *The New York branch and BW&Co. (USA) Inc., sales, asset values, and profits 1919–1940*

Year ending	Sales ($)	Capital ($)	Trading profit (loss) before tax ($)	Trading profit (loss) before tax (£)
1919	696,290	390,961	3,688	838
1920	907,088	432,109	144,247	40,068
1921	1,014,874	409,415	129,348	34,049
1922	1,131,426	355,214	181,481	41,246
1923	1,332,230	889,147	229,321	49,852
1924	1,549,931	1,265,594	241,652	54,921
1925	1,785,968	1,498,291	266,820	55,588
1926	2,044,681	2,132,029	327,711	66,879
1927	2,176,183	2,468,132	392,210	80,004
1928	2,338,627	2,844,780	431,283	88,017
1929	2,525,477	3,230,543	492,094	100,427
1930	2,398,939	3,386,382	226,919	46,310
1931	2,363,010	3,123,736	309,396	(68,755)
1932	2,147,797	3,036,407	245,816	70,233
1933	2,000,306	2,979,197	200,494	47,737
1934	2,085,219	2,843,077	158,839	31,768
1935	2,204,015	2,964,167	139,516	28,473
1936	2,501,708	2,885,214	276,668	56,463
1937	2,756,491	2,848,146	361,878	73,853
1938	2,553,288	2,822,635	203,025	41,434
1939	2,688,816	2,820,775	250,193	51,060
1940	2,966,526	2,869,267	384,310	85,402

The sterling profit figure for 1931 is an estimate necessitated by a substantial fall in the dollar–sterling exchange rate from $4.9 to $3.7 in September. GWHC, BW&Co. (USA) Inc., Coll. 107, Public affairs, 'Brief analysis'.

CHAPTER FOURTEEN

A failing business?
The nature and origins of decline

Interpretations and explanations

Four different perspectives have been offered by those historians who have examined the history of the Foundation, the life of Henry Wellcome, the history of the Wellcome Trust, and the history of BW&Co. Historians have differed in the emphasis they have attached to the various factors adduced by the Trustees to explain stagnation or decline of the business. Macdonald's centennial celebratory history of the Wellcome Foundation detected a loss of 'commercial drive' after Wellcome created the Foundation in 1924, when the 'old magic of motivation and leadership from the top' disappeared and parsimonious Pearson was left to manage a stagnating business.[1] Rhodes James, Wellcome's biographer, remarked on an 'increasingly eccentric approach to the business during the later years of his life and his failure to appoint others of high calibre to manage it for him as he grew older'. He concluded that this weakness, together with Wellcome's prodigal expenditure on matters wholly unconnected with the business, resulted in the company's diminishing competitive strength and declining profits.[2]

Measurement is almost entirely missing from both of these studies, likewise in the analysis offered in Hall and Bembridge's history of the Wellcome Trust, in which they identified 1929 as the year after which the company ceased to grow.[3] Robson's unpublished PhD thesis is the most recent treatment of the history of BW&Co. albeit presented in a brief chapter devoted to the company's performance between the wars. Robson employed quantitative data showing (at least) relative decline, but the data he used were seriously incomplete and his conclusions, therefore are flawed. Like his predecessors, he was hampered by the absence of financial and sales data. The series of home and foreign sales figures he reproduced from a Wellcome Foundation archive source (in which he admitted having little confidence) were limited to the period 1919 to 1929.[4] His reservations were well-founded, for the discovery of a second source which spans the period between 1905 and 1940 reveals the figures presented by Robson to refer to home sales plus export sales originating in London only. Sales from the overseas companies and their predecessors and from BW&Co.'s own overseas distributing agencies – in New York, Sydney, Cape Town, Buenos Aires, Montreal, Bombay, Shanghai, and Milan – are excluded. The result, of course, is a distorted view of the history of the sales of BW&Co. and the Wellcome Foundation and a neglect of the financial dimensions of the multinational company. For the history of overseas branches and subsidiaries described above shows the importance for the business in London and Dartford of the investments in these companies and of their profitability. The new source reveals that beginning in 1920, overseas sales (including exports dispatched direct to wholesalers from London plus goods supplied to overseas depots and branches) persistently exceeded sales in the home market. During the 1920s and 1930s, home sales fluctuated at levels between one-half and two-thirds of sales overseas. It is also possible to analyse both the geographical distribution and composition of sales (though within a limited number of broad product categories). When an almost complete set of balance sheets and profit and loss accounts is added to these data, a reliable quantitative basis exists for judging conclusions drawn by contemporaries and by subsequent commentators alike, not only about the company in Britain, but also about its multinational dimensions.

Another criticism of previous accounts of the business is the lack of an external frame of reference, whether with regard to general contemporary economic trends or specifically to the drug industry and the firms therein. Among contemporary commentators, only Pearson argued that the company's difficulties resulted from external factors. While not the whole explanation for the deteriorating trading position of the company during the 1930s, they were undoubtedly adverse and affected the trade generally. Home and overseas sales of BW&Co. fell after 1929, but so too did those of other drug companies; the depression of the 1930s was accompanied by falling prices and a contraction of the market for drugs. Stone and Rowe's drug price index declined from 130.6 in 1922 to 100 in 1931, reaching the low point of 90.8 in 1935 before reversal began. Stone and Rowe's estimates for consumer expenditure on drugs and medicines reveal a similar fall from £20.4 million in 1922 to a low of £14.1 million in 1930. The 1922 level was not surpassed until 1935. A sharp increase in 1937 to £24.3 million marked a substantial change in trend.[5]

The fall in home sales occurred at a time of international depression, declining prices, and increasing competition. The British market for drugs was also affected by the implementation of the NHI scheme in which one effect of state spending on medicines was to reduce consumers' spending. At the same time, the depression may also have checked expenditure on the relatively more expensive drugs, a development to which BW&Co. was especially vulnerable because of a policy that ensured Tabloids were more highly priced than similar unbranded products.[6] As a crude indicator of performance, a comparison of Stone and Rowe's consumer expenditure figures with BW&Co.'s home sales suggests a rising share of the home market during the 1920s from 1.9 per cent to a peak of 3.3 per cent in 1930. The subsequent gradual decline to 2.9 per cent in 1934 was followed by a sharp reduction to 1.8 per cent in 1937, evidence of the onset of a decline in the company's competitiveness in the 1930s. At the level of product categories, the most striking trend is for general goods sales to decline while sales of sera and vaccines rose during the 1930s. By 1940 anti-diphtheria preparations were sold by four other licensed companies in Britain, although BW&Co. supplied the highest proportion of such sera.[7] Sera sales overseas accounted for roughly one half of the total during the late 1920s and early 1930s. As overseas sera sales stagnated thereafter, such relatively limited growth that did occur was in the home market where sales rose from barely £100,000 to around £150,000 from the mid-1930s.[8] This was possibly the result of immunological and bacteriological advances in the WPRL, which established the foundations of public health immunisation measures around the world.[9] Why this scientific achievement did not translate into a greater commercial success was examined in chapter 11.

The extent of the failure of the general goods trade has been greatly exaggerated by previous historians. Hall and Bembridge interpret the figures for gross profit from general goods, sera, and vaccines sold overseas in 1937, not only as proxies for sales but also as indicative of a possible ratio of the value of sera and insulin sales to those of general goods, which they estimated to be roughly 1 to 6 under 'normal' market conditions.[10] As comparable estimates for the home market produced a 1 to 1 ratio, Hall and Bembridge concluded that this was a measure of the failure of general goods sales (implying that they should have been 6 times as much as those of sera and insulin).[11] No evidence is presented to justify the use of profits as a proxy for sales, yet they imply the same profit margins for different categories of product, an assumption not intuitively plausible. No justification is offered for assuming identical consumption propensities for general goods, sera, and vaccines in home and overseas markets, and no defence is presented to support the assumption that competitive conditions at home and abroad were similar. The actual sales data show a ratio of sera and vaccines to general goods of 1 to 3 in the home market rather than 1 to 6.[12] The ratio of gross profits to sales of products supplied by the WPRL shows a similar ratio. Within the general goods category, sales of both Kepler goods and Tabloids declined during the 1930s, though it is not possible to quantify the extent to which each suffered. Estimates of the production and sales of Tabloids also indicate a fall, while the adverse impact of competitors' vitamin research and development on the sales of Kepler goods was described in chapter 12. One significant contribution to the check on production of both of these staple goods was the expansion of the manufacture of Kepler products, first in Australia and from the mid-1920s in the US, the result of which was a diminishing export base provided hitherto by two important markets.

Apart from the effects of the NHI that were specific to Britain, sales in overseas sales by BW&Co. companies were affected by adverse international trading conditions and restrictive commercial policies introduced in certain countries to protect domestic industry. Australia, the US, and Canada continued to be largest markets for BW&Co.'s products until the 1930s when sales in the US, supplied almost entirely from Tuckahoe, dwarfed those in Australia, hitherto the largest. Following the buoyancy in the demand for Australian manufactured goods during the First World War the market entered a period of stagnation triggered by the collapse of primary product prices.[13] The potentially protective effect of high tariffs introduced by the Australian government during the Depression does not appear to have compensated for the deflated level of internal demand.

In Canada, too, the annual sales by BW&Co. fell. Exceeding £100,000 during the late 1920s, they dropped to levels fluctuating between £70,000 and £90,000 thereafter. The Shanghai company's record was better, although sales did not exceed £50,000 until 1928/29. Despite a fall in all British exports to China (temporarily enjoying the benefit of remaining on the silver standard), the company maintained annual levels exceeding £60,000 during the 1930s. South African sales did not recover from the Depression. Average annual sales between 1922 and 1930 of approximately £25,000 dropped to around £15,000 during the rest of the decade. Even more spectacular was the collapse of sales in Italy, hitherto BW&Co.'s longstanding major market in Europe. Since the war, sales from the Milan business ran at three times the levels of the pre-war years, rising from approximately £22,000 from 1912 and, during the war, to a peak of £77,746 in 1924/25. That year was a turning point, the deflationary policy introduced by the fascist government in 1926 having an immediately adverse effect on exports entering Italy. Rising tariffs, exchange controls, and devaluation of the lira in 1936, components of the policy intended to achieve autarky, rendered international trade increasingly problematic. So too, did the policy of implementing bilateral agreements to reorient trade away from historically important European countries (including Britain) to favour Germany.[14] Sales from the company in Milan plummeted from £77,746 in 1924/25 to £20,860 in the following year, fell steadily to £10,614 in 1934/35, and during the rest of the decade averaged £3,800. Partly compensating for this dramatic loss in Italian trade was the performance of the business in Buenos Aires. Averaging no more than £10,000 per annum until the international financial crisis in 1929/30, sales almost doubled in the following year and rose steadily to a peak of £36,324 in 1938/39. The more spectacular success of the American company was described in chapter 13.

Disaggregation of the financial performance of the companies that made up the Foundation reveals the extent of the financial failure of the English company – and of the smaller overseas subsidiaries – during the 1930s. While sales by the South American branch rose, the enterprise ran at a net loss (£907) from the formation of the Foundation until 1936, the period for which data have survived; profits were recorded in only four years.[15] BW&Co. (South Africa) Ltd, also suffered a net loss of £2,628 between 1923 and 1938 during which time profits were returned in six years.[16] No data have survived for the Canadian business. These losses, which precluded remittances to London (except for £2,400 distributed as the South American company's first dividend payments in 1938 and 1939), did not represent a serious drain on the parent company's resources. They were more than offset by the profitability of BW&Co. (Australia) Ltd.[17] and BW&Co. (USA) Inc., the dividends from which shored up the finances of the business in London.[18]

Table 14.1 *BW&Co. dividends from overseas subsidiaries, 1924–1940 (£)*

	BW&Co. Australia	BW&Co. USA	BW&Co. South America
1924	9,665	31,650	
1925	0	0	
1926	0	0	
1927	30,000	0	
1928	0	0	
1929	0	0	
1930	30,000	0	
1931	22,500	100,979	
1932	15,000	57,602	0
1933	15,000	62,918	0
1934	18,750	58,530	0
1935	20,625	14,102	0
1936	20,625	29,821	0
1937	20,625	67,849	0
1938	20,625	40,246	1,200
1939	22,500	54,782	1,200

WFA, F/FA/328, trading and profit and loss accounts

Fluctuating within narrow limits, the gross profits of the Australian company averaged £59,341 per annum between 1924 and 1936. Dividends distributed to the parent company during the 1920s amounted to £39,665 in total. During the 1930s, dividends for the decade totalled £206,250 in addition to the £69,920 paid to London as annual fees for 'management services'. The contribution of the American company to BW&Co.'s finances was on an altogether larger scale buttressing the parent company's weakening finances at a time of restricted liquidity during the late 1930s. Dividends transferred to London between 1930 and 1940 amounted to £497,970. Furthermore, although since the formation of the business the American company had been in perpetual negative balance with London, amounting to an annual average of roughly £49,000 until 1936, thereafter inter-company balances recorded an annual average surplus for the New York business of £42,000, providing further support to the English company's weakening financial position.

The effect of the diverse sales trends in the various companies was to show relatively stable total overseas sales which fluctuated around slightly more than one-half of the aggregate sales of all BW&Co. companies from 1923/24 until the Second World War. These trends and fluctuations presented similar difficulties for the overseas trade of pharmaceutical companies in compe-tition with BW&Co. Among Allen & Hanburys' overseas companies (none of which possessed manufacturing capacity) loss-making in the US, Canada, and Australia which led to closure or divestment, more than outweighed successes in South Africa and the Far East.[19] Similarly, the record of May & Baker's overseas companies achieved indifferent results. By comparison with BW&Co. and Allen & Hanburys, May & Baker were late in making overseas investments. These began in the 1920s in Canada, Australia, and in India. Like Allen & Hanburys, May & Baker made such investments for trading purposes only. These, too, were beset by problems resulting from the prevailing trends in prices and commercial policies until the improved economic environment of the late 1930s.[20] Aggressively competitive in the British market, Nathan & Co. were either more cautious or more perceptive (or both) in approaching overseas developments; they showed a reluctance to commit substantial resources into Glaxo's overseas companies estab-lished in Canada, Australia, Argentina, India, Italy and Greece. With the exception of the Indian company, Glaxo's largest and greatest success, the overseas enterprises experienced unspectacular growth at best.[21] None of them succeeded in developing business in the US market, one of the most difficult to penetrate because of strong, long-established indigenous drug companies. The success of BW&Co. (USA) Inc., while diminishing the English company's export market added to the company's financial position from the late 1920s, offsetting losses elsewhere by a substantial margin. Viewed within a worldwide economic environment and in an industry-wide context, therefore, BW&Co.'s sales performance overseas was at least satis-factory and at best (exemplified by the record of the Argentinian, Australian, and American companies' sales records) a success. In terms of profit, however, only the American company was successful, though Australia succeeded in meeting its dividend obligations. Placed in a comparative context, therefore, it is difficult to be critical of the conduct of the overseas companies belonging to BW&Co., the management of which became increasingly independent of London. Adverse international economic and financial influences, as

Pearson had argued, created difficulties for the company, but its competitors endured the same problems.

BW&Co. in the British pharmaceutical industry

During the First World War, the equity capital in BW&Co. more than doubled from barely £0.5 million in 1914 to more than £1 million by 1918. The next substantial rise occurred during the boom of the late 1920s, the figure increasing to almost £1.8 million by 1931, at which level it remained during the depression until 1940. Fixed assets rose roughly in line with equity capital during this period, reducing the ratio of working to fixed capital from roughly one-half to about one-fifth. By the standards of European and American pharmaceutical companies – and other British consumer goods manufacturers – BW&Co. remained no more than a medium sized company; it employed fewer than 3000 people at the pre-war peak in 1930.[22] Its historic British rival, Allen & Hanburys, had been capitalised at £850,000 in 1920, though paid up capital was barely 60 per cent of this. This compared with Evans Sons Lescher & Webb, the long-established manufacturer of fine chemicals, capitalised at £400,000 in 1913, and with May & Baker at £252,250 in 1924, which in 1927 the French company, Poulenc Frères, purchased for £376,958. In the previous year, sales by May & Baker were valued at £491,953.[23] A more direct competitor with BW&Co. was British Drug Houses (BDH). Formed in 1908 from a merger of old-established retailing and wholesale chemists, BDH had begun to manufacture fine chemicals in 1914. When the business was floated on the Stock Exchange in 1926, the firm employed 1200 workers and asset value was £642,000,[24] which increased to £750,000 in 1935.[25] Equivalent to less than half of the capitalisation of BW&Co. in 1926 and in 1935, none the less, BDH had rapidly joined Allen & Hanburys as the largest challengers to BW&Co. in the home market. It is true that the capitalisation of Boots exceeded even that of BW&Co. in the early 1920s (£1.4 million), but the assets of Boots Pure Drug Co. were primarily directed towards funding the retail and wholesale activities of the numerous small subsidiaries owned by the holding company.[26]

Sales by Allen & Hanburys were slightly greater than those of BW&Co. during the war when they exceeded £1 million, but whereas Allen & Hanburys' sales had fallen back to below £1 million by the mid-1920s, the sales of BW&Co. rose to roughly £1.5 million, where they remained until 1940.[27] The difference between the sales history of the two companies is almost entirely explained by BW&Co.'s superior record overseas. May & Baker's sales were roughly one-third of those recorded by BW&Co. in 1926, immediately before the company was taken over by Poulenc Frères,[28] though sales figures are not available for the 1930s (and not at all for BDH).

Though we cannot compare sales, it is possible to compare the profits earned by BW&Co.'s main competitors. During the 1920s, Allen & Hanburys' net profits fluctuated (synchronous with those at BW&Co.) at levels between £50,000 and c.£130,000, dropping to well below £100,000 during the 1930s before recovery began in 1938. In contrast, apart from the exceptional loss of £104,554 in 1921, BW&Co.'s net profits fell below £100,000 only twice between 1922 and 1940. The average between 1922 and 1930 was £215,400 (a rate of return on sales between 1922 and 1926 below 8 per cent) compared with £120,500 during the 1930s. May & Baker's profits between 1922 and 1930 averaged £20,400, though shortly after the merger profits had risen by one quarter. Between 1934 and 1938 the comparable average was £46,278, though this excludes the average annual payment of £12,290 to the French owners; even so, the figures were well below the revenues generated by either BW&Co. or Allen & Hanburys. May & Baker's profits did rise, however, as did those of BDH. Between 1922 and 1930 BDH's profits averaged £51,935, increasing to £66,789 during the 1930s.[29] The rising profitability was in contrast to the records of Allen & Hanburys and BW&Co.

On all measures available, employment, sales and levels of profit, it appears that BW&Co. remained the largest in the industry. There are, however, reasons to suppose that BDH was the most rapidly developing company. Glaxo, an even more recent newcomer to compete with BW&Co., emerged from a reconstruction of the capital of the Nathan company in 1926 with an almost identical figure for a capitalisation of £1,231,341, though in the years immediately following it achieved rates of return on sales in single figures.[30] The incorporation of Glaxo Laboratories as a separate private limited company in 1935 with a capital of £400,000 coincided with the appointment of Harry Jephcott as chairman and general manager. This heralded a shift in the direction of the firm's activities away from food products and via vitamins into other pharmaceuticals.[31] For the remainder of the 1930s until 1939 the sales of food products continued marginally to exceed those of pharmaceuticals. Importantly however, 'net income' generated from the sale of pharmaceuticals averaged 62 per cent, indicating a higher profitability compared with that produced by food products.[32]

Lack of data prevents a comparison of rates of return between the companies, the most instructive measure of the efficiency of the use of corporate resources. Those calculated for BW&Co. reveal rates of return on capital and rates of return on sales indicative of declining performance. Comparable return on (London-based) sales during each of the two interwar decades were 30.9 per cent and 17.7 per cent. Whereas the average rate of return on capital was 21.6 per cent during the 1920s this fell to 7.9 per cent during the 1930s. The financial history of the company, therefore, is evidence of a business in decline.

FIGURE 14.1
The
Wellcome
Research
Institution
being built
on the
Euston Road,
London, 16
October 1931.

Financial dimensions; profits, investment, and Wellcome's diverse expenditures

None of the explanations which have been offered for the company's problems refers specifically to financial and investment policy, though Rhodes James referred to Wellcome's 'prodigality of … expenditure in his later years on matters wholly unconnected with medical research'.[33] While this might be interpreted as implying under-investment, his assertion is unspecific, indicating neither the magnitude nor the precise chronology of the diversion of Wellcome's wealth away from the business. During the First World War, his withdrawals as a percentage of net profits fell from the high pre-war levels to single figures. The high levels of withdrawal before the war were sustainable because they coincided with years of rapid growth in sales and levels of profitability of the business which allowed both substantial withdrawals and increased investment.[34] After the war, until the formation of the Foundation in 1924 when trading conditions were more difficult, annual withdrawals averaged £20,649, roughly 20 per cent of net profits. As sole owner and Governing Director of the Foundation, Wellcome received an annual fee of £24,000 plus an annual dividend.

Table 14.2 *Wellcome's income from BW&Co., 1925–1936 (£)*

	Dividends	Director's fee
1925	76,048	24,000
1926	70,642	24,000
1927	90,000	24,000
1928	108,000	24,000
1929	130,000	24,000
1930	136,600	24,000
1931	116,250	24,000
1932	112,500	24,000
1933	9,3750	24,000
1934	95,000	24,000
1935	96,875	24,000
1936	114,331	24,000

WFA, F/FA/328, WFL trading and profit and loss accounts. BW&Co.

FIGURE 14.2 The Wellcome Research Institution being built on the Euston Road, London, 26 January 1932.

As a percentage of the company's net income, dividend payments fluctuated between 28 per cent and 62 per cent, with an average of 41 per

cent between 1925 and 1930. Dividend payments dropped thereafter, but not as sharply as net profits. Between 1931 and 1935, before Wellcome's death, dividends amounting to £102,875 represented an average 82 per cent of net profit.

Net profits were under pressure from two or possibly three sources. First, competition was unavoidable and contributed to the company's static sales and a squeeze on trading profitability. Second, construction of the Wellcome Research Institution on Euston Road added significantly to the company's

FIGURE 14.3
Entrance
hall of the
Wellcome
Research
Institution,
with statue
of Asclepius,
c. 1932.

fixed assets from £1,108,276 in 1928 to £1,847,037 in 1932. The assets represented by the Institution, however, were not primarily related to research and the business. Neither the Snow Hill office staff nor the scientists of WPRL at Beckenham were brought together in the imposing building on the Euston Road. Accommodation was confined to the WBSR specialising in tropical medicine, the Chemical Research Laboratories, the Library, Wellcome Historical Medical Museum (WHHM), and Wellcome Museum of Medical Science (WMMS), of which only the first two contributed directly (though minimally) to the company's trading position. By contrast, the WPRL was a source of both profitability and reputation for the business. However, limited by space and staff shortages, annual research expenditure at the WPRL averaged £26,698 between 1920 and 1933 compared with roughly £60,000 spent on advertising.[35] Figures for research expenditure (including the WPRL, WCRL, and WBSR) in 1935 and 1938 were £30,547 and £25,665. Non-business expenditure which was born of Wellcome's passion for collecting and which initially was paid from his own pocket is the third source limiting profits. His income from the business increased hugely after the Foundation was formed in 1924. Between 1925 and 1936, Wellcome received £1,239,996 in dividends plus £288,000 in director's fees. During the same period, £216,278 was spent on collections for the WHMM and £125,898 on acquisitions for the Library.

Table 14.3 *Expenditures on library and museums, 1919–1937 (£)*

	Library expenditure	*Museum expenditure*	*Total*
1919	4,342	21,764	26,088
1920	567	7,673	8,240
1921	272	2,485	2,757
1922	540	2,652	3,192
1923	957	2,214	3,171
1924	1,459	11,274	12,733
1925	893	3,996	4,889
1926	1,861	35,351	37,212
1927	5,750	27,111	8,461
1928	10,120	18,911	29,031
1929	24,124	40,595	64,719
1930	14,923	18,117	33,040
1931	22,122	50,130	72,252
1932	14,415	22,508	36,923
1933	10,624	21,882	32,506
1934	10,460	24,907	35,367
1935	5,938	22,768	28,706
1936	3,209	2,634	5,843
1937	195	455	650

WFA, Acc. 96/47, BW&Co., trading and profit and loss accounts; WFA, F/FA/328, WFL trading and profit and loss accounts.

An additional project was the Lachish archaeological expedition in Palestine begun in 1932, for which Wellcome provided much of the funding.[36] How much of this non-business expenditure was debited to his personal account is unknown as there is no mention in the company accounts. This contrasts with the appearance in the annual capital accounts of asset valuations (from which annual expenditures are derived) for the Library and the collections. A note in the accounts for 1925 records the payment from the company to Wellcome of £30,000 to purchase his private collection of 'curios, relics, armour, furniture, etc. and all other chattels belonging to Mr Wellcome'.[37] This entry, together with annually recorded asset valuations strongly suggests that at least after the formation of the Foundation in 1924, purchases for the Libraries and museums were funded by the company rather than from Wellcome's personal resources. In 1927 Pearson was critical of the publications funded by the company in connection with the activities of the WHMM (in addition to those of the WBSR), which he felt heavily handicapped the firm's business publications and advertising.[38]

Table 14.4 *Laboratory and asset values, 1929–1939 (£)*

	Total laboratory asset values	Total research expenditure
1929	28,410	28,411
1930		29,838
1931	23,838	31,241
1932	31,241	30,937
1933	30,931	30,547
1934	25,171	
1935	30,547	30,547
1936	38,735	
1937	35,420	
1938	35,850	25,665
1939	37,334	18,808

WFA, Acc. 96/47, BW&Co. trading accounts and profit and loss accounts; WFA, F/FA/328, WFL trading and profit and loss accounts. Disaggregated figures have not been found.

A diversion of resources into non-business expenditure and a withdrawal from management signalled neither a waning of interest in business on Wellcome's part, nor any diminution in his appreciation of the relationship between business expansion, business strategy, and investment. However, data relating to development expenditure reveal that following an upturn in laboratory asset values during the early 1920s, they fell and remained below the levels of the mid-1920s. Research expenditure rose slightly but was barely sustained in the 1930s.

Table 14.5 *Marketing expenditure, 1914–1939 (£)*

	Advertising	*Travellers' salaries*	*Travellers' expenses*	*Total*
1914	95,918	25,694	27,723	149,335
1915	n/a	n/a	n/a	n/a
1916	36,872	22,914	23,105	82,891
1917	35,676	21,616	21,293	78,585
1918	n/a	n/a	n/a	n/a
1919	32,246	n/a	n/a	n/a
1920	40,348	28,230	28,339	96,917
1921	n/a	n/a	n/a	n/a
1922	50,877	30,894	29,821	111,592
1923	50,926	35,205	34,362	120,444
1924	45,051	12,969	14,105	72,125
1925	49,622	13,334	15,694	78,650
1926	51,235	13,099	13,791	78,125
1927	58,837	13,549	13,752	86,138
1928	61,065	14,057	13,701	88,823
1929	72,562	15,205	14,491	102,258
1930	80,395	15,862	15,171	111,428
1931	81,618	16,899	16,085	114,602
1932	85,310	18,741	17,592	121,643
1933	76,710	18,103	17,052	111,865
1934	n/a	n/a	n/a	n/a
1935	73,914	17,857	16,507	108,278
1936	n/a	n/a	n/a	n/a
1937	n/a	n/a	n/a	n/a
1938	73,808	18,787	16,489	109,084
1939	n/a	n/a	n/a	n/a

WFA, F/FA/328, trading and profit and loss accounts.

Expenditure on marketing dropped sharply from levels reached during the peak years of 1910–14 (see Table 14.5) and were not repeated either in the 1920s or 1930s, though they reached roughly 80 per cent of the pre-war level. This check to development expenditure identified in the 1920s coincided with Wellcome's commitment of the company's resources to support the development and expansion of the business in North America. This distraction (as it was perceived by Pearson and Moore in London), may have resulted partly from Wellcome's growing sense of isolation in London following his divorce and the death of close confidants, and the influence of his upbringing in the US where he retained many friends. He spent increasing amounts of time there during the 1920s and 1930s.[39] However, Wellcome's commitment to the American business also reflected his conviction that under Nevin, his long held ambition for the American company would be successful. Between 1922 and 1929, capital invested increased by roughly £554,000 and at the same time, the American company ran annual average negative balances with London of £53,000. It is possible that the diversion of resources away from London, Dartford, and Beckenham might have had adverse effects on the capacity of the company in England to invest more in research and development, the expansion of plant, and the increase in staff. That was the strategy pursued by Nevin at Tuckahoe to which Wellcome gave his personal approval and to which he committed both time and resources. However, notwithstanding Wellcome's profligate non-business expenditure and his heavy investment in the American business, the argument that investment in the English company was constrained as a result should be seen in the context of its financial reserves (see Table 14.6).

Table 14.6 *BW&Co. reserves, 1924–1939 (£)*

1924	45,000
1925	177,326
1926	277,326
1927	357,326
1928	457,326
1929	545,000
1930	595,000
1931	670,000
1932	725,000
1933	735,000
1934	745,000
1935	770,000
1936	785,000
1937	770,000
1938	770,000
1939	785,000

WFA, F/FA/328, trading and profit and loss accounts.

Even though net profits fell sharply after 1929, reserves rose until 1932. From £177,326 in 1925, they increased to £545,000 in 1929 and to £725,000 by 1932, equivalent to six times the net profit. Reserves continued at a slightly higher level for the rest of the decade. At the same time, during the 1930s the English company received remittances from Australia totalling £276,170 and from the American company £497,970. Added to these were surplus balances held in London, which also buttressed the company's liquidity (see Table 14.7, below).

Marketing policies

The foregoing analysis suggests that the key to interpreting the company's relative decline during the interwar period is not primarily an absence of financial resources, though limitations imposed on investment were important. Among the Directors, Oakes and Moore were critical, in retrospect, of a lack of enterprise in introducing new products and of delay in adopting modern methods of advertising and marketing. An 'unpopular system of trading terms' was also adduced as another major factor contributing to deteriorating trading results resulting from declining sales of general goods in the home and overseas markets since 1928/29.[40]

Although it is impossible to construct a continuous series of financial data measuring marketing expenditure, it is possible to draw some conclusions from the data that does exist. Between 1911 and 1914, total expenditure on travellers' salaries and expenses and advertising averaged £137,626 per annum compared with an average of £109,965 in 1920, 1922, and 1923.[41] As a percentage of London-based sales, the average marketing expenditure for 1911/14 was 33 per cent and 23 per cent of total sales. Comparable figures for the early 1920s were 17 per cent and 9 per cent. The accounts produced by the Foundation after 1924 excluded salary and expenses paid to travellers employed in overseas subsidiaries; consequently, comparisons of total expenditure before and after 1924 cannot be made. Between 1924 and 1933, for which there are continuous data, the average total marketing expenditure was £96,657. An average of £80,772 for the five years beginning in 1924 rose to £112,652 over the succeeding five years – though expenditure remained well below the Edwardian average.[42] The figures, however, do not reveal the change in policy, dating from 1928, which resulted in substantially increased advertising expenditure. Comparison with the Edwardian period is again instructive. Average advertising expenditure between 1910 and 1914 was £85,868, representing 21 per cent of London-based sales and 14 per cent of total sales; the comparable figure between 1924 and 1928 was £53,162; 7 per cent of London-based sales and 4 per cent of total sales. The average between 1929 and 1933 was £79,319; 11 per cent of London based sales and 5 per cent of total sales. After a peak of £85,310 in 1932, the figures available for 1935 and 1938 were £73,914 and £73,808 respectively. Again, therefore, even though resources to support advertising were increased from the low base of the 1920s, levels during the 1930s were below those in the Edwardian period. Travellers' salaries and expenses remained broadly static, averaging £27,610 between 1924 and 1928. Between 1929 and 1933, the figure was £33,040. Expenditure on travellers' salaries and expenses as a proportion of total marketing expenditure fell from an average of 34 per cent between 1924 and 1928 to 29 per cent between 1929 and 1933.

The contrast with the American business that outperformed the parent company is clear. From incorporation in 1924, marketing expenditure as a percentage of US sales rose steadily. An increase of 42 per cent between 1924/28 and 1929/33 was followed by a further 26 per cent increase in the average for the succeeding quinquenniun. As a proportion of sales, marketing expenditure accounted for 16 per cent in 1924/28, 19 per cent in 1929/33, and 22 per cent in 1934/38. Representatives' salaries and expenses also accounted for a higher percentage of marketing expenditure, 80 per cent in 1924/28 and 71 and 72 per cent in the subsequent two quinquennia. At the same time, annual average advertising expenditure doubled between 1920/23 and 1924/28, doubled again in 1929/33, and increased by 23 per cent in the following quinquennium. The contrast in the relative levels of expenditure on marketing and the balance between supporting a sales force in the field and advertising, highlights the different managerial approaches at Tuckahoe and London.

Central to marketing policy, and especially damaging to the company's home sales was the implementation of the long-established principle of refusing to concede substantially greater discounts to wholesalers than to retailers. This was in the belief that strict loyalty to retailers was necessary in order to enforce resale price maintenance. Retail price maintenance was suspended during the War but on its reintroduction in 1925 it was accompanied by a policy of direct sales to retailers on the condition that they sold to the public at the current list price plus ten per cent.[43] This policy did not, however, extend to multiple retail chemists which represented a rapidly growing share of the trade in proprietary medicines, healthcare, and related toiletry products. They were excluded, partly because outlets such as Boots, Taylors, and Timothy Whites expected wholesale discounts but also fundamentally because BW&Co. chose not to regard them as proper wholesalers. The general multiple stores, the Army and Navy Store, the Co-op, and especially Woolworth's, were also rapidly expanding outlets for general goods. These included toiletries and cosmetics and such non-prescription over the counter items as oil and malt extracts, analgesics, and laxatives.[44] Allen & Hanburys adopted a similar policy.[45] Both companies thereby excluded themselves from the fastest growing sector of the pharmaceutical trade.[46]

The growth in advertising and the trend towards increasingly direct appeals to consumers through the mass media presented the company with another problem. Should it depart from another long-established principle not to produce popular, well-advertised products in existing markets? The company faced up to this dilemma in 1933, when the success of Reckitt & Sons' Dettol, an innovative high-quality disinfectant promoted for personal, surgical (and later for household use) both directly at the medical profession and in the popular press, triggered a discussion as to whether BW&Co. should reverse its current policy of not advertising to the public. The STC explored the technical possibility of replicating such a product, though this would be intended only for the hospital market where BW&Co.'s reputation might be exploited. Dartford succeeded in producing a similarly effective disinfectant, though creating an acceptable odour proved difficult. The project was aborted, partly for this reason but also because of increasing recognition of the strong first mover advantage possessed by Reckitt & Sons through branding and heavy national advertising.[47] This is indicative of a recognition within the company, even before Wellcome's death, that the business was at the crossroads, with respect both to product development and to advertising policy.

Advertising policy; ethical medicines and over the counter proprietary products

This new perception of advertising as a *barrier* to the company's entry into product markets amounted to a complete reversal of the historic role of advertising since the earliest years of the company's existence. However, recognition of the problem was not accompanied by action until T.R.G.Bennett's appointment as Managing Director in 1940. This was followed by the creation of the executive position of Distribution Director who, together with an executive staff, assumed responsibility for product policy and development including advertising.[48]

As for the company's policy regarding advertising methods, analysis can be divided into an examination of the target recipients, the choice of media, and content. All decisions with respect to the possibilities each of these offered were constrained by the company's marketing dilemma presented in extreme form by Kepler goods, still the major single line that was sold both on and off prescription. The problem arose because as a prescribed 'ethical' product, advertising had been limited to the trade and the profession, whereas over-the-counter sales were increasingly supported by advertising by competitors willing to promote products directly to the public.

While the overall objective was to expand sales, maintaining a high

FIGURE 14.4
Blotter 'for the medical profession only', advertising Kepler Malt Extract with chemical food, *c.*1926.

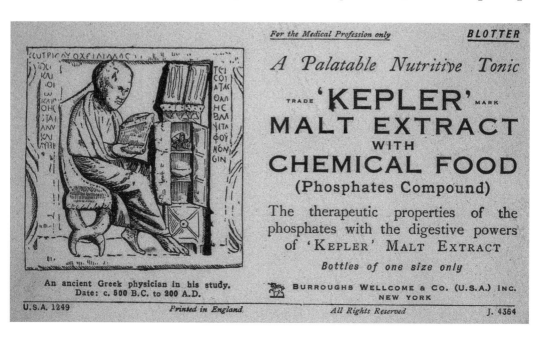

reputation was considered to be the primary means of achieving them. An item entitled 'Truth in advertising' that appeared in the Monthly Memoranda in 1927 underlined this approach: 'One secret of the reputation which Burroughs Wellcome & Co. have with the medical profession is undoubtedly the dignified restraint observed in making claims for their products. No definite therapeutic value is claimed unless ample and authentic evidence is available.'[49] This message was repeated in essence in 1930 and again in 1932 when an article entitled 'Reputation' underlined the importance of ethical selling: 'A business organisation, if it possesses any vitality at all, acquires "personality". It attaches to itself a reputation in the same manner and with precisely the same effect as a man. It is valued according to its associates and their opinion of it'.[50]

From time to time, BW&Co.'s advertisements drew attention to the deficiencies of competing products, though avoiding actually naming the culprits. For example, an advertisement for Tabloid ammoniated quinine referred to the appearance of unnamed competitors' advertisements that referred to 'tablets labelled "ammoniated quinine" [which] had been found to contain ammonium sulphate, calcium carbonate, and quinine and supported by a claim that they kept well under adverse conditions; 'Probably they do – but … so far as therapeutic effect of free ammonia in association with quinine is concerned, such tablets are useless. Tabloid ammoniated quinine is an honest product.'[51] BDH was criticised for making excessive claims for Danish sera and attention drawn to the fact that a printed endorsement by the Health Committee of the League of Nations that had initially been included in that company's advertisements subsequently became 'conspicuous by its absence.'[52]

The rapidly expanding market for vitamin-rich health foods presented the company with a dilemma. WPRL scientists regarded the current methods of testing for vitamins to be 'practically valueless' and the extravagant claims made by competitors which appeared to offer guaranteed health benefit to families therefore false. In 1927 a pamphlet entitled 'The story of vitamins' was produced for issue to the medical profession and for the use of representatives as a briefing document intended to enable them to expose 'the fairy stories' appearing in competitors' advertisements. Representatives were urged to memorise the collection of published items which provided evidence to refute competitors' claims. Described as more than 'a weapon

FIGURE 14.5
Bookmark in Wellcome Medical Diary & Visiting List 1939 (Australian edition), advertising Tabloid insulin.

of defence', it claimed to supply 'munitions for assault – hard scientific facts stated with moderation ... a business-getting publication ... all the better because its contents are accurate and its language restrained. In fact it is a Burroughs Wellcome publication'.[53]

With respect to the measurement of vitamin content, O'Brien cautioned against specific quantification expressed in so-called 'blue units'. Although the colometric method of determining Vitamin A was accepted by the League of Nations to be consistent with biological methods, the units could provide only a rough indication of the value of cod liver oil. However, acknowledging to Jowett that the company would suffer commercially from a self imposed handicap if no claims at all were made for Kepler products and specifically if no reference was made to testing, O'Brien approved a compromise which would permit references to testing but only within strict limits, avoiding a precision that might be open to criticism by nutritionists and the medical profession.[54] In 1933 a new advertising campaign was launched informing the profession and the trade that the cod liver oil used in Kepler products conformed to a Vitamin A standard of _no fewer_ than 10 blue units. A new Kepler booklet issued in 1933 as part of the company's fight back in the battle for vitamins contained a chapter entitled 'The limitations of vitamin concentrates'.[55] Another, aimed primarily at the trade, introduced a new advertising campaign using the logo, 'Ramparts of health'. A multi-coloured, three dimensional window display measuring three feet by two presented three columns of armed men bearing banners showing vitamins A, B, and D. Separate cameo images showed on the right, infants and sturdy children and the benefits of growth to be obtained by taking Kepler Cod Liver Oil and Malt Extract; in the cameo on the left, attention was drawn to the restorative properties for convalescent adults, care-worn businessmen, and the elderly: 'virility to the weak and strength in advancing years. Its strong forces of contained VITAMINS sally forth to combat the hostile hosts of infection, damp, fog, or cold; weak bones and teeth; lack of nutrition'.[56]

The Monthly Memoranda continued to print critiques of competitors' advertisements, sometimes reproducing articles from the trade journals. Such a critique focused on advertisements for Ostelin, containing

Vitamin D, which had appeared in the *Lancet*. The attention of representatives was drawn to inconsistencies regarding the levels of concentration of the extract claimed for the product. The author wondered: 'Is it possible that Ostelin, like wine, grows stronger with age?'. Representatives were reminded that cod liver oil contained vitamin A as well as D, that the benefits to be derived from oil resided in its value as a foodstuff. Therefore the claim that Ostelin superseded cod liver oil was wholly misleading. They were advised to refer to the flawed advertisements when in discussion with clients.[57] Such vigilance continued in the 1930s. In 1935 advertisements for food supplements in competition with Kepler products showed diagrams and charts based on dietary experiments conducted with rats. They purportedly indicated superior growth-inducing properties of the product. Monthly Memoranda reported the results of other researchers that undermined such a claim. Representatives were also informed that one of the chemists who had conducted the original experiment was employed by the makers whereas similar rat experiments conducted for BW&Co. were undertaken by independent researchers.[58]

'OZOZO'
TRADE MARK

Brightens Pale Complexions

Concern that unsubstantiated claims should not appear in the company's literature is also illustrated by the approach to advertising animal substance products to the medical profession. The company's researchers classified animal medicaments in three categories: proved, unproved, and doubtful. Price lists excluded category three preparations. Category two products contained in the lists were accompanied by a statement to the effect that proof of their therapeutic value did not exist and that their inclusion was in response to requests from medical men who wished to obtain high-quality preparations for clinical trial.[59]

For BW&Co., ethical marketing consisted of strict adherence to truth in advertising, the avoidance of unsubstantiated claims for products, and observance of its traditional division between methods and content of advertising intended for medical professionals and those employed in advertising directed at chemists and druggists. Some competitors had departed from these principles and from the distinction between advertising for the profession and for the trade. The development, initially by American pharmaceutical companies, of advertising directly to the public began also in Britain in the mid-1920s. Through the pages of the Monthly

Memoranda, BW&Co. accused Parke Davis of unethical advertising because Parke Davis had transgressed the principle that no firm should attempt to advertise concurrently to the prescriber and the prescriber's patient.[60] Parke Davis defended the new policy announced in 1928 as essentially educative, designed to acquaint the public 'not only with what we are doing, but concerning matters of scientific interest, the discussion of which will promote helpful relations between physician and patient'. The company emphasized the limited nature of the campaign that was restricted to advertising in a few 'high class' publications. BW&Co.'s travellers were urged to let medical practitioners know that the company 'will not weaken in their loyal attitude to the medical profession. If physicians tend to lose confidence in leading houses ... they may still rest assured that Burroughs Wellcome & Co. will stand firmly by their old policy and will continue to play the game'.[61] By 1930 a wider relaxation of traditional policy prompted an accusation that competitors had become 'consumer-minded', pursuing 'new-fangled' advertising and distribution policies. Criticism was levelled against firms whose advertisements (like those of Parke Davis) contained very general institutional messages presented with 'a detached editorial swing' suitable for over-the-counter preparations and genuine proprietary compounds but not for listed medical preparations which hitherto had been dispensed only on physicians' prescriptions.[62] By the early 1930s, direct advertising to the public of purgatives, painkillers, vitamin concentrates and various patent foods as cures for certain diseases and conditions appeared in daily and weekly newspapers in Britain as well as in the US. The more extravagant claims typically made in those media contrasted with the scientific or semi-scientific language of advertisements for the same items appearing in the pages of the medical press where claims were more modest. The blurring

FIGURE 14.8 Hazeline Snow packaging, 1925.

of prescription and over-the-counter medicines and healthcare products brought a further development in advertising imagery and copy. Direct testimonials from medical professionals endorsing a specific product, a feature of advertising when BW&Co. began, had long been regarded as unethical. Indirect approaches to invoking medical authority began to appear in the form of images of doctors and nurses addressing patients or potential patients, to whom were attributed relevant quotations designed to promote a product. Reckitt & Co.'s national advertising campaign to promote Dettol featuring a 'Tell me doctor' series, beginning in the mid-1930s,[63] illustrates the closing of the circle between manufacturer, retailer, and consumer in which the medical practitioner was seen to deliver the message.[64]

BW&Co. persisted with an ethical advertising policy to the medical profession, advertised over-the-counter preparations and proprietary products to the retail trade, but not directly to consumers. Brand names were adopted only when it was considered necessary for the mutual protection of the prescriber and the company, but unlike in the firm's early history, 'snappy' names that patients could memorize from prescriptions and re-order from the chemist or recommend to their friends were avoided (though not by the American business). The company's policy on packaging was consistent with this approach with respect to ethical products. Even Tabloid products were packaged in a way that prevented identification by shape, colour, or design. No directions or suggestions appeared on containers or packages, leaving these to the doctor to suit circumstances and individual patients. Neither were diseases mentioned. Increasingly, however, other competitors adopted the reverse of this anonymising policy in attempts to secure instant recognition of products when prescribed by doctors, a practice which facilitated repeat self-dosage. This was criticised by BW&Co. for transforming ethical products into 'pseudo-ethical products' and using doctors for an ulterior purpose to connect them more directly with the patient as consumer. In an item entitled 'Ethical marketing' concern was expressed that newly qualified doctors seemed to be unaware of this form of exploitation by manufacturers in search of increased sales.[65] This did not, however, rule out the use of slogans in the company's advertising of general goods and selected Tabloids; for example, 'Used at night keeps the skin bright' to advertise Hazeline Snow, and 'The bark that never bites' to describe the non-griping qualities of Tabloid Cascara. More widely applicable, 'B.P. or better', emphasized the quality of the company's products that were shown never to fall below the official standard and often to exceed it.[66]

Whether BW&Co.'s advertisements were less 'modern' than those of competitors, a criticism levelled by the Trustees in the latter half of the 1930s and later by Robson, is open to question. It is true that the educational sub-texts and images narrating pharmaceutical history since ancient times, introduced on Wellcome's initiative in the 1890s, persisted into the 1930s.

FIGURE 14.10

Apologies, used in an advertisement, from an Indian company for infringing BW&Co.'s 'Tabloid' copyright (*Chemist & Druggist*, 21 February 1925).

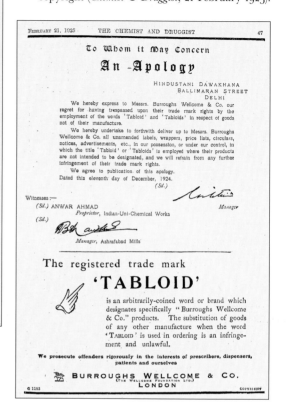

FIGURE 14.9

Advertisement for Hazeline cream (*Chemist & Druggist*, 27 January 1923). Note the use of the same artwork as that in Figure 12.9 (page 371).

However, images associated with science and modernity had also been a feature from the beginning, the company's advertisements including white-coated scientists at work, showing rats before and after dosing on Kepler Cod Liver Oil and Malt Extract, accompanied by graphs and tabulated data. Moreover, the existence of imitators suggests that competitors did not perceive the company's advertisements to be behind the times. Fraudulent imitations (especially overseas) of the company's advertisements were met with legal action against importers and manufacturers, many of whom discontinued the infringement only after the printing of an apology in journal or newspaper.[67]

Product innovation in a competitive environment

The company's record of product innovation is difficult to assess. The only available basis for an attempt to draw up even the most tentative conclusions consists of data published in the *British Medical Journal* in a regular column that included reports and analyses of 'new preparations and inventions' entering the market for the first time. The data are flawed by such shortcomings as the identifiable omission of some new preparations and the impossibility of distinguishing levels of therapeutic effectiveness or financial success of the various items. However, in the absence of any other measure of innovative activity, they provide a basis on which it is possible to suggest levels of innovative activity over time and to make limited comparisons with the record of other companies. Underlying the decision to use the data is the assumption that an incentive existed for companies to report new preparations entering the market to achieve free publicity in the leading major medical journal. A long-term perspective reveals that the opening of the research laboratories in the 1890s coincided with the highest ever number of new preparations launched by BW&Co.: seven in 1895, ten in 1896, eight in 1897. The average between 1888 and 1902 was 4.25 compared with 1.2 between 1903 and 1927, by which time, in Jowett's view, BDH was establishing leadership status in the industry.[68]

On the measures reported here, therefore the propensity for product innovation appears to have declined. The importance, therapeutically and commercially, of the products introduced (notably sera) during the early period also far exceeded those introduced during the interwar period.[69] Whereas the war appears not to have substantially altered the flat-lining evident from 1903, a sharp upward trend developed from the mid-1920s when the annual average for the period between 1927 and 1937 was 5.4. Commencing shortly after the formation of the STC in 1925, the rise might be interpreted as evidence that the efforts of the STC to revive the company's capacity for innovation were successful.

Judgement of innovativeness, however, requires comparisons for which the *BMJ* data offer a basis. The other pharmaceutical companies whose new products were listed in the *BMJ* were BDH, Allen & Hanburys, Boots, May & Baker, and Parke Davis & Co. None compared with the levels of innovative activity recorded for BW&Co. Before the war, only Allen & Hanburys and Parke Davis figure, though neither barely averaged a single reported innovation in any year. Not until the mid-1920s do any of the companies approach the figures recorded for BW&Co. The second best record was that of BDH, though even during the most prolific period the company recorded an annual average of only 2.3 between 1926 and 1932. Otherwise, during that period and throughout the inter-war years, the remaining companies trailed both BDH and BW&Co. Many of BW&Co.'s entries during the surge in innovations in the late 1920s and early thirties were biologicals, including sera, insulin and test kits, and vitamin D, developed in the WPRL. Digoxin and new insulin preparations represented the most innovative of the drugs developed by the company in this period.

Commentaries on the lists recorded in the *British Medical Journal* convey the impression that the innovations recorded for BDH, notably insulin and vitamin D, were major, whereas those recorded for BW&Co. were reformulations of known drugs or announcements of the issue of Tabloids made up in different strengths.[70] So far as both insulin and vitamin D are concerned, BDH's claim to be first to develop them is disputed, although judged on promotional and commercial criteria BDH's managers proved to be more adroit, moving into production on a commercial scale more rapidly that did BW&Co. On the other hand, Digoxin, marketed from 1934, was developed completely in-house by BW&Co., as were the several sulphonamide preparations placed on the market in the late 1930s. Both ergometrine and canine distemper vaccine were developed from research undertaken elsewhere (as was the insulin initially produced by both companies, and likewise vitamin D) but marketed by BW&Co. Judged on the basis of research-led innovation therefore, BDH does not appear to have usurped the leading position held indisputably in all respects by BW&Co. before the First World War. BDH was, however, catching up by the mid-1920s, evidence for which is an invitation issued in 1927 to both BW&Co. and BDH to take part in an MRC inquiry into the use of liver extract in the treatment of pernicious anaemia which required large-scale testing outside the laboratory.[71] In terms of research capacity and commercial application, BDH remained the principal British competitor to BW&Co. until the Second World War. The *BMJ* lists also reveal an increasing convergence of the types of drugs produced by all of the pharmaceutical companies, in chemicals, pharmaceuticals, and biologicals. A striking example is the simultaneous introduction in 1937 of zinc protamine insulin by four manufacturers, including BW&Co., which in the same year also announced Sulphonamide-P, as did BDH. This evidence underlines the highly competitive nature of R & D in the industry.

This also applied to sera and vaccines. In 1940, in addition to BW&Co., anti-diphtheria preparations were sold by four companies in Britain each holding a licence to manufacture. However, BW&Co. claimed the largest market share.[72] This resulted from the company's policy of diversification in this direction following the near collapse of the market for Salvarsan, Salvarsan substitutes and anti-gas-gangrene serum after 1918. Demand for anti-tetanus preparations depended increasingly upon preparations resulting from research into veterinary diseases and, most importantly, the development of diphtheria toxoid introduced in 1924 and sold in an improved, more effective form in 1926.[73] Sera sales had doubled between 1914 and 1929 and doubled again by 1936; actual sales, however, remained modest. At peak production in 1939 sales reached £150,000 out of a total sales turnover of £1.6 million (£1.03 million London-based sales).[74] Whereas during the 1920s gross profits on sera averaged 42 per cent of sera sales, competition and price reductions more than halved that figure during the 1930s.[75]

The increasing relative importance of sera and vaccines to the company was a consequence of the market difficulties that its other products experienced. The inability to increase sales reflected not only competition but more fundamental difficulties in the British market for sera and vaccines. The commercial payoff for sera and vaccines depended not merely on persuading the medical profession of the quality of the products to meet patients' need, as was the case with other science-based medicines. General practitioners were slow to show interest in the laboratory diagnostic test of diphtheria that would have generated a demand for standardised toxin for the purpose or in inoculation.[76] The Ministry of Health was not at all proactive, with respect for example to a standardised prophylactic, leaving officers and practitioners to choose a vaccine from several competing suppliers. In the absence of national intervention to implement public health policy and denied financial support, the responsibility for public health in the country resided with Medical Officers of Health (MOsH), only a minority of whom took the initiative to provide a free service. Lewis concluded that excessive time and energy they spent on clinical work and the administration of maternal and child welfare centres was at the expense of preventative medicine. The effect of these structural, attitudinal, and behavioural influences left Britain well behind extensive immunisation programmes in Canada and continental Europe.[77]

Yet of all the sera and vaccines sold by the company, those for the testing and treatment of diphtheria offered the largest potential market and absorbed the greatest amount of effort to overcome the limitations resulting from the apathy of practitioners and the inactivity of the Ministry of Health. In an attempt to achieve a breakthrough the company offered its products to MOsH for use in clinical trials and guidance from WPRL staff on testing and immunisation techniques.[78] Through this network, thousands of children from vulnerable populations in hospitals, Board schools, Barnardo homes, and asylums, were tested and immunised where necessary. The clinical data this provided added to cumulative laboratory experience thereby advancing analytical techniques and simultaneously promoted the company's products. This entire process of developing a market was expensive, absorbed the time and energies of personnel, and incurred costs; the fees offered for the services of the WPRL staff were donated to charity.[79]

The broader question is: why did a company which, at least until the mid-1920s, was acknowledged by contemporaries to possess the best equipped research laboratories in the industry in Britain and staffed by some outstanding scientists, produce no major medical breakthroughs and only a single important product innovation during the 1930s? A failure to diversify and to develop new lines of general goods raises a similar question: why did a hitherto highly successful, and profitable firm lose ground to competitors? There is no single explanation. Answering both questions requires a

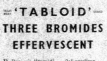

FIGURE 14.11 'Nerves – a vital war-time problem', (*BMJ*, 28 October 1939), promoting three bromides effervescent, empirin, and empirin with codeine, for use in 'cases of nervous disorder attributable to shock and acute tension'.

consideration of the fundamental structure, organisation, and philosophy underlying the formation and development of BW&Co. in relation to knowledge and reputation, trust, and profit, the subject of chapter 15.

Wellcome's legacy: The Wellcome Trust

Wellcome died on 25 July 1936. For several years he had spent large parts of his time visiting friends in the US, where he also received medical treatment for a cancerous condition at the Mayo Clinic.[80] Wellcome's Will required the creation of a Trust to administer the legacy he bequeathed: the Wellcome Foundation Ltd and his personal fortune. As the inheritors of the Foundation, the Trustees became responsible for managing the business and research laboratories, the museums, the library, and the multifarious other dimensions of his activities. These included the scientific and archaeological work in the Sudan and, in accordance with Wellcome's wishes, encouragement and funding of medical research and medical historical studies. While Wellcome personally selected his inaugural Trustees, his Will also prescribed the composition of the Trust: at least two should be qualified in medicine or allied sciences and two others 'of wide business experience, at least one of whom should be a lawyer with exceptional experience in the administration of large estates.'[81] These specifications and their implementation proved to be obscure, complicated further by details contained in an accompanying memorandum intended for the guidance of the Trustees. The prevailing confusion necessitated clarification in the courts.[82] The first Trustees included George Henry Hudson Lyall, who was the first chairman for a year only, and Launcelot Claude Bullock, aged 57. Both were partners in the firm of Markby, Stewart, and Wadeson, longstanding solicitors who had managed the legal aspects of Wellcome's business and other interests. When Lyall died in June 1938, he was succeeded by Sir Henry Dale, then aged 63, the distinguished former Director of the WPRL and eminent physiologist who became a Nobel Laureate in 1936. The other members were Thomas Elliott, FRS, aged 59, Professor of Medicine at University College, London and close friend of Dale, and Martin Price, aged 55, senior partner in the accountancy firm of Viney, Price and Goodyear.[83] Except for the single qualifying share allotted to each director of the Board of the Foundation, the Trustees were the sole shareholders. The Will was unclear with respect to the relationship between the Trustees and the directors. The appointment and remuneration of the directors of the Foundation rested with the Trustees, who possessed the power of final decision in the event of differences between the Trust and the Foundation. Thus, it may be presumed that Wellcome's intention was that the Trustees should possess final authority over the Board. The Trustees had been, in effect, designated as an 'immortal self',[84] while the directors continued to be responsible primarily for managing the business as a commercial enterprise. In order to enable Trustees to monitor activity and ultimately, in theory, to exercise executive power over the Foundation, all accounts and any other information were open to scrutiny by the Trustees at their discretion.[85] They could also attend meetings of the Foundation Board, which they began to do in 1938.[86] By appointing the following additional directors, Wenyon, head of the WBSR; Oakes, formerly head of sales department and personal assistant to Pearson; and Sydney Smith, the scientist responsible for the discovery of digoxin, who acted as Works Manager at Dartford after Jowett's death, the Trustees widened the composition of the board.[87] This measure ensured that views other than those of Pearson were heard in the ensuing investigation of the problems presented by the Foundation in general, and the commercial crisis, which the Trustees perceived BW&Co. to be facing, in particular.

Since its formation in 1924, meetings of the Board of the Foundation had been reported in the barest detail during Wellcome's lifetime when Pearson was General Manager. Minutes of the enlarged Board became noticeably fuller. A resolution passed in February 1938 required 'that details of any proposed capital expenditure at the Dartford Works, the WPRL, and the Wellcome Research Institution, that any proposed heavy or unusual expenditure such as upon advertising at exhibitions, and that any special proposals of the Scientific and Technical Committee should come before the Board as routine matters.'[88] Another decision was to begin to keep records of processes developed at the WPRL, a surprising omission in the laboratories.[89] The Directors also agreed that a priority should be the appointment of a 'a medical man to become thoroughly acquainted with recent developments in pharmacology, therapeutics, research, science etc. and to make new suggestions for new products and for improving [advertising and publicity] literature', almost certainly an indication of the influence of Wenyon and Smith.[90]

Dale was worried by the ambiguity of the Will, concerned that even an indirect link with the firm might compromise the independent status of the Trustees, especially the medical men. At a meeting to discuss the issue the other Trustees and Pearson (nominated by Wellcome as Governing Director of the Foundation), Dale was reassured that in his capacity as a Trustee, he 'should have no personal interest in or responsibility for the business'. The Trustees were 'even prevented from interfering with its policy or that of its attached institutions, except under quite abnormal conditions'.[91] His role was envisaged as one limited to advising on the allocation of funds to promote medical research.[92]

Short of the ultimate sanction through the power to dismiss and appoint directors, the Trustees were not given effective means of influencing the directors' commercial policy. Indeed, in the short term it appeared that the Trustees were denied the power to choose either of the two most senior directors, for the Will included an expressed wish '... that so long as they shall live and be able and willing to act ... George Edward Pearson and Gerald Leslie Moore shall continue Directors' of the Foundation.'[93] Without a definition of how to judge their ability to continue in their respective roles as Governing Director and accountant (*de facto* Deputy Governor), it appears that Wellcome had taken care to protect their position indefinitely; yet in 1936 Pearson had already reached the age of 70 and Moore was 64.

In his memorandum of policy and aims for the guidance of Trustees, Wellcome had left guidelines to be adopted for the future management of the business and of the research laboratories. These advised that: any person regarded as unfit for his role (defined for example, by consuming alcohol before the age of 26 or before the evening meal) should be dismissed; that there should be no material reduction in proportional expenditure on advertising publicity and propaganda; and that heads of scientific laboratories should not be expected to direct or supervise operations in the experimental or manufacturing departments. Lines of research under the authority and direction of the WBSR were to be determined by the Trustees in consultation with the directors of the Foundation, but in order to ensure rapid exploitation of new knowledge and to avoid losing opportunities, he recommended a 'frequent and harmonious exchange of views between all concerned', (another aspiration conspicuously absent in the past).[94] The ambiguity of the relationship between research and business was not resolved. In Dale's view, this was the result of Wellcome's failure to exercise 'steady vision' with particular respect to the Euston Road 'Wellcome Research outfit' which Dale thought risked becoming 'a sham facade'.[95] Later, Pearson's successor as manager of BW&Co., T. R. G. Bennett,[96] echoed this view but applied it to the Foundation as a whole, which he described as 'a facade really amounting to misrepresentation'.[97]

Following Lyall's death in June 1938 and the elevation of Dale to the chairmanship of the Trust, it soon became clear that it was untenable for the Trustees to distance themselves from the firm. Profits were the source of the Trust's funds for disbursement for medical research, to sustain the activities of museums and library, to support, at least temporarily, Wellcome's other commitments and to meet the pressing demands of the Inland Revenue. The purposes to which the allocation should be applied and the relative proportions of expenditure on each to be adhered to after Wellcome's death were contained in the Articles of Association drawn up in 1924. The Articles specified that whereas during his lifetime Wellcome would decide on the appropriation of profits, thereafter profits should be allocated to the following formula: 35 per cent was to be allocated to the 'establishment, maintenance, and development of institutions or organisations of scientific research and study or otherwise for the purpose of scientific research and exploration generally'; 5 per cent was to be allocated to promote the physical or intellectual welfare of staff and employees, and 10 per cent to establish and endow libraries and museums. A capital and business expansion fund as a general reserve was to be financed from 25 per cent of profit, leaving the remainder 'to be applied for such purposes as directors think fit.'[98] This implies a minimum of 50 per cent allocation for activities directly business related, though more through the allocation for scientific research, depending upon the extent to which applied research was accorded priority.

When Pearson sought to claim control for all of the Trust's activities because BW&Co. was the sole source of its funds, Dale told him bluntly that this was not the case, and that the Trustees would not take responsibility for the actions of either Pearson or Johnson-Saint (Conservator of the Wellcome collections) taken without their approval. Underlining the confrontational relationship between the Trust and the directors of the Foundation from the beginning, Dale told Elliott '... they are on the run',[99] and while Dale expressed a wish to improve relations, he soon began to hold special meetings of the Trustees to which Pearson was not invited.[100]

Dale's view was that funding the research laboratories was the Trust's responsibility, though he acknowledged that expenditure would 'for accounting purposes be regarded as a Foundation expense'. He considered that the head of the Wellcome Research Institution should report directly to the Trustees, rather than to the Governing Director.[101] Dale defended this view by referring to Wellcome's insistence that the laboratories and museums were his own personal property and unconnected with the business 'except in so far as they served its interests at his request'.[102] This qualification, however, is important, for its implementation was instrumental in transforming the WPRL as the supplier of sera and vaccine. The WPRL was both a research laboratory and a productive organisation, the value of which increased further from 1940 when Wellcome's diphtheria vaccine became the main brand used in the government's national vaccination scheme. The continuing tensions arising from the fundamental dilemma presented by the research laboratories in relation to production and marketing and of ensuring a favourable perception of the firm by medical men, had long remained unresolved. Dale believed that no authority should be conceded to the Foundation's Governing Director. However, he also acknowledged that the business – and the other organisations within the Foundation – depended on profits.[103] In contrast to the position implied in his reiteration in 1937 of Wellcome's declared views on the separation of the business from the research laboratories, Dale later insisted that there was nothing undignified or humiliating in conducting research for the purpose of advancing industry, an observation prompted by Wenyon's attempt to distance himself from the business, adopting instead the role of pure scientist.[104] Elliott's perception of the relationship between production, marketing and research showed a similar ambiguity. He noted that the 'scientific men, and especially [Sir]Andrew Balfour were always eager to keep themselves and their Bureau disassociated in the public eye from the commercial side of Henry Wellcome's business, even though its profits made their work possible'.[105] Elliott favoured a marketing policy, which emphasised the company's reliance on medical research to which the manufacturing business gave wholehearted commitment and support.[106] He criticised the company's heavy reliance on Tabloids, a demand for which still existed in Asia but which had declined in England. He contrasted Glaxo's vigorous promotion of biological products that, on the evidence of his brother in general practice, were increasingly used by doctors.[107] It is true that the home sales of compressed goods had fallen. However, the contrast is overdone. Historians of Glaxo have emphasized the slow progress of that company in its transition from infant food to pharmaceuticals, even prompting Jephcott, Managing Director, to consider resignation in 1938. In that year, although Glaxo's home pharmaceutical sales exceeded food sales, 54 per cent of 'pharmaceutical turnover' consisted of sales of Glucodin (Glucose, vitamin D).[108]

The Trust's review of BW&Co.

The immediate task of preparing to pay death duties inevitably focused the minds of the Trustees on the health of the business and the origins of the company's declining momentum. Long-term indebtedness had declined since the early 1930s, falling from the all-time peak of £395,505 in 1933 to less than half that level by the end of the decade. Beginning in 1920, the company's pension fund was the other source of debt, virtually the only one between 1922 and 1927 when this figure rose from £110,166 to £172,411. Thereafter, debt on this account did not exceed half the 1927 figure (see Table 14.7).

Table 14.7 *BW&Co., long-term debt and reserves, 1924–1939 (£)*

	Bank loan	Wellcome loan	Pension fund	Sundry	Total	Reserves
1924			150,171	556	150,727	45,000
1925			157,679	976	158,655	177,326
1926			164,993	66	165,059	277,326
1927			172,411	493	172,904	357,326
1928			4,672	965	5,637	457,326
1929			4,072	85	4,157	545,000
1930			4,576	631	5,207	595,000
1931		75,000	15,859	1,193	92,052	670,000
1932		350,000	25,646	1,765	377,411	725,000
1933		390,000	5,505		395,505	735,000
1934		365,000	4,491	15,528	385,019	745,000
1935		320,000	22,963	16,080	359,043	770,000
1936		230,000	30,236		260,236	785,000
1937	133,000		44,805	25,653	203,458	770,000
1938	63,000		62,381	34,871	160,252	770,000
1939	78,000		75,393	28,664	182,057	785,000

WFA, Acc. 90/1, BW&Co. balance sheets; F/FA/328, trading and profit and loss accounts.

However, a major new source of long-term indebtedness, which doubled previous levels, emerged when the company experienced trading and liquidity difficulties during the early 1930s that coincided with the construction of the Wellcome Research Institution on Euston Road. Beginning in 1931, Wellcome's personal wealth was mobilised in the form of a loan to the company of £75,000. This figure rose to £350,000 in 1932, and to £390,000 in the following year. By the year of Wellcome's death the figure had fallen to £230,000, a debt that fell to the Trustees to liquidate. Bank loans contributed to bridging the gap with a loan of £133,000 in 1937, falling to £63,000 in 1938, and £78,000 in 1939. Unlike the investment-related long-term indebtedness of the late 1890s, the early 1900s, the 1920s, and the early 1930s, that incurred by the company after 1932 was not accompanied by rising values of equity capital and fixed assets. Until 1939, working capital also remained at lower levels compared with the period preceding the depression of the early 1930s. This was indicative of lower levels of business activity during the 1930s, just as the change in the relationships between indebtedness and equity capital and fixed assets were symptomatic of a serious weakening in the company's long-term financial position.

Rising profit levels from the mid-1930s masked this underlying financial weakness to some extent, though these concealed a worrying trend in sales, to which Martin Price's review of the business between 1925 and 1939 drew attention. This was the subject of discussion at a special meeting of the Trustees in February 1940. Price reported that total sales had stagnated during this period. Sales of General Goods and of Kharsivan had fallen, offset only by rising serum and vaccine sales preventing a drop in turnover.

The Trustees agreed that the data provided by Price warranted a fundamental inquiry into policy and the administration of the business.[109] At a meeting of the Trustees to which the Directors of the Foundation were invited, the directors were asked to comment on Price's report and to propose remedies for the company's problems. Moore, whose disagreement with Wellcome's American investment had long set them at odds, frequently counselling financial restraint, had already agreed that some reorganisation of the business was desirable, notably levels of expenditure on selling and advertising.[110] Surprisingly, because both Moore and Oakes were both closely identified with Pearson's approach to management, they concurred in attributing 'trading decline' to 'a general loss of initiative and an unprogressive policy in the conduct of the business since 1929'.[111] They referred to the absence of new products, to delay in adopting modern methods of advertising and marketing, and the continuance of 'a complicated and unpopular system of trading terms'.[112] Perhaps the departure in 1929 of six of the company's fully trained medical representatives who had been recruited by British Colloids Ltd contributed to the directors' later sense of a loss of marketing momentum.[113] There was also a problem of managerial succession resulting from the lack of younger people qualified to promote to positions of responsibility. At a joint meeting of Trustees and directors in August to plan the future, the directors recorded their views that considerably greater efforts should be made to develop new lines of productive research for which additional personnel, buildings, and equipment should be provided, and that constructive effort on a large scale was needed to improve the marketing methods and organisation of the Foundation.[114] Drs Wenyon and Smith defended the research organisation against any charge of lack of initiative and enterprise, though they conceded that further expansion along 'lines more directly at practical therapeutic developments was greatly to be desired'.[115] Pearson was even more defensive, emphasising external causes: the impact of the worldwide slump in business since the Wall Street crash of 1929, the breakdown of the gold standard, and 'the rapid and unexpected decline' in the demand for certain staple products, particularly for Kepler goods.[116] In pointing only to external factors as the source of the company's problems, however, Pearson was isolated. The new Board referred to the urgent need for reconstruction at Snow Hill and Dartford and proposed

> that every effort be made to break down the existing isolation and lack of co-operation between departments, and to develop the team spirit between the various organisations and departments and to encourage exchange of information between them.[117]

However, without awaiting the directors' proposals for reform, the Trustees drew up their own plan. Their immediate priorities were first, a reorganisation of the distributive section of the business and second, improved 'co-ordination of departmental aims and activities'.[118] Furthermore, they decided that the creation and implementation of a new business strategy required the appointment of a new manager immediately. Despite Wellcome's confirmation of Pearson as the Governing Director in perpetuity, the Trustees believed that a complete break with the past was necessary, deciding to replace Pearson with 'an expert possessing the necessary technical and executive qualifications and experience'.[119]

On Price's suggestion, the Trustees interviewed T. R. G. Bennett. One of his previous employers was a competitor, Johnson & Johnson, the large American manufacturer of proprietary pharmaceutical goods, notably plaster and bandage products. Another previous employer was Urwick Orr & Partners Ltd, management consultants, for whom he was chief marketing and selling consultant, development manager, and subsequently principal partner. Testimonies from both companies referred to Bennett's thorough knowledge of the theory and practice of marketing, his business acumen and capacity for initiative.[120] The Trustees agreed that Pearson could continue as Chairman and Governing Director of the Foundation, though limiting his duties to chairing Board meetings and being available during Bennett's induction period should he require advice.[121] Bennett assumed full managerial responsibilities within weeks. Pearson offered his formal resignation from the positions of Governing Director and Chairman of the Foundation in July, effective from 31 December 1940; his deputy, Moore also resigned.[122] Wenyon, Director of the WBSR, followed shortly after. One of Bennett's first decisions as Managing Director was to examine the company's problems and analyse their origins, the outcome of which was contained in a report to departmental heads within months of his appointment.[123] It is significant that in analysing the problems that the company faced in 1940, historical factors loomed large.

CHAPTER FIFTEEN

Themes and perspectives: BW&Co., the pharmaceutical industry, and medical research

Scientific ethic, reputation and profitable business

Between 1880 and 1895, Burroughs and Wellcome created an organisational culture rooted in mutual distrust, dictatorial with respect to managers and departmental heads, and paternalistic towards employees. Especially during the early years, the culture was also innovative. Burroughs introduced 'detailing' as a method of marketing drugs in Britain. Wellcome established laboratories to which he recruited scientists who were encouraged to conduct pure scientific research adhering to a scientific ethic. This development was unique to the industry at the time. As a young man Wellcome had contributed articles to the *American Journal of Pharmacy* and the *Pharmacist*, and later revealed a capacity to combine academic interest in scientific development with a flair for salesmanship and the exercise of discipline in business administration. Surprisingly, not until 1928 was he awarded an honorary degree at Edinburgh University, a tardy recognition of his contribution to medical research which may have reflected a lingering distrust of commercial activity on the part of the medical professional establishment[1]. However, in 1932, he received a knighthood, was elected to the Royal Society, and became an Honorary Fellow of the Royal College of Surgeons. Recognition for his contribution to medicine through the advancement of scientific knowledge by the Wellcome laboratories signalled the achievement of one of his twin aims for the company. The other aim was to harness scientific advances for commercial gain, thereby, he had claimed as far back as 1905, generating profit for the business and stemming Britain's loss of important industries.[2]

Wellcome's knowledge, entrepreneurial skills, and reputation for setting high standards in production equipped him to lead effectively, not only staff employed in the office and factory, but also research scientists in the laboratories. His willingness to listen and to be persuaded by Dale, when

457

he was director of the WPRL, was a departure from his characteristically dictatorial approach to management but proved to be a critically important decision in creating an organisational culture attractive to scientists.[3] The calibre of the scientists he succeeded in recruiting in competition with university departments reflected not only levels of salary but also research facilities in a well-funded laboratory under conditions which offered a freedom unknown in other commercial organisations. Wellcome explained that his firm would not conduct business 'seeking gold for the sake of gold' but would reinvest, for the advancement of science, whatever gold accrued.[4] In an appreciation, Dale later confirmed the truth of Wellcome's rhetoric; he had indeed chosen 'to spend his wealth in supporting research as another man might choose to spend on a racing stable'.[5] This was a mission wholly consistent with the professional ethic of scientists and physicians. Wellcome's contribution to medical science was recorded by W. J. Simpson, Professor of Hygiene and Public Health at King's College, London, who knew him for twenty years. He described Wellcome as 'the first in this country to place the chemical industry relating to medical preparations on a scientific basis. Through his success and high esteem among the medical profession, the unsatisfactory and wasteful medical equipment of our army has changed and [been] placed on a scientific basis. The WPRL became a training school for men interested in research.' Simpson referred to his own experience of research during two years spent at the WPRL where facilities were superior to those at his own college: 'the special laboratory equipment, animals, and a trained assistant were placed at my disposal and it never cost me a penny, all expenses defrayed by Mr Wellcome'.[6]

Following the formation and development of the laboratories during the 1890s, Wellcome's strategy, which combined scientific integrity and the production and sale of products of the highest quality with ethical marketing, remained crucial to the company's reputation. The effect of this personal triumph for Wellcome was to create a high level of trust in the business among the medical profession and the trade.[7] Once established, however, trust within the organisation proved, after a while, to be increasingly fragile. Even before the First World War, increasing commercial pressures intensified the potential for conflict between strict adherence to scientific ideals and the pursuit of lower costs, larger sales, and increasing profits. As Wellcome began to play a diminishing role in decision-making, divisions of opinion between scientists at Beckenham and managers in the London office over ethical advertising provide evidence of a continuing divergence of interests and divisions over policy.

Ensuring adequate clinical testing, while at the same time minimising cost and delay in launching a new product, presented a challenge to all pharmaceutical manufacturers. Failure to strike the correct balance could damage a company's reputation. One example of this is the premature issue of a canine distemper vaccine into the market in 1929 that resulted in several dog deaths. O'Brien admitted that he had been 'too economical' in organising the verification and reproduction of work carried out initially at the NIMR. Hampered by staff shortages when the demand for diphtheria anti-toxins was rising, O'Brien's request for investment in building, plant, equipment, and staff had been rejected by Pearson. Parish, head of bacteriological research at the WPRL, suggested that O'Brien might have accepted a lower standard for veterinary products.[8] Dale considered O'Brien to have been in too much of a hurry to boost the sales of a living virus vaccine to treat dog distemper.[9] More dead dogs prompted Pearson and O'Brien to discuss the withdrawal of the product in 1930, though after a costly interim scheme involving free extra doses from the laboratory, an improved, commercially successful product entered the market in the following year. This episode reveals the possible conflict between resourcing and commercial exploitation on the one hand and scientific development on the other. The Ring case in 1936, which involved a human fatality, presented a potentially even more damaging problem. Though the company was acquitted, investigation of the case revealed contamination risk and mismanagement of the laboratories; it also culminated in O'Brien's resignation in 1940.[10] Both cases revealed the risk to reputation as a result of compromising ethical policy in the pursuit of commercial interests in a competitive market.

Entrepreneurship, management, and under-investment; personalities and policies

Under-investment emerges as an enduring problem after the First World War and appears to have developed from the managerial culture that prevailed early on in the history of the organisation. Even before the creation of the research laboratories, Wellcome had been reluctant to risk undertaking capital expenditure in the late 1880s when Burroughs had purchased the Phoenix Mill from personal resources.[11] Carr later claimed to have resigned from BW&Co. in 1914 because of Wellcome's refusal to invest in buildings and plant to expand the production of chemicals. During the mid-1920s, Jowett, Wenyon, and O'Brien had expressed concern that resourcing was inadequate if the company was to develop. Wellcome, however, told Wenyon that the firm had 'no reason to fear rivalry ... Fair competition is beneficial and promotes progress.'[12] However, this coincided with his commitment to substantial investment in the Tuckahoe plant in New York, a decision explicable as much by Wellcome's complete confidence in Nevin, the Irish-Canadian manager, as by his assessment of the American market. It is pertinent to contrast Nevin's success in persuading Wellcome to invest in the American business regardless of Pearson's views with the evident failure of Jowett, Wenyon, and O'Brien to persuade either Wellcome or Pearson to support the case for increased investment in Britain.

Beginning in 1896, extensive travels to the Continent in search of artefacts, books, and curios for his collection as well as his extended visits to Africa, where he became involved in Sudanese archaeology, removed the crucial decision-maker from London for months at a time. Time spent touring Europe by motor car starting in 1907 and frequent trips to the US for recuperation and to visit family also explain his prolonged absences from England. The business absorbed less and less of his time. In 1910 his wife Syrie observed that since their marriage in 1901 most of their time had been spent in travelling to collect curios, a life which she hated.[13] It is true that until 1908, Wellcome was a prolific correspondent with the London office. For example, in five months during 1907–08, writing from abroad, he sent 502 letters plus cables and private letters.[14] Thereafter, either correspondence dropped suddenly to insignificant levels or it has not survived. It is probably significant that correspondence diminished shortly after the 1905 office re-organisation intended to relieve Wellcome of managerial responsibility. A longer term absence of communication may also have been a consequence of the deeply wounding effect of the breakdown of his marriage in 1910. Haggis described Wellcome as having been plunged into a condition of 'morbid misery and withdrawal.'[15] An anonymous critic within the company remarked on Wellcome's frequent absences, his 'remoteness', and consequent isolation from employees.[16] A junior manager in the buying department spoke of Wellcome's eccentric behaviour on his occasional visits to the office when he would present an employee with a personal item, 'perhaps a pair of exotic braces, demand its immediate and identical replacement, and walk out again – just like that'.[17] More serious, however, is Haggis' assessment that between the wars a tendency to procrastinate was added to intolerance and obstinacy. He would only deliver a judgement or take a decision when he could be persuaded that action was 'vital'.[18] Furthermore, his adherence to a principle reported to be 'never tell anyone what you propose to do until you've done it'[19] proved frustrating to his deputy and contributed to the general lack of communication which characterised the organisation during and after the period of Wellcome's active managerial role.[20] Macdonald's observation that business success was greatest between 1895 and 1920 when Wellcome 'was in the driving seat and the company prosperous at home and abroad',[21] is wide of the mark. He was in the driving seat as the *owner* until 1936; evidence of his role as governing director, however, indicates a sharply declining contribution to the management of the business from the early 1900s.

This withdrawal was planned, as was the promotion of Pearson to become General Manager and his 'personal deputy' in 1905. These appointments followed a record of extreme loyalty to Wellcome. In 1896 Pearson had demonstrated his commitment to Wellcome in spectacular fashion when he planned and implemented the live lamb and cod exhibits at the BMA annual conference.[22] As a successful traveller at home and overseas, in 1902 he became head of the newly created Foreign and Colonial Department after he had masterminded the establishment of trading branches in Milan, Cape Town, and Sydney. The significance of his promotion may be inferred from Wellcome's message of appreciation to Pearson in 1916. Writing from Alaska, Wellcome, then aged 63, expressed the hope that Pearson would carry on as deputy for many more years 'to promote the continued development and prosperity of the great institutions under your control and direction and to safeguard the welfare of the large army of faithful workers of all ranks.'[23] This is an explicit indication of Wellcome's abdication since 1905 and of his intention to continue to transfer power to Pearson to control strategic decision-making and management of the entire organisation.

The reality of the managerial situation, however, was more complicated. A combination of Wellcome's frequent absences, procrastination, and a failing memory, though at the same time occasionally concerning himself with detailed execution of policy, had serious implications for the role played by his 'personal deputy' and General Manager. Pearson told Haggis in 1940 that such a combination had 'often made things extremely difficult for his responsible officials'. Wellcome's absences left a vacuum. The hierarchical structure of the company and a dictatorial management style that came naturally to Wellcome had created a corporate personality and set the tone of managerial style in the organisation. However, Pearson's judgement that Wellcome had lost the capacity and determination to carry out big tasks[24] does not apply to the period before the early 1930s, as Wellcome's involvement in the development of new strategies for the American company show.[25] Pearson's shortcomings cannot be laid entirely at Wellcome's door; Pearson was not equipped to fill Wellcome's role even during the period of Wellcome's advancing age and frailty. When Pearson became General Manager in 1905, he was said to have lacked Sudlow's 'happy facility for making subordinates feel at ease'.[26] Internal criticism was aimed at his introduction of increasing numbers of rules affecting managerial, supervisory, and other staff and of an inflexible implementation that produced inter-departmental friction.[27] He was uncommunicative, his managerial style described as 'abrupt'. He apparently delighted in rudeness in his dealings with departmental heads. His practice of summoning heads of departments to his office where he would deliver an address did not make him popular and seems unlikely to have engaged their enthusiasm and support.[28] Even before 1914, regarding his dealings with the laboratories, the Director of the WPRL described him as a nuisance. Typically Pearson declined to take decisions necessary for work in the laboratories when Wellcome was away.[29] Even when, on Wellcome's infrequent visits to the laboratories, he made verbal promises of funding, Pearson ignored them. He earned a reputation for always refusing requests for funding, whether to expand accommodation, add more equipment, or to undertake new research. Parish attributed this posture to Pearson's misguided (in the long term) loyalty to Wellcome, concluding that 'Wellcome's considerable fortune was partly the result of Pearson's parsimony'.[30]

Pearson's generally negative approach in his role of Deputy Governor may have reflected his lack of self-confidence. Without the knowledge or personality that Wellcome possessed, he was unable to manage the organisation in Wellcome's image. Nevertheless, from 1905, this was Pearson's task. There is no evidence before the war either whether Wellcome noticed Pearson's negativity and unpopularity or whether he chose to disregard his weaknesses. Acknowledging Pearson's record during 25 years of service to the company, Wellcome praised his 'loyal and efficient service and unwavering devotion to duty'.[31] That both men interpreted duty as a personal matter is suggested by the perception of others that 'if Wellcome wanted anything, Pearson got it'.[32] A dutiful and hard-working manager, Pearson possessed neither vision nor a sense of strategy, weaknesses which, especially after the war, Wellcome's absences from office, factory and laboratories exposed.[33] It was left to Jowett to comment on the resulting vulnerability of the organisation. As competition intensified after the war, Jowett identified a lack of integration between office, factory, and laboratories as a crucial deficiency. His criticism referred specifically to the British enterprise. Relations between the British company and the North American business reveal further fundamental deficiencies in the whole organisation, a growing tension between senior managers, and renewed intervention by Wellcome.

Owner-entrepreneur and managers; more dysfunctional relationships

Relations between Wellcome and Pearson are illuminated in valuable though limited correspondence which has survived between Wellcome, Pearson, Nevin, and Lang. The exchanges primarily concerned strategy and management with respect to the American and Canadian subsidiary companies after the First World War. This correspondence throws additional light on the development of the two companies. However, in the context of analysing the history of the management of BW&Co. in its entirety, the importance of this correspondence lies in the revelation of the lack of trust prevailing between Pearson and Nevin, and Pearson and Lang. It also exposes levels of distrust between Pearson and Wellcome which had implications for strategic policy affecting the company in Britain as well as the overseas subsidiaries. The deterioration in relations between the two men appears to have originated during the war; the catalyst was the issue of policy affecting the future of business in North America after war ended. Wellcome's aspirations for the American business which he articulated forcefully in 1917, were not shared by Pearson. In response to Wellcome's prediction that the US would become the most profitable field of operations,[34] Pearson drew attention to the unprofitable record of the American branch since its formation in 1906, an observation based on the calculations from the trading accounts prepared by C. Leslie Moore, BW&Co.'s accountant at Snow Hill. They showed an accumulated negative aggregated balance on capital and current account plus an imputed accumulation of foregone interest. Adjustments taking into account profits accrued in London on wholesale sales to New York, suggest that the business was probably profitable from 1915, though the accounting system used by Moore and Pearson continued to show deficits until 1926.[35] After the war, Nevin perceived Pearson to be frustrating his ambitions (and those of Wellcome) to expand the American business through investment in manufacturing and vigorous marketing. Pearson imposed drastic reductions in Nevin's marketing budget, denied carry over of unspent balances, and refused to replace the second hand machinery then in use.[36] A reorganisation of the New York Works in 1920, intended to integrate and improve utilisation of the limited amount of manufacture introduced by Nevin, precipitated a clash with Pearson who, without consulting Nevin, dispatched a person from London to manage the changes. Nevin's complaint that his qualifications and experience showed him to be unsuitable for the task soon proved to be justified. In the dispute with Pearson that followed, Wellcome backed Nevin's appointment of his own man to superintend the reorganisation.[37]

The restructuring of BW&Co. to form the Wellcome Foundation in 1924, conceded almost no independence to the new subsidiary companies. The companies were still branches in all but name; proprietary rights remained with the Wellcome Foundation. All decisions regarding product range, formulae, recipes, and production methods to be employed depended on decisions made in London – in practice by Pearson, though subject to Wellcome's final diktat should he choose to make one. In 1925 Nevin finally persuaded Wellcome to invest in manufacture on a scale which the manager of the American business believed was justified by expanding sales and potential for development. Wellcome became personally involved in the acquisition of extensive manufacturing premises at Tuckahoe, NY, which could accommodate 1200 workers. Pearson disapproved of this development and advised re-selling part of the site, advice that Wellcome ignored.[38] Pearson also reminded Nevin that decisions affecting alterations in products or manufacturing processes, even affecting those lines peculiar to the American market, would be initiated by London.[39] Wellcome took a different view, accepting Nevin's argument that the Americanisation of the business was vital to success and in 1926, signalled that this process should begin. When Pearson continued to try to restrict Nevin's scope for innovation in this respect, Wellcome backed Nevin, notably over the manufacture of malt extract using local inputs.[40]

The issue of pricing, of longstanding concern to Nevin in the US, surfaced again in Canada in 1927 when Wellcome, then aged 74, was on a visit to Detroit to attend the Lister Centenary and Clinical Congress. There he met Canadian and American surgeons and physicians who praised his company's high ethical reputation and the scientific excellence of its products but criticised the high prices and their cost to consumers. For that reason they were reluctant to prescribe or recommend hospitals to purchase. Wellcome's attention was also drawn to evidence of the fierce competition the Canadian company was facing, principally from American companies located in Canada. The Canadians claimed that standards set for the *United States Pharmacopoeia* were superior to those of the *British Pharmacopoeia* and as a consequence, American companies were supplying superior products. Concern led Wellcome to travel to Toronto, London Ontario, and Ottawa and to the subsidiary company in Montreal where he met J. S. Lang, the recently appointed manager.[41] He told Wellcome that the restrictive price list adjustment formula set in London was adversely affecting competitiveness. Whereas the New York business had benefited from a war-induced stimulus to sales and production in volumes that reduced the impact of the pricing restrictions, no such shock had galvanised the Canadian house into manufacturing.

Lang informed Wellcome that his own appeal against pricing (and marketing) policy had been ignored by the London office which he thought showed a lack of appreciation of the gravity of the situation. Wellcome's next step was to instruct Lang to assemble all relevant documentation and correspondence between the Montreal and London offices relating to prices, terms, and other matters at issue in connection with the development of the Canadian business. After scrutinising the evidence and discussing the issues Wellcome expressed confidence in Lang's ability to combat competition, but acknowledged that this would depend on strong support from London – which he did not believe the Canadian company had been given. Wellcome encouraged Lang to manage the business more independently, the same advice he had given to Nevin.

Wellcome also demanded that staff in the Foreign and Colonial Department at Snow Hill re-read all the correspondence between London and Montreal, to reconsider pricing policy and also the proposal (presumably from Lang) to establish a manufacturing base in Canada. Outlining his views forcefully to Pearson, he pointed out that American companies promoted their products in the Canadian market as 'just as good at half the price'. This explained why BW&Co.'s prices were provoking intimations of profiteering, an allegation particularly wounding to Wellcome who found it embarrassing and difficult to answer.[42] On the subject of pricing, it can be assumed that Moore advised Pearson on the policy towards Canada, as he had with regard to New York. Wellcome discovered a memorandum from London (almost certainly originating from Moore, though possibly written by Pearson) which included the sentence: 'actuarial reckoning shows that it is customary for the curve of increase to fall when following a period of exceptional rise'. Wellcome noted: 'Responsible managerial reports of definite concrete facts of injury caused by high prices and urgent necessity of prompt action to prevent further losses are of far greater weight than actuarial theoretical curves'.[43]

Pearson's response to the proposal to establish manufacturing in Montreal was that the heavy capital outlay required could not be justified unless demand increased enormously: 'the whole yearly output for Canada could be manufactured in a few months and the works would, therefore, remain idle for the rest of the year'.[44] Revealing a more sympathetic approach, Wellcome commented that the relation between sales and plant capacity was obvious but that so far as logistical considerations in the early years were concerned, the frequency of batches could be varied and workers transferred from one department to another to occupy their time, as had been the practice during the early years of the London business.[45] He drew a direct parallel between the contemporary state of the Canadian business and the pre-manufacturing stage of the New York Works. Indeed, 'a special extra profit' [tax] claimed and held in London and not credited to Montreal imposed an even heavier handicap on the Canadian business than had been applied to the American firm.[46] He insisted that a revision of prices was urgent and that it was equally necessary that plans for manufacturing in Montreal should be prepared forthwith: 'This correspondence does not impress me as indicating that the Foreign and Colonial Department … have (sic) a better understanding of the conditions and needs of the firm's Canadian business than the management in Montreal. Nor do they appear to have shown superior judgement with the case presented.'[47] Wellcome inspected sites, chose La Salle, on the island of Montreal, and instructed Pearson to cable Lang to authorise immediate purchase. On Wellcome's instructions, Nevin acted as adviser to Lang during the planning process project.[48]

In the course of his review of the relationships between London and overseas branches in 1927, Wellcome offered a remarkable detailed critique of Pearson's approach. Wellcome decided that Moore's eccentric accounting system must be reformed, arguing that the system and the pricing policy associated with it had contributed to undermining his own higher volume, lower cost, and lower price philosophy by giving all the advantage to Dartford and London. He reminded Pearson that one reason why he had rejected repeated requests to 'abandon the US enterprise as hopeless' was that the accounts were discovered to be flawed (indicating a belated acceptance of Nevin's analysis). The other explanation was that '... an accountant's view that immediate profits are the all-essential points for consideration in promoting the development and best interests of the business may not prove to be the most practical policy in building up a successful business, especially in pioneer fields.'

Diverging views and a lack of trust between Wellcome and Pearson became even more serious in relation to Nevin's ambition to diversify the business through scientific research. Nevin's aspiration for BW&Co. (USA) Inc. was to achieve a reputation independent of that established by the company in Britain. He explained to Pearson that in order to cultivate a favourable reputation with the American medical profession it would be necessary to develop a research department comparable with those of American competitors. With respect to medical practice, Nevin referred to the need to respond quickly to sudden changes in treatment which the American medical profession was prone to make. The research route was necessary to retain status and in practical terms to satisfy American universities where most medical research was conducted. It was important that the company should be able to manufacture new products to standards acceptable to university faculty rather than be merely (as he later observed) 'a tablet-making outfit'.[49] Two further arguments were advanced to defend the research policy. The first was the increasing severity of government restriction and legal requirements for which demonstrable pharmaceutical research alongside manufacture was a necessity. The second, the 'buy American first' campaign that originated during the depression meant that it was important to present an unambiguously American identity for the company thereby preventing competitors to describe it as foreign.[50]

Pearson was not persuaded by these arguments; unlike Wellcome, who privately gave Nevin wholehearted support and in 1928 committed BW&Co.'s resources to establish the Tuckahoe Experimental Research Laboratories. Pearson was a stubborn critic, opposed to the Americanisation of the company and to any idea that pure research might take place outside Britain.[51] Several years later, when Wellcome was 82 and visiting the US for medical treatment,[52] he wrote to Pearson providing a detailed justification for the formation of the Tuckahoe Experimental Research Laboratories, a justification which echoed Nevin's initial proposal.[53] With Wellcome's private agreement, Nevin had chosen as his first Research Director, Dr C. S. Leonard, assistant professor of pharmacology and toxicology at Yale. Writing to Pearson in the summer of 1928 to secure the approval required for new appointments, Nevin had described Leonard as a person 'capable to ensure that the Works' standards were maintained to a degree in every respect comparable to the Chief Works standards'. His familiarity with the requirements of the US Government would also enable him to suggest product improvements in line with them.[54] Nevin mentioned neither the research laboratory nor the undertaking that he and Wellcome had given to Leonard to provide him and other research staff with facilities for fundamental research and opportunities for publication. The impression conveyed to Pearson, that research was not part of Leonard's remit appears, therefore, to have been intentionally misleading. Leonard's curriculum vitae, sent by Nevin to Pearson only after the appointment had been made, opened Pearson's eyes, though he remained unaware, as yet, of Wellcome's connivance.

Pearson replied that while Leonard's appointment was as an 'expert chemist' his specialist training was in pharmacology and his salary (approved by Wellcome), signified a more senior role than that suitable for the post he understood was being created.[55] He regarded Leonard as more suited to pure laboratory-based scientific research of the academic kind and likely to become dissatisfied with routine duties.[56] Pearson was even more surprised when, in June 1929, the *Chemist & Druggist* reported the appointment of Dr J. S. Buck, formerly Professor of Chemistry at Duke University, to the company's new experimental research laboratory to be opened at Tuckahoe in September. Pearson also discovered the first entry in the New York accounts referring to 'research laboratories'. An expenditure equivalent to £3,850 rose to £11,222 in 1930, equal to roughly two-thirds of the annual cost of the WBSR. Tuckahoe research expenditure increased to £25,602 in 1938; this compared with the WBSR figure of £35,850.[57]

In 1929 Pearson expressed his concern that such expenditure had been incurred, objected to the appointments made, and complained to Nevin that this was the first intimation he had received either of the appointment or of the new research laboratories.[58] In reply, Nevin explained that Wellcome had been fully consulted on the laboratory project, its expenditure, staffing, the nature of Leonard's duties, and on the direction research should take.[59] On Wellcome's instructions Nevin had visited the finest research laboratories in the US to assist in choosing equipment. His intention was to equip them 'in the most up-to-date, practical but strictly scientific and ethical manner … The apparatus and atmosphere of these laboratories must be thoroughly scientific and ethical but at the same time thoroughly practical.'[60] Not until this had been completed in the autumn of 1929 did Nevin inform Pearson that the research laboratory was equipped to commence research and that Dr L. Reiner, who had been involved in the preparation of the laboratory on a temporary basis since 1928, had become a permanent member of the research staff.[61] Another omission was the appointment of Dr Julia B. Paton to lead vitamin research.[62] At Pearson's request Wenyon, chairman of the STC, produced a report critical of the laboratories which strengthened Pearson's objection. He conceded only that a limited amount of experimentation might be desirable of the kind undertaken in the Experimental Department at Dartford and that 'a distinct tendency' for scientists at

Tuckahoe to undertake academic research should be resisted. Pearson was critical of heavy expenditure associated with laboratory staff and equipment. He drew attention to spare capacity for research existing at Beckenham (which many scientists there would have vehemently denied) where he believed research conducted at Tuckahoe could be carried out as well or better. He criticised expenditure on an animal house built without receiving authorisation from London, and objected to the publication of scientific papers by American staff which made no mention of BW&Co.[63] Nevin informed Pearson that Wellcome had undertaken to deal personally with the various issues arising from policy at Tuckahoe on his return to London.[64] The effect of Wellcome's intervention was to enable Nevin to resist further interference in the management of the American business.[65]

Underlying Pearson's criticisms was resentment at the conspiratorial manner in which the laboratories had been created, staffed, and encouraged to engage in pure research. He complained to Wellcome that the first time he had been informed of the activities of the Tuckahoe research laboratories was by letter in August 1934.[66] Here Pearson seems to have drawn distinctions between three sources of information. In 1929 he had discovered an entry for expenditure on the laboratories in the trading accounts. He learned of the laboratories' existence from Nevin shortly before research began, but only later was he informed directly by Wellcome that he had been personally responsible for deciding on the expenditure. Later, Nevin told Bennett, Pearson's successor, that the laboratories 'were equipped and staffed and gotten under way by Sir Henry himself without consultation with either the general manager of BW&Co. or the WRI staff.'[67] He also remarked that when Pearson visited Tuckahoe to inspect the laboratories his 'attitude and talk almost resulted in 100 per cent resignations.'[68] Wenyon did not visit Tuckahoe until 1939, a brief and unproductive event which did nothing to promote inter-laboratory cooperation.[69]

Organisational culture, trust and corporate sclerosis

Whereas Wellcome moderated and finally ended Pearson's managerial negativity as it affected the development of the American business, Pearson's management of the British company appears to have remained undisturbed. Wellcome's engagement with the American business contrasted with his increasing distance from the management of the British company. The consequences were an ossified organisational culture and advancing corporate sclerosis which Jowett believed seriously weakened the capacity of the company to achieve full potential. Further evidence of a continuing absence of organisational integration was reported by G. H. Warrack who had joined Parish as a research assistant at the WPRL in 1929, subsequently completing a PhD while working there. She referred to a continuing mistrust between heads of departments at the WPRL and those at the Dartford factory: 'Dartford thought that Beckenham were a lazy lot – that they did not have much to show for their research work.'[70] Divisions between the laboratories and the rest of the organisation, between the work ethic of scientists and others, however, were symptomatic of fundamental differences. References later to the 'University of Beckenham' by former employees of BW&Co. and of the Wellcome Trust[71] convey the élite character of the culture of the laboratories in contrast to office and factory. The scholarly ethos had been established in the research laboratories, first under Power and Dowson, and between 1906 and 1914 under Dale, even before the WPRL was moved to Beckenham in 1921. Dale's style of management was open and encouraging to his staff, depending upon personality rather than authority to exercise leadership.[72] His successor, O'Brien, perpetuated the scholarly ethos, organising senior staff meetings, not for discussing policy but to conduct seminars.[73] Researchers were encouraged (and funded) to communicate with other scientists and, like academics, to participate in discussions at scientific meetings and to publish papers.[74]

Unlike employees in office and factory who were strictly controlled by rules rigidly enforced, scientists at Beckenham enjoyed a high degree of freedom. Warrack recalled that 'so long as the routine work was done you could do as much research as you wanted'.[75] Members of staff working in the laboratories were considered to be 'on a higher plane'. She observed colleagues who were enjoying a pleasant life, rewarded by adequate pay, job security, and freedom from the strict regime within BW&Co. This, she believed, bred a snobbery which others resented.[76] This perception of the working lives of those at Beckenham, however, differed from that presented by Parish who referred to O'Brien's use of 'fear and economy' in managing the WPRL.[77] Geographically distant from London and Dartford and regarded as an élite, members of the WPRL were insulated from the business environment because O'Brien ensured that the laboratory staff had minimal contact with other employees of BW&Co. This was not difficult to achieve as senior managers at Snow Hill and the Dartford Chemical Works rarely visited Beckenham. Except for O'Brien, who visited Snow Hill as the 'intermediary' between laboratory staff and other managers, Beckenham scientists neither met nor spoke to their opposite numbers in 'the firm'.[78] The logic of this policy of isolation is revealed in O'Brien's intimation to Wenyon (just before the formation of the STC in 1924) expressing his fear that collaboration between the WPRL and Dartford might gradually crowd out 'pure research' completely.[79] Parish regarded O'Brien's refusal to discuss the financial and other difficulties affecting his role as director of the WPRL as having attracted more criticism than might otherwise have been the case.[80] O'Brien's senior, Charles Wenyon, took a similar view of the role of the laboratories. He became increasingly obsessed with maintaining the scientific independence of the Research Laboratories and was 'firmly opposed to any encroachment of business interests on its scientific activities'.[81] This attitude caused more problems for the company during the interwar period. Wenyon was Director in Chief of the Research Laboratories and Chairman of the STC when he was charged with improving productive collaborative research within the organisation. After Wellcome's death, Wellcome Trustee Henry Dale, former director of the WPRL and a Nobel Laureate and President of the Royal Society, was the first to criticise Wenyon openly for his attitude to the business.[82]

An environment in which croquet on the lawn and common room conversation seemed appropriate was conducive to the distancing of the WPRL from the factory and the counting house. However, divisions also existed within the laboratories because of real or perceived differences in status. Warrack referred to the hierarchical seating conventions at lunch when research directors and other senior staff sat at the heads of tables around which sat graduate researchers, physicians, and veterinary scientists.[83] In keeping with an ethos associated with academic communities, under O'Brien's regime, senior researchers enjoyed independence; no committees of management existed to enable departmental heads in the WPRL to exchange views and discuss policy.[84] Parish recalled: 'Heads would be told in strictest confidence and instructed to refrain from discussion with other heads who might be involved'.[85] O'Brien was believed to adopt reticence in order to avoid trouble, but this resulted in misunderstandings, suspicion, and friction. In the absence of a formal structure for communication between departmental heads, personality assumed an increased importance in the management of the organisation.

In 1942, two years after Bennett was appointed as general manager, he conducted a review of the business and reported his conclusions at a meeting of departmental heads. He perceived under-investment to be the major problem, attributable, he believed, to a managerial policy based on a prevailing historical practice, throughout the organisation, of 'splendid isolation' which he described as 'stupid.' He found a 'fantastic state of affairs' prevailing at Snow Hill. 'Each man … shut himself in a sort of rabbit hutch, pulled down the blinds, and [did] his work, often very well, but without co-operation'.[86] Bennett also expressed amazement that, except for travelling to Germany at his own expense, the Head of the Overseas Department had never been abroad.[87]

Although clashes of personality undoubtedly resulted in tension during the 1920s, the more difficult economic environment of the 1930s introduced further pressure. The potential conflict between the scientific ideal of producing and testing medicines to the highest standards and that of commercial interest faced the scientists with increasingly difficult decisions. The organisation was not well placed to cope with these developments, not least because of O'Brien's insistence on the independence of the laboratories from the commercial enterprise. O'Brien reproved members of his staff and even visitors for referring to the WPRL as Burroughs Wellcome. Parish recalled that O'Brien told his staff that BW&Co. 'did not make our appointments and had no control over our research work or other activities. We were employees of Mr Wellcome's private laboratories entirely independent and unconnected with any selling organisation ... O'Brien led us to believe that sales were not very important, and he was hesitant in putting new products on BW's list.'[88] The purely commercial activities of the organisation were seldom discussed. Although not all other scientists approved of O'Brien's ultra-cautious approach to product development and clinical testing (Parish, for example, referred to it as procrastination), O'Brien's approval was necessary before a commercial launch could take place. It is probable that when O'Brien divulged details of the company's use of Schick testing tests in South Africa to a competing research laboratory in 1928,[89] he may have been ignorant of BW&Co.'s attempt to develop a market in that country. If that was the case, then it is indicative at least of a communications failure between Snow Hill and Beckenham and is consistent with Bennett's 'isolation' model of the company's corporate culture. Otherwise, O'Brien's action was in accordance with the scholarly promotion of the dissemination of knowledge.[90]

It was also consistent with another aspect of the culture which so surprised Bennett when he first joined the company. He pointed to the perversity of pursuing an altruistic policy regardless of commercial interests, citing as an example the handling of the development of Alum Precipitated Diphtheria Toxoid (APT) by A.T.Glenny and C.G.Pope and Pope's method of purifying anti-toxin. The publication of their findings enhanced the laboratories' reputation but they were used subsequently by competing organisations to their commercial advantage and to the disadvantage of BW&Co.[91] An earlier example of conflicting views between scientists and head office occurred during the period 1928 to 1930, when O'Brien and the WPRL scientists opposed the introduction of the company's policy (hitherto long practised by Parke Davis) of replacing vets with retail chemists as exclusive distributors for all veterinary products. This betrayal of the medical profession, as O'Brien regarded it, was implemented in 1930, but only after a wrangle with the profession generated adverse publicity.[92]

O'Brien's approach, entirely consistent with the professed ideal expressed by Wellcome, endured not only after Wellcome's death but also long after Trevan had succeeded O'Brien in 1940.[93] When Sir Michael Perrin became Chairman of the Wellcome Foundation in 1953, he discovered an organisation split in two, in which the laboratories continued a traditional emphasis on research, the cultivation and maintenance of special relationships with the medical profession, and 'a distinctly un-industrial and un-commercial

FIGURE 15.1
George
Pearson, no
date.

outlook. The company tended to look at its job as if it were almost itself a philanthropic operation in the field of the highest quality medical research out of which from time to time some product might come'.[94] His perception implied that the culture that Wellcome deliberately created in the laboratories regarding the relations between them, the factory, and office eventually paralysed the commercial functions of the business. Bennett, too, was critical of Wellcome's inclusion of the Wellcome Research Institution within the Foundation. By so doing, non-business related activities became a direct charge against the company's profits. He observed that 'Wellcome had little or no conception of the kind of organisational form that would be required, either before or after the Second World War, to enable an international business to be directed, managed, and developed.'[95]

The responsibility for this lay squarely with Wellcome when, in effect, he withdrew his unique combination of entrepreneurial skills and scientific credibility which Pearson was not equipped to provide. Wellcome also neglected the question of managerial succession at other levels. No attention was paid to training a younger generation of managers in an organisation which, during the 1930s, was managed at all levels and in every department and laboratory by people whose main experience was either that of commercial success or of scientific achievement. It seems likely that on the birth of his son, Henry Mounteney Wellcome in 1903 when Wellcome was 50, he perceived his son as his successor, following a model historically beloved by autocratic entrepreneurs. This cannot, however, explain Wellcome's disregard for management planning. By 1916, when Mounteney was 13, often alone in a dysfunctional household and inclined to prefer the peace and tranquillity of the countryside, Mounteney's learning disability was unmistakable, both to professionals and Wellcome. Understandable but at once a cause for sadness and deep disappointment to Wellcome, Mounteney's chosen path was farming rather than a life dedicated to business.[96]

Perhaps the distractions resulting from a failed marriage and a son of limited mental capacities explain why Wellcome ignored the fact that his senior managers were ageing and ill-equipped to respond effectively to an increasingly challenging market environment. These limitations certainly applied to Pearson, yet in effect, Wellcome's guidance to the Trustees in setting up the Trust made Pearson his successor in the management of the business, a measure of protection understandable only as a reciprocation of Pearson's longstanding loyalty. An alternative, and far more credible choice, would have been Nevin whose leadership qualities and business judgement had led to Wellcome's commitment to financing the expansion and development of the American company even though he neglected his firm in England. Having made a spectacular success of the American company, Nevin is known to have aspired to lead the entire organisation.[97] Without the increasingly vital financial support from the American business, the very survival of the English company after 1945 would have been even more problematical than it was to prove to be.

Viewed in the long term, adopting a wider perspective beyond the personal shortcomings and failures detectable within the factory, offices, and laboratories and the defective interaction between them, the role of trust emerges as a central theme.[98] The creation and subsequent erosion of trust helped to explain the rise of BW&Co. between 1880 and the First World War and its incipient decline thereafter. In different forms, trust was the key to effecting the transition from a small-scale enterprise supplying proprietary medicines (several of which were barely distinguishable from patent medicines) and dietetic foods to become a major innovator and supplier of ethical medicines. Initially achieved through strict attention to quality of product, ethical advertising followed up by detailing physicians, and chemists and druggists, proved to be an effective strategy between 1880 and the 1890s. Building on this, as a manifestation of Wellcome's genuine aspiration to promote scientific research with the intention of advancing medical knowledge and its practical contribution to mankind, the laboratories he created and the investment made by the company were fundamental to the corporate image associated with science and modernity. These features, displayed through the company's advertisements and communicated by its salesmen, were accompanied by a transformation of the corporate culture. The important concessions he made to laboratory staff – freedom to publish without censorship and to research in areas which they chose – provided the key to gaining the credibility of Wellcome scientists within the wider scientific community. By so doing, Wellcome signalled that the independence of scientists in the Wellcome laboratories was safeguarded even though they were associated with a commercial organisation. The reputation resulting from such a strategy was the key to conducting successful interactions between the company and the medical profession and with government departments.

After 1905 Wellcome's increasingly distant and intermittent involvement in management encouraged the emergence of two competing philosophies perceived by contemporaries to imply conflicting objectives. These replaced the culture of complementarity within the organisation so carefully constructed by Wellcome beginning in the 1890s.: that of the office and factory where the priorities were production, sales, and profits, and that of the laboratory where the scientific ideal prevailed as a higher priority. Before 1914, the trust which had been established within the medical profession had enabled the company to reach pre-eminence in the industry. As the trading and industrial environment became more difficult during the 1920s, the corporate culture created by Wellcome began to be a handicap as the organisation split into two sub-cultures: commercial and scientific. The cultural divide was to survive the Second World War and present a continuing problem to managers and trustees as financial difficulties threatened the company's very existence.

The history of BW&Co. between 1880 and 1940 is central to an explanation why, after the Second World War, the British pharmaceutical industry was to become one of the most successful of all British industries and a major competitor in international markets. An examination of the company's rise and relative decline also highlights a problem of balancing a policy of adherence to the scientific ethic with the pursuit of profitable business. An imperative which presented a peculiarly challenging problem for pharmaceutical manufacturers, this dilemma also has a wider relevance to business. As the competition faced by BW&Co. increased dramatically between the wars, striking the balance between reputation and the trust associated with it and profit became more difficult and contributed to the company's relative decline.

CHAPTER SIXTEEN

Wellcome's influence on pharmaceutical and medical research in Britain

The relative decline in the company's fortunes must not obscure the major impact it made in founding a modern research-based pharmaceutical industry in Britain and in the advancement of medical research. The product, technical, and marketing innovations introduced by BW&Co. have been described in previous chapters. So, too, has the development of the company's in-house research capabilities in the Wellcome Laboratories beginning in 1894, the first to be set up by a commercial enterprise in the British pharmaceutical industry. By creating quasi-'independent' laboratories devoted primarily to research projects which were neither immediately nor directly related to commercial objectives, Wellcome introduced an entirely new class of activity into the embryonic pharmaceutical industry in Britain.[1] The establishment of these laboratories, the introduction and promotion of the procedures introduced at BW&Co., and the precedents that Wellcome created are important in explaining the development of the industry in Britain. They led to changed attitudes within government bodies and within the medical profession with respect to the kind of research that could be conducted within commercial organisations. While pursuing profitable self-interest on behalf of his own organisation, Wellcome's role was central in affecting legislative changes, which benefited the entire industry in the long term. The impact of these innovations and of the scientists trained in the Wellcome Laboratories who spearheaded the industry's development is clear. Wellcome scientists were also in the vanguard of several advances achieved in medical research and medical practice. This was especially so with respect to public health, partly resulting from their research, but also through the influence they exercised through the institutions to which they belonged.

The law and animal experimentation

Possibly the most important contribution Wellcome made to medical research in Britain was his eventual success with the Home Office in 1901 in securing registration of the WPRL under the 1876 Cruelty to Animals Act. This paved the way for applications by other firms, thereby contributing to the establishment and growth of an R & D based pharmaceutical industry in Britain. A concern harboured by government officials that allowing registration would open the floodgates to applications from other manufacturers proved to be groundless, for it was not until November 1905 that the Home Office received a second 'commercial' application. Brady & Martin, a small manufacturer in Newcastle-upon Tyne, lacked experience of bacteriological or physiological work and was without a qualified licence-holder.[2] Surprisingly, considering a previous determination not to use BW&Co. as a precedent, government officials, who included Sir James Russell, the Home Office Inspector for the North of England and Scotland (who referred to Brady & Martin as 'a purely English company')[3] and Thane, the Chief Inspector, readily accepted this application. Thane remarked: 'Wellcome's laboratories having been registered it is not possible to refuse the demand of another manufacturing chemist who makes satisfactory arrangements as to place & person.'[4] Further Home Office memoranda acknowledge that Wellcome's precedent carried important implications for future applications from other British companies and their ability to counter the development and supply of toxin from Germany and the US.[5]

Wellcome's breakthrough was enormously significant for the industry. In 1910 the Runcorn Research Laboratories, indirectly associated with the Evans Medical Company, also achieved registration. Started by Charles Sherrington and other colleagues in Liverpool, these were used to study comparative pathology and the raising of anti-toxins and sera.[6] It was not until the First World War that another pharmaceutical company initiated an application, though May & Baker's laboratories in Wandsworth, South London, were registered in 1916 in very different circumstances to those of both Wellcome and Brady & Martin.[7] Already possessing well-organised chemical laboratories May & Baker responded to wartime demand by embarking on the manufacture of Salvarsan substitutes that required toxicity tests on experimental animals. The company's suitability for registration was not a matter debated within the Home Office. It seems highly unlikely that May & Baker would have been granted registration without the precedent set by the WPRL. Several premises, such as military hospitals and laboratories were granted registration at this time, but only for the duration of the war.[8] In 1919 the laboratories of two more 'commercial' premises were registered: Nathan and Company (the forerunner of the Glaxo Company) and Lever Brothers. These were followed by five more such premises including the new WBSR at Endsleigh Gardens in central London and their separate field laboratories in the following year. Home Office records reveal that all such applications were regarded as routine and considered alongside those from hospitals and university departments.

Registration under the 1876 Act allowed several companies to take immediate advantage of post-war developments, such as insulin, vitamins, and new synthetic drugs, to undertake their own innovative investigative research and to contribute to national and international attempts to standardise medicines, all of which required animal experimentation. Without Wellcome's lead, it seems unlikely that these developments would have been possible. Had Wellcome not been successful, BW&Co. would probably have developed research capabilities on the Continent or in North America. During the protracted negotiations with the Home Office, Wellcome informed his staff: 'I shall seriously consider the question of establishing physiological testing laboratories abroad if we finally fail to get justice at home' and Milan *had* been suggested as a suitable site.[9] Had he done so, undoubtedly other companies would have followed his example with the consequence that a major twentieth century industry would have been lost to Britain.[10]

Standardisation: innovation and diffusion[11]

From the beginning of their partnership in 1880, the production of drugs of consistent content and reliable effect had been a priority for the two partners. Clearly inherited from their American colleagues and former employers, these concerns came into their own once BW&Co. began manufacturing. To ensure quality control of their products, procedures had to be developed and implemented in the factory. These techniques

FIGURE 16.1 Unidentified event, possibly at WPRL, Beckenham, *c*. mid 1920s. Standing fourth from the left in the second row is Henry Dale (with buttonhole); to his left is J. H. Burn; to his left is Percival Hartley.

required the employment, first in the factory and after 1896 in the WCRL, of chemists professionally trained in routine production control and in development work. Although chemical techniques could assess the purity of the majority of the constituents of BW&Co.'s products and confirm the correct formulation and weight of manufactured goods, such methods could not measure the biological efficacy or toxicity of their products. The physiological research expertise that, uniquely, Wellcome introduced into the company ensured a high degree of product reliability. The urgent need for such physiological testing had been a central theme of Wellcome's application for Home Office registration.[12] The production of anti-sera and the need to test and 'measure' accelerated Wellcome's emphasis on stand-ardisation. The skill and experience that his staff subsequently developed led to the creation and improvement of several new techniques. These laboratory procedures were immediately translated into the market. Sera and other goods, such as ergot and digitalis, were advertised as 'physi-ologically standardised'. Product purity and efficacy also became the selling points of the successful 'Wellcome Brand Chemicals' launched in 1902. The Wellcome laboratories, individually and collectively, provided ideal condi-tions for the development of both theoretical concepts and practical testing techniques of standardisation. Uniquely in BW&Co., expertise built up in an environment where commercial requirements for safe, reliable medicines that would sell well were juxtaposed with innovative research into a range of new compounds and therapies. It was an expertise that BW&Co. was to export unwillingly to other companies and to the MRC.

Not until the early 1920s did concerns about therapeutic standards and legislation achieve wider currency in Britain. These were stimulated largely by two pharmacological developments, both involving BW&Co. The first was the urgent wartime need to produce Salvarsan replacements and to ensure stringent toxicity and efficacy testing. Staff from the Works and the research laboratories collaborated closely with the MRC to develop, refine, and establish the requisite manufacturing methods and testing techniques, most of which were later incorporated into national legislative standards for Salvarsan and its derivatives.[13] The second stimulus was the discovery and introduction of insulin. The MRC, which was in charge of national insulin production, soon realised that the initial diversity of measurement techniques combined with major production difficulties experienced by manufacturers trying to produce the hormone, necessitated the introduction of some degree of conformity. Such advances would undoubtedly have occurred without Wellcome, but they would have been much delayed. Without Wellcome's vision there would have been limited practical expertise in standardi-sation in Britain. This would have hampered British companies' ability to take advantage, for example, of the discovery of insulin. The advances of foreign companies, especially Parke, Davis & Co., might well have proved

unchallengeable had not BW&Co. developed effective biological standardisation processes in the WPRL before the First World War.

The weaknesses exposed by war stimulated others to address issues of
pharmaceutical standardisation and testing. The priorities were to develop
collaborative mechanisms to devise workable, agreed standards of toxicity
and efficacy and to formulate appropriate clinical tests of new medicines.
In a memorandum to the Government's Reconstruction Committee, the
MRC called for the establishment of official standards for a limited number
of preparations. In 1919 the Local Government Board (soon to be part of
the new Ministry of Health) asked the MRC to elaborate the requirement
for a national biological standardisation scheme. The following year,
the Ministry of Health decreed that the National Institute for Medical
Research (NIMR) should assume national responsibility for biological
standardisation.[14] Such obligations were undertaken by Dale's Department
of Biochemistry and Pharmacology, the work being shared among all staff
members, although initially Dale and Harold Burn performed most of the
testing experiments. The workload gradually increased to such an extent
that in 1923, Dale recruited Percival Hartley from the WPRL to head a
separate Department of Biological Standards.[15] Dale, Burn, and Hartley had
learned, developed, and refined their analytical techniques at the WPRL,
where they had also been in close contact with the realities of commercial
conditions. Indeed, Dale, who had had his eye on Hartley four years earlier
but was unable to offer him a position, directed him towards the WPRL,

convinced that experience there would
'strengthen his equipment for dealing with
these biological standards'.[16] For men such
as Dale and Wellcome, biological standardisation was not merely an academic exercise
but a critical adjunct of pharmaceutical
manufacture.

Considerable pressure to do something
also came from the industry. In early 1923,
the Association of British Chemical Manufacturers (ABCM), of which BW&Co. was a
member, wrote to the MRC about the possibility of improving co-operation between
manufacturers and clinicians in the testing
of new products.[17] The ABCM suggested that
medical men 'lose caste in the eyes of their
professional brethren' because association
with industry was regarded as 'not quite the
correct thing' in a country and at a time
when 'the correct thing' was of considerable

FIGURE 16.3
Sir Andrew
Balfour.

importance. However, they also pointed to an anomalous situation which was to trouble the WPRL several times during the interwar period.[18] In a clear reference to the Lister Institute and the Inoculation Department of St. Mary's Hospital, the ABCM complain that some 'medical' institutes undertake 'purely commercial investigations and work in close association with industrial firms' without damaging their prestige, whereas those openly and explicitly associated with industrial firms were often stigmatized.[19] The ABCM's appeals to the MRC for help in resolving these tensions went unheeded at the time.

Several other plans and schemes were afoot. The MRC's calls for regulation were partly answered by the passing of the Therapeutic Substances Act in 1925. A limited range of biological materials, including sera, vaccines and hormones and also Salvarsan, were required to reach specified standards of purity, efficacy, and toxicity, many of which had been devised in the laboratories of BW&Co. In the summer of the same year, the DSIR approached several companies, including BW&Co., to discuss collaboration in the large-scale manufacturing of previously imported chemical intermediaries that were required only in small quantities by individual drug firms. Henry, Director of the WCRL, told the STC that 'no success could attend any co-operative effort to encourage and stimulate scientific research and the best way is to allow each firm to make their own arrangement'. He added that it was not in BW&Co.'s interest to share expertise with lesser companies.[20] Other companies seem to have been equally unenthusiastic. Although the DSIR tried to engage the interest of the MRC in the plan, nothing further came of the suggestion.

By 1926, the MRC and the DSIR appointed a Joint Chemotherapy Committee to test new therapies. Eight companies were allowed to submit compounds: BDH, Boots, May & Baker, Howards, Allen & Hanbury, Martindale, John Bell & Croydon, and BW&Co.[21] Once more, BW&Co. expressed considerable reservations about getting involved because of its disproportionately large investment in research. The STC advised that the company should not take part on equal terms with 'some of the small people on the list given who have spent possibly nothing on research'.[22] On the other hand, the STC recognized that if a team of clinicians supported by the

MRC became available to test and validate new compounds, the company would be 'hopelessly handicapped if it rigidly stood aside', as rival companies were now rapidly following its lead on standardisation and testing. The company's cautious reply to the ABCM expressed a 'readiness when the time comes to consider sympathetically any scheme for the co-operation of representatives of manufacturers in some central organising committee'.[23]

In 1927 the Chemotherapy Committee (CC) was formally constituted 'to explore the field for general researches in chemotherapy'. Three of the nine members were former Wellcome staff: Andrew Balfour, George Barger, and Henry Dale who was its chairman, while Harold King (Secretary) had also been employed previously by Wellcome. The objects of the Committee were to 'supervise and correlate' the work of both chemical and biological workers and to liaise with chemical manufacturers in

FIGURE 16.4
Dr Harold
King.

the development and testing of suitable therapeutic compounds.[24] By 1930, of the four companies which had submitted compounds for testing, three were headed by current or former Wellcome staff: BW&Co. (Henry), May & Baker (Ewins), and Boots Pure Drug Co. Ltd (Pyman).[25] However, the CC was criticised for failing to satisfy the original requirements and expectations of the pharmaceutical manufacturers. Delays in getting material tested were considerable; reports from clinicians did not necessarily provide the information manufacturers wanted while 'the development of new medicinal products [was] being seriously handicapped' by the continuing difficulties of arranging proper clinical tests.[26] In early 1931, the company awaited the testing of 16 products, a delay which prompted the STC to try to organise separate trials.[27] Now the problems of pioneering such work became apparent, as the CC, which was already overwhelming sympathetic clinicians with material for testing, viewed such 'independent' trials unfavourably. The MRC's response to pressures from companies was to establish a further body, the Therapeutic Trials Committee (TTC), which reported to the CC and which was charged with the more direct and speedy organisation of trials. The TTC was responsible for organising the widespread testing of digoxin and co-ordinating other trials of the company's products.[28]

People and networks

Wellcome's contribution, direct and indirect, to medical research derived from the training which scientists received in his laboratories, many of those who benefited proceeded to fill senior roles in the profession. One of the comments following his obituary in *The Times* drew attention to Wellcome's shrewdness in choosing staff. By the end of the 1930s, many of those trained in the Wellcome research laboratories and in the factory had moved into every area of medical research in academic, governmental, and industrial settings.[29] We have attempted, in diagrammatic form, to illustrate the influence and impact of a group of Wellcome scientists, among whom are those who held several of the most senior positions in British biomedical science. Figure 16.5 presents a 'snapshot' of British biomedicine

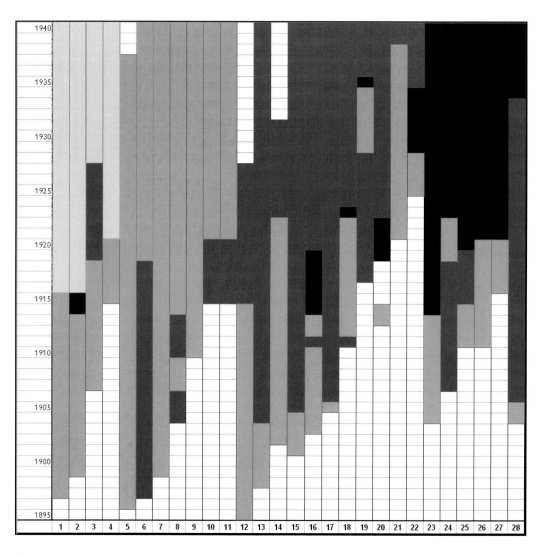

in 1939, showing the careers of 28 scientists, of whom 25 were still alive. Each numbered vertical line represents a named individual who had spent part, or in some cases all, of his career in BW&Co. The list includes one Nobel Laureate, seventeen Fellows of the Royal Society (one of whom also became President), and the then Secretary of the MRC. It also included the heads of research or research divisions of five pharmaceutical companies, the Director, Deputy Director, and three departmental heads of the NIMR, and nine university professors in subjects ranging from chemistry to clinical medicine. Several were awarded civilian honours including seven knighthoods: Balfour (14), Dale (23) who was knighted at the same time as Wellcome, Dalling (21), Gaddum (22), Hartley (24), Laidlaw (25), and Edward Mellanby (28). The diagram also shows the movement of Wellcome staff into different institutional arenas of research and indicates potential for influence extending into several medical areas.

FIGURE 16.5
A diagram-
matic repre-
sentation of
the careers
of selected
scientists
who worked
at BW&Co.
between
1895 and
1939. Each
numbered
vertical line
represents one
man's career.

Key to Figure 16.5

1. F. H. Carr — Experimental Dept.
2. A. J. Ewins — WPRL
3. F. Pyman — Experimental Dept., then WCRL
4. A. Bacharach — WCRL, then Experimental Dept.
5. H. Jowett — WCRL, then Wellcome Chemical Works
6. T. Henry — WCRL
7. A. Glenny — WPRL
8. C. Wenyon — WTRL, then WBSR
9. R. O'Brien — WPRL
10. S. Smith — Experimental Dept.
11. J. Trevan — WPRL
12. F. B. Power — WCRL
13. S. Schryver — WCRL
14. A. Balfour — WTRL, then WBSR
15. J. Mellanby — WPRL
16. G. Barger — WPRL
17. T. R. Elliott — WPRL
18. J. B. Buxton — WPRL
19. E. Hindle — WBSR
20. J. H. Burn — WPRL
21. T. Dalling — WPRL
22. J. H. Gaddum — WPRL
23. H. H. Dale — WPRL
24. P. Hartley — WPRL
25. P. P. Laidlaw — WPRL
26. H. King — WPRL, then Experimental Dept.
27. C. Dobell — WBSR
28. E. Mellanby — WPRL

Wellcome Laboratories

Other pharmaceutical companies

Academic institutions

MRC/NIMR

Companies and industry

Both the model of commercial research laboratories and the techniques of standardisation that Wellcome scientists devised were important influences on the course of the industry's development. However, the success with which BW&Co.'s innovations were emulated by other companies depended to a great extent on aspirant competitors' effectiveness in acquiring 'ready-made' research staff from the Wellcome Laboratories. By 1940 the research directors of no fewer than four other leading pharmaceutical manufacturers had been employed previously by Wellcome. These were Francis Carr at BDH, Arthur Ewins at May & Baker, Frank Pyman at Boots, and Alfred Bacharach at Glaxo (see Figure 16.5).

The process by which this transfer of scientific and management resources occurred and the reaction within BW&Co. were described in chapter 10. The significance of the exodus of senior scientific staff as an explanation of the difficulties experienced by BW&Co. has been referred to above. The importance of the migration for the development of the industry warrants more detailed commentary. Carr's (1 in Fig 16.5) departure to Boots in 1914 was an important trigger for other departures.[30] Marmaduke Barrowcliff, who had left BW&Co. in 1909 for the Department of Agriculture in the Federated Malay States, returned to join Carr at Boots early in 1915. He was later a co-author with Carr of the influential postwar textbook, *Organic Medicinal Chemicals*, which acknowledged the wartime efforts of British chemical companies to synthesise important chemicals, but also re-worked all the chemical processes to maximise economy and yield.[31] Barrowcliff's skill in organic chemical synthesis, largely honed in the Experimental Department at Dartford, enabled him to manufacture saccharine at Boots, for which he was awarded the MBE in 1920. He became Research Manager of ICI in 1931.[32]

As a director at Boots from 1914, Carr continued to be in touch with Barger (16), Ewins (2), Pyman (3), and Dale (23) in trying to resolve problems of the large-scale manufacture of fine chemicals during the war. Carr's efforts, which had been aided by others who had originated from BW&Co., were rewarded with a CBE. His work was instrumental in transforming Boots into a major pharmaceutical manufacturer and a serious rival to BW&Co.[33] In 1920 Carr left Boots to join British Drug Houses, again as a director, retaining his position until retirement in 1951. Yet again, he attracted former colleagues from BW&Co. to join him. After leaving BW&Co. Stanley Underhill qualified in medicine at Guy's Hospital before re-joining Carr at BDH to become director of the 'A&B' insulin production laboratory. In that capacity he ensured regular supplies of the hormone at a time when BW&Co. were sorely in need of such skills. His work on vitamin A was another area of expertise missing from BW&Co. following his departure. Carr's own talents in synthetic procedures, and particularly in the scaling up of laboratory research to industrial manufacture at BW&Co., then at Boots, and finally at BDH, was a unique contribution to the expansion and diversification of the pharmaceutical industry in Britain.

Carr's success and pivotal role in the development of research in the industry often overshadows the contributions of another significant figure in pharmaceutical history. Frank Pyman (3) joined the Experimental Department under Jowett (5) at the Wellcome Chemical Works in 1906. Located within an organisation that also supported its own research laboratories at the WCRL, the Experimental Department might have become a centre for the routine working-up of laboratory procedures to a manufacturing scale. That was not, however, Wellcome's intention, nor was it interpreted in this way by Jowett and Pyman. Separately, jointly, and in collaboration with scientists throughout the organisation, they investigated the relationship between chemical constitution and pharmacological action.[34] This work led to several marketable compounds and it was Pyman's early work with Reynolds, Barrowcliff, and Remfry on arsenical compounds that gave BW&Co. a head start in developing Salvarsan during the First World War.[35] After several years as a Professor in Manchester, during which time he was elected FRS in 1922, Pyman accepted the offer to return to the pharmaceutical industry as Director of Research at Boots in 1927. Thereafter, he continued to establish lines of research and to initiate other projects. Several originated from work begun at BW&Co., especially research on glyoxalines that formed the basis of several manufacturing processes. He also discovered an amidine that, in the hands of his former colleague, Arthur Ewins at May & Baker, proved to be a particularly effective anti-protozoal.[36] Pyman's contributions to pharmaceutical science in Britain were described by one obituarist as 'outstanding'.[37]

A third important figure, Alfred Bacharach (4), was somewhat carelessly discarded by BW&Co. He joined WCRL as a chemist when war began and was moved shortly after to a temporary position in the analytical department of the chemical works because of the severe manpower shortage. In 1919 he returned to the WCRL, where Henry, its Director, sternly reminded Bacharach of his temporary status and told him that no permanent positions were available at the laboratory. Not surprisingly Bacharach left to join Joseph Nathan & Co., later Glaxo Laboratories, where he worked as analyst, chemist, and head of the nutrition department.[38] In particular, he pioneered the standardisation of Glaxo's vitamin products and uniquely became an expert in breeding the homozygous strains of laboratory animals necessary for such assay work.[39] Drawing on his experience in the Wellcome Laboratories, Bacharach's work was enormously important in transforming Glaxo from a food manufacturer into a leading pharmaceutical company.[40]

Arthur Ewins (2) was one of the earliest members of staff at the WPRL, recruited as a schoolboy with Alexander Glenny (7) in 1899. In 1914 he left

C. M. Wenyon

FIGURE 16.6
Dr Charles
Wenyon.

with Dale and Barger to join the Central Research Laboratory (later the NIMR) of the MRC. He took particular responsibility for testing Salvarsan, initially made only by BW&Co., and then later by May & Baker. The high quality of his work, already well known to his former Wellcome colleagues, particularly impressed Robert Blenkinsop of May & Baker and in 1917, led to Ewins's appointment as Director of Research.[41] It was under his immediate direction that May & Baker made their major discovery of the anti-streptococcal agent 'M&B 693' (sulphapyridine) in 1937. Dale described this breakthrough as 'an invaluable contribution to the progress of medicinal chemistry in this country and … research on the chemo-therapy of infections'.[42]

Among those scientists who spent <u>all</u> their careers with the Wellcome organi-sation were Alexander Glenny (7), Henry Parish, and Charles Wenyon (8). Glenny was the schoolboy recruited to the WPRL with Arthur Ewins (2) in 1899, and by the time he was elected FRS in 1944, he had probably done more than anyone else to promote immunisation in Britain, with the possible exception of O'Brien. One commentator claimed that Glenny showed '… [that] first rate research work could be done in a commercial institution, and not only that, but it paid the institution to get it done'.[43] Parish joined the bacteriology department in 1923 to work with Glenny and O'Brien on immunisation. He officially retired nearly 40 years later, after which he devoted himself to historical studies, including an unpublished account of the Wellcome laboratories. Wenyon (8) moved from the London School of Hygiene and Tropical Medicine (LSHTM) where he had spent a year on secondment in the Wellcome Laboratories in Khartoum. After joining the WBSR in 1914, he succeeded Balfour (14) as Director in Chief of the Research Laboratories in 1924 and in 1932, became Director of Research to the Wellcome Foundation. He was elected FRS in 1927 for his contributions to tropical medicine and is credited by some with raising the international reputation of the WBSR to equal that of the LSHTM, an accolade not universally accepted.[44]

Academe

Despite the frequent expression of ambivalent attitudes to the 'commercial' nature of the laboratories, notably by government bodies, the return of several of Wellcome's scientific staff to positions in academic life suggests an absence of prejudice among university scientists. Chemists from the WCRL and, to a lesser extent the Works, had moved easily between industrial and academic laboratories since the beginning of the twentieth century. Several junior staff also passed through the Wellcome laboratories.

The first senior chemist to leave was Power (no. 12 in Figure 16.5), who resigned as the first Director of the WCRL shortly after Balfour was appointed Director-in-Chief of Wellcome's research laboratories, to return to the US as Chemist at the department of Agriculture in Washington, DC. In the UK experienced research staff were particularly needed as new educational establishments were created. These include Samuel Schryver who became Lecturer in Physiological Chemistry at UCL after leaving the WPRL in 1901. Subsequent appointments at the Cancer Institute London and the Imperial College of Science culminated in a Professorship of Biochemistry at Imperial College in 1920. He was elected FRS eight years later.[45] Similar opportunities opened up for Harold Rogerson who had worked for seven years with Power at the WCRL on plant products before moving to Guy's Hospital at the beginning of 1914 as Lecturer in Chemistry, and after the war was recruited to help develop the chemistry department at the expanding University of Liverpool.[46] George Barger (16), the chemist at the WPRL had a less straightforward relationship to academe. In 1908 he became head of Chemistry at Goldsmith's College, and four years later Professor of Chemistry at Royal Holloway College. Throughout he retained a 'part time consulting connexion' with the WPRL, and was still regarded as a member of staff.[47] It may well be that the professorial salaries were insufficient (this was still an age of pluralism for many academics, as salaries were so poor), or the facilities for research inadequate or non-existent, but Barger continued to be on the BW&Co. payroll until 1914. From the Experimental Department at the Works, Frank Pyman (3) became Professor of Technological Chemistry at the University of Manchester in 1919. The reasons for Pyman's move after thirteen years with

FIGURE 16.7
Dr Frederick
Belding
Power.

BW&Co. are obscure: an obituarist hints at 'certain irksome features which he never confided to his staff turned his mind to a professional career'.[48] What were those 'irksome features'? By 1919 the chemical expertise within BW&Co. had been greatly depleted, yet the demands had intensified, and having born a heavy burden throughout the war years, Pyman may have desperately wanted a change. Whatever the reasons, yet another senior, distinguished, dedicated Wellcome scientist departed BW&Co. at a critical time. He was soon to return to the pharmaceutical industry, but to Boots, not BW&Co.

Unlike chemists who, as a profession, had a longer history of undertaking industrial work, medically qualified staff had no such tradition of movement into and out of commercial companies. The view offered to Dale (23) when he was considering an appointment at the WPRL in 1904, was that he would be selling his birthright 'for a mess of commercial pottage', a judgement which epitomises anti-business prejudice.[49] However, researchers from the WPRL found that they could move easily between BW&Co. and medical academe. An early example was John Mellanby (15), who was employed as the first physiologist at the WPRL in 1900 before leaving three years later to complete his clinical training. Mellanby, later Professor of Physiology at St. Thomas' Hospital and later still at Oxford, explained to Wellcome how he valued that early training and experience.

> I should like to thank you for the great facilities which I enjoyed in your laboratories at Brockwell Hall. I retain the pleasantest recollections of my work there and I am certain that my contributions to Medical Science are largely due to my original experiences in your Research Laboratories.[50]

The quotation begs a question: would John Mellanby have become a distinguished professional scientist without that early experience? His comments certainly suggest that working for BW&Co. significantly affected his career trajectory, as it did those of several of the other scientists included in Figure 16.5.

Veterinarians, too, encountered no opposition when transferring from the Wellcome Laboratories to university posts or to their efforts to influence professional bodies. One of the most distinguished was Thomas Dalling

(20) who succeeded Basil Buxton (18) at the WPRL in 1923, and later became Professor of Animal Pathology at Cambridge in 1937.[51] It was to Dalling, for his work at the WPRL, that Northumbrian sheep farmers proposed erecting a golden statue.[52]

The reputation of BW&Co.'s laboratories was such that it also attracted staff from established university positions. These included Thomas Henry (6) and Clifford Dobell (27), both of whom moved to the WCRL after several years at the Imperial Institute. John Trevan's (11) academic career began at Bedford College before moving to the WPRL in 1920 and Edward Hindle (18) brought particular recognition to the laboratories as the first Beit Fellow allowed to work in a non-University setting. These transfers and movements provide clear evidence that working at BW&Co. was not considered as a 'stop-gap' before achieving more respectable employment, but offered a desirable career opportunity. In addition to formally contracted staff, the Wellcome laboratories played host to several scientists, often at the beginning of their professional careers. An early beneficiary was Edward Mellanby (27), who spent some weeks whilst a Cambridge medical student working with his brother John at the WPRL. That first exposure to an active laboratory engaged on a number of different investigations and projects profoundly influenced Mellanby, directing his career towards a lifetime in medical research. He became Professor of Pharmacology at the University of Sheffield, was elected FRS in 1925, and was Secretary of the Medical Research Council. Writing to Wellcome in 1931, Mellanby recalled his period at the WPRL:

> ... It stands as a kind of landmark in my life ... because I had my first experience of research there. More than any other experience it helped in the crystallisation of my very amorphous mind and led me to a career of physiological and medical research.[53]

FIGURE 16.9
Professor John
Mellanby.

FIGURE 16.10
Dr John
Trevan.

Another visitor to the WPRL at the beginning of his career was Thomas Elliott (17), elected FRS in 1913. He became Professor of Medicine at University College London.[54] Never a BW&Co. employee but a grateful beneficiary of Wellcome's hospitality at an early stage of his career, Elliott had been a student of J.N. Langley at Cambridge. He worked on the physiological effects of adrenaline and collaborated at the WPRL on significant experiments with Henry Dale who was then beginning his own research career. Dale later recorded his indebtedness to Elliott: '... you gave me, at a rather critical juncture, much needed encouragement, advice and even personal collaboration, in the week which first put me on the track for all that has followed'.[55] Elliott became a member of the MRC and, of particular relevance to BW&Co., became one of the first two scientific trustees of the Wellcome Trust. The joint acceptance of such duties in 1936 by Elliott and Dale owed much to their friendship and mutual respect, which began with those early experiments at the WPRL. Dale's later recollections of facing the obligations put upon them by Wellcome's Will specifically stress the importance of Elliott '... I felt already that the association with you [Elliott] was the only condition, which would make it possible for me to share such a new kind of responsibility'.[56] As Wellcome Trustees, Dale and Elliott played decisive roles in the future of the Wellcome Laboratories that had, of course, played a decisive part in their own careers.[57]

The Royal Society and other professional organisations

Fellowship of the Royal Society has long been regarded as the highest national accolade a scientist can achieve in Britain. Seventeen of the 28 individuals depicted in Figure 16.5 became Fellows, an astonishing record for any organisation.[58] Whatever reservations there may have been in some quarters about the suitability of Wellcome scientists, there were none whatsoever at the Royal Society when it came to assessing the quality of their work. In 1914 Dale was the first to be so honoured, shortly before he left the WPRL.[59]

Although many achieved Fellowship after employment with Wellcome: Pyman (3), Schyrver (13), both Mellanbys (15 & 27), Barger (16), Hindle (18),

Burn (19), Gaddum (21), Hartley (23), Laidlaw (24), and King (25) all achieved the recognition for work either completed or begun in the Wellcome laboratories. Like Dale, several achieved the distinction while employed by Wellcome. These include Glenny (7), Wenyon (8), Trevan (11), and Dobell (26); only Ewins (2) did so whilst a member of another pharmaceutical company. Arthur Ewins's case clearly emphasises the importance of the Wellcome phase of his career during which he wrote 30 papers. Thereafter, he produced only nine publications, some of which Dale described as 'left over, as it were, from … earlier collaboration in the Wellcome Laboratories', and it was for that early work that he was honoured.[60]

Several of these Fellows in Figure 16.5 achieved further merit within the Royal Society by serving on the Council, delivering a noteworthy eponymous lecture to the Society, or receiving one of the Society's medals, all signs of even higher distinction. Dale achieved the highest honour the Society had to offer when he became President in 1940. The President admitted two new Fellows, Glenny (7) and Ewins (2), who had been his former colleagues at the WPRL. In later years, Dale and Elliott also proposed Wellcome for election under special statute for his services to science. In suggesting the move, Dale acknowledged 'I, of course, have very special reason for personal gratitude to him … [election] would give him more pleasure than anything else the world could give.'[61] Wellcome was elected FRS in 1932.[62]

Another area of influence of Wellcome 'graduates' can be measured by the roles they played in academic societies and committees, for example, in chemical research the Council of the Chemical Society, the premier chemical

FIGURE 16.12
Scientific staff of the WPRL, 1914, shortly after Henry Dale's election to the Royal Society. Standing: G. S. Walpole, A. T. Glenny (FRS 1944), J. H. Burn (FRS 1942), J. B. Buxton, A. J. Ewins (FRS 1943); Seated: G. H. K. MacAlistair, George Barger (FRS 1919), Henry Dale (FRS 1914), R. A. O'Brien and H. J. Sudmersen.

FIGURE 16.13
Election of
Sir Henry
Wellcome as
FRS, signed
by Henry
Dale, then
one of the
Secretaries
of the Royal
Society, 1932

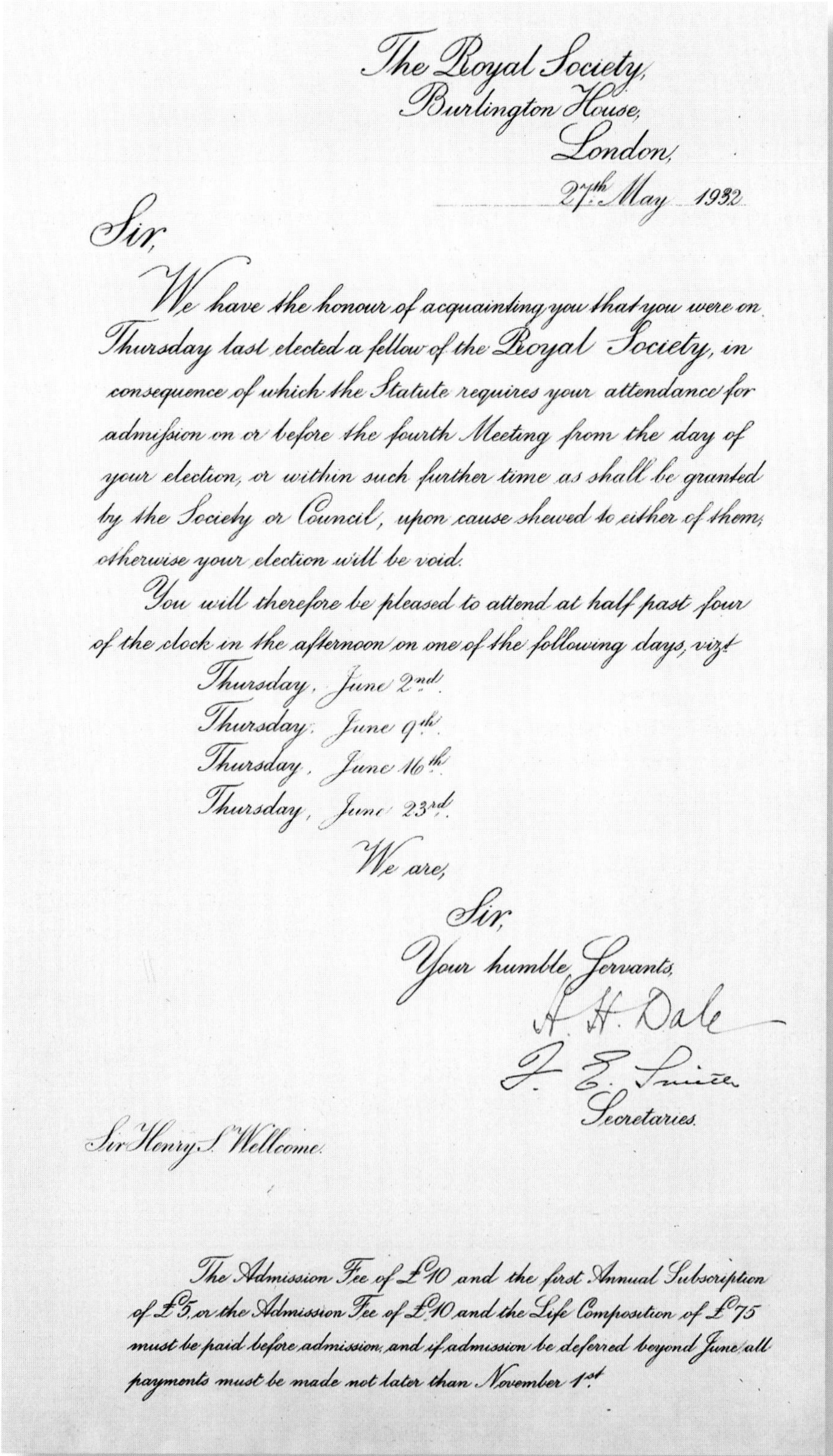

The Royal Society,
Burlington House,
London,
27th May 1932

Sir,

We have the honour of acquainting you that you were on Thursday last elected a fellow of the Royal Society, in consequence of which the Statute requires your attendance for admission on or before the fourth Meeting from the day of your election, or within such further time as shall be granted by the Society or Council, upon cause shewed to either of them; otherwise your election will be void.

You will therefore be pleased to attend at half past four of the clock in the afternoon on one of the following days, vizt

Thursday, June 2nd.
Thursday, June 9th.
Thursday, June 16th.
Thursday, June 23rd.

We are,

Sir,

Your humble Servants,

H. H. Dale
F. E. Smith
Secretaries.

Sir Henry S. Wellcome.

The Admission Fee of £10 and the first Annual Subscription of £5, or the Admission Fee of £10 and the Life Composition of £75 must be paid before admission, and if admission be deferred beyond June all payments must be made not later than November 1st.

body in the UK, included a member, or former member, of BW&Co. for more than 20 years: Jowett (1906–09), Barger (1913–17, 1937–39), Henry (1917–30), Carr (1920–23), and Pyman, (1916–19, 1924–27, 1930–33).[63]

The Medical Research Council and the National Institute for Medical Research

The single main beneficiary of the research experience and grounding fostered by the Wellcome laboratories was undoubtedly the Medical Research Committee (Council). Indeed, it could be argued that the Wellcome laboratories, the WPRL in particular, provided the prototype for the National Institute for Medical Research, the leading research establishment of the MRC. By 1939 several former BW&Co. staff occupied senior positions there: the Director was the Nobel Laureate Sir Henry Dale (23), and the Deputy Director was Sir Patrick Laidlaw (25). The Head of Biological Standards was Sir Percival Hartley (24), and present or past senior staff included Ewins (2); Barger (16); Dobell (27); King (26); Burn (20); Buxton (18), and Gaddum (22).

An early decision of the MRC, created in 1913 as a consequence of the National Insurance Act of 1911, was to establish its own Central Research Institute, and to which Dale, Barger and Ewins of the WPRL were all recruited just before the First World War.[64] Not surprisingly, the personal and professional connections between former Wellcome staff continued. An early illustration concerned the wartime supply of flavine which Dale had identified as an effective antiseptic. A dye company was asked to produce a supply for the MRC, which they agreed to do, on condition that no other company was involved. After considerable delay, Dale received a consignment of the dye labelled 'Avalon' and with a trade-mark pending: the unidentified company had delayed production until they had almost acquired trade-marked protection. Dale was furious, and immediately contacted Francis Carr, by then head of research at Boots. Carr rapidly produced a supply of the antiseptic and applied to the Controller of Patents for a trade-mark, thus confounding the original application and stopping a monopoly supply of a substance originally identified by the MRC. Dale's experiences working at the WPRL clearly informed his actions in this situation. Not only was he confidently knowledgeable about the relevant patent legislation, he also had the personal and professional contacts to circumvent what he saw as underhand behaviour.

The post-war research programme at the NIMR was largely determined by work that Dale had started at the WPRL. The departure of Dale, Barger and Ewins had completely depleted the physiological/chemical resources of the WPRL, and the type of work they had initiated there on the physiologically active constituents of ergot was not continued. By the end of the First World War both Dale's co-workers had moved elsewhere: Ewins to May &

Baker, and Barger to be Professor of Medicinal Chemistry at the University of Edinburgh. To fill these vacancies Dale recruited Harold Dudley, a British chemist then working in New York, and Harold King, yet another Wellcome employee.[65] King (25 in Fig 16.5) had spent most of his Wellcome career in the Works' Experimental Department, apart from a few months in 1913 at the WPRL when he first joined the organisation. Then he had joined Dale and Barger in their ergot work, and continued the collaboration after transfer to the Works.[66] Much of his work for the MRC, from which he retired in 1950, stemmed from his days at BW&Co. and were entirely in keeping with the research agenda that Dale developed for his department: studies on arsenical compounds and Salvarsan; and the isolation of active alkaloids including the discovery of muscarine and tubocurarine. For many years King also served as the chemical secretary of the Chemotherapy Committee.[67]

Dale continued to recruit former WPRL colleagues for other areas of the NIMR's work. Patrick Laidlaw (25), the schoolboy he had known whilst a student at Cambridge and whom he later employed at the Wellcome laboratories, was appointed to the NIMR in 1922. There Laidlaw and Dale resumed work they started at the WPRL on histamine and anaphylactic shock. Laidlaw's work on canine distemper vaccine was also of critical importance, despite the setbacks referred to in Chapter 12. When Dale recruited yet another WPRL employee, Buxton (18), to assist in the distemper work, he drew an anguished protest from the WPRL Director, R.O'Brien, 'I am getting a bit scared about raids on the WPRL staff'.[68]

FIGURE 6.14
Sir John
Gaddum.

J.H.Gaddum (21) also came to the NIMR from the WPRL, and was to occupy several major positions in academic pharmacology. He was a 'second generation' recruit from the WPRL – he had not been there in Dale's time. It was Sir Frederick Gowland Hopkins, a frequent behind-the-scenes figure in the history of BW&Co., who had directed him towards the WPRL.[69] From January 1925, Gaddum assisted Trevan, who initiated him into pharmacological research just as he was re-aligning his own work after years of regularising BW&Co.'s insulin production.[70] Two years later Gaddum took the already well-worn route to the NIMR to join Dale's department in Hampstead, before becoming successively Professor of Physiology at Cairo, Professor of Pharmacology at UCL, and then Professor of Pharmacology at the College of the Pharmaceutical Society in 1938. He became renowned for his work on lysergic acid diethylamide (LSD) and its effects on brain, work clearly following in the research tradition established by Dale at the WPRL before the First World War. After war service Gaddum became Professor of Materia Medica at Edinburgh, and then Director of the Agricultural Research Council's Institute of Animal Physiology in Babraham, Cambridge in 1958. Elected FRS in 1945, he served on the Royal Society's Council from 1954–6, was a member of the Medical Research Council from 1948 to 1951, and was knighted in 1964.

These sample careers are testimony to the impact of Wellcome's scientific enterprise on medical research, which his establishment of the Wellcome Trust was to perpetuate to a degree which Wellcome could hardly have imagined. The history of BW&Co. is the history of a business which created a modern, research-based pharmaceutical industry and which, albeit in the longer run, generated the wealth that enabled the Trust to become the largest private funder of medical research in Britain.

Notes and references

Notes to Chapter 1: From trading to manufacturing; S. M. Burroughs & Co. and Burroughs Wellcome & Co., 1878–1888

1. Robert Rhodes James, *Henry Wellcome* (The Wellcome Trust and Hodder & Stoughton, 1994), pp. 71–5.
2. Tom Mahoney, *The Merchants of Life, An Account of the American Pharmaceutical Industry* (Harper & Brothers, New York, 1959), p. 32.
3. Ibid.
4. Ibid., pp. 38–46; 48–9.
5. See below pp. 15–17.
6. Nathan Rosenberg (ed.), *The American System of Manufactures* (Edinburgh University Press, 1969), Introduction.
7. Jonathan Liebenau, *Medical Science and the Medical Industry. The Formation of the American Pharmaceutical Industry* (Macmillan, Basingstoke, 1987), p. 20.
8. L. G. Matthews, *History of Pharmacy in Britain* (E. and S. Livingstone, Edinburgh, 1962), pp. 319–21.
9. Jonathan Liebenau, 'Marketing high technology: educating physicians to use innovative medicines', in J. P. T. Davenport-Hines (ed.), *Markets and Bagmen* (Aldershot, 1986), pp. 82–6. However, Liebenau places this development in the 1890s, whereas we show that these marketing methods were being employed in the US in the 1870s; Landau, R., B. Achilladelis, and A. Scriabine, *Pharmaceutical Innovation: Revolutionising Human Health* (London, Chemical Heritage Press, 2000), pp. 48–51.
10. Idem, 'Ethical business: the formation of the pharmaceutical industry in Britain, Germany, and the United States, before 1914', *Bus. Hist.*, XXX (1988), pp. 116–20.
11. Mahoney, *Merchants of Life*, p. 31.
12. Ibid.
13. WFA, Horton LB40, 283, Horton to Heselton, 22 April 1895.
14. Archives of the University of the Sciences in Philadelphia, College of Pharmacy Box, John Wyeth to Prof Robert Bridges, 24 Feb., 1877; manila envelope. Burroughs was said to have been with the firm 'almost continuously since October 1869 and has exhibited a laudable interest in this business and has conducted himself in every way satisfactorily'.
15. John Davies, 'Silas M. Burroughs, Part 1: The Early

Years From Medina to Medicines', *Wellcome Journal*, Feb. 1991, pp. 10–11.
16. Archives of the University of the Sciences in Philadelphia, College of Pharmacy Box, Silas Mainville Burroughs, 'An inaugural essay on the compression of medicinal powders', pp. 1–8.
17. WFA, Acc. 82/1 Box 15, John Wyeth to Burroughs, 13 April 1881.
18. Rhodes James, *Henry Wellcome*, pp. 71–2.
19. *The British and Colonial Druggist*, 8 Feb. 1895.
20. WFA, Acc. 82/1 Box 15, John Wyeth to Burroughs, 13 April 1881
21. Ibid.
22. See below, chapter 2, pp. 62–6. For a more detailed account of the history of Burroughs' firm and an evaluation of his contribution to the trade in Britain see Roy Church, 'The British market for medicine in the late nineteenth century; the innovative impact of S. M. Burroughs & Co.', *Med. Hist.*, 2005, 49, pp. 281–98.
23. The practice and its further development is examined in detail in chapter 2.
24. WFA, Acc. PP110, 'Medical formulae of new and improved chemical preparations', 1881. The list and accompanying text refer to several products supplied before 1880.
25. Wellcome's evidence in the Tabloid case is reported fully in *Med. Times & Gaz.*, 19 Dec. 1903, p. 812.
26. Such a policy also avoided Stamp Duty which was to cause a major change in the partnership's approach to business during the 1880s, see below, pp. 34–7. Burroughs' claim to be the first to introduce compressed medicine into Britain appears in a letter written to the *Chem. & Drug.*, 40, May 1892, p. 75. Tweedale's account of the introduction of compressed medicine by Allen & Hanbury, who placed orders for an American rotary machine in 1876, raises the possibility that this company was ahead of Burroughs by one or possibly two years. Geoffrey Tweedale, *At the Sign of the Plough, Allen & Hanburys and the British Pharmaceutical Industry, 1715–1990* (Glaxo Pharmaceuticals Ltd and John Murray, 1990), p. 81.
27. Quoted in 'Medical formulae', WFA, PB 110, p. 32.

28. Rhodes James, *Henry Wellcome*, p.72.
29. Geoffrey Tweedale, *At the Sign of the Plough*, chapters 3 and 4.
30. *Commissioner of Patents Journal*, 11 Dec. 1877, p.1391.
31. WFA, Acc. 99/6/7, 30 Dec. 1878.
32. Ibid.
33. WFA, Acc. 99/6/7, Memorandum of Association, 22 Oct. 1879.
34. Ibid.
35. WFA, Acc. 99/6/7, Lockwood to BW&Co. 22 Oct. 1879, 9 April 1881; WFA, Acc. 99/6/7, Memorandum of Association, 20 Oct. 1879.
36. WFA, Acc. 90/1 Box 149, BW&Co., Balance Sheets Aug. 1880–Aug. 1939. See below, chapter 4.
37. See below, chapter 5.
38. WFA, Burroughs LB35, Box 523, Burroughs to Wyeth, 13, 19 June 1878.
39. Ibid., Burroughs to Kelley, 22 Oct. 1878; WFA, Acc. 82/1, Box 15, John Wyeth to Wellcome, 9 July 1880.
40. WFA, Burroughs LB36, Box 523, Burroughs to L.W.Warner & Co., NY, 18 March 1879.
41. WFA, Acc. 99/6/7, KMEC balance sheets, WFA.
42. Rhodes James, *Henry Wellcome*, p.141, footnote.
43. See chapter 3, pp.73–4.
44. Tweedale, *At the Sign of the Plough*, p.81.
45. *Chem. & Drug.*, 32, 28 Jan. 1888, pp.104–6.
46. Ibid.
47. Rhodes James, *Henry Wellcome*.
48. Joseph W. England (ed.), *The First Century of the Philadelphia College of Pharmacy* (Philadelphia College of Pharmacy and Science, 1922), pp.207–8.
49. The following paragraph is based on Rhodes James, *Henry Wellcome*, chapter 2.
50. Ibid., pp.68–9.
51. Rhodes James refers to a holiday, *Henry Wellcome*, p.71 whereas, writing in 1920, Joseph W. England of the College of Pharmacy referred to a joint venture. England (ed.), *The First Century*, pp.207–8.
52. WFA, Wellcome LB3, 9, Wellcome to Fred Wellcome, 1 Jan. 1895.
53. WFA, Wellcome PE/C 12, A.W. Haggis, 'The life and work of Sir Henry Wellcome' unpublished typescript [hereafter, Haggis, 'Life and work'] pp.80–99; Rhodes James, *Henry Wellcome*, chapter 3.
54. Quoted by Haggis, 'Life and work', p.80.
55. Rhodes James, *Henry Wellcome*, pp.82–3.
56. Ibid., p.86.
57. Anne Hardy, *Medicine in Britain Since 1860* (Palgrave, 2001), pp.22–8; P. Weindling, 'Changing patterns of sickness in the nineteenth century', in Andrew Wear (ed.), *Medicine in Society: Historical Essays* (Cambridge, 1992), pp.305–6.
58. Christopher Lawrence, *Medicine in the Making of Modern Britain, 1700–1920* (1994), p.64.
59. Landau, Achilladelis, and Scriabine (eds), *Pharmaceutical Innovation*, pp.26–9; Jordan Goodman, 'Pharmaceutical industry', in R. Cooter and J. Pickstone (eds), *Medicine in the Twentieth Century* (Amsterdam, Harwood Academic, 2000), p.143.
60. Miles Weatherall, *In Search of a Cure: A History of Pharmaceutical Discovery* (Oxford, 1990), pp.36–37.
61. W. Bynum, *Science and the Practice of Medicine* (Cambridge, 1994), pp.119, 141, 226.
62. Landau, Achilladelis, and Scriabine, *Pharmaceutical Innovation*, p.38.
63. The largest German company, Bayer, established a laboratory solely for the purpose of product innovation in 1885 (the last of the German fine chemical manufacturers to do so), which was replaced by a larger Main Laboratory in 1891, regarded as the most modern company laboratory at that time. Pharmaceutical and Bacteriological Laboratories were built in 1902. Ulrich Marsch, 'Strategies for success: research organisation in German chemical companies and I.G. Faben until 1936', *History and Technology*, 12, 1994, pp.25–31; Ernst Homburg, 'The emergence of research laboratories in the dyestuffs industry, 1870–1900', *British Journal for the History of Science*, 25 (1992), pp.91–102.
64. Landau, Achilladelis, and Scriabine, *Pharmaceutical Innovation*, pp.30–4.
65. Judged by the criterion of therapeutic outcomes, apart from the new pain-killing and fever-reducing drugs, the results of medical research before 1880 were limited. They indicate, however, the discernible trends current at the time and the nature of changes to the environment when BW&Co. first began to manufacture medicines. Anne Hardy, *Health and Medicine in Britain Since 1860*, pp.22–8.
66. Hardy, *Health and Medicine*, p.180, table 1.
67. Anne Digby, *Making a medical living: doctors and patients in the English market for medicine, 1720–1911'* (Cambridge, Cambridge University Press, 1994), table 1.1.
68. S. D. Chapman, *Boot of Boots the Chemists* (1974), pp.11–30; T. A. B. Corley, 'The British Pharmaceutical Industry since 1851', unpublished paper.
69. Anne Digby, *The Evolution of British General Practice* (Oxford, OUP, 1999), p.192.
70. Hardy, *Health and Medicine*, p.35.
71. Harmke Kamminga, 'Nutrition for the people, or the fate of Jacob Moleschott's contest for a humanist science', in Harmke Kamminga and Andrew Cunningham (eds), *The Science and Culture of Nutrition, 1840–1940* (Rodopi, Amsterdam-Atlanta, GA, 1995), pp.15–34; Mark R. Finlay, 'Early marketing of the theory of nutrition: the science and culture of Liebig's Extract of Meat', in ibid., pp.48–66.
72. F. Peckel Moller, *Cod Liver Oil and Chemistry* (Peter Moller, 1895, London, Norway, New York and Copenhagen), pp.lv–lviii.
73. G. Tweedale, *At the Sign of the Plough*, pp.74–9.
74. Finlay, 'Early marketing of the theory of nutrition', pp.48–66.
75. Liebenau, 'Ethical business', pp.116–29.
76. *Chem. & Drug.*, 26, 26 June 1886, p.630.
77. Digby, *Evolution*, p.37.

78. The following paragraphs are based on the excellent thesis by Anna Simmons, 'The chemical and pharmaceutical activities of the Apothecaries' Hall', unpublished PhD thesis (Open University, 1993), chapters 5 and 6.

79. Deduced from Simmons, thesis, based on Graphs B and C, Appendix D.

80. Ibid., p. 240.

81. S. W. F. Holloway, *Royal Pharmaceutical Society of Great Britain, 1841–1991: A Political and Social History* (Pharmaceutical Press, 1991), pp. 34–45.

82. Simmons, thesis, pp. 287–8.

83. Judy Slinn, 'Research and development in the UK pharmaceutical industry from the nineteenth century to the 1960s', in Roy Porter and Mikulas Teich (eds) *Drugs and Narcotics in History* (Cambridge, 1995), pp. 168–86.

84. Jonathan Liebenau, 'Thomas Morson', in David J. Jeremy (ed.), *Dictionary of Business Biography*, 4 (Butterworth, 1985), pp. 346–7. WFA, T. Morson & Son Ltd, papers, SA/MOR/F2 (1–3), Box 7, Private Ledgers; MOR/F/1–10 Box 6, Accounts, 1878–97; Jonathan Liebenau, 'Sir Thomas Morson', in Jeremy (ed.), *Dictionary of Business Biography*, 4 (Butterworth, 1986), pp. 346–7.

85. See below, chapter 2.

86. These included hydrochloric and nitric acid, crystalline silver nitrate, trinitrate of bismuth, camphor, calomel, sulphate of zinc, precipitates of mercury, acetate of potash and zinc, sulphate of zinc and chlorate of potash. Judy Slinn, *A History of May & Baker, 1834–1984* (Hobsons, Cambridge, 1984), chapter 2.

87. Ibid., p. 57.

88. Jonathan Liebenau, 'Whiffen', in David J. Jeremy (ed.), *Dictionary of Business Biography*, 5 (Butterworth, 1986), pp. 763–4; Tweedale, *At the Sign of the Plough. Allen & Hanburys and the British Pharmaceutical Industry, 1715–1990* (John Murray, 1990), pp. 83–5.

89. Tweedale, *At the Sign of the Plough*, p. 91.

90. Rhodes James, *Henry Wellcome*, p. 86.

91. WFA, Acc. 90/1, Account ledger; Acc. 82/1 Box 28, Sales of BW&Co.

92. WFA, PB/110, *Med. Press & Circ.*, 3 Aug. 1881.

93. Ibid.

94. WFA, Wellcome LB10, 18, Sudlow to Wellcome, 16 Dec. 1881. In the event, external funds were not needed, 22, Sudlow to Wellcome, 31 Dec. 1881.

95. WFA, Wellcome LB1, Wellcome to Bishop, 22 Oct. 1883.

96. WFA, Acc. 82/1 Box 16, Burroughs to Wellcome, 16 Sept., 25 Sept. 1884.

97. Rhodes James, *Henry Wellcome*, p. 141; WFA, Acc. 82/1, Box 28, Sales of BW&Co.

98. WFA, Acc. 82/1 Box 28, Burroughs v. Wellcome memorandum; WFA, Acc. 90/1, Account ledger.

99. WFA, Wellcome LB10, 62–8, Wellcome to Burroughs, 16 Feb. 1882; WFA, Acc. 82/1 Box 13; WFA, Wellcome LB10, 110, Wellcome to Burroughs, 26 May 1882 '... now doing business for over £1,500 per month, and nearly this we are paying out for goods and expenses ...'

100. Obituary, 'A leader among men', *Pharm. Era*, 21, 6 June 1895, pp. 720–2; WFA, Acc. 82/1 Box 23. During the first four years of the partnership, whereas Wellcome withdrew £4,146, Burroughs' withdrawals amounted to £71,468.

101. WFA, Acc. 82/1 Box 15, Wyeth to Burroughs, 13 April 1881, 'We thought that ... as soon as Mr Wellcome became associated with you that he would exert an influence and keep you in check in the matter of unnecessary expenditure in circular matter etc ...'

102. WFA, Acc. 82/1 Box 13, Burroughs to Wellcome, 19 June 1882.

103. WFA, Acc. 99/6/7, Memorandum of Association, 1 Jan. 1881; 'Kepler Malt Extract Co.'.

104. Ibid.

105. WFA, Acc. 99/6/7, Lockwood to Garner, 18 March 1881; Lockwood to Burroughs Wellcome, 9 April 1881; Lockwood to Garner, 13 April 1881.

106. Ibid., Burroughs to Kepler Board of Directors, 1881.

107. Ibid.

108. Ibid., Burroughs to Gardner, 20 April 1881.

109. Ibid., Lockwood to Burroughs Wellcome, 25 May 1881.

110. WFA, Acc. 82/1, Box 16, Augustine Birrell, 'Legal opinion', 2 Nov. 1881.

111. WFA, Acc. 99/6/7, Box 16, Augustine Birrell, 'Legal opinion', 14 July 1881.

112. WFA, Wellcome LB2, 3, Wellcome to Burroughs, 6 Dec. 1881.

113. PP/SMB/6, Burroughs to Wellcome, 25 April 1882.

114. Ibid.

115. WFA, Wellcome LB5, Wellcome to Burroughs, 6 Dec. 1881.

116. WFA, Acc. 82/1 Box 16. KMEC Special Meeting, 21 Aug. 1882.

117. Ibid.

118. WFA, Acc. 99/6/7, Smith to Wellcome, 1908, 8 Dec. 1909.

119. WFA, Acc. 82/1 Box 13, Sudlow to Wellcome.

120. WFA, Acc. 82/1 Box 13, Pearson, 'A Chronology', p. 2; WFA, Wellcome LB1, 34, Wellcome to Burroughs, 19 Sept. 1882.

121. WFA, Wellcome LB1, 50, Wellcome to Buck, 26 Oct. 1882.

122. WFA, Wellcome LB10, 18, Sudlow to Wellcome, 22 Dec. 1881; WFA: Wellcome LB1, Wellcome to Burroughs, 30 Sept. 1882.

123. Quoted by Rhodes James, *Henry Wellcome*, p. 108.

124. WFA, Wellcome LB10, 115. Wellcome to Burroughs, n.d.

125. See above p. 22. WFA, Acc. 82/1, Box 19, 'Sites', London memo, 17 March 1914. Acc. 82/1, Box 19; Wellcome to Burroughs, 6 Dec. 1881. WFA Wellcome LB10, 4; Wellcome to Bishop, 18 Aug. 1882. WFA, Wellcome LB10, 155.

126. WFA, Wellcome LB1, 36, Wellcome to Burroughs, 30 Sept. 1882.

127. Rhodes James, *Henry Wellcome*, pp. 107–8.

128. Ibid. pp.107–9.

129. WFA, Wellcome LB1, 84–107, quote on p.99, Wellcome to Burroughs, 27 Jan. 1883.

130. See below, chapter 3, pp.73–8.

131. The cumulative expenditure Wellcome described as 'the cause of our little pinch'. Rhodes James, *Henry Wellcome*, p.109.

132. WFA, Wellcome, LB1, 173, Wellcome to Bishop, 22 Oct. 1883.

133. WFA, Wellcome, LB10, 18, Sudlow to Wellcome, 22 Dec. 1881; WFA, Acc. 82/1, Box 16, Burroughs to Sudlow, 25 Sept. 1884.

134. WFA, Acc. 82/1 Box 16, Burroughs to Wellcome, 17 Sept., 16 Oct. 1884.

135. PP/SMB/6, Partnership indenture, 1885.

136. Quoted by Haggis, 'Life and work', p.150.

137. WFA, Wellcome LB10, 567–8, BW&Co. to Shepperson, 30 July 1889.

138. WFA, Rhodes James, *Henry Wellcome*, p.141; WFA, Acc. 82/1 Box 28, Burroughs v Wellcome memorandum, WFA, Acc. 90/1, Box 149, account ledger, BW&Co. As no significant increase in the range of products (other than McKesson & Robbins's pills) occurred when Wellcome joined the business, it is reasonable to suppose that the sales figure for the first six months trading (implying an annual figure of £35,622) probably indicates a level possibly somewhat in excess of the level of turnover reached by S. M. Burroughs & Co. by the time the partnership was formed. Sales by BW&Co. were: 1881/82, £33,158; 1882/83, £57,165; 1883/na; 1884/85 £52,184; 1885/86 £55,724; 1886/87 £72,147; 1887/88, £81,846; 1888/89, £99,339.

139. Trading profits were £6,648 in 1885/86 which, considering the general depression in the economy, Wellcome regarded as sufficient justification for mutual congratulations. WFA, Wellcome LB1, 389–390, Wellcome to Burroughs, 24 July 1885.

140. WFA, Acc. 90/1 Box 149, account ledger, BW&Co; WFA, Acc. 96/45, BW&Co. sales book 2.

141. WFA, Acc. 82/1 Box 28, sales memorandum, BW&Co.

142. '... the question of a larger factory and larger machinery demands immediate attention.' Quoted by Haggis, 'Life and work', p.176.

143. WFA, Acc. 82/1 Box 16, Burroughs to ?, 1890; Box 13, Wellcome to Burroughs, 22 Oct. 1889. WFA, Acc. 82/1 Box 13, Pearson, 'A chronology', p.4.

144. Haggis, 'Life and work', quoting a letter from Wellcome to Searl, p.225.

145. WFA, Acc. 82/1 Box 13, Wellcome to Burroughs, 22 Oct. 1889.

146. H. A. Phillips, 'Kepler Time is Winter Time', *Foundation News*, 2, Oct. 1952, pp.6–8.

147. Ibid.

148. WFA, Wellcome LB10, 18–21, Sudlow to Wellcome, 22 Dec. 1881.

149. WFA, PB 110, Trade Price List, 1885.

150. BW&Co.'s Advertisements mentioned laboratory work from Spring 1881, though probably referred to that owned by the Fellows' business (suppliers to BW&Co. of hypophosphite) in the US. *Chem. & Drug.*, 24, 19 March 1881.

151. WFA, Wellcome LB1, 65, Wellcome to various correspondents, 16 Jan. 1883; Wellcome to Witte, 20 Jan. 1883.

152. WFA, Acc. 82/1 Box 8, Sudlow to Wellcome, 9 Dec. 1886.

153. WFA, Wellcome LB10, 381–7, Wellcome to Burroughs, 9 July 1885; 489–91, Wellcome to Witte, 15 May 1886.

154. WFA/PB 110, *Lancet*, extract, Oct. 1887, *London Medical Record*, extract, 1887.

155. Referred to in the company's account of 'Progress in Pharmacy', *Chem. & Drug.*, 28 Jan. 1888, pp.104–6. According to Pearson, however, the production of a truly high diastase malt extract eluded the firm until 1893.

156. WFA, Wellcome LB1, 533–7, Wellcome to Ben and Ann [Fairchild], 10 Aug. 1887.

157. A mechanic who obtained a machine to repair and copy demanded £2,000 from the partners for its return. Damage to the company was avoided when the plot was discovered. Dr Witte was confronted with the evidence, dismissed, and all the machines retrieved. *Chem. & Drug.*, 32, 28 Jan. 1888, pp.104–6.

158. WFA, Wellcome LB10, 526–8, Wellcome to Smith, 19 Oct. 1888; Wellcome to Smith, n.d., *c.* 18 May 1889.

159. WFA, Wellcome LB2, 193, Wellcome to manager, Dartford branch of London & County Bank, 17 March 1890; ibid., Wellcome to Burroughs, 17 March 1890; ibid., LB10, 580, Burroughs to Wellcome, 26 March 1890.

160. WFA, Acc. 87/33, Burroughs to Wellcome (1882, n.d.). Note that this letter refers to Wellcome's agreement with a proposal *by Burroughs* to give notice that at some stage the partners would manufacture products formerly supplied by Wyeth. Rhodes James (following Haggis) referred only to Wellcome's espousal of such a policy. Rhodes James, *Henry Wellcome*, p.105.

161. WFA, Acc. 87/33, Burroughs to John Wyeth, 12 Feb. 1883.

162. Ibid., John Wyeth to BW&Co., 21 Feb. 1882; Draft agreement, March 1882, 17 April 1882. WFA, Acc. 82/1, Box 15, Burroughs Wellcome to John Wyeth; 12 July 1882.

163. WFA, Wellcome LB1, 76–82, 107–8, Wellcome to Burroughs, 27 Jan. 1883; Wellcome LB1, 1–3, Wellcome to Burroughs, 15 March 1883.

164. WFA, Acc. 82/1 Box 16, Burroughs to Wellcome, 7 Aug. 1884, complaining that Somerset House was 'hunting us'.

165. Though it would be surprising if the generation of revenue to meet war expenditure was not a factor considered when the 1812 Act was framed. The 1812 legislation had replaced the Act of 1775 when stamp duty was first introduced. WFA, Wellcome LB1, 23, Wellcome to Hobbins, 14 Feb. 1884.

166. Rhodes James, *Henry Wellcome*, p.105.

167. H. E. Chapman, 'Proprietary Medicines-the Present Position', *Pharm. J.*, 175, Sept. 1955, p. 207.

168. Ibid., p. 207.

169. WFA, Wellcome LB10, 169–75, BW&Co. to Wyeth, 27 Sept. 1882.

170. Ibid., 319–323, BW&Co. to Melville, 7 Nov. 1883.

171. WFA, Wellcome LB1, 231, Wellcome to Hobbins (?), 14 Feb. 1884.

172. Ibid., 224, Wellcome to Burroughs, 6 Dec. 1883.

173. This remark was prompted by Somerset House taking action over the hypodermic tablets which had Wyeth's name on the label and therefore believed by Customs to be American goods whereas in fact these were manufactured by BW&Co., WFA, Wellcome LB10, Burroughs to Wellcome, 7 Aug. 1884.

174. WFA, Wellcome LB10, 363–7, BW&Co. to Melville, 26 July 1884.

175. Ibid., 371, 7 Aug. 1884.

176. Ibid., 368, BW&Co. to Melville, 26 July 1884.

177. Ibid., 371, 7 Aug. 1884.

178. WFA, Wellcome LB10, 399–400, Sudlow to Burroughs, 13 Aug. 1884.

179. Ibid.

180. Ibid., 504–7, BW&Co. to Melville, 17 Sept. 1887.

181. Ibid., 509–10, BW&Co. to Melville, 11 Oct. 1887.

182. In May 1888 Wellcome wrote to the editor of the *Lancet* to draw his attention to an exchange in the House of Commons when the Chancellor appeared to concede that, regardless of the argument concerning patent versus other, including foreign, medicines, the consequence of exemption would 'destroy the greater part of the produce of the duties', an unwitting acknowledgement of the strength of the case being advanced by BW&Co. and proprietors of similar firms. Wellcome believed this was 'a very important admission' which gave the *Lancet* 'a magnificent text upon which to found a very powerful leader, and ammunition with which the authorities should be given a vigorous rap over the knuckles'. Ibid., 524–5, Wellcome to Wakley, 19 May 1888. Exemption was finally secured in 1903.

183. WFA, Wellcome LB1, 69, Wellcome to Witte, 20 Jan. 1883. The reference to the new plans for malt manufacture (which he instructed Dr Witte to be kept secret) suggests that this development would make space to accommodate tablet-making machinery, perhaps in another building.

184. WFA, Wellcome LB10, 170–2, BW&Co. to Wyeth, 27 Sept. 1882.

185. Ibid., BW&Co. to Wyeth, 27 Sept. 1882.

186. WFA, Wellcome LB10, 169–173, BW&Co. to Wyeth, 27 Sept. 1882. Ibid., 169–73; Wellcome to Burroughs, 27 June 1883. Rhodes James refers to machinery being transferred to London at the end of 1882, though no source is given to support this assertion. *Henry Wellcome*, p. 105. Even the abortive draft 1883 agreement with Wyeth for the supply of compressed tablet machines post-dated the date of delivery according to Rhodes James who also quotes Wellcome, writing to Burroughs in 1883, that prompt steps must be taken to manufacture capsuled pills. Ibid., pp. 106–7. Wellcome informed Burroughs on 27 June 1883: '… compressed tablet machines arrived from Philadelphia, setting them up and hope to have in working order soon'. WFA, Wellcome LB10, 279.

187. Ibid.

188. WFA, Acc. 82/1 Box 16, Burroughs to Wellcome, 26 Aug. 1884.

189. An account of the negotiations can be found in WFA, Wellcome LB10, 532, BW&Co. to John Wyeth, 5 Nov. 1888.

190. WFA, Acc. 82/1 Box 16, Burroughs to Wellcome, 15 Aug. 1884; WFA, Wellcome LB10, 279, Wellcome to Burroughs, 27 June 1883.

191. WFA, Wellcome LB10, 59–60, BW&Co. to Wyeth, 8 March 1882.

192. WFA, Wellcome LB1, 19, Wellcome to Burroughs, 6 Sept. 1882; Wellcome to Burroughs, 27 Jan. 1883.

193. WFA, Wellcome LB10, 386, Wellcome to Burroughs, 7 Aug. 1884.

194. WFA, Acc. 82/1 Box 16, Burroughs to Wellcome, 29 Sept. 1884.

195. WFA, Wellcome LB1, 438–9, Wellcome to Wyeth, 8 Jan. 1886.

196. WFA, Acc. 82/1, Box 76, 'Information for representatives', 1914. WFA, Wellcome LB10, 530–2, Wellcome to John Wyeth, 5 Nov. 1888.

197. WFA, Wellcome LB10, 530–2, Wellcome to John Wyeth, 5 Nov. 1888.

198. WFA, Wellcome, LB2, 26, Burroughs to Wellcome, 5 Nov. 1888.

199. WFA, Wellcome LB10, 530–2, Wellcome to Wyeth, 5 Nov. 1888.

200. Ibid.

201. Ibid.

202. WFA, Wellcome LB10, 530–2, Wellcome to Wyeth, 5 Nov. 1888; ibid., 632, Burroughs to Wyeth, 25 April 1893.

203. *Chem. & Drug.*, 32, 28 Jan. 1888, pp. 104–6.

204. 'A leader among men', *Pharm. Era*, 21, 6 June 1895, pp. 720–2.

Notes to Chapter 2: Americanisation of the British drug trade: product innovation and 'creating a demand'

1. WFA, PB 110, Medical formulae of new and improved chemical and pharmaceutical preparations, 1881.

2. Ibid., p. 19.

3. Burroughs responded by proposing that in the short term the name 'capsulets' or 'pil-ovids' should replace 'pills'.

4. WFA, Acc. 87/33, 43, 73, Burroughs to Wellcome,

20 April 1883; n.d. 1883. WFA, Wellcome LB10, 632–4, Burroughs to Wyeth, 25 April 1893.

5. The agency for McKesson & Robbins was not renewed when it expired shortly before February 1886. WFA, Wellcome LB1, 448a, Wellcome to Sam Fairchild, 4 Feb. 1886.

6. WFA, Acc. 85/16, 'Trade Marks Burroughs Wellcome & Co., 1879–1893'.

7. Ibid.

8. The agreement was initially for three years, but was extended to 1893 when it was renewed in modified form, and to 1897 when a fourteen year agreement commenced. The terms were typical of other agency agreements. The preparations were shipped and supplied in bulk free to BW&Co. in London. The English company to meet the actual costs of production, thereafter prices were charged to be 15 per cent above cost price. At the firm's expense, BW&Co.'s travellers would carry samples and exhibit to the medical profession and advertise frequently in the medical press. The partners undertook not to manufacture competing products nor sell similar products from other companies during the period of the agreement. The 1897 agreement was superseded in 1899 whereby Fairchild's products were to be priced as per BW&Co.'s price list less discounts of 40 per cent for the London firm, goods also to be supplied to BW&Co.'s Sydney warehouse. That discount was reduced when sales exceeded the £15,000 annual sales threshold in any consecutive twelve months. WFA, Acc. 83/3, Fairchild Bros. Agreement 1884.

9. WFA, Acc. 99/6/7, Agreement between BW&Co. and Benno Jaffe Darmstaedter, 29 July 1886.

10. WFA, Acc. 85/16, Trade Marks, Burroughs Wellcome & Co.

11. PP/SMB/6, Burroughs to Wellcome, 10 May 1882; WFA, Acc. 87/33/16, Burroughs to Wellcome, 23 Dec. 1882.

12. Ibid.

13. WFA, Acc. 87/33/44, Burroughs to Wellcome 20 April 1883; WFA, Wellcome LB1, 85, 180–2, Burroughs to Wellcome (1883?).

14. WFA, Acc. 85/16, Trade Marks, Burroughs Wellcome & Co.

15. PP/SMB/6, Burroughs to BW&Co., 2 Feb. 1882.

16. PP/SMB/6, Burroughs to Phillips & Co., n.d. 1882.

17. WFA, Acc. 87/33, Burroughs to Wellcome, n.d. 1883.

18. WFA, Wellcome LB10, 634, Burroughs to Wyeth, 25 April 1893.

19. WFA, Wellcome LB1, 88, Wellcome to Burroughs, 27 Jan. 1883; Wellcome LB10, 385–92 Burroughs to Wellcome, 7 Aug. 1884.

20. WFA, Wellcome LB11, 112–13, BW&Co. to Jaffe & Darmsteidter, 23 Oct. 1897.

21. WFA, Wellcome LB10, 463–5, BW&Co. to Warner, n.d. 1883.

22. WFA, Acc. 82/1 Box 17, Burroughs to Wellcome, 13 March 1883.

23. WFA, Acc. 87/33/35e Burroughs to Wellcome, 13

March 1883; Acc. 85/16, 'Burroughs Wellcome & Co. Trade Marks.' c. 1897. Macdonald, In Pursuit of Excellence (1980), p. 12.

24. Lancet, ii, 4 July 1885, p. 36; WFA, Acc. 82/1 Box 14. Initial use was limited to direct applications to ocular surfaces and to mucus membranes in nasal, oral, and laryngeal surgery and later used in general surgery. The chemical works began to prepare synthetic cocaine from 1904. After the introduction of regulation in 1914, the company was one of the first to be granted a licence from the Home Office.

25. Chem. & Drug., 25, 15 Dec. 1885.

26. Such was the procedure, for example, in response to a suggestion relating to a blood-purifying burdoch decoction applied to boils. WFA, Wellcome LB29, 868, BW&Co. to ?, 2 May 1905; Wellcome LB11, 82, BW&Co. to Reynolds & Branson, 14 Sept. 1898.

27. 'Medicine making up to date', Talk, 21 July 1893.

28. WFA, Acc. 99/6/4, Charles Weld, 'Statement', 1902.

29. WFA, PB 110, Price List, 1895.

30. Haggis, 'Life and work', p. 244.

31. The suggestions by Ernest Hart (editor of the BMJ), that added milk and sugar or citrine would enhance the product were explored but not pursued. Wellcome regarded the 12.5 per cent royalty that Hart was asking was excessive. He drew attention to the gross profit on Tea Tabloids at 12.5 per cent which after business expenses implied a loss. WFA, Wellcome LB10, 643–4, BW&Co. to Hart, 30 Jan. 1894; LB38, 52–4. Wellcome to Burroughs, 20 March 1894.

32. WFA, Acc. 82/33/28, Burroughs to Dr Valentine, 20 July 1883; WFA, Acc. 87/33/43, Burroughs to Wellcome, 20 April 1883.

33. WFA, Acc. 87/33/28, Burroughs to Dr Valentine, 20 July 1883.

34. WFA, PB 110, Price list 1899.

35. Haggis, 'Life and work', p. 161.

36. See below p. 60.

37. WFA, Wellcome, LB1, 86e, 93, Wellcome to Burroughs, 27 Jan. 1883.

38. Ibid.

39. WFA, Acc. 87/33/40e, Burroughs to Wellcome, 16 May 1883.

40. WFA, Acc. 82/1 Box 16, 7, 'Chronology of the history of BW&Co. compiled by George E. Pearson 1878–1936.'

41. WFA, Wellcome LB1, 393–7, Wellcome to Burroughs, 7 Aug. 1885; WFA, LB1, 432; Wellcome to Fraser, 19 Dec. 1885; WFA, Acc. 82/1, Box 14. Wellcome to BW&Co., 19 Jan. 1887; Acc. 82/1 Box 7, Home representatives' convention, 1908; Rhodes James, Wellcome, p. 125.

42. WFA, Wellcome LB11, 821, BW&Co. to Dartford, 7 May 1898; BW&Co. to Reynolds, Reynolds, and Branson, 14 Sept. 1898.

43. WFA, Wellcome LB29, 868, BW&Co. to ?, 2 May 1905.

44. WFA, Wellcome LB29, 963, BW&Co. to ?, 24 May 1905.
45. WFA, Wellcome LB11, 38, Wellcome to J.Ward Cousins, 8 July 1897. Though the 1905 Price List included these products. PB/III, p.48.
46. Glaxo Wellcome archive, Toronto, 'From Ergot to Ernutin. An historical sketch', lecture memoranda, Canadian Medical Association meeting, Ottawa, 1908.
47. See, for example, the price list for 1906, WFA, PB/III, p.ix.
48. WFA, Acc. 82/1 Box 7, Report on home representatives' convention 1907, Greig, p.57; Matthews, pp.60–1; Curry, 78; Jowett, pp.115–17.
49. Chem. & Drug., 41, 19 Nov. 1892, supplement p.xxxl.
50. Chem. & Drug., 38, 7 Feb. 1891, p.13.
51. Chem. & Drug., 40, 5 March 1892, p.339.
52. Chem. & Drug., 39, 22 Aug. 1891, pp.297–8; 40, 30 April 1892, supplement, p.xxxi.
53. WFA, Wellcome LB12, 395, Snow Hill to Dartford, 23 May 1899.
54. WFA, Wellcome LB30, 47, BW&Co. to Dartford, 27 Dec. 1905.
55. See chapter 8.
56. WFA, Acc. 82/1 Box 15, Wyeth to BW&Co., 21 Feb., 1 March 1882; Burroughs Wellcome to Wyeth, 17 April, 12 July 1882.
57. PP/SMB/6, Burroughs to Wellcome, 1 April 1882. The financial returns suggest this was an exaggeration, though only net profit figures (£383 on £9,631 sales) have survived for 1882. WFA, Acc. 99/6/7, KMEC balance sheets.
58. PP/SMB/6, Burroughs to Wellcome, 1 April 1882.
59. WFA, Acc. 82/1 Box 16, Burroughs to Wellcome, 29 Sept. 1884.
60. Ibid.
61. WFA, PB/110, Price List 1887, 1890.
62. WFA, Wellcome LB1, 438–9, Wellcome to Wyeth, 8 Jan. 1886.
63. WFA, PP/110, Price list 1887.
64. WFA, Acc. 82/1 Box 4, 'Anti-cutting correspondence', BW&Co. to Dundee Chemists' and Druggists' Association, 6 Nov. 1902.
65. See below, chapter 5, pp.138–9.
66. WFA, Wellcome LB10, 559, Burroughs Wellcome to Casala (?), 19 July 1889.
67. WFA, Wellcome LB12, 5, BW&Co. to Wellcome, 22 Feb. 1898; WFA, Wellcome LB36, 9, BW&Co. to Lt. Col. Western, 2 Jan. 1899.
68. WFA, Wellcome LB17, 13, Wellcome to Curry, 22 Jan. 1901.
69. WFA, Wellcome LB13, 552, BW&Co. to medical officer, Brompton Hospital, 28 April 1900; WFA, Wellcome LB12, 268; Wellcome to Rogers, 29 March 1899.
70. WFA, Wellcome LB11, 399–400, BW&Co. to Wellcome, 19 Feb. 1898.
71. WFA, Acc. 87/33/35b, n.d. 1883. 'Prices in the colonies'.
72. WFA, Acc. 87/33/2, Burroughs to Fellows, n.d. 1882.
73. Ibid.
74. The estimated cost of advertising is based on individual contracts placed with journals and magazines. Expenditure does not include samples, cards, and circulars etc. WFA, Acc. 82/1 Box 78, Advertising Book 1, 1881–84.
75. Chem. & Drug., 40, 20 Feb. 1892, p.266.
76. WFA, F/FA/328, trading and profit and loss accounts.
77. WFA, Acc. 82/1 Box 78, Advertising book 1, 1881–84, F 1–8, 20–47.
78. WFA, Acc. 82/1 Box 16, Burroughs to Wellcome, 16 Aug. 1884.
79. Ibid.
80. WFA/M/GB, Cuttings book, 1888–1892, pp.2, 8, 23–4.
81. Ibid.
82. Chem. & Drug.., 27, 27 Jan. 1894, p.113.
83. Two examples are contracts with the Chemists' Journal and the Mercantile Shipping Register. WFA, Acc. 82/1 Box 78, Advertising Book 1, 1881–84, F 51.
84. Ibid.
85. WFA, PP/SMB/6, Burroughs to Wellcome, 2 Feb. 1881.
86. WFA, Wellcome LB10, 25, Wellcome to Burroughs, 26 May 1882.
87. WFA, Acc. 82/1 Box 13, Burroughs to Wellcome, 19 Feb. 1882.
88. WFA, Wellcome LB10, 957–8, BW&Co. to Fairchild, 24 March 1897.
89. Ibid.
90. WFA, Wellcome LB10, 90–1, BW&Co. to Harwicker, 27 April 1882.
91. WFA, Wellcome LB10, 92, BW&Co. to Murrell, 1 May 1882.
92. WFA, Wellcome LB10, 97, BW&Co. to Whitmarsh, 5 May 1882.
93. WFA, Wellcome LB10, 183–6, BW&Co. to Luland (?), n.d. 1882.
94. WFA, Acc. 87/33/37a, Burroughs to Wellcome, 26 March 1883.
95. WFA, Wellcome LB10, 544–7, BW&Co. to Holman, 26 March 1889.
96. Chem. & Drug., 38, 17 Jan. 1891, p.85.
97. Chem. & Drug., 46, 20 April 1895, pp.553–4.
98. See, for example, Burroughs Wellcome & Co., Anglo Saxon Leechcraft (1912), 115–37.
99. Med Press & Circ. 1881, quoted in Wellcome News, Feb. 1952, p.11.
100. WFA, PB/III, 1906 Price List, p.ii.
101. See chapter 1, pp.3–97.
102. Ron Champion, 'Wellcome in Australia', Wellcome News, Dec. 1986, p.4.
103. WFA, Acc. 99/6/1, Dompe to Wellcome, 1 Nov., 2 Dec. 1895.
104. WFA, GB 32/2, Records of travellers' calls on medical men at home and abroad, 1881–87; WFA, Wellcome LB10, 216, Sudlow to Wellcome, 13 March 1883. ibid., 427–31, Sudlow to Wellcome, 7 June 1884; Wellcome LB1, 341, Wellcome to

Fairchild, 11 April 1885; ibid., 235–42, Wellcome to Burroughs, 3 Feb. 1884; ibid., 396, Wellcome to Burroughs, 7 Aug. 1885; ibid., 383, Wellcome to Burroughs, 9 July 1885; ibid., Wellcome to Burroughs, 9 July 1883; Wellcome LB10, 698, BW&Co. to Loxton, 25 Sept. 1895. Champion, 'Wellcome in Australia', *Wellcome News*, Dec. 1986, p. 4.

105. WFA, Acc. 84/10, Salaries ledger.
106. *Chem. & Drug.*, 38, 28 Feb. 1891, p. 307.
107. WFA, Wellcome LB10, 613–17, Wellcome to Burroughs, 29 April 1892.
108. WFA, Wellcome LB1, 202–3, Wellcome to Burroughs, 17 Nov. 1883.
109. WFA, Acc. 84/10, Salaries ledger, WFA, Wellcome LB10, 613–17, Wellcome to Burroughs, 29 April 1892.
110. Digby, *Making a Medical Living*, pp. 144–5.
111. Ibid. This figure from table 5.2 was calculated from the gross incomes from which 16 per cent has been deducted for expenses. That is Digby's lower figure for expenses which ranged up to 25 per cent.
112. WFA, Wellcome LB1, 213, Wellcome to Burroughs, 6 Dec. 1883.
113. WFA, Wellcome, LB1, 179, Wellcome to Burroughs, 26 Oct. 1883.
114. WFA, PB/110, *Med. Press. & Circ.*, 3 Aug. 1881.
115. *Chem. & Drug.*, 32, 25 Feb. 1888, pp. 104–6.
116. WFA, Wellcome LB16, 556, BW&Co. to all travellers, 9 Oct. 1901.
117. PP/SMB/6, 30 March 1882.
118. WFA, Acc. 87/33/69, 'Instructions to travellers'.
119. Ibid.
120. WFA, Wellcome LB10, 32, Wellcome to Burroughs, between 23 Jan. and 16 Feb. 1882.
121. WFA, Acc. 87/33/2, Burroughs to Wellcome, 27 Feb. 1883.
122. WFA, Wellcome LB10, 279, Wellcome to Burroughs, 27 June 1883.
123. WFA, GB 32/2, Records of travellers' calls on medical men at home and abroad, 1881–87, book 2.
124. WFA, GB 32/2, Records of travellers' calls upon medical men at home & abroad, 1881–87, book 2, 26 Feb. 1883, 15 March 1883.
125. Ibid.
126. Michael Worboys, *Spreading Germs. Disease Theories and Medical Practice, 1865–1900* (Cambridge, University Press, 2000), pp. 20, 284–8.
127. Ibid., p. 284.
128. WFA, GB 32/1 Records of travellers' calls upon chemists and druggists at home and abroad, 1881–85, book 1.
129. WFA, Wellcome LB11, 78, Wellcome to Hastings, 7 Sept. 1897.
130. WFA, Wellcome LB11, 616, 617, BW&Co. to Hull and Francis, 23 May 1898.
131. WFA, Acc. 87/33/2, Burroughs to Fellowes, 1882 n.d.
132. WFA, Wellcome LB11, 502–4, BW&Co. to Wellcome, 25 March 1898.
133. WFA, Wellcome LB12, 830, BW&Co., Wellcome to Pearson, 13 Nov. 1899.
134. Ibid., 864, BW&Co. to D, 20 Nov. 1899.
135. WFA, Wellcome LB13, 812, BW&Co. to BW&Co., Sydney, 15 June 1900.
136. *Chem. & Drug.*, 40, 2 Jan. 1892, p. 19, T. H. Parke to editor, *Chem. & Drug.*, 41, 3 Sept. 1892, p. 374.
137. WFA, Wellcome LB10, 718, Wellcome to Lloyd Williams, 18 Nov. 1895; Ibid., 725, Wellcome to QMG to the Forces, 9 Dec. 1895.
138. Ibid.
139. *Chem. & Drug.*, 55, 23 Dec. 1899, pp. 1016–17.
140. WFA, Wellcome LB11, 309, BW&Co. to Wellcome, 22 Jan. 1898; LB13, 793, Snow Hill to Dartford, 18 June 1900; LB16, 517, 4 Oct. 1901.
141. *Chem. & Drug.*, 55, 23 Dec. 1899, pp. 1016–17.
142. WFA, Wellcome LB5, 236, Wellcome to General Potter (US Army surgeon), 28 Feb. 1900.
143. WFA, Wellcome LB13, 769, Snow Hill to Dartford, 11 June 1900; WFA, Wellcome LB13, 812, BW&Co. to BW&Co., Sydney, 15 June 1900.

Notes to Chapter 3: 'Quality for profit' through 'science and industry'; management and organisation, labour policies, and finance

1. WFA, PB/110 'Perfection in pharmacy'.
2. *Chem. & Drug.*, 56, 2 June 1900, p. 926.
3. Rhodes James, *Henry Wellcome*, pp. 133, 160.
4. Ibid., p. 172.
5. Ibid., pp. 120, 153, 160.
6. WFA, Wellcome LB10, 610, Wellcome to Lloyd Williams, 9 March 1892; ibid., 718, Wellcome to Lloyd Williams, 18 Nov. 1895.
7. Tansey and Milligan, 'The early history', pp. 91–2.
8. WFA, Acc. 82/1 Box 13, extract of an article prepared for publication in 'Talks', 21 July 1893.
9. WFA, GB/29/25, 'Dartford cuttings book 1899–1936.' Obituary of Lloyd Williams in *Chemical Trade Journal*, 20 Jan. 1900.
10. J. Donnelly, 'Defining the industrial chemist in the United Kingdom, 1850–1921', *J. Soc. Hist.*, 29, 1996, pp. 779–96.
11. WFA, Wellcome LB3, 354, Wellcome to Lloyd Williams, 28 Nov. 1896.
12. WFA, Wellcome LB11, 2, Wellcome to Lloyd Williams, 24/7 May 1897; WFA, Wellcome LB4, 182, A-C, Wellcome to Miss Leake, 18 June 1897.
13. Chapman, *Jesse Boot*, pp. 67–9.
14. WFA, Wellcome LB10, 610, Wellcome to Lloyd Williams, 9 March 1892; ibid., 718, Wellcome to Lloyd Williams, 18 Nov. 1895.
15. WFA, Wellcome LB3, 293c, Wellcome to Searl, 9 Jan. 1896; LB11, 24, Wellcome to Lloyd Williams, 27 May 1897; Lloyd Williams to Wellcome, 12 June 1897.

16. WFA, Acc. 96/41, H. A. D. Jowett, re. works history; WFA, PB/78, obituary. See below chapter 6, pp. 193–5.
17. WFA, PB/78, obituary in *J. Chem. Soc.*, 1936.
18. WFA, Acc. 82/1 Box 27, Works chronology, 1884–1928.
19. WFA, Acc. 89/57:2, J. A. Hogg, 'Organisation of the Wellcome chemical works, Dartford', vol. 3, pp. 2–4.
20. With the exception of the Tea Tabloid department. WFA, Acc. 96/41, 'Some notes on buildings, people, and methods at Pheonix Mills, Dartford, from 1894 onwards'.
21. WFA, Acc. 82/1 Box 7, H. A. D. Jowett, 'History of an industry', *East Kent Advertiser*, 21 March 1924.
22. WFA, GB/31/1, Instructions sent to foreign manufacturing houses, 1898–1932, Standing order 102, 19 Jan. 1898, p. 74. Even with the strict regulations in place, complaints were received from two customers who found a doorknob and a beetle in bottles of Kepler. WFA, Wellcome LB15, 864, BW&Co. to Dartford, 28 May 1901; LB28, 234, 4 Jan. 1905.
23. WFA, Acc. 82/1 Box 7, Proceedings of the convention of home sales representatives of BW&Co., henceforward Representatives' Convention, 1907.
24. WFA, Acc. 82/1 Box 7, H. A. D. Jowett, 'History'.
25. WFA, Wellcome, LB10, 731, Wellcome to Searl, 30 Jan. 1895; WFA, Wellcome LB13, 293a, Wellcome to Searl, 9 Jan. 1896.
26. WFA, Wellcome LB10, 700–1, Wellcome to Searl, 10 Oct. 1895, pp. 700–1.
27. WFA, Wellcome LB11, 615, BW&Co. to Dartford, 21 May 1898.
28. WFA, Wellcome LB11, 615, BW&Co. to Dartford, 21 May 1898. WFA, GB/31/1, Instructions sent to foreign manufacturing houses: no. 18, 29 Nov. 1898.
29. WFA, Wellcome LB11, 175, BW&Co. to Dartford, 2 Dec. 1897; 189, 8 Dec. 1897, 76, 3 Jan. 1898, 298–9, 19 Jan. 1898.
30. Imperial College archives, B/Carr/6, F. H. Carr's papers, conversations recorded by Mr Gunther, winter, 1966/67.
31. WFA, GB 31/1, Analytical Department instructions sent to foreign manufacturing houses, 1898–1932, p. 4.
32. WFA, Acc. 82/1 Box 13, Control measures employed in the manufacture and packaging of Tabloid and Soloid products (*c.* 1914).
33. Given Wellcome's familiarity with the American industry, it is possible that the new system may have been modelled on the practice of Parke Davis observed a commentator from Britain who described it as an 'almost perfect system of checking to prevent mistakes', *Chem. & Drug.*, 29 Jan. 1898, pp. 182–3.
34. WFA, GB 31/1, Instructions sent to foreign manufacturing houses, 1898–1932, re returns and rejections at Sydney and New York Works, 14 July 1914, p. 38. These were based on those in place in Dartford from 1898.
35. WFA, GB/31/2, General instruction book no. 17 (first issued 1909).
36. WFA, Wellcome LB11, 37, BW&Co. to Dartford, 8 July 1897.
37. The existence of a drawing office is indicative of the continuing process of construction and reconstruction at Dartford from the 1890s until 1914.
38. WFA, Acc. 96/41, 'Some notes on buildings, people, and methods at Phoenix Dartford from 1894 onwards' (*c.* 1920), n.p.; WFA, Acc. 89/57:2, Hogg, 'Organisation'; WFA, Acc. 82 Box 16, Pearson 'Chronology', p. 4.
39. WFA, Acc. 89/57:2, Hogg, 'Organisation' II, 'Tabloid manufacturing dept'.
40. WFA, Acc. 82/1 Box 38, 'Behind the scenes by observer' (typescript, n.d.).
41. WFA, Wellcome LB32, Wellcome to BW&Co., 2 March 1906.
42. WFA, Wellcome LB16, 701, BW&Co. to Dartford, 23 Oct. 1901; WFA, Wellcome LB13, 794, Wellcome to Smart (Dartford), 13 June 1900.
43. WFA, Wellcome LB16, 740–1, Sudlow to Hill, 28 Jan. 1901.
44. WFA, Wellcome LB16, 772–3, BW&Co. to Wellcome, 29 Oct. 1901; 886, BW&Co. to Wellcome, 30 Oct. 1901.
45. WFA, Wellcome LB12, 143–4, BW&Co. to Smart, 21 Feb. 1899.
46. WFA, Wellcome LB15, 518, Head Office to Dartford, 1 April 1901; 190, BW&Co. to Fairchild, 6 March 1901.
47. WFA, Wellcome LB19, 501, BW&Co. internal memo, 16 July 1902; 506, 18 Sept. 1902.
48. WFA, Wellcome LB40, 398, Horton to Lewis, 13 May 1895.
49. WFA, Wellcome LB15, 625, BW&Co. to Dartford, 23 April 1901; 523, BW&Co. to Dartford, April 1901.
50. WFA, Wellcome LB15, 389, BW&Co. to Wellcome, 15 March 1901.
51. WFA, Wellcome LB16, 488, BW&Co. to Wellcome, 28 Sept. 1901; 538, BW&Co. to Wellcome, 8 Oct. 1901.
52. WFA, Wellcome LB15, 625, BW&Co. to Dartford, 23 April 1901.
53. WFA, Wellcome LB15, 388, BW&Co. to Dartford, 19 March 1901.
54. WFA, Wellcome LB15, 388, BW to Wellcome, 15 March 1901.
55. WFA, Wellcome LB12, 76, BW&Co. to Dartford, 23 Jan. 1899.
56. WFA, Wellcome LB19, 468–9, BW&Co. to Sydney, 11 July 1902; 485, BW&Co. internal memo, 13 July 1902; 501, 23 July 1902; 617, 8 Aug. 1902.
57. WFA, Wellcome LB19, 468–9, BW&Co. to Sydney, 11 July 1902.
58. Ibid.
59. Ibid.
60. WFA, Wellcome LB15, BW&Co. to Dartford, April 1901.

61. WFA, Wellcome LB19, 163, BW&Co. internal memo, 31 May 1902. It is not clear whether this policy was adopted, but consideration shows the sensitivity to costing.

62. WFA, Wellcome LB19, 858–9, BW&Co. internal memo, 8 Sept. 1902.

63. WFA, Wellcome LB19, 179, BW&Co. internal memo, 2 June 1902.

64. Haggis, 'Life and work', p.368.

65. WFA, Wellcome LB32, 71, Wellcome to BW&Co., 2 March 1906.

66. WFA, Acc. 89/58/3, 'Organisation' IV; WFA, Acc. 82/1 Box 27, 'Items of interest', 1884–1926.

67. WFA, GB/31/8, Works Manager's Instructions Book no. 1, Jowett to Vineall, 23 Jan. 1907, 5 Jan. 1907, 15 Jan. 1912.

68. Ibid.

69. Ibid., Jowett, 'Re Checking', 2 Feb. 1912.

70. WFA, GB/31/1, Instructions sent to foreign manufacturing houses, 1898–1932, 'J.' re Scheme for securing efficiency in packing rooms – New York Works, 9 Jan. 1912, p.89.

71. WFA, GB/24/5, Works Manager's Instruction Book 1, 1907–1913, 'Re New Lines', 10 Feb. 1909, p.85.

72. Ibid., Jowett, Re Experimental Work – New Substances, 17 July 1912, p.143.

73. Ibid., Jowett, marked private and confidential, 5 May 1909.

74. For further discussion see chapter 15, pp.468–74.

75. WFA, Acc. 82/1 Box 7, H. A. D. Jowett, 'A local industry', *East Kent Advertiser*, 28 March 1924.

76. WFA, GB/29/24, Dartford cuttings book 1, *Dartford Advertiser*, 1890.

77. WFA, Acc. 82/1 Box 13, *Talk*, 21 July 1893.

78. WFA, Wellcome LB34, 194, Memo, 25 April 1899. It is not clear whether this figure includes salesmen, of whom there may have been a dozen.

79. LSE archives, Charles Booth Collection, LSE/279/vol.B93, interviews and questionnaires, pp.31–5.

80. WFA, Wellcome LB8, 450, Wellcome to J.Y.W. McAllister, 29 June 1904.

81. LSE archives, Charles Booth Collection, LSE/279/vol.B93, interviews and questionnaires, pp.31–5.

82. WFA, Acc. 89/57/3, Organisation of Chemical Works, Dartford, IV, pp.6–10.

83. Burroughs' disc was number 1, which he used regularly when he visited the factory. WFA, Acc. 96/41, 'Some notes on buildings', p.17.

84. See WFA, GB/31/6, Drug stock standing orders, 1897–1915; WFA, GB/31/2, Works manager's instruction book, 1907–1912.

85. WFA, Acc. 82/1, box 19, Instruction, June 1904.

86. WFA, GB/31/6, Drug stock standing orders, 1897–1915, 'Cleanliness', 18 July 1913, p.108; WFA, GB/31/1, Instructions sent to foreign manufacturing houses, 1898–1932. 'Compressing machines', 2 March 1914, pp.10–14.

87. WFA, GB/31/1, Instructions sent to foreign manufacturing houses, 1898–1932, p.10, 'Granulating room regulations', Oct. 1897.

88. WFA, GB/31/9, Works Manager's Instruction Book 1, 1907–1913, 'Notice', 2 July 1907, p.75.

89. WFA, GB/31/6, Standing order 318, 20 Dec. 1900/1908. Drug stock standing orders, 1897–1915, 31 June; Standing orders 4 and 292, 28 Dec. 1927; WFA, GB/31/1, Instructions sent to foreign manufacturing houses, 1898–1932, p.83.

90. WFA, GB/31/9, 'Works Manager's Instruction Book 1, 1907–1913', 'Notice', 2 July 1907, p.75.

91. WFA, GB/31/2, 'Works Manager's Instruction Book 1, 1907–1912', p.2, Jowett to Wilson, 23 Jan. 1907.

92. Ibid.; WFA, Acc. 89/57/3, Organisation of Chemical Works, Dartford, IV, pp.6–10.

93. WFA, PB 63, 89/27, 'Punctuality'; WFA, PB 63, 87/14, 'General Rules and instructions for the employees of Burroughs Wellcome & Co.'.

94. WFA, Acc. 82/1, reminiscences of Miss Freeman; WFA, Acc. 82/1 Box 38, 'Behind the scenes by observer' (typescript, n.d.).

95. WFA, Acc. 82/1 Box 38, 'Behind the scenes' (typescript).

96. For extended discussion of management after 1914, see below chapter 15, pp.459–62.

97. WFA, Wellcome LB8, 400, 3 June 1904, BW&Co. to M. Sadler.

98. WFA, Acc. 82/1 Box 19, *West Kent Advertiser*, 28 Jan. 1905.

99. LSE archives, Charles Booth Collection, LSE/279/vol.B93, interviews and questionnaires, pp.31–5.

100. WFA, Acc. 82/1 Box 27, 'Items of interest', 1884–1928.

101. Ibid.

102. Ibid.

103. WFA, Acc. 82/1, P. Gambler to Folder, 28 July 1975.

104. Haggis, 'Life and work', p.309; WFA, Acc. 82/1, Box 19, Staff general, 1884–1948, Box 38, *West Dartford Advertiser*, 21 July 1895.

105. Haggis, 'Life and work'. p.308; Rhodes James, *Henry Wellcome*, p.170.

106. Haggis, 'Life and work', p.309. WFA, Acc. 82/1 Box 19, Staff general, 1884–1948, Box 38, *West Dartford Advertiser*, 21 July 1895.

107. WFA, Acc. 82/1 Box 24, interview with Miss Juster, p.1. This contrasted with the policy of Allen & Hanbury where in the Booth survey of 1893 it was reported that 25 per cent of girls employed were discharged during summer months when the factory was usually slack. '… notes are made of their working capability and in this way the idle and troublesome are weeded out'. Ibid., pp.67–71.

108. *Pharm. Era*, 16, Feb. 1890, p.25.

109. WFA, Acc. 82/1 Box 19, letter to BW&Co.

110. *Chem. & Drug.*, 43, 8 July 1893.

111. P. A. Joyce, *Work, Society and Politics. The Culture of the Factory Worker in Later Victorian England* (Brighton, 1980), pp.140, 180.

112. Tweedale, *At the Sign of the Plough*, pp.91, 118.

113. WFA, Wellcome LB10, 613–17, Wellcome to Burroughs, 29 April 1892.

114. Her animosity may have originated from Wellcome's advice to Burroughs to postpone his

marriage, expressing the fear that Burroughs was vulnerable to women who flattered to deceive. Rhodes James, *Henry Wellcome*, pp. 126–7.

115. Haggis, 'Life and work', chapter 7; HSBC archives, Acc. 339/10, Pollock's daybook, 24 March 1899.
116. WFA, Acc. 90/1 Box 149, Balance sheets.
117. WFA, Wellcome LB10, 642, Kirby to Wellcome, 30

Aug. 1893.
118. Because the profit figures are net, however, all ratios understate the true level. Allen & Hanbury's rate of return on sales (also based on net profit figures) between 1912 and 1914 was roughly 15 per cent. Tweedale, *At the Sign of the Plough*, p. 118.

Notes to Chapter 4: 'Friend and brother' in dysfunctional partnership: Burroughs *versus* Wellcome

1. *Chem. & Drug.*, 25, 25 Jan. 1888, pp. 104–6.
2. *Pharm. Era*, 16, Feb. 1890, p. 24.
3. See below, pp. 120–4.
4. *Pharm. Era*, 21, 8 Feb. 1895, p. 190.
5. WFA, Acc. 82/1 Box 15, John Wyeth to Burroughs, 13 April 1881.
6. WFA, Wellcome LB1, 192, Wellcome to Burroughs, 26 Oct. 1883.
7. WFA, Wellcome LB10, 32–3, Wellcome to Burroughs between 23 Jan. and 1 Feb. 1882.
8. PP/SMB/6, Burroughs to Wellcome, 2 March 1882; WFA, Acc. 19, Burroughs to Wellcome, June 1882.
9. WFA, Wellcome LB1, 204, Wellcome to Burroughs, 17 Nov. 1883.
10. WFA, Acc. 87/33/51, Burroughs to Wellcome, n.d., 1883.
11. Burroughs to Wellcome, 18 June 1882, quoted in A.W. Haggis, 'Life and work', pp. 188–9.
12. Burroughs to Wellcome, 9 Aug. 1882, quoted in Haggis, 'Life and work', p. 191.
13. WFA, Wellcome LB1, 1–15, Wellcome to Burroughs, 25 Aug. 1882.
14. Ibid.
15. Ibid.
16. Ibid.
17. Wellcome to Burroughs, 25 Aug. 1882, quoted in Haggis, 'Life and work', pp. 197–8.
18. WFA, Acc. 82/1 Box 13, Burroughs to Wellcome, 10 Aug. 1882.
19. WFA, Wellcome LB1, 19, Wellcome to Burroughs, 6 Sept. 1882.
20. WFA, Wellcome LB1, 213–30, Wellcome to Burroughs, 6 Dec. 1883.
21. Ibid.
22. WFA, Wellcome LB1, Wellcome to Burroughs, 6 Dec. 1883, 6 Feb. 1884; WFA, Wellcome LB10, Wellcome to Burroughs, 6 Sept. 1884; Haggis, 'Life and work', p. 204.
23. WFA, Acc. 82/1 Box 16, Burroughs to Wellcome, 25 Sept. 1884.
24. Ibid.
25. Ibid., Burroughs to Wellcome, 16 Oct. 1884.
26. Quoted in Rhodes James, *Henry Wellcome*, p. 141.
27. PP/SMB/6, partnership indenture, 1885.
28. Ibid.
29. Ibid.
30. WFA, Acc. 90/1, BW&Co. balance sheets, 1880–1939.
31. Rhodes James, *Henry Wellcome*, p. 143.

32. Burroughs to Wellcome, 1 May 1887, quoted in Haggis, 'Life and work', pp. 177–8.
33. Ibid., p. 179, Wellcome to Burroughs, 2 May 1887.
34. Ibid., Burroughs to Wellcome, 26 May 1887.
35. Ibid., pp. 180–1, Wellcome to Burroughs, 28 July 1887.
36. Ibid.
37. Ibid.
38. WFA, Wellcome LB1, 533–7, Wellcome to Ben and Ann Fairchild, 10 Aug. 1887.
39. Haggis, 'Life and work', pp. 209–11.
40. WFA, Wellcome LB19, Shepperson to Burroughs, 19 Dec. 1887.
41. WFA, Acc. 82/1 Box 38, Radford & Frankland to Wellcome, 27 July 1887.
42. WFA, Acc. 82/1 Box 13, 8 March 1888.
43. Wellcome to Ann and Sam Fairchild, 11 April 1888, quoted in Haggis, 'Life and work', p. 214.
44. *Chem. & Drug.*, 49, 24 July 1896; WFA, GB/29/10, Reports book 1, 1892–99.
45. WFA, Acc. 82/1 Box 14, 4 June 1888. See the statement by William Kirby, first appointed by Burroughs as bookkeeper in 1879.
46. Ibid.
47. WFA, Acc. 82/1 Box 13, Burroughs v Wellcome: questions in case for the opinion of counsel, 1889.
48. Haggis, 'Life and work', p. 217.
49. WFA, Acc. 82/1 Box 13, Wellcome to Markby & Stewart, 21 Aug. 1889.
50. Ibid., 'Judgement of the Court in Burroughs v Wellcome', 23 June 1889.
51. Haggis, 'Life and work', pp. 218–20.
52. For a detailed account see Rhodes James, *Henry Wellcome*, pp. 169–71.
53. WFA, Wellcome LB2, 171, Wellcome to Burroughs, 22 Oct. 1889.
54. Wellcome to Burroughs, 12 March 1890, Haggis, 'Life and work', p. 266.
55. WFA, Wellcome LB2, 216–31, Wellcome to Burroughs, 22 March 1890.
56. PP/SMB/6, copy by Markby Stewart & Co. on behalf of Wellcome to Burroughs, 16 Nov. 1891.
57. Wellcome to Burroughs, 10 May 1892; Burroughs to Wellcome, 12 May 1892, quoted in Haggis, 'Life and work', p. 270.
58. WFA, Acc. 82/1 Box 13, Wellcome to Markby Stewart & Co., 21 Aug. 1889, Agreement.
59. WFA, Acc. 82/1 Box 13, Markby Stewart & Co. to Burroughs, 9 Jan. 1893.

60. WFA, Acc. 82/1 Box 16, Radford & Frankland to Burroughs, 4 July 1892.
61. WFA, Acc.82/1 Box 13, Markby Stewart & Co. to Burroughs, 9 Jan. 1893.
62. Ibid.
63. Ibid.; Haggis, 'Life and work', p. 268.
64. WFA, Wellcome LB38, 55–8, Wellcome to Burroughs, 20 March 1894.
65. Haggis, 'Life and work', p. 268, Markby Stewart & Co. to Burroughs, 9 Jan. 1893.
66. WFA, Acc. 82/1 Box 19, Wellcome to Burroughs, 14 March 1893.
67. PP/SMB/6, Wellcome to Burroughs, 25 July 1894.
68. PP/SMB/6, Wellcome to Burroughs, 11 Aug. 1893.
69. WFA, Acc. 82/1 Box 19, Wellcome to Sudlow, 3 Sept. 1893.
70. WFA, Wellcome LB37, 56–9, Wellcome to Burroughs, 29 Sept. 1893 (marked 'not sent').
71. Ibid.
72. Haggis, 'Life and work', p. 274.
73. PP/SMB/6, Burroughs to Clark, 14 Dec. 1894.
74. WFA, Wellcome LB10, 658, Wellcome to Fairchild, 2 March 1895.
75. The correspondence is reproduced in Rhodes James, *Henry Wellcome*, pp. 124–7.
76. Haggis, 'Life and work', chapter 7; Pollock's daybook, 24 March 1899, HSBC archives, Acc. 339/10.
77. Haggis, 'Life and work', p. 298.
78. The first, the Physiological Research Laboratories set up in 1894, reflected Wellcome's new priorities, though it seems unlikely that Burroughs would have been unaware of this development. See chapter 6, pp. 168 et seq.
79. Wellcome to Mrs Wellcome, 21 Aug. 1889, quoted in Haggis, 'Life and work', p. 195.
80. Haggis, 'Life and work', pp. 97–8.
81. Burroughs to Wellcome, Aug. 1879, quoted in Haggis, 'Life and work', p. 80.
82. Burroughs to Wellcome, 20 Oct. 1879, quoted in Haggis, 'Life and work', p. 81.
83. Wellcome to Burroughs, 27 Jan. 1883, quoted in Haggis, 'Life and work', p. 148.
84. WFA, Wellcome LB10, 6, Wellcome to Burroughs, n.d. 1882.
85. WFA, Wellcome LB10, 35, 6–9, BW&Co. to Burroughs, 9 July 1884.
86. See below p. 129.
87. WFA, Wellcome LB1, 181, Wellcome to Burroughs, 26 Oct. 1883.
88. Burroughs to Wellcome, Aug. 1879, quoted in Haggis, 'Life and Work', p. 80.
89. Ibid., p. 77.
90. There has also been some suggestion that the Wyeth family displayed an eccentric tendency, though there is no evidence relating to the two brothers with whom Burroughs was associated. Mahoney, *Merchants*, p. 32; *Chem. & Drug.*, 46, 1895, p. 213, where a business acquaintance referred to 'initial trade and national prejudice' against Burroughs' new products and 'unconventional methods': 'Burroughs made his own road and it has become a highway'.
91. Rhodes James, *Henry Wellcome*, pp. 91–2.
92. Haggis, 'Life and work', pp. 99–100.
93. Ibid., pp. 77, 82–3, 89–90.
94. Ibid., p. 90.
95. WFA, Acc. 87/33, Burroughs to Wellcome, 20 April 1883.
96. See above, chapter 2, pp. 66–9.
97. WFA, Wellcome LB1, 448a, Wellcome to Fairchild, 4 Feb. 1886. The agreement was terminated through a public statement to which McKesson & Robbins objected, giving rise to tart exchanges with Wellcome who insisted that the 'very unfriendly expressions' critical of BW&Co. were entirely unwarranted. Rhodes James, *Henry Wellcome*, p. 152.
98. Macdonald, *In pursuit of excellence*, p. 41.
99. Jonathan Liebenau, 'Marketing high technology; educating physicians to use innovative medicines', in R. P. Davenport-Hines (ed.), *Markets and Bagmen. Studies in the History of Marketing and British Industrial Performance, 1830–1939* (Aldershot, Gower, 1986), p. 91.
100. For a more detailed assessment of Burroughs' contribution before the formation of BW&Co., see Roy Church, 'The British market for medicine in the late nineteenth century: the innovative impact of S. M. Burroughs & Co.', *Med. Hist.*, 49, 2005, pp. 281–98.

Notes to Chapter 5: The 'new crusade': Burroughs Wellcome & Co. *versus* the retail trade

1. Reported in *Chem. & Drug.*, 38, 24 Jan. 1891, p. 114; WFA, Acc. 2/1 Box 17, typescript (anon.), 'Re-substitution and price cutting', 18 March 1903; WFA, Acc. 82/1 Box 6, 'Proceedings at the conference between the deputation from the London Chemists' Association etc. and Burroughs Wellcome & Co.', 1906, Wellcome, p. 54.
2. WFA, Acc. 82/1 Box 17, typescript (anon.), 'Re-substitution and price cutting', 18 March 1903.
3. *Chem. & Drug.*, 39, 15 Aug. 1891, p. 13.
4. WFA, Acc. 82/1 Box 17, typescript (anon.), 'Re-substitution and price cutting', 18 March 1903, p. 36.
5. Ibid., p. 16.
6. Ibid.; *Chem. & Drug.*, 38, 24 Jan. 1891, p. 114.
7. Ibid., pp. 16, 40.
8. The company received intelligence that the agitation stirred up had been sustained by some tablet-making competitors. WFA, Wellcome LB20, 541, BW&Co. to Burnett, 28 Nov. 1902.
9. WFA, Acc. 2/1 Box 17, typescript (anon.), 'Re-substitution and price cutting', 18 March 1903.

10. WFA, Wellcome LB1, 19, Wellcome to Burroughs, 6 Sept. 1882.

11. WFA, Wellcome LB1, 19, Wellcome to Burroughs, 6 Sept. 1882; WFA, Wellcome LB1, 88, Wellcome to Burroughs, 27 Jan. 1883; WFA, Wellcome LB10, 223–32; BW&Co. to Coffin, 29 March 1883; WFA, Wellcome LB1, 113, Wellcome to ?, n.d, 1883.

12. WFA, Acc. 99/6/1, Horton to Wyeth, 2 Nov. 1897.

13. WFA, Acc. 99/6/1, Raffo Dalmazzo & Co. to BW&Co., 10 Oct. 1900; Appeal Court Decision, 26 March 1902; Elkin & Dixon to Giuseppe Forzani, 8 Aug. 1902; 'SM' to Forzani, 17 Oct. 1903; memo re Dompe, 2 Oct. 1903.

14. WFA, Wellcome LB20, 300, BW&Co. to J.W., 15 Feb. 1899; WFA: Wellcome LB12, 126, BW&Co. to Elkin Esq., 15 Feb. 1899; BW&Co. to Bailey, 11 April 1904.

15. WFA, Wellcome LB19, 956, Wellcome to Beecham, 25 Sept. 1902; *Chem. & Drug.*, 38, 10 Jan. 1891, p.51.

16. WFA, Acc. 82/1 Box 17, typescript (anon.), 'Re-substitution and price cutting', 18 March 1903, p.36.

17. WFA, Acc. 82/1 Box 14, BW&Co. to ?, 1 Dec. 1902.

18. *Chem. & Drug.*, 38, 10 Jan. 1891, p.10, 30 May, 1891, pp.18–21.

19. *Chem. & Drug.*, 39, 19 Dec. 1891, p.23.

20. WFA, Wellcome LB20, 552, BW&Co. to Burnett, 3 Dec. 1902.

21. WFA, Acc. 82/1 Box 7, Representatives' convention 1907, Curry, p.79, Smith, p.134.

22. WFA, Wellcome LB19, 413, BW&Co. to Villars, 4 July 1902.

23. WFA, Wellcome LB26, 219, BW&Co. to Blanch-flower, 30 March 1904.

24. WFA, Wellcome LB19, 731, BW&Co. to Burnett, 26 Aug. 1902.

25. WFA, Wellcome LB26, 56, BW&Co. to Moore, 11 March 1904.

26. WFA, Acc. 82/1 Box 7, Representatives' convention 1908, Pearson p.79.

27. WFA, Acc. 82/1 Box 17, Statement for the plaintiff by Ralph Neville K.C., 'The Tabloid case', *Medical Times and Hospital Gazette*, 19 Dec. 1903 (hereafter Tabloid case), 810; Wellcome's evidence, p.812.

28. Rhodes James, *Wellcome*, pp. 211–12, 292.

29. WFA, Acc. 82/1 Box 17, Tabloid case, pp.810–49.

30. Rhodes James, *Wellcome*, p.293.

31. Ibid., pp.120–1.

32. WFA, Wellcome LB20, 293, BW&Co. to Fletcher, 10 Nov. 1902.

33. WFA, Acc. 82/1 Box 17, Tabloid case, p.815.

34. WFA, Wellcome LB20, 375, BW&Co. to Slater, Heelis & Co., 18 Nov. 1902; WFA, Wellcome LB20, 969, BW&Co. to Markby Stewart&Co., 8 Jan. 1903.

35. WFA, Acc. 82/1 Box 17, The Tabloid case, p.816.

36. Ibid., p.813.

37. Ibid.

38. WFA, Wellcome LB25, 842, BW&Co. to Burnett, copied to all travellers, 18 Feb. 1904.

39. Ibid.

40. WFA, Wellcome LB25, 842, BW&Co. to Moore, 25 Feb. 1904; WFA, Wellcome LB29, 954, 29 Feb. 1904.

41. WFA, Acc. 82/1 Box 7, Report of home representatives' convention 1908, Linstead, p.49.

42. WFA, Wellcome LB19, 871, BW&Co. to McBride, 10 Sept. 1902.

43. WFA, Wellcome LB26, 249, BW&Co. to McBride, 6 April 1904.

44. WFA, 'BW&Co. home sales representatives at the 1896 British Medical Association Meeting, Carlisle'; WFA, Acc. 82/1 Box 7, Representatives' convention, 1907.

45. WFA, Wellcome LB26, 249, BW&Co. to McBride, 6 April 1904; 333, 13 April 1904.

46. WFA, Wellcome LB26, 331, BW&Co. to Moore, 13 April 1904.

47. WFA, Acc. 82/1 Box 4, Burnett (?) to Wellcome, 1 March 1899.

48. WFA, Wellcome LB12, 199a, BW&Co. to Burnett, 6 March 1899.

49. WFA, Wellcome LB20, 761, BW&Co. to Kirkpatrick, 23 Dec. 1902.

50. Ibid.

51. WFA, Acc. 82/1 Box 4, Barnsley and District Chemists' Association to BW&Co., 1 Nov. 1902.

52. WFA, Acc. 82/1 Box 4, 'Anti-cutting correspondence'; WFA, Wellcome LB20, 551, BW&Co. to Burnett, 1 Dec. 1902.

53. WFA, Acc. 82/1 Box 4, 'Substitution and price cutting'.

54. WFA, Wellcome LB19, 983–7, BW&Co. to Chairman of Federation, 29 Sept. 1902. To which response from the company was 'We are sorry that your organisation has been seriously misled and that at your next meeting they will unanimously pass a resolution disapproving of pirates and piracy, substitutors and substitution, and thus render a real service to the general drug trade'. See also voluminous correspondence from individual chemists printed in issues of the *Chem. & Drug.* during this period.

55. WFA, Acc. 82/1 Box 14.

56. WFA, Acc. 82/1 Box 17, BW&Co. to FLPCA, 4 Sept. 1902.

57. WFA, Wellcome LB20, 153, BW&Co. to Rogers, 21 Oct. 1902.

58. WFA, Acc. 82/1 Box 4, Wellcome to Sixsmith, 22 July 1905.

59. Ibid.

60. Ibid.

61. WFA, Acc. 82/1 Box 21, Houfton to BW&Co., 3 Oct. 1906.

62. WFA, Wellcome LB28, 687, BW&Co. to Allard, 27 March 1905.

63. WFA, Acc. 82/1 Box 6, 'Proceedings at the conference between the deputation from the London Chemists' Association etc. etc. and Burroughs Wellcome, 1906', henceforward 'Proceedings at the conference', pp.44, 46.

64. WFA, Acc. 82/1 Box 21, Reid to BW&Co., 12 Jan.

65. 1906.
Ibid.
66. WFA, Acc. 82/1 Box 6, 'Proceedings at the conference', p.46.
67. Ibid., Gibbs and Wellcome, p.10.
68. WFA, Wellcome LB32, 35–9, Wellcome to BW&Co., 9 Feb. 1906.
69. Ibid.
70. WFA, Wellcome LB32, 57–66, Wellcome to BW&Co., 1 March 1906.
71. WFA, Acc. 82/1 Box 6, 'Proceedings at the conference', p.9.
72. Ibid., pp.15–18, 38.
73. Both are to be found in 'Anti-cutting correspondence', WFA, Acc. 82/1 Box 4. See also, Wellcome's evidence contained in 'Proceedings at the conference', pp.23–4, WFA, Acc. 82/1 Box 6.
74. WFA, Acc. 82/1 Box 6, 'Proceedings at the conference', p.45.
75. Ibid., pp.47–9.
76. Ibid., p.51.
77. Ibid., p.55.
78. Ibid., p.6.
79. Chem. & Drug., 69, 22 Sept. 1906, p.468.
80. Ibid., 27 Oct. 1906, p.660.
81. WFA, Acc. 82/1 Box 21, Beeston to BW&Co., 2 Oct. 1906, Cockburn to BW&Co., 1906, Battle & Son to BW&Co., 3 Oct. 1906, Froggitt to BW&Co., 5 Oct. 1906.
82. WFA, Acc. 82/1 Box 21, Thornber to BW&Co., 2 Oct. 1906.
83. WFA, Acc. 82/1 Box 21, Poingdestre to BW&Co., 2 Oct. 1906.
84. WFA, Acc. 82/1 Box 21, Kemsey-Bourne to BW&Co., 29 Sept. 1906.
85. Chem. & Drug., 68, 6 Oct. 1906, p.525; 14 July 1906, p.51.
86. WFA, Acc. 82/1 Box 7, 'Representatives' convention', 1907, Curry, pp.74–5, 82.
87. Ibid., McBride, p.37.
88. Ibid., Clark, p.43, Carmichael, p.49.
89. J.B.Jefferys, Retail Trading in Great Britain, 1850–1950 (Cambridge, 1954), pp.388–9; B.S.Yamey, 'The origins of resale price maintenance', Economic Journal, LXII, 1952, pp.522–33.
90. S.D.Chapman, Jesse Boot of Boots the Chemists (1974), chapter 5.
91. S.W.F.Holloway, Royal Pharmaceutical Society of Great Britain, 1841–1991. A Political and Social History (Pharmaceutical Press, 1991), pp.311–20.
92. Yamey, 'Origins', p.538.
93. Jefferys, Retail Trading, p.390.
94. Ibid., p.390.
95. Holloway, Royal Pharmacetical Society, p.319.
96. Holloway refers to Allen & Hanbury's and BW&Co. having 'tried' their own price control schemes but is silent on whether they succeeded. Holloway, Royal Pharmaceutical Society, pp.312, 319.
97. WFA, Acc. 82/1 Box 7, 'Representatives' convention', 1907, p.39.
98. Ibid., Curry, p.71.

99. Ibid., Sixsmith, pp.13–17, Rogers, p.37. Monthly Memoranda, Points for Propaganda, hereafter Monthly Memoranda.
100. WFA, Wellcome LB28, 128, BW&Co. to Parkin, 19 Dec. 1904.
101. WFA, Wellcome LB30, 349, BW&Co. to Sydney, 26 March 1906.
102. Chem. & Drug., 27, 28 April 1894, p.574.
103. WFA, Acc. 82/1 Box 7, 'Representatives' convention', 1907, p.52.
104. Ibid.
105. See above, p.133.
106. WFA, Wellcome LB11, 357, Reports to Wellcome, 5 Feb. 1898. Another traveller in Ireland was similarly rebuked. On each of four days, he had visited three chemists and five medical men; on the fifth day he called on institutions in Dublin, and on the final day, seven chemists and 11 medical men. The Snow Hill response was: 'let us have your response by early post; need to more effective'.
107. Ibid., 509.
108. WFA, Wellcome LB25, 238, BW&Co. to Burnett, 7 Jan. 1904.
109. WFA, Wellcome LB26, 324, BW&Co. to Blanch-flower, 13 April 1904.
110. WFA, Wellcome LB19, 871, BW&Co. to McBride, 10 Sept. 1902.
111. WFA, Wellcome LB20, 428, BW&Co. to Sixsmith, 28 Nov. 1902.
112. Ibid., 555, BW&Co. to Sixsmith, 4 Dec. 1902.
113. WFA, Wellcome LB23, 943, BW&Co. to Hull, 16 Sept. 1903.
114. WFA, Wellcome LB25, 1, BW&Co. to Blanchflower, 17 Dec. 1903.
115. Ibid., 88, BW&Co. to Blanchflower, 25 Dec. 1903.
116. WFA, Wellcome LB27, 253, BW&Co. to Blanch-flower, 26 July 1904.
117. WFA, Acc. 82/1 Box 7, 'Representatives' convention', 1908, Jowett, 91.
118. WFA, Acc. 82/1 Box 7, 'Representatives' convention', 1907.
119. For a detailed examination of this issue see Roy Church, 'The British market for medicine in the late nineteenth century: the innovative impact of S.M.Burroughs & Co., Med. Hist., 2005, 49, pp.281–98.
120. Jonathan Liebenau, Medical Science and the Medical Industry. The Formation of the American Pharmaceutical Industry (Macmillan, Basingstoke, 1987).
121. WFA, Acc. 82/1 Box 7, 'Representatives' convention', 1907, Greig, p.55. He addressed those attending the convention as if all had worked 'behind a chemist's counter', which equipped them to avoid bluster and swagger as well as the 'sleekit "Uriah Heep" approach' to chemists.
122. Ibid., Jones, p.65.
123. Ibid., Weld, p.88.
124. Ibid., p.70.
125. Ibid., Clark, p.5.
126. Ibid., Overton, p.61.
127. WFA, Acc. 82/1 Box 7, 'Representatives'

convention', 1908, Curry, p.78. 'How such a doctor would be startled into attention if he were told that a medical man might be sued for damages in a court of law if he lost a case of P.P.H. [post partum haemorrhage] as he had not used Ernutin. Not to do so is culpable negligence. I do not suggest that you can tell a doctor this in so many words, but you can exert the full power of your will and state your case with such conviction that he is bound to listen to you.'

128. Ibid., Curry, p.18.
129. Ibid., Curry, p.78.
130. Ibid., Curry, pp.72–4.
131. Ibid., Kirkpatrick, p.67.
132. Ibid., Curry, pp.15–19.
133. Ibid., p.25.
134. Ibid., pp.73–5.
135. WFA, Wellcome LB25, 859, BW&Co. to Bailey, 19 Feb. 1904; WFA, Wellcome LB25, 921, Feb. 1904.
136. Ibid., Curry, p.37.
137. WFA, Acc. 82/1 Box 7, 'Representatives' convention', 1908, p.22.
138. WFA, Acc. 82/1 Box 7, 'Representatives' convention', 1907, Grieg, p.57.
139. Ibid., Blanchflower, p.31; Rogers, p.33.
140. Ibid., day 2, Curry, pp.4–5.
141. Ibid., McBride, pp.7–8.
142. Ibid., Jowett, pp.1–2.
143. WFA, Acc. 82/1 Box 7, 'Representatives' convention', 1908, Curry, p.8.
144. Ibid., pp.1–5.
145. Ibid., Blanchflower, p.7.
146. Ibid., Clark, p.12.
147. Haggis, 'Life and work', p.483.
148. Ibid.
149. WFA, Acc. 82/1 Box 7, 'Representatives' convention', 1908, Johnson, pp.50, 52.
150. Ibid., p.53.
151. Ibid., Turnbull, p.120; Curry and Hill, p.121.
152. WFA, Wellcome LB10, 544–7, BW&Co. to Holman, 26 March 1889.
153. WFA, Wellcome LB16, 607, BW&Co. to Wellcome, 16 Oct. 1901.
154. See Liebenau's account of the campaign mounted by the American Mulford Co. in J. Liebenau, 'Marketing high technology: educating physicians to use innovative medicines', in J. R. T. Davenport-Hines (ed.), *Markets and Bagmen, 1830–1939* (Aldershot, Gower, 1986), pp.87–9.
155. Ibid., Holland, pp.39–40; Curry, p.44; Weld, p.45.
156. Ibid., Curry, p.44.
157. Ibid., Linstead, pp.46–7.
158. WFA, Wellcome LB32, 22–4, Wellcome to BW&Co., 29 Jan. 1906.
159. Ibid.
160. In 1913 he became the first curator of the Wellcome Historical Medical Museum. See Haggis, 'Life and work', pp.403–4.
161. Ibid. These included *Anaesthetics, Ancient and Modern* (1907).
162. WFA, Acc. 82/1, Box 7 'Representatives' convention', 1907, Greig, p.99.
163. Ibid., Clark, p.42.
164. Ibid., Burnage, p.41.
165. Ibid., Holland, pp.37–40; Hill, p.42; Greig, p.57.
166. WFA, Guard Book B1/22, Circulars book 21, 1914.
167. Rhodes James, *Henry Wellcome*, p.222.
168. *Pharm. Era*, 16, Feb. 1890, p.24. In 1893 Kepler goods were described as the firm's staple products. WFA, Acc. 82/1 Box 13, *Talks* (1893), 21 July 1893.
169. LSE archives, Charles Booth Coll., LSE/279/ vol. B93, industry, interviews, and questionnaires.
170. WFA, Wellcome LB10, 783, BW&Co. to Weld, 26 June 1896.
171. WFA, PB III, BW&Co. price lists.
172. WFA, Acc. 96/45, BW&Co. sales book 2, 1905–44.
173. This record may be compared with that of Allen & Hanbury's. In 1911 turnover was £383,211 (excluding sales by overseas subsidiary companies which may have approached £100,000) against the figure for BW&Co. of £575,756 (including £187,294 sales from branches overseas). Measured in terms of employment, however, the number of workers employed by Allen & Hanbury's did not exceed 500 until 1914, a figure below the numbers employed by BW&Co. even before 1890. Tweedale, *At the Sign of the Plough*, p.118.

Notes to Chapter 6: Creating products, producing knowledge, and gaining respect: research laboratories, 1894–1914

1. See chapter 1, pp.31–4, for details of early laboratory work within the factory.
2. D. S. L. Cardwell, *The Organisation of Science in England* (Heinemann, London, 1972), pp.175–6.
3. See H. Power, *Tropical Medicine in the Twentieth Century: A History of the Liverpool School of Tropical Medicine, 1898–1990* (Kegan Paul, London, 1998); L. Wilkinson and A. Hardy, *Prevention and Cure: The London School of Hygiene and Tropical Medicine – A Twentieth-century Quest for Global Public Health* (Kegan Paul, London, 2001).
4. Wellcome's applications for Home Office registration are detailed in E. M. Tansey, 'The Wellcome Physiological Research Laboratories, 1894–1904: the Home Office, pharmaceutical firms and animal experiments', *Med. Hist.*, 33, 1989, 1–41.
5. TNA, HO45/11092/B21744/1, Home Office (hereafter HO) to BW&Co., 4 May 1896; ibid., Wellcome to HO, 17 July 1896.
6. Neither 'experiment' nor 'calculated to cause' pain were defined in the Act, and were open to interpretation.
7. TNA, HO45/11092/B21744/3, Bokenham to Home Secretary, 1 Sept. 1896. See also ibid., HO Memo,

4 Sept. 1896 and TNA: PRO, HO45/11092/
B21744/4, Bokenham to Home Secretary, 7 Sept.
1896.

8. See chapter 7, pp. 207–10.

9. C. L. Oakley, 'Alexander Thomas Glenny,
1882–1965', *Biog. Mems. FRS Lond.*, 12, 1966, 163–80,
RS 93HD, 65.5, 'Brockwell Hall 1952–1967',
'Observations recently reported to Sir Henry Dale,
as having been made by technicians working in
the Wellcome Physiological Research Laboratories,
before he himself arrived there in 1904', an undated
manuscript, c.1960.

10. WFA, Acc. 83/3/28, typescript draft, 'The
Wellcome Physiological Research Laboratories',
undated.

11. TNA, HO45/11092/B21744/8, Dowson to Ridley,
15 and 22 Feb. 1900; WFA, Acc. 83/3/28, HO to
Dowson, 16 and 23 Feb. 1900, 13 and 15 March
1900.

12. TNA, HO45/11092/B21744/28, undated draft for
Law Officer's Opinion, and Digby to Attorney
General, 7 Jan. 1901.

13. WFA, Acc. 83/3/28, draft of petition from
Wellcome to Charles Ritchie, Secretary of State for
Home Affairs, 25 Feb. 1901; TNA, HO45/11092/
B21744/30, page 2, Wellcome to HO, 25 Feb. 1901.

14. Ibid., Appendix A, pp. 8–11.

15. Ibid.

16. TNA, HO45/11092/B21744/34, HO Minute by
Thane, 12 June 1901, and note by Digby, 15 June
1901.

17. WFA, Wellcome LB16, 281, BW&Co. to Dowson,
14 Aug. 1901, and BW&Co. to Thane, 15 Aug.
1901; ibid., 282, BW&Co. to Dowson, 14 Aug. 1901;
ibid., 280, BW&Co. to Thane 15 Aug. 1901; TNA,
HO45/11092/B21744/34, HO memo by Thane, 20
Aug. 1901.

18. Ibid., 768, HO to Wellcome, 5 Sept. 1901; WFA,
Acc. 83/3/28, Dowson to BW&Co., 6 Sept. 1901,
and BW&Co. to Wellcome, 6 Sept. 1901. TNA,
HO156/14, 784, Anti-vivisectionists were also told
that the laboratories had been registered, e.g. HO
to International Anti-vivisectionist Council, 26
Sept. 1901.

19. *Chem. & Drug.*, 61, 1901, 412.

20. WFA, Wellcome LB32, 25, Wellcome to BW&Co.,
c. Feb. 1906.

21. WFA, Wellcome LB7, 399, Wellcome to Starling, 2
June 1904.

22. H. H. Dale, 'Autobiographical sketch', *Perspec. Biol.
& Med.*, 1, 1958, 125–37.

23. W. S. Feldberg, 'Henry Hallett Dale', *Biog. Mems.
FRS Lond.*, 16, 1970, 77–174, quote on p. 94.

24. WFA, Acc. 84/10 Box 5, salary details from
Management Salary Book, c. 1897–1955.

25. Ibid.

26. WFA, Acc. 82/1 Box 38, Dowson to Wellcome, 27
Feb. 1905.

27. Missing Wellcome Papers, Dowson to Wellcome, 11
Feb. 1904.

28. H. A. D. Jowett and F. L. Pyman, 'Relations between

chemical constitution and physiological action in
the tropeines', *J. Chem. Soc.*, 91, 1907, 92–8; *idem*,
Part II, ibid., 95, 1909, 1020–32.

29. E.g. WFA, Acc. 82/1, 'Wellcome Physiological
Research Laboratories, 1895–1922', Wellcome to
Mellanby, 1 Jan. 1902, and Mellanby to Wellcome,
15 Jan. 1902.

30. RS, 93HD, 36.4.29, Sir Henry Dale papers,
'T. R. Elliott', Dale to Elliott, 6 June 1958.

31. WFA, Wellcome LB17, 126, memo 1097, BW&Co.
to Wellcome, 3 Dec. 1901; ibid., 329, memo 1207,
BW&Co. to Wellcome, 28 Dec. 1901.

32. WFA, Wellcome LB17, 735, memo 1461, BW&Co.
to Wellcome, 31 Jan. 1902.

33. Ibid., 675, Wellcome to A. K. Gracie (WPRL), 30
Jan. 1902.

34. See e.g. WFA, Wellcome LB13, 529, BW&Co. to
Dowson, 4 April 1900 (*re.* thyroid glands); WFA,
Wellcome LB15, 36, BW&Co. to Dowson, 1 Feb.
1901 (*re.* Beef Juice); Dowson did pursue some
research projects, including an investigation of
shallow burial, see L. J. Picton, *Thoughts on Feeding*
(Faber & Faber, London, 1946), pp. 17–19.

35. WFA, Wellcome LB26, 964, Wellcome to Dowson,
13 June 1904.

36. Ibid.

37. WFA, Wellcome LB13, 22, Sudlow to Dowson, 9
Jan. 1900.

38. Anon., 'The conference in London', *Chem. & Drug.*,
56, 1900, 1035.

39. WFA, Wellcome LB8, 448, BW&Co. to Dowson, 11
May 1905.

40. WFA, Wellcome LB8, 188, Wellcome to Dowson,
31 Oct. 1904. RPS 'Minutes of Executive
Committee 1887–1911', 318, Executive Committee, 8
July 1907.

41. WFA, Wellcome LB15, 84–9, BW&Co. to
Wellcome, 8 Feb. 1901.

42. G. Oliver, 'On the therapeutic employment of the
supra-renal glands', *BMJ*, ii, 1895, 653–5.

43. WFA, Wellcome LB3, 354, Wellcome to Lloyd
Williams, 28 Nov. 1896.

44. WFA, Technical Journal Advertisements 3, '1893–
1905', Box 108, p. 145, *London Figaro*, 3 Jan. 1895.

45. WFA, Wellcome LB11, 330–1, memo 103, BW&Co.
to Wellcome, 28 Jan. 1898.

46. WFA, Wellcome LB10, 732, Wellcome to Searl, 1
Jan. 1896.

47. Anon., 'Animal remedies', *Chem. & Drug.*, 48, 1896,
853.

48. WFA, Wellcome LB11, 957, BW&Co. (Snow Hill) to
BW&Co. (Dartford), 1 Dec. 1898.

49. WFA, Wellcome LB11, 330–1, memo 104, BW&Co.
to Wellcome.

50. E.g. Anon., 'Report of work on Tabloid Lymphatic
Gland, and Three Glands preparation', *Chem. &
Drug.*, 83, 1913, 355, 874.

51. WFA, Wellcome LB16, 895, BW&Co. to Mr Curry,
11 Nov. 1901.

52. WFA, Wellcome LB31, 1–2, Wellcome to Dowson,
19 Dec. 1901.

53. WFA, Wellcome LB16, 725, BW&Co. to Dowson, 24 Oct. 1901.

54. H. H. Dale, 'On some physiological actions of ergot', *J. Physiol.*, 34, 1906, 163–206.

55. H. H. Dale, *Adventures in Physiology* (Wellcome Trust, London, 1965), p. 51.

56. H. H. Dale, 'The action of extracts of the pituitary body', *Biochem. J.*, 4, 1909, 427–47.

57. W. Blair-Bell, 'The pituitary body and the therapeutic value of the infundibular extract in shock, uterine atony and intestinal paresis', *BMJ*, ii, 1909, 1609–13.

58. W. Blair-Bell and P. Hick, 'Observations on the physiology of the female genital organs. IV. Uterine contractions', *BMJ*, i, 1909, 777–83.

59. The words adrenaline and adrenalin were used interchangeably in the correspondence. This section is based on E. M. Tansey, 'What's in a name? Henry Dale and adrenaline, 1905', *Med. Hist.*, 39, 1995, 459–76.

60. Missing Wellcome Papers, Wellcome to Dowson, 25 Feb. 1906, and Wellcome to Dale, 25 Feb. 1906. Annotated carbon copies of both in WFA, Acc. 82/1 Box 23, 'WPRL 1895–1922'.

61. Missing Wellcome Papers, telegram, Wellcome to Dowson, 27 Feb. 1906, and letter, Wellcome to Dowson, 27 Feb. 1906.

62. There are two extant copies of this letter, Dale to Wellcome, 6 March 1906: the carbon copy from the company files was in Missing Wellcome Papers; the original, heavily annotated by Wellcome in WFA, Acc. 82/1 Box 12.

63. WFA, Acc. 82/1 Box 23, 'WPRL 1895–1922', Report of Chune Fletcher's opinion by Pearson to Wellcome, undated, but *c.* early March 1906.

64. Several further items of correspondence, querying the precise wording of the footnote, dated between 8 and 10 March 1906, were in Missing Wellcome Papers. See also H. H. Dale, 'On some physiological actions of ergot', *J. Physiol.*, 34, 1906, 163–206, quote on p. 169.

65. WFA, Acc. 82/1 Box 23, 'WPRL 1895–1922', Dale to Wellcome, 14 March 1906.

66. WFA, Wellcome LB32, 78, Wellcome to BW&Co., n.d. but between 3 and 7 March 1906.

67. Anon., 'Recent patents', *Pharm. J.*, 12, 1901, 583.

68. WFA, Wellcome LB32, 25, consecutive undated notes, Wellcome to BW&Co., *c.* Feb. 1906, emphasis as in the original.

69. W. S. Feldberg, 'Henry Hallett Dale', *Biog. Mems. FRS Lond.*, 16, 1970, 77–174, quote on page 98.

70. WFA, Acc. 82/1 Box 182, Barger to Wellcome, 13 Sept. 1905, on the receipt of a cutting from the *Chemist & Druggist* about yet another new ergot preparation.

71. WFA, Wellcome LB8, 607, BW&Co. to Dowson, 16 March 1905, enclosing specimen #36, batch #5533 of supra-renal granules, for testing and report.

72. H. H. Dale, *Adventures in Physiology* (London, Wellcome Trust, 1965), p. xi.

73. WFA, Wellcome LB8, 637 and 638, BW&Co. (Snow Hill) to BW&Co. (Dartford Works), 17 March 1905; ibid., BW&Co. to Dowson, 18 March 1905, with a specimen from the same batch (#5533).

74. Wellcome Library, Wellcome Library Film and Audio Collection, 395V, unbroadcast interview, 1960, 'A talk with Sir Henry Dale' conducted by Stephen Black.

75. W. S. Feldberg, 'Henry Hallett Dale', *Biog Mem FRS*, 16, 1970, 77–174.

76. G. Barger, F. H. Carr, and H. H. Dale, 'An active alkaloid from ergot', *BMJ* ii, 1906, 1792; G. Barger and H. H. Dale, 'Ergotoxine and some other constituents of ergot', *Biochem. J.*, 2, 1907, 240–99.

77. 'Trade notes', *Chem. & Drug.*, 70, 1907, 830.

78. F. H. Carr, 'Experimental work in an English herb garden', *Am. J. Pharm.*, 83, 1913, 487–96.

79. See above, pp. 183–5.

80. F. Kraft, 'Ueber das Mutterkorn', *Archiv der Pharmazie*, 204, 1906, 336–59.

81. WFA, Acc. 84/7/14, Dale to Wellcome, 16 Oct. 1906; WFA, Missing Wellcome Papers, Wellcome to Dale, 17 Oct. 1906.

82. G. Barger and G. S. Walpole, 'Isolation of the pressor principles of putrid meat', *J. Physiol.*, 38, 1909, 343–52.

83. See chapter 10, pp. 309–12.

84. See e.g. H. H. Dale, *The Wellcome Physiological Research Laboratories. Guide and Catalogue with a Description of the Exhibits of these Laboratories at the Franco-British Exhibition* (BW&Co., London, 1908).

85. WFA, Acc. 82/1, Box 7, Report on Home Representatives' Convention, 1908, at which Dale spoke on 'Modern Therapy'.

86. RS, 93HD, 65.5, 'Brockwell Hall 1952–67', Dale to Fowler, 20 June 1960.

87. RS, 93HD, 64.2, 'Personal file II. Correspondence 1904–48', Elliott to Dale, 20 Dec. 1940.

88. RS, 93HD, 36.4.29, 'T. R. Elliott', Dale to Elliott, 6 June 1958.

89. H. H. Dale, *The Wellcome Physiological Research Laboratories* (BW&Co., London, 1910), pp. 9–10; see also J. R. Vane, 'The Research Heritage of Henry Wellcome', *Pharm. Hist.*, 10, 1980, 2–8.

90. Missing Wellcome Archives, Wellcome to Power, 14 Feb. 1895.

91. Ibid., Wellcome to Power, late 1882 or early 1883.

92. WFA, Wellcome LB3, 33, Wellcome to Power, 9 April 1895.

93. Ibid., 333, Wellcome to Power, 12 Dec. 1896.

94. Ibid., 384, Wellcome to Power, 2 May 1896; *Chem. & Drug.*, 48, 1896, 57.

95. The celebrations were reported at length in the *Pharmaceutical Journal*, 57, 1896, 78–9.

96. *Pharm. J.*, 57, 1896, 78–9.

97. WFA, D3 WCRL, Power to BW&Co., 22 Jan. 1907; WFA, Acc. 83/3, PB80, F. B. Power, *The Wellcome Chemical Research Laboratories* (BW&Co., London, 1900).

98. WFA, Wellcome LB13, 871, BW&Co. to the editor, *Pall Mall Gazette*, 4 July 1900. Copies also to the editors of *The Times, Daily Graphic, Daily Chronicle,*

Daily Mail, Daily News, Daily Telegraph, Globe, Morning Post and *Standard*.

99. WFA, Wellcome LB4, 29, 39, Power to Wellcome, 11 and 14 Dec. 1896.

100. WFA, Wellcome LB1, 103–104, J.C.Smith to Wellcome, 7 Oct. 1897.

101. WFA, Wellcome LB11, 132, 133, 138–139, 150–151, various reports, BW&Co. (Snow Hill) to BW&Co. (Dartford), Nov. 1897.

102. WFA, Wellcome LB4, 231–2, Wellcome to Moulton, 26 Oct. 1897.

103. WFA, Wellcome LB11, 152, BW&Co. (Snow Hill) to BW&Co. (Dartford), 15 Nov. 1897; ibid., 312, memo 88, BW&Co. to Wellcome, 22 Jan. 1898.

104. Ibid., 271–2, memo 48, BW&Co. to Wellcome, 11 Jan. 1898.

105. Ibid., 384–9, memo 157, BW&Co. to Wellcome, 12 Dec. 1898; ibid., 441–4, memos 218, 219, BW&Co. to Wellcome, 5 March 1898.

106. Ibid., 535–7, memo 282, BW&Co. to Wellcome, 7 April 1898.

107. WFA, Wellcome LB18, 794, memo 2074, BW&Co. to Wellcome, 23 April 1902.

108. [Burroughs, Wellcome & Co.] *The Wellcome Chemical Research Laboratories. With a Description of the Exhibits of these Laboratories at the Anglo American Exposition, London, 1914* (BW&Co., London, 1914), p.7.

109. H. A. D.Jowett, 'Some new gold salts of hyoscine, hyoscyamine and atropine', *J. Chem. Soc.*, 71, 1897, 679–82.

110. WFA, Acc. 83/3, PB/786 and PB/102, *Wellcome Research Laboratories: Publications*.

111. Missing Wellcome Papers, Power to Wellcome, 15 Jan. 1900.

112. J.Gorvin, 'The early development of chemical research in the Wellcome laboratories', in L.Goodwin, E.Beveridge and J.H.Gorvin, *Wellcome's Legacies* (Wellcome Trust, London, 1998), pp.54–92, especially 56–8.

113. WFA, Wellcome LB11, 953, BW&Co. (Snow Hill) to BW&Co. (Dartford), 30 Nov. 1898.

114. Gorvin, op. cit., note 112.

115. WFA, Wellcome LB15, 401, BW&Co. to Wellcome, 23 March 1901; F. B. Power, 'A soluble manganese citrate and compounds of manganese with iron', *Pharm. J.*, 67, 1901, 135.

116. BW&Co., *British Alkaloids and Fine Chemicals* (BW&Co., London, 1914).

117. WFA, Acc. 82/1 Box 25, 'Private and confidential report on formulae and secret processes, dated 13 January 1916' WFA, B3, 'Chronology 1880–1936'.

118. E.g. WFA, Wellcome LB34, 187, BW&Co. to Lloyd Williams, 31 Aug. 1898.

119. WFA, Wellcome LB4, 178, Wellcome to Carr, 11 June 1897; WFA, Wellcome LB11, 60, BW&Co. to Carr, 3 Aug. 1897.

120. Ibid., 263–7, BW&Co. to Wellcome, 8 Jan. 1898; ibid., 300, BW&Co. (Snow Hill) to BW&Co. (Dartford), 19 Jan. 1898.

121. Ibid., 679, BW&Co. (Snow Hill) to BW&Co. (Dartford), 2 July 1898.

122. E.g. ibid., 913, BW&Co. (Snow Hill) to BW&Co. (Dartford), 5 Nov. 1898; ibid., 921, BW&Co. (Snow Hill) to BW&Co. (Dartford), 8 Nov. 1898; ibid., 953, BW&Co. (Snow Hill) to BW&Co. (Dartford), 30 Nov. 1898.

123. Anon., 'Obituary: William Lloyd Williams', *Chem. Trade J.*, 26, 1900, 52.

124. WFA, Wellcome LB17, 277–282, memo 1167, BW&Co. to Wellcome, 19 Dec. 1901.

125. S. B. Schryver and F. H. Lees, 'Researches on morphine, part 1', *J. Chem. Soc.*, 77, 1900, 1024–40; *idem*, 'Researches on morphine, part 2', ibid., 79, 1901, 563–80.

126. WFA, Acc. 82/1 Box 19, 'The essential features of the method adopted for the synthesis of codeine from morphine', document dated 19 June 1899, deposited with Markby Stewart & Co.; WFA, Wellcome LB14, 384, BW&Co. (Snow Hill) to BW&Co. (Dartford), 7 Nov. 1900.

127. F. B. Power and F. H. Gornall, 'The constituents of chaulmoogra seeds', *J. Chem. Soc.*, 85, 1904, 838–51; *idem*, 'The constitution of chaulmoogric acid, Part 1', ibid., 851–61; M. Barrowcliff and F. B. Power, 'The constitution of chaulmoogric and hydnocarpic acids', ibid., 91, 1907, 557–78.

128. Anon., 'Dr F. B. Power, Obituary', *Nature*, 119, 1927, 573.

129. See chapter 10, pp.423–6.

130. E.g. P. E. F. Pérrèdes, 'A contribution to the pharmacognosy of official strophanthus seed', *Yearbook of Pharmacy*, 1900, 366; *idem*, *London Botanic Gardens* (WCRL, London, 1906).

131. WFA, Wellcome LB17, 823–8, memo 1540, BW&Co. to Wellcome, 8 Feb. 1902.

132. WFA, Wellcome LB18, 14–16, BW&Co. to Pérrèdes, 26 Feb. 1902; ibid., 831, BW&Co. to Pérrèdes, 26 April 1902.

133. Pérrèdes, 1900, 'Pharmacognosy of strophanthus'.

134. WFA, Acc. 82/1 Box 50, correspondence between Power and Pérrèdes, and Dale and Pérrèdes, 1905–08.

135. WFA, Acc. 82/1, 'List of drugs available for investigation', undated, c. 1907?, and various notes on plants and seeds, in reply to queries from Power or Pyman.

136. WFA, Acc. 82/1, Pérrèdes to Power, 3 March 1908. See also Anon., 'P. E. F. Pérrèdes, obituary', *Chem. & Drug.*, 153, 1950, 102–3.

137. *The Wellcome Chemical Laboratories*, 1914, 7–8.

138. 'Wellcome' Brand Chemical Price List (1912), *passim*.

139. H. S.Wellcome, *The Story of Metlakahtla* (Saxon, London, 1887).

140. T. Pakenham, *The Scramble for Africa* (Abacus, London, 1991).

141. S. Pasha, *Fire and Sword in the Sudan: A Personal Narrative of Fighting and Serving the Dervishes, 1879–95*, translated by F. R.Wingate (E. Arnold, London, 1899).

142. WFA, Wellcome LB11, 949, Wellcome to Lord Kitchener, 26 Nov. 1898.

143. WFA, Wellcome LB14, 730, BW&Co. to Pearson, 21 Dec. 1900; WFA, Wellcome LB5, 429, L. M. Henry to BW&Co., 30 Jan. 1901.

144. *Gorgas Memorial Laboratory. Hearings before the Committee on foreign affairs, House of Representatives, seventieth congress, first session on HR 8128 to authorise a permanent annual appropriation for the maintenance and operation of the Gorgas Memorial Laboratory* (United States Government Printing Office, Washington, DC, 1928), pp. 32–52, quote on p. 45.

145. WFA, Wellcome LB6, 13, Wellcome to Major Gen. Sir Francis Reginald Wingate, 4 Sept. 1901.

146. Financial details taken from A. A. Abdel-Hameed, 'The Wellcome Tropical Research Laboratories in Khartoum (1903–1934): an experiment in development', *Med. Hist.*, 41, 1997, 30–58, especially pp. 31–2.

147. Wellcome, *'Evidence to Gorgas Memorial Laboratory hearing'*, p. 42.

148. Abdel-Hameed, 'Wellcome Tropical Laboratories', p. 31.

149. WFA, Wellcome LB6, 171–2, Wellcome to Currie, 28 Aug. 1902.

150. WFA, Acc. 90/14:2, Dinner for Dr Balfour; 'Gordon Memorial College Khartoum', *The Times*, 9 Dec. 1902; 'Gordon Memorial College Khartoum', *Daily Chronicle*, 9 Dec. 1902; 'Dinner to Dr Andrew Balfour', *Journal of Tropical Medicine*, 15 Dec. 1902, 390–1.

151. Details of the work of the WTRL taken largely from Wellcome's 'Evidence' to the *Gorgas Memorial Laboratory* (1928).

152. L. Bousfield. *Sudan Doctor* (Christopher Johnson, London, 1954), 71.

153. A. Cruickshank, 'The golden age of tropical medicine and its impact on the modernization of the Sudan', in M. W. Daly (ed.), *Modernization in the Sudan: Essays in Honor of Richard Hill* (Lilian Barber Press, New York, 1985), pp. 85–100. L. Bousfield,

ibid.

154. See e.g. WFA, Wellcome LB25, 584–5, BW&Co. to J. A. Atkinson (rep. in Egypt), 29 Jan. 1904, and various items of correspondence in H. Bell, *Frontiers of Medicine in the Anglo-Egyptian Sudan, 1899–1940* (Oxford Historical Monographs, Oxford, 1999), p. 62.

155. E.g. WFA, Acc. 82/1 Box 26, correspondence between Wellcome and Linstead, Feb. 1906.

156. For considerable correspondence between Wellcome and Balfour, and Wellcome and several artists, especially A. G. E. Terzi, see [March] 1906 in WFA, Wellcome LB32, 95; ibid., 79–82, Wellcome to Balfour, 7 Nov. 1906.

157. WFA, Wellcome LB32, 79–82, Wellcome to Balfour, 7 Nov. 1906.

158. The Wellcome Tropical Research Laboratories survived at Khatan until 1934, although Wellcome's direct, personal links with Balfour did not continue under the next two directors. See Abdel-Hahmeed, 'Wellcome Tropical Laboratories', pp. 56–8.

159. WA/HSW/PE/C, Haggis, 'Life and work', 1939–44, Wellcome to Balfour, 8 Feb. 1913, p. 413.

160. WFA, Acc. 82/1, Box 12, Wellcome to Alsberg, 12 July 1915.

161. WFA, PB/78, Wellcome Research Laboratories Publications.

162. PP/ARC/D.1, Cushny to Abel, 6 Jan. 1913. See J. Parascandola, '"Preposterous provision": The American Society for Pharmacology and Experimental Therapeutics' Ban on Industrial Pharmacologists, 1908–41', in J. Liebenau, G. J. Higby and E. C. Stroud (eds), *Pill Peddlers – Essays on the History of the Pharmaceutical Industry* (American Institute of the History of Pharmacy, Madison, WI, 1990), pp. 29–47.

163. RS, 93HD, 64.2. 'Personal file II. Correspondence 1904–48', Dale to Wellcome, 1 May 1914.

Notes to Chapter 7: Products and prestige: sera and vaccines before the First World War

1. E. von Behring and S. Kitasato, 'Ueber das Zustandekommen der Diphtherie-Immunitat und der Tetanus-Immunitat bei Thieren', *Dtsch. Med. Wochen.*, 16, 1890,1113–14; P. R. E. Roux and A. L. F. J. Martin, 'Contribution a l'etude de la diphterie (serum therapie)', *Ann. Inst. Pasteur*, 8, 1894, 609–39.

2. SA/Lis/I.l.f5, Sir Henry Roscoe to Amand Ruffer, 21 Sept. 1894.

3. H. Chick, M. Hume and M. Macfarlane, *War on Disease – A History of the Lister Institute* (Andre Deutsch, London, 1971), p. 39. SA/Lis/I.1, extracts from a meeting of the Council of the BIPM, 6 Oct. 1894.

4. SA/Lis/A.4, minutes of BIPM Council meeting, 8 Oct. 1894.

5. J. Lister, 'The antitoxin treatment of diphtheria', *The Times*, 31 Oct. 1894. For details of *Le Figaro*'s

appeal see P. Weindling, 'From medical research to clinical practice: serum therapy for diphtheria in the 1890s', in J. V. Pickstone (ed.) *Medical Innovations in Historical Perspective* (Macmillan, Basingstoke, Hampshire, 1992), pp. 72–83.

6. WFA, P2 Acc. 82 Box 46, 35, 1879–1928 Staff Register CA/08; also in WFA, Acc. 82/1 Box 38, 'Notes on early diphtheria serum'.

7. Anon., 'The anti-toxin treatment of diphtheria: the supply of serum', *BMJ*, ii, 1894, 1452; *Chem. & Drug.*, 44, 1894, 736.

8. J. M. Liebenau, 'Public health and the production and use of diphtheria antitoxin in Philadelphia', *Bull. Hist. Med.*, 61, 1987, 216–36.

9. SA/Lis/A.4, minutes of BIPM Council meeting, 8 Oct. 1894.

10. R. Rhodes James, *Henry Wellcome* (Hodder & Stoughton, London, 1994), pp. 134, 247; H. Turner,

Henry Wellcome: The Man, His Collection and his Legacy (Wellcome Trust and Heinemann, London, 1980), pp. 66–72.

11. *Chem. & Drug.* (suppl), 46, 19 Jan., 1895, advert.

12. WFA, Wellcome LB10, 673, BW&Co. to Bokenham, 8 April 1895; ibid., 682, BW&Co. to Bokenham, 29 April 1895.

13. T. J. Bokenham, 'Additional notes on the preparation of anti-streptococcus serum', *BMJ*, ii, 1896, 3–4.

14. Anon., 'The *Lancet* Special Commission on the relative strengths of diphtheria anti-toxic serums', *Lancet*, ii, 1896, 182–95.

15. WFA, Wellcome LB10, 882, Wellcome to Bokenham, 3 Dec. 1896. Ibid., 881, BW&Co. to Kanthack, 3 Dec. 1896; ibid., 883–6, memo, 'Detailed instructions: Antidiphtheritic serum', 3 Dec. 1896.

16. Ibid., 902, BW&Co. to Kanthack, 23 Dec. 1896.

17. For J. W. Washbourn (1863–1902), see *Trans. Epidem. Soc. Lond.*, 21, 1901–02, 151–4; WFA, Wellcome LB10, 903, BW&Co. to Bokenham, 22 Dec. 1896.

18. SA/Lis/M9, 'Early years – notes from Minutes 1891–1900', meetings, 22 Oct. 1897 and 20 Dec. 1898.

19. WFA, Wellcome LB10, 904, BW&Co. to Washbourn, 22 Dec. 1896; ibid., 910, BW&Co. to Lucas, 24 Dec. 1896.

20. Ibid., 915, BW&Co. to Wellcome, 6 Jan. 1897.

21. Ibid., 917, BW&Co. to Bokenham, 12 Jan. 1897.

22. Ibid., 920, BW&Co. to Wellcome, 13 Jan. 1897.

23. Ibid., 915, BW&Co. to Wellcome, 6 Jan. 1897.

24. E.g. WFA, Wellcome LB13, 825, BW&Co. to Dowson, 25 June 1900.

25. The premises were insured for £10,250. WFA, Wellcome LB16, 970–971, BW&Co. to assistant solicitor, LCC, 18 Nov. 1901.

26. See e.g. WFA, Reports and references to BW&Co. and staff, Book 2, 1899–1903, *Chem. & Drug.*, 55, 1899, 780–1; *Pharm. Era*, 30 Nov. 1899.

27. Anon. 'Wellcome Physiological research laboratories', *Chem. & Drug.*, 54, 1899, 780–1.

28. Anon. 'A stranger within our gate', *Chem. & Drug.*, 54, 1899, 896.

29. WFA, Wellcome LB15, 250–61, memo 340, BW&Co. to Wellcome, 1 March 1901.

30. *The Brown Institution Rabies Investigations: A Ledger of Diagnostic Reports etc., from October 1895 to June 1907*, is in the Medical School Library, St Thomas' Campus, King's College London. See also E. M. Tansey, 'Charles Sherrington and the Brown Animal Sanatory Institution', *St Thomas' Hospital Gazette*, 84, 1986, 5–10.

31. H. H. Dale, 'Frederick Gowland Hopkins 1861–1947', *Obit. Notes FRS Lond.*, 6, 1949, 115–45.

32. This data is taken from WFA, Acc. 99/6, 15, a sheaf of letters from the WPRL to BW&Co., dated 23 Oct. 1900–30 March 1901.

33. The total income has been estimated using 2s. 6d. as the unit cost for each case, which is probably an underestimate.

34. WFA, Acc. 99/6, 15.

35. WFA, Wellcome LB18, 394–400, memo 1843, BW&Co. to Wellcome, 25 March 1902. WFA, Acc. 99/6, 15. Ibid., Dowson to BW&Co., 16 March 1901.

36. WFA, Wellcome LB17, 823–8, memo 1539, and 845–7, memo 1560, BW&Co. to Wellcome, 8 Feb. 1902 and 11 Feb. 1902; WFA, Wellcome LB18, 1–5, BW&Co. to Wellcome, 25 Feb. 1902.

37. Ibid., 394–400, memo 1843, BW&Co. to Wellcome, 21 March 1902.

38. E.g. WFA, Wellcome LB17, 313, BW&Co. to Wellcome, 24 Dec. 1901; ibid., 826, memo 1539, BW&Co. to Wellcome, 8 Feb. 1902; New physiological equipment at the WPRL is described in *Chem. & Drug.*, 60, 1902, 768. For Glenny's report, see Wellcome Missing Archives, Dowson to Wellcome, 1 Jan. 1905.

39. WFA, Wellcome LB17, 735–8, memo 1461, BW&Co. to Wellcome, 31 Jan. 1902.

40. WFA, Wellcome LB16, 915–17, memo 959, BW&Co. to Wellcome, 12 Nov. 1901.

41. WFA, Wellcome LB17, 634, BW&Co. to Dowson, 27 Jan. 1902.

42. Ibid.

43. E. C. Bousfield, 'Diphtheria antitoxin in private practice', *Lancet*, ii, 1898, 1544–5.

44. WFA, Wellcome LB21, 175 and 211, Wellcome to Dowson, 29 Jan. 1903 and 31 Jan. 1903.

45. WFA, Wellcome LB24, 938–9, Wellcome to Dowson, 11 Dec. 1903.

46. WFA, Wellcome LB25, 166, Wellcome to Bousfield, 1 Jan. 1904.

47. E.g. see Bousfield's entries, *Medical Directories* 1900–06.

48. WFA, GB 30/2, Monthly memoranda, March 1923.

49. WFA, Wellcome LB15, 251, memo 339, BW&Co. to Wellcome, 1 March 1901.

50. Many of the original 'horse-cards' are in WFA, Acc. 84/7/3; Glenny's earliest notebook, 1899–1900, is in Glaxo Smith Kline Archives, Stevenage, (WFA, Acc. 84/7/7), and provides details of testing anti-typhoid serum, monitoring sterile air supplies for contamination and lab experiments on bacterial cultures.

51. C. L. Oakley, 'Alexander Thomas Glenny, 1882–1965', *Biog. Mems. FRS Lond.*, 12, 1966, 163–80.

52. WFA, Wellcome LB14, 859–62, memo 183, BW&Co. to Wellcome, 11 Jan. 1901.

53. WFA, Wellcome LB17, 735–8, memo 1461, BW&Co. to Wellcome, 31 Jan. 1902.

54. WFA, Wellcome LB18, 394–400, memo 1843, BW&Co. to Wellcome, 21 March 1902.

55. WFA, Wellcome LB17, 735–8, memo 1461, BW&Co. to Wellcome, 31 Jan. 1902.

56. WFA, Acc. 99/6, 15, Dowson to BW&Co., 19 March 1901.

57. WFA, Wellcome LB27, 847, Wellcome to Dowson, 31 Oct. 1904; WFA, Wellcome LB33, 175–186, memo 309, BW&Co. to Wellcome, 11 Jan. 1905.

58. WFA, Acc. 82/1 Box 38, Dowson to Wellcome, 1

Jan. 1905.

59. Ibid.

60. Editorial, 'Diphtheria antitoxin', *J. Royal Army Med. Corps*, 2, 1904, 601–2.

61. SA/Lis/I.6, documents mostly concerned with supply of anti-plague serum, correspondence with Local Government Board and Colonial Office, Aug. 1903–05.

62. SA/Lis/I.12.f2.

63. See e.g. Cape Town Industrial Exhibition, November 1904; *Chem. & Drug.*, 63, 1905, 41.

64. Allen & Hanburys had originally established two agencies in North America, one in Toronto, one in New York, these were converted into a subsidiary company in 1902. See D. Chapman-Huston and E. C. Cripps, *Through a City Archway: The Story of Allen & Hanburys, 1715–1954* (John Murray, London, 1954), p. 254.

65. SA/Lis/I.11.f2, Lloyd Wood, Allen & Hanburys, Toronto to Allen & Hanburys, London, 2 Oct. 1905.

66. SA/Lis/I.11.f4, Lloyd Wood, Allen & Hanburys, Toronto to Allen & Hanburys, London, 6 Jan. 1905.

67. SA/Lis/I.11.f8, Allen & Hanburys, London, to Lloyd Wood, Toronto, 17 Oct. 1905.

68. SA/Lis I.11.f4, Charles A. Hodgett, Secretary of the Provincial Board of Health, Canada to C. J. Martin, Lister Institute, 25 Jan. 1905.

69. SA/Lis/I.11.f4, Allen & Hanburys, London, to Lloyd Wood, Toronto, 20 Jan. 1905; Lloyd Wood, Toronto, to Allen & Hanburys, London, 30 Jan. 1905.

70. SA/Lis/I.11.f6, Lloyd Wood, Toronto, to Allen & Hanburys, London, 22 May 1905.

71. SA/Lis/I.11.f5, Lloyd Wood, Toronto, to Allen & Hanburys, London, 4 April 1905.

72. Ibid.

73. SA/Lis/I.11.f7, Allen & Hanburys, London, to Lloyd Wood, Toronto, 14 June 1902.

74. SA/Lis/I.11.f8, Allen & Hanburys, London, to Lloyd Wood, Toronto, 17 Oct. 1905.

75. WFA, Wellcome LB30, 363, BW&Co. (Snow Hill) to BW&Co. (Australia), 26 March 1906.

76. E.g. *Brit. & Col. Drug.*, 37, 1900, 16.

77. R. T. Hewlett, *Serum Therapy, Bacterial Therapeutics and Vaccines* (J. A. Churchill, London, 1903), p. 258.

78. SA/Lis/I.10, Notes of interview, 27 July 1904, 'Serum and vaccine lymph, special advertisements 1905'.

79. WFA, Acc. 82/1 Box 38, Dowson to Wellcome, 1 Jan. 1905.

80. RS, 93HD, 65.5 'Brockwell Hall, 1952–67', Dale to Fowler, 20 June 1960, and Fowler to Dale, 28 June 1960.

81. W. S. Feldberg, 'Henry Hallett Dale 1875–1968', *Biog. Mems. FRS Lond.*, 16, 1970, 77–174, especially p. 101.

82. E.g. WFA, Wellcome LB28, 6, 11, requests for anti-puerperal preparations, BW&Co. to Dowson, 26 Nov. 1904 and 29 Nov. 1904.

83. WFA, Wellcome LB33, 148–55, memo 252, BW&Co. to Wellcome, 23 Dec. 1904.

84. These figures do not include diphtheria anti-toxin production, WFA, Acc. 86/72 Box 74.

85. WFA, PB, *Price List of Fine Products*, 1913, 113–14, 157–8.

86. WFA, Wellcome LB15, 52–53, BW&Co. to Raffo, Dalmazzo & Co., 6 Feb. 1901.

87. Allen & Hanburys, *General List of Drugs, Pharmaceuticals, and the 'Allenburys' Specialities* (Allen & Hanburys, London, 1908). See also F. Vannozzi, *Sienna, la città laboratorio: Dall'innesto del vajuolo ad Albert Sabin* (Protagon Editore Toscani, Siena, 1999).

88. WFA, Wellcome LB15, 52–3, BW&Co. to Raffo, Dalmazzo & Co., 6 Feb. 1901.

89. WFA, Wellcome LB10, 356–9, Wellcome to Burroughs, 9 July 1884.

90. H. J. Parish, *Victory with Vaccines: The Story of Immunization* (E. and S. Livingstone, Edinburgh and London, 1968), p. 42.

91. WFA, Acc. 83/3, 29, memo, BW&Co. to Wellcome, 22 Feb. 1901, and Wright to BW&Co., 17 Feb. 1901.

92. M. Dunnill, *The Plato of Praed Street* (RSM Press, London, 2000), pp. 95–7. See also, W. Chen, 'The laboratory as business: Sir Almoth Wright's vaccine programme and the construction of penicillin', in A. Cunningham and P. Williams (eds), *The Laboratory Revolution in Medicine* (Cambridge University Press, Cambridge and New York, 1992), pp. 245–92.

93. W. C. Bosanquet and J. W. H. Eyre, *Serums, Vaccines and Toxins in Treatment and Diagnosis* (Cassell, London, 1909), pp. 354–5.

94. WFA, Wellcome LB11, 591, BW&Co. (Snow Hill) to BW&Co. (Dartford), 7 May 1898; WFA, Wellcome LB16, 175, BW&Co. (Snow Hill) to BW&Co. (Dartford), 22 July 1901; Veterinary Tabloids, *Chem. & Drug.*, 55, 1899, 682.

95. WFA, Wellcome LB19, 54, BW&Co. (Snow Hill) to BW&Co. (Cape Town), 16 May 1902.

96. WFA, Wellcome LB18, 233–4, BW&Co. to Dowson, 13 March 1902; WFA, Wellcome LB20, 13, 181, BW&Co. to Hon. Sec., Poultry & Ornithological Society of Jersey, 16 Oct. 1902 and 24 Oct. 1902.

97. WFA, Wellcome LB18, 394–400, memo 1843, BW&Co. to Wellcome, 21 March 1902.

98. For notes on BIPM's early production, see SA/Lis/M9, 'Early years – notes from minutes, 1891–1900' and SA/Lis/P.13, '*Tuberculin and mallein for veterinary use*', in Allen & Hanburys 1904 Price List, 29–30.

Notes to Chapter 8: In search of overseas markets; agencies, depots, branches, and multinational enterprise

1. WFA, Wellcome LB10, 116, Burroughs to Wellcome, 5 April 1883; Rhodes James, *Henry Wellcome*, p.141fn.
2. PP/SMB/6, Burroughs to BW&Co., 2 Feb. 1881; WFA, Acc. 87/33/5, Burroughs to Fellows, 27 July 1882; John Davies, 'Burroughs into Europe', *Wellcome World*, Aug. 1992, pp.5–17.
3. See above chapter. 2, pp.62–3.
4. WFA, Wellcome LB10, 55, Wellcome to Buck, 26 Oct. 1882.
5. WFA, Wellcome, LB10, 34–5, Wellcome to Burroughs, n.d. 1882.
6. WFA, Wellcome, LB1, 213–22, 243, Wellcome to Burroughs, 6 Dec. 1883.
7. WFA, Wellcome, LB10, 32, 34–5, Wellcome to Burroughs, n.d. 1882; WFA, Wellcome LB10, 62–82, March 1882. Wellcome was particularly incensed by an agreement with Ballantyne as a traveller in India without obtaining references.
8. Rhodes James, Henry Wellcome, pp.72–3.
9. WFA, Wellcome LB10, 116, Burroughs to Wellcome, 5 April 1883.
10. WFA, Wellcome LB10, 219, Wellcome to Burroughs, 6 Dec. 1883; WFA, Wellcome LB1, 381, Wellcome to Burroughs, 9 July 1885.
11. WFA, Wellcome LB25, 50, BW&Co. to Ross, 21 Dec. 1903; WFA, Wellcome LB25, 634, 2 Feb. 1904.
12. WFA, Wellcome LB11, 273, BW&Co. to Linkenheil, 13 Jan. 1898; WFA, Wellcome LB11, 284–5, 287; BW&Co. to Wellcome, 15 Jan. 1898. WFA, Wellcome LB11, 337–8, BW&Co. to A.K., 1 Feb. 1898.
13. WFA, Wellcome LB12, 27, BW&Co. to Prof. Liebrich, 29 Dec. 1898.
14. WFA, Wellcome, LB13, 331, BW&Co. to ACF, 17 March 1900; WFA, Wellcome LB13, 335, Burroughs Wellcome to Linkenheil, 17 March 1900.
15. WFA, Acc. 91/14.
16. WFA, Wellcome LB10, 456–60, BW&Co. to Christie, 14 April 1885.
17. WFA, Acc. 99/6/1, Wellcome to Burroughs, 2 March, 5 Dec., 15 Dec. 1892; Wellcome to De Giovanni, 1 March 1894.
18. WFA, Acc. 99/6/1, Dalmazzo to BW&Co., n.d. 1896?
19. See chapter 5, p.132.
20. WFA, Wellcome LB28, 609, BW&Co. to J.Collett Smith, 15 March 1905; WFA, Wellcome LB28, 702, 29 March 1905.
21. WFA, Wellcome LB12, 564; 23 May 1905; WFA, Wellcome LB29, 951, BW&Co. to Kris, 28 July 1899.
22. WFA, PB/111, BW&Co., 'Quarter century: past, present and future', 1906 price list.
23. PP/SMB/6, Burroughs to Wellcome, n.d. 1882.
24. PP/SMB/6, Burroughs to Wellcome, 10 May 1882.
25. WFA, Wellcome LB14, BW&Co. to Wellcome, 11 Jan. 1901.
26. Ibid. Burroughs was especially enthusiastic having experienced 'good results' in his own case and in those of acquaintants.
27. WFA, Acc. 87/33/66, Burroughs to Wellcome, n.d. 1882.
28. WFA, Wellcome LB29, BW&Co. to Humphreys, 12 April 1905; *Foundation News*, 1, 6 Dec. 1951.
29. WFA, PB/111, BW&Co., 'Quarter century: Past, Present and Future', 1906 price list.
30. WFA, Acc. 82/1 Box 13, memo, 8 July 1930, re G.Pearson.
31. WFA, Wellcome LB15, 609–18, BW&Co. to Wellcome, 19 April 1901.
32. WFA, Wellcome LB18, 33–8, BW&Co. to Wellcome, 27 Feb. 1902; WFA, Acc. 82/1 Box 38, Pearson (?), 'Pros and cons re the establishment of a branch in South Africa'.
33. WFA, Wellcome LB15, 609–18, BW&Co. to Wellcome, 19 April 1900.
34. WFA, Wellcome LB20, 440, BW&Co. to Cape Town, 20 Nov. 1902; WFA, Wellcome LB20, 508–9, BW&Co. to Cape Town, 25 Nov. 1902.
35. WFA, Wellcome LB26, 603, BW&Co. to Cape Town, 11 April 1904; ibid., 994, BW&Co. to Cape Town, 11 May 1904.
36. WFA, Wellcome LB30, 611, BW&Co. to Cape Town, 18 Dec. 1906.
37. WFA, Wellcome LB28, 70–1, BW&Co. to Cape Town, 9 Dec. 1904.
38. WFA, Acc. 96/45, BW&Co. sales book no. 2.
39. Gregory Haines, *Three Grains and Threepenn'orths of Pharmacy in New South Wales, 1788–1976* (Lowden P.C.Kilmore, Australia, 1976), pp.70–1.
40. WFA, Wellcome LB10, 116, Wellcome to Burroughs, May 25 1882. Burroughs found that in Tasmania 'all of the chemists except one drunken good-for-nothing fellow are going for our goods and the doctors as users are all delighted.'
41. WFA, Acc. 87/33/35e, Burroughs to Wellcome, 12 March 1883, 13 March 1883. However, some local doctors objected to the name of Beef and Iron Wine, deeming it unsuitable as language for a prescription. Burroughs suggested a change to Elixoid.
42. *Aust. Chem. & Drug.*, VI, 61, May 1883; 62, June 1883; 63, July 1883; 64, Aug. 1883.
43. *Aust. Chem. & Drug.*, VI, 63, July 1883.
44. Ron Champion, 'Wellcome in Australia', *Wellcome News*, 7, Dec. 1986, p.4.
45. Haines, *Three Grains*, p.71.
46. Ibid.
47. These amounted to £629 between 1889 and 1896. WFA, Wellcome LB26, 657, Re-finance, BW&Co. to Sydney office, 13 May 1904; Champion, 'Wellcome', p.4; Haines, *Three Grains*, p.71.
48. Champion, 'Wellcome', p.5.
49. Glaxo Wellcome Historical Records, GSK, Melbourne, 007523/88–8–30b, note on

A. B. Hector.

50. Haines, *Three Grains*, p. 84.
51. WFA, Wellcome LB18, 520, BW&Co. to Sydney, 16 Jan. 1902.
52. Ibid.
53. Ron Champion, 'Wellcome in Australia', *Wellcome News*, 7, Dec. 1986.
54. WFA, Wellcome LB16, 568, 570 [747] BW&Co. to Sydney, 11 Oct. 1901; WFA, Wellcome LB17, 40–4 [1052]; 121, BW&Co. to Wellcome, 22 Nov. 1901.
55. WFA, Wellcome LB16, 548, BW&Co. to Wellcome, 1901 n.d.; WFA, Wellcome LB25, 987, BW&Co. to Sydney, 2 March 1904.
56. WFA, Wellcome LB19, 140, BW&Co. to Sydney, 26 May 1902, 150, 28 May 1902, 187, 30 May 1902.
57. Champion, 'Wellcome', p. 6.
58. WFA, Wellcome LB17, 194–6, BW&Co. to Wellcome, 9 Dec. 1901. London's attitude to re-building and refurbishment was to minimise expense and not to insist (in contrast to the policy for buildings in England) upon the best or most permanent work, WFA, Wellcome LB18, 723, BW&Co. to Sydney, 18 April 1902.
59. WFA, Wellcome LB17, 148–9, BW&Co. to Sydney, 4 Dec. 1901.
60. WFA, Wellcome LB19, 329, BW&Co. to Sydney, 19 June 1902.
61. WFA, Wellcome LB20, 920, BW&Co. to Sydney, 5 Jan. 1903.
62. WFA, Wellcome LB20, 784, 15 Feb. 1907.
63. WFA, Wellcome LB17, 711–714, BW&Co. to Wellcome, 31 Jan. 1902.
64. WFA, Wellcome LB19, 47, BW&Co. to Sydney, 16 May 1902; ibid., 79, BW&Co. to Sydney, 22 May 1902.
65. WFA, Wellcome LB19, 468–9, BW&Co. to Sydney, 11 July 1902; WFA, Wellcome LB21, 123, BW&Co. to Sydney, 16 Dec. 1902.
66. WFA, Guard book 31/6, Drug standing orders.
67. WFA, Wellcome LB16, 570 [747], BW&Co. to Wellcome, 11 Oct. 1901.
68. WFA, Wellcome LB16, 701, BW&Co. to Dartford, 23 Oct. 1901.
69. WFA, Wellcome LB16, 701, BW&Co. to Dartford, 23 Oct. 1901; ibid., 800–2, 1 Nov. 1901, BW&Co. to Wellcome.
70. WFA, Wellcome LB17, 950–1, BW&Co. to Hill, 20 Feb. 1902.
71. WFA, Wellcome LB19, 14, BW&Co. to Sydney, 12 May 1902.
72. WFA, Guard book 31/6, Drug stock standing orders, 1897–1915. See 'A short account of the manufacturing process at the works, Dartford', dispatched to Sydney on 14 April 1902 in connection with the manufacture of Tabloid and Soloid products.
73. WFA, Wellcome LB19, 349, BW&Co. to Sydney, 14 Nov. 1902,
74. WFA, Wellcome LB20, 488–9, BW&Co. to Sydney, 25 Nov. 1902; WFA, Wellcome LB19, 838, BW&Co. to Sydney, 4 Sept. 1902; WFA, Wellcome LB20,

488–90, BW&Co. to Sydney, 25 Nov. 1902.
75. WFA, Wellcome LB20, 488–90, BW&Co. to Sydney, 25 Nov. 1902.
76. WFA, Wellcome LB21, 555, BW&Co. to Sydney, n.d. 1903.
77. WFA, Wellcome LB20, 334, BW&Co. to Sydney, 14 Nov. 1902.
78. WFA, Wellcome LB25, 373, BW&Co. to Sydney, 15 Jan. 1904; ibid., 455, 14 Dec. 1903.
79. WFA, Wellcome LB18, 490, BW&Co. to Sydney, 27 March 1902.
80. WFA, Wellcome LB25, 656, BW&Co. to Sydney, 29 Dec. 1903.
81. WFA, Wellcome LB30, 903, BW&Co. to Sydney, 28 March 1906.
82. WFA, Wellcome LB25, 455, BW&Co. to Sydney, 14 Dec. 1903, n.d.; WFA, Wellcome LB17, 610, HO to Dartford memo, 24 Jan. 1902.
83. Sales of goods (excluding Fairchild's and Lanoline) from London to Sydney were: 1898/99 – £13,356; 1899/00 – £13,773; 1900/01 – £17,869; 1901/02 – £18,572; 1902/03 – £16,615 WFA, F/FA/328, profit and loss accounts.
84. WFA, Wellcome LB26, 657, BW&Co. to Sydney, 13 May 1904.
85. Ibid.
86. WFA, Wellcome LB27, 294, BW&Co. to Sydney, 29 July 1904.
87. WFA, Wellcome LB29, 233, BW&Co. to Sydney, 9 Jan. 1906.
88. WFA, Wellcome LB26, 427, BW&Co. to Sydney, 22 April; ibid., 991, 17 June 1904.
89. WFA, F/FA/328, profit and loss accounts.
90. WFA, Acc. 96/45, BW&Co. Sales Book 2.
91. Over the long term, the war and postwar boom conditions carried sales to new heights, reaching £131,228 in 1919/20, peaking at £141,694 in 1924/25, the first year of BW&Co. (Australia) Ltd.
92. 'Montreal arrival', *Foundation News*, 31 Oct. 1981, p. 13.
93. WFA, Wellcome LB19, 443, BW&Co. to Kirkpatrick, 9 July 1902.
94. WFA, Wellcome LB9, 744, BW&Co. to Nicholl & Co., 2 June 1905.
95. WFA, Wellcome, LB28, 166, BW&Co. to Kirkpatrick, 21 Dec. 1904; ibid., 424, 8 Feb. 1905.
96. For example, WFA, Wellcome LB29, 744, BW&Co. to Nicholls & Co., 5 April 1905.
97. WFA, Wellcome LB30, 70, BW&Co. to Kirkpatrick, 2 Jan. 1906.
98. WFA, Wellcome LB32, 14–17, Wellcome to BW&Co., 27 Jan. 1906.
99. Glaxo Wellcome Heritage Center, Raleigh Durham, NC, USA archives, Coll 107, Public Affairs, 'A brief analysis, 1959', reproduction of paper presented by Creasy to a Foundation Board Meeting, 6 Jan. 1959. Hereafter GWHC, coll 107, 'Brief analysis'.
100. WFA, Wellcome LB27, 86, BW&Co. to Forbes & Havilland, 29 June 1904; ibid., 94, BW&Co. to Fairchild, 1 July 1904.

101. It is possible, of course, that this was a hoax perhaps intended to ridicule the wide range of Tabloid products advertised by BW&Co.

102. Potentially more serious was the advertising for Wilson's 'Tabuloids', which again led Wellcome to call on Fairchild for advice. WFA, Acc. 99/6/1, Fairchild to Wellcome, 6 Oct. 1899.

103. WFA, Wellcome LB27, 172, BW&Co. to M. Kallman, 13 July 1904.

104. Ibid.

105. WFA, Wellcome LB32, 30, Wellcome to BW&Co., n.d., 1906.

106. WFA, Wellcome LB32, Wellcome to BW&Co., 27 Jan. 1906.

107. Philadelphia College of Physicians archives, ID: PACVMTEO, 125-A, Medical trade ephemera, advertisements and pamphlets, BW&Co., 1906–30.

108. Glaxo Wellcome Heritage Center, Raleigh Durham, NC, USA, BW&Co. Public affairs, publications, Tabloid Monthly Memoranda, 107.07/07.05, (hereafter Tabloid Monthly Memoranda), Feb. 1942, p. 54; May 1942, p. 232.

109. *Chem. & Drug.*, 52, 29 Jan. 1898, pp. 182–3.

110. Philadelphia College of Physicians archives, ID: PACVMTEO, 125-A, Medical trade ephemera, advertisements and pamphlets, BW&Co., 1906–30.

111. WFA, Wellcome LB30, 815, BW&Co. to NY, 12 Feb. 1907.

112. WFA, Wellcome LB30, 768, BW&Co. to NY, 1 Feb. 1907.

113. Ibid., 830, BW&Co. to NY, 28 Feb. 1907.

114. Ibid., 770, BW&Co. to NY, 13 Feb. 1907.

115. Jan Tanner, 'The New York venture', *Foundation News*, June 1981, p. 12.

116. Ibid., pp. 12–14.

117. WFA, Acc. 82/1 Box 20, 'Moves', 1924; Tanner, 'New York venture', p. 12.

118. WFA, F/FA/328, Report on NYB accounts, 10 Dec. 1908.

119. Ibid.

120. Tanner refers to his request for a rise for his staff on account of extra travel expenses, a request apparently conveyed to Wellcome whose response is not known. We do not know whether the two are linked. Tanner, 'New York venture', p. 13.

121. WFA, F/FA/328, Report on NYB Accounts, 30 June 1910.

122. Ibid.

123. Ibid., 18 Sept. 1913.

124. Ibid., 18 Sept. 1913.

125. Ibid., 26 Oct. 1914.

126. Ibid., 15 Dec. 1909.

127. Ibid., 10 Dec. 1908.

128. Tanner, 'New York venture', p. 13.

129. GWHC, coll 107, 'Brief analysis'.

130. WFA, Acc. 82/1 Box 38, Pearson to Nevin, 13 Oct. 1914; GWHC, coll 107, 'Brief analysis'.

131. *Foundation News*, April 1984, p. 15.

132. Ibid.

133. Ibid.

134. WFA, F/FA/328, NYB Accounts for 1914, 26 Oct. 1914.

135. Ibid., Accounts for 1913, 18 Sept. 1913.

136. Ibid., 30, 1909/10 accounts; 5 March 1920, 1918/19 accounts.

137. Ibid., 15 Dec. 1909.

138. WFA, F/FA/328, WFL accounts, NYB, 28 Oct. 1914. The Works did, however, attain profitability, albeit modest, by 1914.

139. WFA, Acc. 82/1 Box 38, Pearson to Nevin, 13 Oct. 1914.

140. Ibid., GWHC, coll 107, Public affairs, 'A brief analysis'.

141. Ibid., 26 Oct. 1914.

142. Ibid.

143. Ibid.

144. Ibid.

145. WFA, Acc. 87/56, Wellcome to Pearson, 12 Dec. 1927.

146. Ibid.

147. Ibid.

Notes to Chapter 9: The impact of war: innovation and transformation from laboratory research to factory production

1. *Chem. & Drug.*, 84, 12 Dec. 1914, pp. 53–5; 19 Dec., p. 47.

2. M. Robson, 'The British pharmaceutical industry and the first World War', in J. Liebenau (ed.), *The Challenge of New Technology: Innovation in British Business Since 1850* (Gower, Aldershot, 1988), p. 88.

3. 'The war and the supply of drugs; a memorandum on the special measures taken by the NHI Commissioners in relation to the supply of drugs and other medicinal stores during the war', PP, 1919, Cd. 183, paras 2–3, 7.

4. Ibid.

5. Royal Commission on Venereal Diseases 1916, Cd. 8189, p. 16.

6. E.g., F. L. Pyman and W. C. Reynolds, 'Aromatic and arsenic acids', *J. Chem. Soc.*, 93, 1901, p. 1180.

7. Anon. 'Arylarsonates', *Chem. & Drug.*, 73, 22 Aug. 1908, pp. 323–24.

8. *Chem. & Drug.*, 84, 19 Sept. 1914, p. 51.

9. Details of work carried out at WCRL are taken principally from monthly reports of the Director. WA/BSR/BA/Crl/A: WCRL reports, July 1914–Dec. 1922.

10. H. H. Dale, C. F. White, J. H. Burn, F. M. Durham, J. E. Marchal, and C. H. Mills, 'Report on an experimental and clinical comparison of the therapeutic properties of different preparations of 914 (neosalvarsan)', *Lancet*, i, pp. 779–83.

11. A. L. Thomson, *Half a Century of Medical Research*, vol 2, 'The programme of the Medical Research

Council UK, (MRC)', pp. 245–6.

12. E.g., WA/BSR/BA/Crl/A, WCRL report, Nov. 1916, July 1914–Dec. 1922.

13. Quoted in 'The story of the Foundation' – 3 'In the cause of healing', *Foundation News*, 2, Oct. 1952, pp. 3–4.

14. Ibid.

15. WA/BSR/BA/Crl/A, WCRL reports, March, April 1915.

16. *Lancet*, i, March 1920, p. 673.

17. Haggis, 'Life and work', p. 468.

18. All production figures for sera are taken from WFA, Acc. 86/72 Box 74.

19. *Chem. & Drug.*, 85, 19 Sept. 1914, p. 51.

20. W. G. Macpherson, *History of the Great War Based on Official Documents: Medical Services, General History*, vol. 1 (HMSO, 1921), p. 179.

21. Chapman, *Boots*, p. 96.

22. WA/BSR/BA/Crl/A, War work at the WRCL, 1 Jan. 1919. This product was discontinued after the war, probably because of the additional strictures imposed by the Dangerous Drugs Act of 1920, which governed the production, storage, and marketing of such drugs. For details regarding cocaine, ergot, salvarsan, and strophanthus, see WFA, Acc. 82/1 Box 14, miscellaneous papers.

23. WFA, Acc. 82/1 Box 78, WCRL correspondence with Vickers, 1922.

24. Chapman, *Boots*, p. 82.

25. Ibid., pp. 73, 90, 94–5.

26. Ibid., chapter 6, 'Finance'.

27. Boots Pure Drug Co. archives, 321/3, 'Reminiscences of C. E. Coulthard', c. 1963.

28. Boots Pure Drug Co. archives, 341/1, unpublished ms, 'Reminiscences of three old members of the Analytical Dept, London Road'.

29. Ibid., WFA 82/1 Box 9, typescript, 'Notes on the move of F. H. Carr and other Dartford chemists to Boots, 1915'; Chapman, *Jesse Boot*, pp. 96–8.

30. Chapman, *Jesse Boot*, pp. 97–8.

31. Imperial College archives, B/Carr/6, F. H. Carr's papers, conversations recorded by Mr Gunther, winter, 1966/67.

32. Ibid.

33. WFA, Acc. 82/1 Box 9, typescript, 'Notes on the move of F. H. Carr and other Dartford chemists to Boots, 1915'.

34. Boots Pure Drug Co. archives, 321/3, 'Reminiscences of C. E. Coulthard', c. 1963. WFA/CW/27/01, 'Notes of interest'.

35. WFA 82/1 Box 9, typescript, 'Notes on the move of F. H. Carr and other Dartford chemists to Boots, 1915'.

36. Chapman, *Jesse Boot*, p. 97.

37. Ibid.

38. Ibid.

39. Ibid.

40. Boots Pure Drug Co. archives, 321/3, 'Reminiscences of C. E. Coulthard', c. 1963.

41. Chapman, *Jesse Boot*, p. 97.

42. Boots Pure Drug Co. archives, 321/3, 'Reminis-

43. Chapman, *Jesse Boot*, p. 96. BW&Co. had drawn attention to its achievements in this respect during the war in full page cartoon advertisements in the medical and trade press, see above pp. 265–8.

44. Chapman, *Jesse Boot*, pp. 97–8.

45. Robson 'British Pharmaceutical Industry', p. 192.

46. WFA, Acc. 82/1 Box 9, Notes on the move of F. H. Carr. The 'widow's clause' refers to the provision in the Acts which while excluding from dispensing and selling medicines those unqualified to do so, was *intended* to protect the right of pharmacists' widows to own and conduct their deceased husband's business (roughly 200 were listed in the 1869 register). Reference to 'other persons' rather than specifically to widows, provided Boot with a loophole. Holloway, *Royal Pharmacetical Society*, p. 261.

47. H. Turner, *Henry Wellcome, The Man, His collections and his Legacy* (London, 1980).

48. Hall and Bembridge, *Physic and Philanthropy*, p. 42.

49. *Chem. & Drug.*, 57, 2 June 1900, p. 926.

50. Rhodes James, *Henry Wellcome*, p. 333.

51. WA/BSR/BA/Crl/A, WCRL report.

52. WA/BSR/BA/Crl/A, WCRL reports, 15 April, July 1914–Dec 1922; E. M. Tansey, 'Illustrations from the Wellcome Institute Library: Sir Henry Dale's laboratory notebooks, 1914–1919', *Med. Hist.*, 34, 1990, pp. 199–209.

53. WFA, Acc. 83/3, 128, WBSR report, 'Services rendered by the WBSR during the war', a.d.c. Dec. 1918; WA/BSR/RP/Mon/A 2, e.g. fee for Wenyon.

54. L. G. Goodwin and E. Beveridge, 'Sir Henry Wellcome and tropical medicine', in L. G. Goodwin, E. Beveridge, and J. H. Gorvin (eds), *Wellcome's Legacies* (Wellcome Trust, 1988), pp. 21–2.

55. W. G. Macpherson, W. P. Herringham, T. R. Elliott, and A. Balfour, *History of the Great War Based on Official Documents: Medical Services, Diseases of the War* (HMSO, two vols, 1923).

56. WFA, GB/31/9, Works Manager's Instruction Book 2, p. 21, 4 Dec. 1914.

57. Ibid.

58. Ibid., 7 June 1918, p. 50; 25 Feb. 1918, p. 48.

59. WFA, Acc. 82/1 Box 38, Wellcome to Pearson, 19 Oct. 1917.

60. WFA, GB/31/9, Works Manager's Instruction Book 2, pp. 23–5, 3 Feb. 1915, 9 Feb. 1915, 4 Feb. 1915; p. 35, 5 Oct. 1915.

61. Ibid., 13 Jan. 1916, 22 Feb. 1916, pp. 35–7.

62. WA/BSR/BA/Crl/A, WCRL reports, July 1914–Dec. 1922.

63. WA/BSR/BA/Crl/A, WCRL reports, May 1916.

64. Ibid.

65. *Therapeutic Sera, Vaccines, and Tuberculins* (BW&Co., 1922).

66. WA/BSR/BA/Prl/A1, WPRL reports, 1914–18, 10 May 1915.

67. WFA, Acc. 86/72 Box 74, Anti-toxic serum production, excepting diphtheria, Sept. 1914–Dec. 1917.

68. Rhodes James, *Henry Wellcome*, p.331.
69. WA/BSR/BA/Prl/A1, WPRL reports, May 1915–Jan. 1919.
70. WA/BSR/BA/Prl/A1, WPRL reports, May 1915.
71. WA/BSR/BA/Prl/A1, WPRL reports, May 1915.
72. J.S.G. Blair, *In Arduis Fidelis: Centenary History of the Royal Army Medical Corps* (Scottish Academic Publishing, 2001), p.205.
73. See 'British Union of Anti-vivisection', 1916 annual report; R.M. McLeod, 'Law medicine, and public opinion: the resistance to public health legislation, 1870–1907', *Public Law*, 106, 1967, pp.188–211; Anon, 'Mr Churchill has no use for serums', *Vacc. Inq.*, 36, 1914, p.252.
74. W.G. Macpherson, W.G. Leishman, S.L. Cummins, *History of the Great War Based on Official Documents: Medical Services: Pathology* (HMSO, 1923), p.225.
75. F.S. Brereton, *The Great War and the RAMC* (Constable & Co., London, 1919), pp.259–62.
76. Ibid., p.260.
77. Macpherson *et al.*, *History of the Great War* (1923), p.181, fn 9.
78. W.G. Macpherson, *History of the Great War: Medical Services. General Services*, vol.1 (HMSO, 1921), pp.182–3.
79. Ibid.; see also Macpherson *et al.*, *History of the Great War*, vol.1, chapter VII, pp.151–68.
80. Blair, *In Arduis*, p.205.
81. L.J. Blenkinsop and J.W. Rainey, *History of the Great War Based on Official Documents: Veterinary Services* (HMSO, 1925), p.508.
82. Ibid., p.673.
83. German and French armies had used gas gangrene serum to a limited extent from the beginning. Macpherson *et al.*, *History of the Great War, Surgery of the War*, vol.1 (HMSO, 1922), p.147.
84. Macpherson, *History of the Great War Based on Official Documents: Medical Services: General History*, vol.1 (HMSO, 1921), pp.182–3, 414.
85. WFA, GB/31/9, Works manager's instruction book no. 2, 26 March 1914, p.10; 20 July 1924, p.16; 12 Aug. 1919, p.19.
86. WFA, PB 63, 87/14, Rules and Regulations and Instructions for employees of Burroughs Wellcome, 1917.
87. Judy Slinn, *A History of May & Baker, 1834–1984* (Cambridge, 1984), pp.93, 100.
88. Ibid., pp.92–4.
89. Chapman, *Jesse Boot*, p.141.
90. Ibid.
91. *Chem. & Drug.*, 78, 21 Jan. 1911, pp.133–9.
92. Ibid.; *The Times*, 25 Feb. 1926, p.20; *Pharm. J.*, 161, 12 April 1941, p.155.
93. WA/BSR/LA/Sci/2, 'Chemical Works', STC report, 17 Dec. 1926.
94. Chapman, *Jesse Boot*, p.96–7.
95. Michael Robson, 'The pharmaceutical industry in Britain and France, 1919–1939' (unpublished PhD thesis, University of London, 1989), pp.192–3.
96. Jowett was equally resentful that whereas Carr was a member of the government's principal Trade Mission to Germany after the War, he had not been included, though he was invited to join a visiting group of less important business leaders. Robson, thesis, p.193–4.
97. Ibid., pp.193–4.
98. WA/BSR/LA/STC/3, O' Brien to Wenyon, 4 Nov. 1927.
99. See chapter 10, 'Formation of the Scientific and Technical Committee', pp.293–5.
100. Tweedale, *At the Sign of the Plough*, pp.103, 116.
101. Ibid., p.122.
102. Slinn, *History of May & Baker*, pp.41, 55, 62–3.
103. WFA, Acc. 96/45, BW&Co. sales book no. 2.
104. WFA, Acc. 82/1, 38, Wellcome to Pearson, 17 Oct. 1917.
105. *Lancet*, i, 20 March 1920, p.673; Haggis, 'Life and work', p.468.
106. Haggis, 'Life and work', pp.468, 484.
107. WFA, Acc. 82/1 Box 38, Wellcome to Pearson, 17 Oct. 1917.
108. See below, chapter 10, pp.288–9.
109. HSBC archives, Acc. 81/3, Reference book, p.41. Regard for Wellcome at the bank had been manifested in 1910 when Holden, manager of the City Bank, had supported his application for naturalisation. HSBC archives Acc. 26/8, managing director's diary, 2 Sept. 1910.
110. Quoted in *Chem. & Drug.*, 94, 9 April 1921, p.477.
111. *Pharm. J.*, 121, 26 Feb. 1921, p.165.
112. Imperial College archives, Carr papers, B, p.93.
113. Robson, 'British pharmaceutical industry', p.101.
114. Royal Commission on Veneral Disease, Cd. 8189, xvi, Q. 2915.
115. Ibid., p.157.
116. WFA, Acc. 96/40/1; Acc. 96/6/14.
117. WFA, Acc. 96/45, BW&Co. Sales book no. 2 and see above, pp.270–2.
118. Ibid.
119. Only gross profits are recorded for sera and these were in addition to net profit declared in the balance sheets. WFA, F/F 328, WFL trading and profit and loss accounts.
120. Ibid.
121. Ibid., p.316.
122. WFA, Acc. 96/45, BW&Co. Sales book no. 2.
123. Stone and Rowe, *Consumer Expenditure in Britain* (1966), p.51.
124. Haggis, 'Life and work', p.485.
125. Rhodes James, *Henry Wellcome*, p.348.
126. WFA, File 5/CS/205/3: LF 110/5D, Price Waterhouse to Wellcome, 2 April, 17 May 1923.
127. Ibid., Pearson to Wellcome, n.d. 1923.
128. WFA, SCS 281, Board minute book 1, 1924–1940.; WFA, Acc. 83/3/1, AGM agendas, 1924–1940.
129. WFA, 99/6/12, f3, Meeting of British Association of Insulin Manufacturers, 30 July 1946.

Notes to Chapter 10: Policy formation, research and development

1. WA/BSR/BA/Prl/A1, WPRL Reports, Sept. 1919; WA/BSR/BA/Prl/A2, WPRL Reports, June 1920.
2. WFA: PB/78, Wellcome Research Laboratories Publications; Parke, Davis & Co., *Collected papers from the Research Laboratory* (Detroit, Parke, Davis & Co, n.d.).
3. WA/BSR/BA/Prl/A2, WPRL Reports, 1920–21. O'Brien also estimated £15 as the average price of a horse used for routine injections, which is three times higher than the figures calculated for 1901.
4. WFA, Acc. 83/3/35, Wellcome to O'Brien, 3 May 1923.
5. Ibid.
6. WFA, Acc. 86/45, *Typescript History of Brockwell Park*.
7. *Chem. & Drug.*, 94, 1921, 680, 757.
8. WFA, Box 184, 'Beckenham', 1922 onwards; Anon., 'Opposition to proposed laboratory', *Chem. & Drug.*, 94, 1921, 639.
9. Anon., 'Ministry of Health enquiry', *Chem. & Drug.*, 94, 1921, 639.
10. *Chem. & Drug.*, 94, 1921, 801, 862.
11. This brief summary is taken from WA/BSR/BA/Crl/.
12. WA/BSR/BA/Crl/A, 'WCRL Reports, July 1914–Dec. 1922', April 1919 and Aug. 1920.
13. H. Paget, 'Reminiscences', 1975, quoted in J. Gorvin, 'The early development of chemical research in the Wellcome laboratories' in L. G. Goodwin, E. Beveridge and J. Gorvin, *Wellcome's Legacies* (London, Wellcome Trust, 1998), pp. 54–92, quote on p. 65.
14. WA/BSR/LA/Sci/2, 'Minutes of the STC', 17 Dec. 1926.
15. See e.g. C. M. Wenyon, *Protozoology: A Manual for Medical Men, Veterinarians and Zoologists* (Ballière, Tindall & Cox, London, 1926); C. A. Hoare, *The Trypanosomes of Mammals: A Zoological Monograph* (Blackwell, Oxford, 1972).
16. E.g. J. A. Goodson, T. A. Henry and J. W. S. Macfie, 'The action of the cinchona and certain other alkaloids in bird malaria', *Biochem J.*, 24, 1930, 874–90.
17. WA/BSR/BA/Crl/A, 'WCRL Reports, July 1914–Dec. 1922', WCRL reports, April and Dec. 1919.
18. Ibid., WCRL report, Aug. 1920.
19. WFA, PB 112, Price list 1921–22.
20. See also correspondence about producing Yatren, an anti-amoebic, in WA/BSR/LA/Sci/4, 'Minutes of the STC', 23 March 1928, e.g. T. A. Henry and H. C. Brown, 'Observations on reputed dysentery remedies', *Trans. R. Soc. Trop. Med. Hyg.*, 17, 1924, 378–85; W. H. Brindley and F. L. Pynam, 'The alkaloid of ipecacuanha. Part IV', *J. Chem. Soc.*, 10, 1927, 1067–77. For treatment of bacterial dysentery see chapter 9, pp. [360–62].
21. For references to early work on tartar emetic see L. G. Goodwin, 'Pentostam® (Sodium stibogluconate), a 50-year personal reminiscence', *Trans.*

R. Soc. Trop. Med. Hyg., 89, 1995, 339–41. For development in BW&Co., see WA/BSR/BA/Crl/A, 'WCRL reports July 1914–Dec. 1922', Jan. 1922.
22. W. H. Gray and J. W. Trevan, 'Experiments on antimony compounds used in the treatment of bilharzia disease and kala-azar', *Trans. R. Soc. Trop. Med. Hyg.*, 25, 1930, 147–52.
23. WA/BSR/LA/Sci/1, STC minutes, 13 Feb. 1925. Some of the material used in this chapter was also examined, but from a different perspective, by Keith Williams in his PhD thesis '*The history of the Wellcome Chemical Laboratory and clinical trials in Britain in the interwar period*' (University of Manchester, 2004).
24. WA/BSR/BA/Prl/A2, 'WPRL Reports, 1920–21', O'Brien to Stammers, 30 Sept. 1921; ibid., O'Brien to Balfour.
25. WA/BSR/LA/Sci/1, STC minutes, 13 Feb. 1925.
26. WA/BSR/LA/Sci/2, STC minutes, 29 Oct. 1926, re: confidential anonymous memo, 'The relation of the Foundation to research workers'.
27. See below, pp. 297–9.
28. WA/BSR/BA/Adm/A-2, Wellcome to Balfour, 21 March 1915.
29. See chapter 6, pp. 183–5, and also Tansey, 'What's in a name?'.
30. For more on research activities and for continuing ambivalence about the nature of the laboratories, see chapter 11, especially pp. 347–9.
31. WFA, Acc. 83/3/44, British Medical Association to O'Brien, 15 March 1928.
32. Ibid., O'Brien to Dr A. Macpherson, BMA, 17 March 1928.
33. O'Brien was critically aware of the importance of networking of this kind, see for example WFA, Acc. 83/3/47, O'Brien to Wenyon, 11 March 1929.
34. WFA, Acc. 83/3/34, O'Brien to Wellcome, 25 Aug. 1923.
35. WFA, Acc. 83/3/34, O'Brien to Daukes, 18 July 1924.
36. Ibid., copy of memo, M. A. to O'Brien, 15 July 1924; Daukes to O'Brien, 22 July 1924.
37. Robson, 'British pharmaceutical industry', p. 197.
38. WA/BSR/LA/Sci/1, R. A. O'Brien, *Note on Pharmacology in Relation to the Wellcome Foundation*; WA/BSR/LA/Sci/1, STC minutes, 13 Feb. 1925, 20 Jan. 1926.
39. WA/BSR/LA/Sci/1, STC, Jowett, Procedure to be followed before consideration of any new research, 19 May 1925.
40. WA/BSR/LA/Sci/1, STC, Pearson to L, 9 July 1925.
41. Ibid.
42. WA/BSR/LA/Sci/1, STC, Pearson to L, 8 July 1925.
43. WA/BSR/LA/Sci/1, STC, Henry, Memo and discussion, 17 Dec. 1926.
44. See M. Bliss, *The Discovery of Insulin* (Macmillan, Basingstoke, 1982).

45. WA/BSR/LA/Sci/1, STC minutes, 25 Feb. 1925, notes by Wenyon, Henry, Jowett, and O'Brien, Jan. 1925. See also WFA, Acc. 83/3/38.

46. TNA: FD1/7066, Minute Book 2, '1915–26', Minutes of the MRC, 21 July 1922, 17 Nov. 1922, 17 July 1925.

47. TNA: FD1/949, H.H. Dale and H.W. Dudley, 'Report to the MRC of our visit to Canada and the United States'. See also J. Liebenau 'The MRC and the pharmaceutical industry: the model of insulin', in J. Austoker & L.M. Bryder (eds), *Historical Perspectives on the Role of the MRC* (Oxford, Oxford University Press, 1989), pp. 163–80.

48. TNA: FD1/918, 'Insulin: Enquiries from producers and companies'. D.N. Paton to W.M. Fletcher, 23 Nov. 1922.

49. Liebenau, 'The MRC', p. 174.

50. NIMR 740, 'Insulin: Circular letters and memos', Dale to Meakins, 9 Jan. 1923.

51. NIMR 754/2, 'Insulin: Commercial enquiries, 1922–23'.

52. TNA: FD1/7066, MRC Minute Book 2, '1915–26', 12 Jan. 1923, p. 276, Minute 3.

53. H. Maclean, 'An address on the present position of diabetes and glycosemia, with observations on the new insulin treatment', *Lancet*, i, 1923, 1039–46, quote on p. 1044.

54. H.W. Dudley, 'The purification of insulin and some of its properties', *Biochem. J.*, 17, 1923, 376–90.

55. J.R. Wright, 'From ugly fish to conquer death: J.R.R. Macleod's fish insulin research, 1922–24', *Lancet*, 359, 2002, 1238–42. See also NIMR 756, 'Fish Insulin'.

56. Wellcome Library, Medical Film and Audio Collections, 501V, Testimony of Mr Richard Fox, *From Mincers to Microbes* (Wellcome Foundation promotional film, c. 1983).

57. WA/BSR/Prl/A3, 'Minutes of the STC'. For early availability of insulin see editorials and adverts, e.g. in *Chem. & Drug.*, 98, 1923, 508–50; ibid., 99, 1923, 736.

58. NIMR 740, 'Insulin: circular letters and memos', several items of correspondence, Dale to the licensed firms, various dates in 1923.

59. Ibid., Dale to pharmaceutical manufacturers, 22 March 1923.

60. J. Murnaghan and P. Talalay, 'H.H. Dale's account of the standardization of insulin', *Bull. Hist. Med.*, 66, 1992, 440–50. C. Sinding, 'Making the unit of insulin: standards, clinical work and industry (1920–25)', ibid., 76, 2002, 231–70.

61. Anon., 'Insulin', *Chem. & Drug.*, 98, 1923, 508.

62. WFA, Guard Books GB/30/02; GB/30/03, Monthly Memoranda, e.g. May and July 1923, Jan. and Feb. 1924.

63. WA/BSR/LA/BWc/3, 'Burroughs Wellcome', BW&Co. (S. America) memoranda to BW&Co. (Snow Hill), Jan. to Aug. 1926.

64. NIMR 776, 'Insulin: Ministry of Health', G.F. McLeary to Dale, 13 Sept. 1923 and 16 Oct. 1923, and 'weekly sales of insulin'.

65. NIMR 755, 'Insulin: Evans, Lescher and Webb', various correspondence between H.A. Mitchell and H.H. Dale, 1922–28.

66. Women were expected to give up work on marriage, and were not regarded as offering long-term solutions to staffing problems.

67. WA/BSR/BA/Prl/A2, 'Reports from WPRL 1920–21', Correspondence between O'Brien and Stammers, June–Sept. 1921.

68. WFA, Acc. 83/3/33, correspondence, 3 July 1923 to 29 Jan. 1924.

69. E.g. for Eli Lilly, see H.A. Shonle and J.H. Waldo, 'Some chemical reactions of the substance containing insulin', *J. Biol. Chem.*, 58, 1992, 731–6; for BDH, see F.H. Carr, K. Culhane, A.T. Fuller and S.W.F. Underhill, 'A reversible inactivation of insulin', *Biochem. J.*, 23, 1929, 1010–21.

70. WFA, Acc. 83/3/31, O'Brien to Wenyon, 15 Aug. 1924.

71. Tweedale, *At the Sign of the Plough: Allen & Hanburys and the British Pharmaceutical Industry 1715–1990* (John Murray, London, 1990), 128–30.

72. WA/BSR/BA/Prl/A2, 'WPRL reports 1920–21', O'Brien to Stammers, 1 Sept. 1921.

73. Ibid., WPRL report, Jan. 1920.

74. TNA: FD1/930, 'Insulin: Boots Pure Drug Co. Nov. 1922–Jan. 1933'.

75. NIMR 783/1(a), Charles Best to Dale, 10 Dec. 1936.

76. Liebenau, 'The MRC', p. 175.

77. NIMR 622, 'O'Brien', Dale to O'Brien, 8 and 19 Nov. 1924; ibid., O'Brien to Dale, 25 Nov. 1924. A.H. Lacey, 'The unit of insulin', *Diabetes*, 16, 1967, 198–200. See also pp. 301–2 above.

78. C.R. Harington and D.A. Scott, 'Observations on insulin, Part One: Chemical observations', *Biochem. J.*, 23, 1929, 384–97. K. Culhane, J.H. Marks, D.A. Scott, and J.W. Trevan, 'Observations on insulin, Part Two: Physiological assay', ibid., 397–409.

79. WFA, Acc. 83/3/49, correspondence between O'Brien and Wenyon, April and Oct. 1929; WFA *Monthly Memoranda*, Oct. 1929, pp. 9–10.

80. O'Brien also complained that advertising claims of BW&Co.'s insulin as keeping better in tropical conditions than rival preparations were totally unsustainable.

81. WFA, Acc. 83/3/51, correspondence between O'Brien and Wenyon, and Wenyon and Pearson, March and April 1930.

82. Anon., 'Official inquiry on imported insulin', *Chem. & Drug.*, 118, 1933, 652–3; ibid., 739–41.

83. NIMR 771/2, 'Leo insulin 1930–34', Dale to Thomson, 27 April 1932.

84. See e.g. G.A. Wrenshall, G. Hetenyi and M. Feasby, *The Story of Insulin: Forty Years of Success Against Diabetes* (Bickley Head, London, 1962), esp. 'Modern insulins', pp. 102–8.

85. NIMR 783/1(a), 'Report on meeting of Insulin manufacturers', 10 Dec. 1936; ibid., Dale to Charles Best, 31 Dec. 1936.

86. NIMR 783/1(c), 'Protamine insulin', H.P. Marks

to Dale, 30 Nov. 1936; ibid., Mrs Cutts to Dale, 11 Dec. 1936.

87. NIMR 783/1(a), Trevan to Dale, 24 Dec. 1936; ibid., Dale to Trevan, 25 Jan. 1937; WFA, Acc. 83/3/376, 'Nordisk Insulinlaboratorium 1937–39', several items of correspondence.

88. The role that insulin played in stimulating similar collaborations between companies and academic scientists in the US is discussed by J. H. Swann, 'Insulin: a case study in the emergence of collaborative pharmacomedical research, Parts 1 and 2', *Pharmacy in History*, 28, 1986, pp. 3–13, 65–74.

89. WFA, Acc. 83/3/38, O'Brien to Pearson, 5 Feb. 1925.

90. WA/BSR/LA/Sci/1, 'Minutes of the STC', 8 May 1925.

91. WFA, Acc. 83/3/38, O'Brien to Pearson, 5 Feb. 1925.

92. Ibid.

93. WFA, Acc. 83/3/37, O'Brien to Ref L (Linstead), 25 Aug. 1925.

94. WA/BSR/LA/Sci/1, 'Minutes of the STC', 21 Oct. 1925, and associated correspondence.

95. BW&Co., 'Phamacopoeia revision: the report on ergot', *Pharm J. & Pharmacist*, 74, 1932, 19; F. Wokes and H. Crocker, 'Biological and spectroscopic tests on ergot alkaloids, with notes on the Maurice Smith colour test', *Q.J. Pharm. Pharmacol.*, 4, 1931, 420–43.

96. See e.g. A. Bourne and J. H. Burn, 'The dosage and action of pituitary extract and of ergot alkaloids on the uterus in labour, with a note on the action of adrenaline', *Pharm J. & Pharmacist*, 10, 1927, 485–90, esp. p. 488.

97. See e.g. correspondence about ergamine in NIMR 622, 'O' Brien', O'Brien to Dale, 13 Dec. 1920; NIMR 482, 'Enquiries 1921–28', Dale to G. Slot, 21 Sept. 1926; see E. M. Tansey, 'Henry Dale, histamine and anaphylaxis: reflections on the role of chance in the history of allergy', *Stud. Hist. Phil. Biol. Biomed Sci.*, 34, 2003, 455–72.

98. WFA, Acc. 83/3/47, O'Brien to Wenyon, 15 April 1929, and draft, O'Brien to Clarke (Snow Hill), 9 April 1929.

99. F. L. Brown and H. H. Dale, 'The pharmacology of ergometrine', *Proc. R. Soc. Lond.*, 118 B, 1935, 446–77.

100. C. Moir, 'Clinical comparison of ergotoxine and ergotamine: a report to the Therapeutic Trials Committee of the Medical Research Council', *BMJ*, i, 1932, 1022–4.

101. C. Moir, 'The action of ergot preparations on the puerperal uterus', *BMJ*, i, 1932, 1119–22.

102. H. W. Dudley and C. Moir, 'The substance responsible for the traditional clinical effect of ergot', *BMJ*, i, 1935, 520–3.

103. These disputes are detailed in E. M. Tansey, 'Ergot to ergometrine: an obstetric renaissance?' in L. Conrad and A. Hardy (eds), *Women and Modern Medicine*, Wellcome Institute for the History of Medicine series (Amsterdam, Rodopi, 2001), pp. 195–215.

104. RS 93HD 39.25.4, Dale to Chauncey Leake, 15 Oct. 1935.

105. Ibid., G. L. Brown and H. H. Dale, 'The pharmacology of ergometrine', *Proc. R. Soc. Lond.*, 118B, 1935, 446–7, esp. p. 447.

106. BELRA undertook a range of preventive, local control and treatment work around the world. See M. Worboys 'The colonial world as mission and mandate: Leprosy and Empire 1900–1940', *Osiris*, 15, 2001, 207–18.

107. PP/ROG/C.13/210, memo, dated 1925, in response to BELRA questionnaire, 1924.

108. E.g. WA/BSR/LA/Sci/1, 'Minutes of the STC', 3 April 1925.

109. PP/ROG/C.13/258, 'Minutes of the British Empire Leprosy Relief Association', 7 Oct. 1926; WFA, Acc. 83/3, 133, WCRL report. See also PP/ROG/ C.13/313–29, L. Rogers, 'Memorandum on the present position of prophylaxis against leprosy in relation to recent improvement in treatment'.

110. PP/ROG/C.13/266, Note on 1927 expenditure, BELRA. This appears to be the production cost of Alepol.

111. PP/ROG/C.13/287, Appendix to memo on the Leprosy problem in the British Empire, Sept. 1927; WA/BSR/LA/Sci/5, 'Minutes of the STC', minutes of meeting, 1 Nov. 1929.

112. L. Rogers, 'Recent advances in the treatment and prophylaxis of leprosy', *BMJ*, ii, 1929, 961–2. WA/ BSR/LA/Sci/5, 'Minutes of the STC', minutes of meeting, 8 Feb. 1929.

113. PP/ROG/C.13/313–29, typewritten draft, 'Memorandum on the present position of prophylaxis against leprosy in relation to recent improvement in treatment', prepared for the Leprosy Conference, Jan. 1931.

114. E.g. WA/BSR/LA/Sci/6, 'Minutes of the STC', minutes of meeting, 24 Oct. 1930; WA/BSR/LA/ Sci/7, 'Minutes of the STC', minutes of meeting, 23 Jan. 1931. See also several WCRL reports in WFA, Acc. 83/3/138.

115. E.g. ibid.

116. WA/BSR/LA/Sci/8, 'Minutes of the STC', minutes of meeting, 19 Feb. 1932.

117. See e.g. ibid., 138–41, 'Monthly Reports of WCRL 1931–34'.

118. E.g. WFA, Acc. 83/3/138, WCRL monthly report, Nov. 1931, work on a new plant oil from Malaya, and a copper salt of hydnocarpus.

119. WFA, Acc. 83/3/31, O'Brien to Wenyon, 8 Aug. 1924.

120. Ibid.

121. Ibid., O'Brien to Wenyon, 12 Aug. 1924.

122. Ibid.

123. WFA, Acc. 83/3/43, O'Brien to Wenyon, 25 Nov. 1927.

124. WFA, Acc. 83/3/46, O'Brien to Dr Bennet [probably from Beckenham Council], 26 Oct. 1928.

125. WFA, F/FA/328, WFL trading accounts and profit and loss.

126. WFA, Acc. 83/3/52, O'Brien 'Future of the

WPRL', memo, 4 Oct. 1930.

127. WFA, Acc. 83/3/54, O'Brien to Ref P [Pearson], 'Further accommodation at Langley Court', 28 Jan. 1931; ibid., O'Brien WPRL requirement of more accommodation, memo, 6 March 1931; ibid., O'Brien to Wenyon, 7 March 1931.

128. Ibid., O'Brien to Ref P [Pearson], 28 Jan. 1931.

129. Ibid., O'Brien to Ref P [Pearson], 28 Jan. 1931.

130. See chapter 11, pp. 353–6

131. WFA, Acc. 83/3/34, Jowett to O'Brien, 16 July 1928; ibid., O'Brien to Jowett, 24 July 1928.

132. WA/BSC/LA/Sci/8, Henry to Wenyon, 13 Jan. 1932.

133. Ibid.

134. WA/BSR/LA/Sci/10, Wenyon to Pearson, 23 Oct. 1934; Henry to Wenyon, 25 Oct. 1934, 15 Nov. 1935.

135. WA/BSR/LA/Sci/10, Wenyon to Pearson, 23 Oct. 1934; Henry to Wenyon, 25 Oct. 1934.

136. WA/BSR/RP/Mon/B6, Feb. 1930. See, however, chapter 11, pp. 342–3, for the successful resolution of this work.

137. Robson, 'British Pharmaceutical Industry', p. 215, fn 92.

138. WA/BSR/LA/Sci/ STC/3, Wenyon to BW&Co., 8 July 1927.

139. WA/BSR/LA/Sci/STC/3, Wenyon to BW&Co., 8 July 1927.

140. WFA, Acc. 84/6 Box 1 (3), typescript by H. J. Parish, 'History of the WRPL and immunization', chapter 6.

141. Ibid.

142. WFA, F/FA/328, trading and profit and loss accounts.

143. Exceptions include patent applications made for antimony compounds, soluble and insoluble Phoagene, Neostam, and Avenyl. WA/BSR/LA/ Sci/7, 23 Jan. 1931.

144. *BMJ*, 1927, i, p. 888; J. M. Liebenau, 'Patents and the chemical industry' in J. M. Liebenau (ed.) *The Challenge of New Technology* (Aldershot, Gower, 1988), pp. 135–50.

145. WFA, Monthly memoranda, Jan. 1934, p. 4.

146. WFA, Acc. 85/20/1 'Historical notes'.

147. WFA: PB/78, Wellcome Research Laboratories Publications.

148. WFA, Acc. 83/3, 227, Minutes of the Therapeutic

149. Robson claimed that the number of papers produced from BW&Co. was inflated by including publications from all scientists who worked at the Wellcome Foundation, whether or not they were employed there. Robson, thesis, p. 206. However, the only identifiable external researcher working in the laboratories and whose publications are listed by the company was Hindle, a Beit Fellow. All his research expenses were met by BW&Co. and his collaborators were Wellcome staff. The figure for BW&Co.'s publications is from table 10.3 above.

150. WFA, PB 81, 'typescript, 'The Wellcome Foundation', 13 June 1945', pp. 37–8.

151. In 1893, thyroid Tabloids were listed in the *BMJ*. New preparations and inventions column.

152. WA/BSR/LA/Sci/3, minute, 28 March 1927; WA/BSR/LA/Sci/6, minute, 24 Jan. 1930.

153. WA/BSR/LA/Sci/3, Henry to Wenyon, 14 Dec. 1926.

154. Ibid.

155. WA/BSR/LA/ Sci/9, minute, 31 March 1933.

156. WA/BSR/LA/Sci/10, minute, 14 Dec. 1934.

157. Ibid., O'Brien to Wenyon, 16 June 1934.

158. WFA, SCS 283, WFL minute book 2, 21 Sept. 1944. Those from 1940 onwards these remain with GlaxoSmithKline.

159. WA/BSR/LA/Sci/9, Jowett to Wenyon, 15 March 1933.

160. Ibid., Henry to Wenyon, 20 Feb. 1934.

161. WA/BSR/LA/Sci/9, O'Brien to Wenyon, 16 Feb. 1934.

162. See above, pp. 314–15.

163. WA/BSR/LA/Sci/9, O'Brien to Wenyon, 16 Feb. 1934; minute, 12 July 1935; 15 Nov. 1935.

164. Ibid., Pearson to O'Brien, 3 June 1936.

165. WFA, Acc. 83/3:31, O'Brien to Wenyon, 12 Aug. 1924.

166. WFA, F/FA/328, WFL accounts.

167. WFA, Monthly Memoranda, March 1932, p. 333.

168. WFA, Monthly Memoranda, June 1922, p. 106.

169. Ibid., p. 107.

170. WFA, Monthly Memoranda, April 1923, p. 198.

171. *BMJ*, 5 June 1920, p. 1137.

172. WFA, *Monthly memoranda*, Dec. 1933, p. 496.

173. Ibid.

Notes to Chapter 11: Academic reputation counters commercial stigma: sera and vaccines 1918–1940

1. See e.g. the discussions of the Medical Society of London, 'The prophylactic and therapeutic value of vaccines', *BMJ*, ii, 1930, 734–6.

2. H. J. Sudmersen and A. T. Glenny, 'Immunity of guinea-pigs to diphtheria toxin, and its effects upon the offspring. I.', *J. Hyg.*, 11, 1911, 220–34; idem, II., ibid., 11, 1911, 423–42; idem, III., ibid., 12, 1912, 64–76.

3. A. T. Glenny and H. J. Sudmersen, 'Notes on the

production of immunity to diphtheria toxin', *J. Hyg.*, 20, 1921, 176–220.

4. A. Zingler, 'Results of active immunization with diphtheria toxin–antitoxin', *JAMA*, 78, 1922, 1945–52; J. Lewis, 'The prevention of diphtheria in Canada and Britain, 1914–45', *J. Soc. Hist.*, 20, 1986, 163–76; P. A. Bator and A. J. Rhodes, *Within reach of Everyone: A history of the University of Toronto School of Hygiene and the Connaught Laboratories*, vol. 1, 1927–55

(Canadian Public Health Association, Ottawa, 1990), especially pp. 31–70.

5. See considerable correspondence between Dale and O'Brien, NIMR 622 'O'Brien'.

6. E.g. NIMR 622, 'O'Brien', O'Brien to Dale, 17 Nov. 1925.

7. A. T. Glenny and H. J. Sudmersen, 'Notes on the production of immunity to diphtheria toxin', *J. Hyg.* 20, 1921, 176–220.

8. A. T. Glenny and B. E. Hopkins, 'Duration of passive immunity', *J. Hyg.*, 21, 1922, 142–8.

9. WFA, Acc. 84/6/6, H. J. Parish, handwritten notes towards his 'History of the WPRL, vol. 2', c.1960. Marked 'To be censored drastically', henceforward 'Parish notes, c.1960'.

10. For a detailed bibliography, see C. L. Oakley, 'Alexander Thomas Glenny, 1882–1965', *Biog. Mems. FRS Lond.*, 12, 1966, 163–80.

11. WFA, Acc. 84/6,'Parish notes, c.1960'.

12. Ibid.

13. WFA, Acc. 83/3/41, O'Brien to Wenyon, 25 Oct. 1926.

14. S. F. Dudley, P. M. May and J. A. O'Flynn, *Active Immunization Against Diphtheria: Its Effect on the Distribution of Anti-toxic Immunity and Case and Carrier Infection* (HMSO, London, 1934), acknowledges O'Brien, Parish, Glenny and Pope for their assistance, pp. 5–6.

15. E.g. J. C. Saunders, 'Alum-precipitated toxoid', *Lancet*, i, 1935, 402; A. Hutchinson, 'Treatment of diphtheria with refined antitoxin', *BMJ*, i, 1939, 384; J. T. Lewis, 'Diphtheria prophylaxis: a review of the antigens and methods available', *BMJ*, ii, 1939, 1226–7.

16. WFA, Acc. 84/6:6, H. J. Parish, 'A typescript history of the Wellcome Physiological Research Laboratories', c.1960, chapter 7. 'Diphtheria'.

17. NIMR, 622 'O'Brien', O'Brien to Dale, 14 Dec. 19(23?).

18. G. Bousfield, *A Practical Guide to the Schick Test and Diphtheria and Scarlet Fever Immunization* (J. & A. Churchill, London, 1929).

19. G. Bousfield, 'Diphtheria immunisation: a plea for the immediate abandonment or control of "one-shot" treatment', *Med. Officer*, 57, 1937, 15–16; idem, 'Diphtheria prophylaxis: an investigation into the comparative merits of one or two injections of alum-precipitated toxoid', ibid., 59, 1938, 5–8.

20. 'Parish notes c.1960'.

21. G. Bousfield, 'Restoration of diphtheria immunity without injections: Toxoid pastilles by mouth', *BMJ*, i, 1945, 833–5.

22. 'Parish notes c.1960'.

23. WFA, Acc. 83/3/45, copy of memo, BW&Co. (South Africa) to BW&Co. (Snow Hill), 12 Apr. 1928, sent to O'Brien.

24. Ibid.

25. E.g. R. Swyer, 'Antigenic properties of diphtheria toxoid–antitoxin floccules', *Lancet*, i, 1931, 632–4; J. C. Saunders, 'Observations on the use of alum-toxoid as an immunising agent against diphtheria',

ibid., ii, 1932, 1047–50; G. Chesney, 'Immunization against diphtheria with alum-precipitated toxoid: efficiency, duration and grade of immunity', *BMJ*, i, 1937, 807–8.

26. E.g. Editorial, 'Communal immunization against diphtheria', *BMJ*, i, 1932, 671; Editorial, 'Prophylaxis of diphtheria', ibid., ii, 1936, 723; Editorial, 'Compulsory immunisation', *Lancet*, ii, 1938, 737.

27. E. H. R. Harries, 'Diphtheria', *Lancet*, i, 1939, 45–8, quote on p. 45 referring to J. G. Fitzgerald, D. T. Fraser, N. E. McKinnon, and M. A. Ross, 'Diphtheria – A preventable disease', ibid., i, 1938, 391–7. See also J. Lewis, 'Prevention of diphtheria', 1986, op. cit., note 4.

28. Ministry of Health, *Production of Artificial Immunity Against Diphtheria*, Ministry of Health memorandum, 170/Med, see *Pharm. J.*, 144, 1940, 74.

29. B. Schick, 'Kutanreaktion bei impfung mit diphtherietoxin', *Münch. med. Wschr.*, 55, 1908, 504–6; A. T. Glenny, K. Allen and R. A. O'Brien, 'The Schick reaction and diphtheria prophylactic immunisation with toxin–antitoxin mixture', *Lancet*, i, 1921, 1236–7.

30. WA/BSR/BA/Prl/A1, WPRL reports 1914–1919, WPRL Report, Nov. 1919.

31. E. M. Hammonds, *Childhood's Deadly Scourge: The Campaign to Control Diphtheria in New York City, 1880–1930* (Johns Hopkins University Press, Baltimore, MD, 1999), pp. 179–88.

32. Glenny et al., 'The Schick reaction', 1921.

33. E.g. WFA, Acc. 83/3/34, O'Brien to Balfour, 11 July 1923, and O'Brien to Stammers, 15 Aug. 1923; ibid., 31, O'Brien to Wenyon, 9 Sept. 1924.

34. E.g. H. J. Parish and J. Wright, 'The Schick test and active immunisation in relation to epidemic diphtheria', *Lancet*, i, 1935, 600–4.

35. Any fees were donated to charity. WFA, Acc. 83/3/32, C. A. Powell (Clerk to Metropolitan Asylums Board) to O'Brien, 22 Feb. 1924.

36. G. Newman, *Bacteria, Especially as they are Related to the Economy of Nature to Industrial Processes and to the Public Health* (John Murray, London, 1899); WFA, Wellcome LB12, 944a, BW&Co. to Dowson, 13 Dec. 1899. WFA, Acc. 83/3/32, correspondence between Newman and O'Brien, March 1924.

37. See Anon., 'Parliamentary intelligence', *Lancet*, ii, 1927, 1321; and J. Lewis, 1986, 'Prevention of diphtheria'.

38. NIMR 622, 'O'Brien', O'Brien to Dale, 2 Dec. 1925.

39. Ibid.

40. NIMR 622, 'O'Brien', Dale to O'Brien, 3 Dec. 1925.

41. R. A. O'Brien, 'Active immunisation against diphtheria: the present position', *Lancet*, i, 1926, 616–7.

42. R. Munro, 'The Schick test: its application in an institution for mental defectives', *BMJ*, i, 1927, 506–8; WFA, Acc. 83/3/47, output figures 1923–28, O'Brien to Wenyon, 20 Feb. 1929.

43. H. J. Parish, *A History of Immunization*, (E. &

S. Livingstone, Edinburgh, 1965), pp. 149–55; see also J. Lewis, 1986, 'Prevention of diphtheria'. For a contemporary report see Editorial, 'New Haven's Public Health Research for 1932', *JAMA*, 98, 1932, 819–20.

44. L. Rogers, 'Diphtheria a preventable disease: why not prevented?', *Med. Officer*, 59, 1938, 237–9.

45. Ministry of Health, *Memorandum on the Production of Artificial Immunity Against Diphtheria* (revised) (HMSO, London, 1940); Editorial, 'Diphtheria not prevented', *Lancet*, i, 1940, 273–4.

46. G. F. Dick and G. R. H. Dick, 'A skin test for susceptibility to scarlet fever', *JAMA*, 82, 1924, 265–6; C. C. Okell and H. J. Parish, 'The Dick test in scarlet fever', *Lancet*, i, 1925, 712–14.

47. H. J. Parish, 'Charles Cyril Oakley, 1888–1939', *J. Hyg.*, 39, 1939, 217–23.

48. 'Parish notes, c.1960', chapter 9. 'Scarlet fever in the pre-chemotherapeutic era'; R. A. O'Brien and C. C. Okell, 'Some problems connected with the Dick test', *Lancet*, ii, 1925, 1327–9.

49. H. J. Parish and C. C. Okell, 'The relationship of scarlet fever to other streptococcal infections', *Lancet*, i, 1928, 746–7; *idem*, 'The relationship of scarlet fever to other streptococcal infections', ibid., 748; C. C. Okell and H. J. Parish, 'Two studies of streptococcal infections', ibid., 748–50.

50. G. F. Dick and G. H. Dick, 'Scarlet fever preparations', *JAMA*, 85, 1925, 996. Editorial, 'Patented research', *BMJ*, i, 1927, 479–80.

51. G. F. Dick and G. H. Dick, 'The patents in scarlet fever toxin and antitoxin', *JAMA*, 88, 1927, 1341–2.

52. WA/BSR/LA/Sci/3, '1927 Minutes of the Scientific and Technical Committee', meeting, 25 Feb. 1927.

53. WFA, Acc. 83/3/47, production figures for 1928, sent from O'Brien to Wenyon, 20 Feb. 1929.

54. WFA, Acc. 83/3/42, e.g. O'Brien to Pearson, 16 Mar. 1927.

55. Ibid., O'Brien to Pearson, 19 Mar. 1927.

56. Ibid., undated notes by O'Brien, c. 20 Mar. 1927, and Pearson to Martin, c. 23 Mar. 1927. H. F. Moulton, *The Life of Lord Moulton* (Nisbet & Co., London, 1922).

57. Some American scientists shared the Wellcome staff's view, see note 71 below.

58. WFA,: Acc. 83/3/42, O'Brien to Pearson, 28 Mar. 1927, and O'Brien to Wenyon, 8 Apr. 1927.

59. 'Parish notes, c.1960', chapter 9, 'Scarlet fever'.

60. G. F. Dick and G. H. Dick, 'The patents in scarlet fever toxin and antitoxin', *JAMA*, 88, 1927, 1341–2.

61. WFA, Acc. 83/3/42, O'Brien to Pearson, 8 Apr. 1927, and O'Brien to Kerr (Scarlet Fever Committee), 8 Apr. 1927.

62. Ibid.

63. WFA, Acc. 83/3/47, Gladys Dick to O'Brien, 2 Feb. 1929.

64. Ibid., O'Brien to Wenyon, 11 Mar. 1929, copy of proposed reply, O'Brien to Dick.

65. WFA, Acc. 83/3/47, O'Brien to Warren, 11 Mar. 1929.

66. Ibid. Many journal articles at this time refer specifically to using BW&Co.'s material to carry out Dick testing, see e.g. M. Salmond and B. Turner, 'The Dick test in pregnancy', *BMJ*, ii, 1929, 145–6.

67. WFA, Acc. 83/3/41, O'Brien to Wenyon, 4 Nov. 1926.

68. H. J. Parish and C. C. Okell, 'The titration of scarlet fever antitoxin in rabbits', *Lancet*, i, 1927, 71–2.

69. WFA, Acc. 83/3/47, O'Brien to Warren, 11 Mar. 1929.

70. Ibid.

71. L. P. Rubin, 'Dick, Gladys Rowena Henry', in B. Sicherman, C. H. Green, I. Kantrov and H. Walker (eds), *Notable American Women: The modern period* (Belknap Press, Cambridge, MA, 1980), pp. 191–2.

72. E.g. T. M. Ling, 'Note on the treatment of asthma in children with tuberculin', *Lancet*, ii, 1928, 972–3.

73. See e.g. NIMR 622, 'O'Brien', O'Brien to Dale, 2 Dec. 1925; C. C. Okell, H. J. Parish, R. A. O'Brien, G. Dreyer, R. L. Vollum, S. Lyle Cummins, and J. B. Buxton, 'The standardisation of tuberculin and the precipitin test', *Lancet*, i, 1926, 433–4.

74. A. J. Eagleton and E. M. Baxter, 'Standardisation of tuberculin', *Brit. J. Exp. Path.*, 4, 1923, 289–304.

75. C. C. Okell, H. J. Parish, R. A. O'Brien, G. Dreyer, R. L. Vollum, S. Lyle Cummins, and J. B. Buxton, 'The standardisation of tuberculin and the precipitin test', *Lancet*, i, 1926, 433–4.; H. J. Parish, 'Critical review: the modern outlook on tuberculin', *Tubercle*, 19, 1938, 337–50.

76. 'Parish notes, c.1960', chapter 10. 'Other miscellaneous infections: some Wellcome contributions, 1920–40'; A. T. Doig, G. Gemmill, G. Gregory Kayne, F. V. Linggood, H. J. Parish and J. S. Westwater, 'Laboratory and clinical investigations on tuberculin purified protein derivitive (PPD) and old tuberculin (OT)', *BMJ*, i, 1938, 992–7; R. F. Montgomerie and A. Thomson, 'Tuberculin purified protein derivitive (PPD) in the double intradermal test in cattle – preliminary observations', *Vet. Rec.*, 51, 1939, 229–36.

77. C. Mantoux, 'Intra-dermo-réaction de la tuberculine', *Compt. rend. Acad. Sci. (Paris)*, 147, 1908, 355–7.

78. H. J. Parish, 'Critical review: the modern outlook on tuberculin', *Tubercle*, 19, 1938, 337–50.

79. V. Cameron and E. R. Long, *Tuberculosis Medical Research: National Tuberculosis Association, 1905–1955* (National Tuberculosis Association, New York, 1959), pp. 15–16, 28–9.

80. WA/BSR/BA/Prl/A1, WPRL reports 1914–19, WPRL Report, Nov. 1919.

81. *Chem. & Drug*, 1918, 90: advert 30 Nov, p. 40

82. W. B. Leishman, 'The results of protective inoculation against influenza in the army at home, 1918–19', *Lancet*, i, 1920, 366–8.

83. WFA, Acc. 83/3/30, Topley to O'Brien, 12 Sept, 1924.

84. Ibid., O'Brien to Topley, 13 Sept. 1924.

85. Ibid., Topley to O'Brien, 20 Sept. 1924.

86. WFA, Acc. 83/3/41, O'Brien to Wenyon, 4 Nov. 1926.

87. Ibid.

88. P. C. English, 'Therapeutic strategies to combat pneumococcal disease: repeated failure of physicians to adopt pneumococcal vaccine, 1900–45', *Perspec. Biol. Med.*, 30, 1987, 170–85.

89. 'Parish notes, *c.*1960', chapter 10. 'Other miscellaneous infections: some Wellcome contributions 1920–40'. The problems encountered by Wellcome and other scientists in the 1930s continued to cause difficulties for pneumonia vaccine producers, see D. R. Feikin and K. P. Klugman, 'Historical changes in pneumococcal serogroup distribution: implications for the era of pneumococcal conjugate vaccines', *Clin. Inf. Dis.*, 35, 2002, 547–55.

90. WFA, Acc. 83/3/47, output figures for 1923–28, O'Brien to Wenyon, 20 Feb. 1929.

91. Ibid., O'Brien to Wenyon, 11 Mar. 1929.

92. R. A. O'Brien and A. T. Glenny, 'Production of antitoxin for therapeutic purposes' in Medical Research Council, *A System of Bacteriology in Relation to Medicine*, vol. 3 (HMSO, London, 1929), pp. 353–8.

93. L. Goodwin, 'John Smith Knox Boyd', *Biog. Mems. FRS Lond.*, 28, 1982, 27–57.

94. A. T. Glenny and M. F. Stevens, 'The laboratory control of tetanus prophylaxis', *J. Roy. Army Med. Corps.*, 70, 1938, 308–10.

95. L. Goodwin, 'John Smith Knox Boyd', *Biog. Mems. FRS Lond.*, 28, 1982, 27–57, pp. 35–6.

96. WFA, Acc. 83/3/46, O'Brien to Wenyon, 19 Sept. 1928. WFA, Acc. 83/3/34, two letters, O'Brien to Wenyon, 11 July 1928.

97. E. Hindle, 'An experimental study of yellow fever', *Trans. R. Soc. Trop. Med. Hyg.*, 22, 1929, 406–34.

98. E. Hindle, 'A yellow fever vaccine', *BMJ*, i, 1928, 976–7; idem, 'An experimental study of yellow fever', *Trans. R. Soc. Med. Hyg.*, 22, 1929, 405–34.

99. L. G. Goodwin and E. Beveridge, 'Sir Henry Wellcome and Tropical Medicine' in L. Goodwin, E. Beveridge and J. Gorvin, *Wellcome's Legacies* (The Wellcome Trust, London, 1998), pp. 9–51, esp. pp. 26–7.

100. E. Hindle, 'The transmission of yellow fever', *Lancet*, ii, 1930, 835–42.

101. E. Hindle, 'Yellow fever' in Medical Research Council, *A System of Bacteriology in Relation to Medicine*, vol. 7 (HMSO, London, 1930), 449–62.

102. P. C. C. Garnham, 'Edward Hindle, 1886–1973', *Biog. Mems. FRS Lond.*, 20, 1974, 217–34; S. R. Christophers, 'Sydney Price James', *Obit Notes FRS*, 5, 1945–8, 507–23.

103. Ibid., Garnham, 1974.

104. Goodwin and Beveridge, 'Sir Henry Wellcome and tropical medicine', p. 27; G. Cook, 'Fatal yellow fever contracted at the Hospital for Tropical Diseases, London, UK, in 1930', *Trans. R. Soc. Trop. Med. Hyg.*, 88, 1994, 712–13.

105. Goodwin and Beveridge, 'Sir Henry Wellcome and tropical medicine', p. 28.

106. P. C. C. Garnham, 'Edward Hindle, 1886–1973',

Biog. Mems. FRS Lond., 20, 1974, 217–34.

107. See British Drug Houses, *Price List* (British Drug Houses, London, 1914), p. 54; and Parke, Davis & Co., *Veterinary Materia Medica*, 1928, 2. WFA, Acc. 83/3/34, O'Brien to Wenyon, 31 Oct. 1912.

108. T. Dalling, 'Lamb dysentery: an account of some experimental fieldwork in 1925 and 1926', *J. Comp. Path. Ther.*, 39, 1926, 148–53; T. Dalling, J. H. Mason and W. S. Gordon, 'Lamb dysentery prophylactic in 1927', *Vet. Rec.*, 7, 1927, 451–4.

109. WFA, Acc. 83/3/36, O'Brien to Wenyon, 29 May 1925.

110. WFA, Acc. 83/3/39, O'Brien to Wenyon, 22 Feb. 1926.

111. NIMR 622, 'O'Brien', O'Brien to Dale, 25 July 1925.

112. E.g. papers read at local meetings of veterinary surgeons, H. R. Dalling, H. R. Allen, and J. H. Mason, 'Veterinary biological products – their standardisation and application', *Vet. Rec.*, 6, 1926, 65–70; T. Dalling, 'A consideration of some diseases of animals – the laboratory and field worker', ibid, 7, 1927, 451–4.

113. 'N.F.', Northumberland, 'Lamb dysentery' *Scottish Farmer*, 19 Nov. 1928, 1485; see also WFA, Acc. 83/3/46.

114. 'Parish notes, *c.*1960', chapter 11. 'Veterinary research under Thomas Dalling, 1923–37'.

115. H. J. Parish, *A History of Immunization* (E. & S. Livingstone, Edinburgh, 1965), pp. 149–55; see also J. Lewis, 1986, 'Prevention of diphtheria'. For a contemporary report see editorial, 'New Haven's Public Health Research for 1932', *JAMA*, 98, 1932, 819–20.

116. T. Dalling, H. R. Allen and J. H. Mason, 'Research into certain animal diseases', *Vet. Rec.*, 5, 1925, 561–6.

117. Parke, Davis & Co., *Veterinary Materia Medica*, 1928, 3–4.

118. F. Pickering, 'Letter to the Editor', *Vet. Rec.*, 42, 1929, 922–34; WFA, Acc. 83/3/48, O'Brien to Pearson, 21 Oct. 1929.

119. Ibid., Clarke (BW&Co., Snow Hill) to O'Brien, 21 Oct. 1929.

120. WFA, Acc. 83/3/48, O'Brien to Pearson, 21 Oct. 1929.

121. WFA, Acc. 83/3/49, O'Brien to F. Pickering, 31 Oct. 1929, and O'Brien to Wenyon, 31 Oct. 1929.

122. WFA, Acc. 83/3/52, O'Brien to Pearson, 11 July 1930.

123. See e.g. Editorial, 'Foot and mouth disease', *BMJ*, i, 1924, 25–6.

124. WFA, Acc. 83/3/32, O'Brien to Capt. W. Wragg (Ministry of Agriculture and Fisheries), 10 July 1924.

125. WFA, Acc. 83/3/30, O'Brien to Wenyon, 5 Nov. 1924.

126. Ibid., O'Brien to Wenyon, 10 Dec. and 23 Dec. 1924.

127. WFA, Acc. 83/3/30, O'Brien to Leishman, 20 Dec. 1924.

128. Ibid., O'Brien to Pearson, 23 Dec. 1924. SA/Lis/ K.6, H.G.Richardson (Ministry of Agriculture and Fisheries) to C.J.Martin, 22 July 1924.

129. WFA, Acc. 83/3/30, O'Brien to Pearson, 23 Dec. 1924.

130. Editorial, 'The Tuberculosis conference', *Lancet*, ii, 1925, 105, 296–9; *idem*, 'Tuberculous cattle and sheep', ibid., ii, 1925, 47.

131. For a broader examination of bovine TB and attempts to eradicate it, see K.Waddington 'To stamp out "so terrible a malady": bovine tuberculosis and tuberculin testing in Britain, 1890–1939', *Med Hist.*, 48, 2004, 29–48.

132. WFA, Acc. 83/3/37, W.J.Smart (Ministry of Agriculture) to O'Brien, 11 Nov. 1925.

133. Ibid., W.T.Smart (Ministry of Agriculture) to Cumberland Agricultural Committee, 22 Sept. 1925, and Cumberland County Council to WPRL, 19 Oct. 1925.

134. Ibid., O'Brien to Stockman, 28 Oct. 1925.

135. Ibid., draft, Wenyon to Ministry of Agriculture, 28 Oct. 1925.

136. Ibid., W.J.Smart (Ministry of Agriculture) to R.A.O'Brien, 11 Nov. 1925.

137. C.C.Okell, T.Dalling and L.P.Pugh, 'Leptospiral jaundice in dogs (yellows)', *Vet. J.*, 81, 1925, 1–35.

138. T.Dalling and C.C.Okell, 'Vaccine treatment of canine leptospiral jaundice', *J. Path. Bact.*, 29, 1926, 131; C.C.Okell, L.P.Pugh, and T.Dalling, 'Discussion on canine jaundice: with special reference to leptospiral infection', *Proc. R. Soc. Med.*, 18, 1925, 17–21.

139. Some of this account is taken from E.M.Tansey, 'Protection against dog distemper and Dogs Protection Bills: the Medical Research Council and anti-vivisectionist protest, 1911–33', *Med Hist.*, 38, 1994, 1–26.

140. TNA FD1/1274, 'Approach of Sir Theodor Cook to MRC', Fletcher to Cook, 14 Nov. 1922.

141. A.A.Comerford, 'Two years field experience with the preventative treatment of distemper as advocated by Laidlaw and Dunkin', *Vet. Rec.*, 2 Dec. 1929, reprinted by Hudson & Son, Birmingham, NIMR Pamphlet Collection, P133. See also TNA: FD1/1274, 'Approach of Sir Theodor Cook to MRC'.

142. P.P.Laidlaw, and G.W.Dunkin, 'Studies in dog distemper. V.The immunisation of dogs', *J. Comp.* ibid., 41, 1928, 209–27; Anon., 'Prevention of canine distemper', *BMJ*, ii, 1928, 1100–1. WFA, Circular Book 38, 'Directions for use: Wellcome anti-distemper serum'. WFA, Acc. 83/3/46, O'Brien to Pearson, 9 Aug. 1928.

143. TNA FD1/1277, confidential progress report by Dr P.P.Laidlaw and Dr G.W.Dunkin to Field Distemper Council, 7 Oct. 1926; P.P.Laidlaw, and G.W.Dunkin, 'Studies in dog distemper. IV. The immunisation of ferrets against dog distemper', *J. Comp. Path. & Ther.*, 41, 1928, 1–17.

144. WFA, Acc. 83/3/50, T.Dalling, Unpublished notes of a speech at the Dog Owners' Club, Dec. 1929;

ibid., R.A.O'Brien and T.Dalling, 'Vaccination against dog distemper', *The Field*, (1 Feb), 1930.

145. Ibid., O'Brien to veterinary surgeons, 9 Dec. 1929; WFA, Acc. 83/3/49, O'Brien to Wenyon, 11 Dec. 1929, and related correspondence.

146. WFA, Acc. 83/3/50, O'Brien to Wenyon, 6 Mar. 1930.

147. Ibid., O'Brien to Martin, 7 Mar. 1930, and suggested emendation of Distemper Committee Report.

148. T.Dalling, 'Experiences with distemper immunisation', *Vet. Rec.*, 10, 1930, 225–34; WFA, Acc. 83/3/50, O'Brien to Laidlaw, 31 Mar. 1930; O'Brien to veterinary surgeons, n.d.; and modified Canine Distemper Prophylactive Directions for use, n.d.

149. Letters of complaint about the virus and vaccine issued during this period are in WFA, Acc. 86/91, 2–3.

150. WFA, Acc. 83/3/51, O'Brien to Wenyon, 4 June 1930, and O'Brien to Pearson, 4 June 1930.

151. Ibid., BW&Co. to Martin, 4 June 1930.

152. WFA, Acc. 83/3/52, O'Brien to Laidlaw, 13 June 1930.

153. Ibid., O'Brien to Wenyon, 14 June 1930.

154. Ibid., O'Brien to Ref. P (Pearson), 12 July 1930.

155. Ibid., R.A.O'Brien and T.Dalling, draft letter to the Editor of the *Veterinary Record*, 25 June 1930; R.A.O'Brien, 'Laidlaw–Dunkin distemper prophylactic', *Vet. Rec.*, 29, 1930, 647.

156. See e.g. WFA, Acc. 83/3/52, O'Brien to Laidlaw, 29 July 1930.

157. Ibid, an internal typescript report, 'Canine distemper – recent work: Wellcome Physiological Research Laboratories', details the relevant experimental work.

158. T.A.B.Corley, 'The use of pharmaceutical products in UK veterinary medicine', conference paper, British Society for the History of Medicine, September 2003.

159. E.g. *Willows' Veterinary Diary & Visiting List* 1934, which lists anti-toxin products from the Pasteur (Paris) and Cutter (Philadelphia) laboratories for equine, poultry, swine and bovine diseases.

160. '"M & B" cures Lion', *The World's Fair*, 22 Jan. 1944, p.12, report from the *Glasgow Evening News*, where the circus was performing. We thank Mr Tim Neal, National Fairground Archive, University of Sheffield, for tracking down this reference.

161. For a detailed analysis of the event, see C.Hooker, 'Diphtheria, immunisation and the Bundaberg tragedy: a study of public health in Australia, *Health & History*, 2000, 2, 52–78.

162. Anon., 'Diphtheria immunization: the Queensland fatalities', *BMJ*, i, 1928, 193.

163. WFA, Acc. 83/3/44, O'Brien to N.G.Horner, Editor of the *BMJ*, 1 Feb. 1928, and Daukes to Horner, 1 Feb. 1928, typescript copy of article.

164. Ibid., the Bundaberg disaster – Royal Commission's Report.

165. See Anon., 'Medico-legal: A fatality after

diphtheria immunization', *BMJ*, i, 1937, 1345; Anon., 'Inquest', *Chem. & Drug.*, 127, 1937, 692.

166. See Anon., 'Inoculation damages claim: verdict for the defendants', *BMJ*, i, 1939, 480–6; Anon., 'Tuberculosis after inoculation', *Chem. & Drug.*, 131, 1939, 145.

167. See J.W. Bigger, J.W.S. Blacklock, and H.J. Parish, 'Investigations and observations on inoculation technique', *BMJ*, i, 1940, 79–84.

168. 'Parish notes, *c*.1960', Chap. 13, 'The High Court Case at Dublin'; see Anon., 'Inoculation damages claim: verdict for the defendants', *BMJ*, i, 1939, 480–6;

169. See Anon., 'Medico-legal: A fatality after diphtheria immunization', *BMJ*, i, 1939, 480–6; quote on p. 485; Anon., 'Tuberculosis after inoculation', *Chem. & Drug.*, 131, 1939, 145, 244.

170. J.G. Wilson, 'Diphtheria immunisation', *Med. Officer*, 49, 1933, 150.

171. J.W. Bigger, J.W.S. Blacklock, and H.J. Parish, 'Sterilization of syringes and needles', *BMJ*, i, 1940, 582–3; idem, 'Investigations and observations on inoculation technique', *BMJ*, i, 1940, 79–84.

172. 'Parish notes, *c*.1960', Chap. 13, 'The High Court Case at Dublin'.

173. See e.g. NIMR 622, 'O'Brien', O'Brien to Dale, 18 Nov. 1937, and Dale to O'Brien, 19 Nov. 1937.

174. 'Parish notes, *c*.1960', Chap. 13, 'The High Court Case at Dublin'.

175. WFA, Acc. 83/3/44, O'Brien memo, 'Capital expenditure', 9 Feb. 1928.

176. 'Parish notes, *c*.1960', Chap. 14, 'Two changes of leadership, 1939–40'.

177. Considerable correspondence in the archives of the NIMR attest to their friendship and collaboration NIMR 622, 'O'Brien'.

178. 'Parish notes, *c*.1960', chapter 14, 'Two changes of leadership, 1939–40'.

179. Ibid.

180. For a general account of the development of the sulphonamides, see M. Weatherall, *In Search of a Cure* (Oxford University Press, Oxford, 1990), pp. 150–4.

181. L. Colebrook and M. Kenny, 'Treatment of human peurperal infections, and experimental infections in mice with Prontosil', *Lancet*, ii, 1936, 1279–86; for Buttle's contribution see p. 1280.

182. W.H. Gray, G.A.H. Buttle and D. Stephenson, 'Derivatives of *p*–aminobenzone-sulphonamide in the treatment of streptococcal infection in mice', *Biochem J.*, 31, 1937, 724–30.

183. E.g. A.J. Cokkins, 'Treatment of gonorrhea with oral sulphanilamide', *BMJ*, ii, 1937, 905–9, quote on p. 905, T.F. Cream, 'The use of *Prontosil* in the treatment of gonorrhoea', *Lancet*, ii, 1937, 895–8.

184. See e.g. WFA, Monthly Memoranda (USA), January 1938.

185. Editorial, 'Deaths following elixir of sulfanilimide-Massengill II', *JAMA*, 109, 1937, 1456, 1727; editorial, 'Poisoning by elixir of sulfanilimide', *BMJ*, ii, 1937, 1129–30.

186. 'Parish notes, *c*. 1960', Addendum to chapter 10.

Notes to Chapter 12: Competition and product development between the wars: Tabloids, Kepler, and other 'General Goods'

1. H.A.D. Jowett, 'A local industry', *East Kent Advertiser*, 28 March, 1924.

2. WFA, Acc. 96/40/1, Dartford works production journal; WFA, Acc. 99/6/14, Wellcome Chemical Works production record.

3. WFA, GB 30/1, Monthly Memoranda (Points for Propaganda), hereafter Monthly Memoranda, Sept. 1920, p. 78.

4. H.A.D. Jowett, 'A local industry', *East Kent Advertiser*, 28 March 1924. The other two products he described were Salvarsan and insulin, which suggests that these, too, were among the few most important items measured by production. WFA, GB 30/1, Monthly Memoranda, Nov. 1920, p. 98.

5. WFA, GB 30/3, Monthly Memoranda, June 1924, p. 49; ibid., Nov. 1925, p. 282.

6. WFA, GB 30/8, Monthly Memoranda, Feb. 1935, pp. 210–11.

7. WFA, GB 30/1, Monthly Memoranda, Nov. 1919, p. 3.

8. *Chem. & Drug.*, 90, 19 Oct. 1918. Talc and boric acid were other ingredients used as makeweights.

9. *American Druggist & Pharmaceutical Record*, 18 Jan. 1919.

10. WFA, GB 30/1, Monthly Memoranda, Nov. 1919, p. 3.

11. Ibid., Sept. 1920, pp. 80–1.

12. Ibid., Nov. 1920, pp. 96–7.

13. The tablets and Tabloids tested were: nux vomica, calomel, salol, antipyrene, bismuthated magnesia, soda mint, and aspirin.

14. WFA, GB 30/1, Monthly Memoranda, Sept. 1920, p. 86.

15. Ibid., Sept. 1920, p. 86a.

16. WFA, GB 30/4, Monthly Memoranda, Jan. 1926, pp. 39–40.

17. WFA, GB 30/3, Monthly Memoranda, April 1925, p. 196.

18. WFA, GB 30/7, Monthly Memoranda, July/August 1932, pp. 342–51.

19. WFA, GB 30/9, Monthly Memoranda, Jan. 1936, pp. 14–15.

20. Ibid., pp. 18–19.

21. WFA, GB 30/10, Monthly Memoranda, Jan. 1939, p. 182.

22. WA/BSR/LA/BWC/1/Sci/2, Wenyon to LA, 11 Nov. 1925.

23. WFA, GB 30/3, Monthly Memoranda, Feb. 1924, p. 23; Dec. 1924, p. 168.

24. WFA, GB 30/5, Monthly Memoranda, Sept. 1929, p. 267.
25. Ibid.
26. WA/BSR/LA/Sci/9, Jowett to Wenyon, 15 March 1933, and memo 're Dig', 21 March 1933; WA/BSR/LA/Sci/3, STC minutes, 28 Sept. 1934.
27. WFA, Wellcome LB35, Evans, Lescher & Evans to Burroughs, 13 June 1878.
28. G. Barger and W. V. Shaw, 'The chemical and physiological assay of digitalis tinctures', *Yearbook. Pharm.*, 1904, 541–57.
29. WA/BSR/LA/Sci/1, O'Brien to Wenyon, 27 Mar. 1925; ibid., 'Minutes of the STC', 3 April 1925.
30. Ibid., 'Minutes of the STC', 21 Oct. 1925.
31. A. N. Drury and R. T. Grant, 'Thomas Lewis', *Obit Nots FRS*, 5, 1945–48, 179–202, quote on p. 193.
32. WA/BSR/LA/BWC/1, copy of report from a travelling representative, 26 June 1925.
33. WA/BSR/LA/Sci/3, 'Minutes of the STC', 31 May 1927.
34. WA/BSR/LA/BWC/6, Memo, BW&Co. (Linstead?) to Wenyon, 1 Dec. 1927.
35. WA/BSR/LA/Sci/4, 'Minutes of the STC', Minute of meeting, 5 Oct. 1928.
36. WA/BSR/LA/Sci/4 and 5, minutes of several STC meetings, 1928 and 1929.
37. WA/BSR/LA/Sci/9, 'Minutes of the STC', minutes of several meetings, 1933.
38. E.g. T. East, 'The treatment of persistent auricular fibrillation and flutter', *BMJ*, ii, 1935, 25–6.
39. WA/BSR/LA/Sci/7, 'Minutes of the STC', minute of meeting, 9 June 1931; E. J. Wayne, 'Clinical observations and on two pure glucosides of digitalis, digoxin and digitalinum verum', *Heart*, 1, 1933–34, 63–76.
40. WA/BSR/LA/Sci/10, 'Minutes of the STC', 9 Feb. 1934.
41. WFA, GB 30/1, Monthly Memoranda, Feb. 1920, p. 19.
42. Ibid.
43. Tweedale, *At the Sign of the Plough*, p. 79.
44. Ibid., p. 126.
45. R. P. T. Davenport-Hines and Judy Slinn, *Glaxo: A History to 1962* (Cambridge, 1992), chapters 2 and 3.
46. Tweedale, *At the Sign of the Plough*, p. 145,
47. Rima D. Apple, *Vitamania: Vitamins in American Culture* (Rutgers, New Brunswick, New Jersey, 1996), chapter 2.
48. WFA, GB 30/1, Monthly Memoranda, Jan. 1921. pp. 141–2.
49. Ibid., March 1921, p. 153. Not all salesmen showed a concern to find something new to say about Kepler goods. It was the profit-generating advantage offered by the company's staple products which led an Australian representative to write to Snow Hill enthusiastically, adding: 'I believe so strongly in Kepler that I almost feel I <u>exude</u> it when I am talking about it … I feel and know that I am speaking the truth and selling the <u>very best line.</u> On more than one occasion I have persuaded a chemist to stock only Kepler'. Ibid., p. 206.
50. Ibid.; Sally M. Horrocks, 'The business of vitamins: nutrition science and the food industry in inter-war Britain', in Harmke Kamminga and Andrew Cunningham (eds.), *The Science and Culture of Nutrition, 1840–1940* (Cambridge, 1995), pp. 235–58.
51. WFA, GB 30/2, Monthly Memoranda, May 1922, p. 88.
52. WFA, GB 30/2, Monthly Memoranda, March 1922, p. 37.
53. WFA, GB 30/3, Monthly Memoranda, May 1924, p. 200.
54. Ibid., Jan. 1923, p. 171.
55. Ibid, p. 172.
56. Ibid.
57. WFA, GB 30/3, Monthly Memoranda, Oct. 1925, p. 274.
58. WFA, GB 30/2, Monthly Memoranda, March 1922, p. 37.
59. WFA, GB 30/3, Monthly Memoranda, Oct. 1925, p. 274.
60. Ibid., pp. 268–9.
61. WFA, GB 30/3, Monthly Memoranda, Oct. 1925, pp. 269–70.
62. WFA, GB 30/4, Monthly Memoranda, May 1927, p. 239.
63. Ibid, Feb. 1927, p. 149.
64. WFA, GB 30/3, Monthly Memoranda, Oct. 1925, pp. 269–70.
65. WA/BSR/LA/Sci/1, STC minutes, 13 Feb. 1925.
66. Davenport-Hines and Slinn, *Glaxo*, pp. 71–3.
67. Ibid., pp. 73–9.
68. Ibid., pp. 74–5.
69. Apple, *Vitamania*, pp. 35–49.
70. Jones, *The Business of Medicine*, p. 33.
71. Jephcott is quoted in Jones, ibid.
72. WA/BSR/LA/Sci/3, O'Brien to Pearson/Wenyon, 9 April 1927.
73. *Chem. & Drug.*, 104, 20 Feb. 1926, p. 254.
74. Tweedale, *At the Sign of the Plough*, pp. 147–9.
75. Ibid.
76. WA/BSR/LA/Sci/3, STC minutes, O'Brien to Pearson, 2 April 1927.
77. WFA, GB 30/3, Monthly Memoranda, May 1927, p. 238.
78. WFA, Acc. 83/3/41, O'Brien to Wenyon, 28 Feb. 1927 with draft report.
79. WA/BSR/LA/Sci/3, STC minutes, 25 Feb. 1927, O'Brien to Jowett, 1 April 1927, O'Brien to Pearson, 2 April 1927.
80. WA/BSR/LA/Sci/2, O'Brien to Jowett, 9 Feb. 1927.
81. WFA, Acc. 83/3/43, O'Brien to Wenyon, 31 Oct. 1927; O'Brien to Ref. L (Linstead), 28 Oct. 1927.
82. WFA, Acc. 82/1 Box 21, O'Brien to Wenyon, 5 Feb. 1930.
83. WA/BSR/LA/Sci/5, STC minutes, 8 Feb. 1928.
84. Anon 'Definition of drugs for the purposes of medical benefit: report of the advisory committee', *Lancet*, i 1930, pp. 467–8.
85. WFA, GB 30/5 Monthly Memoranda, March 1928, p. 35.

86. WA/BSR/LA/Sci/1, STC minutes, 25 Feb. 1927.
87. WA/BSR/LA/Sci/4, Wenyon to Pearson, 18 Feb. 1928; Pearson to Wenyon, 20 Feb. 1928; STC minutes, March 1928.
88. WA/BSR/LA/Sci/5, STC minutes, 8 Feb. 1929.
89. They had identified the unsaturated sterol, Ergesterol, as the precursor of Vitamin D. WFA, GB 30/9, Feb. 1926, p. 15–16.
90. Ibid.
91. WFA, GB 30/5, Monthly Memoranda, March 1928, pp. 34–5; April 1928, p. 66–8.
92. WFA, GB 30/5, Monthly Memoranda, Sept. 1929, p. 277–8.
93. Ibid.; WFA, GB 30/6, Monthly Memoranda, July 1930, p. 90.
94. Ibid., Jan., 1930, p. 17.
95. Ibid.
96. Ibid., pp. 80–8.
97. *The Times*, 25 Feb. 1926, p. 20 (BDH Ltd Prospectus).
98. *Chem. & Drug.*, 106, Jan. 1927, p. 74.
99. British Drug Houses Ltd Prospectus, *The Times*, 25 Feb., p. 20; 20 Feb. 1926, *Chem. & Drug.*, 104, p. 254; Guildhall Library, Stock Exchange Collection, British Drug Houses Ltd, Annual Report 1928.
100. WFA, GB 30/7, Monthly Memoranda, Jan. 1933, p. 399.
101. WFA, GB 30/8, Monthly memoranda, March 1934, p. 64.
102. Guildhall Library, Stock Exchange Collection, British Drug Houses Ltd, Annual Report 1928.
103. Ibid, Annual Report, 1929.
104. *Chem. & Drug.*, 116, 14 May 1932, p. 532.
105. WFA, GB 30/8, Monthly Memoranda, March 1934, pp. 48–9.
106. WFA, GB 30/6, Monthly Memoranda, April 1930, p. 46.
107. Ibid., May 1930, p. 91; Oct. 1931, pp. 274–6.
108. Ibid, April 1931, p. 47.
109. Ibid., Oct. 1931, p. 276.
110. Ibid., May 1931, pp. 178–80.
111. WFA, Acc. 82/1 Box 21, O'Brien to Wenyon, 5 Feb. 1930.
112. Ibid., 3 June 1930.
113. WFA, GB 31/1, Instructions Book, Home and Abroad, 2 Oct. 1931; 16 Nov. 1931.
114. WFA, GB 30/6, Monthly Memoranda, June 1931, p. 192.
115. WFA, GB 30/7, May 1932, pp. 330–1.
116. Sir Frederick Gowland Hopkins lecture quoted in ibid., Oct. 1933, p. 474; WFA, GB 30/8, 'Monthly Memoranda', Jan. 1934, p. 21.
117. WFA, GB 30/8, Monthly Memoranda, Feb. 1934, p. 21.
118. Ibid., p. 37.
119. WFA, GB 30/7, Monthly Memoranda, Dec. 1933, p. 491.
120. Tweedale, *At the Sign of the Plough*, p. 153.
121. By 1937/8, home sales of Kepler had dwindled to a mere £13,635; and £25,054 in India and Pakistan. WFA, Acc. 99/6/28, 'Sales of Kepler product, 1937/8–1950.
122. WFA, GB 30/9, Monthly Memoranda, Oct. 1936, p. 193.
123. WFA, GB 30/9, Monthly Memoranda, March 1937, p. 236.
124. Ibid.
125. Ibid., pp. 236–7.
126. WFA, GB 30/10, Monthly Memoranda, Aug. 1939, p. 235.
127. Ibid., Jan. 1939, p. 182.
128. WFA, GB 30/2, Monthly Memoranda, June 1922, p. 67.
129. WFA, GB 30/1, Monthly Memoranda, Dec. 1919, p. 21.
130. Ibid., Jan. 1921, p. 118; WFA, GB 3, Monthly Memoranda, Dec. 1925, p. 131.
131. WFA, GB 30/1, Monthly Memoranda, July/Aug. 1921, p. 183.
132. WFA, GB 30/2, Monthly Memoranda, June 1922, p. 67.
133. Ibid.
134. WFA, GB 30/7, Monthly Memoranda, Feb. 1932, pp. 308, 335.
135. WA/BSR/LA/Sci/9, STC minutes, 9 April 1930, Memo re tannic acid from 'Ref O', 22 June 1932.
136. WFA, GB 30/2, Monthly Memoranda, June 1922, p. 67.
137. WFA, GB 30/8, Monthly Memoranda, March 1934, p. 86; May 1935, p. 252.

Notes to Chapter 13: Wellcome's American agenda; tariffs, war, and the transition to manufacturing and research at the New York branch

1. WFA, Acc. 82/1 Box 38, Wellcome to Pearson, 19 Oct. 1917.
2. GWHC, internal publications, 'Brief analysis accompanying charts pertaining to the USA Business', hereafter 'Brief analysis'.
3. WFA, Acc. 82/1 Box 19, Pearson to Nevin, 4 April 1924.
4. WFA, Acc. 82/1 Box 19, BW&Co. (USA) to Wellcome, 1 July 1927.
5. WFA, Acc. 82/1 Box 19, Nevin to Pearson, 7 Oct. 1924.
6. GWHC, internal pubs., Monthly Letter, 107/07/07.05, May 1942, p. 224.
7. WFA, F/FA/328, WFL accounts, 1918 NYB, Jan. 1919.
8. GWHC, BW&Co. (USA) internal pubs., 107. 08/05.04, Monthly letter, Oct. 1930, pp. 1–2.
9. GWHC, Library ephemeral, vertical files, 107 08/06, 'retirees', interview with Ted Holmes, 1984. Unfortunately no data indicating volume or value of Empirin production has survived.
10. WFA, Acc. 82/1 Box 19, Nevin to Pearson, 12 Dec.

1922; 3 Feb. 1923.

11. Ibid.

12. Ibid., Pearson to Nevin, 15 Dec. 1920.

13. Ibid., Pearson to Nevin, 15 Dec. 1920, 15 April 1921, 31 Aug. 1921; Nevin to Pearson, 7 Sept. 1921.

14. Ibid., Nevin to Pearson, 12 Jan. 1923.

15. Ibid., Nevin to Wellcome, 13 Jan. 1923.

16. Ibid., Nevin to Pearson, 24 Aug. 1923.

17. WFA, File 5/cs/205/3: LF 110/SD, Price Waterhouse to Wellcome, 2 April, 17 May 1923.

18. WFA, Acc. 83/3/22, WFL and BW&Co.

19. WFA, Acc. 82/1 Box 19, Nevin to Pearson, 7 Oct. 1924.

20. WFA, Acc. 82/1 Box 8, Wellcome to Pearson, 12 Dec. 1927; Jan Tanner, 'The New York Venture', *Foundation News*, June 1981, p. 14.

21. Jan Tanner, 'The New York Venture', *Foundation News*, June 1981, p. 14.

22. This guess is based on the figure of 440 in 1936, and taking account of the increased sales between 1925 and 1936.

23. WFA, Acc. 82/1 Box 19, Pearson to Nevin, 3 Nov. 1926.

24. WFA, Acc. 82/1 Box 19, Wellcome to Pearson, 23 Oct. 1926.

25. Ibid., Wellcome to Pearson, 23 Oct. 1926.

26. Ibid., Pearson to Nevin, 10 Nov. 1925.

27. WFA, Wellcome LB32, 44–6, Wellcome to BW&Co., c. Feb. 1906 pp. 44–6.

28. WFA, Wellcome LB32, 14–17, Wellcome to BW&Co., 27 Jan. 1906.

29. WFA, Acc. 82/1 Box 19, Wellcome to Pearson, 23 Oct. 1926.

30. Ibid.

31. Ibid., May 1942, p. 232.

32. WFA, SCS/205/1, Pearson to Wellcome, 23 Sept. 1923.

33. Philadelphia Public Library, Pamphlet Coll. 1895–1932, ID:PACUMTBO 672-A, Solmides, 1925.

34. GWHC, internal pubs, 107. 08/05.04, Monthly letter, Oct. 1927, pp. 6–8.

35. WFA, Acc. 82/1 Box 19, Nevin to Pearson, 28 Jan. 1926.

36. GWHC, internal pubs, 107. 08/05.04, Monthly letter, Oct. 1927. p. 1.

37. WFA, Acc. 82/1 Box 19, Nevin to Pearson, 26 Feb. 1926; Nevin to Pearson, copy to Wellcome, 15 June 1926, 25 March 1927; Wellcome to Pearson, 27 May 1927.

38. Ibid., Nevin to BW&Co., 1 July 1927.

39. Ibid., Pearson to Wellcome, 8 June 1927.

40. Ibid.

41. Ibid., Nevin to Wellcome, 1 July 1927.

42. Ibid.

43. GWHC, internal pubs, 'Brief analysis'.

44. GWHC, internal pubs, 'Brief analysis'.

45. See below, chapter 15, pp. 463–4.

46. WFA, Acc. 82/1 Box 19, Nevin to Pearson, 28 Jan. 1926.

47. GWHC, internal pubs, 'Brief analysis'.

48. WFA, Acc. 82/1 Box 6, Report on North American markets, 1926/27.

49. WFA, Acc. 82/1 Box 6, Pearson to Oakes, 6 May 1926.

50. Thomas S. Jones, *Detailing the Physician* (Romaine Pearson, NY, 1940), p. 46.

51. GWHC, internal pubs, 107.07/07.05, Monthly letter, Oct. 1926, pp. 1–3.

52. Ibid., Monthly Letter, Oct. 1926, p. 2; June 1930, p. 1.

53. Ibid., Monthly Letter, Feb. 1927, pp. 6–7.

54. Ibid., Monthly Letter, Feb. 1926, pp. 7–38.

55. Ibid., Monthly Letter, Oct. 1926, p. 23.

56. GWHC, Library ephemeral, vertical files, 107.08/06, 'retirees', interview with Stuart Jacobs, 1984.

57. GWHC, 107.07/07.01, Monthly Letter, Feb. 1926, p. 4.

58. Ibid., p. 38. In similar vein see 'Success and failure', ibid., Jan. 1927, pp. 12–13.

59. Ibid., Monthly Letter, March, pp. 20–1.

60. Ibid., p. 30.

61. Ibid., Monthly Letter, May 1930, p. 12.

62. Ibid., Monthly Letter, May 1926, pp. 30–2.

63. Ibid., Monthly Letter, Nov. 1926, pp. 3–4.

64. Ibid., Monthly Letter, March 1927, pp. 8–9.

65. Ibid., Monthly Letter, Jan. 1928, pp. 6–8.

66. Ibid., Monthly Letter, Feb. 1927, p. 6.

67. Ibid., pp. 4–9.

68. Ibid., p. 11.

69. GWHC., Library ephemeral, vertical files, 107.08/06, 'retirees', interview with Stuart Jacobs, 1984.

70. Ibid., Monthly Letter, Dec. 1926, pp. 4–5.

71. Ibid., pp. 6–9.

72. Ibid., Monthly Letter, Jan. 1927, pp. 1–5.

73. Ibid., Monthly Letter, March 1927, pp. 2–4.

74. Ibid., pp. 4–5.

75. Ibid., p. 11.

76. Ibid., p. 13.

77. Ibid., Monthly Letter, Jan. 1927, pp. 6–7.

78. Ibid., Monthly Letter, Feb. 1930, p. 9.

79. Ibid., Monthly Letter, Dec. 1926, pp. 14–15.

80. Ibid., Monthly Letter, Sept. 1928, p. 6–7.

81. Ibid., Monthly Letter, Feb. 1929, pp. 1–6.

82. *American Druggist*, 79, 3 Jan. 1929, p. 5; 94, 4 Oct. 1932, p. 10.

83. GWHC, internal pubs, 107.07/07.05, Monthly Letter, Oct. 1928, p. 10.

84. Ibid., Monthly Letter, Jan. 1928, p. 6.

85. *American Druggist*, 79, 2 Aug. 1929, p, 51.

86. GWHC, internal pubs., 107.07/07. 05, Monthly Letter, Oct. 1930, p. 5.

87. *American Druggist*, 76, 5 Nov. 1929, p. 57.

88. GWHC, internal pubs, 10–7.07/07. 05, Monthly Letter, Oct. 1930, p. 5.

89. Ibid., Monthly Letter, Sept. 1929, pp. 10–12.

90. Ibid., Monthly Letter, Jan. 1931, pp. 12–13.

91. Ibid., Monthly Letter, Feb. 1933, pp. 44–7.

92. Ibid., Monthly Letter, Feb. 1930, p. 2; March 1930, pp. 3, 5.

93. Ibid., Monthly Letter, Jan. 1928, pp. 15–18.

94. Ibid., Monthly Letter, July/Aug. 1930, pp. 19–20; Oct. 1930, pp. 23–4.

95. Ibid., Monthly Letter, May 1928, p. 12.

96. Ibid., Monthly Letter, May 1929 p. 22.

97. Ibid., Monthly Letter, Jan. 1930, p. 22.

98. Ibid., Monthly Letter, May 1929, p. 25; Feb. 1930, p. 28.

99. Ibid., Monthly Letter, June 1929, p. 13.

100. Ibid., Monthly Letter, Jan. 1928, pp. 20–1.

101. Ibid., Monthly Letter, March 1928, pp. 15–18.

102. WFA, Acc. 82/1 Box 19, Wellcome to Nevin, 23 Oct., 1926. See below chapter 15, [pp. 640–650].

103. WFA, Acc. 82/1 Box 20, Kellaway, 'Review', quoting Wellcome to Nevin, July 1928.

104. GWHC, internal pubs, 10–7.07/07. 05, Monthly Letter, June 1933, p. 167.

105. Ibid., Monthly Letter, June 1934, pp. 169, 207.

106. Ibid., Monthly Letter, March 1935, pp. 105–6.

107. GWHC, Public Affairs, 107.07/07.05; Monthly Letter, Feb. 1935, pp. 55–65.

108. Ibid., March 1935, pp. 105–6.

109. Ibid., Sept. 1932, p. 278.

110. Ibid.

111. Ibid., Nov. 1932, p. 356–64, 374–7.

112. Ibid., Dec. 1932, pp. 410–11.

113. Ibid., Monthly Letter, Jan. 1934, pp. 11–14.

114. WFA, Acc. 99/6/12, 29 May 1946.

115. WFA, Acc. 99/6/12 f3, British Association of Insulin Manufacturers, 30 July 1946, 29 May 1946.

116. For further details of research issues and the disagreements arising see chapter 15.

117. GWHC, 107.01/01, President's correspondence, notebook of F. Coe.

118. GWHC, 107.08/06, Library ephemeral, vertical files, 'retirees', Ted Holmes interview, 1984.

119. GWHC, 107.07/07.01, *Wellcome News*, Winter 1968, pp. 3–6.

120. Ibid.

121. Ibid., Monthly Letter, April 1930, p. 1.

122. Quoted from the *JAMA*. 23 March, 1935, p. 1005; WFA, GB 30/8, Monthly Memoranda April/May 1935, pp. 210–11.

123. Ibid., p. 212.

124. See below, pp. 412–14.

125. GWHC, 107.07/07.05, Monthly Letter, Jan. 1931, p. 8.

126. Ibid., April 1931, pp. 38–9.

127. Ibid., Jan. 1932, pp. 27–9.

128. Ibid.

129. Ibid., May 1931, pp. 33–4.

130. Ibid.

131. Ibid., July 1931, p. 8.

132. Ibid., Dec. 1931, p. 2.

133. Ibid., March 1933, pp. 92–5.

134. William J. Hartmann Collection, History of advertising, Duke University, NC, J. Walter Thompson archives, reel 257, 'Confidential facts on the pharmaceutical business', Sharpe and Dohme, NY., 1932.

135. Ibid., reel 257, 'Trends in the drug business 1919–1929', NY., 1932.

136. Ibid., Oct. 1932, p. 339.

137. Ibid., May 1933, pp. 154–5.

138. Ibid., March 1933, p. 78; Dec. 1936, p. 400.

139. Ibid., May 30, 1930, p. 20.

140. Ibid., March 1932, pp. 116–18.

141. Ibid., June 1933, p. 200.

142. Ibid., April 1930, pp. 6–7, May 1930, p. 22.

143. Ibid., May 1930, p. 9.

144. Ibid., Feb. 1935, pp. 51–2.

145. Ibid.; GWHC, 107.08/06, Library ephemeral, vertical files, 'retirees', Ted Holmes interview, 1984.

146. Ibid., Oct. 1932, p. 321; April 1932, pp. 131–2.

147. Ibid., Monthly Letter, Dec. 1932, pp. 393–402.

148. Ibid.

149. *American Druggist*, 93, Oct. 1936, p. 34.

150. Ibid., 95, April 1938, p. 9.

151. E.g. Abbott and Parke Davis & Co., *American Druggist*, 94, 9 April 1937 p. 10, 86, 3 Sept. 1932, pp. 20–1.

152. GWHC, 'Brief analysis'.

153. GWHC, 'Brief analysis'.

154. GWHC, 107.07/07.05, Public affairs, Monthly Letter, Feb. 1934, pp. 37–8.

155. Ibid., Monthly Letter, Nov. 1936, p. 372.

156. Ibid.

157. Ibid., Monthly Letter, Jan. 1933, pp. 5–6; Aug. 1933, pp. 225–6.

158. Ibid., Monthly Letter, Sept. 1935, p. 298.

159. Ibid., Monthly Letter, May 1934, pp. 151–4.

160. Ibid., Monthly Letter, Feb. 1930, pp. 10–11.

161. Ibid.

162. GWHC, 107.07/07.05, Public affairs, Monthly Letter, Jan. 1935, pp. 1–4.

163. Ibid., Monthly Letter, Jan. 1938, p. 3.

164. Ibid., Monthly Letter, June 1935, p. 238; May 1936, p. 141–2.

165. Ibid., Monthly Letter, Dec. 1934, pp. 397–8.

166. WFA, F/FA/328, Wellcome Foundation Ltd accounts (Moore's report), 1935, 12 Dec. 1935.

167. Tanner, 'The American Story, New York Venture' *Foundation News*, June 1981, p 13; GWHC, 107.07/07.05, Public affairs, Monthly Letter, May 1934, p. 156.

168. GWHC, 107.07/07.05, Public affairs, Monthly Letter, Oct. 1933, p. 295.

169. Ibid., Monthly Letter, Oct. 1933, pp. 295–6.

170. GWHC, 'Brief analysis'.

171. Ibid., Monthly Letter, April 1935, pp. 141–8. The decision to commence group subscription to the *JAMA* in 1936 and the advice to representatives on how to use it to their best advantage is another indicator of the company's concern to ensure that on their visits to physicians and pharmacists in hospitals and elsewhere they should be well informed of the scientific aspects of the products on the list. Ibid., Monthly Letter, June 1936, pp. 79–82. On the subject of American 'ergot', see above, chapter 10, pp. 309–12.

172. Ibid., Monthly Letter, May 1934, pp. 182–3; ibid., Dec. 1932, pp. 393–402.

173. Ibid., Monthly Letter, Aug. 1936, p.326; Sept. 1936, pp.295–6; Nov. 1936, pp.354–5.
174. Ibid., June 1936, pp.207–8.
175. Ibid., March 1937, p.117; Feb. 1937, p.77.
176. Ibid., March 1937, pp.117–18.
177. Ibid., Jan. 1938, p.4.
178. Ibid., Jan. 1937, pp.39–42.
179. Ibid., Feb. 1937, p.73.
180. Ibid., Feb. 1938, p.96.
181. Ibid., June 1939, pp.302–3.
182. Ibid., Jan. 1938, p.1.
183. Ibid., June 1937, pp.263–4; Jan. 1938, pp.1–2.
184. Ibid., June 1936, pp.203–4.
185. Ibid., March 1935, p.124.
186. Ibid., pp.124–6.
187. Ibid., May 1935, p.215.
188. Ibid., Oct. 1935, pp.363–4.
189. Ibid., April 1937, pp.164–5.
190. Ibid., Oct. 1938, pp.484–5.
191. Ibid., March 1935, p.100.
192. Ibid., May 1938, pp.269–71; June 1934, pp.216–17.

Notes to Chapter 14: A failing business? The nature and origins of decline

1. Macdonald, *In pursuit of excellence*, p.29.
2. Rhodes James, *Henry Wellcome*, p.373.
3. They show figures for the Foundation's profits in 1937/38 and 1938/39 and gross profits on General Goods, insulin, and sera in home and overseas markets for 1937 only. Hill and Bembridge, *Physic and Philanthropy* (Cambridge, Cambridge University Press), pp.30, 43, 45.
4. Robson, thesis, p.195, Table 5.1.
5. Stone and Rowe, 'Consumer spending on drugs and other medicines, 1920–1938', *National Institute of Economic and Social Research, Vol. II* (Cambridge, Cambridge University Press, 1966), p.51, table 21. The consumer spending figure excludes NHI drugs. The authors also estimate the turnover of patent medicines in 1937 at between £16 million and £20 million, p.45, n.2.
6. Robson, thesis, p.221.
7. See above chapter 11, pp.325–31.
8. WFA, Acc. 96/45, BW&Co. sales book 2.
9. See above chapter 11, pp.331–9.
10. Hall and Bembridge, *Physic and Philanthropy*, p.45. Their calculations are based on figures for 1937 which show 'gross profits' on sales at home and abroad of £610,000, yet the gross trading profit figures recorded in the amalgamated Wellcome Foundation accounts for 1937 were £375,554.
11. Ibid.
12. WFA, Acc. 96/45, BW&Co. sales book no. 2.
13. Barrie Dyster and David Meredith, *Australia and the International Economy in the Twentieth Century* (Cambridge, 1990), pp.72–164.
14. A. James Gregor, *Italian Fascism and Developmental Dictatorship* (Princeton, 1979), pp.140–79; Phillip Morgan, *Italian Fascism* (Basingstoke, Macmillan, 1995), pp.88–92, 107–30.
15. WFA, F/FA/328, WFL accounts, BW&Co. (South America) Ltd.
16. WFA, F/FA/328, WFL accounts, BW&Co. (South Africa) Ltd.
17. WFA, F/FA/328, WFL accounts, BW&Co. (Australia) Ltd.
18. GWHC, BW&Co. (USA) Inc., Coll 107, Public affairs, 'Brief analysis'.
19. Tweedale, *At the Sign of the Plough*, pp.115, 119, 157. In Russia, the company's assets were seized during the Revolution.
20. Davenport-Hines and Slinn, *Glaxo*, pp.108–9, 119.
21. Ibid., chapter 5.
22. WFA, Acc. 82/1 Box 38, typescript, 'Historical notes on Burroughs Wellcome & Co.', 1930.
23. *Chem. & Drug.*, 82, 26 July 1926, p.144; Slinn, *A History of May & Baker*, pp.95–6.
24. *Chem. & Drug.*, 104, 20 Feb. 1926, p.7.
25. Guildhall Library, Stock Exchange records, BDH annual report and balance sheets, 1926, 1935.
26. Chapman, *Boots*, p.131, table 8.
27. Tweedale, *At the Sign of the Plough*, p.125.
28. Slinn, *A History of May & Baker*, p.118, table 1.
29. Guildhall Library, Stock Exchange records, BDH balance sheets, 1926–39.
30. Davenport-Hines and Slinn, *Glaxo*, p.51.
31. Ibid., chapter 4.
32. Net income is not defined but is assumed to bear some relationship to profit. Davenport-Hines and Slinn, 1930 *Glaxo*, chapter 5, table 1.
33. Rhodes James, *Henry Wellcome*, pp.373–4.
34. See above chapter 9, table 9.5, p.280.
35. The detailed financial data regarding expenditure and withdrawals are taken from WFA, F/FA/328, trading and profit and loss accounts.
36. Rhodes James, *Henry Wellcome*, pp.350–1.
37. WFA, Acc. 96/47, trading and profit and loss accounts, 3 Sept. 1925.
38. WFA, Acc. 87/56:1, Pearson to Wellcome, 10 Nov. 1927.
39. Rhodes James, *Henry Wellcome*, p.367.
40. Hall and Bembridge, *Physic and Philanthropy*, p.46.
41. Figures for travellers' expenses are missing between 1906 and 1910.
42. WFA, F/FA/328, trading and profit and loss accounts.
43. WFA Acc. 82/1 Box 22, Items of interest, p.30; Haggis, 'Life and work', p.484.
44. Tweedale, *At the Sign of the Plough*, p.153; J. B. Jefferys, *Retail Trading in Great Britain, 1850–1950* (Cambridge, 1954), pp.382–95.
45. Tweedale, *At the Sign of the Plough*, p.153.
46. J. B. Jefferys, *Retail Trading in Great Britain, 1850–1950* (Cambridge, 1954), pp.382–95.
47. WA/BSR/LA/SCi/9, STC, 24 Nov. 1933.
48. WFA, PB 81, T. R. G. Bennett, 'The Wellcome

Foundation', draft typescript, 13 June 1945.

49. WFA, GB 30/4, 'Monthly Memoranda', April 1927, p.175.
50. WFA, GB 30/6, 'Monthly Memoranda', June 1930, p.56; GB 30/37, April 1932, p.330.
51. WFA, GB 30/3, 'Monthly Memoranda', Feb. 1924, p.23; Dec. 1924, p.168.
52. WFA, GB 30/3, 'Monthly Memoranda', Nov. 1924, p.273.
53. WFA, GB 30/4, 'Monthly Memoranda', Dec. 1927.
54. WA/BSR/LA/Sci/1, Henry to Wenyon, 20 Jan. 1925; O'Brien to Jowett, 9 Feb. 1927.
55. WFA, GB 30/7, 'Monthly Memoranda', Oct. 1933, p.481.
56. WFA, GB 30/7, 'Monthly Memoranda', Oct. 1933, p.482.
57. WFA, GB 30/4, 'Monthly Memoranda', May 1927, p.209.
58. WFA, GB 30/8, 'Monthly Memoranda', Dec. 1935, p.304.
59. WFA, GB 30/8, 'Monthly Memoranda', Dec. 1934, p.145.
60. WFA, GB 30/5, 'Monthly Memoranda', July 1928, p.107.
61. Ibid., p.108.
62. WFA, GB 30/6, 'Monthly Memoranda', April 1930, p.56.
63. Basil N. Reckitt, *The History of Reckitt & Sons Ltd* (Hull, 1952), p.85.
64. WFA, GB 30/7, 'Monthly Memoranda', Dec. 1932, p.388.
65. WFA, GB 30/10, 'Monthly Memoranda', April 1939, p.229.
66. WFA, GB 30/7, 'Monthly Memoranda', Oct. 1933, p.475.
67. WFA, GB 30/9, 'Monthly Memoranda', Feb. 1937, pp.227–8.
68. H. A. D. Jowett, 'Memo re scientific societies', 12 Oct. 1926, quoted in Robson, thesis, p.192.
69. Curiously the company's sera were not included in the *BMJ* columns in 1894/95, neither were those marketed by Allen & Hanburys for the BIPM, even though sera appeared extensively and repeatedly in the advertisements carried by the journal. Their omission does not, however, invalidate the overall conclusion regarding trends in innovative activity.
70. Robson, thesis, pp.200–1.
71. WA/BSR/LA/Sci 3, STC minutes, O'Brien to Wenyon, 4 Nov. 1927.
72. See chapter 11, p.331.
73. See chapter 11, p.327.
74. WFA, Acc. 96/45, BW&Co. sales book 2.
75. WFA, F/FA/328, WFL trading accounts and profit and loss.
76. See chapter 11, pp.331–9.
77. H. J. Parish, *A History of Immunisation* (E. and S. Livingstone, Edinburgh, 1965), pp.149–55; J. Lewis, 'The prevention of diphtheria', pp.163–76. See also chapter 11 above, pp.331–3.
78. Ibid.
79. Ibid.

80. Rhodes James, *Henry Wellcome*, pp.368–70.
81. A. R. Hall and B. A. Bembridge, *Physic and Philanthropy*, p.19. Elliott had been named as 'reserve' in the event that Wellcome's first nominee, Sir Walter Morley Fletcher, Secretary of the MRC, predeceased him.
82. Ibid.
83. Ibid., p.18.
84. Ibid., p.34.
85. Ibid., pp.18–20.
86. WFA, GW SCS 298, Wellcome Foundation minute book 1, 2 Feb. 1938.
87. Ibid., 29 Jan. 1939. For Smith's work see chapter 12, pp.366–9.
88. Ibid., 2 Feb. 1938.
89. Ibid., 10 March, 27 April 1938.
90. Subsequently under Pearson's successor, Smith was released from works management to concentrate on hormone research, for which he was given assistance in support and space at Beckenham, WT/Tru/Min/1–2, 23 Sept. 1940.
91. Hall and Bembridge, *Physic and Philanthropy*, p.24.
92. Ibid.
93. Ibid., p.20.
94. Hall and Bembridge, *Physic and Philanthropy*, p.7.
95. Quoted from letters written by Dale, Nov. 1941 and Spring 1942, in Hall and Bembridge, *Physic and Philanthropy*, p.52–3.
96. See below, p.456.
97. Quoted in Hall and Bembridge, *Physic and Philanthropy*, pp.54–5.
98. WFA, Acc. 83/3, Articles of Association, BW&Co., 1924.
99. Quoted in Hall and Bembridge, *Physic and Philanthropy*, p.34.
100. Ibid., p.35.
101. Ibid., pp.34, 42–3. Hall and Bembridge maintain that Wenyon did not command Dale's respect, though Dale supported Wenyon for a Fellowship of the Royal Society, see below chapter 15. Wenyon's heart attack in 1932 at the age of 60 may have had some relevance to the change.
102. Ibid., p.34. Dale's earlier role as director of the WPRL is testimony to this view. See chapter 6.
103. Ibid., p.43.
104. Quoted in Hall and Bembridge, *Physic and Philanthropy*, p.52.
105. Ibid., p.43.
106. Ibid.
107. Ibid.
108. Davenport-Hines and Slinn, *Glaxo*, pp.136, 154.
109. WT/Tru/Min/1–2, Trustees Minutes, 19 June 1939; 26 Feb. 1940.
110. Ibid., 11 March 1940.
111. WFA, SCS/281, Directors' minutes, 10 April 1940.
112. Ibid., 15 April 1940.
113. WFA, Acc. 82/1 Box 16, 6 Dec. 1929.
114. Ibid., 19 Aug. 1940.
115. WT/Tru/Min/1–2, Trustees Minutes, 1 April 1940.
116. Ibid.
117. WFA/SCS/128, Board minutes, 15 April 1940.

118. WT/Tru/Min./1–2, Minutes of Trustees, 1 April 1940.
119. Ibid., 17 April 1940.
120. WFA, Acc. 82/1 Box 16, Fleetwood C. Pritchard to Messrs Viney, Price, and Goodyear, 25 April 1940; L. Urwick to Martin Price, 25 April 1940.
121. WT/Tru/Min/1–2, Trustees Minutes, 1 April 1940.
122. Ibid., 20 May 1940. The Trustees agreed to allow Pearson to continue the traditional directors' perk of leaving income on deposit (then standing at £112,000) with the company at beneficial non-commercial interest rates until the end of his directorship.
123. See below chapter 15, p. 470.

Notes to Chapter 15: Themes and perspectives: BW&Co., the pharmaceutical industry, and medical research

1. Or possibly anti-American prejudice, although during his early years in Britain Wellcome had denied experiencing such a sentiment.
2. WFA, R1/10, *Dartford Express*, 14 July 1905.
3. E. M. Tansey, 'What's in a name? Henry Dale and adrenaline, 1905', *Med. Hist.*, 39, pp. 459–76.
4. *Chronicle and District Times*, 5 Dec. 1899.
5. *The Times*, 1 Aug. 1936.
6. WFA, Box 72, BE/65, 'Statement by Prof. Simpson', which was probably written on Wellcome's death.
7. However, regardless of the reputation enjoyed by BW&Co.'s scientists and the quality of their research and the standing of the company with practising vets, Wellcome and his senior staff did not succeed entirely in overcoming a prejudice against research laboratories owned by a commercial organisation. See, for example, the continuing problems of the WPRL, chapter 11, Foot and mouth disease, and tuberculosis: the commercial taint continued, pp. 347–9.
8. WFA, Acc. 84/6 folder 2, H. J. Parish, 'Sidelights on Mr Pearson and Dr O'Brien.'
9. WFA, Acc. 84/6 Box 1 (9), brief hand-written note of meeting with Dale by Parish (1964?).
10. See chapter 11, pp. [485–89].
11. Though Wellcome's concern over Burroughs' increased ownership of the equity capital was an important factor contributing to his caution on that occasion. See chapter 4, pp. 121–2.
12. Quoted in Haggis, 'Life and work', p. 588.
13. Rhodes James, *Henry Wellcome*. p. 269.
14. Haggis, 'Life and work', p. 377.
15. Ibid., p. 392.
16. WFA, Acc. 82/1 Box 38, typescript, Observer, 'Behind the scenes' n.d.
17. *Foundation News*, 25, 10 Oct. 1975, p. 6.
18. Haggis, 'Life and work', p. 587.
19. Ibid., p. 576.
20. Most evidently with respect to Wellcome's role in developing the American business.
21. Macdonald, *Excellence*, p. 29.
22. WFA, 82/1 Box 13, memo, Pearson, July 1930.
23. WFA, 82/1 Box 13, Wellcome to Pearson, 15 June 1916.
24. Haggis quoting Pearson, reproduced in Rhodes James, *Henry Wellcome*, p. 357.
25. See below pp. 466–8.
26. WFA, Acc. 84/6 folder 2, typescript, H. J. Parish, 'Sidelights on Mr Pearson and Dr O'Brien.'
27. WFA, Acc. 82/1 Box 38, typescript, by Observer, 'Behind the scenes', n.d; WFA, Acc. 84/6, folder 2, H. J. Parish, 'Sidelights on Mr Pearson and Dr O'Brien'.
28. WFA, Acc. 84/6 folder 2, typescript, H. J. Parish, 'Sidelights on Mr Pearson and Dr O'Brien.'
29. Ibid.
30. Ibid.
31. WFA, Acc. 82/1 Box 13, Wellcome to Pearson, 15 June 1916.
32. WFA, Acc. 87/14/5 Box 79, interview with W. Solomon, 1984.
33. WFA, Acc. 82/1 Box 38, typescript, Observer, 'Behind the scenes', n.d; see also WFA, 84/6 folder 2, typescript, H. J. Parish, 'Sidelights on Mr Pearson and Dr O'Brien.'
34. WFA, Acc. 82/1 Box 38, Wellcome to Pearson, 19 Oct. 1917.
35. GWHC, internal publications, 'Brief analysis'.
36. WFA, Acc. 82/1 Box 19, Nevin to Pearson, 12 Dec. 1922; 3 Feb. 1923.
37. WFA, Acc. 82/1 Box 19, Nevin to Pearson, 12 Dec. 1922; 3 Feb. 1923; Pearson to Nevin, 15 Dec. 1920.
38. WFA, Acc. 82/1 Box 19, Wellcome to Pearson, 23 Oct. 1926.
39. WFA, Acc. 82/1 Box 19, Pearson to Nevin, 3 Nov. 1926.
40. WFA, Acc. 82/1 Box 19, Nevin to Pearson, 26 Feb. 1926; Nevin to Pearson, copy to Wellcome, 15 June 1926, 25 March 1927; Wellcome to Pearson, 27 May 1927.
41. The history of the Canadian company and its relations with London were examined by Wellcome in a 15-page letter to Pearson, on which the following paragraphs are based. WFA, Acc. 87/56/1, Wellcome to Pearson, 12 Dec. 1927.
42. Ibid.
43. WFA, Acc. 87/56/1, London to BW&Co., Montreal, 16 June 1927.
44. Ibid.
45. Ibid.
46. Ibid.
47. Ibid.
48. WFA, Acc. 87/56/1, Lang to Wellcome, 24 Feb. 1928.
49. WFA, Acc. 82/1 Box 20, Nevin to Pearson, 1 June 1934; WFA, Acc. 82/1 Box 20, Nevin to Bennett, 19, 30 July 1941.

50. WFA, Acc. 82/1 Box 20, Nevin to Pearson, 1 June 1934.
51. This division of opinion surfaced in the course of appointing the first director of the laboratory in 1928. Kellaway, 'Review', WFA, Acc. 82/1 Box 20, quoting Nevin to Wellcome, 28 Feb. 1928; Pearson to Nevin, 20 April 1928; Nevin to Pearson, 25 June 1928.
52. Rhodes James, *Henry Wellcome*, pp. 368–9.
53. WFA, Acc. 82/1 Box 20, Pearson to Nevin, 18 March 1935.
54. WFA, Acc. 82/1 Box 20, Nevin to London, 2 April 1928; Nevin to Pearson, 25 June 1928.
55. WFA, Acc. 82/1 Box 20, Kellaway, 'Review', p. 1.
56. WFA, Acc. 82/1 Box 20, Kellaway, 'Review', quoting Pearson to Nevin, 20 April 1928.
57. GWHC, 'Brief analysis'.
58. WFA, Acc. 82/1 Box 20, Kellaway, 'Review', quoting Pearson to Nevin, 4 July 1929.
59. WFA, Acc. 82/1 Box 20, Kellaway, 'Review', quoting Nevin to Pearson, 25 June 1928, 1 June 1934.
60. Ibid., quoting Wellcome to Nevin, July 1928.
61. WFA, Acc. 82/1 Box 20, Kellaway, 'Review', quoting Nevin to Pearson, 4 July 1929; quoting Reiner to Nevin, 8 Nov. 1929; quoting Nevin to Pearson, 26 Dec. 1929.
62. WFA, Acc. 82/1 Box 20, Kellaway 'Review' quoting Nevin to Pearson, 26 Dec. 1929.
63. WFA, Acc. 82/1 Box 21, Wenyon report, 21 Nov. 1933, quoted in Pearson to Nevin, 21 Dec. 1933.
64. WFA, Acc. 82/1 Box 21, Nevin to Pearson, 7 March 1935.
65. WFA, Acc. 82/1 Box 19, Nevin to Pearson, 28 Jan. 1926.
66. Ibid.
67. WFA, Acc. 82/1 Box 20, Kellaway, 'Review', quoting Nevin to Bennett, 19, 30 July 1941.
68. Ibid.
69. WFA. Acc. 82/1 Box 20; Kellaway, 'Review', quoting Wenyon to Nevin, 26 July 1939.
70. WFA, Acc. 87/14:5 Box 79, interview with G. H. Warrack, 1984.
71. WFA, transcripts of interview with Peter Williams, 2003.
72. WFA, Reminiscences, Box 1, taped interview with Richmond, 1963.
73. WFA, Acc. 84/6 Box 1, typescript, H. J. Parish, 'The Wellcome Research Laboratories and immunisation: historical survey and personal memoir'.
74. WFA, Wellcome LB17, 420–6, BW&Co. to Wellcome, 8 Jan. 1902; WFA, Acc. 87/14/5, interview with Warrack, 1984.
75. Ibid.
76. WFA, Acc. 87/14/5, Box 79, interviews with W. Solomon, and Warrack, 1984; WFA, Acc. 84/6, folder 2, typescript, H. J. Parish, 'Sidelights on Mr Pearson and Dr O'Brien'.
77. WFA, Reminiscences, Box 1, taped interview with Richmond, 1963.
78. WFA, Acc. 87/14/5 Box 79, taped interview with W. Solomon, 1984; WFA, Acc. 84/6 folder 2, typescript, H. J. Parish, 'Sidelights on Mr Pearson and Dr O'Brien.'
79. WFA, Acc. 83/3/30, O'Brien to Wenyon, Dec. 1923.
80. WFA, Acc. 84/6/1 (9), typescript, H. J. Parish, 'The Wellcome Research Laboratories and immunisation: a historical survey and personal memoir', chapter 4.
81. C. A. Hoare 'Charles Morley Wenyon', *Obit Nots FRS*, 6, 1948–49, 627–42, quote on page 633.
82. Hall and Bembridge *Physic and Philanthropy*, pp. 52–3.
83. WFA, Acc. 87/14/5 Box 79, interview with G. H. Warrack, 1984.
84. WFA, Acc. 84/6/1 (9), typescript, H. J. Parish, 'The Wellcome research laboratories', chapter 5.
85. Ibid.
86. Ibid.
87. Ibid.
88. Ibid.
89. See above, chapter 11, pp. 329–30.
90. The memo was forwarded from Snow Hill to O'Brien. WFA, Acc. 83/3/45, BW&Co. (SA) to BW&Co., 12 April 1928.
91. WFA, Acc. 99/6/11; WFA, PB 81, T. R. G. Bennett, 'The Wellcome Foundation', typescript, 13 June 1945.
92. See above chapter 11.
93. A replacement described by a colleague as one poor administrator for another whose managerial skills were even worse. WFA, Acc. 84/6, folder 2, typescript, H. J. Parish, 'Sidelights on Mr Pearson and Dr O'Brien.'
94. Quoted in *Foundation News*, 21, 1 Jan. 1971, p. 3.
95. Quoted in Hall and Bembridge, *Physic and Philanthropy*, p. 54. In 1947 the Trustees were to reject his proposal advanced to the Trust at the time of a financial crisis, the intended effect of which was to separate the business from the WRI and its building, for which the Trust would be directly responsible.
96. Rhodes James, *Henry Wellcome*, pp. 336–7.
97. Captain Peter Johnson-Saint, curator of the Wellcome museum, reported that during his visit to Wellcome in Florida in February 1936, Wellcome had spoken of Nevin in the highest terms, and had declared his intention that on his return to London Nevin would be appointed general manager of the entire business activities of BW&Co. in England and overseas. According to family descendants, Nevin and his wife had agreed to move to England for this purpose. However, Wellcome returned, and died after a grave illness, six months later. Neither his will, nor the memorandum for the guidance of testators (both signed in February 1932), mentioned Nevin. Johnson-Saint to Robert Wallace Nevin (Thomas Nevin's nephew), 7 Jan. 1965, communicated to the authors by e-mail by Linda Nevin, USA, 22 July 2002.

98. For a review of the social science and management literature dealing with trust in relation to business as a context for the case of trust in the history of Burroughs Wellcome & Co., see Church, 'Trust, Burroughs Wellcome & Co., pp. 376–98.

Notes to Chapter 16: Wellcome's influence on pharmaceutical and medical research in Britain

1. Elsewhere we suggested that Burroughs must have agreed to this departure. However, his death shortly after its inauguration left the direction, organisation, work, and ultimately the achievements of these laboratories solely to Wellcome. See chapter 7, pp. 205–6.
2. TNA, HO144/738/114089/2, Martin to HO, 8 Nov. 1905.
3. Although this nationalistic attitude may have played a part in Wellcome's difficulties, there is no explicit evidence of anti-American prejudice affecting the Home Office's deliberations in 1900–01.
4. TNA, HO144/738/114089/2, HO Minute by Thane, 17 Nov. 1905.
5. Ibid., Internal Home Office memorandum, 21 Nov. 1905. The Newcastle company made limited use of their authorization, in that William Martin performed the occasional experiment in the next few years. From 1914, however, the company's premises no longer appear in the Home Office's list of approved premises. See the Home Office, *Experiments on Living Animals, Annual Returns for 1906–1914*, PP (HMSO, London), various.
6. Ibid., *Annual Returns 1911*, PP (HMSO, London), 1913, 68, p. 149.
7. Ibid.
8. Such premises included, for example, the School of Army Sanitation, Aldershot; the Kitchiner India Hospital, Brighton; the Ontario Military Hospital, Orpington; and the Central Military Hospital, Chatham. For lists of wartime registered premises that were not re-registered, see Home Office, *Experiments on Living Animals, Annual Returns for 1915*, PP (HMSO, London), 22, Session 1916, p. 389; Ibid., *Annual Returns for 1916*, PP (HMSO, London), 1918, 38, p. 221; Ibid., *Annual Returns for 1919* 42, p. 361; Ibid., *Annual Returns for 1919–20*, Parliamentary Papers (HMSO, London, 1920), 40, p. 589.
9. See chapter 6, pp. 172–5.
10. For details of later pharmaceutical company registrations and the impact on animal experimentation statistics see E. M. Tansey, 'The Wellcome Physiological Research Laboratories 1894–1904: the Home Office, pharmaceutical firms and animal experiments', *Med Hist.*, 33, 1989, 1–41, esp. 37–41.
11. The word 'standardisation' refers to the methods employed to characterize a biologically active substance. Biological responses of a drug within a given range are identified as being standardized and drug preparations responding outside this range are rejected. The procedure ensures a certain degree of reproducibility and reliability in the compounds thus standardised, although, as it depends on comparisons between variables it is not an exact science, but based on probability. See D. Bangham, *A History of Biological Standardisation, The Characterization and Measurement of Complex Molecules Important in Clinical and Research Medicine* (Society for Endocrinology, Bristol, 1999), esp. pp. 7–12.
12. See chapter 6, pp. 172–5.
13. F. M. Durham, J. H. Gaddum, , J. E. Marchal (1929) *Reports on Biological Standards II. Toxicity tests for Novarsenobenzene (Neosalvarsan)* HMSO; London, 1929, esp. pp. 13–14, 28–30.
14. TNA FD/1, MRC Minute Book 2, MRC Minutes of meeting, 3 Jan. 1919, item 11.
15. H. H. Dale, 'Percival Hartley', *Biog. Mems. FRS. Lond.*, 3, 1957, 81–100, esp. 85–6, 87–91; NIMR 622, O'Brien to Dale, 30 Nov. 1923.
16. H. H. Dale, 'Percival Hartley', *Biog. Mems FRS Lond.*, 3, 1957, 81–100, quote on page 88.
17. WA/BSR/LA/Sci/2, typescript [ABCM], Co-operation in research between medical investigations and fine chemical manufacturers, 13 Feb. 1923, in STC Minutes, 29 Dec. 1926.
18. See e.g. the prohibition against allowing the WPRL to participate in either foot and mouth disease or TB research, chapter 11, pp. 347–9.
19. WA/BSR/LA/Sci/2, typescript [ABCM], Co-operation in research between medical investigations and fine chemical manufacturers, 13 Feb. 1923, in STC Minutes, 29 Dec. 1926.
20. WFA, Acc. 83/3/34, T. A. Henry to A. W. Crossley, 9 July 1925.
21. WA/BSR/LA/Sci/2, Woolcock (ABCM) to Dale, 9 Dec. 1926; Dale to Woolcock (ABCM), 16 Dec. 1926, STC Minutes, 29 Dec. 1926.
22. WA/BSR/LA/Sci/2, Pearson to Wenyon, 23 Dec. 1926; O'Brien to Pearson, 31 Dec. 1926, draft by O'Brien, all in STC Minutes, 29 Dec. 1926.
23. Ibid.
24. NIMR Archives, Typescript Report on the work of the Chemotherapy Committee (1927–30), 8 Dec. 1930.
25. Ibid. The fourth company was Ilford Ltd, headed by Dr Frances Hamer.
26. NIMR 588/6/3, 'Chemotherapy Committee and ABCM', J. Davidson Pratt to Sir Walter Fletcher, 28 Nov. 1930; Pratt to Henry Dale, 28 Nov. 1930; Pratt to Editor, *Lancet*, draft, 28 Nov. 1930. J. Davidson Pratt, The clinical trial of medicinal products, *Lancet*, ii: 1930, 1264.
27. WA/BSR/LA/Sci/7, Minutes of STC, 27 March 1931.

28. See chapter 12, p.369.
29. H. E. Armstrong, 'Sir Henry Wellcome', *The Times*, 3 Aug. 1936, p.12.
30. WFA, Box 184, papers re Carr's departure – 'Typescript history of the WCRL'. See chapter 10.
31. M. Barrowcliff and F. H. Carr, *Organic Medicinal Chemicals Synthetic and Natural* (London, Ballière, Tindall & Cox, 1921). WFA, Box 184, 'Typescript history of WCRL'.
32. C. J. T., 'Cronshaw Marmaduke Barrowcliff – Obituary', *J. Chem. Soc.*, ii, 1948, 1475–6.
33. F. J. Griffin, 'Francis Howard Carr, 1874–1969,' *Chem. & Ind.*, 7, 15 Feb. 1969, 196.
34. Pyman's numerous contributions to the field during this period are listed in the bibliography in H. King, 'Frank Lee Pyman', *Obit Nots. FRS.*, 4, 1942–44, pp.681–97.
35. See chapter 9, p.256.
36. See e.g. Pyman, F., Easson, A. P. T., Boots Pure Drug Co. Ltd, Manufacture of (therapeutically valuable) amidines. British Patent 343, 577, 1927; F. H. Carr and T. A. Henry, 'Frank Lee Pyman', *J. Chem. Soc.*, ii, 1944, 563–70.
37. King, op. cit., note 34 above, p.691.
38. WFA, Acc. 83/3/151, Henry to Balfour, 8 April 1919; Henry to Bacharach, 1 April 1919, Bacharach to Henry, 15 April 1919.
39. 'SFW' & 'ELS', 'Obituary – Alfred Louis Bacharach', *BMJ*, ii, 1966, 308–9.
40. E. Jones, *The Business of Medicine* (Profile, London, 2001), pp.30, 64–6; R. P. T. Davenport Hines and J. Slinn, *Glaxo: A History to 1962* (Cambridge, Cambridge University Press, 1992), pp.47–9, 71–3, 79–83.
41. H. H. Dale, 'Arthur James Ewins, *Biog Mems FRS*, 4, 1958, 81–91.
42. Ibid, p.90.
43. C. L. Oakley, 'Alexander Glenny', *Biog Mems FRS*, 12, 1966, 163–180, quote on p.168.
44. Hall and Bembridge, *Physic and Philanthropy*, pp.52–3. Dale had, however, earlier been one of Wenyon's proposers for election to the Royal Society, RS EC/1927/15.
45. Harden, A., 'Samuel Barnett Schryver: obituary', *J. Chem. Soc.*, i, 1930, 901–5.
46. WFA, Box 184, 'Typescript history of the WCRL'. See also H. Rogerson, 'Chemical examination of the root of *Lasiosiphon meissnerianus*', *Amer. J. Pharm.*, 83, 1911, 49–55.
47. H. H. Dale, 'George Barger', *Obit Nots FRS*, 3, 1939–1941, 63–85, quote on p.69.
48. H. King, 'Frank Lee Pyman', *Obit Nots FRS.*, 4, 1942–1944, 681–97, esp. 687.

49. See chapter 7, p.175.
50. Wellcome Missing Archives, 'Sir Edward Mellanby etc.', John Mellanby to Wellcome, 12 Nov. 1931.
51. Sir Thomas Dalling (1892–1982), *Who Was Who* (A&C Black, London, 2003).
52. Chapter 11, p.346.
53. Wellcome Missing Papers, 'Sir Edward Mellanby etc.', Edward Mellanby to Wellcome, 8 Nov. 1931.
54. H. H. Dale, Thomas Renton Elliott (1887–1961), *Biog. Mem. FRS. Lond.*, 7, 1961, 53–74.
55. Wellcome Trust Archives, 'Sir Henry Dale correspondence with Professor T. R. Elliott 1937–1955, Mr L. C. Bullock 1937–1957, Dale to Elliott', 14 Nov. 1955.
56. Ibid., Dale to Elliott, 23 Aug. 1944.
57. See Hall and Bembridge, *Physic and Philanthropy*, 48–65. 'Pure' research has, however, been continuously fostered by the commercially neutral Wellcome Trust, see e.g. Wellcome Trust Annual Reports.
58. WFA, Acc. 82/1 Box 81, 'List of Wellcome FRSs', includes the note, 'not proper to count Dorothy Hodgkin who worked in our chemistry lab when she was 13'.
59. See chapter 6, pp.201–2 for more details of his election and his departure.
60. H. H. Dale, 'Arthur Ewins', *Biog Mems FRS*, 4, 1958, 81–91, quote on p.87.
61. RS 93 HD 36.4.4.7, 'T. R. Elliott', Dale to Elliott, 26 Nov. 1931.
62. C. M. Wenyon, 'Henry Solomon Wellcome', *Obit Nots FRS*, 2, 1936–38, 229–238.
63. T. S. Moore, J. C. Philip, *The Chemical Society, 1841–1941* (Chemical Society, London, 1947), pp.219–26.
64. For the creation and early history of the MRC see A. L. Thomson, *Half a Century of Medical Research*, 2 vols (London, HMSO, 1973 and 1975) and the essays in J. Austoker and L. Bryder, *Historical Perspectives on the Role of the MRC* (Oxford, Oxford University Press, 1989). See also, TNA FD1/5254, MRC Minutes Book 1, '1913–1914', Meetings of the MRC, 22–23 Nov. 1913; 11 Dec. 1913; 26 Feb. 1914.
65. WFA, Acc. 88/3/144.
66. See e.g. the list of publications produced whilst at BW&Co. in Harington, C. R., 'Harold King', *Biog Mems FRS*, 2, 1956, 157–71, p.167.
67. T. C. Gray, 'Harold King: a notable contributor to anaesthesia', *Anaesthesia*, 41, 1991, 679–82.
68. NIMR/622, 'O'Brien', O'Brien to Dale, 30 Oct. 1922.
69. W. Feldberg 'John Henry Gaddum', *Biog Mems FRS*, 13, 1967, 57–77.
70. See chapter 10, pp.300–5.

Bibliography

Abdel-Hameed, A. A., 'The Wellcome Tropical Research Laboratories in Khartoum (1903–1934): an experiment in development', *Medical History*, 41 (1997), 30–58.

Allen & Hanburys, *General List of Drugs, Pharmaceuticals, and the 'Allenburys' Specialities* (Allen & Hanburys, London, 1908).

Anon., 'J. W. Washbourn (1863–1902) – obituary', *Transactions of the Epidemiological Society of London*, 21 (1901–02), 151–4.

Anon., 'Mr Winston Churchill has no use for serums', *Vaccinator Inquirer & Health Review*, 36 (1914), 252.

Anon., 'Gordon Memorial College Khartoum', *The Times*, 9 Dec. 1902.

Anon., 'Gordon Memorial College Khartoum', *Daily Chronicle*, 9 Dec. 1902.

Anon., 'Dinner to Dr Andrew Balfour', *Journal of Tropical Medicine*, 15 Dec. 1902, 390–1.

Anon., 'Dr F. B. Power, Obituary', *Nature*, 119 (1927), 573.

Anon., '"M & B" cures Lion', *The World's Fair*, 22 Jan. 1944, 12.

Anon., 'P. E. F. Pérrèdes, obituary', *Chemist & Druggist*, 153 (1950), 102–3.

Anon., 'Obituary: William Lloyd Williams', *Chemical Trade Journal*, 26 (1900), 52.

Apple, Rima D., *Vitamania: Vitamins in American Culture* (Rutgers University Press, New Brunswick, NJ, 1996).

Armstrong, H. E., 'Sir Henry Wellcome', *The Times*, 3 Aug. 1936, 12.

Austoker, J. and L. Bryder, *Historical Perspectives on the Role of the MRC* (Oxford University Press, 1989).

Bangham, D., *A History of Biological Standardisation, The Characterization and Measurement of Complex Molecules Important in Clinical and Research Medicine* (Society for Endocrinology, Bristol, 1999).

Barger, G. and H. H. Dale, 'Ergotoxine and some other constituents of ergot', *Biochemical Journal*, 2 (1907), 240–99.

Barger, G., F. H. Carr, and H. H. Dale, 'An active alkaloid from ergot', *British Medical Journal*, ii (1906), 1792.

Barger, G. and G. S. Walpole, 'Isolation of the pressor principles of putrid meat', *Journal of Physiology*, 38 (1909), 343–52.

Barrowcliff, M. and F. B. Power, 'The constitution of chaulmoogric and hydnocarpic acids', *Journal of the Chemical Society*, 91 (1907), 557–78.

Barrowcliff, M. and F. H. Carr, *Organic Medicinal Chemicals Synthetic and Natural* (Ballière, Tindall & Cox, London, 1921).

Bartripp, P. W. J., *Mirror of Medicine: A History of the British Medical Journal* (Clarendon Press, Oxford, 1990).

Bator, P. A. and A. J. Rhodes, *Within Reach of Everyone: A History of the University of Toronto School of Hygiene and the Connaught Laboratories. Vol. 1, 1927–55* (Canadian Public Health Association, Ottawa, 1990).

Bell, H., *Frontiers of Medicine in the Anglo-Egyptian Sudan, 1899–1940* (Oxford Historical Monographs, Oxford, 1999).

Bigger, J. W., J. W. S. Blacklock, and H. J. Parish, 'Investigations and observations on inoculation technique', *British Medical Journal*, i (1940), 79–84.

Bigger, J. W., J. W. S. Blacklock, and H. J. Parish, 'Sterilization of syringes and needles', *British Medical Journal*, i (1940), 582–3.

Blair, J. S. G., *In arduis fidelis: Centenary History of the Royal Army Medical Corps* (Scottish Academic Publishing, Edinburgh, 2001).

Blair-Bell, W., 'The pituitary body and the therapeutic value of the infundibular extract in shock, uterine atony and intestinal paresis', *British Medical Journal*, ii (1909), 1609–13.

Blair-Bell, W., and P. Hick, 'Observations on the physiology of the female genital organs. IV. Uterine contractions', *British Medical Journal*, i (1909), 777–83.

Bokenham, T. J. 'Additional notes on the preparation of anti-streptococcus serum', *British Medical Journal*, ii (1896), 3–4.

Bosanquet, W. C. and J. W. H. Eyre, *Serums, Vaccines and Toxins in Treatment and Diagnosis* (Cassell, London, 1909).

Bousfield, E. C., 'Diphtheria antitoxin in private practice', *Lancet*, ii (1898), 1544–5.

Bousfield, G., *A Practical Guide to the Schick Test and Diphtheria and Scarlet Fever Immunization.* (J. & A. Churchill, London, 1929).

Bousfield, G., 'Diphtheria immunisation: a plea for the immediate abandonment or control of "one-shot" treatment', *Medical Officer*, 57 (1937), 15–16.

Bousfield, G., 'Diphtheria prophylaxis: an investigation into the comparative merits of one and two injections of alum-precipitated toxoid', *Medical Officer*, 59

(1938), 5–8.

Bousfield, G., 'Restoration of diphtheria immunity without injections: Toxoid pastilles by mouth', *British Medical Journal*, i (1945), 833–5.

Bousfield, L., *Sudan Doctor* (Christopher Johnson, London, 1954).

Boyce, Gordon, 'A professional association as network and communicating node: the Pharmaceutical Society of Australia', *Australian Economic History Review*, 39 (1999), 258–83.

British Drug Houses, *Price List* (British Drug Houses, London, 1914).

Burroughs, Wellcome & Co. *The Wellcome Chemical Research Laboratories. With a Description of the Exhibits of these Laboratories at the Anglo American Exposition* (BW&Co., London, 1914).

Burroughs, Wellcome & Co., *British Alkaloids and Fine Chemicals* (BW&Co., London, 1914).

Bynum, W., *Science and the Practice of Medicine* (Cambridge University Press, 1994).

Cameron, V. and E. R. Long, *Tuberculosis Medical Research: National Tuberculosis Association, 1905–1955* (National Tuberculosis Association, New York, 1959).

Cardwell, D.S.L., *The Organisation of Science in England* (Heinemann, London, 1972).

Carr, F.H., 'Experimental work in an English herb garden', *American Journal of Pharmacy*, 83 (1913), 487–96.

Carr, F.H. and T.A. Henry, 'Frank Lee Pyman'. *Journal of the Chemical Society*, ii (1944), 563–70.

Champion, Ron, 'Wellcome in Australia', *Wellcome News*, Dec. 1986.

Chapman, H.E., 'Proprietary medicines – the present position', *Pharmaceutical Journal*, 175 (1955), 207–10.

Chapman, S.D., *Jesse Boot of Boots the Chemists: A study in business history* (Hodder & Staughton, 1974).

Chapman-Huston, D. and E.C.Cripps, *Through a City Archway: The Story of Allen & Hanburys 1715–1954* (John Murray, London, 1954).

Chen, W., 'The laboratory as business: Sir Almoth Wright's vaccine programme and the construction of penicillin', in A. Cunningham and P. Williams (eds), *The Laboratory Revolution in Medicine* (Cambridge University Press, 1992), 245–92.

Chesney, G., 'Immunization against diphtheria with alum-precipitated toxoid: efficiency, duration and grade of immunity', *British Medical Journal*, i (1937), 807–8.

Chick, H., M.Hume and M.Macfarlane, *War on Disease – A History of the Lister Institute* (Andre Deutsch, London, 1971).

Christophers, S.R., 'Sydney Price James', *Obituary Notices of Fellows of the Royal Society London*, 5 (1945–8), 507–23.

Church, Roy, 'The British market for medicine in the late nineteenth century: the innovative impact of S. M. Burroughs & Co.', *Medical History*, 49 (2005), 281–98.

Church, Roy, 'Trust, Burroughs Wellcome & Co., and the foundation of a modern pharmaceutical industry in Britain', *Business History*, 48 (2006), 376–98.

'C.J.T.', 'Cronshaw Marmaduke Barrowcliff – Obituary', *Journal of the Chemical Society*, ii (1948), 1475–6.

Cokkins, A.J., 'Treatment of gonorrhea with oral sulphanilamide', *British Medical Journal*, ii (1937), 905–9.

Colebrook, L. and M. Kenny, 'Treatment of human peurperal infections, and experimental infections in mice with Prontosil', *Lancet*, ii (1936), 1279–86.

Comerford, A.A., 'Two years' field experience with the preventative treatment of distemper as advocated by Laidlaw and Dunkin', *Veterinary Record*, 9 (1929), 83–93.

Cook, G., 'Fatal yellow fever contracted at the Hospital for Tropical Diseases, London, UK, in 1930', *Transactions of the Royal Society of Tropical Medicine and Hygiene*, 88 (1994), 712–13.

Corley, T.A.B., 'Interactions between the British and American Patent Medicine Industries, 1708–1914', *Business and Economic History* 16 (1987), 111–29.

Corley, T.A.B., 'The Beecham Group in the world's pharmaceutical industry, 1914–1970', *Zeitschrift fur Unternehmensgchichte*, 39 (1994), 18–30.

Corley, T.A.B., 'The use of pharmaceutical products in UK veterinary medicine' (Conference paper, British Society for the History of Medicine, September 2003).

Cream, T.F., 'The use of Prontosil in the treatment of gonorrhoea', *Lancet*, ii (1937), 895–8.

Cruickshank, A., 'The golden age of tropical medicine and its impact on the modernization of the Sudan', in M.W.Daly (ed.), *Modernization in the Sudan: Essays in honor of Richard Hill* (Lilian Barber Press, New York, 1985), 85–100.

Dale, H.H., 'On some physiological actions of ergot', *Journal of Physiology*, 34 (1906), 163–206.

Dale, H.H., *The Wellcome Physiological Research Laboratories. Guide, and catalogue with a description of the exhibits of these laboratories at the Franco-British exhibition* (BW&Co., London, 1908).

Dale, H.H., 'The action of extracts of the pituitary body', *Biochemical Journal*, 4 (1909), 427–47.

Dale, H.H., *The Wellcome Physiological Research Laboratories* (BW&Co., London, 1910).

Dale, H.H., 'George Barger', *Obituary Notices of Fellows of the Royal Society London*, 3 (1939–41), 63–85.

Dale, H.H., 'Frederick Gowland Hopkins 1861–1947', *Obituary Notices of Fellows of the Royal Society London*, 6 (1949), 115–45.

Dale, H.H., 'Percival Hartley', *Biographical Memoirs of Fellows of the Royal Society London*, 3 (1957), 81–100.

Dale, H.H., 'Autobiographical sketch', *Perspectives in Biology & Medicine*, 1 (1958), 125–37.

Dale, H.H., 'Arthur James Ewins', *Biographical Memoirs of Fellows of The Royal Society London*, 4 (1958), 81–91.

Dale, H.H., 'Thomas Renton Elliott (1887–1961)', *Biographical Memoirs of Fellows of the Royal Society London*, 7 (1961), 53–74.

Dale, H. H., *Adventures in Physiology* (Wellcome Trust, London, 1965).

Dalling, T., 'Lamb dysentery: an account of some experimental fieldwork in 1925 and 1926', *Journal* of *Comparative Pathology and Therapeutics*, 39 (1926), 148–53.

Dalling, T., 'A consideration of some diseases of animals – the laboratory and field worker'. *Veterinary Record*, 7 (1927), 451–4.

Dalling, T., 'Experiences with distemper immunisation', *Veterinary Record*, 10 (1930), 225–34.

Dalling, T., H. R. Allen and J. H. Mason, 'Research into certain animal diseases', *Veterinary Record*, 5 (1925), 561–6.

Dalling, T., H. R. Allen, and J. H. Mason, 'Veterinary biological products – their standardisation and application', *Veterinary Record*, 6 (1926), 65–70.

Dalling, T., J. H. Mason and W. S. Gordon, 'Lamb dysentery prophylactic in 1927', *Veterinary Record*, 7 (1927), 451–4.

Dalling, T., and C. C. Okell, 'Vaccine treatment of canine leptospiral jaundice', *Journal of Pathology and Bacteriology*, 29 (1926), 131.

Daly, M. W. (ed.), *Modernization in the Sudan: Essays in honor of Richard Hill* (Lilian Barber Press, New York, 1985).

Davenport-Hines, R. P. T. and Judy Slinn, *Glaxo: A History* (Cambridge University Press, 1992).

Davidson Pratt, J., 'The clinical trial of medicinal products' *Lancet*, ii (1930), 1264.

Davies, John, 'Silas M. Burroughs, Part 1: The early years from Medina to medicines', *Wellcome Journal*, Feb. 1991, 10–13.

Dick, G. F. and G. R. H. Dick, 'A skin test for suscepti-bility to scarlet fever', *Journal of the American Medical Association*, 82 (1924), 265–6.

Dick, G. F. and G. H. Dick, 'Scarlet fever preparations', *Journal of the American Medical Association*, 85 (1925), 996.

Dick, G. F. and G. H. Dick, 'The patents in scarlet fever toxin and antitoxin', *Journal of the American Medical Association*, 88 (1927), 1341–2.

Digby, Anne, *Making a Medical Living: Doctors and patients in the English market for medicine, 1720–1911* (Cambridge University Press, 1994).

Digby, Anne, *The Evolution of British General Practice* (Oxford University Press, 1999).

Doig, A. T., G. Gemmill, G. Gregory Kayne, F. V. Linggood, H. J. Parish and J. S. Westwater, 'Laboratory and clinical investigations on tuberculin purified protein derivitive (PPD) and old tuberculin (OT)', *British Medical Journal*, i (1938), 992–7.

Donnelly, James, 'Defining the industrial chemist in the United Kingdom, 1850–1921', *Journal of Social History*, 24 (1996), 3–30.

Dudley, S. F., P. M. May and J. A. O'Flynn, *Active Immuni-zation Against Diphtheria: Its effect on the distribution of anti-toxic immunity and case and carrier infection* (HMSO, London, 1934).

Dunnill, M., *The Plato of Praed Street* (RSM Press, London, 2000).

Durham, F. M., J. H. Gaddum, J. E. Marchal, *Reports on Biological Standards. II. Toxicity Tests for Novarse-nobenzene (Neosalvarsan)* (HMSO, London, 1929).

Dyster, Barrie and David Meredith, *Australia and the International Economy in the Twentieth Century* (Cambridge University Press, 1990).

Eagleton, A. J. and E. M. Baxter, 'Standardisation of tuberculin', *British Journal of Experimental Pathology*, 4 (1923), 289–304.

Edgerton, D. E. H., and S. M. Horrocks, 'British industrial research and development before 1945', *Economic History Review*, 47 (1994), 213–38.

Editorial, 'Diphtheria antitoxin', *Journal of the Royal Army Medical Corps*, 2 (1904), 601–2.

Editorial, 'New Haven's Public Health Research for 1932', *Journal of the American Medical Association*, 98 (1932), 819–20.

Editorial, 'Deaths following elixir of sulfanilimide – Massengill II', *Journal of the American Medical Association*, 109 (1937), 1456, 1727.

England, Joseph W. (ed.), *The First Century of the Phila-delphia College of Pharmacy* (Philadelphia College of Pharmacy and Science, Philadelphia, 1922).

English, P. C., 'Therapeutic strategies to combat pneumococcal disease: repeated failure of physicians to adopt pneumococcal vaccine, 1900–45', *Perspectives in Biology and Medicine*, 30 (1987), 170–85.

Feikin, D. R. and K. P. Klugman, 'Historical changes in pneumococcal serogroup distribution: implications for the era of pneumococcal conjugate vaccines', *Clinical Infectious Diseases*, 35 (2002), 547–55.

Feldberg, W. S., 'John Henry Gaddum', *Biographical Memoirs of Fellows of the Royal Society London*, 13 (1967), 57–77.

Feldberg, W. S., 'Henry Hallett Dale', *Biographical Memoirs of Fellows of the Royal Society London*, 16 (1970), 77–174.

Finlay, Mark R., 'Early marketing of the theory of nutrition: the science and culture of Liebig's Extract of Meat', in Harmke Kamminga and Andrew Cunningham (eds), *The Science and Culture of Nutrition, 1840–1940* (Rodopi, Amsterdam-Atlanta, GA, 1995), 48–74.

Fitzgerald, J. G., D. T. Fraser, N. E. McKinnon, and M. A. Ross, 'Diphtheria – a preventable disease', *Lancet*, i (1938), 391–7.

Foreman-Peck, J., *Smith & Nephew in the Health Care Industry* (Elgar, Cheltenham, 1995).

Galambos, Louis, and Jane E. Sewell, *Networks of Innovation: Vaccine development at Merck, Sharpe & Dohme and Mulford, 1895–1995* (Cambridge University Press, 1995).

Garnham, P. C. C., 'Edward Hindle, 1886–1973', *Biographical Memoirs of Fellows of the Royal Society London*, 20 (1974), 217–34.

Glenny, A. T., K. Allen and R. A. O'Brien, 'The Schick reaction and diphtheria prophylactic immunisation with toxin–antitoxin mixture', *Lancet*, i (1921), 1236–7.

Glenny, A. T. and B. E. Hopkins, 'Duration of passive immunity' *Journal of Hygiene*, 21 (1922), 142–8.

Glenny, A. T. and M. F. Stevens, 'The laboratory control of tetanus prophylaxis', *Journal of the Royal Army Medical Corps*, 70 (1938), 308–10.

Glenny, A. T. and H. J. Sudmersen, 'Notes on the

production of immunity to diphtheria toxin', *Journal of Hygiene*, 20 (1921), 176–220.

Goodman, Jordan, 'Pharmaceutical industry', in R. Cooter and J. Pickstone (eds), *Medicine in the Twentieth Century* (Harwood Academic, Amsterdam, 2000), 141–54.

Goodwin, L., 'John Smith Knox Boyd', *Biographical Memoirs of Fellows of the Royal Society London*, 28 (1982), 27–57.

Goodwin, L.G., and E. Beveridge, 'Sir Henry Wellcome and tropical medicine', in L.G. Goodwin, E. Beveridge, and J.H. Gorvin (eds), *Wellcome's Legacies* (Wellcome Trust, London, 1998), 9–51.

Goodwin, L.G., E. Beveridge and J. Gorvin, *Wellcome's Legacies* (Wellcome Trust, London, 1998).

Gorvin, J., 'The early development of chemical research in the Wellcome laboratories', in L. Goodwin, E. Beveridge and J.H. Gorvin, *Wellcome's Legacies* (Wellcome Trust, London, 1998), 54–92.

Gray, W.H., G.A.H. Buttle and D. Stephenson, 'Derivatives of p–aminobenzone-sulphonamide in the treatment of streptococcal infection in mice', *Biochemical Journal*, 31 (1937), 724–30.

Gray, T.C., 'Harold King: a notable contributor to anaesthesia', *Anaesthesia*, 41 (1991), 679–82.

Gregor, A. James, *Italian Fascism and Developmental Dictatorship* (Princeton University Press, 1979).

Griffin, F.J., 'Francis Howard Carr 1874–1969', *Chemistry & Industry*, 7 (1969), 196.

Hall, A.R., and B.A. Bembridge, *Physic and Philanthropy: The Wellcome Trust, 1936–86* (Cambridge University Press and the Wellcome Trust, 1986).

Hammonds, E.M., *Childhood's Deadly Scourge: The campaign to control diphtheria in New York City, 1880–1930* (Johns Hopkins University Press, Baltimore, MD, 1999).

Harington, C.R., 'Harold King', *Biographical Memoirs of Fellows of the Royal Society London*, 2 (1956), 157–71.

Harden, A., 'Samuel Barnett Schryver: obituary', *Journal of the Chemical Society*, pt I (1930), 901–5.

Hardy, Anne, *Health and Medicine in Britain Since 1860* (Palgrave, Basingstoke, 2001).

Harries, E.H.R., 'Diphtheria', *Lancet*, i (1939), 45–8.

Hewlett, R.T., *Serum Therapy, Bacterial Therapeutics and Vaccines* (J. & A. Churchill, 1903).

Hindle, E., 'A yellow fever vaccine', *British Medical Journal*, i (1928), 976–7.

Hindle, E., 'An experimental study of yellow fever', *Transactions of the Royal Society of Tropical Medicine and Hygiene*, 22 (1929), 406–34.

Hindle, E., 'The transmission of yellow fever', *Lancet*, ii (1930), 835–42.

Hindle, E., 'Yellow fever' in Medical Research Council, *A System of Bacteriology in Relation to Medicine*, vol. 7 (HMSO, London, 1930), 449–62.

Hoare, C.A., 'Charles Morley Wenyon', *Obituary Notices of Fellows of the Royal Society London*, 6 (1948–49), 627–42.

Holloway, S.W.F., 'The orthodox fringe: the origins of the Pharmaceutical Society of Great Britain', in W.F. Bynum and Roy Porter (eds), *Medical Fringe and Medical Orthodoxy, 1750–1850* (Croom Helm, 1987), 129–57.

Holloway, S.W.F., *Royal Pharmaceutical Society of Great Britain, 1841–1991, A Political and Social History* (Pharmaceutical Press, London, 1991).

Homburg, Ernst, 'The emergence of research laboratories in the dyestuffs industry, 1870–1900', *British Journal for the History of Science*, 25 (1992), 91–111.

Homberg, Ernst, Anthony Travis, and Harm Schroter, (eds), *The Chemical Industry in Europe, 1850–1914: Industrial growth, pollution, and professionalisation* (Kluwer Academic Publishers, Dordrecht, 1998).

Hooker, C., 'Diphtheria, immunisation and the Bundaberg tragedy: a study of public health in Australia', *Health & History*, 2 (2000), 52–78.

Horrocks, Sally M., 'The business of vitamins: nutrition science and the food industry in inter-war Britain', in Harmke Kamminga and Andrew Cunningham (eds.), *The Science and Culture of Nutrition, 1840–1940* (Cambridge University Press, 1995), 235–58.

Hutchinson, A., 'Treatment of diphtheria with refined antitoxin', *British Medical Journal*, i (1939), 384.

Rhodes James, R., *Henry Wellcome* (Hodder & Stoughton, 1994).

Jefferys, J.B., *Retail Trading in Great Britain, 1850–1950: A study of trends in retailing with special reference to the development of co-operative, multiple shop and department store methods of trading*, National Institute of Economic and Social Research, Economic and social studies no. 13 (Cambridge University Press, 1954).

Jones, G.E., *British Multinationals: Origins, management, and performance* (Gower, Aldershot, 1986).

Jones, Edgar, *The Business of Medicine. The extraordinary history of Glaxo, a baby food producer which became one of the world's most successful pharmaceutical companies* (Profile Books, London, 2000).

Jones, Thomas S., *Detailing the Physician* (Romaine Pearson, New York, 1940).

Jowett, H.A.D., 'Some new gold salts of hyoscine, hyoscyamine and atropine', *Journal of the Chemical Society*, 71 (1897), 679–82.

Jowett, H.A.D., 'History of an industry', *East Kent Advertiser*, 21 Mar. 1924.

Jowett, H.A.D. and F.L. Pyman, 'Relations between chemical constitution and physiological action in the tropeines', *Journal of the Chemical Society*, 91 (1907), 92–8.

Jowett, H.A.D., and F.L. Pyman, 'Relations between chemical constitution and physiological action in the tropeines Part II', *Journal of the Chemical Society*, 95 (1909), 1020–32.

Joyce, P.A., *Work, Society, and Politics. The culture of the factory worker in later Victorian England* (Harvester Press, Brighton, 1980).

Kamminga, Harmke, 'Nutrition for the people, or the fate of Jacob Moleschott's contest for a humanist science', in Harmke Kamminga and Andrew Cunningham (eds), *The Science and Culture of Nutrition, 1840–1940* (Rodopi, Amsterdam and Atlanta, GA, 1995), 15–34.

King, H., 'Frank Lee Pyman', *Obituary Notices of Fellows*

of the Royal Society London, 4 (1942–44), 681–97.

Kraft F., 'Ueber das Mutterkorn', Archiv der Pharmazie, 204 (1906), 336–59.

Laidlaw, P. P. and G. W. Dunkin, 'Studies in dog distemper. IV. The immunisation of ferrets against dog distemper', Journal of Comparative Pathology & Therapeutics, 41 (1928), 1–17.

Laidlaw, P. P. and G. W. Dunkin, 'Studies in dog distemper. V. The immunisation of dogs', Journal of Comparative Pathology & Therapeutics, 41 (1928), 209–27.

Landau, R., B. Achilladelis, and A. Scriabine, Pharmaceutical Innovation: Revolutionising human health. (Chemical Heritage Press, London, 2000).

Lawrence, Christopher, Medicine in the Making of Modern Britain, 1700–1920 (Routledge, 1994).

Leishman, W. B., 'The results of protective inoculation against influenza in the army at home, 1918–19', Lancet, i (1920), 366–8.

Lewis, J., 'The prevention of diphtheria in Canada and Britain, 1914–1945', Journal of Social History, 20 (1988), 163–76.

Liebenau, Jonathan, 'Industrial R & D in pharmaceutical firms in the early twentieth century', Business History, 26 (1984), 329–46.

Liebenau, Jonathan, 'Sir Thomas Morson', in D. Jeremy (ed.), Dictionary of Business Biography, 4 (Butterworths, 1985), 346–7.

Liebenau, Jonathan, 'Marketing high technology: educating physicians to use innovative medicines', in J. P. T. Davenport-Hines (ed.), Markets and Bagmen: Studies in the history of marketing and British industrial performance 1830–1939 (Gower, Aldershot, 1986), 82–101.

Liebenau, Jonathan, 'Thomas Whiffen', in David J. Jeremy (ed.), Dictionary of Business Biography 5 (Butterworths, 1986), 763–5.

Liebenau, Jonathan, 'The MRC and the pharmaceutical industry: the model of insulin', in Austoker, J. and L. Bryder, Historical Perspectives on the Role of the MRC (Oxford University Press, 1989), 163–80.

Liebenau, J. M., 'Public health and the production and use of diphtheria antitoxin in Philadelphia', Bulletin of the History of Medicine, 61 (1987), 216–36.

Liebenau, Jonathan, Medical Science and the Medical Industry. The formation of the American pharmaceutical industry. (Macmillan, Basingstoke, 1987).

Liebenau, Jonathan, G. H. Higby, J. Gregory, and Elaine C. Stroud (eds), Pill Peddlers: Essays on the history of the pharmaceutical industry (American Institute for the History of Pharmacy, Madison, WI, 1990).

Ling, T. M., 'Note on the treatment of asthma in children with tuberculin', Lancet, ii (1928), 972–3.

Macdonald, G., In Pursuit of Excellence (Wellcome Foundation, London, 1980).

Lister, J., 'The antitoxin treatment of diphtheria', The Times, 31 Oct. 1894.

McLeod, R. M., 'Law medicine, and public opinion: the resistance to public health legislation, 1870–1907', Public Law, 106 (1967), 188–211.

Macpherson, W. G., History of the Great War based on

Official Documents: Medical services, general history (HMSO, London, 1921).

Macpherson, W. G., W. P. Herringham, T. R. Elliott, and A. Balfour, History of the Great War based on Official Documents: Medical services: Diseases of the war (HMSO, London, 1923).

Macpherson, W. G. Leishman, S. L. Cummins, History of the Great War based on Official Documents: Medical services: Pathology (HMSO, London, 1923).

Mahoney, Tom, The Merchants of Life, An Account of the American Pharmaceutical Industry (Harper & Brothers, New York, 1959).

Mantoux, C., 'Intra-dermo-réaction de la tuberculine', Comptes rendus de l'Académie des sciences, 147 (1908), 355–7.

Marsch, Ulrich, 'Strategies for success: research organisation in German chemical companies and I. G. Faben until 1936', History and Technology, 12 (1994), 25–31.

Matthews, L. G., History of Pharmacy in Britain (E. and G. Livingstone, Edinburgh, 1962).

Milligan, R. C. E., 'Henry Solomon Wellcome', in D. J. Jeremy (ed.), Dictionary of Business Biography 5 (Butterworths, London, 1996), 728–36.

Milligan, R. C. E., and E. M. Tansey, 'The early Wellcome Research Laboratories, 1894–1914', in J. Liebenau, G. J. Higby and E. C. Stroud (eds), Pill Peddlers – Essays on the History of the Pharmaceutical Industry (American Institute of the History of Pharmacy, Madison, WI, 1990), 91–106.

Möller, F. Peckel, Cod Liver Oil and Chemistry (Peter Möller, London, Norway, New York and Copenhagen, 1895).

Montgomerie, R. F. and A. Thomson, 'Tuberculin purified protein derivitive (PPD) in the double intra-dermal test in cattle – preliminary observations', Veterinary Record, 51 (1939), 229–36.

Moore, T. S. and J. C. Philip, The Chemical Society, 1841–1941 (Chemical Society, London, 1947).

Morgan, Phillip, Italian Fascism (Macmillan, Basingstoke, 1995).

Moulton, H. F., The Life of Lord Moulton (Nisbet & Co., London, 1922).

Munro, R., 'The Schick test: its application in an institution for mental defectives', British Medical Journal, i (1927), 506–8.

Newman, G., Bacteria, especially as they are Related to the Economy of Nature to Industrial Processes and to the Public Health (John Murray, London, 1899).

'N. F.' Northumberland, 'Lamb dysentery', Scottish Farmer, 19 Nov. 1928, 1485.

O'Brien, R. A., 'Active immunisation against diphtheria: the present position', Lancet, i (1926), 616–7.

O'Brien, R. A., 'Laidlaw–Dunkin distemper prophylactic', Veterinary Record, 29 (1930), 647.

O'Brien, R. A., and T. Dalling, 'Vaccination against dog distemper', The Field, 1 Feb. 1930.

O'Brien, R. A. and A. T. Glenny, 'Production of antitoxin for therapeutic purposes' in Medical Research Council, A System of Bacteriology in Relation to Medicine, vol. 3 (HMSO, London, 1929), 353–8.

O'Brien, R.A., and C.C.Okell, 'Some problems connected with the Dick test', *Lancet*, ii (1925), 1327–9.

Okell, C.C., 'Two studies of streptococcal infections', *Lancet*, i (1928), 748–50.

Okell, C.C., and H.J.Parish, 'The Dick test in scarlet fever', *Lancet*, i (1925), 712–14.

Okell, C.C., T.Dalling and L.P.Pugh, 'Leptospiral jaundice in dogs (yellows)', *Veterinary Journal*, 81 (1925), 1–35.

Okell, C.C., L.P.Pugh, and T.Dalling, 'Discussion on canine jaundice: with special reference to leptospiral infection', *Proceedings of the Royal Society of Medicine*, 18 (1925), 17–21.

Okell, C.C., H.J. Parish, R.A. O'Brien, G.Dreyer, R.L.Vollum, S.Lyle Cummins, and J.B.Buxton, 'The standardisation of tuberculin and the precipitin test', *Lancet*, i (1926), 433–4.

Oakley, C.L., 'Alexander Thomas Glenny, 1882–1965', *Biographical Memoirs of Fellows of the Royal Society London*, 12 (1966), 163–80.

Oliver, G., 'On the therapeutic employment of the supra-renal glands', *British Medical Journal*, ii (1895), 653–5.

Pakenham, T., *The Scramble for Africa* (Abacus, London, 1991).

Parascandola, J., '"Preposterous provision": The American Society for Pharmacology and Experimental Therapeutics' Ban on Industrial Pharmacologists, 1908–41', in J.Liebenau, G.J.Higby and E.C.Stroud (eds), *Pill Peddlers – Essays on the History of the Pharmaceutical Industry* (American Institute of the History of Pharmacy, Madison, WI, 1990), 29–47.

Parish, H.J., 'Critical review: the modern outlook on tuberculin', *Tubercle*, 19 (1938), 337–50.

Parish, H.J., 'Charles Cyril Oakley, 1888–1939', *Journal of Hygiene*, 39 (1939), 217–23.

Parish, H.J. *A History of Immunisation* (E. & S. Livingstone, Edinburgh, 1965).

Parish, H.J., *Victory with Vaccines: The Story of Immunization* (E. & S. Livingstone, Edinburgh and London, 1968).

Parish, H.J. and C.C.Okell, 'The titration of scarlet fever antitoxin in rabbits', *Lancet*, i (1927), 71–2.

Parish, H.J. and C.C. Okell, 'II. The relationship of scarlet fever to other streptococcal infections', *Lancet*, i (1928), 748–50.

Parish, H.J. and J.Wright, 'The Schick test and active immunisation in relation to epidemic diphtheria', *Lancet*, i (1935), 600–4.

Parke, Davis & Co., *Veterinary Materia Medica*, 6th edn (Parke, Davis & Co., London, 1928).

Pasha, S., *Fire and Sword in the Sudan: A personal narrative of fighting and serving the dervishes, 1879–95*, translated by F.R.Wingate (E. Arnold, London, 1899).

Pérrèdes, P.E.F., 'A contribution to the pharmacognosy of official strophanthus seed', *Yearbook of Pharmacy* (1900), 366.

Pérrèdes, P.E.F., *London Botanic Gardens* (Wellcome Chemical Research Laboratories, London, 1906).

Pickering, F., 'Letter to the Editor', *Veterinary Record*, 42 (1929), 922–34.

Pickstone, J.V. (ed.), *Medical Innovations in Historical Perspective* (Macmillan, Basingstoke, Hampshire, 1992).

Picton, L.J., *Thoughts on Feeding* (Faber & Faber, London, 1946), 17–19.

Porter, Roy, and Mikulas Teich (eds), *Drugs and Narcotics in History* (Cambridge University Press, 1995).

Power, F.B., 'A soluble manganese citrate and compounds of manganese with iron', *Pharmaceutical Journal*, 67 (1901), 135.

Power, F.B., *The Wellcome Chemical Research Laboratories* (BW&Co., London, 1900).

Power, F.B. and F.H.Gornall, 'The constituents of chaulmoogra seeds', *Journal of the Chemical Society*, 85 (1904), 838–51.

Power, F.B. and F.H.Gornall 'The constitution of chaulmoogric acid, Part 1', *Journal of the Chemical Society*, 85 (1904), 851–61.

Power, H., *Tropical Medicine in the Twentieth Century: A History of the Liverpool School of Tropical Medicine 1898–1990* (Kegan Paul, London, 1999).

Pyman, F., Easson, A.P.T., and Boots Pure Drug Co. Ltd, *Manufacture of (therapeutically valuable) Amidines* (British Patent 343577, 1927).

Reckitt, Basil N., *The History of Reckitt & Sons Ltd* (A. Brown & Sons Ltd, Hull, 1952).

Robson, Michael, 'The British pharmaceutical industry and the First World War', in Jonathan Liebenau (ed.), *The Challenge of New Technology: Innovation in British Business since 1850* (Gower, Aldershot, 1988), 83–105.

Robson, Michael, 'The Pharmaceutical Industry in Britain and France, 1919–1939' (unpublished PhD thesis, University of London, 1989).

Rogers, L., 'Diphtheria a preventable disease: why not prevented?', *Medical Officer*, 59 (1938), 237–9.

Rogerson, H., 'Chemical examination of the root of *Lasiosiphon meissnerianus*', *American Journal of Pharmacy*, 83 (1911), 49–55.

Rosenberg, Nathan (ed.), *The American System of Manufactures* (Edinburgh University Press, 1969).

Rubin, L.P., 'Dick, Gladys Rowena Henry', in B.Sicherman, C.H.Green, I.Kantrov and H.Walker (eds), *Notable American Women: The modern period* (Belknap Press, Cambridge, MA, 1980), 191–2.

Saks, Mike, *Alternative Medicine* (Clarendon Press, 1992).

Salmond, M. and B.Turner, 'The Dick test in pregnancy', *British Medical Journal*, ii (1929), 145–6.

Saunders, J.C., 'Alum-precipitated toxoid', *Lancet*, i (1935), 402.

Saunders, J.C., 'Observations on the use of alum-toxoid as an immunising agent against diphtheria', *Lancet*, ii (1932), 1047–50.

Schick, B., 'Kutanreaktion bei impfung mit diphtherietoxin', *München medicinische Wochenschrift*, 55 (1908), 504–6.

Schryver, S.B., and F.H.Lees, 'Researches on morphine, part 1', *Journal of the Chemical Society*, 77 (1900), 1024–40.

Schryver, S. B. and F. H. Lees, 'Researches on

morphine, part 2', *Journal of the Chemical Society*, 79 (1901), 563–80.

'SFW' & 'ELS', 'Obituary – Alfred Louis Bacharach', *British Medical Journal*, ii (1966), 308–9.

Sicherman, B., C.H. Green, I. Kantrov and H. Walker (eds), *Notable American Women: The modern period* (Belknap Press, Cambridge, MA, 1980).

Simmons, Anna, 'The Chemical and Pharmaceutical Activities of the Apothecaries' Hall' (unpublished PhD thesis, Open University, 1993).

Slinn, Judy. *A History of May and Baker, 1834–1984* (Hobson's Ltd, Cambridge, 1984).

Slinn, Judy, 'Research and development in the UK pharmaceutical industry from the nineteenth century to the 1960s', in Roy Porter and Mikulas Teich (eds), *Drugs and narcotics in history* (Cambridge University Press, 1995), 168–86.

Smith, David F. (ed.), *Nutrition in Britain: Science, scientists and politics in the twentieth century* (Routledge, 1997).

Stone, Richard and A.D. Rowe, 'Consumer spending on drugs and other medicines, 1920–1938', in *The Measurement of Consumer Expenditure and Behaviour in the United Kingdom, 1920–1938*, vol. II (Cambridge University Press, 1966), PAGES.

Sudmersen, H.J. and A.T. Glenny, 'Immunity of guinea-pigs to diphtheria toxin, and its effects upon the offspring. I.', *Journal of Hygiene*, 11 (1911), 220–34.

Sudmersen, H.J. and A.T. Glenny, Immunity of guinea-pigs to diphtheria toxin, and its effects upon the offspring. II.', *Journal of Hygiene*, 11 (1911), 423–42.

Sudmersen, H.J. and A.T. Glenny, Immunity of guinea-pigs to diphtheria toxin, and its effects upon the offspring. III.', *Journal of Hygiene*, 12 (1912), 64–76.

Swyer, R., 'Antigenic properties of diphtheria toxoid–antitoxin floccules', *Lancet*, i (1931), 632–4.

Tanner, Jan, 'The New York Venture', *Foundation News*, June 1981, 1–21.

Tansey, E.M., 'Charles Sherrington and the Brown Animal Sanatory Institution', *St Thomas' Hospital Gazette*, 84 (1986), 5–10.

Tansey, E.M., 'The Wellcome Physiological Research Laboratories, 1894–1904: the Home Office, pharmaceutical firms, and animal experiments', *Medical History*, 33 (1989), 1–41.

Tansey, E.M., 'Protection against dog distemper and Dogs Protection Bills: the Medical Research Council and anti-vivisectionist protest, 1911–33', *Medical History*, 38 (1994), 1–26.

Tansey, E.M., 'What's in a name? Henry Dale and Adrenaline, 1906', *Medical History*, 39 (1995), 459–76.

Thomson, A.L., *Half a Century of Medical Research. 1. Origins and policy of the Medical Research Council (UK).* (HMSO, 1973).

Thomson, A.L., *Half a Century of Medical Research. 2: The Programme of the Medical Research Council (UK)* (HMSO, 1975).

Turner, H., *Henry Wellcome: The man, his collection and his legacy* (Wellcome Trust and Heinemann, London, 1980).

Tweedale, Geoffrey, *At the Sign of the Plough, Allen & Hanburys and the British pharmaceutical industry,*

1715–1990 (Glaxo Pharmaceuticals Ltd and John Murray, 1990).

U.S. House of Representatives, 70th Congress, first session, Committee on Foreign Affairs, *Gorgas Memorial Laboratory, Hearings on H.R. 8128 to authorize a permanent annual appropriation for the maintenance and operation of the Gorgas Memorial Laboratory.* (United States Government Printing Office, 1928).

Vane, J.R., 'The research heritage of Henry Wellcome', *Pharmaceutical Historian*, 10 (1980), 2–8.

Vannozzi, F., *Sienna, la città laboratorio: Dall'innesto del vajuolo ad Albert Sabin* (Protagon Editore Toscani, Siena, 1999).

Vaughan, Paul, '"Secret remedies" in the late nineteenth and early twentieth centuries', in M. Saks (ed.), *Alternative Medicine in Britain* (Continuum, London, 1992), 101–11.

Waddington, K., 'To stamp out "so terrible a malady": bovine tuberculosis and tuberculin testing in Britain, 1890–1939' *Medical History*, 48 (2004), 29–48.

Wear, Andrew (ed.), *Medicine in Society: Historical essays* (Cambridge University Press, 1992).

Weatherall, Miles, *In Search of a Cure: A history of pharmaceutical discovery* (Oxford University Press, 1990).

Weindling, P., 'Changing patterns of sickness in the nineteenth century', in Andrew Wear (ed.), *Medicine in Society: Historical essays* (Cambridge University Press, 1992), 305–6.

Weindling, P., 'From medical research to clinical practice: serum therapy for diphtheria in the 1890s', in J.V. Pickstone (ed.) *Medical Innovations in Historical Perspective* (Macmillan, Basingstoke, Hampshire, 1992), 72–83.

Wellcome, H.S., *The Story of Metlakahtla* (Saxon, London, 1887).

Wenyon, C.M., 'Henry Solomon Wellcome', *Obituary Notices of Fellows of the Royal Society of London*, 2 (1936–38), 229–38.

Wilkinson, L., and A. Hardy, *Prevention and Cure: The London School of Hygiene and Tropical Medicine – A twentieth-century quest for global public health* (Kegan Paul, London, 2001).

Williams, Keith, 'The History of the Wellcome Chemical Laboratory and Clinical Trials in Britain in the Interwar Period' (Unpublished PhD thesis, University of Manchester, 2004).

Willows' *Veterinary Diary & Visiting List* (Willows, London, 1934).

Wilson, J.G., 'Diphtheria immunisation', *Medical Officer*, 49 (1933), 150.

Worling, P.M., 'Pharmaceutical wholesale distribution in the UK, 1950–1990', *Pharmaceutical Historian*, 28 (1998), 53–8.

Worboys, Michael, *Spreading germs. Disease theories and medical practice, 1865–1900* (Cambridge University Press, 2000).

Yamey, B.S., 'The origins of resale price maintenance', *Economic Journal*, LXII (1952), 522–45.

Zingler, A., 'Results of active immunization with diphtheria toxin–antitoxin', *Journal of the American Medical Association*, 78 (1922), 1945–52.

Journals

In addition to specific articles listed above, numerous anonymous trade notes, editorials, news features, advertisements and other items have been used.

Relevant runs of several journals have been examined, including:

British Medical Journal (1879–1940)
British & Colonial Druggist (1885–1915)
Chemist & Druggist (1879–1940)
Lancet (1879–1940)
Medical Press & Circular (old series 1879–1938, new series 1939–1940)
Medical Times & Gazette (1879–1885)
Pharmaceutical Journal (4th series, 1895–1940)
Pharmaceutical Journal and Transactions (3rd series, 1879–1895)
Pharmaceutical Era (1895–1902)

Official publications

1919:   National Health Insurance Commission (England). Memorandum on the Special Measures taken by the National Health Insurance Commission (England) in relation to the Supply of Drugs and Other Medicinal Stores during the War. Cd. 183. London: HMSO, PP, 1919, xxxix. Waldorf Astor, Chairman.

1896–1906:   Home Office, Annual Returns of Experiments [HO Returns]. London: HMSO.

1916:   Royal Commission on Venereal Diseases, Final Report, Cd. 8189, PP, 1916, xvi.

1940:   Ministry of Health, Memorandum on the production of artificial immunity against diptheria.

                   Revised edition. Memo. 170/Med. (HMSO, London).

Wellcome printed sources

Foundation News   *Tabloid*
Monthly Letter   *Wellcome Diaries*
Monthly Memoranda   *Wellcome News*
Price Lists   *Wellcome World*

Index

Page numbers given in *italics* refer to illustrations

mechanisation 38–9, 77–8, 83–5, 88
nineteenth-century advances 4–5
packing girls at work *79, 219, 330*
serum anti-toxins *205*, 206, 209–10, 213–16, 220,
    272, 325
Tabloids 77, 235
in the USA 245, 390–1, 393–4, 463
at Wandsworth 27–8, 30
see also quality control
Markby Stewart & Co. (solicitors for BW&Co.),
    London 121, 135, 449
marketing
advertising 21–2, 55–61, 159–63, 306–8, 402–3,
    438–44
    see also advertisements
to chemists 57, 59–60, 65, 68–9, *68*, 158–9, 401–2
detailing 7, 11, 66–9, 129, 150, 397
to doctors 56–9, 65–8, 151, 157–8, 162, 323–4,
    399–400, 419, *438*
ethical 55–63, 159, 306–8, 376–7, 402–3, 409,
    438–44
exhibitions *see* exhibitions
expenditure 55, 319, 434–5, *436*
free samples and gifts 57–8, 400, *438*
to the general public 162–3, 404–5, 414, 437–8,
    441–3
to the government/military 70–1, 228–9, 416–18
Hazeline products 56, 59, 163, 383
to hospitals 53–4, 65–6
Kepler products 23–4, 51, 56, 163, 369–81, 402,
    438–41
market research 66–9, *68*, 414
policies contributing to decline 435–8
pricing *see* pricing policies
propagation (demonstrations) 152–7, 369–70
salesmen *see* travelling salesmen
serum anti-toxins 215, 217–19, 447
Tabloids, 361, 364–6
and the transition to manufacturing 39–40
in the USA 388, 394, 396–405, 406–7, 408–19,
    436–7
veterinary products 159, 343–4, 346–7, 412
vitamin concentrates 379, 382–3
Martin, Charles 336, 377
Materia Medica farm, Dartford, Kent 80, 186, *367*
May & Baker 20
ex-BW&Co. staff at 486
financial data 276, 426, 427, 428
medicines for syphilis 274, 476
publications 320
sulphonamides 352
May, Earl 406
Mayo, William Worrall 12
McBride, Mr 144, 147, 154
McCarthy, D.T. 353
McKesson & Robbins 4, 13, 14, 41, 69, 128–9
meat extracts *see* Beef and Iron wine
Medical Diary 58, 190, *439*

Medical Formulae of New and Improved Chemical and
    Pharmaceutical Preparations 21, 57–8, *226*
medical kits *see* first aid kits
medical press
advertisements in 21–2, 55, 56–8, 159
attitude to substitution 136, 139
endorsements of BW&Co. products 22, 33, 44, 58–9
see also individual journals
Medical Press & Circular 21, 63
medical profession *see* doctors; hospitals
Medical Research Committee (1913–22); Medical
    Research Council (1922–) (MRC); *see also* NIMR
canine distemper vaccines 349–50
diphtheria anti-sera and vaccines 327
ergosterol 378
ergot and 312
ex-BW&Co. staff at 289, 479, 481, 493–4
First World War activities 256–7, 264
insulin and 299–300, 301, 305, 308
standardisation 305, 479
testing of new therapies 479–81
Medical Times & Gazette 136
medicine chests *see* first aid kits
Medicines Stamp Act (1812) 31, 34–7
Melbourne (Australia) 218, 232–3
Mellanby, Edward 380, *482–3*, 489, 490, *490*
Mellanby, John *482–3*, 488, *489*, 490
meningococcus anti-sera 272
Menthofax 383
menthol snuff 48, 154–6
Merkley, Mr 242
midwives 158–9
Milan 132, 226–7, 238, 277, 424
military usage
Apothecaries' Hall products 19
BW&Co. products 70–1, 228–9, 256, 258, 270–3,
    342
milk, dried *112*, 370–1, 375, 406–7
missionaries, products for 46, 228, *245*
Moir, John Chassar 312
Montreal office *237*
    see also Canada, BW&Co.
Moogrol (chaulmoogra) 194, 269, 312–14, 317
Moore, G. Leslie
US branch accounts and 242, 243–5, 246–7, 248–9,
    250, 395
Wellcome Foundation and 286, 451, 455, 456
Moore, Thomas Henry 136, 241, 243, 250
morphine 15, 194
Morris, William, catalogue of early printed books *160,*
    161
Morson, Thomas 20
Moulton, Fletcher (Snr) 134, 207
Moulton, H. Fletcher (Jun.) 336
MRC *see* Medical Research Committee/Council
museums 432, 433

perfumes 43, 127, 131
Pérrèdes, Paul 194–5
Perrin, Sir Michael 471
personnel *see* employees
Peters, Rudolph 377, 378
pharmaceutical industry
    American 3–5, 410–11
    British 18–20, 175, 276, 422, 426–8, 475, 479–81
    effect of WWI 255, 275–9, 280–1
    nineteenth-century 3–5, 15–20
    see also competitors; *individual companies*
Pharmaceutical Society 173, 175, 180
pharmacists *see* chemists
Philadelphia 3, 5, 12, 242
Phoenix Mills factory *see* Dartford Phoenix Mills
    factory
phosphate drinks 43
photographic chemicals 48, 70, 383–4, *384*
Physic and Philanthropy (Hall and Bembridge,
    1986) 421, 423
pills *see* Tabloids
Pinkus, Stanislaus 172
pituitary gland products 183, *183*, 304, 401
pneumonia *340*, 341
    Churchill and a lion cured by M&B 693 352
poisons 81, 140
Pope, C. G. 328
Power, Frederick Belding 12, *190*, 487
    career progression *482–3*, 487
    at the WCRL 189–90, 191–2, 201
Prevost, Mr 119
Price, Martin 449, *450*, 454
Price Waterhouse 286
price lists *52, 153, 227, 228, 239*
pricing policies
    effect of competition 39, 51–4, 165, 297, 305
    overseas 230, 234, 236, 247, 250, 464–5
    retail (resale) price maintenance 53, 130–1, 136–9,
        140–5, 437
    see also discounts
product range
    Hazeline products 42–3, 164
    Kepler products 49–50, 164
    nineteenth-century 17, 21–2, *23*, 41–51, 164
    serum anti-toxins and vaccines 218, 221, 222, 223,
        270
    Tabloids 44–6, 48–9, 50, 360–1
    twentieth-century 280–1, 383–6
    WCRL innovations 193, 194
product support 80–2, 195
    see also quality control
production *see* manufacturing
profit-sharing 100, 123
profits
    1880–1914 103
    1898–1914 106, 166
    1914–1918 276, 279
    1914–1923 278

compared with competitors' 276, 428
    nineteenth-century 11, 30
    overseas branches 236–8, 246–9, 395, 419–20
    serum anti-toxins 166, 279, 357–8
    see also sales
promotion *see* advertisements; marketing
Proom, Harry 328
propagation (sales demonstrations) 152–7, 369–70
Proprietary Articles Trading Association (PATA) 138–
    9, 140, 145
Protamine Insulin Zinc 309
public health 16
    British reluctance to start immunisation and surveil-
        lance campaigns 204, 270, 330–1, 332–3, 339,
        447
public safety fears about biomedical research 288, 343
publications 180–1
    all laboratories compared 201, 288, 320
    for children *379*
    formulae books *21*, 57–8, *226*
    from the museums 433
    from the WCRL 192
    from the WPRL 183–4, 306–8
    from the WTRL 199–200
    information booklets 160–2, *162*, *245, 246, 304*, 310,
        384, 385, 440
purgatives *see* laxatives
Pyman, Frank
    career progression 201, *482–3*, 485, 487–8, 490, 493
    research 256, 292
    role in defection of Carr to Boots, 260

quality control
    by Apothecaries' Hall 19
    at McKesson & Robbins 13
    problems with anti-sera and vaccines 207–8, 214,
        218, 219–20, 353–5
    procedures 78–82, 84–5, 88–90, 477–8
    Tabloids 81, 84–5, 191–2
quinine 14
    Chinese labelling *375*
    manufacture 47, 193, 258
    marketing 154, 365, 439

Radio Malt 379–80
Raisin, Mr 84
Rasmusen, Henry C. 245
Rational Obstetrics 310
raw materials 80, 186, 193–4, 235
    see also Wellcome Brand Chemicals
regulation
    nineteenth-century 17, 19
    testing of new products by the MRC 479–81
    in the USA 220, 241
    see also standardisation
Reid, James 140

Reiner, L. 467
Remington, Joseph 5
Reports from the Khartoum Laboratories 199–200
research laboratories 168–9
    collaborations between 178, 193, 195, 292, 314–17
    in the Dartford factory 81–2, 193–4, 195, 320, 367, 485
    government prejudice against 170, 172–5, 347–9
    post-WWI constraints 287–90, 315–17, 355, 371–2, 432, 433, 459
    relations with commercial side of the business 168–9, 183–5, 188–9, 294–7, 337, 346–7, 468–9, 473–4
    STC 293–4, 298–9, 317–18, 321, 377, 445, 480–1
    in the USA (Tuckahoe) 396, *396*, 406, 407–8, 466–8
    Wellcome Trust and 452–3
    see also individual laboratories (entries at Wellcome)
respiratory diseases 16, *22*, 340–1, *340*
retail chemists *see* chemists
Richardson, Sir Albion 288
rickets 16, 372, 375, 378, 380
Ring case 353–5, 459
Robert & Cie 225
Robson, Mr 421
Roger, Mr 45
Rogers, Mr 153, 159
Rogers, Sir Leonard 313
Rogerson, Harold 487
Roscoe, Sir Henry 203
Royal College of Physicians of London 173, 175
Royal College of Surgeons of England 173, 175
Royal Society Fellowships 490–1, *492*
Runcorn Research Laboratories 476
Russell, Sir James 476
Russia, price lists *227, 228*
Ryzamin-B 382, *382*

salaries *see* pay
sales
    1881–1914 103, 231
    1914–1918 276
    1914–1923 278
    1920–1940 360
    General Goods 164–5, 232, 238, 280–1, 423–4
    KMEC 10–11
    overseas 166–7, 231–2, 237–8, 247, 249, 277, 419–20, 424–6
    sera and diagnostic services 211, 281, 357–8, 360, 423
    Tabloids 359–60, 361, 363
    Wellcome Brand Chemicals 166, 232, 238, 281, 360
    see also profits
salesmen *see* travelling salesmen
salicylic acid *see* aspirin
Salodent *see* Opa
Salvarsan 256

Saxon & Co. 116, 119
scarlet fever 334–9, *338, 339*
Schaack, H. John van 63, 113–14
Schäfer, Edward 172
Schick test 329–30, 331–3
schistosomiasis (bilharzia) 317–18
Schryver, Samuel 194, *482–3*, 487, 490
Scientific and Technical Committee (STC) 293–4, 298–9, 317, 321, 377, 445, 480–1
Searl, Albert 75, 76
Second World War
    advertising in *382, 448*
    bombing of Snow Hill 315
    insulin supply 309, *309*
    tetanus immunisation 342
secrecy, policies of 80, 83, 96, 234
self-medication 17, 46, 56, 63–4, 233, 364
serum anti-toxins 203, 325
    animal experimentation registration 170, 172–5
    BIPM and 203–4
    competitors 204, 210, 216–18, *218*, 221, 222, 337–8
    diphtheria 206–9, *207*, 215, *215*, 270, 325
    dysentery 264
    end of production 357
    financial data 166, 211, 279, 281, 357–8, 360, 423, 446
    First World War and 269–73
    Lancet special commission 207
    manufacturing *205*, 206, 209–10, 213–16, 220, 272, 325
    marketing 215, 217–19, *218, 338, 339, 340*, 447
    packing *219*
    product range 218, 221, 223, 270
    quality problems 207–8, 214, 218, 219–20
    respiratory diseases 340–1, *340*
    streptococcal infections 206, 219, 272, 334–5, 337–8, *338, 339*
    tetanus 209, 223, 270–2, 342
    veterinary 222–3, 272
    see also diagnostic services; vaccines
sex steroids 321–2
Shanghai office 229, 238, 277, 424
Sharp, T. M. *291*
Shaw, Vernon 212, 366
sheep, diseases of 344–6
Sheldon, Mrs French, palanquin designed by Wellcome *196*
Shepperson, William 62, 232
Simpson, W. J. 458
Sixsmith, Mr 140, 148
Sketofax 383, *383*
sleeping sickness 293, 318
Smart, Mr 83
S. M. Burroughs & Co. (SMB&Co.) 6, 7–9
smelling salts 153, 412
Smith, Dr 113
Smith, A. P. 33–4
Smith, Sydney *367*, 368, 449, *482–3*